The Canadian City:
Essays in Urban and Social History

Edited by
Gilbert A. Stelter and Alan F. J. Artibise

Revised and Enlarged

CARLETON UNIVERSITY PRESS
OTTAWA — CANADA
1984

THE CARLETON LIBRARY SERIES

A series of original works, reprints, and new collections of source material relating to Canada, issued under the supervision of the Editorial Board, Carleton Library Series, Carleton University Press Inc., Ottawa, Canada.

GENERAL EDITOR
Michael Gnarowski

EDITORIAL BOARD
Bruce Cox (Anthropology)
J. Keith Johnson (History)
David B. Knight (Geography)
John de Vries (Sociology)
T.K. Rymes (Economics)
Maureen A. Molot (Political Science)
Margaret H. Ogilvie (Law)

© Carleton University Press Inc. 1984
ISBN 0-88629-018-X (paperback)

Printed and bound in Canada

Canadian Cataloguing in Publication data

Main entry under title:
    The Canadian City

(The Carleton library; no. 132)
Bibliography: p.
ISBN 0-88629-018-X

1. Cities and towns—Canada—History—Addresses,
essays, lectures. I. Stelter, Gilbert A., 1933-
II. Artibise, Alan F.J., 1946- III. Series.

HT127.C33 1984   307.7'6'0971   C84-090212-3

Distributed by:
    Oxford University Press Canada
    70 Wynford Drive
    DON MILLS, Ontario, Canada, M3C 1J9
    (416)441-2941

ACKNOWLEDGMENT

Carleton University Press gratefully acknowledges the support extended to its publishing programme by the Canada Council and the Ontario Arts Council.

Cover photo: St. George's Square, Guelph, Ontario, 1908.
Courtesy: Guelph Civic Museum

CONTENTS

Preface to the Second Edition

This volume represents a shift in emphasis from the first edition published in 1977, for we have added a number of new articles that deal with the question of urban society. Thus there is a new emphasis on subjects such as family, social structure, immigration and religion. Other sections of the volume have been revised as well, with new articles in several areas. The editors have provided new introductions to each section with indications of recent literature available. This volume, with its concentration on urban society, is a companion to two other Carleton Library books — *The Usable Urban Past: Planning and Politics in the Modern Canadian City* (No. 119, 1979) which emphasizes the nature of urban government and the evolution of modern planning, and *Shaping the Urban Landscape: Aspects of the Canadian City-Building Process* (No. 125, 1982), which stresses the formation of the urban environment, with articles on factors in urban growth, land speculation and development, the subdivision process, building and architecture, and internal transportation.

This edition is dedicated to the members of the Urban History Group of the Canadian Historical Assocation. Since 1971 this committee of historians, geographers, planners and archivists has met regularly at the annual Learned Societies meetings in June and in the fall in a succession of cities to promote the study of urban history. Through conference planning and organization and through the sponsorship of the *Urban History Review*, this group has been a vital force in the development of the historical dimension of urban studies in Canada.

Gilbert Stelter, Guelph
Alan Artibise, Winnipeg.

I.   General Introduction: What is Urban History?

"Urban history," according to H.J. Dyos, one of the pioneers of the field in Britain, "is the most newly discovered continent and into the scramble for it goes every kind of explorer."[1] In Canada, the rush was relatively late compared to that in the United States and Great Britain, but the activity has been intense since the early 1970s. For example, a major bibliography published in 1981, *Canada's Urban Past*, contains more than 7,000 entries for books, articles and theses, most of them the product of the past decade, indicating the wealth of material now available to the researcher and student.[2] As well, there are a number of articles which serve as guides to the general concepts of urban history or to specific themes such as urban growth, land development, architecture and building, and urban society.[3] For up-to-date information on what is going on in the field in Canada, readers should regularly consult the *Urban History Review*, a periodical which is now published by the Institute of Urban Studies, University of Winnipeg.

In spite of all of this activity, defining urban history in a precise way remains a difficult task, partly because the subject matter is so complex. To most of those who consider themselves urban historians, urban history is not a single discipline or subdiscipline in any exclusive sense; rather, it is a field of knowledge in which many disciplines converge.[4] Thus geographers, planners, architects, political scientiests and a good many others as well as historians can be said to "do" urban history when they deal with the urban past. In general terms, urban history is an attempt to explain some of the most basic phenomena of modern history — the growth of cities and the urbanization of society. Its approach is closely related to those who study major elements of social change such as class and family formation; the specific contribution it makes to questions such as these is a concern for grounding these questions in specific places.

As a result, the growth of urban history as a self-conscious field of study is tied to the general increase of interest in local history. Is urban history really just another name for the local history of towns and cities? The answer is yes if a local study is put into the perspective of regional or general community development. What often characterizes local history, however, is an antiquarian interest in specific details and events, without any concern for whether these represent unique or typical occurrences. The urban historian's approach thus tends to fall between that of the local historian and that of the social scientist. What this amounts to, in practice, on the one hand, is an interest in particular places and in the extent to which people — individuals and groups — can and do affect events; and, on the other hand, an awareness of general patterns and large-scale forces over which the people of a specific community have little or no control.

In some respects the study of urban history in Canada is simply a logical development of some of the traditional interpretations of Canadian history. The so-called Laurentian school of historians — including Harold A. Innis, Donald G. Creighton, and A.R.M. Lower — brought a metropolitan focus to their work on the staples trade. Their books still provide a necessary background for an understanding of the growth of the dynamic entrepreneurial cities of the 18th and 19th centuries.[5] The relationship between city development and the staples industries was made more explicit in a seminal examination of the concept of metropolitanism by J.M.S. Careless in 1954.[6] A second stage of urban history was ushered in during the 1960's and early 1970's when much of the stimulation for the study of urban history was due to the importation of American concepts and methodology. Particularly influential were the ideas of Sam Bass Warner on the social consequences of suburbanization and those of Stephan Thernstrom on social mobility. Unfortunately, Canadian scholars often treated Canadian cities as though they were merely extensions of American society without even asking if the national border made a difference. By the late 1970s a reaction against these rather uncritical importations was reflected in a greater concern for what was indigenous to the Canadian experience. The first national conference in Canadian urban history in 1977 served as a kind of barometer of a changing climate. By the kinds of questions asked, and by the sources used, Canadians consciously declared their independence of American urban history and its concentration only on a limited set of social processes such as mobility.[7]

Despite the growing sophistication of the study of urban history the field is still in its infancy in many respects. Some of the promising new directions are listed below but these are by no means exhaustive. First, there is an increasing recognition that the urban dimension makes sense only when seen as one part of a total society. What this means is that towns and cities are subsystems of a larger political and social system and have to be examined from the perspective of that larger system. Urban and rural history thus could be regarded as different sides of the same scholarly coin.[8] Second, there is a new interest in how the power structure of society is related to the formation of cities and how it affects the nature of urban society. As one observer has put it, "the urban history of the 1980s calls for an analysis of institutionalized urban political and economic power in all of its facets — not only as it is expressed and implemented by those who rule, but also how it is interpreted by the powerless who must live with or combat these rules."[9] Third, there are signs that urban historians are looking beyond one national setting and asking comparative questions. What seems especially possible at this stage of development are comparisons with urban development in countries which, like Canada, are "regions of recent European settlement" — the United States, Australia, and several Latin American nations. We may then be able to begin to distinguish between what is more generally typical of urban development and what is the product of a particular societal context.[10]

NOTES:

1. "Agenda for Urban Historians," in H.J. Dyos, ed., *The Study of Urban History* (London, 1968), p. 6.

2. Alan F.J. Artibise and Gilbert A. Stelter, *Canada's Urban Past, A Bibliography to 1980 and Guide to Canadian Urban Studies* (Vancouver, 1981).

3. For general assessments of Canadian urban history see Gilbert A. Stelter, "The Historian's Approach to Canada's Urban Past," *Histoire sociale/Social History*, 7 (May, 1974), pp. 5-22; Stelter, "Urban History in North America: Canada," *Urban History Yearbook*, 1977 (University of Leicester, England), pp. 24-29; and John Weaver, "Urban Canada: Recent Historical Writing," *Queen's Quarterly*, 86 (1979), pp. 75-97. For an analysis of development in Quebec see Annick German, "Histoire urbaine et histoire de l'urbanisation au Québec," *Urban History Review*, 3-78 (February, 1979), pp. 3-22. The contributions made by geographers are outlined in James T. Lemon, "Study of the Urban Past: Approaches by Geographers," Canada Historical Association, *Historical Papers* (1973), pp. 179-190 and in John U. Marshall, "Geography's Contribution to the Historical Study of Urban Canada," *Urban History Review*, 1-73 (May, 1973), pp. 15-24. The literature on urban growth is summarized in Elizabeth Bloomfield, "Community, Ethos and Local Initiatives," *Urban History Yearbook* (1983); that on land development in Michael Doucet, "Urban Land Development in 19th Century North America: Themes in the Literature," *Journal of Urban History*, 8 (May, 1982), pp. 299-342; that on building and architecture in Deryck Holdsworth, "Built Forms and Social Realities: A Review Essay of Recent Work on Canadian Heritage Structures," *Urban History Review*, 9 (October, 1980), pp. 123-138; that on urban society in Chad Gaffield, "Social Structure and the Urbanization Process: Perspectives on Nineteenth Century Case Studies," in this volume. For informal discussions about the growth of urban history, see Bruce Stave, *The Making of Urban History: Historiography through Oral History* (Beverly Hills, 1977) and two Stave interviews, "Urban History in Canada: A Conversation with Alan F.J. Artibise," *Urban History Review*, 8 (February, 1980), pp. 110-143 and "A Conversation with Gilbert A. Stelter: Urban History in Canada," *Journal of Urban History* 6 (February, 1980), pp. 177-210.

4. Perhaps the clearest statement is H.J. Dyos, "Urbanity and Suburbanity," in David Cannadine and David Reeder, eds., *Exploring the Urban Past: Essays in Urban History by H.J. Dyos* (Cambridge, 1982), pp. 19-36.

5. This approach is well described in Carl Berger, *The Writing of Canadian History* (Toronto, 1976).

6. "Frontierism, Metropolitanism, and Canadian History," *Canadian Historical Review*, 35 (March, 1954), pp. 1-21.

7. David B. Knight and John H. Taylor, "Canada's Urban Past: A Report on the Canadian Urban History Conference," *Urban History Review*, 2-77 (October, 1977), pp. 72-86; Stelter and Artibise, "Urban History Comes of Age: A Review of Current Research," *City Magazine*, 3 (No. 1, 1977), pp. 22-36.

8. Robert Swierenga, ''Toward the 'New Rural History': A Review Essay,'' *Historical Methods Newsletter*, 6 (1973), pp. 111-122.

9. Daniel Shaffer, ''A New Threshold for Urban History: Reflections on Canadian-American Urban Development at the Guelph Conference,'' *Planning History Bulletin*, 4 (No. 3, 1982), pp. 1-8.

10. For some suggestions in this regard see Richard M. Morse, ''The Urban Worlds of Latin and Anglo America: Prefatory Thoughts,'' in Woodrow Borah, Jorge Hardoy and Gilbert Stelter, eds., *Urbanization in the Americas: The Background in Comparative Perspective* (Ottawa, 1980), pp. 1-6.

II CITIES IN THE NEW WORLD: CANADIAN URBAN HISTORY BEFORE 1850

The tiny communities of early Canada have been relatively neglected or downgraded in significance by scholars. A typical assumption is that of A. R. M. Lower: "A History of Canada, any history, must have much to do with untamed nature and with the countryside. Cities will come into it, but late."[1] Lower's view might be considered the Canadian equivalent of Richard Hofstadter's oft-quoted statement that "the United States was born in the country and has moved to the city."[2] But there is increasing evidence to suggest that urban life was a significant feature of Canadian development long before the dramatic urban growth of the late 19th and early 20th centuries. In fact, the basic essentials of the present network of cities in eastern and central Canada were firmly established by 1850. By this time the tiny outposts of the French and British empires had developed into dynamic commercial centres, had won metropolitan hegemony over sizeable hinterlands, and were beginning to produce some of the goods that were formerly imported. The major cities had achieved a degree of autonomy through city charters, and their leadership had shifted from an aristocratic elite based on representatives of imperial governments to an elite based on commerce. The cities were still relatively compact communities with commercial, residential, and industrial functions mixed together. But in the largest cities, specialization of areal functions had begun with the growth of industrial and residential suburbs, and residential segregation by class and ethnicity had made its appearance.

The manner in which cities and urban life originated in Canada was due to a process almost as old as civilization itself. Great empires, with dynamic metropolises as their hearts, expanded by establishing colonial outposts. The Roman Empire provides one of the clearest examples of the use of urbanization as an instrument of expansion. Even with the collapse of the

Roman Empire and the general decline in urban life in the medieval period, new towns continued to be founded, especially as frontier posts on the borderlands. From the 16th century, young aggressive nation-states of western Europe — centred in Madrid, Lisbon, Amsterdam, Paris, and London — began a worldwide competition for hegemony by founding colonial towns in the Americas and Southeast Asia.[3] The colonial towns planted in early Canada were part of this large-scale phenomenon and they served as agents of the urban metropolitan centres. Economically, they served to exploit the colony's staples; culturally, they represented the metropolis in the transmission of the metropolitan centre's style of life to a new frontier; in terms of military and administrative functions, they were often the means of occupying and holding the colony. The economic function is particularly basic to the relationship. The towns were generally entrepôts, collecting staples from their region for shipment to the metropolitan centre for final processing and, in turn, distributing the manufactured goods from the metropolis.[4]

The colonial towns of the French and British colonies often preceded the general settlement of a region. They could thus be regarded as constituting an "urban frontier," a term used by Carl Bridenbaugh and Richard Wade to describe a similar process in early American development.[5] The future growth and prosperity of the colonial towns depended, of course, on the potential of their hinterlands. The relationship between the colonial town and its region appears to fit into a pattern in early Canadian history. In the initial phase, the towns acted as channels for the development of the region. During this period they contained a relatively high proportion of the population. In the second phase, however, a process of decentralization set in. The town's proportion of the total population dropped, even though the towns tended to grow rapidly. The smaller secondary centres which emerged developed a good deal of autonomy during this second phase because the primitive transportation system left them isolated, and because the original town of the region did not yet have the necessary facilities to dominate all aspects of life of the region. This decentralization process was ultimately reversed during a third phase when colonial towns such as Quebec, Montreal, Toronto, and Halifax became major urban centres in their own right. The colonial towns also played a significant role as agents for the transportation of social and cultural institutions from the metropolis to the frontier.

Another characteristic of the colonial town was its lack of significant connections with other colonial towns, even with those of its own region. The primary connection and concern of the colonial town was the overseas metropolis. The beginning of regional and inter-regional connections represented the end of the colonial phase, as towns began to produce goods and services for not only themselves but also for the entire region. In the urban development of Canada in the period prior to 1850 however, this phase had barely begun.

NOTES

1. *Canadians in the Making* (Toronto, 1958), p. 1.
2. *The Age of Reform* (New York, 1956), p. 23.
3. The process is described in Gideon Sjoberg, *The Pre-Industrial City Past and Present* (New York, 1960); Ervin Galanty, *New Towns: Antiquity to the Present* (New York, 1975); Jorge E. Hardoy, *Urbanization in Latin America: Approaches and Issues* (New York, 1975).
4. For a general discussion of the process in Canada see Gilbert A. Stelter, "The Urban Frontier in Canadian History," *Canadian Issues*, vol. 1 (Spring, 1973), pp. 99-114, reprinted in A.R. McCormack and Ian MacPherson (eds.), *Cities in the West* (Ottawa, 1975). See also John W. Reps, *Town Planning in Frontier America* (Princeton, 1969) and J. David Wood, "Grand Design on the Fringes of Empire: New Towns for British North America," *Canadian Geographer*, 26 (No. 3, 1982), pp. 243-255.
5. *Cities in the Wilderness* (New York, 1938); *The Urban Frontier* (Cambridge, Mass., 1959). Perhaps the strongest theoretical statement of what could be called "urban primary" is Jane Jacobs, *The Economy of Cities* (New York, 1969), particularly chap. 1 entitled "Cities First — Rural Development Later."

The Political Economy of Early Canadian Urban Development

GILBERT A. STELTER

The towns and cities of early Canada were part of a large-scale phenomenon whereby western European empires expanded to the Americas and southeast Asia by establishing colonial outposts. Urban life thus became a significant feature of the Canadian experience long before the dramatic urban growth of the late nineteenth and early twentieth centuries. In fact, the basic essentials of the present network of cities in eastern and central Canada were firmly established by 1850. The manner in which the urban environment was shaped during this early period furnishes clues not only to the nature of early urban development but to the character of colonial life in larger terms. These towns and cities were physical and social entities whose form and structure were determined by a variety of factors which can be regarded as independent variables. I will concentrate particularly on decisions affecting land use. I intend to sum up the key variables with the term "political economy", which has a long tradition of usage in Canadian history (in the works of Harold Innis, for example) simply because I find it difficult to divorce "politics" and "economics" in early Canadian history.[1]

In regard to the significance of the political economy in city-building, several perspectives are particularly useful. One involves the place of the town or city within the larger society. Gideon Sjoberg has effectively argued that cities should be seen as nodes or subsystems within state organizations,

SOURCE: This article is a revised and enlarged version of "The Political Economy of the City-Building-Process: Early Canadian Urban Development", in Derek Fraser and Anthony Sutcliffe, eds., *The Pursuit of Urban History* (London: Edward Arnold, 1983). Reprinted by permission of the editors and the publisher.

8

and that urban types and even physical form will vary with the political and economic differences exhibited by different kinds of nation-states. Sjoberg's claim that political factors such as the rise and fall of empires are among the most important elements in determining the pattern, spread and decline of cities in the pre-industrial world seems to be borne out by early Canadian history.[2] Sjoberg's model is less useful for dealing with another question — the evolution of communities through successive types. A commercial phase is obviously the missing ingredient in his analysis of the transition from feudal to industrial society. While there were traces of feudalism in the foundations of the French Empire in North America, the essential characteristic of the period was commercial. It is important to make a distinction between two stages of commercialism, even though these are not yet clearly definable. The first could be designated as the mercantile commercial phase: towns and cities of early Canada essentially were colonial entrepôts, serving as agencies of imperial trade and control. As in Latin America, the emphasis was on an export economy. In the American colonies, on the other hand, staple production relative to overall production declined in the eighteenth century, because of a new emphasis on production for domestic consumption. I don't have a handy label for the second stage, but it was characterized by interregional and localized trade and artisanal manufacturing for a local market. During this second phase, the largest urban places won a measure of autonomy from direct imperial and provincial control through charters of incorporation. The transition to this second level was clearly evident only by the 1820s in British North America, as much as a century later than similar developments in American cities only a few miles to the south.

Some of the reasons for these different rates of development are suggested by the recently elaborated "dependency theory", worked out to explain the effects of American domination of parts of Latin America, but demonstrated to be relevant for other societies as well.[3] A central point is, that an imperial power literally develops "underdevelopment" in its colonies by using its political and economic power to prevent the emergence of modern forms of government or enterprises inimical to its own interests. Advanced technology and organization are applied to those aspects of development most desirable to imperial interests. The benefits of this arrangement go both to the advanced society and to a small client class within the colony. Direct political control becomes less necessary after the client class is firmly established, for their decisions are made in the context of their dependence.[4]

Towns were the key elements in this process as they became vanguards of French and British imperial expansion to North America from the seventeeth to the early nineteeth centuries. Most of these towns were "planted" in the sense that they were consciously conceived to precede and stimulate more general settlement. Like colonial towns of earlier eras, notably those of Rome and the medieval bastides, early Canadian towns were fairly regular in form, in sharp contrast to the relatively spontaneous and unplanned form of the mother cities of Paris and London.[5] While current European planning ideas were exported to some extent in laying out these colonial towns, this regularity represented the purely functional motives of central control. They were not regarded as works of art.[6] As these places developed, they remained subservient to a strong central state, either French or British, which continued to determine their function and their form in most cases, developing a tradition quite unlike that in the American colonies (and eventually the United States), where local residents and private capitalists were more influential. No one seems to have consciously planned anything as limited as towns or villages in early Canada: they always felt they were founding cities, and named them as such, even when they literally had no population. Most of these places dominate the regional hierarchies of the urban system to the present day, much like the early Viking settlements of southern Ireland, illustrating the long-term stability of an established network.[7] The rural population followed, as did secondary centres of an "organic" nature but these seldom rose very high in the hierarchy.

In the following pages I will outline three stages in the evolution of Canadian cities before 1850 in an attempt to show how urban development was related to changes in the context of the prevailing political economy. These are: (1) the French colony of New France, (2) imperial rivaly and conflict: the conquest of New France and the impact of the American Revolution, (3) British North America within a changing British Empire. Each of these stages represents a distinct approach to two key issues — decision-making and land assignment — which were directly relevant to the formation of the urban environment. As to the question of who makes decisions, it is probably valid to argue that leadership within the social hierarchies of early Canada was determined by the extent to which access to power led directly to the ownership of the means of production, especially land.[8] The place of land was crucial in shaping social relationships. In a study of a portion of the colony of Upper Canada, Leo Johnson has concluded that land "became the medium through which policy makers attempted to change not only the manner in which land was acquired and held, but also the very nature of society itself."[9]

Urban life in Canada began with the tiny settlements planted by the French along the St. Lawrence River early in the seventeenth century (see Map 1). The French had no direct overseas experience in town building when they began to colonize New France, but they had a strong tradition of new town building within their own territory with the "villes neuves" of the eleventh and twelfth centuries, the bastides of the twelfth and thirteenth centuries, and the Renaissance towns. During the seventeenth century the state became more directly involved in the building or redesigning of towns and cities, as in Colbert's founding of Rochefort as an arsenal and naval base or in the rebuilding of La Rochelle, the main port for Canada, as a fortified site along the lines recommended by the great military engineer and planner, Sebastian Vauban.[10] Although the towns of New France were outposts in the North American wilderness, they resembled French provincial towns; informed observers compared Quebec City, for example, with the second rank of French cities: "It is not as nice as Montpellier, but better than Béziers, Nîmes, etc." wrote one of the most celebrated generals, Montcalm.[11] By the mid eighteenth century, Quebec had become a fairly impressive city of 8,000 occupying a magnificent site overlooking the St. Lawrence. For much of the seventeenth and eighteenth centuries, Quebec and Montreal, a western mission post and fur trading centre, represented more than 20 per cent of the colony's total population. This high percentage of urban population was the consequence, as in Latin America, of a highly centralized military, administrative and religious establishment and the centralization resulting from a one-industry economy.

These towns were founded, however, by private companies engaged in the fur trade prior to the state's direct intervention. As such, they could aspire, according to one critical commentator, "to no higher fortune that to be made a storehouse for the skins of dead animals."[12] When Samuel de Champlain founded Quebec on a narrow strand of the St. Lawrence, beneath a great cliff, he regarded it as a temporary, fortified trading post, and such it remained for more than 20 years. His long-term plans called for a city which would serve as a capital of a great empire he envisaged in the interior of the continent. This proposed city, to be located on flat terrain near Quebec, was to be called Ludovica, in honour of the king who would hopefully subsidize its development. Champlain wrote that it was to be "almost as large as St. Denis",[13] a reference to the abbey town near Paris, associated with the monarchy in its problems with the nobility and with Paris. But the monarchy was uninterested in the colony at this stage and the proposed city never materialized. Instead, the temporary site of Quebec developed in an informal manner. By the 1630s, residents "had built houses and were continuing to build houses here and there according to the desires and means of each", but a new governor was determined that "all building hereafter shall be done systematically."[14]

Serious attempts to impose regularity were more evident after the establishment of direct royal control of the colony in the 1660s. Colbert's rigid regulation of French provincial cities like Rochefort was paralleled in New France with new initiatives to redirect what appeared to officials to be scandalously disorganized places. In the absence of municipal institutions, provincial civil officials directed a host of royal surveyors, inspectors and engineers in regulatory and planning functions. From France, Vauban advised local officials that "it is certain that if orders are not laid down to group houses in designated locations, and to organize them into orderly small towns, cities and villages, where properties are enclosed, you will never manage to establish good social control, let alone maintain it."[15] But royal power in this regard in Quebec was limited by the nature of the original land assignment, for the trading company had been granted seigneurial rights and had given or sold land in relatively large parcels to religious institutions and individuals. What amounted to an official general plan could therefore only confirm the existing rough grid in the heavily developed Lower Town. The city above the cliff, Upper Town, was still more manageable, allowing the drawing of a simple baroque design of radiating streets where possible on what looked like an informal medieval system of land use dominated by large institutions (see Figure 1).

The desire for order and symmetry led to a series of regulations concerning the future alignment of streets and houses, as in Paris, whose civil laws were the basis of these regulations in the colonies. An Overseer of Highways, appropriately called the Grand Voyer, was to provide an official alignment before a resident began construction of a building. Judging by the number of times the provincial council passed these regulations, they probably were usually ignored.[16] A concern about the dangers of fire and disease also led to a great number of regulations concerning the quality and material of construction, but some by-laws regulating the height of building and even stylistic details were consciously designed to improve the appearance of the city.[17]

The role of the crown in the internal organization of space was most clearly seen in defining the relationship between fortifications and physical expansion. In spite of attempts to keep the community compact, there was constant pressure for suburban expansion because a good deal of vacant land within the town was held by speculators and institutions. In the late seventeenth century, Governor Frontenac appears to have recognized the impracticality of a major wall around the entire city; he concentrated instead on fortifying his own residence, making it a "shelter where I and what this colony has by way of important people, would be secure."[18] The increasing threat of imperial conflict with the British in the eighteenth century forced a greater commitment to fortifications and renewed efforts to reallocate land within the walls if owners did not use it for building within a specified time. As a result, the religious communities conceded some land for private development. Approved suburban expansion beyond the walls took place in an orderly fashion near the St. Charles River in an area known as St. Roch (see Figure 11). Other suburbs grew by accretion however, near the gates of the city, following the major access routes. Because the defences were to have a clear line of fire for a considerable distance, some buildings in this area were demolished when attacks were expected.[19]

The form of Montreal corresponded more closely than did that of Quebec to what officials regarded as an ideal town, even though the state played only a minor role in its development. Founded in 1642 as a mission post, the town evolved in a spontaneous manner on a relatively level plain next to the St. Lawrence. As the entire area of the town and surrounding region had been granted as a seigneury to the Suplician Order, religious leaders influenced the early form. In the 1670s, the Sulpician superior formalized the rectangular design by laying out several new streets roughly parallel to existing streets, thereby creating a pattern reminiscent of the bastides[20] (see Figure 2). Similar designs were later adopted in the case of Mobile, New Orleans and St. Louis where planning may have imitated consciously the Montreal plan.[21]

Of the major towns of New France, Louisbourg (Figure 3) best represented the planning philosophy of French officials. Chosen as the site of France's Atlantic naval fortress early in the eighteenth century, Louisbourg was planned and built according to the principles of Vauban with an elaborate series of fortifications surrounding a gridiron street pattern and lot sizes, which were kept small, in order to give priority to military and government functions. Louisbourg became the quintessential baroque city — the army barracks replaced the monastery, the open square was a parade ground, not a market as at Quebec or Montreal. The fortifications surrounding the governor's residence, as at Quebec, sometimes gave the impression of protecting imperial officials from the local population as well as protecting the town in general. Most of the wage labourers associated with the fishery lived in informal suburbs beyond the wall, near the cod drying platforms, while their employers lived within the city itself.[22]

A second stage of town building in early Canada began with the intensification of the imperial rivalry between Britain and France. The founding of Halifax in 1749 symbolized the attempt to create a countervailing force to Louisbourg. In the manner of the plantation towns of Ulster, Halifax was also designed to subjugate and assimilate a hostile, non-urban local population, in this case the Acadian French and Indians of Nova Scotia. The overall scheme was planned and directed by officials in Britain who induced over 2,000 settlers to accompany a military contingent to the defensible harbour at Chebucto Bay. Government engineers laid out a small gridiron in the baroque fashion; in the centre was a square — the Grand Parade — as a setting for the spectacle of drilling troops (see Figure 4). The result was an instant, State-built town and fortress. Within less than a year, the local governor proudly outlined his version of imperial town building to his superiors.

> . . . without money you could have no Town — no Settlement and indeed no Settlers. Tis very certain that the public money cleared the ground, built the town, secured it . . . The money is laid out in building Forts, Barracks, Storehouses, Hospitals, Church, Wharf, Public Works, all that seem absolutely necessary.[23]

Land in the townsite was to be divided equally, in the manner of the medieval bastides: in this case it was drawn for by lot by heads of households and single residents. The governor soon reported lots were worth 50 guineas because of the stimulation of public works spending; without it, he wryly estimated, "lots would be given for a Gallon of Rum."[24] Because the townsite was the product of military surveyors with their own priorities, subsequent development was hampered by the narrow blocks and the small dimensions of the building lots. Then too, residents later charged that the military laid excessive claim to land within and surrounding the townsite for military purposes.[25]

Power within the community was concentrated in an alliance of the military leaders, imperial administrative officials and a closely associated wholesale merchant class. The latter two groups dominated the provincial government, imposing a highly centralized rule of the Halifax elite over the province. An example was the prohibition of the development of a form of town government in the interior of the province settled by New Englanders, with the requirement that all local officials be appointed by the Courts of Quarter Sessions which were made up of magistrates appointed from Halifax.[26] The spatial organization of the town reflected its social structure; as at Quebec, Montreal and Louisbourg, remnants of an older tradition were reflected in the social geography. The elite and its activities were concentrated at the centre while the lower classes spread into the outskirts of the town.[27]

The culminations of the British-French rivalry had dramatic consequences for the towns of New France. Louisbourg was captured after a long siege and bombardment, its elaborate fortifications destroyed, its population dispersed. Quebec fell after a siege and the destruction of many of its major buildings. Montreal capitulated and emerged virtually unscathed. The full-scale social implications of the Conquest were not to be felt until the massive British immigration of the nineteenth century. During the eighteenth century, the small number of British conquerors allowed the French Canadians to keep their language, religion, civil law and land system because the ties of aristocratic, monarchial tradition were stronger with the French Canadians than were the ties of blood and language with the increasingly rebellious colonies to the south. Ironically, Quebec and Montreal became British imperial strongholds, the lynchpins in a net set of armed conflicts. During the 1770s, invading Americans captured Montreal but Quebec remained firm; the conservative French Canadians did not join the Americans in their attempt to throw off the British yoke.

The conquest of French Canada provided the first major component of what would become the Canadian people. The second was the product of the American Revolution for that conflict resulted in a large influx of refugees politically opposed to American republicanism. They founded a host of new towns and a new province in the Atlantic region as well as a new province on the western frontier, Upper Canada. The political propensities of these loyalist refugees corresponded closely to that of the ruling British officials, and together they set the tone for the development of British North America for the next 50 years. The bulk of the almost 40,000 refugees landed in Nova Scotia, where British officials aided them in setting up several instant towns. Gridiron town plots were hastily subdivided and refugees drew for both town lots and agricultural land in the interior. In some cases these camps became successful commercial centres. Saint John, located at a strategic site at the mouth of the St. John River, became the commercial centre of a new province, New Brunswick, although the capital was located in a loyalist outpost in the interior, Fredericton, more consciously designed to represent a combination of military, administrative and commercial elements. Other instant towns such as Shelburne, St. Andrew's and Sydney did not achieve significant commercial success in spite of considerable government support and overblown local optimism.

Because Saint John seemed to have the greatest potential as a town, competition for space there was intense. About 10,000 refugees had registered by 1784 for the food, shelter, tools and building materials the government provided. The town had been surveyed into two grids (see Figure 5) despite the rocky terrain, with the first lots of a generous size. As more refugees flooded in, officials subdivided some of the original lots, in some cases reducing lots to one-sixteenth of their original size, but some of the more influential early arrivals were able to maintain their hold on the highly desirable waterfront lots.[28] The failure to redistribute land equitably became a source of bitter factionalism to the point where the provincial governor granted a charter of incorporation, the first in British North America, as a means of putting an end to disturbances and to promote law and order. He assured his superiors that "My object therefore was to obtain this end without conceding such liberties as might tend to abridge the Royal Prerogative."[29]

The loyalist settlement of the western frontier, Upper Canada, was not channelled through towns to the same extent as in the Atlantic provinces.

Kingston (see Figure 6) was founded as a refugee centre but most arrivals went directly to a pioneering rural existence. Even by 1821, the urban population of Upper Canada (based on those in places of 1,000 or more) was only 3.6 per cent of the provincial total.[30] And yet, urban development in Upper Canada was more consciously planned, both at the level of the entire system and at the specific site level, by imperial officials than was the case in other provinces of British North America. The first general scheme was an effort to combine town and country planning in a systematic fashion as in some American precedents, notably Savannah, Georgia. From his headquarters in Quebec, the Governor of the Canadas instructed his surveyors to lay out a series of townships 10 miles square incorporating towns one mile square[31] (see Figure 7). The rigid model quickly became unworkable in the realities of the wilderness, forcing the local provincial official, Lt-Governor John Graves Simcoe, to devise his own "system", as he called it (see Figure 8). He believed that a network of towns, combining military and civilian settlement, would "create a solid and permanent system, which would never spring up merely from Agriculture, and be late indeed, if left to the culture of Mercantile Monopoly."[32] The answer was to be found in the ancient tradition of town building through military establishments, he wrote to his superiors: "Following the great Masters of the World, the Romans of old, I propose to consider the Winter Stations of these companies as the Germs of so many well affected Colonial Cities."[33] Actual settlement patterns corresponded fairly closely to Simcoe's proposed network of towns and connecting roads, even though his superiors did not always accept his designation of function for particular places, demanding, for example, that Toronto (York) become the provincial capital and that the major naval base be located at Kingston.

The original townsite of Kingston had been drawn up in the ubiquitous grid with lots of equal size, but when Toronto was laid out as a meagre grid of 10 blocks, almost 10 years later, the system of land assignment incorporated Simcoe's desire to re-establish the British class system in North America. Lots at the front of the town facing the harbour were the largest and were granted to the most important government and military officials. Control was to be exercised over the size and the architectural styles of houses on these lots. Only "in the backstreets and alleys", wrote one sarcastic critic, "would the tinkers and tailors . . . be allowed to consult their taste and circumstances in the structure of the habitations, upon lots of one-tenth of an acre."[34] In addition to organizing the grid itself, Simcoe also ensured a measure of government control over future expansion by reserving large contiguous tracts for public and military purposes. Perhaps most significant, however, was the creation of a suburban plan whereby future expansion of Toronto would contribute to the creation of a hierarchically structured society. Some 32 park lots of 100 acres each, located immediately to the north of the townsite, were granted to government and military leaders (see Figure 9). When the town grew in the nineteenth century, the profits from the development of this land did in fact help create the elite that Simcoe believed this society required.[35]

As in other parts of British North America, officials were reluctant to grant any measure of local self-government to these new communities, for they were guided by the belief that local autonomy had precipitated the American Revolution. Although they admitted that the incorporation of towns "might be directed to very useful purposes which could not so well be obtained by any other medium", incorporation was simply too dangerous "after the Experience we had at Home during Lord Shaftebury's time and in the dawn of Jack Wilke's patriotism."[36] The form imposed, therefore, was the traditional English system of magistrates, closely tied to a centralized power structure in Toronto through patronage. This form of government proved totally inadequate to meet the needs of growing communities, but petitions from urban places for more autonomy were consistently turned down before the 1830s.

Compared to American cities after the Revolution, most Canadian urban places were heavily fortified, with large garrisons integrally connected to the community's economy and social life. Much of this preoccupation with defence was based on the well-founded fear of American invasions, such as during the War of 1812 when Toronto and Niagara were captured and burned. Defensive strategy centred on the power of the Royal Navy, operating out of Halifax, and the impregnability of Quebec's walls, built to withstand a major assault. Most of the fortifications at Halifax were built after 1790 on citadel hill and were designed to command the harbour (see Figure 10). Quebec's defences also included a citadel overlooking the St. Lawrence, but an elaborate wall and gates made it the most heavily defended spot in North America (see Figure 11). Kingston was chosen as the military centre of Upper Canada; a series of defensive structures centred on Fort Henry, constructed across the harbour from the town (see Figure 13). The significance of the military presence for the development of these communities has not been analysed in any detail as yet, but it might be noted that the earliest major city in each region became the defensive centre, but in each case was surpassed in size by more commercially oriented places with only minor military establishments. Montreal dismantled its wall in the early nineteenth century to facilitate expansion, while Saint John and Toronto had garrisons posted in small forts in their vicinity.

The defensive concerns of Canadian communities reflected the vulnerable position of the British North American colonies in relation to the United States. It also pointed to the inescapable fact that these colonies were artificially maintained as a separate entity from the United States by the British imperial presence. In economic terms these colonies did not appear to be a natural unit, but seemed to be merely what was left over after the American Revolution had been completed. The towns of Upper Canada, for example, were forced to maintain transatlantic ties via a circuitous internal route, the St. Lawrence, frozen for almost half of each year, even though communication with Britain and Europe could be made more quickly and inexpensively through American ports.

A third stage of town and city building slowly emerged in the period from 1820 to 1850, characterized by significant developments in the political economy, in population growth and in the technology of transportation and the workplace. Britain's move to free trade abandoned those colonial clients whose wealth depended on operating within a protected system, and its move to reform the colonial legislatures after the rebellions of 1837 loosened the hold of the imperially oriented oligarchies. Increased immigration from Britain led to more rapid urban growth — the urban proportion reached 14 per cent of the total population in most of the provinces — providing a larger local market for trade and for artisanal manufacturing. Technological improvements such as the steam-boat made the river west of Montreal a more viable internal link and opened up other parts of the interior to rural and urban settlement. As a sign of their new maturity, cities such as Montreal, Toronto and Halifax became less dependent on their roles as colonial entrepots and aggressively sought to increase their own commercial sphere of influence.[37]

The changes in the structure of local government were an indication of what was changing and what remained of an older order. The need to move beyond the traditional system of justices of the peace was most urgently felt in the largest centres such as Quebec, Montreal and Halifax, but the major break-through came in the newest province, Upper Canada. Toronto's achievement of incorporation was standardized at the provincial level in successive stages, the 1841 and 1849 Acts, ending the administration by appointed justices and thereby reducing central administrative control over local affairs.[38] Much the same provisions were adopted for the cities of Lower Canada and in Halifax where incorporation was finally granted after a bitter struggle between reformers and the local oligarchy. But the coming of municipal government is not to be equated with the introduction of American majoritarian democracy. The property qualifications were high enough to restrict the franchise to a minority of adult males. The prevailing political philosophy continued to emphasize a balanced social order, a tradition of deference to authority, and especially a rejection of popular sovereignty of the American type.[39]

Government involvement in land assignment and planning appears to have diminished during this period, but the direction of development was influenced by previous decisions and traditions. In Montreal (see Figure 12), the long, narrow shape of the original seigneurial grants affected the street and block pattern of the suburbs. While the French Canadian majority had been substantially reduced (to 54 per cent in 1825) and had been effectively shut out of high-level commerce and industry by an English-speaking elite, they held two-thirds of the real estate and made their mark by influencing the nature and timing of physical expansion.[40] In Toronto, the pattern of suburban growth was determined by the previous grants to a non-commercial administrative elite. Each park lot was developed individually, some with small lots and narrow streets, others with large amounts of public space and wide avenues (see Figure 14). In the newer towns on the western frontier, like Hamilton, the elite which originally owned most of the land in and around the city sold their holdings to promoters who in turn sold to small-scale developers and builders. With no regulations, and with lots dispersed over a wide area, development was a decentralized process resulting in a fragmented pattern of urban growth.[41] Exceptions to the monotonous grid, which proved popular both with the colonial administration and the land speculator, were rare, but included places such as Guelph, 60 miles west of Toronto, and Goderich, another 100 miles further west (see Figure 15), designed by the Canada Company in 1827 and 1829 to stimulate development of their extensive land holdings.

It is difficult to generalize about the internal organization of mid nineteenth-century Canadian cities because they represented diverse ages, functions and cultural backgrounds. What they had in common included the general political system, which, incidentally, produced standardized, rather pompous government buildings in each provincial capital. All the major places were ports with most of their economic activity concentrated at the harbour. In an age of commerce, their commitment to it varied, however, for the fortified places were partially dependent on their military function. In terms of social geography, elements of the mercantile town lingered well into the nineteenth century in the older cities, while spatial segregation based on class was less apparent in the newer cities of the frontier.

My central argument in this paper has been that the political economy of a society is a key independent variable in urban development. Although I have not attempted any full-scale comparison with American cities here, it seems clear to me that the border did make a difference in the building of cities, particularly in the nature of land assignment and in local decision-making. This leads me to question some general assumptions in the historical and social science literature about the existence of a North American city type, with the Canadian portion at most a minor variant, with perhaps a time-lag of a generation or so.[42] I have dealt with an early period in which the differences are clear, and it could be argued that because of the close connections for the past century, these differences have become blurred.[43] But as Jim Dyos and Michael Wolff put it, "inertia is part of the dynamic of urban change: the structures outlast the people who put them there, and impose restraints on those who have to adopt them to their own use."[44] Obviously the early surveys and divisions of land and the original locations of residential and commercial properties imposed a measure of permanence on the form of the city. So, too, did the political structures and values rooted in the initial period of rapid urbanization. Taking these more seriously in our study of the city-building process appears to be a necessary task.

NOTES

1. For a balanced description of the political economy of Harold Innis, see Carl Berger, *The Writing of Canadian History* (Toronto: Oxford University Press, 1976), pp. 85-111. During the past decade a growing body of literature has been spawned by an effort to combine the insights of Innis and Marx; some of the most important examples are R.T. Naylor, "The Rise and Fall of the Third Empire of the St. Lawrence," in Gary Teeple, ed., *Capitalism and the National Question in Canada* (Toronto: University of Toronto Press, 1972), pp. 1-42 and C.B. Macpherson, "By Innis Out of Marx: The Revival of Canadian Political Economy," *Canadian Journal of Political and Social Theory*, 3 (No. 2, 1979.) For a recent rejection of the viability of this theoretical combination, see David McNally, "Staple Theory as Commodity Fetishism: Marx, Innis and Canadian Political Economy", *Studies in Political Economy*, No. 6 (Autumn, 1981), pp. 35-63.

2. "The Rise and Fall of Cities: A Theoretical Perspective", *International Journal of Comparative Sociology* 4 (1963), 107-8; *The Preindustrial City* (New York: Free Press, 1960).

3. Paul Baran, *The Political Economy of Growth* (New York: Monthly Review Press, 1974).

4. A.G. Frank, "The Development of Underdevelopment", in Robert Rhodes, ed., *Imperialism and Underdevelopment* (New York: Monthly Review Press, 1970).

5. James E. Vance, Jr., *This Scene of Man: The Role and Structure of the City in the Geography of Western Civilization* (New York: Harper's, 1977), p. 230.

6. The Latin American tradition was even stronger in terms of regularity and context. See for example, Jorge Hardoy, "European Urban Forms in the Fifteenth to Seventeenth Centuries and Their Utilization in Latin America", in R.P. Schaedel, J.E. Hardoy, and N.S. Kinzer, eds., *Urbanization in the Americas from its Beginnings to the Present* (The Hague: Mouton, 1978); and Woodrow Borah, "European Cultural Influence in the Formation of the First Plan for Urban Centres that has Lasted to our Time", in R.P. Schaedel, *et al.*, *Urbanizacion y proceso social en America* (Lima: Instituto de Estadios Peruanos, 1972). See also, for the larger colonial context, Anthony D. King, "Exporting 'Planning': The Colonial and Neo-Colonial Experience", *Urbanism Past and Present* 5 (1977-78), pp. 12-22.

7. For a discussion of the stability of the Canadian urban system, see James Simmons, "The Evolution of the Canadian Urban System", in Artibise and Stelter, eds., *The Usable Urban Past: Planning and Politics in the Modern Canadian City* (Toronto: Macmillan, 1979), pp. 9-33.

8. Latin American historians have interpreted social structure in these terms for some time. See for example, Richard Morse, "The Urban Worlds of Latin and Anglo America: Prefatory

Thoughts'', in Woodrow Borah, Jorge Hardoy and Gilbert Stelter, eds., *Urbanization in the Americas: The Background in Comparative Perspective* (Ottawa: National Museum of Man, 1981).

9. "Land Policy, Population Growth and Social Structure in the Home District, 1793-1851", *Ontario History*, 63 (1971), pp. 41-60.

10. Josef Konvitz, *Cities and the Sea: Port City Planning in Early Modern Europe* (Baltimore, Johns Hopkins, 1978), 112-22.

11. Letter of Montcalm, 16 April, 1757, in *Report of the Public Archives of Canada* (Ottawa: King's Printer, 1929), p. 55.

12. Father Lejeune, 1636, in R.G. Thwaites, *Jesuit Relations* (New York: Pagent [1896-1901], 1959) IX, p. 132.

13. H.P. Biggar, ed., *The Works of Samuel de Champlain* (Toronto: 1922-26), II, p. 327.

14. *Jesuit Relations* IX, p. 136.

15. L. Dechêne, ed., *La correspondance de Vauban relative du Canada* (Quebec: Ministere des Affaires culturelles, 1968), p. 11.

16. Peter Moogk, *Building a House in New France* (Toronto: McClelland and Stewart, 1977), pp. 13-18.

17. Marc Lafrance, "Evolution physique et politiques urbaines: Quebec sous le regime française," *Urban History Review* 3-75 (February, 1976), pp. 3-22.

18. Cited in William Eccles, *Frontenac: The Courtier Governor* (Toronto McClelland and Stewart, 1958), p. 245.

19. Lafrance, *op. cit.*, and Moogk, *op. cit.*

20. Dollier de Casson, *History of Montreal, 1640-72* (London: Dent, 1928). Jean-Claude Marsan, *Montreal en evolution* (Montreal: Fides, 1974), chap. 1.

21. John Reps, *Town Planning in Frontier America* (Princeton: Princeton University Press, 1969), pp. 70-105.

22. Margaret Fortier, "The Development of the Fortifications at Louisbourg", *Canada, An Historical Magazine* 1 (June, 1974), pp. 16-31.

23. Governor Cornwallis to Lords of Trade and Plantations, April 30, 1750, in *Selections From the Public Documents of Nova Scotia* (Halifax, 1869), p. 608.

24. *Ibid.*

25. T.B. Akins, *History of Halifax City* (Belleville: Mika, 1973 reprint of 1895 edn.), p. 67.

26. D.C. Harvey, "The Struggle for the New England Form of Township Government in Nova Scotia", Canadian Historical Association, *Annual Report,* 1933, pp. 15-22.

27. Based on my analysis of the 1792 assessment rolls for Halifax and vicinity, located in the Public Archives of Nova Scotia, Halifax.

28. J.S. MacKinnon, "The Development of Local Government in the City of Saint John, 1785-1795", MA thesis (University of New Brunswick, 1968), p. 19.

29. Cited in *ibid.*, p. 30.

30. For a more detailed account, see G.A. Stelter, "Urban Planning and Development in Upper Canada", in Borah, Hardoy and Stelter, eds., *Urbanization in the Americas*.

31. *Seventeenth Report of the Department of Public Records and Archives of Ontario, 1928* (Toronto: King's Printer, 1929), pp. 63-7, 108, 200.

32. Simcoe to Henry Dundas, June 21, 1794, in E.A. Cruikshank, ed., *The Correspondence of Lt. Gov. John Graves Simcoe* (Toronto: Ontario Historical Society 1923-31), vol. II, p. 284.

33. Simcoe to Dundas, 12 August, 1791, *ibid.*, vol. I, p. 44.

34. C.E. Cartwright, ed., *Life and Letters of the Late Hon. Richard Cartwright* (Toronto: Belford 1876), pp. 54-5.

35. Peter Goheen, *Victorian Toronto, 1850-1900: Pattern and Process of Growth* (Chicago, University of Chicago Geography Series, 1970), pp. 53-4.

36. Chief Justice Osgoode to Simcoe, 30 January, 1795, cited in J.H. Aitchison, "The

Development of Local Government in Upper Canada, 1783-1850'', PhD thesis (University of Toronto, 1953), p. 548.

37. J.M.S. Careless, ''Metropolis and Region: The Interplay Between City and Region in Canadian History Before 1914'', *Urban History Review* 3-78 (February, 1979), pp. 99-118.

38. J.H. Aitchison, ''The Municipal Corporations Act of 1849'', *Canadian Historical Review* 30 (1949), pp. 107-22.

39. W.L. Morton, ''The Extension of the Franchise in Canada, A Study in Democratic Nationalism', Canadian Historical Association *Annual Report*, 1943, pp. 72-81.

40. Paul-Andre Linteau and Jean-Claude Robert, ''Land Ownership and Society in Montreal: An Hypothesis'', in this volume.

41. Michael Doucet, ''The Role of the *Spectator* in Shaping Attitudes Towards Land in Hamilton, Ontario, 1847-1881''. *Histoire sociale* 11 (1979), pp. 431-43.

42. This is the assumption of an otherwise excellent work, Michael Katz, *The People of Hamilton, Canada West* (Cambridge, Mass., Harvard University Press, 1975).

43. For an effective argument that differences continue to exist because of differing historical traditions, see John Mercer, ''On Continentalism, Distinctiveness, and Comparative Urban Geography: Canadian and American Cities'', *Canadian Geographer* 23 (1979), pp. 119-39.

44. H.J. Dyos and Michael Wolff, eds., *The Victorian City* (London: Routledge and Kegan Paul, 1973), II, p. 893.

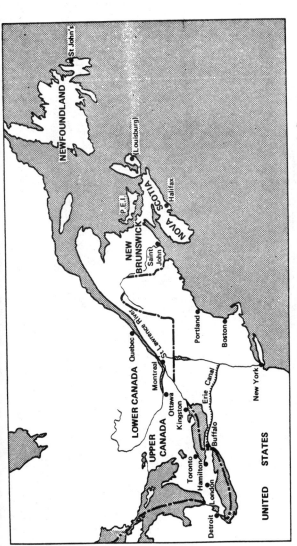

Major Urban Centers of British North America in the Early Nineteenth Century

The provinces of Lower and Upper Canada were created from the province of Quebec (originally New France) and its western frontier in 1791. The province of Upper Canada officially became Canada West in 1841 and Ontario in 1867 with the confederation of the provinces into the Dominion of Canada. Lower Canada became Canada East in 1841 and reverted to the name Quebec in 1867. In the following pages, urban development is illustrated in three stages.

  I   The First Stage: Town Building in New France
 II   The Second Stage: Town Building as an Aspect of British Colonization.
III   The Third Stage: British North American Towns and Cities.

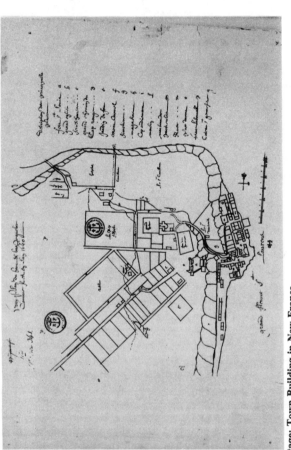

I.   The First Stage: Town Building in New France

1. *A fur trading post becomes a colonial capital: Quebec in 1660*
   Founded in 1608 by a private fur company, the town of Quebec developed first in a haphazard fashion in Lower Town, below the cliff (below). Major religious and political institutions later located above the cliff in Upper Town. This plan, drawn in 1660 by Jean Bourdon, a government engineer, surveyor and public works administrator, was an attempt to establish regularity in the manner of contemporary European baroque styles.

Source: Reproduced from a copy in the National Map Collection, Public Archives of Canada, of the original in the Archives nationales de France.

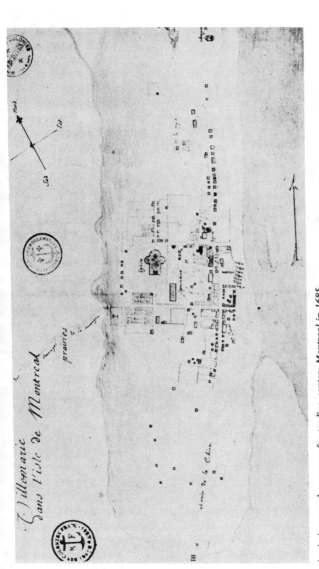

2. *A mission post becomes a fur trading center: Montreal in 1685* Montreal was founded by a French missionary society in 1642 and developed somewhat more regularly than Quebec, perhaps because of the level site. The rectangular shape of the town site was formalized in 1673 by the Sulpician superior, Dollier de Casson, who supervised the laying out of several new streets such as Notre Dame, parallel to the original street, St. Paul's. This map shows the prominent position of the first parish church, Notre Dame, in the evolving community.

Source: Reproduced from a copy in the National Map Collection, Public Archives of Canada, of the original in the Archives nationales de France.

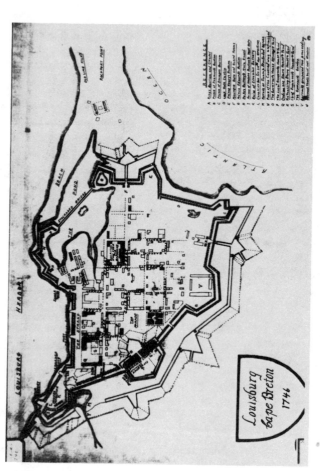

3. *France's colonial fortress, Louisbourg*

This heavily fortified town was France's major outpost in the Atlantic region and corresponded closely to what government officials thought a colonial town should look like. It was begun about 1714 to combine strategic and commercial functions. Captured by British forces in 1745 it is shown here while it was under occupation. Restored to the French in 1748, it was recaptured in 1758 and destroyed.

Source: Detail of "Louisbourg, Cape Breton, 1746". Reproduced from a 1912 transcript in the National Map Collection, Public Archives of Canada.

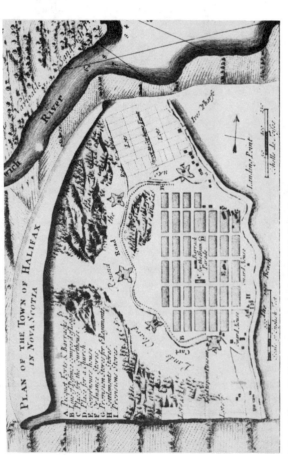

PLAN OF THE TOWN OF HALIFAX
IN NOVA SCOTIA

A Trigonct Forts Barracks
B Line for the temporary Hospitals
C Place for the Church
D Place for a Church
E Governours house
F Ordnance Stores
G Ground laid out for Remnants
H Settlements Stores
I Provisions Stores

II. The Second Stage: Town Building as an Aspect of British Colonization

4. Britain's colonial fortress: Halifax in 1750

Halifax was designed by British officials in 1749 to counter the power of Louisbourg and to spearhead the British colonization of Nova Scotia. It represented the current Georgian style of British planning with a regular grid focussing on a central square called the Grand Parade. This map shows some of the developments which had taken place during the first year, including a ring of rough fortifications, a church on the square and suburban lots laid out to the north.

Source: Detail of a map of Halifax's immediate surroundings published by John Rocque, in 1750 and reproduced in an atlas in Nuremburg, 1756. National Map Collection, Public Archives of Canada.

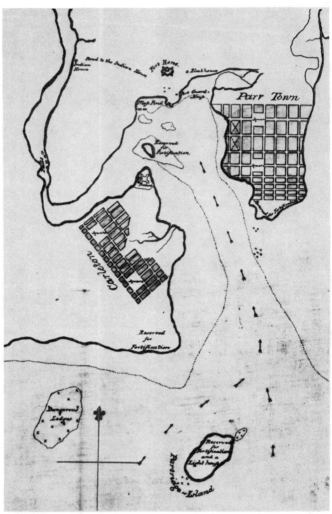

5. *A loyalist town in the Atlantic colonies: Saint John in 1784*
   Saint John was hastily laid out as two grids in 1783 to accommodate the more than
   5,000 refugees from the American Revolution who arrived at the harbour that year.
   Its primary function was commercial; fortifications were limited to two small forts.
   Source: Detail of ''Plan of St. John's Harbour; c. 1784.'' Reproduced from a
   transcript in the National Map Collection, Public Archives of Canada, the original
   in the British Museum.

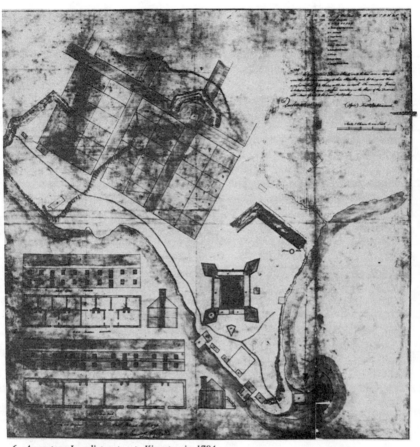

6. *A western Loyalist outpost: Kingston in 1784*
Kingston was laid out in 1784 to act as a staging area for loyalists taking up agricultural land in the western portion of what remained of Britain's North American colonies after the American Revolution. The tiny grid was located next to the old French Fort Frontenac but was quickly expanded as Kingston became the main commercial centre on the western frontier.

Source: "Plan of Old Fort Frontenac and Town Plot of Kingston", Public Archives of Ontario, Toronto.

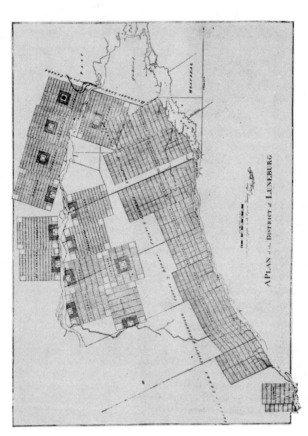

A PLAN of the District of LUNEBURG

7. *A utopian scheme for settling the frontier*

This plan for the general settlement of what became western Lower Canada and eastern Upper Canada came from the governor's office in the colonial capital, Quebec City, in the late 1780s. It was an attempt to combine town and country planning formally, with town plots of one mile square set within townships ten miles square. Shown here are proposed towns/townships north of the Ottawa River (top); those townships along the St. Lawrence (below) presumably were already partially settled on more conventional patterns. The scheme proved too rigid and was quickly abandoned.

Source: Public Archives of Ontario

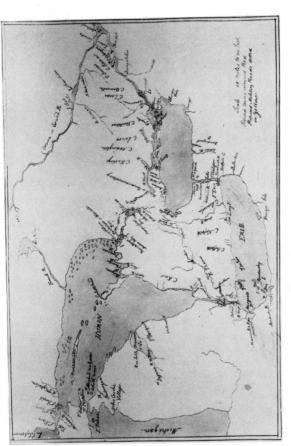

8. *Simcoe's "system" of towns and cities for Upper Canada*

This rough sketch may be Lt. Governor John Graves Simcoe's earliest conception of his plan for Upper Canada. It accompanied his report No. 19 of January 27, 1794 to colonial officials in Britain. It was a conscious attempt to emulate the ancient Roman tradition of frontier settlement by means of semi-military towns connected with roads. His proposed towns were underlined in red and included the recently laid out York (Toronto), London, Chatham and Pennatanga (Penetanguishene). Proposed roads were indicated by dotted yellow lines and indicated Yonge Street north from York and Dundas Road west from York to London. Note the distorted conception Simcoe had of the shape of the western Ontario peninsula which made him think the site of London was more central than it was in reality.

Source: A small sketch simply identified as "Map of Ontario 1794", Public Record Office, London.

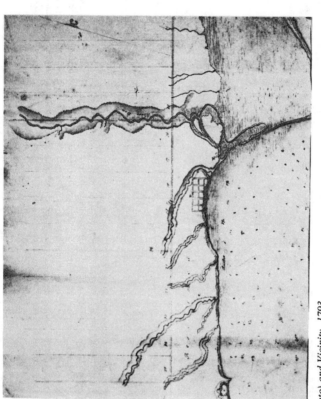

9. *Plan of York (Toronto) and Vicinity, 1793*

This compact little ten-block grid (D) was laid out on orders from Lt. Governor Simcoe on a much more modest scale than had earlier been envisioned. The site was located on a well protected harbour and was to be guarded by a fort to be built at the western entry to the harbour (C). To the north of the townsite can be seen the faint outlines of some of the 32 park lots of 100 acres each which were granted to government and military officials.

Source: Detail of ''Plan of York Harbour, 1793 by A. Aitken,'' Public Record Office, London.

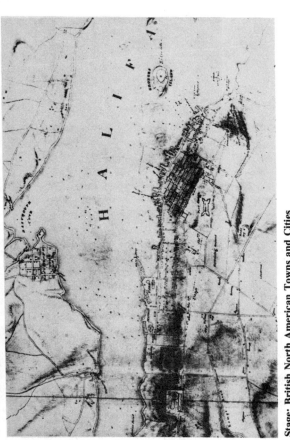

III. The Third Stage: British North American Towns and Cities

10. *Britain's Atlantic fortress: Halifax in 1826*

As a garrison town and naval base, Halifax was closely tied to the ebb and flow of imperial defense requirements during a series of wars — the Seven Years War, The American Revolution, the Napoleonic Wars and the War of 1812. New construction projects for military buildings and fortifications included the massive works at the citadel, (named Fort George in this map), the Naval Yard and other harbour installations. By 1851 Halifax had also established itself as a commercial centre heavily involved in the carrying trade, with a population of 20,749. On this map residential growth to the south (right) and especially to the north (left) is evident and Dartmouth has emerged across the bay.

Source: Detail of ''Halifax and Dartmouth in 1826,'' Public Record Office, London.

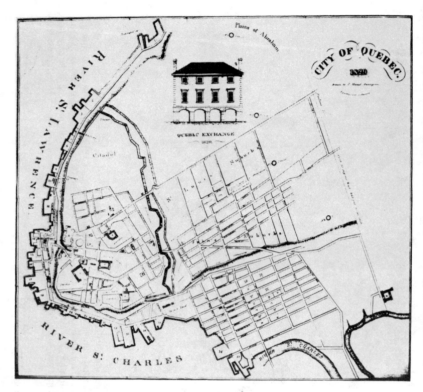

11. *Quebec City in 1829*

During the early nineteenth century Quebec's basic functions were the export of fish products, the maintaining of a large military garrison, and shipbuilding. The map clearly illustrates the spatial dimensions of these functions; the dense system of wharves along the St. Lawrence River in Lower Town (left); the walled Upper Town (centre), with much of the space reserved for the military, such as the citadel, or by religious institutions; the residential suburbs to the west (right), including St. Roch, where the workers in the city's ship yards were concentrated. Quebec, with a population of about 25,000 in 1829, was being supplanted as the major city in British North America by its rival to the west, Montreal.

Source. "City of Quebec, 1829, drawn by J. Hamel, surveyor," in George Bourne, *The Picture of Quebec* (Quebec; D. and J. Smillie, 1829).

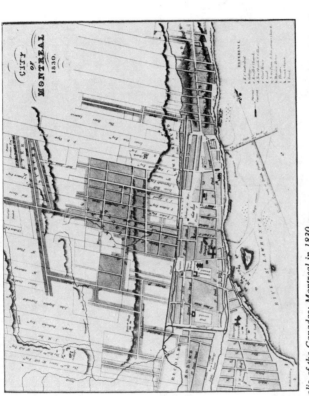

12. *The future metropolis of the Canadas: Montreal in 1830*
Montreal's rapid growth was the product of its commercial expansion. On the map shown here, the wharves are still small and primitive, but the introduction of the steamboat, which overcame the problems of down-stream navigation, allowed Montreal to become an ocean port during the next two decades. By 1851 its population was over 57,000. The map of 1830 indicates the extent to which suburban development beyond the original townsite was shaped by the long, narrow plots of the original seigneurial grants.

Source: Joseph Bouchette, *The British Dominions in North America*, vol. I (London, 1831), p. 217.

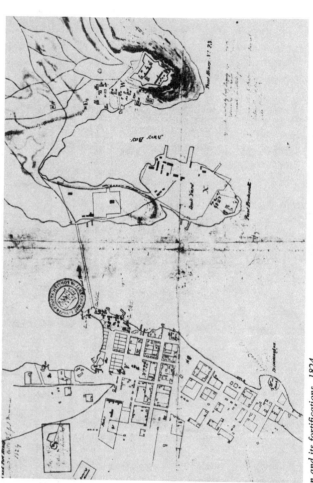

13. *Kingston and its fortifications, 1824*

During the first twenty-five years of the nineteenth century, Kingston was not only Upper Canada's major defensive site, it was also the leading commercial center, closely tied to Montreal and its growing empire. The map indicates the location and extent of fortifications in the harbour at Point Frederick and especially, the immense Fort Henry. A second grid had been added to the townsite, forming a triangular space between the grids which was used for a market place and church.

Source: Detail of "Plan of Kingston, Upper Canada, showing the site proposed for constructing a bridge between that place and Fort Henry", National Map Collection, Public Archives of Canada.

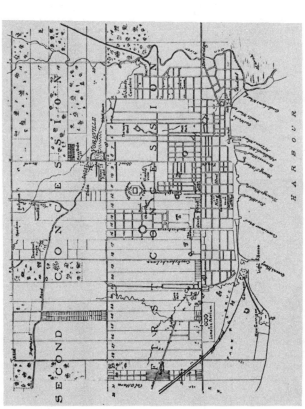

14. *The new western metropolis: Toronto in 1851*
    The city shown here had a population of over 30,000. It was a provincial capital but also a major commercial center, serving the requirements of a growing agricultural hinterland. The city had developed in an inverted T shape, with King and Queen Streets the major thoroughfares parallel to the harbour, and Yonge Street extending north beyond the city limits to the village of Yorkville. As each park lot was developed independently, a wide variety of block sizes and street patterns had emerged.

Source: Detail of "Part of York, 1851," drawn by J.A. Brown. Reproduced from a transcript in the Metropolitan Toronto Public Library.

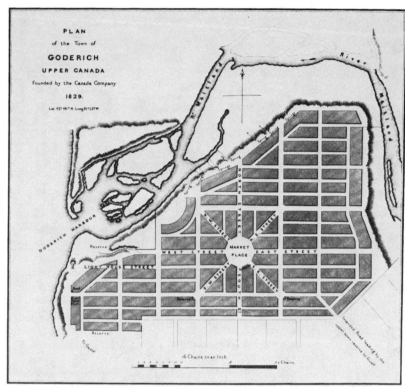

15. *The design of a land company town: the Goderich plan of 1829*
   Most Canadian towns and cities were laid out on a grid pattern. Exceptions include the
   Canada Company towns of Guelph and Goderich, shown here, designed by the
   superintendent of the land company, John Galt. Galt probably chose these relatively
   unconventional plans in order to attract attention to his company's land holdings in Upper
   Canada. As Galt was very impressed with the commercial success of mid-western American
   cities, he may have used the plan of Indianapolis as a model for Goderich, and the plan of
   Buffalo as a model for Guelph. The plans were generous enough in size to accommodate
   growth in each place for more than a century.

   Source: Bouchette, *British Dominions*, I, p. 117.

Land Ownership and Society in Montreal: An Hypothesis*

PAUL-ANDRÉ LINTEAU AND JEAN-CLAUDE ROBERT

The question of land ownership in cities is a neglected aspect of Quebec history. Historians have dealt with the questions of capital investment in trade and manufacturing, but have not analyzed that portion of capital used for the acquisition of land in Quebec's urban areas.[1] One of the reasons for this neglect is that the study of land ownership and its relation to social structure requires prolonged and painstaking work and the deployment of considerable resources. Despite these difficulties, however, research in this area is essential to an understanding of urban development in Quebec. This article presents a hypothesis on the role of land ownership in Montreal and examines the part played by the French-Canadian bourgeoisie in investments in this sector. The article is intended as a point of departure for other researchers; it will need verification and refinement through the application of specific case studies.

The article is divided into four parts. First, the question of land ownership

SOURCE: This study is a product of the Research Group on Montreal Society in the Nineteenth Century, directed by Jean-Paul Bernard, Paul-André Linteau, and Jean-Claude Robert of the Department of History of the University of Quebec at Montreal. It was first published as "Propriété Foncière et Société à Montréal: une hypothèse," *Revue d'histoire de l'amérique française*, Vol. 28, no. 1 (juin, 1974). The translated version of the article presented here is published by permission of the authors and the original publisher.

* The research for this article was made possible by a grant from the Quebec Ministry of Education. The authors also wish to thank Jean-Paul Bernard, Louise Dechêne and Normand Séguin for their valuable comments.

in Montreal is placed in the judicial framework of early nineteenth century Quebec. This is followed by a description of the most important sources for the study of property ownership. The third part is an examination of property ownership in Montreal in 1825, a year for which fairly accurate data exists.[2] Finally, a hypothesis concerning the role of capital investment in land in Montreal is stated.

THE JUDICIAL FRAMEWORK

The judicial framework for property ownership in Montreal was the seigneurial regime, regulated by the *Coutume de Paris*. This system remained until the second half of the nineteenth century, when a new framework came into existence with the abolition of the seigneurial regime and the passage of a new Civil Code. The city of Montreal was part of the seigneury of the same name, from 1663 the property of the Seminary of Saint-Sulpice of Paris and, from 1764, of the Seminary of Saint-Sulpice of Montreal.[3]

Under the seigneurial regime, land was subject to two types of ownership. The first, called *domaine utile*, corresponded to the property of the *censitaire*, who received the product of the land. The second, known as *domaine direct* (or more simply *la directe*), was the basis of seigneurial rights. Beginning in the fourteenth century, however, the *censitaire* was recognized as a proprietor in the more modern sense of the word.[4] *Domaine direct* brought the seigneur only the benefit of fixed rights (*cens et rentes*) and casual rights (of which the best known and most profitable were the *lods et ventes*).[5] Thus within the city of Montreal the *censitaires* could dispose of their property almost as they pleased, subject only to the payment of certain seigneurial dues, most notably those of *mutation*. Certain seigneurial privileges remained (*banalités*, etc.), but they did not inhibit the sale of property. The *mutation* dues, however, being proportional to the sale of property, soon were regarded by the Montreal bourgeoisie as a severe burden, as were certain of the *banalités*. After the dismissal in 1816 of a law suit brought by the seigneurs against a man named Fleming, the seigneurs were reluctant to press any attempt to recover *lods et ventes* or even *cens et rentes*.

The principal effect of the seigneurial regime on the Montreal landscape, however, is not to be found in the question of the precarious nature of the seigneurial rights of the Sulpicians. It is found in the pattern of the sub-division of lots. To understand this question, it is necessary to determine how the lots were cut up and then to compare the various practices of the holders of Montreal sub-fiefs. Generally, the latter divided their land into smaller parts, and divided it sooner, than was the case elsewhere.

SOURCES FOR STUDY OF PROPERTY OWNERSHIP

While sources for the study of land ownership in Montreal are numerous, they are difficult to use. Among the best known sources are the registers of notaries. They contain a large number of contracts and various deeds which are useful for understanding property transfers, the sale value of properties, the uses that were made of land, the buildings that were constructed, and so on. These documents are invaluable at the micro-historical level for the study of particular lots or the holdings of particular property owners, and often give a picture of the state of the property market at a specific moment. But they are not sufficient for a reconstruction of a general picture of landed property for the entire city. They are only complementary sources, useful for rounding out data obtained from other sources.

The archives of the land titles offices are more useful than the registers of notaries.[6] In Montreal, the land titles offices were established in 1842, before the completion of the land survey register which officially recorded the boundaries and area of each property. Previously, the only existing register (*terrier*) was that created for the Sulpicians, the seigneurs of the Island of Montreal. Entries in this document extend from the origins of Montreal to the 1860's. Compared to data from the registration offices of a later period, the information from the Suplician's register is often very vague; the dimensions and boundaries are imprecise, the quantity of data small. Land titles office records are useful for micro-historical studies but are not very amenable to the study of land ownership in the entire city at any particular time.

The inadequacies of the registers and land titles records leads the researcher to a third and more satisfactory source: the assessment rolls (*rôles d'évaluation*) drawn up annually in Montreal from 1847, and their predecessors, the *rôles de cotisation*. These registers were born of the need to tax, for road work, the property owning class in proportion to the value of their holdings. The assessment rolls were mentioned first in the "Act to build, repair and improve the roads and bridges in this province, and for other works";[7] a law which formed the basis for the parish and municipal administrations which governed Lower Canada until the establishment of a municipal system in 1855.

In the section on *cotisation*, the 1796 law distinguished between *cotisation* and *corvée*. The *corvée* was an obligation falling on all males between the ages of 18 and 60; the only exceptions were apprentices and students, men responsible for families of "young children," men who fell victim to disease or disability during the year, and the military with the curious exception of the officers of the general staff. It was possible to substitute lump sum payments in lieu of the *corvée*. In such cases one paid for the number of days of *corvée* decreed by the inspector of roads or by his assistant. *Cotisation*, in contrast to *corvée*, was levied solely on landed property. Each year five assessors, or to quote the law, "five respectable householders" (*domiciliés honnêtes*) undertook to evaluate the annual revenue of every property within the city limits. Assessors were named by judges responsible to the administration. The evaluation made by the assessors could be appealed, otherwise it was assumed to be correct. The *cotisation*, fixed in 1796 at four pence in the pound (*cours d'Halifax*), was then levied and collected by the deputy inspector.

Only a few categories of property were exempt from *cotisation:* properties with a value below £5; properties of religious communities; and plots of land which were outside the fortifications but inside the city limits and serving as meadows, pastures or grain fields. It may be noted also that the law provided no exemptions for churches or for government properties.

The law was amended in 1799.[8] The changes included provision for a rise in the rate of *cotisation* from four to six pence in the pound, and the repeal of the exemptions on plots outside the fortifications.

Other taxes in Montreal during this period included those levied against owners of horses and public houses. After 1823 the city also added a tax on vehicles, drinking houses, auctioneers, and another tax on horses.[9] This sharp increase in taxes explains why Jacques Viger, in a letter to a nephew, finished the list of various taxes with "etc., as new kinds of revenues are created."[10]

In 1825, the rate of the *cotisation* was six pence per pound of assessed revenue, the equivalent of 2.5 percent. This rate and the amount paid in taxes were entered in a register called the *cotisation* book.

While the assessment rolls of the city of Montreal dating from 1847 to the present have been well preserved, the same cannot be said for those from the preceding period. Registers undoubtedly existed before 1847, if not in a continuous series at least for certain years. Jacques Viger, for example, has confirmed the existence of a *cotisation* roll for 1825, and the roll's subsequent disappearance.[11] Fortunately, before this roll disappeared, Viger was able to use it to establish precise statistics on property and on the property owners of Montreal.[12] Based only on a single year, Viger's compilation obviously does not give an impression of the dynamics of property ownership in Montreal over a long period. But it does permit a deeper study of the question at a particular moment in time. It is possible to produce a general description of property ownership in Montreal in 1825. The description, certainly, is an incomplete one; the information collected supplies only the name and ethnic origin of the property owner, along with the number and value of his holdings,[13] all presented in terms of the city's administrative division (the old walled city and the suburbs). Missing from the data are elements essential to any definitive study of property ownership such as the areas of individual plots of land, and the number and quality of buildings erected on them.

PROPERTY IN MONTREAL IN 1825

In 1825, the city of Montreal[14] had 2,698 assessed properties, with a total annual revenue valued at 88,594 pounds. The average annual revenue per property was 33 pounds,[15] a rather unimpressive figure.

The distribution of property between the old walled city and the suburbs closely followed population patterns. The walled city had 23.7 percent of the total population and 22.7 percent of the properties; the suburbs had 76.2 percent of the population and 77.2 percent of the properties. In terms of average annual revenues, however, there were significant differences between the walled city and the suburbs. While the annual revenue for the two areas together was 33 pounds, this was derived from a rate of 82 pounds in the walled city and a mere 18 pounds in the suburbs. This differential is not surprising; it could easily have resulted from differences in building materials (stone in the walled city and wood in the suburbs), or from urban regulation, always less constrictive in the suburbs than in the older portions of urban areas. What is unusual is the magnitude of the difference, which indicates an average value for walled city properties of more than four times suburban property.

In the suburbs, the lowest average property value was in the Faubourg Quebec, with 16 pounds, and the highest in Faubourg Sainte-Anne, with 23 pounds. La Point-à-Callière, which later became part of the Faubourg Sainte-Anne, must be treated separately. At first glance, the situation in Sainte-Anne seems unusual; with 2.7 percent of the total population, the suburb had only .7 percent of the properties. Yet the suburb had an average revenue per property of 90 pounds. These 1825 figures reflect the opening of the Lachine Canal and the influx of the Irish into the area.

The number of occupants per house in the suburbs was high; against an average figure of 7.7 occupants per house in the walled city, the Pointe-à-Callière had 18.2. Even eliminating the General Hospital of the Grey Nuns (155 people), the average is still 13.7 people, roughly double the rate for the rest of the city.

This combination of high population density and high property revenues is a classic one for nineteenth century urban property, particularly in areas populated by immigrants. Except for Point-à-Callière, and to a lesser extent for Sainte-Anne, a large percentage (68%) of land in the suburbs was divided into very small properties: that is, properties with less than 18 pounds of

FIGURE 1

Percentage distribution of estimated revenue of property owners of Montreal in 1825

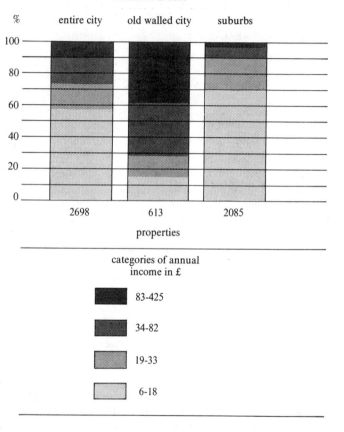

annual income. In Sainte-Anne this type of property represented only 55 percent of the total, possibly because this suburb had been recently established and the area had not yet been fully subdivided.

Figure I shows the percentage distribution of property values and gives an impression of the structure of land ownership in the city. The first column represents the entire city, with 2,698 properties, while the other columns represent the walled city (613 properties) and the suburbs (2085 properties). The average annual value of property in the three areas — 33 pounds in the city, 82 pounds for the walled city, and 18 pounds for the suburbs — have been used to delimit four categories of annual revenues.

It is obvious that the high property values of the walled city were counter-balanced by low property values in the suburbs. While the walled city had 613 properties worth between 6 and 425 pounds per year, the suburbs had 522 properties worth only 6 pounds, effectively holding the average to a low figure. At the same time, the proportion of high-income properties (above 100 pounds) is quite small. There were 230 such properties, amounting to only 8.5 percent of the total, and concentrated to the extent of 87 percent within the walled city. So marked is the difference between the figures for the walled city and the suburbs, that they appear to be referring to two different cities.

Another important aspect in an analysis of land ownership is the type of material used in building construction. In property assessment in Montreal, buildings were evaluated jointly with the land on which they stood. In theory, there should be a correlation between the value of the property and the kind of building material used. This statement cannot be proven, however, because of a lack of information. The wood-stone pairing is only a very crude indicator, since there were wooden houses of high value and stone houses of low value.

In the Montreal region, the predominant building material was wood. It was used in 64.3 percent of the assessed houses while 31.8 percent used stone. In 1825 brick was making a first appearance; it was used in 3.7 percent of the houses, either alone or in combination with wood.

Figures for the division of construction materials between the walled city and the suburbs show the overwhelming predominance of stone in the walled city, since 86.5 percent of the buildings were of stone and 6.3 percent of wood. The walled city did not hold a monopoly on stone buildings, for 38.3 percent of all such buildings in the entire city were in the suburbs. Generally, however, suburban buildings were wood (81.2 percent of the buildings). It should be noted that there was a greater degree of variety in the suburbs than in the walled city for while wood predominated, it did so to a lesser extent that did stone in the walled city.

A broad outline of the physical distribution of economic activity in the city is possible through an examination of the census of workshops, factories, shops and clearing houses. Montreal had 161 of these buildings in 1825. Again, the predominant position of the walled city is apparent; 58 percent of these buildings were in this area, with the remaining 42 percent scattered throughout the suburbs. Buildings of this kind were found in all of the suburbs, but particularly in Saint-Laurent, Sainte-Anne, and Pointe-à-Callière.

That, for the moment, is what can be drawn from a brief analysis of land

TABLE 1

TABLE 2

DISTRIBUTION OF PROPERTY OWNERS BY CATEGORIES OF LAND VALUES, MONTREAL IN 1825

Value of annual income (pounds)	French-Canadians			Anglo-Canadians			British and Foreigners			Total
	No.	% horizontal	% vertical	No.	% horizontal	% vertical	No.	% horizontal	% vertical	No.
600 and over	3	60.0	0.3	1	20.0	1.1	1	20.0	0.2	5
500-599	2	50.0	0.2	0	0	0	2	50.0	0.4	4
400-499	3	30.0	0.3	1	10.0	1.1	6	60.0	1.2	10
300-399	13	44.8	1.2	3	10.3	3.2	13	44.8	2.7	29
200-299	23	46.9	2.1	7	14.3	7.5	19	38.8	3.9	49
100-199	77	49.7	6.9	15	9.7	16.1	63	40.6	12.9	155
50-99	103	47.0	9.2	25	11.4	26.9	91	41.6	18.6	219
25-49	188	60.8	16.9	15	4.9	16.1	106	34.3	21.7	309
20-24	80	63.0	7.2	6	4.7	6.5	41	32.3	8.4	127
15-19	116	70.7	10.4	10	6.1	10.8	38	23.2	7.8	164
10-14	155	75.3	13.9	4	1.9	4.3	47	22.8	9.6	206
6-9	117	86.7	10.5	2	1.5	2.2	16	11.8	3.3	135
6	233	82.3	20.9	4	1.4	4.3	46	16.3	9.4	283
TOTAL	1,113			93			489			1,695

NOTE: This table includes a substantial amount of duplication, for individual land owners were counted each time their name appeared in various sections of the city.

SOURCE: Files of Viger-Verreau, 46, no. 9, Archives of the Seminary of Quebec.

ownership. Two major conclusions emerge: first, the distinction between walled city and suburbs at all levels — rental value, quality of buildings and economic activity; second, the magnitude of the difference in property values between the two parts of the city.

THE PROPERTY OWNERS

One of Jacques Viger's famous statistical tables concerns the owners of assessed real estate (Table 1). Viger began by dividing the property owners according to categories of income for each part of the city; eliminating double counts, he then compiled a list for the city as a whole. His tables establish beyond doubt that income from land in Montreal was very unequally distributed. There were many small properties; 18.3 percent had an income estimated at 6 pounds, and more than half the total (56.4 percent) drew less than 25 pounds per year from their real estate. Income categories of 25 to 50 pounds and 50 to 100 pounds accounted for 16.2 percent and 10.9 percent respectively. Finally, property owners enjoying a fairly substantial income (100 pounds or more), while in a minority, accounted for a full 16.4 percent. The very wealthy — those earning 500 pounds or more — numbered only 28, about 2 percent of the total.

Some 1,390 different property owners were identified by the assessors in the city. As the city included, according to Viger's census, 4452 heads of families[16] not more than 31 percent of the heads of families could have been property owners. Evidently, Montreal in 1825 was already a city of tenants.

Viger made some interesting calculations concerning the ethnic origins of the property owners. He divided the owners into three groups — Canadiens (francophones), Anglo-Canadians, and British and foreigners — and provided figures which make it possible to establish the relative importance of each group. The French-Canadians, representing 54.4 percent of the Montreal population, accounted for two-thirds of the property owners and held two-thirds of the real estate. They received, however, only 52.1 percent of the assessed revenue, an indication that Canadians were already concentrating in low-income properties. The Anglo-Canadians (12.6 percent of the population) accounted for only 6.2 percent of the property owners and 4.8 percent of the real estate, but drew 9.6 percent of the city's rental income. A more significant group, the British and other foreigners (32.0 percent of the population), made up 27.5 percent of the land owners, held 28.4 percent of the property, and collected 38.3 percent of the total revenue.

The average annual income for the three groups was as follows: Canadiens, 50 pounds; Anglo-Canadians, 127 pounds; British and foreigners, 86 pounds. A simple average, however, does not give an accurate idea of the complexities of the situation. A more refined analysis according to categories of income is necessary. Table 2 shows small property concentrated in the hands of the French-Canadians, who are strongly over-represented in the categories below 50 pounds. There is a different distribution in the high-income categories; here the French-Canadians are under-represented, but, with the exception of one otherwise insignificant category, they account for at least 46 percent of the membership of each group. British and foreigners are concentrated in the upper categories, and have a larger place in them than warranted by their share of the population. The Anglo-Canadians, while sometimes found in the higher revenue brackets, are generally under-represented in them.

This table, however, is only the sum of the figures for each category from all sections of the city combined. It contains a good deal of duplication, since many property owners held land in more than one section of the city. By using Viger's data, this source or distortion can be eliminated from the revenue categories of 100 pounds and upward. These upper income levels are also much more likely to contain property owners who were genuinely interested in investment in land, as opposed to those whom merely wanted to own their own houses. Table 3 gives the revised figures for distribution of property, with the properties of each owner grouped together to avoid duplication.

While limited in scope, the data on the ethnic composition of the property owners suggests some interesting conclusions. When we combine the Anglophones (Canadian-born and foreign-born), we find that they formed a majority of the large property owners, and were in consequence over-represented in relation to their percentage (45 percent) of the total population. The dominant position of the English-speaking bourgeoisie in Montreal's economic life during this period is not surprising. The distinction drawn by Viger between Canadian-born and other English-speaking residents is also noteworthy. In the Anglophone group, those born outside the country occupied a very important position, a tangible sign that immigrants were making a dynamic contribution to the city's economy.

The case of French-Canadian property owners is of particular interest. As indicated above, French-Canadians received 52.1 percent of the city's total income from property. Certainly, the majority of them held low-income properties, a reflection of the fact that most of them, as natives of the country, merely wished to own a house of their own, and did not regard property as an investment. However, there were also large numbers of French-Canadians among property owners with assessed revenues of 100 pounds or more. At first sight French-Canadians, who comprised 46.9 percent of this group, still appear under-represented. However, if their position in other fields is considered — according to Fernand Ouellet's calculations, they accounted for only about 35 percent of businessmen and 40 percent of professional men[17] — it is apparent that what appears as under-representation was in fact over-representation. Evidently, the French-Canadian bourgeoisie tended to prefer investments in land to other kinds of investments.

Making up a final category are a very few large land-owners who accounted for a substantial proportion of the city's property revenue. Twelve persons or institutions headed the list of major Montreal property owners, that is, owners of properties with rental values of 600 to 1,000 pounds or more. They were the following: Pre Berthelet (£2,129), D-B Viger (£1,334), the Crown (£1,187), Austin Cuvillier (£907), J. Molson Sr. (£910), The Seminary (£912), David Ross (£880), the Widow Platt (£717), M. Lunn (£754), the David estate (£638), Bte. Castonguay Sr. (£682), Félix Souligny (£680).

TABLE 3

Distribution of Property Owners with Incomes of more than 100 Pounds, City of Montreal, 1825

Amount of Assessed Annual Income (pounds)	French Canadian		Anglo-Canadian		British and Foreigners		Total
	no.	%	no.	%	no.	%	no.
600 and more	6	50.0	3	25.0	3	25.0	12
500-599	5	31.2	2	12.5	9	56.3	16
400-499	13	56.5	0	0	10	43.5	23
300-399	9	45.0	2	10.0	9	45.0	20
200-299	18	42.9	5	11.9	19	45.2	42
100-199	56	48.7	14	12.2	45	39.1	115
TOTAL	107	46.9	26	11.4	95	41.7	228

NOTE: Individuals who owned property in different parts of the city are only counted once.

It is not possible in the context of this article to make a detailed study of these major property owners; we can, however, examine the character of some of the holdings of French-Canadian owners. From the list of major property owners, the "Canadiens" have been singled out — P. Berthelet, D.-B. Viger, A. Cuvillier, B. Castonguay and Félix Fouligny — and the name of Toussaint Pothier (578 pounds) has been added. All of these men had certain characteristics in common. One was the physical dispersion of their properties; in every case they held property in at least two of the suburbs, and more often in three. Secondly, with a single exception, their holdings were all rooted in the walled city, where the highest property values were concentrated. Finally, all of them lived in the walled city on one of their own properties.

The largest property owner was Berthelet. According to Viger's census, 23 of Berthelet's properties, distributed among three suburbs outside the city, were rented to 61 people. Within the walled city, five of his properties were rented for commercial and industrial uses: a shop where combs were manufactured, a hair dresser's shop, a chair factory and two factories which made brushed and iron wire products. In the Faubourg Saint-Laurent, his premises were used by the British and Canadian School. He also exploited the immigrants crammed together in the Pointe-à-Callière where he owned three properties, one of them housing 43 tenants, a very high figure for the period. The diversity of his holdings makes him appear as authentic real-estate entrepreneur. He was also involved in a business that had an indirect connection with housing. As the owner of about 300 cast-iron stoves, he carried on a lucrative business renting out the useful devices over the winter to people who lacked the means to purchase their own.[18]

The second largest property owner, Denis-Benjamin Viger, operated in a very similar fashion. Like Berthelet, he rented commercial properties; in addition, he owned a tract of land with a garden and orchard in the suburbs, perhaps with an eye to future speculative profit. The rental operations of Cuvillier, Castonguay and Souligny were similar.

Unlike the above, Toussaint Pothier had no commercial premises. He also had a significant number of vacant lots among his holdings. He did, however, own three houses with gardens in the walled city.

From this brief inventory of large Canadien property owners, it is not possible to develop a typology of the internal structure of industry. Not only is a wider range of cases necessary, but a careful analysis of the origin and composition of the various holdings would be needed. Nonetheless, this initial over-view of land ownership does give a feeling for the vigour and importance of this sector in the economic life of Montreal.

Two major conclusions emerge from this study of the 1825 data. One is the importance of property ownership, which was at this time was already beginning to show a degree of concentration. Everyone who counted for anything in Montreal in the realm of commerce and industry appears high on the list of property owners, and the sums invested in land were often very large. On the other hand, we have also noted a substantial French-Canadian participation in this sector, even in the upper categories of rental value, a participation which is somewhat surprising in view of the dominance of Anglophones in the commercial sector. The behaviour of Berthelet and the other large French-Canadian property owners seems to leave little doubt about the capitalistic character of their activities.

These conclusions are tentative. They were developed on the basis of generalized results, and their verification will require a more detailed analysis both of the sources used here and of other documents of the period. This procedure, however, will be little more than a methodological exercise if it is not integrated into a coherent and more generalized scientific framework. In our view, the data presented here makes it possible to formulate a more general hypothesis concerning the role of landed capital in the urban setting, and of the place occupied by the French-Canadian bourgeoisie in that context.

A GENERAL HYPOTHESIS

Under the influence of British and American historiography, historians of the Canadian economy have set a high value on the entrepreneur, and in particular on the English model of the entrepreneur, i.e., the bold innovator who set modern industry in motion. The shortcomings of this model as applied to the Canadian situation have been discussed by Alfred Dubuc.[19]

In this kind of interpretive framework the French-Canadian bourgeoisie assumes the role of poor relation. Historians have focussed their attention exclusively on the small number of French-Canadian industrialists, and on the limited scale of their operations.[20] A dichotomy has been created between industrial investment, assumed to have been a sign of economic vigour and progress, and landed or real estate investment, which is thought of as a conservative, security-seeking activity analagous to the purchase of government bonds in the twentieth century. An article by Norman Taylor provides an illustration of this kind of interpretation.[21]

The presentation of the case by the dominant interpretation in Canadian histiography does not take into account the complexity of the economic situation. Aside from finance, industrial and commercial capital, landed capital had a specialized function of its own; it served to organize and administer, if not to control, urban space. It thus provided the necessary conditions for production and exchange.

In the urban context this type of investment tends to be too closely identified with land speculation. It was in fact a much more complex phenomenon; while the investor was a speculator, he often went much farther, creating the conditions that would drive up the value of his properties. Historically, investors in land have effectively acted as urban developers. They exploited their real estate in a thoroughly capitalistic manner, constructing buildings in which they housed the largest possible number of tenants in order to maximize profits; they strove to concentrate their property the better to organize its development; they attempted to attract commercial users, industries, railways and other enterprises whose presence would increase the value of the surrounding properties. They manipulated, or at the very least exerted strong pressure on, municipal councils to ensure that political decisions conformed to their economic interests. They negotiated with the directors of public utilities (water, gas, street railways, and electricity) whose collaboration was essential to the success of their construction projects. The vital role of these promoters in most of the great cities of the United States has been studied by American historians.[22] Thus, we are dealing with an economic activity that is obviously bound to the progress of commerce and industry, but which also had an impact of its own.

Our hypothesis is that the French-Canadian capitalists, while a minority among financial, commercial, or industrial capitalists, found their true economic footing in the land-owning sector. Furthermore, far from regarding land investment as a necessarily conservative and passive activity, they attempted to exploit their land holdings in a capitalistic manner.

If this interpretation proves correct, it will resolve the apparent contradiction between the ideological control this bourgeoisie exerted over the French-Canadian masses, and the weakness of its economic foundation in the industrial sector. Landed capital, like other forms of capital, is a source of power and dominance. In another context — that of an agricultural and forest economy — Normand Séguin has shown how the settlers of the Lac Saint-Jean area were effectively evicted at the end of the nineteenth century.[23] In that case we see the bourgeoisie monopolizing the soil and using it to gain a greater degree of social control.

Certainly, French Canadians were not the only investors in land, but their wielded much more influence in that sector than they did elsewhere. They probably had access to certain sources of information about land which would all too often be closed to them in the commercial and industrial sectors.

Evidence of the importance of landed capital to the French-Canadian bourgeoisie can be found in several areas. The case of Montreal in 1825, which we have discussed in this article, is itself very significant. Also of interest are the activities of one Barthélemy Joliette, who, faced with stagnating seigneurial revenues, established a wood-cutting industry and brought about the urbanization of his village of Industrie.[24] At the end of the nineteenth century, the question of the construction of port installations in the east end of Montreal divided the French and English bourgeoisie into two warring camps,[25] an incident which illustrates the importance of French-Canadian property ownership in that part of the city. Finally, in studying the development of the city of Maisonneuve, on the outskirts of Montreal, we have been able to examine the activities of a few French-Canadian promoters. Owners of large tracts of land, they succeeded in reaping windfall profits on them by controlling the municipal council, and by

bringing about the adoption of an industrial policy favouring expansion of population.[26]

These few examples are inadequate to prove our hypothesis, and other more detailed studies are needed. Research is in progress in this area, however, and we have reason to hope that we will soon have a better understanding of the role of land ownership in the Quebec economy.

NOTES:

1. Among the rare studies on the subject are an article by Louise Dechêne, "La croissance de Montréal au XVIIIe siècle." *RHAF*, Vol. 27, No. 2 (Sept. 1973), 163-79, and the book by the same author entitled, *Habitants et marchands de Montréal au XVII^6 siècle* (Paris, 1974). At the methodological level, mention must be made of the work currently being undertaken at the University of Quebec at Chicoutimi by the Groupe de recherche sur la propriété foncière au Saguenay. See Pierre Houde and Normand Séguin, *Rapport d'activité du Groupe de recherche sur la propriété foncière au Saguenay pour l'année de subvention mai 1973 à mai 1974* (November, 1974), 53 pp. (mimeographed).

2. The documents used come from the Viger-Verreau collection in the Archives of the Seminary of Quebec. We wish to thank the staff of the archives, and in particular its director, Mr. l'Abbé Honorius Provost, for his assistance.

3. See G.-E. Baillargeon, *La survivance du régime seigneurial à Montréal* (Montréal, Le Cercle du Livre de France, 1968).

4. Jean-Philippe Lévy, *Historie de la propriété* (Paris, P.U.F., 1972), p. 46. An excellent discussion of the seigneurial regime is R.C. Harris, *The Seigneurial System in Early Canada: A Geographical Study* (Quebec and Madison, Wis., 1967). Most of the terms used here are explained in detail in the Harris study.

5. On the question of rights and of the establishment of the seigneurial regime in Montreal, see: Louise Dechêne, "L'évolution du régime seigneurial au Canada," *Recherches Sociographiques*, Vol. XII, No. 2 (May-August, 1971), pp. 143-83; and Yves F. Zoltvany, "Esquisse de la Coutume de Paris", *RHAF*, Vol. 25, No. 3 (December, 1971), pp. 372-73.

6. For a description of this type of source, see Gérard Bouchard and Normand Séguin, "Pour une historie de l'occupation du sol et de la propriété foncière au Saguenay," *Protée* Vol. 1, No. 3 (December, 1971), pp. 33-39; and Gilles Durand, "Sources manuscrites pour l'histoire de la vallée du Hant-Saguenay et du Lac Saint-Jean", *Protée*, Vol. 2, No. 1 (April, 1972), pp. 103-12.

7. *Statutes of Lower Canada*, 36 George III (1796), chp. 9.

8. *Ibid.*, 39 George III (1799), chp. 5.

9. *Ibid.*, 3 George IV (1823), chp. 6.

10. Jacques Viger to Pre Auger, December 31, 1825, *Saberdache* (Bleue), Vol. 8, pp. 275-76.

11. *Ibid.*, vol. 6 and 7, correspondence, *passim*. The books of *cotisation* were conserved by the *cotiseurs* but were not found at the Greffe de la Cour.

12. These documents are to be found in the Viger-Verreau files of the Archives of the Seminary of Quebec. The principal sources used are: Recensement de Montreal en 1825, Livre de dépouillement par Jacques Viger (015A), Recensement de la Ville de Montréal fait par Jacques Viger en 1825 pour Louis-Jos. Papineau (Carton 46, no. 9); Documents sur la propriété foncière (Carton 46, no. 9); Tablettes statistiques du Comté de Montréal 1825 (017). The last have been analyzed briefly and completed in J.-P. Bernard, P.-A. Linteau et J.-C. Robert, "Les tablettes statistiques de Jacques Viger (1825)," Groupe de recherche sur la société montréalaise au 19e siècle, *Rapport 1972-1973* (Montréal, Université du Québec à Montréal, 1973), 42 pp. (mimeographed).

13. Throughout this article the expression "annual revenue" designates the estimates established by the assessors of the amount that a property owner might draw annually from his real estate holdings. This must not be confused with the actual revenues, which may have been different, and which are not known to us. It is evident that the estimates used here must be considered as indicators allowing us to make comparisons but which do not take account of the price which a particular piece of land might command on the market.

14. Three terms recur frequently in the 1825 texts to designate Montreal: "Cité de Montréal," "ville de Montréal," and the "faubourgs" (translated here as "the city" or "the entire city," "the walled city," and "suburbs"). "Cite" and "ville" are easily confused, but refer to different entities. "Cité" designated the administrative unity deliniated and created by the proclamation of 1792, and includes the city and its suburbs, "Ville de Montréal" is applied solely to the area circumscribed by the perimeter of the old fortifications; it is the old city of the French regime. The suburbs (faubourgs) grew up from the 18th century onward, and by 1825 there were seven of them, if we include the Pointe à Callière. The six others are Sainte-Anne, Saint-Joseph or des Récollets, Saint-Antoine, Saint-Laurent, Saint-Louis, and Sainte-Marie or Québec. For more details, see P.-A. Linteau and J.-C. Robert, "Les divisions territoriales à Montréal au 19ᵉ siècle," Groupe de recherche sur la société montréalaise au 19ᵉ siècle, *Rapport 1972-1973* (Montréal, Université du Québec à Montréal, 1973), 32 pp. (mimeographed).

15. Rounded off to the nearest whole number.

16. "Tablettes statistiques du comté de Montréal, 1825," Archives of the Seminary of Quebec, Viger-Verreau Files 017.

17. Fernand Ouellet, "Structure des occupations et ethnicité dans les villes de Québec et de Montréal (1819-1844)," *Eléments d'histoire Sociale du Bas-Canada* (Montréal, HMH, 1972), pp. 180-192.

18. *Montréal fin de siècle: histoire de la métropole du Canada au dix-neuvième siècle* (Montréal, The Gazette Printing Company, 1899), p. 23.

19. Alfred Dubuc, "Thomas Molson, entrepreneur canadien, 1791-1863," Thèse de doctorat d'Etat (Paris, 1969); "Les classes sociales au Canada," Annales ESC, Vol. 22, No. 4 (July-August, 1967), pp. 829-44.

20. See René Durocher and P.-A. Linteau, *Le "retard" du Québec et l'infériorité économique des Canadiens français* (Montréal, Boréal Express, 1971), 127 pp.

21. Norman W. Taylor, "L'industriel canadien-francais et son milieu," R. Durocher et P.-A. Linteau, *op. cit.*, pp. 43-74.

22. See C. N. Glaab and A. T. Brown, *A History of Urban America* (Macmillan, 1967), pp. 107-132; D. J. Boorstin, "The Businessman as an American Institution," A. B. Callow, ed., *American Urban History* (New York, Oxford University Press, 1969), pp. 136-43.

23. Normand Séguin, "Hébertville au Lac Saint-Jean (1850-1900), un exemple québécois de colonisation au XIXᵉ siècle," Canadian Historical Association, *Historical Papers 1973*.

24. Jean-Claude Robert, "Un seigneur entrepreneur, Barthelemy Joliette et la fondation du village d'Industrie (Joliette), 1822-1850," *RHAF*, Vol. 26, No. 3 (December, 1972), pp. 375-95; by the same author, L'activité économique de Barthelemy Joliette et la fondation du village d'Industrie (Joliette) 1822-1850, Master's thesis, Dept. of History, University of Montreal, 1971, 183 pp.

25. Paul-André Linteau, "Le développement du port de Montréal au début du 20ᵉ siècle," Canadian Historical Association, *Historical Papers 1972*, pp. 181-85.

26. Paul-André Linteau, *Maisonneuve, Comment des promoteurs fabriquent une ville* (Montréal: Boréal Express, 1981).

Metropolitanism and Toronto Re-examined, 1825-1850[1]

FREDERICK H. ARMSTRONG

I

In recent years Canadian historiography has concentrated upon the influence of the metropolis rather than the frontier, upon the spread of civilization and commerce from the centres along the St. Lawrence and the Great Lakes. Innis, Creighton and Careless have laid the basis of what has generally come to be called the Laurentian School of Canadian historiography. In spite of this interest in metropolitanism, however, there has been very little work done on the actual growth of the metropolitan centres themselves; as is typified by the lack of a detailed scholarly history of either Toronto or Montreal, although for Toronto Masters and Firth have studied parts of the last century and Kerr and Spelt have written a geographic survey. Most of the writing on urban history has been done by amateurs; some of it has reached a very high level, but it is frequently antiquarian rather than historical in nature.

If, as the supporters of the Laurentian school claim, the cities have played such a dominant role in our development, organizing the frontier, rather than being organized by it, urban history is of the utmost importance; without studies of metropolitan development many questions on broader subjects must remain only partly answered. As the second metropolis of the nation, and the greatest city of English-speaking Canada, Toronto has a key role in the national history. Yet so little accurate work has been done on Toronto's evolution that it is difficult to even state which eras were crucial in the city's development.[2]

A complete history of Toronto is well in the future; for the present the

SOURCE: "Metropolitanism and Toronto Re-examined, 1825-1850," *Canadian Historical Association Papers* (1966), pp. 29-40. Reprinted by permission of the author and Canadian Historical Association.

historian must concentrate on detailed studies of short segments of the city's past. In this way the most important developments can probably be pinpointed, and the major trends arranged in connected sequence. For the earliest periods of Toronto's history some of this work has already been done. The late Percy J. Robinson examined the French Regime in his detailed study that was published in 1933[3] and Edith Firth has written the history of the Town of York, which Simcoe established in 1793.[4] It is to the next major period in the history of the city that this paper is directed: the few years after 1825 which saw the village of York turn into the city of Toronto. This metamorphosis, which resulted from the great influx of population from the British Isles that began in the mid-1820's, was a sudden one. Within a decade the population of the city increased from 1,500 to 10,000, and the nature of the town changed in all its aspects: political, administrative, social, and economic.

The change is most strikingly symbolized by the incorporation of York as a city in 1834, with the concurrent return to the original name of Toronto, but it is the economic readjustment that concerns us here; there is no time to examine the social and political aspects in a paper of this length. Economically, Toronto in 1825 was a village; ten years later it was well on the way to becoming an important metropolis. This development has been little examined by historians. Canon Henry Scadding in his monumental *Toronto of Old*, published in 1873, was chiefly interested in the earlier period. D. C. Masters' *Rise of Toronto 1850-1890*, which appeared in 1947, deserves great credit as one of the first studies of a specific period in the history of a Canadian city and the first to bring in an interpretive framework, but it begins just before the railway boom, and only touches briefly the city before the early 1850s.

Certainly, Toronto did not attain a very large population until a later date, it was about 30,000 in 1850, but the entire province was thinly populated, and the city, in spite of its small size, was assuming the appearance of a fledgling metropolis by the time of the Rebellion. It is, then, the contention of this paper that the date for the emergence of Toronto as an important economic centre should be placed in the 1830 period. A great economic boom unquestionably followed the opening of the railways in 1853-55; but it could be regarded as the second great economic upswing rather than the beginning of Toronto's metropolitan economy. In the years between the beginnings of the British immigration and the panic of 1837, the city underwent its first period of expansion. Thus the date 1825 is a better starting point for a study of Toronto's metropolitan growth than the year 1850.

The economic events that took place in what might be called "Mackenzie's Toronto" — though many leading citizens of the era would shiver in their graves at the thought — have been overshadowed by the political ones. Mackenzie and the events of the Rebellion are colourful topics for discussion, routine details of commerce are not. Because of these political events, however, Toronto is usually seen as a provincial capital rather than an economic centre and an important aspect of its development has been obscured. The fact that almost from the first Toronto was the provincial capital naturally had an affect on its development, but this effect can easily be exaggerated after the 1820s. Of course being the capital meant that many provincial activities were focused in the city, and that the organizations inherent in a capital would locate themselves in York. Such institutions as the provincial courts, centres of church administration, and land companies, each in their way helped to focus economic as well as political concentration on the capital. This factor became less important, however, as Toronto grew in size and its hinterland developed; in the end, losing the seat of government in 1841 had little adverse affect on the city.

Another factor that may have tended to lessen the attention on Toronto's early economic development has been the fairly rigid application of N.S.B. Gras's metropolitan thesis to the city. This thesis, based on the growth of London, England, which he presented in his *Introduction to Economic History* in 1922, divides metropolitan evolution into four phases: first there is a concentration of commercial facilities, then the development of manufacturing, thirdly the evolution of transportation, and finally the achievement of financial maturity. The strict application of this thesis to North American metropolitan centres, as Gras notes himself, should be undertaken with a certain amount of caution. There are differences in marketing conditions between London and the North American cities, but these do not affect the first phase of development too greatly as it is really based on the extension of existing village facilities, such as the enlargement of markets, rather than on new technological developments. The real divergence takes place between the second and third stages as they evolved in England and on this continent. Both these phases are based on changes in an expanding technology, and in England, where manufacturing systems preceded communication improvements, these stages followed each other to a large extent. In London, metropolitan communications could not be improved until McAdam had perfected his road surfacing methods and Symington his steamboat; in North America this was simply not the case. Technological innovations that preceded the opening up of the interior of North America could naturally be applied immediately. Further, new ideas and processes were constantly being adopted while the cities grew. Gras notes an example of the resulting duality of development in the evolution of Minneapolis-St. Paul (the centre that he examined in the most detail) where he decided the second and third phases appeared together in the years 1870-1900. He concluded as follows:

> While in older districts, for instance, in England and the Atlantic states of America, the Industrial Revolution preceded the revolution in transportation, in the American Northwest these two movements were synchronous.[5]

Unfortunately Gras did not elaborate upon this point, but specifically, it meant that there was a very different course of evolution in the metropolitan areas of North America; a difference which became more and more apparent as civilization moved west and technology advanced. One other variation should also be noted, and it is a most important one. In many North American regions not only do the second and third stages come together, but they also tend to infringe on the first stage, for manufacturing and communications appear before the phase of market evolution is complete.

The development of young York-Toronto, therefore, did not follow the same basic pattern as that of the great European metropolitan cities such as London. The first stage was still under way in 1830; however, at that time the second and third stages had begun and were reaching a fair level of advancement by the time of the Rebellion, although they were not to come into full blossom until after the railways were completed in the mid-1850s. Gras's model should thus be used with care in discussing the development of Toronto. At the same time, however, it provides a convenient basis for examination of the economic growth of the city, and thus will be employed to guide the following discussion.

II

The first stage of metropolitan economy, characterized by the appearance of all the institutions necessary to service a large agglomeration of people — wholesalers, specialist merchants, warehousing, extended civic facilities — was well advanced in York by the early 1830's. The growing commercial importance of the town was particularly characterized by the appearance of several new wholesale firms, some established by local residents, other branches opened by mercantile houses in Montreal or Kingston. Although the development of branches of Montreal firms in the city might be taken as evidence of the continuing domination of that centre, it can also be seen as an indication that the trade of Toronto could no longer be obtained by merely waiting for the city's merchants to place orders in Montreal. Also, the selection of Toronto as a branch office site by Montreal firms was a confirmation of that city's growing place in the western Upper Canadian economy. That the citizens of Toronto regarded these new wholesalers as evidence of emancipation from Montreal can be seen from an editorial which appeared in the *Courier of Upper Canada* on October 20, 1832. The editor announced that there were now four Montreal wholesalers in the city as well as five local wholesale firms and added "with all these numerous and extensive concerns, it will be obvious that Country merchants need no longer think of going to Montreal, since every article of Merchandise can be obtained at York, in equal abundance and variety, and upon Montreal terms." Further evidences that Toronto was attempting to break away from Montreal control are the advertisements of such merchants as George Monro and Isaac Buchanan, who boasted that they had established direct connections with the Old County, and the many signs that a large volume of trade was being carried on with the United States.[6]

Paralleling the growth of the wholeslaers was an equally rapid expansion of specialist firms. Various merchants had claimed to be specialist dealers in the earlier years of the town, but by 1830 large, sound businesses were making their appearance, such as Watkins & Harris hardware, and the printing and publishing firm operated by Henry Rowsell. There were also a great variety of minor concerns: silversmiths, book stores, druggists, hatters, even a cigar store and a used clothes shop. Many of these businesses, of course, were ephemeral, but others were to grow and play a leading role in the city for decades.

Whether the new stores were wholesale or retail, Montreal-controlled or Toronto-owned, they all had one thing in common: the desire to develop business both in the city itself and in its hinterland. Their advertisements frequently contained instructions for local papers in other parts of the province to copy them, and by studying these we can gain a good idea of the extent of the commercial influence of Toronto of the period. Most of the places where Toronto merchants solicited business were in the western part of the province, or in the Niagara peninsula: such centres as Hamilton, London, St. Thomas, Niagara (-on-the-Lake), and St. Catharines. In addition, the names of central Lake Ontario villages, such as Cobourg, were to be found on occasion. That there were also Toronto trade connections to Lake Simcoe in the north is evident as early as 1832 when the firm of Murray, Newbigging & Company were operating a wagon route to that area[7] and had at least three co-partnerships there located at Holland Landing, Newmarket, and the Narrows of the Lake (Orillia).

The counterpart of this expansion of inbound trade, the place of Toronto as a port of export for its hinterland, is more difficult to establish. The only merchant's correspondence that survives from the period, the letters from John S. Baldwin to his partner Jules Quesnel in Montreal, is quite fragmentary, but still shows that shipments of wheat and potash played a major role in business. This evidence is corroborated by evidence that the farmers of the Home District founded their own co-operative store on the Ontario lakefront as early as 1824, as a centre for both exporting from and trading in the town of York, and operated it successfully for some years.

Another aspect of Toronto's commercial development was the flourishing newspaper enterprise that had grown up in the city; an activity that was particularly important in spreading the capital's influence throughout the hinterland. York had had a newspaper since the official *Upper Canada Gazette* had moved from Niagara in 1798, but the *Gazette* remained the only paper until 1820. After that date new sheets began to appear rapidly, and, though many of them failed, by the early 1830's there were usually about six papers being published in the town. Beginning with the *Courier of Upper Canada* in 1829, these tended to become semi-weekly, and the *Royal Standard*, which flourished briefly in 1836-37, was the first daily in the province.

Newspapers were particularly important to the growth of the city's influence, for most papers of province-wide interest tended to locate in Toronto. The *Gazette*, not surprisingly, had followed the capital from Niagara; Mackenzie's *Colonial Advocate* came from Queenston in 1824; Thomas Dalton's *Patriot* from Kingston in 1832; and George Gurnett moved his operations to York from Ancaster in 1829. Of the two denominational papers, the Methodist *Christian Guardian* settled in Toronto and the Anglican *Church* was sometimes published there.

The circulation range of these papers is difficult to establish. Mackenzie, whose paper must have been one of the most influential in the province, once published a list of 52 agents scattered over a very wide area,[8] but the fact that he had appointed an agent for a particular village does not necessarily mean that he had subscribers living there. Another paper with a wide circulation was the *Christian Guardian*, for every travelling circuit rider of the faith was automatically an agent. On a more limited basis the *Courier* had subscribers in the Gore, London, and Western Districts, which was almost the exact area where the commercial houses of the provincial capital circulated their advertisements, and this may well represent the limit of influence of most Toronto journals.

In addition to this development of commercial enterprises, there is another aspect of Gras's first stage of development, which he touches upon but does not elaborate, and that is the organization of public services to handle the needs of the growing population. This can also be seen in the city of the period. The very reason for incorporation was the inability of the appointed magistrates who governed the Home District, which included Toronto, to deal with the problems posed by the continuing waves of immigration. The preamble to the city's Act of Incorporation of 1834 stated the problem clearly: "whereas from the rapid increase of the Population, Commerce and Wealth, of the Town of York, a more efficient system of Police and Municipal Government has become obviously necessary."[9] In the years before incorporation the local magistrates had made valiant, but unsuccessful, efforts to expand municipal services to meet the growing demands of the population. Two wells for the town water supply were dug in 1823, a volunteer fire service was organized in 1826, and a new court house and jail opened in 1827. The inadequacies of these last buildings demonstrate the problem facing the government authorities. When they were first planned in 1820 the population of the Home District was 13,000; when they were finished seven years later it was 21,000, and by 1835 there were 57,000 inhabitants, 9,250 of them in Toronto.[10] By the mid-1830's new buildings were under consideration and a new jail was opened in the city in 1841.

In spite of the financial load imposed by the court house and jail, and a taxation system that was far from fair or adequate, the district magistrates were next forced to build a new market for the city to replace the old one, which had become hopelessly overcrowded. This was done in 1830-32, but the costs involved (over £9,000) were the final difficulty that brought on incorporation for Toronto, because some new system of governing and financing simply had to be found. The provincial government had also attempted to aid the fast-growing city, and Governor Sir John Colborne was largely responsible for the opening of the first hospital there in 1829.

William Lyon Mackenzie, as first Mayor in 1834, proved to be singularly ineffective in alleviating the problems facing the new city of Toronto, partly because the Tories and Reformers on the City Council were more interested in battling each other than undertaking constructive measures, but mainly because of his own incompetence as an organizer, administrator and leader. After Mackenzie and his Reformers were decisively defeated in the election of 1835, however, civic government took a decided turn for the better, Robert Baldwin Sullivan, the Tory second mayor, began an organized municipal financial system, appointed an Inspector of Nuisances to clean up the streets,[11] and, most important, started the construction of a sewer system. The Reformers returned to power the next year under an able new leader, Dr. Thomas D. Morrison, and began the macadamization of the city streets. At the very end of his term, in January, 1837, Morrison also played a part in the establishment of the first House of Industry in the city, evidence that a Reform mayor could be effective.

In the years that followed, the city's sewers and paved roads were gradually extended, and a gas supply and water supply system were begun in the early 1840's, though neither worker very well for some years. Thus by the mid-1830's the basic civic services of the period had made their appearance in Toronto, and in municipal organization too, the city was well advanced in the first stage of metropolitan development.

III

The second stage of metropolitan evolution Gras dubbed simply ''Industrial

Development." Masters, in discussing Toronto in 1850, correctly noted that, though the city had made considerable progress, it had not as yet reached that stage where it could be called a manufacturing centre.[12] The same statement might well be applied to the mid-1830's. Though Toronto was not to become an important manufacturing city until after the railway boom of the mid-1850's, enough progress had been made by the time of incorporation that it seems safe to say that the city had already entered into the second phase of metropolitan development. Some of the local manufactories were located in the centre of Toronto's downtown area, but others, including many varieties of mills, spread along the Don and Humber Rivers. One of the most important of these was the mill complex developed at Todmorden on the Don by the Helliwell, Eastwood, and Skinner families.

In the central area there were a wide variety of enterprises by the 1830's: Jesse Ketchum's tannery; Peter Freeland's soap factory, one of the main landmarks on the shoreline for many years; the famous furniture manufactory of Jacques & Hay; and various brick-makers, breweries and distilleries. These last categories provided some of the most stable firms in the city including Copland's brewery, founded in 1830 and sold to Labatt's of London in 1946, and Gooderham & Worts, which was established in 1832. Heavier industry was also beginning to make its appearance and the largest manufacturing operation in Toronto was probably the foundry of Sheldon, Dutcher & Company which was employing eighty men by 1833.[13] Thus the manufacturing stage, though still in its beginning, was plainly in evidence in Toronto before the "market" stage was completed.[14]

Toronto was also making definite steps forward in the same period of the 1830's towards Gras's third phase, the development of transportation. We have seen how the roads were being improved within the city. By 1833 similar macadamization projects were being undertaken in the surrounding townships, and stretches of macadamized highway were gradually being extended along Yonge and Dundas Streets and Kingston Road. Vehicles for the transportation of both goods and people were also making their appearance. Carters were available in the city, and the first cab was built in 1837.[15] For travel beyond the city scheduled stagecoach itineraries had been established as early as 1816, and by 1833 there were regular runs of coaches from Toronto to all the main neighbouring centres. In the winter almost daily connections were available west to Hamilton, via both the Lakeshore Road and Dundas Street, east to the Bay of Quinte and Montreal, and north to Holland Landing on Lake Simcoe. Toronto was thus developing an effective system of communication with its agricultural hinterland.

The main lines of transportation outside the city were, however, by boat, whenever the seasons permitted. Water connections had developed rather earlier than land transportation and by 1826 one newspaper had been able to report that there were no less than five steamboats on the lake and "the routes of each are so arranged that almost every day of the week the traveller may find opportunities of being conveyed from one extremity of the Lake to the other in a few hours."[16] In 1834 there were seven boats running from Toronto, five making a full circuit of the lake, which usually took a week, and two more providing more localized connections: the one with Niagara (-on-the-Lake), the other with Rochester. Between them, these boats connected Toronto with the stage routes leading onward to Montreal and major American cities, as well with transit routes along the Rideau Canal in one direction and to the Upper Great Lakes in the other.

The focal position of Toronto in water transportation in the years that followed incorporation is well shown by the number of piers built in its harbour. The 1833 Directory showed only the government dock, two small piers, and a third commercial wharf which was still under construction. By 1842, when James Cane engraved the Sir Charles Bagot Plan of the city, there were no less than four new private wharfs. Nearly all of these, including the three that were the main commercial piers of the city, were in use by the time of the 1836 Rebellion.

Although Toronto was thus a major shipping centre it was never the scene of much shipbuilding. Its merchants were, however, shareholders in many of the ships built around the lake, and Torontonians such as Hugh Richardson and the Macintosh brothers commanded many of the most notable vessels. The merchants and leading citizens were also interested in any canal building measures that would expand the commerce of the capital. The connection between the Family Company and the Welland Canal Company is well known, and many leading Torontonians, including William Lyon Mackenzie, who is not often thought of as a capitalist, were involved with the Desjardins Canal venture.

Not satisfied with their steamer and stage connections, in the years 1834-38 the merchants of the city made their first attempt to improve communications with their hinterland to the north and north-west of the city by planning a railway. The surveys originally called for a line to Lake Simcoe, but later this was altered so that it would have run to Lake Huron, and so to the American west beyond. The idea failed to materialize because of the depression of 1836, but it was to be revised when times had improved in 1844, and would eventually become the Northern Railway.

In general, then, it could be said that Toronto had established quite adequate connections with a considerable hinterland region, considering the level of technology of the period, about the time of its incorporation. Moreover, the merchants of the city were already looking ahead to any new means, such as railways or canals, to spread its sphere of influence farther. In fact, Toronto's development in communications was, if anything, ahead of its advance in manufacturing. Thus even though it had not quite completed phase one of its metropolitan development it was entering phases two and three simultaneously, to become both a centre of manufacturing and a hub of communications.

IV

Toronto was still far from the fourth stage of metropolitan development in the years we are discussing; but, as Gras noted, financial evolution of a rudimentary sort takes place during the earlier phases, and such changes can be seen in Toronto at the incorporation period. Like the city's other activities, the financial advance was accelerated considerably by the growth of population and commerce.

The merchants of the city had always been alive to investment possibilities and, though there was as yet no stock market, a considerable trade in stock had developed by the early 1830's. This was carried on partly by opening books for subscription to new enterprises, partly by banks handling stock transactions, and partly by various dealers in a variety of businesses also selling stock. The city was further a centre for the sale of land both within its limits and in its hinterland. As the seat of government it was the location of the Crown Lands office. It was also a centre of control of the powerful Canada Land Company, and of various independent land agents, one of whom, Joseph Talbot, even published a weekly newspaper devoted almost exclusively to land sales in 1834-35.[17]

Banking in Toronto also underwent a major boom period in the years preceding the panic of 1837. For a decade the government-allied Bank of Upper Canada was the only bank in the city. Its first real rival was the Commercial Bank of the Midland District, founded at Kingston in 1832 and partly controlled by Toronto interests, which soon opened an office in Toronto.[18] Because, like the Bank of Upper Canada, it was a Tory organization, it did not stop Reform demand for an independent bank. As the Reformers soon quarreled among themselves, however, they ended up with two new banks in Toronto, not one: the Farmers' Joint Stock & Banking Company, founded in May, 1835, and the Bank of the People, established in November of the same year. The latter was run by a somewhat more radical group than the former. Meanwhile, two English financiers had chosen Toronto as the site for a banking operation and opened the Agricultural Bank there in the spring of 1834. This institution was the only one willing to underwrite the first Toronto loan, and the first to pay interest (three percent) on deposits.[19] Rather more enterprising in its policy than the banks dominated by the Reformers, it was also the only bank to go under in the panic of 1837. Before the depression temporarily put a stop to banking expansion, there also appeared the English-direct Bank of British North America, which chose Toronto as the site of its first office in June, 1837. Except for the Upper Canada and the Commercial, all these banks were partnerships rather than chartered companies.

That the Toronto banks were generally able to survive the troubles of the later 1830's showed that the financial expension of the city was not premature. From this time on Toronto was unquestionably the financial centre of the province, and was recognized as such even beyond the provincial boundaries. The collapse of the Agricultural Bank, moreover, was brought on in 1837 by overexpansion in New York State, and not because of its Toronto banking operations.

Another facet of Toronto's contemporary financial growth was the appearance of local insurance companies. Prior to this time the insurance business in the city had been handled by agents of English and American firms; but in 1832-34 a group of prominent citizens founded the British America Fire & Life Assurance Company, which still continues in business today. Although there were members of the Reform party in this group other leading Reformers in the city decided to found a second company, and the Home District Mutual Fire Insurance Company was accordingly set up in 1837.

A final evidence of Toronto's metropolitan growth, perhaps, was the beginning of labour troubles there — though these were of a very minor nature. The printers established a union in 1832, and in October of 1836 staged an unsuccessful strike, calling down upon themselves the wrath of Mackenzie, who uttered statements worthy of the most unreconstructed tycoon when faced with a strike himself.[20] The printers' strike was followed almost immediately by an equally unsuccessful tailors' strike. Although organized labour made little progress during the period, the apprentices in the stores had some success, for the merchants agreed to an 8 p.m. closing in August, 1836,[21] and a 7 p.m. closing in November 1840.[22] Sundays were, of course, excepted.

V

Thus, by the 1830's, Toronto, in spite of its small population and the lack of developmental funds, was on the way to becoming much more than a market centre. If we accept Gras's terminology, the city had gone beyond the first stage and entered phases two and three of metropolitan economic growth, even though the great boom in both these stages would not come until the railways were completed in the mid-1850's. The city was also the centre of a growing hinterland which extended throughout most of the settled areas of the province to the north and west, and financially, to an extent, as far as Kingston in the east.

In any case, leaving Gras's terminology aside, we may say that by 1834 Toronto was already much more to Upper Canada than simply the political capital and the focus of provincial society; it was also becoming the prime focus of its business. Some of this business activity was admittedly concentrating there because Toronto was the seat of government, but by this very concentration the city was developing into something more than an administrative centre, while losing its dependence on being such a centre at the same time. In fact, Toronto had grown beyond the stage of dependence on the government and become a substantially powerful economic community on its own with a growing hinterland. This transition had manifestly taken place between the late 1820's and the Rebellion. Thus, in the economic as well as the political sense, these years were ones of critical transition, when the Town of York became the City of Toronto, and its village economy began to assume a metropolitan character.

NOTES:

1. The writer would like to thank Professor J. M. S. Careless, University of Toronto, Miss Edith G. Firth of the Metropolitan Toronto Central Library, and his colleague Professor A. M. J. Hyatt, who all read the original manuscript and made many helpful suggestions.

   Since this paper was written a decade ago, urban studies have made almost unbelievable strides in Canada, as elsewhere, and the Gras thesis, on which this article is based, has been greatly amplified by the work of such historians as Eric Lampard. In view of the fact that this is a reprint, however, the original structure has been left as it stands, although changes have been made in some points and additional footnotes added.

2. Recent work has, of course, greatly changed this picture. G. P. de T. Glazebrook has provided us with the first overall analytical survey of the city's development in *The Story of Toronto* (Toronto, 1971) and many of the important issues in the city's development are being examined by a number of scholars using a wide variety of techniques.

3. Robinson's book was reissued, with extra appendices, by the University of Toronto Press in 1965.

4. See her two excellent volumes: *The Town of York, 1793-1815* (Toronto, 1962) and *The Town of York, 1815-1834* (Toronto, 1966).

5. N. S. B. Gras, *An Introduction to Economic History* (New York, 1922), p. 402.

6. The Macaulay Papers in the Ontario Archives provide many interesting examples of this trade.

7. *Courier of Upper Canada*, September 29, 1832.

8. *Constitution*, November 7, 1836. He had set up an elaborate agency system even before he left Queenston in 1824.

9. Upper Canada, *Statutes*, 4 William IV, c. 23, (1834).

10. Minutes of the Quarter Sessions of the Peace of the Home District, March 26, 1936 (Public Archives of Ontario and Metropolitan Central Library).

11. Toronto City Council Papers, May 6, 1835 (Public Archives of Ontario).

12. D. C. Masters, *The Rise of Toronto 1850-1890* (Toronto, 1947), p. 15.

13. *Courier of Upper Canada*, April 27, 1833.

14. John E. MacNab examined the manufacturing growth of Toronto in "Toronto's industrial growth to 1891," *Ontario History*, Vol. XLVII (1955), p. 59-80, coming to much the same conclusions for this period.

15. J. R. Robertson, *Landmarks of Toronto*, 6 vols. (Toronto, 1894-1914), Vol. II, p. 677.

16. Henry Scadding, *Toronto of Old* (Toronto, 1873), p. 548.

17. *The Upper Canada Land, Mercantile and General Advertiser*, published June, 1834–August, 1835.

18. *Patriot*, February 1, 1833.

19. *Advocate*, June 26, 1834.

20. See F. H. Armstrong, "Reformer as Capitalist: William Lyon Mackenzie and the Printers' Strike of 1836," *Ontario History*, Vol. LIX, No. 3 (September, 1967), pp. 187-196.

21. *Patriot*, August 9, 1836.

22. *Mirror*, November 20, 1840.

III METROPOLITAN GROWTH AND THE SPREAD OF THE URBAN NETWORK, 1850-1930

The question of urban growth in Canada since 1850 has received a considerable amount of attention from historians and geographers. A variety of factors have been isolated, such as location, initial advantage, internal leadership, outside government or corporate decisions and a rich hinterland. It is extremely difficult, of course, to weigh precisely the relative merits of any of these factors for cities in general or even for any particular place, for that matter. But some of the descriptive and analytical problems become more manageable when one realizes that scholars usually operate at one of at least three different scales of explanation, the local, the regional, or the national. All are closely related but will be discussed separately here. The first level is that of the individual city or town which is often treated in biographical form; that is, the community as a whole is treated as a personality with distinguishable characteristics. Peter Goheen's essay on Toronto in this section is a good example, for the author has successfully related several of the complex facets of a city. Much of the literature on the growth of individual cities tends to emphasize the initiative of elites, either through private entrepreneurial action, or through group efforts such as Boards of Trade or municipal councils. Some of this activity has been termed "boosterism" as leaders aggressively promote their community in the hopes of raising its status, or at least maintaining it within the regional or national urban hierarchy.[1]

A second level of description and analysis involves urban growth in a regional context such as the West, Ontario, Quebec or the Maritimes and includes the articles by W.T. Acheson and Alan Artibise in this section. Discussions at this scale usually concentrate on the economic base of the region and especially, the region's location within the larger Canadian context, for urban development was closely related to a particular region's function and location. For example, national policies on tariffs and transportation seemed designed to strengthen the growth of manufacturing in cities of the central regions, while cities in the Maritimes and the West remained subject to the international market in staples and to outside government and corporate decisions.[2]

A third scale of explanation is that of the national urban system. In comparison with the work that has been done on other levels, this is the least developed area of study except for the pioneering work of J.M.S. Careless and James Simmons.[3] Both stress the ''openness'' of the Canadian urban system — that is, the extent to which it is influenced by external forces. To a large extent, the economic function of Canadian cities has always involved the export of raw materials from fur and fish in the earliest years to lumber and wheat in the nineteenth century to minerals in the twentieth. Fluctuations in the international demand for these products has had an immediate and direct effect on urban growth. Another characteristic of the Canadian urban system is the extent to which cities represent an integral component of what has come to be known as a heartland — hinterland or core-periphery explanation of Canadian development. Some of the basic essentials of the urban system in central and eastern Canada were established by the middle of the 19th century. By 1851 the nine largest cities — Montreal (with a population of over 50,000), Quebec City, Saint John (including Portland), Toronto, Halifax, Hamilton, Kingston, Ottawa, and London — had developed into dynamic commercial centres and had won metropolitan hegemony over sizeable hinterlands.

The completion of the urban network and the emergence of the modern Canadian city took place in the later portion of the period from 1851 to 1921. In most respects the changes in the system in the first three decades after 1851 were relatively minor adjustments. Toronto replaced Quebec as the second city, and several manufacturing towns in Southern Ontario grew to almost 10,000 in population (Guelph, St. Catharines, Brantford, and Belleville), forming a second tier of cities behind the original nine. The changes in the urban hierarchy were more dramatic and basic after 1881. Perhaps the most significant was the relative growth of the two largest cities. Montreal and Toronto previously had been only marginally larger than those ranked third and fourth, but after 1851 these two began to assume some of the characteristics of primate cities, outdistancing their nearest rivals by three and four times. Equally dramatic was the sudden appearance of the western cities, led by Winnipeg and Vancouver, which mushroomed to third and fourth place by 1921, soon to be closely followed by two other young giants, Calgary and Edmonton. These spectacular developments signalled the relative decline of Quebec and Kingston in central Canada and of Saint John and Halifax in the Atlantic provinces.[4]

NOTES:

1. Some of the best examples are, D.C. Masters, *The Rise of Toronto, 1850-1890* (Toronto [1947] 1974); Jacob Spelt, *Toronto* (Toronto, 1973); Paul-André Linteau, *Maisonneuve: Comment les promoteurs fabriquent une ville* (Montreal, 1981); David Sutherland, "The Personnel and Policies of the Halifax Board of Trade, 1890-1914," in L.R. Fischer and Eric Sager, eds., *The Enterprising Canadians: Entrepreneurs and Economic Development in Eastern Canada* (St. John's, 1979); L.D. McCann, "Staples and the New Industrialism in the Growth of Post-Confederation Halifax," in Gilbert Stelter and Alan Artibise, eds., *Shaping the Urban Landscape: Aspects of the Canadian City-Building Process* (Ottawa, 1982); Alan Artibise, *Winnipeg: A Social History of Urban Growth, 1874-1914* (Montreal, 1975); Paul Voisey, "Boosting the Small Prairie Town, 1904-1931," in Artibise, ed., *Town and City, Aspects of Western Canadian Urban Development* (Regina, 1981).

2. Examples are Jacob Spelt, *Urban Development in South Central Ontario* (Toronto, 1972); John U. Marshall and W.R. Smith, "The Dynamics of Growth in a Regional Urban System: Southern Ontario, 1851-1971, *Canadian Geographer*, 22 (1978), pp. 22-40; T.W. Acheson, "The Maritimes and Empire Canada", in D.J. Bercuson, ed., *Canada and the Burden of Unity* (Toronto, 1977); J.M.S. Careless, "Aspects of Metropolitanism in Atlantic Canada", in Mason Wade, ed., *Regionalism in the Canadian Community, 1867-1967* (Toronto, 1969); Careless, "Aspects of Urban Life in the West, 1870-1914," in A.W. Rasporich and H.C. Klassen, eds., *Prairie Perspectives 2* (Toronto, 1973); Alan Artibise, "City-Building in the Canadian West: From Boosterism to Corporatism," *Journal of Canadian Studies*, 17 (Autumn, 1982), pp. 35-44.

3. Careless, "Metropolis and Region: The Interplay Between City and Region in Canadian History," *Urban History Review*, No. 3-78 (February, 1979), pp. 99-118; Simmons, "The Evolution of the Canadian Urban System," in Alan Artibise and Gilbert Stelter, eds., *The Usable Urban Past: Planning and Politics in the Modern Canadian City* (Toronto, 1979); L.D. McCann, ed., *Heartland and Hinterland: A Geography of Canada* (Scarborough, Ont., 1982).

4. For a general discussion of these trends, see Gilbert Stelter, "The City-Building Process in Canada," in Stelter and Artibise, eds., *Shaping the Urban Landscape*.

Currents of Change in Toronto, 1850-1900

PETER G. GOHEEN

During the half century following 1850 Toronto welcomed the age of iron and steam, experienced the revolution of industrialization, and outgrew both its old shell and perhaps its old ways. The colonial city which had been isolated by dint of geography and politics from the mainstreams of economic life on the continent became a commercial and industrial capital of first rank. The new city was distinguished from the old by its size, by its communications, and by its social and economic organization. Toronto in 1851 housed 30,775 persons; in 1901 the figure was 208,040,[1] a population increase of almost 700 percent within fifty years.

Among the most important innovations which appeared in the urban landscape during these fifty years were those features around which the economic system of production reorganized itself. Additionally, a few remarks indicating what can be gleaned from already available information about the social landscapes of the city throughout the period. Scadding anticipated the social importance of change in defining the character of the city after mid century when, in 1873, he perceptively titled his book *Toronto of Old*.[2] The new Toronto was only beginning its history of transition in the 1870's; the process would continue for the remainder of the century.

THE ECONOMIC DIMENSIONS OF CHANGE

By mid-century, certain old and respected realities of Canada's commercial life had been fundamentally altered. The system of trade and the organization of the commerce of Britain's northern American colonies had

SOURCE: Peter G. Goheen, *Victorian Toronto, 1850 to 1900* (Chicago: University of Chicago, Department of Geography, 1970), pp. 58-92. Reprinted by permission of the author.

been shattered. The commercial aggressiveness of the colonies' southern neighbour, in concert with the revocation by the British of the concept of commercial protection for colonial goods, as witnessed in the repeal of the Corn Laws and the subsequent abrogation of the Navigation Acts, served to kill the old arrangements of trade and commerce by which the Canadian commercial system had so long survived. In particular, the system of commerce by which Montreal had been granted privileges amounting to a monopoly on the export trade of Canada was ended. Of this ending, Creighton has written:

> With the repudiation of its past and this denial of its ancient principles, the history of the Canadian commercial state comes to a close. . . . 1849 meant the conclusion of an entire drama. . . . The commercial empire of the St. Lawrence was bankrupt. . . . The failure to win the international commercial empire of the west and the forfeiture of part of the trading monopoly of western Canada had come home to a commercial generation whose historic weapons were broken in their hands and whose traditional support had vanished. . . . The design of the St. Lawrence, as the Canadian merchants had always conceived it in the past, had been shattered beyond redemption. . . . Canada had ceased to be an imperial trade route which sought its source of supply in the international American west, which built its political structure in the interests of commerce and which found its markets and its final court of appeal in the ample resources of the British Empire.[3]

In this collapse of an old Imperial design lay the possibilities for Toronto's rise; Toronto was provided with an opportunity to challenge the Montreal merchants for control of their old Empire up and down the St. Lawrence valley. To meet this challenge meant that new communications would be required and this, in the middle years of the nineteenth century, meant railways.

The Promise of the Rails

> Railroad iron is a magician's rod in its power to evoke the sleeping energies of land and water.[4]

The story of the railroads introduces Toronto at the point when its first energies were about to be directed toward creating those conditions that would make possible its eventual and successful rise to the status of a great city. The transformation of the city from a quiet commercial centre into a metropolis in which the commerce of the province would concentrate and the industry of a great city would prosper may date from the collapse of the old strategy of trade which had worked so well against the interests of Toronto and so fitfully for the commercial growth of Montreal. The destruction of the old commercial system of the ''Empire of the St. Lawrence'' presented Toronto with new opportunities to exploit its long appreciated geographical position and its newly developed relationships with the Canadian West, with New York, and with Ontario.

Most importantly, an opportunity now arose for alternate systems of transportation to contest the monopoly previously enjoyed by Montreal as a port for shipping the staples of the interior to the market of Britain. Now there were no laws insisting that exports destined to Britain cross the Atlantic in British bottoms, now the possibilities of using the Erie Canal and New York as a route to European markets were available. This alternative was attractive because the costs of shipping from New York to Europe were considerably less than the costs from Montreal to the same markets. Without the protection of the old British mercantile system, Montreal was subject to direct competition for the exports of the West. Further, although shipping costs from the West to Montreal were less than those from the West to New York, New York enjoyed a great advantage in overseas shipping rates.[5] New York's competitive position for the trade from the Canadian and United States agricultural interiors was greatly enhanced when British ports were opened to commodities shipped from American ports and in American ships as well as goods arriving from Canadian ports in British ships. Toronto was in an ideal position to take advantage of these new opportunities. For some time, Toronto had been able to import directly from New York, but now she was able to explore the possibilities of exporting via that port as well.

Toronto's competitive position as the Canadian terminal for trade from the West and from Ontario was now greatly enhanced. She could herself compete for some benefits from the carrying trade. As one author put it, the "Toronto Carrying Place" was now becoming, once again as in the days of the French traders, a route of trade. Exports from Toronto increased greatly, and the exportation was predominantly through the United States. In 1859, only two percent of the shipments of wheat and flour from Toronto went to Montreal and Quebec, the rest went out by Oswego and the American ports.[6] A sign of the increasing importance of this trade to Toronto is the increasing number of merchants engaged in the import and export of various items, including lumber, grain, livestock, hardware, and consumer goods.[7] This trade was possible in good measure because of the railroads which were being built to Toronto.

Building the Railways

Toronto's desire for trade made it necessary to build railroads. Toronto's campaign for trade from the St. Lawrence basin and from the opening West was pursued by the construction of railway lines which were built first into peninsular Ontario in an attempt to capture the trade of this growing area, then to Ontario ports in an effort to funnel the Western trade via the upper Great Lakes into the city, and finally to a few United States ports in an effort to create cheap routes along which to channel the exports of the great Western hinterland destined eventually for overseas markets. Toronto's greatest enthusiasm in the optimistic days of the early and mid 1850's was reserved for those lines which would extend the city's influence into the hinterland of Ontario and the West. George Brown, editor of *The Globe*, perhaps Toronto's leading newspaper, was convinced that the city's commercial influence would spread along the rail lines.[8]

The city's first railway was incorporated in August of 1849 under the name of the Toronto, Simcoe, and Huron Railway Company. The first sod was turned on October 15, 1851 and on 15 May 1853, the road was first opened to the public. The Northern Railroad, as it became known, opened the 53 miles from Toronto to Barrie in 1853, and on June 2, 1855, the route was complete to Collingwood, a port on Georgian Bay some 95 miles distant from Toronto.[9] Toronto's first railway sought to exploit those particular advantages of the city's situation which had been appreciated from the earliest days of European settlement along the shores of Lake Ontario.[10] An old understanding was being realized, belatedly, under the impulses of a new policy.

The railway was built by city businessmen in an effort to secure the trade of Ontario and more especially of the West, thereby gaining an advantage in the competition for this trade over Buffalo and New York.[11] Brown saw in this the splendid realization of the strategy of Simcoe; that the Toronto Passage would be an important overland route for trade. The wealth of the western continent would ''come pouring down its rails to a mighty Toronto entrepôt.''[12] The dreams were realized, though not immediately. Collingwood was a terminus for trade gathered from the Upper Great Lakes on both sides of the international border. By 1861, Collingwood maintained a tri-weekly steamer service to Lake Michigan ports. So successful was this port in siphoning the trade of the lakes and funnelling it on to Toronto that the new town was moved to protest its status as a mere outport of the larger city. Grain now moved from Chicago to Toronto with great efficiency, untouched by human hands.[13] For the first time since the French regime, the Toronto Passage was a significant route and Toronto was beginning to realize advantages others had long seen in its situation.

The second railway to enter the city provided it with links to the American ports. In early December of 1855 Toronto was connected with the Great Western Railway system. Now the city had direct rail connections with Buffalo and Windsor. The Great Western was designed to be part of a system which would carry traffic from Michigan to New York state, passing on the shortest route between these points. That route, it happened, lay through

Ontario along the north shore of Lake Erie. Toronto interests had not sponsored this line nor had they supported it financially to the degree that they had invested in the Northern Railway. This was not Toronto's businessmen's brainchild, but nevertheless the city's connection with the trunk line proved to be very important from a variety of perspectives. This railway was particularly important for Toronto, not only for its long distance connections, but because it linked the city with the major competitor for trade in South Central Ontario. This was the city at the head of the lake, Hamilton. Toronto was now able directly to challenge the commercial position of Hamilton in peninsular Ontario. Although Hamilton had enjoyed rail connections with the Great Western before Toronto had, the stronger commercial interests in the larger city asserted their position with the consequence that Hamilton suffered from the competition. The Great Western was the principal instrument for the early extension of Toronto's commercial hinterland into rapidly growing Southern Ontario.[14] It is significant in this context that Toronto was connected with New York state by rail before it had similar ties with Montreal. In part, this advantage over its Canadian sister city helped Toronto perserve its trading area against the competitive powers of the largest city of Canada. This was particularly true for the development of a substantial wholesaling business in Toronto, for the city aggressively sought the job of supplying the merchants of Ontario. Further, Toronto continued to import through New York, avoiding dependence upon Montreal and the expense of transport on the St. Lawrence River.

The third railway to enter Toronto arrived in the autumn of 1856. At last Toronto was connected by rail with Montreal. The railway had been largely designed as a substitute for the inconvenience and inefficiencies caused by the canal system of the St. Lawrence River, which was icebound several months of every year. The railway would, it was hoped, overcome the need to transship cargo *en route* to Montreal. The line was extended to Sarnia from Toronto in late 1859, further aiding the Ontario city in its efforts to establish itself as the undisputed commercial centre of agricultural Ontario. The Grand Trunk Railway was predominantly a Montreal venture and was an important expression of that city's effort to extend its commercial hinterland to the limits of the old commercial empire of the Saint Lawrence. The railway was not an immediate success. Progress toward creating an effective system by which to capture the trade of the new West was extremely slow. It was not until early in 1880 that the Grand Trunk developed direct connections with Chicago, for example. In 1882 the Grand Trunk and the Great Western systems merged in a belated effort to improve their financial positions.[15] By this time the prospects of the trunk railways had been reappraised and were found not to be so promising. One reason why the trunk lines failed to meet the expectations of their success was that they never succeeded in attracting the inbound trade which continued to reach most of Canada via New York. Furthermore, as was soon realized, the railways of Ontario were not so much complementary to the canal system of the St. Lawrence as they were competitive with it.[16]

The attention of Toronto's businessmen continued to focus on the opportunity to capture the trade of the growing hinterland of Southern Ontario. The Great Western had revealed the possibilities afforded by direct rail connections with a growing hinterland and had further revealed the ability of Ontario's first city to compete with any other provincial towns for

TABLE 1

POPULATION AND INDUSTRIAL GROWTH OF TORONTO, 1860 TO 1901

Year	Population	Industrial Statistics		
		Number of Establishments	Employees	Value of Articles Produced (in dollars)
1860	44,821[a]			
1870	56,092[b]	497[f]	9,400	13,686,093
1880	86,415[c]	932[g]	12,708	19,100,116
1890	144,023[d]	2,109[h]	24,480	42,489,352
1901	208,040[e]	847[i]	42,515	58,415,498

[a] Canada, Board of Registration and Statistics, *Census of the Canadas, 1860-61*, I, 48.

[b] Canada, Department of Agriculture, *Census of Canada, 1870-71*, I, 16-17.

[c] Canada, Department of Agriculture, *Census of Canada, 1880-81*, I, 73.

[d] Canada, Department of Agriculture, *Census of Canada, 1890-91*, I, 66.

[e] Canada, Census and Statistics Office, *Fourth Census of Canada, 1901*, I, 22.

[f] The industrial statistics for 1870 are derived from the *Census of Canada, 1870-71*, III, 290-445.

[g] The industrial statistics for 1880 are given in the *Census of Canada, 1880-81*, III, 503.

[h] The industrial statistics for 1890 are given in the *Census of Canada, 1890-91*, III, 385.

[i] The industrial statistics for 1901 are given in the *Fourth Census of Canada, 1901*, III, 329. These statistics refer only to establishments employing five or more persons.

commercial dominance. The building of local lines was, therefore, indulged in at great expense and with even greater hopes. It was thought that a well developed system of feeder rail lines focusing on Toronto would offset the weaknesses of the canal and railway system which had largely failed to secure for the city a major role in the handling of through traffic. In 1868 the Toronto and Nipissing was chartered under the guiding influence of George Laidlaw, a prominent Toronto investor. The railroad was designed to tap the timber stands, which would bring trade to Toronto from east of Lake Simcoe and Georgian Bay. In 1872 it had reached as far as Coboconk, east of Lake Simcoe. At about this time the railway promoters were busy with schemes designed to tap the Lake Huron trade as well. Among others, the Grey and Bruce was undertaken reaching from Toronto to Owen Sound. Likewise, the Wellington, Grey, and Bruce Railway was built to tap the Ontario hinterland. Meanwhile, the Northern was being extended along Georgian Bay from Collingwood to Meaford, another small port.

Within twenty years of the first line into Ontario the province was crisscrossed by railroads; some were trunk lines designed to carry through traffic and sprout towns along the way, others were designed to trap the local trade of their regions and funnel this into the metropolis. By 1880 the enthusiasm for new lines was dying.[17] Toronto was not the only city to have been active in spawning rail lines, and eventually the network was overextended. Numerous lines were later to be consolidated in the effort to reduce losses, but in the meantime, there had sprung into existence a well articulated system of transport which could be used to collect the produce of the land and to distribute in return the commerce and, later, the manufacturers, of the city. In 1860 the united provinces of Canada were traversed by 1,880 miles of track. In 1875-76, the figure was 5,157 miles, under the control of no less than 37 companies.[18] The system was substantially complete. Its importance was not unappreciated, for as one Toronto writer put it: "no other one thing has contributed so materially in building up the city. It has made it really the metropolis . . . the mart of Ontario."[19]

The Growth of Industries

The growth of industries in Toronto in the last decades of the nineteenth century provided further evidence of a new era in the life of the town. The industrial establishments which intruded into the old urban landscape were but the bulkiest symbols of the process by which the life of the city was being reorganized.

Two sets of statistics document the changing economic complexion of the city: in 1870, 9,400 industrial employees produced articles valued at $13,093; in 1901, 42,515 industrial employees produced goods valued at $58,415,498.[20] Industrial growth during these thirty years was not steady and there remains some mystery as to how the industrialization of the city proceeded so rapidly during a period of general economic depression.[21] Nonetheless, the achievement of an industrialized economy by 1900 cannot seriously be questioned. Industry was by 1900, perhaps, the single most important source of employment and of income in the city.

The growth of employment in industry and the development of the factory system were the fruits of patient labouring. The momentum of change built up slowly. The first industrial production-lines in the city date from no later than 1850 and perhaps much earlier. By 1856, however, factory operatives were beginning to be conspicuous among the artisans and craftsmen who formerly had monopolized industrial employment within the city.[22] The factory system was first adopted in the manufacture of materials and products the demand for which was created by the newly developed nineteenth-century technology. Steam and iron were responsible for creating the first factory-industry in the city. The Toronto Locomotive Works, established in 1852, was among the first major industrial establishments to be organized as a large scale factory.[23] In 1860 the city was still properly characterized as a place of craftsmen and artisans. These skilled workers were the last to abandon their well established system of production in favour of the regimentation and scale economies achieved by the factory. Gradually, however, the jobs of the skilled were reorganized.

As the population of the city grew, so also did the number of industries. In 1871, a city of just over 56,000 people was the home of 497 industries. By 1881, 932 manufacturing establishments were located in a city of over 86,000 population (Table 4). Despite the numerical increase of establishments, evidence suggests that no fundamental change in the scale of manufacturing operations had taken place in the decade prior to 1880. In 1871, there were, on the average, 19 employees per establishment; in 1881 the number remained about the same, declining to roughly 13 per establishment. The large-scale factory continued to be a somewhat exotic feature in the economic landscape, although the number and size of these establishments continued to increase. In its annual review of commerce in Toronto, *The Globe*, in February of 1886 noted the existence of a number of large factories in the city.[24] This review identified several firms employing over one hundred persons. Among these were the Toronto Rolling Mills, manufacturing nails and employing, according to *The Globe*, some 300 men; for another, a boiler and still factory employed 120 men. By this time, several factories not engaged in metal fabricating were large as well. The Gooderham and Worts Distillery employed 160 hands, Jacques and Hay cabinet factory had 400 men working, and a meat packing plant was said to have 300 workers.

The first signs of rapid industrial growth in the city were noted during the succeeding decade, from 1880 to 1890, when the real turn in the fortunes of the city occurred. The population of the city almost doubled in the decade and the value of articles produced more than doubled. By 1890, over forty million dollars value came from the factories and shops of the city (Table 1). The number of employees per factory, averaged over the entire range of industry, remained small, but important new large-scale industrial establishments were now in operation. Of these, one of the most noteworthy was the Massey Manufacturing Company. Daniel Massey had established an agricultural implement business in nearby Newcastle in 1847. In 1879, the entire business was moved to Toronto.[25] By 1890, the census taker recorded that at the one firm in the city manufacturing agricultural implements there were 575 persons employed.[26]

By 1900, the factory system had been introduced to Toronto not only as a means of organizing the production of those materials the demand for which was created by new uses of iron and steam but also as the system for manufacturing those goods which had for many years constituted the industrial product of the city but which had until now been manufactured in small workshops by craftsmen and artisans. A whole new scale of production was now becoming evident through a process by which the factory replaced the small scale shop. The scale shifts in manufacturing are revealed in the statistics for 1890, 1901, and 1905. In 1901, an average of 50 men laboured in each city factory, defined for census purposes as a manufacturing establishment employing five or more persons (Table 1). A special 1905 census of manufacturing confirms the trend to large-scale factory production. In that year, when all establishments of every size were enumerated, 38 persons on the average were employed per work place.[27] When compared with the 11 or 12 workers per plant averaged in 1890, the dimensions of the change begin to be clear. This represented a second stage in the industrialization process. In the first, the value of products manufactured had increased greatly, along with a rise in the number of establishments in the city, but without a change in the overall scale of the unit of production. The second stage, the period in which the number of employees per establishment increased dramatically, corresponded with the adoption by many kinds of manufacturing enterprises of the factory system of production. This process involved not only enlarging the scale of production but also the consolidation of many small workshops into larger factories.

Toronto's industrial growth began slowly and had a late start. Among the possible explanations for this, two of the most important relate to her difficulties in securing economical ties with the West and the correlation between her own prosperity and that of the Ontario hinterland. Toronto's efforts to secure for herself a portion of the trade of the West were marked by much frustration following the initial success at appropriating a share of the grain trade of the Lakes via Collingwood and the Northern Railway. Subsequent to this, attempts to gain access by rail to Chicago were delayed until 1880 and the completion of Grand Trunk, by which time the coast advantage formerly enjoyed by the Toronto-Montreal route over New York for grain shipment from Chicago had been reversed.[28] To a considerable degree, the inefficiencies of the St. Lawrence canal system contributed to the uncompetitive character of the Canadian route. Furthermore, Toronto was deprived of her important Georgian Bay timber hinterland after 1883 when the tolls on the Erie Canal were removed without similar steps being taken to end Welland Canal charges.[29] Ontario timber then took the American route to Europe. No precise analysis has been made of Toronto's reliance upon her own immediate hinterland as a source of trade and as a market, but there have been suggestions that the city's commercial and industrial prosperity was linked to the growth of Southern Ontario which, by the 1880's boasted a dense network of small rail lines many of which radiated out from Toronto.[30]

In her struggle to win a share of the Canadian West's trade Toronto experienced considerable difficulty. Initially, Toronto interests were unsuccessful in securing the charter for the Canadian Pacific Railway which was to connect British Columbia with central Canada. After the original charter for the railway was cancelled and a new company organized for the same purpose in 1880, Toronto business interests again failed to win the contract. Montreal became, in fact, the eastern terminus for the Canadian Pacific Railway, although a feeder line was built northward from Toronto to connect the city with the transcontinental line. Having experienced difficulty securing good overland connections with the West, Toronto's business community displayed interest in the Great Lakes. In 1886 when grain elevators were built at Port Arthur on Lake Superior, Owen Sound became a grain port providing Toronto with the shortest possible route between the Great Lakes and the St. Lawrence River outlet.[31] Symptomatic of Toronto's improving competitive position by the end of the decade, foreign imports to the city rose substantially between 1884 and 1889.[32]

Toronto's industrial prosperity would have been impossible without the system of transportation which made it possible for the city's industries to serve efficiently and compete for a sizeable trading hinterland. The success of the city in the competition for markets is revealed in statistics showing localization of manufacturing in the city. Even before 1880 the advantages offered by Toronto as a convenient and cheap transportation hub were appreciated by at least a few industrialists. The availability of low cost transportation and its attendant advantages in the search for markets have been cited as inducements attracting the Massey Company to Toronto in 1879.[33] As other factories found Toronto convenient and attractive because of access to the Ontario markets, both urban and rural, numerous types of industry began to localize within the city. In particular, the manufacture of consumer goods became localized in the city. Clothing, secondary wood products, and non-ferrous metal products became increasingly localized in the city as did such services as printing and publishing. By contrast, in such resource processing activities as primary food and beverage production and

TABLE 2

VALUE ADDED IN MANUFACTURING, BY INDUSTRY, FOR YORK COUNTY, IN 1870, 1880 AND IN 1890[a]

Industry	Value Added, in Thousands of Dollars, by Year		
	1870	1880	1890
Clothing (textiles and furs)	844	1,362	4,037
	(11.0)[b]	(11.6)	(17.7)
Iron and steel production	1,313	2,791	3,481
	(17.0)	(23.7)	(15.2)
Food and beverages (secondary)	1,526	1,282	2,593
	(19.8)	(10.9)	(11.4)
Printing and publishing	653	1,158	2,332
	(8.5)	(9.9)	(10.2)
Wood products (secondary)	364	500	1,282
	(4.7)	(4.2)	(5.6)
Non-metallic mineral products	178	362	1,161
	(2.3)	(3.1)	(5.1)
Leather products	822	851	996
	(10.6)	(7.2)	(4.4)
Textile products	86	273	928
	(1.1)	(2.3)	(4.1)
Wood products (primary)	390	641	922
	(5.0)	(5.5)	(4.0)
Chemical and allied products	85	336	919
	(1.1)	(2.9)	(4.0)

[a] Data are given in Edward J. Chambers and Gordon W. Bertram, "Urbanization and Manufacturing in Central Canada, 1870-1890," in *Papers on Regional Statistical Studies*, ed. Sylvia Ostry and T. K. Rymes, Canadian Political Science Association: Conference on Statistics, 1964 (Toronto: University of Toronto Press, 1966), pp. 242-53.

[b] Statistics in parentheses indicate the value added as a percentage of the total value added for York county.

the handling of primary wood products, Toronto was of declining importance.[34] When evaluated in the context of the industrialization of Central Canada, Toronto's growth is impressive. For York County, in which Toronto was situated, the ratio of value added in all manufacturing over value added in all manufacturing in Central Canada was 9.72, 11.09 and 13.45 in 1870, 1880 and 1890.[35]

If we look at the relative importance of the various manufacturing sectors to the county itself it can be seen that the same generalizations apply (Table 2). Clothing ranks first in 1890 while other consumer and service sectors contribute heavily to the total of value added. The Table reveals the declining significance for Toronto of such industry groups as primary wood products, leather products and iron and steel production. Primary food and beverages, not shown on the table, also declined in their importance to the creation of value added in manufacture in Toronto.

What these statistics index is the growing importance of Toronto as an industrial centre of Canada and the growing significance for the city itself of manufacturing industry by the end of the century.[36] Whereas Toronto in 1850 was a small trading center, by 1900 she had achieved the rank of a great manufacturing and industrial centre.

ELEMENTS OF THE SOCIAL LANDSCAPES

Street Railways

The symbol of progress and pride perhaps most widely adopted by cities and towns in the latter half of the nineteenth century was the street railway. This visible and dramatic innovation in mass transit had appeared on the streets of several American cities by the early 1850's and was to be seen in Toronto after 1861. Toronto was among the first cities on the continent to grant a charter for construction of a street railway and to witness its building.[37]

When the rails were laid on the streets of Toronto in the early 1860's, they did not initiate public transportation in the city. In 1850 there already were several omnibus lines radiating out from the centre of the city in various directions. The omnibuses had been in operation in the city since at least the early 1840's, but soon ceased operation after the introduction into the city of the first street car.[38]

In October of 1860, Alexander Easton, an Englishman resident of the suburb of Yorkville applied to the Toronto city council for a license granting him exclusive rights to build and operate a street railway in the city. In March of 1861 the council was pleased to grant the license and a thirty-year franchise for the operation of a street railway under certain conditions stipulating the frequency of service and routing of the lines. Three lines were to be built: along Yonge Street, from King to Bloor (the northern boundary of the city), along Queen Street from Yonge to the Asylum in the western part of the city, and along King Street from the Don River in the east to Bathurst Street in the west. The company was duly incorporated in May of 1860 and began operations in September of the same year. The first company report, dated December 31, 1861, indicated that six miles of track had been laid. On Yonge Street, tracks stretched from King Street to the suburban Yorkville Town Hall, on Queen from Yonge to Dundas Street (Ossington Street today), and on King Street the few blocks from the St. Lawrence Market to Yonge Street. The same report indicated that the average daily passenger load numbered 2,000 persons.[39]

Despite this early activity and construction, the railway soon proved to be unremunerative and the company asked for financial relief. In 1869 an act for the relief of the Toronto Street Railway Company was passed and the property sold to new owners. The transfer of ownership brought no rapid expansion of the system which was not yet operating all of the lines called for in the initial contract of 1861. It was not until 1874 that any more building of lines was undertaken.[40] In that year a cautious expansion was undertaken in order to improve service to the more prosperous northern suburbs of the city. By 1880, nineteen miles of track had been laid in Toronto. The railway still was far from serving the whole city. The stimulus for rapid expansion of the network was still largely absent, but expansion of the system had begun.

The decade of 1880-1890 saw a remarkable growth in the population of the city and it was during this ten years that the street railway system first realized expansion on a large scale. Despite the difficulties occasioned at the end of the decade, owing to the expiration of the franchise and the reluctance of the company prior to the termination of their charter in 1891 to extend the company lines, the decade witnessed a rapid growth in service. By 1891 there was a total of 68½ miles of track traversing the city. Every part of the city was now within reasonable easy access of the railway. The system carried over 16 million revenue passengers in 1890, or an average of between 50,000 and 60,000 every working day of the week.[41] At least by 1890, there was no question that the street railway was a vital part of the transportation system of the city, without which its economic life could hardly have been carried on.

Exercising its rights of purchase, the city bought the street railway company at the expiry of the thirty-year franchise in 1891. Late the same year the company was sold to a group of private interests who were granted another 30 year franchise. From 1891 to 1894, in accord with the terms of the franchise agreement, the entire system was electrified.[42] From 1891 to 1897 new additions were made to the system, but disagreements arose as to the legal responsibilities of the company to extend lines to areas of the city incorporated after the date of franchising of the company. The company was upheld by the Privy Council in its interpretion that it had no legal obligation to extend its lines beyond the boundaries of the city as they were defined in 1891. As a result, the expensive job of laying new lines into the newer suburbs of the city was left to subsidiary companies which, subsequently, were purchased and operated by the city.[43] By 1900, numerous companies were operating lines to all areas of the city. The requirements of a growing population were being met by a series of companies; no longer could the indifference of a single traction company deny the city the service it demanded.

The story of street railways in large cities has been told as a serial success story. The rails created the divided city, they exercised a "moral influence"[44] over the townspeople. Such were the accomplishments of the suburbanization made possible by the streetcar ride into the country. In contrast, the story of the building of the street railway in Toronto is told as a series of legal battles and bankruptcies and interruptions to service. The eventual destruction of most of the records of the main traction company leaves many details of the history unavailable for all time. Despite an unquestionably unhealthy climate of operation which was created in part by the thirty-year franchises which were in the habit of expiring at just those times when major investments were called for, and despite the late beginning of rapid population growth which resulted in the early unprofitability of the lines, there is reason to believe that the streetcar lines were of great importance to Toronto. A few threads of evidence on the passenger use of the facilities suggest this. Other evidence points to the early service afforded the better suburban districts of the city. It is of more than passing interest that the first franchise holder was a resident of Yorkville, Toronto's first high class suburb, an area of some settlement already in 1860. The first impulses came more from a desire for service in the suburbs than from a realization of the potential impact of the lines on the mobility habits of the central city population. Thus, Toronto is thoroughly typical in that the desire to gain access to the centre of the city on the part of a few well-to-do suburbanites preceded the desire to escape the city by its residents.

A substantial expression of enthusiasm for suburban living was only to materialize when the city spawned a growing middle class which could afford the luxury in cost and time of reaching the outer limits of the city. But it was this ground swell of enthusiasm, created many years after the initial laying of the rails, which was to turn the crude system into a modern, efficient, and profitable one. In the years following the middle class use of the rails, the working people of the city gained the habit as well. The first evidence which is available for Toronto to suggest that the streetcar had become a route of access for labouring people comes in 1891 at the time when the city had exercised its right to purchase the expired franchise of the railroad. As a condition of contract, the city instructed the corporation to whom it leased the lines for operation that working-class reduced fares were to be instituted in the early morning and early evening hours.[45] This thread of evidence is virtually all that remains to indicate that before the end of the century Toronto's street railways were used by all classes as an economic necessity. Clarification of the role of the railways and of their impact will be obtained from an evaluation of the evidence provided in the course of examining the growth of Toronto in detail. It is impossible to "test" a hypothesis of railway determinism in any precise way, for the railway was only one of the significant innovations altering the way people lived in the city in the late nineteenth century. It is possible, however, to evaluate in some statistically less precise manner the patterns of development and the availability of the city's first rapid and mass transportation system. It is reasonable to expect that this was, indeed, as important an innovation as many authors have claimed it to be.[46]

The Population: Its Changing Composition and Enduring Mood

The social map of Toronto during the last half of the nineteenth century remains almost completely unencumbered with meaning. The grosser features of the changing landscape have been recognized and the institutions which created them have been briefly investigated. There is no correspondingly simple procedure, however, by which to assess the changing ways in which people lived in the city, and no evidence now survives which would permit a simple evaluation of the impact of each of these developments upon the changing modes of city life.

Toronto was, in 1860, and, at the turn of the century, continued to be a British city. This fact provides perhaps the most important clue to the social character of the place. Indeed, Toronto might be thought to have been exclusively British, so great was the proportion of the total population that was of British stock. In 1860, out of a population of roughly forty thousand, less than five thousand of the city's inhabitants traced their origins outside of Britain (Table 3). There were less than one hundred persons resident in Toronto in 1860 who were born in France. Roughly half of the city's population of that year was native to Canada, but of this number a mere four hundred were of French extraction. What was true of Toronto in 1860 remained true for the rest of the century. In 1870, of a total population of roughly fifty-six thousand, some twenty-eight thousand were native to Canada. Of these, only a thousand were from the province of Quebec, while but a few hundred had immigrated to Toronto from France. By 1901, out of a total of 208,040 people in the city, some 94,021 were of English origin and a further 96,070 were of Scottish or Irish descent. A mere three thousand and fifteen traced their roots to France. Germans comprised the only other numerically significant minority group in the city in 1900.

The immigration to the city which occurred toward the end of the century failed to upset the British quality of Toronto even though the migrants came from many countries of Europe. The migration late in the century created subtle and important changes, however. The first massive migration to the city had been a result of the Irish famines of the late 1840s. This mass movement had profound effects on the city. A revealing statistic for Toronto in 1860 shows that, in that year, the city contained more persons who were by birth Irish than who were born English. At that time the city houses few persons of Scottish ancestry. The immigration of the 1860s and later years changed this balance and by 1870 the Irish no longer outnumbered the English in the city. The Census of Origins in 1880 reveals that at that date there were still almost as many Irish as English, however. By 1890 the immigrant population was distinctly more English than Irish. Thus, following the initial flood of immigrants out of Ireland, the city was a destination for persons from all parts of the British Isles. Nevertheless, the early characterization of the town as an Irish city was to have lasting consequences in attitudes developed and long maintained during subsequent years when conditions were much changed.

As an immigrant city, Toronto was unique within Canada. Immigration contributed a much larger proportion of people to total population of the city than was the case for any other major urban place in the country. Whereas in 1890 there were 50,861 foreign born in Toronto out of a total population of 144,023, in Montreal the foreign born numbered only 31,843 of a total city population of 182,695.[47] Thus, to be correct, Toronto must be characterized both as a peculiarly British city and also as a city of newcomers. None of the cities of Ontario or Quebec rivalled it as the destination for immigrants.[48] In large part, its attractiveness to migrants may be considered to be owing to the rapid growth of industry and a strong demand for labour in the city. At a time when the interior of the provinces was still absorbing new immigrants it is probable that there was no surplus of farm sons to fill city jobs, whereas labour was obtainable from the ships as they landed.[49] The continuing immigrant character of Toronto is of great importance if one is to understand the development in the city of a set of attitudes which explain the persistence of some of the important institutions of the time. Whereas the citizens of the city shared British backgrounds and constituted a homogeneous group by most standards, they did not share a history of common experience in this city. There was no very substantial tradition of Canadian life for many, indeed, for the majority, of those living in the city. The divisions were transferred from Europe along with its population.[50]

The religious composition of the city shows a weave of finer strands. The Church of England and the Roman Catholic Church were, in 1860, the two large religious groups in the city (Table 3). The Roman Catholic populations had only very recently arrived. In 1850 there had been but 7,940 Catholics in Toronto and by 1860 that number had increased to 12,135.[51] This rate of growth in the decade 1850 to 1860 was by far the highest in the city. Presbyterians and Methodists were present in substantial numbers as well, but at this time were small confessional groups in comparison with the two leading denominations. As immigration from Ireland to Toronto slackened and a greater proportion of the immigrants came from the other parts of Britain, the proportion of the total population which was Catholic shrank correspondingly. In 1870 there were over 20,000 Anglicans in the city and only 11,881 Catholics, an actual drop in their numbers during the decade. By this time, Methodist and Presbyterian numbers had swelled so that they were each about as large as the Catholic group. This trend continued for the rest of the century. By 1880 there were more Methodists than Catholics in the city and by 1890 both the Methodist and Presbyterian churches claimed more adherents than did the Roman Catholic Church. By this time, then, the Protestant and English Church groups dominated the religious scene. Among these, the Anglicans were by far the largest group, constituting over a quarter of the total population.

Given the increasingly Protestant character of the city one might expect that a measure of religious toleration would be achieved in the city. Evidence suggests that, with respect to the Catholics of Toronto, this was not the case. The first signs of the Orange Order in the city had already been noted. This organization, embodying as it did religious zeal and bigotry, played an important and conspicuous role in the life of the city in the late decades of the century. There is no evidence that the Order lost vigor as the Catholic population of the city declined in proportion to the total. The answer to the continuing vitality of the Orangemen can perhaps be found in the immigrant spirit of the city in the late nineteenth century. The early support for the Order derived from the antipathy felt by the Protestant Irish toward the Irish Catholics, and most of the Catholics in Toronto at that time were Irish.[52] The verve of this organization was to manifest itself in rather spectacular ways at various moments from 1860 to 1900. In 1860, the visit to Toronto of the Prince of Wales, a figure well revered by all the city's British population, was interrupted by crowds of Orangemen jeering the Catholics of his entourange. The Duke of Newcastle, in charge of the Prince's itinerary, was Catholic.[53]

The Orange Order responded to external stimuli as well as to local opportunities. The Red River Insurrection was a case in point. A most uneasy relationship existed in the Red River settlements between the

TABLE 3

**POPULATION OF TORONTO, 1860 TO 1901,
BY ORIGIN AND RELIGION[a]**

	1860	1870	1880	1890	1901
Total population	44,821	56,092	86,415	144,023	208,040
By religion:					
Anglican	14,125	20,668	30,913	46,084	62,406
Baptist	1,288	1,953	3,667	8,223	11,898
Congregational	826	1,186	2,018	3,102	3,658
Jews*	153	157	534	1,425	3,083
Lutheran	167	343	494	738	972
Methodist	6,976	9,606	16,357	32,505	48,278
Presbyterian	6,604	8,982	14,612	27,449	41,659
Roman Catholic	12,135	11,881	15,716	21,830	28,994
Other and unspecified	2,547	1,316	2,104	2,677	7,092
By origin:					
English			34,608		94,021
Irish			32,177		61,527
Scotch			13,754		34,543
Other British					785
French			1,230		3,015
German			2,049		6,028
Other			2,597		8,121
By nativity:					
English	7,112	11,089		22,801	
Irish	12,441	10,366		13,347	
Scotch	2,961	3,263		6,347	
French	66	61		114	
German	336	336		799	
Native to Canada	19,202	28,424		93,162	
Other	2,703	2,553		7,435	

[a] Sources for this table are the following: Canada, Board of Registration and Statistics, *Census of the Canadas, 1860-61*, I, 48-49, 128-29; Canada, Department of Agriculture, *Census of Canada, 1870-71*, I, 114-17, 266-67; Canada, Department of Agriculture, *Census of Canada, 1880-81*, I, 276-77, 174-75; Canada, Department of Agriculture, *Census of Canada, 1890-91*, I, 282-83, 345; Canada, Census and Statistics Office, *Fourth Census of Canada, 1901*, I, 218-19, 222-23, 344-45, 348-51.

* The term used in the Censuses.

Canadians from Upper Canada, who were, in the 1860's, beginning to populate the region, and the Métis who comprised most of the population. The surveying of the area by parties sent out by the Canadian government led to much friction because the surveyors abused the local settlers. Amid the tensions of the time, an "Ontario Orangeman, Thomas Scott,"[54] was murdered. This event, in distant Manitoba, inspired the protests of Toronto Orangemen who demanded that the murder of a Protestant Orangeman by the forces of Catholicism must quickly be repaid with "justice." The slow speed at which the Dominion government acted prompted a Toronto Orange Lodge to insist that "the blood of Scott should not pass unavenged."[55] In this murder a singularly noted Canadian Catholic, Louis Riel, was implicated. The case of Riel made the event "the most determinative specific political incident between Confederation and the Great War."[56] It also preluded the most notable outburst of anti-French and anti-Catholic feeling in Toronto in the late nineteenth century. The same raw edges of Western expansionism which touched off the Red River troubles in 1870 recurred in the West on the Prairies in the 1880's. The same man, Riel, returned to lead a new group of local Prairie dissidents in 1885. The eventual result of the encounter between the federally sponsored troops and the protesting Saskatchewan Métis was that the militia, "after losing nearly all the skirmishes to the rebels, crushed them by sheer weight."[57] Riel surrendered. Here was fresh kindling for the highland Ontario temperament, as the Orangemen of Toronto once again revealed their stripes. To be a supporter of Riel meant, in their interpretation, that one was "bent upon precipitating a war of the races."[58] It is probable that most of Toronto shared in the sentiment that Riel had to be found guilty.

In contrast with the anti-Catholic sentiment which lasted throughout the nineteenth century, Toronto showed little hostility toward its miniscule but growing Jewish community. The Jewish population of the city remained small throughout the century, increasing from 153 persons in 1860 to 3,083 in 1901 (Table 3). This small group represented one of the important clusters of Jewry in Canada in the nineteenth century, comprising roughly 20 percent of the Canadian total by 1901.[59] In 1860, the Jewish population of Toronto was composed of immigrants from Britain, the German states, and the United States predominantly. The community spoke English and adopted pro-English, or pro-British attitudes. Relations were developed with London and not with New York or Cincinnati. Many members of the Jewish community in the city were British educated; British rabbis were appointed to the synagogue and, in numerous ways, Anglophile attitudes were encouraged.[60]

Migration in the 1880s brought to the city the first Jewish people from Eastern Europe and Russia. These immigrants were not Anglicized and came from a culture which was altogether unlike that of Toronto. Despite this introduction into Toronto of a most foreign cultural group, the overt hostility which characterized the Protestant attitude toward Catholics was not directed toward them. The reason for this may perhaps be found in the steps taken within the Jewish community itself to assure the harmonious integration into the life of the city of the Russian Jews. In the beginning, as one author has pointed out, Toronto's Jews were "Jews by religion and not by culture."[61] When, soon after the arrival in the city of large numbers of Russian Jews, a new and orthodox synagogue was formed, its membership included, in addition to most of the recent immigrants to the city, some of the established families of the city. These members withdrew from the original synagogue after reforms had been instituted there. This small group of English-speaking Jews played a very important role in the new congregation; they "gave to an immigrant congregation that stemmed from the Russian political and cultural sphere a handy core-group already trained in British parliamentary procedure and possessing a reorganized status, assets that were to become of much value in the development of Toronto's other great congregation."[62] This "stroke of fortune" many have had much to do with the maintenance within the Toronto Jewish community of a common effort toward social and economic betterment and of a common identity. As it was perceived by the city, the community maintained its old identity and there were no serious problems of assimilation. The middle class, Anglophile tag had been firmly affixed to the group and apparently remained as the characterization, in the eyes of the city, of Jewish Toronto up until 1900.

Evidence of the social prestige of the various religious groups within the city is scant, but it is true to say that the importance socially of some religious groups was notably above that of others. The Anglican Church included in its confession the families of old Toronto, the early leaders in the city. Many of the first families of the city continued to belong to this group. The immigration, late in the century, of many English people, added a working-class element to it, however Presbyterianism was directly associated with the Scottish population of the city, and counted among its members some of the prominent socially. By contrast, Methodism was more identified with the working class population of Toronto. "To become a member of that Church was to some extent to lose caste. . . . There were very few professional men connected with the body, and none who were wealthy."[63] Methodism claimed only the Masseys. The Baptists and Congregationalists also apparently failed to share with the Church of England the connotation of prestige. The hostility toward Catholics manifested in the Orange Order was most probably an amalgam of religious prejudice and feelings of social superiority on the part of the Protestants. In the absence of concrete evidence, however, no conclusions can be drawn from these snips of information. Instead, these scanty data concerning

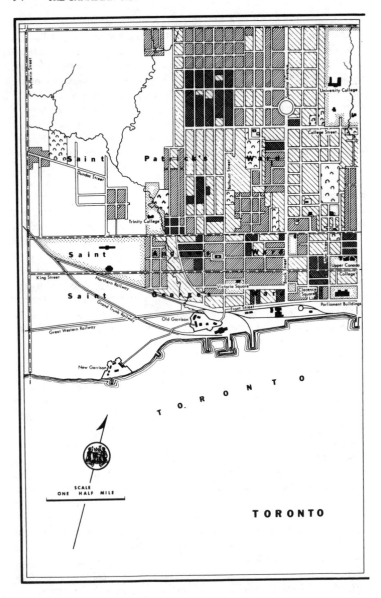

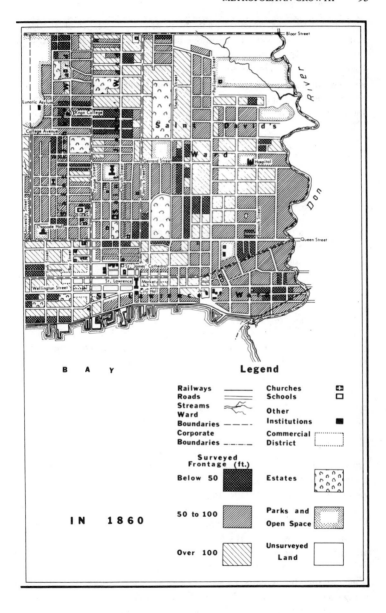

Legend

Railways
Roads
Streams
Ward
Boundaries
Corporate
Boundaries

Churches
Schools
Other
Institutions
Commercial
District

Surveyed
Frontage (ft.)

Below 50

50 to 100

Over 100

Estates

Parks and
Open Space

Unsurveyed
Land

IN 1860

hostilities and bias provide some hints which suggest that regligious denominationalism warrants serious consideration as a probable means of identification of various groups in the latter part of the nineteenth century. Religion was important in that era, investment in real estate and buildings along would convince any observer of that fact, but the task remains to find out in what ways religion influenced and was correlated with the broader social and economic issues of the time.

The Social Imprint on the Map

The maps of Toronto in the years from 1860 to 1900 suggest three important attributes of the changing landscapes of these years. These features are the changing scale of the city, the changing heterogeneity of small areas within the city, and a changing orientation of the physical landscape.

The city in 1860 was small in area, comprising a patchwork of old patterns and new developments (Figure 1). The city was still seen at its best when reached from the lake which remained, as in the earliest of days, the principal avenue of approach and the main entrance route for new arrivals to the city. By 1860 the first railway tracks had been laid on the Esplanade, but the consequences of this action for the amenities of the waterfront were not yet fully realized. Toronto in 1860 extended along the north shore of the lake for a distance of about three miles, reaching westward from the mouth of the Don River toward Bathurst Street, a concession line surveyed through the former Garrison Reserve. The encroachment on the former Reserve lands continued, some fields still awaiting their absorption into the land-consuming process of city-building. To the north, the city had struggled almost to the bottom of the line of bluffs, the most distinct break in the generally flat plain on which the city was being built. The bluff, marking the eroded shorelines of the enlarged lake which in glacial times overspilled the limits of Lake Ontario, long proved to be a difficult obstacle in the northward expansion of the city. The town boundaries had been extended as far north as Bloor Street, one and a quarter miles north of Queen Street and about a mile and a half from the shoreline in 1860. To the north of this line small suburbs had risen, spreading along the main streets and struggling over the brow of the bluffs whence the finest prospects of the city were to be seen once the amentities of the waterfront had been despoiled by the greatest of the mid-century's symbols of progress. Yonge Street had been surveyed in Simcoe's time but remained a slow axis of expansion; the city preferred to sprawl along the lakeshore flats, tending to avoid the minor streams which provided the only major barriers to construction along the shoreline.[64]

Within the roughly four square miles which comprised the built-up city in

1860, about fifty thousand people lived, worked, maintained their warehouses and constructed the institutions around which they organized their society. What is most notable about this compact city is not the density of the settlement, for this was not particularly high, but rather the heterodox quality of the map. By comparison with the end of the century, the city was a jumble of confusion in 1860. Commerce, industry and high class residential properties were tightly intermixed. The central commercial district was also the focus for the larger industrial plants of the city. Intermixed with these were the main institutions of the city and many of the estates of the wealthiest and most prominent citizens. The map of Toronto in 1860 reveals clearly this mix of land uses. The Anglican Cathedral was constructed on some of the city's most valuable real estate in the centre of the most prosperous commercial development, along King Street.[65] Factories along the quays were immediately adjacent to the commercial district and workshops occupied many commercial lofts.

Immediately adjacent to the commercial and institutional core of the city and to the west was located one of the high prestige residential areas of the city, localized around some of the most important of the urban institutions, the Parliament Building and the private preparatory school, Upper Canada College. Here the Bishop's Palace was located along with some large estates, shown on Figure 1. This district was the first of many tracts laid out as the town expanded, and the generous lot sizes combined with the amenities provided by the lake created a high social valuation in the district. In 1860 some of this prestige remained despite the incursions of commerce, waterfront industry and railways. To illustrate this, the occupations of persons living on several blocks of Wellington Street are listed below. Wellington Street, on the north side from Clarence to John Streets contained the homes of the following: a barrister, a professor, a surgeon, a merchant, a widow, a boarding housekeeper and an accountant. On the south side of the street between Peter and Bay Streets there lived 3 gentlemen, 3 merchants, a professor, a broker, a registrar, a civil engineer, an auctioneer and a widow. In addition, at the corner of Bay and Wellington Street, in the heart of this district, there were already several prestigious commercial developments, notably barristers' offices and a bank. This range of occupations typified the high class district's main streets. By contrast, and to emphasize the characteristic diversity to be found even in the districts of wealth in the city, the occupations of persons living on a small side street just one block away from the previous example are listed: 6 labourers, 2 widows and a tailor, a shoemaker, a cooper, a moulder, an innkeeper, a clerk and a carver.[66] This social and economic diversity within a small area was characteristic of the waterfront area, but less forceful examples could be drawn from other parts of the city as well. The pattern of segregation appears to have been finely

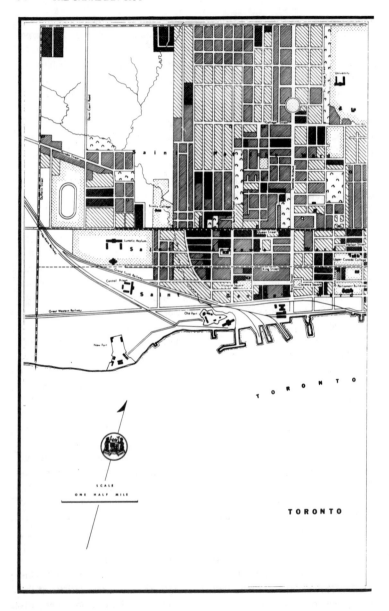

TORONTO

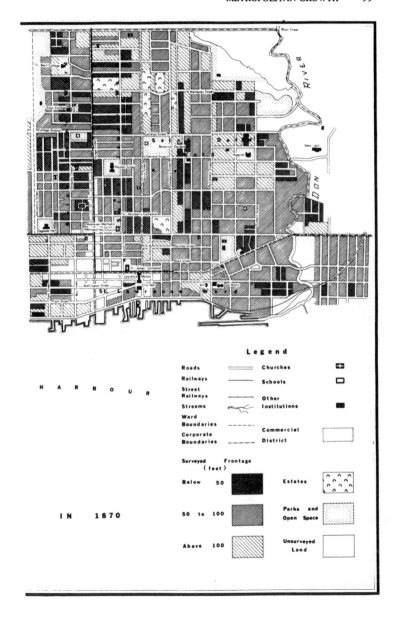

Legend

Roads   Churches

Railways   Schools

Street
Railways   Other
                                          Institutions
Streams

Ward
Boundaries

Corporate   Commercial
Boundaries   District

Surveyed   Frontage
            (feet)

Below   50   Estates

50 to 100   Parks   and
                                          Open   Space

Above   100   Unsurveyed
                                          Land

H A R B O U R

I N   1 8 7 0

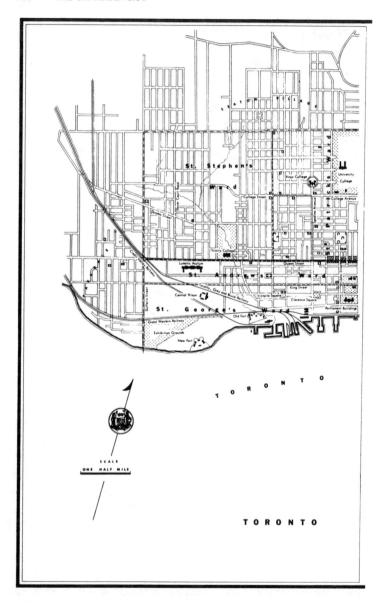

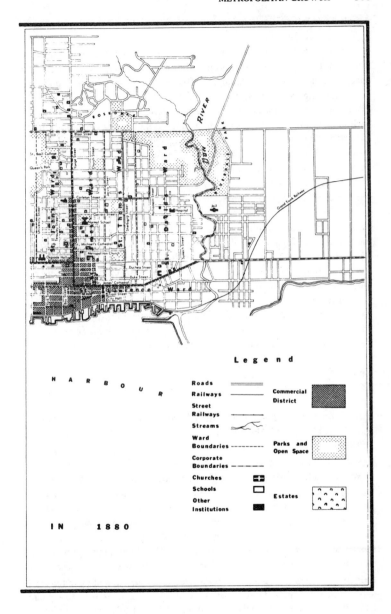

Legend

Roads

Railways

Street
Railways

Streams

Ward
Boundaries

Corporate
Boundaries

Churches

Schools

Other
Institutions

Commercial
District

Parks and
Open Space

Estates

H A R B O U R

IN   1880

detailed and to have been responsive to the variations in prestige attached to very precisely defined sites.

Another highly visible aspect of the large-scale complexities of the urban map of 1860 is the multitude of unco-ordinated surveys, each of which was characterized by an individual and frequently deranged street plan plus accompanying lot surveys. The map north of Queen Street is covered with evidence of these speculative surveys undertaken at different times and various scales for numerous entrepreneurs. Adding to this collage of surveys and plans were the efforts at overbuilding the old surveys by subdividing properties to ensure the maximum use of land. South of Queen Street and east of Yonge ample evidence of this process was to be found in the development of tiny streets lined by tinier lots. North of Queen Street there remained, in 1860, a random scattering of undivided land and of remnant estates. In contrast to the general confusion of development was the property owned by the Allan family, originally a park lot. By 1860 only this one property, located just west of Sherbourn Street, extending from Queen to Bloor Streets, reveals the dimensions of the original park lots, most of the one hundred acres of the original grant still being unsubdivided. The old park lots were consumed not only by housing but also by the institutional acreages of a growing city. The landscape was speckled with church sites, many donated for particular purposes and needs. Educational institutions occupied the largest fragments of several old estates, however. By 1860, University College had been built in the northwestern quarter of the city adjacent to the old King's College which after 1856 saw service as a Lunatic asylum. The University of Trinity College was established on the southern portion of another park lot after 1851. Most of the nineteenth-century institutions established in Toronto after the first years of settlement eventually came to occupy property in this area north of Queen Street, and the pattern of institutional land use in this part of the city remained in 1960 about as it was in 1860.

Whereas the development north of Queen Street of educational complexes served to localize institutions of higher learning in the city for over a century, the intrusion of other activities onto Toronto's waterfront destroyed old patterns and altered dramatically the social valuation of this part of the city. The residual prestige still attached to this district in 1860 was to be short lived. The death of the waterfront as an amenity was part of the gradual reorientation of the city away from the lake. The new high status districts were located in the northern suburbs. The waterfront was destroyed by the railways and their attendant industry as well as by the expanding commercial activity of this entrepot town. By 1870 the small estates had disappeared from the lakeshore and only the old Parliament Buildings, the Bishop's

Palace and Upper Canada College survived as ossified remainders of a vanished district (Figure 2).

Other subtle indications of the changing orientation of the city can be gleaned from the maps. For some time the new religious establishment had been avoiding the lake front. St. Basil's and St. Michael's Colleges were begun in 1856 at the northern edge of the city. Knox College moved from Front Street to quarters in the northern fringes after 1856 as well. These only add to the examples already mentioned. St. Michael's Cathedral, begun in 1848, was located north and east of the old waterfront district on part of the same park lot on which the Metropolitan (Methodist) Church was built in

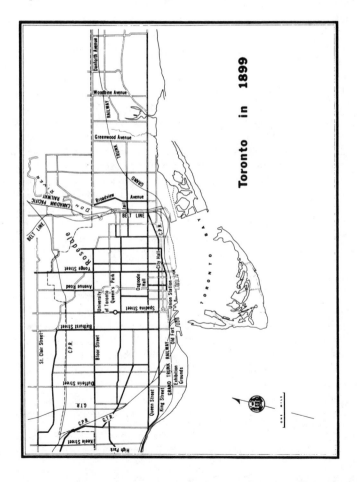

1872. Investment in amenities unconnected with religion also reflected the changing direction of growth and prestige. The first street railway in the city was constructed, not along the broad east-west waterfront axis of the city, but along the shorter north-south spine to the fashionable northern periphery. In all, these trends probably contributed significantly to the abandonment by the citizens of the old districts and to the new orientation of the city. The town no longer focused on the waterfront. Here the commerce and industry of the city remained and expanded, but by 1870 residential growth had taken a different direction.

The map of 1880 reveals, in a general manner, the continuation of the trends discerned already (Figure 3). The waterfront was becoming more industrialized and the commercial core was continuing to expand yet further into the old western suburb. The institutions previously planted in the northern part of the city were flourishing and expanding while the remnant estates in the old city continued to shrink. Land south of Bloor Street continued to be parceled out under the influence of the speculative subdividers so that by 1900 the process was virtually complete. The same procedures were then reiterated in all the newer and more distant suburbs. The city continued to grow by the piecemeal plans of speculative realtors.

The changing scale of the city becomes quite apparent when the map of 1889 is compared with that of 1860 (Figures 4 and 1). In 1889 the new and expanded plan was being held together by the growing mileage of streetcar lines. Following the old design, the lines first reached into the northern suburbs and only later were they built to the more distant but less fashionable areas of the city. In 1880 the best served district in Toronto was the newly fashionable northern area just south of Rosedale. By 1899, however, the major achievement of the transport system was that it had effectively reached to the limits of the populated areas of the city, tying the sprawling new metropolis together.

Industrial development, population growth, and the changing system of internal transportation were three of the most conspicuous agents of change in the late nineteenth-century urban landscape of Toronto. Each created opportunities, influenced the character of the new city, and provided the broad context within which the city grew. The social characteristics of different parts of the city developed not only within these broad constraints but also under the more intimate influences of social taste and the prevailing definition of prestige. The attributes of these social worlds were a product of the interplay of the general economic context of life in the city and of the more particularistic conceptions which were derived from the immediate urban environment.

NOTES:

1. Canada Board of Registration and Statistics, *Census of the Canadas, 1851-52*, I, p. 30; Canada, Census and Statistics Office, *Fourth Census of Canada*, 1901, I, pp. 218-19.
2. Henry Scadding, *Toronto of Old* (Toronto: Oxford University Press, 1966).
3. D.G. Creighton, *The Commercial Empire of the St. Lawrence* (Toronto: Ryerson Press, 1937), pp. 382-84.
4. Ralph Waldo Emerson, quoted in Asa Briggs, *Victorian Cities* (Harmondsworth, England: Penguin Books Ltd., Pelican Books, 1968), p. 13.
5. The costs of shipping from Montreal to Europe as against the costs from New York to Europe were the subject of investigation in Canada. New York already controlled the bulk of the import trade into Canada, and had for some time been able to do this because of relaxation of the Navigation Laws as they applied to shipping on the Great Lakes. Thus, there was special urgency in the investigation. The findings and later reports are discussed by Innis in H.A. Innis and A.R.M. Lower, eds., *Select Documents in Canadian Economic History* (Toronto: University of Toronto Press, 1933), p. 473.
6. Innis and Lower, *op. cit.*, p. 492.
7. A discussion of the various merchants engaged in the trade is found in D.C. Masters, *The Rise of Toronto, 1850-1890* (Toronto: University of Toronto Press, 1947), p. 60.
8. The attitudes of Toronto's leading editor, who was also an avid railway supporter, toward the railways are discussed in J.M.S. Careless, *Brown of the Globe*, Vol. I: *The Voice of Upper Canada, 1818-1859* (Toronto: Macmillan Co. of Canada, 1959), pp. 211-12.
9. These details are according to *The Handbook of Toronto* (Toronto: Lovell and Gibson, 1859), pp. 201, 221.
10. Details of the gateway functions of early settlements near Toronto are given in Percy J. Robinson, *Toronto During the French Regime, 1615-1793* (Toronto: Ryerson Press, 1933).
11. Careless, *op. cit.* p. 229; Innis and Lower, *op. cit.*, p. 489.
12. The words are those of Careless describing Brown's idea. Careless, *op. cit.*, p. 212.
13. Details of this trade may be found in Innis and Lower, *op. cit.*, p. 494.
14. *Ibid.*, p. 664.
15. *Ibid.*, p. 490.
16. *Ibid.*, p. 493.
17. Masters, *op. cit.*, pp. 178-80.
18. Of this total trackage, 228 miles were operated in the United States. Innis and Lower, *op. cit.*, p. 497.
19. C. Pelham Mulvany, *Toronto: Past and Present* (Toronto: W.D. Caiger, 1884), p. 59.
20. Figures given are in the *Census of Canada, 1870-71*, and the *Fourth Census of Canada, 1901*. For the complete statistics for the thirty years, see Table 1.
21. D.C. Masters discusses the general depression that hung in the rooms of the business community. See Masters, *op. cit.*, pp. 142-72. The general argument of a depression is countered by Chambers and Bertram who dispute the evidence offered concerning a prolonged business malaise. See Edward J. Chambers and Gordon W. Bertram, "Urbanization and Manufacturing in Central Canada, 1870-1890," in *Papers on Regional Statistical Studies*, ed. Sylvia Ostry and T.K. Rymes, Canadian Political Science Association: Conference on Statistics, 1964 (Toronto: University of Toronto Press, 1966), pp. 225-58.
22. An inspection of the city directory published by William Brown for 1856-57 led Guillet to the conclusion that factories had begun to "supplant" the city's small tradesmen. See Edwin C. Guillet, *Toronto — From Trading Post to Great City* (Toronto: Ontario Publishing Co., 1934), p. 273.
23. *Ibid.*, p. 268.
24. Quoted in D.C. Masters, *op. cit.*, pp. 61-62.

25. John E. McNab, "Toronto's Industrial Growth to 1891," *Ontario History*, XLVII (1955), p. 73.

26. Canada, Department of Agriculture, *Census of Canada, 1890-91*, III, p. 385.

27. Canada, Census and Statistics Office, Bulletin 2: *Manufacturers of Canada*, 1907.

28. Innis and Lower, *op. cit.*, p. 477.

29. Masters, *op. cit.*, p. 173.

30. *Ibid.*, p. 147. Masters suggests that the growth of Toronto's hinterland may have played an important role in the timing of its late prosperity.

31. *Ibid.*, p. 172. In efforts to control the trade of Georgian Bay, Toronto interests had built a railway connecting Owen Sound with the larger city. The significance of this line was enhanced once the C.P.R. had finished its line to Fort William-Port Arthur. Innis and Lower, *op. cit.*, p. 490.

32. Masters, *op. cit.*, p. 172.

33. Innis and Lower, *op. cit.*, pp. 596-97.

34. For a fuller discussion of industrial localization and specialization in Toronto and in Central Canada from 1870 to 1890, see Edward J. Chambers and Gordon W. Bertram, "Urbanization and Manufacturing in Central Canada, 1870-1890," in Ostry and Rymes, *op. cit.* pp. 225-58.

35. *Ibid.*, p. 258.

36. Chambers and Bertram cite statistics for the percent of value added in manufacturing within Ontario and Quebec accounted for by York county. These data are as follows: 1870 — 9.72 percent; 1880 — 11.09 percent; 1890 — 13.45 percent. See Chambers and Bertram, *op. cit.*, pp. 244, 248, 252.

37. Street railway lines had been installed in only seventeen cities in America prior to the construction of Toronto's first line. Dates of construction of street railways in the cities of the United States and Canada are given in Arthur J. Krim, "The Innovations and Diffusion of the Street Railway in North America" (unpublished Master's dissertation, Department of Geography, University of Chicago, 1967), p. 63.

38. Guillet, *op. cit.*, p. 121.

39. *Ibid.*, pp. 121-31.

40. Louis H. Pursley, *Street Railways of Toronto, 1861-1921*, Interurbans Special: Interurbans, Vol. XVI, No. 2 (Los Angeles: Electric Railway Publications, 1958), p. 7.

41. *Ibid.*, p. 9.

42. According to Pursley, the agreement had called for the electrification of the system within one year of franchising. The first electric line was installed in the city of August of 1892, on Church Street, leading to a fashionable northern suburb. *Ibid.*, p. 16.

43. *Ibid.*, p. 22.

44. The words are those of Henry M. Whitney of Boston, quoted in Sam B. Warner, *Streetcar Suburbs* (Cambridge, Mass.: Harvard University Press, 1962), p. 26. A moderate interpretation of the impact of local railways is found in D.A. Reeder, "A Theatre of Suburbs: Some Patterns of Development in West London, 1801-1911," in *The Study of Urban History*, ed. H.J. Dyos (London: Edward Arnold, 1968), pp. 253-71.

45. This fact is mentioned in Frederic W. Speirs, *The Street Railway System of Philadelphia: Its History and Present Condition*, Johns Hopkins University Studies in Historical and Political Science, Vol. XV (Baltimore: John Hopkins Press, 1897), pp. 70-71.

46. Some of the more important works discussing the role of street railways in reforming the morphology of cities are listed in Goheen, *Victoria Toronto*, p. 74, footnote 2.

47. Canada, Department of Agriculture, *Census of Canada, 1890-91*, I, pp. 349, 357.

48. Since Toronto was the second city of the country, it is not surprising that there should be more migrants there than in smaller places. By comparison, in 1890, Hamilton contained 15,596 foreign-born as against 31,649 Canadian-born residents, a proportion close to Toronto's ratio.

Ottawa numbered 6,431 foreign-born and 30,838 Canadian-born residents in the same year. *Ibid.*, pp. 343, 347.

49. There is at present no information on this procedure relating to Toronto in the nineteenth century. The process was not, however, unusual. Details of its application in Boston are given in Oscar Handlin, *Boston's Immigrants* (New York: Atheneum, 1968).

50. The recency of the arrival in Canada of Toronto's population is given added support by numbering children of foreign-born fathers as well as the foreign-born population itself. In 1890, there were 111,489 in these categories, only 32,534 being born in Canada of native fathers. Canada, Department of Agriculture, *Census of Canada, 1890-91*, II, p. 230.

51. Figures quoted in Masters, *op. cit.*, p. 33.

52. *Ibid.*, p. 37.

53. *Ibid.*, p. 85.

54. Arthur R.M. Lower, *Colony to Nation, a History of Canada* (Toronto: Longmans Canada, 1946), p. 352.

55. Quoted from the *Globe*, Feb. 18, 1871, in Masters, *op. cit.*, p. 128.

56. Lower, *op. cit.*, p. 352.

57. *Ibid.*, p. 382.

58. Remarks of the *Orange Sentinel* were reprinted in the paper *Week*, Oct. 1, 1885 and are quoted from Masters, *op. cit.*, p. 192.

59. In 1901, 18.9 percent of the Jewish population of Canada lived in Toronto, Louis Rosenberg, "A Study of the Changes in the Geographic Distribution of the Jewish Population in the Metropolitan Area of Toronto, 1851-1951," *Canadian Jewish Population Studies, Jewish Community Series,* II (1954), p. 1.

60. Ben Kayfetz, "The Jewish Community in Toronto," in *A People and Its Faith*, ed. by Albert Rose (Toronto: University of Toronto Press, 1959), pp. 14-29.

61. Sidney S. Schipper, "Holy Blossom and Its Community," *Ibid.*, p. 31.

62. *Ibid.*, p. 34.

63. Quoted in Guillet, *op. cit.*, p. 376. Remark made in 1914.

64. For several decades scholars have followed Griffith Taylor in his assertions that these tiny streams have controlled the early development in Toronto. Taylor asserts that, "the evolution of the city of Toronto . . . [is] determined by the minor topographic features" of the plain. Griffith Taylor, "Topographic Control in the Toronto Region," *Canadian Journal of Political Science*, II (1936), p. 493.

65. St. James Cathedral was actually constructed on land set aside for the purpose in the plans for the enlargement of the city plot drawn up by The Honorable Peter Russell soon after the founding of the town. Not all of the land so designated, however, was preserved by the Church for its own use.

66. This street is Melinda Street, one block long and extending west of Yonge Street south of King. The descriptions of the occupations are taken from the "Assessment Roll for the Ward of St. George, City of Toronto, 1860," pp. 14-18, p. 22.

Sources of the Figures:

Figure 1 is drawn from the "Plan of the City of Toronto Showing the Government Survey and the Registered Subdivision into Lots According to Plans Filed in the Office of the City Registrar," made by H.J. Browne under the direction of J.O. Browne, Civil Engineer and P.L. Surveyor in 1862. Details have been corrected for 1860 from the Assessment Rolls of that year.

Figure 2 is drawn from "Wadsworth and Unwin's Map of the City of Toronto," compiled by Maurice Gaviller, C.E. and P.L.S. from plans filed in the Registry Office and the most recent surveys in 1872, and corrected for 1870 from the Assessment Rolls of 1870.

Figure 3 is drawn from a map titled "City of Toronto," published in Toronto by R.L. Polk and Co., 1887, and corrected for 1880 from the Assessment Rolls, City of Toronto, 1880.

Figure 4 is derived from an untitled map in the collection of the Baldwin Room, Toronto Public Library, drawn in 1899 by J.G. Foster and Co.

The National Policy and the Industrialization of the Maritimes, 1880-1910

T.W. ACHESON

The Maritime provinces of Canada in 1870 probably came the closest of any region to representing the classic ideal of the staple economy. Traditionally shaped by the Atlantic community, the region's industrial sector had been structured to the production and export of timber, lumber products, fish and ships. The last was of crucial significance. In terms of the balance of trade, it accounted for more than one-third of New Brunswick's exports at Confederation. In human terms, the manufacture of ships provided a number of towns with large groups of highly skilled, highly paid craftsmen who were able to contribute significantly to the quality of community life. Against this background, the constricting British market for lumber and ships after 1873 created a serious economic crisis for the area. This was not in itself unusual. Throughout the nineteenth century the region's resource-based economy had suffered a series of periodic recessions as the result of changing imperial policies and world markets. Yet, in one respect, this crisis differed from all earlier, while the lumber markets gradually returned in the late 1870's, the ship market did not. Nova Scotians continued to build their small vessels for the coasting trade, but the large ship building industry failed to revive.

In the face of this uncertain future the National Policy was embraced by much of the Maritime business community as a new mercantilism which would re-establish that stability which the region had enjoyed under the old British order. In the first years of its operation the Maritimes experienced a dramatic growth in manufacturing potential, a growth often obscured by the stagnation of both the staple industries and population growth. In fact, the

SOURCE: *Acadiensis: Journal of the History of the Atlantic Region*, Vol. I, No. 2 (Spring 1972), pp. 3-28. Reprinted by permission of the author and the Department of History of the University of New Brunswick.

decade following 1879 was characterized by a significant transfer of capital and human resources from the traditional staples into a new manufacturing base which was emerging in response to federal tariff policies. This development was so significant that between 1881 and 1891 the industrial growth rate of Nova Scotia outstripped all other provinces in eastern Canada.[1] The comparative growth of the period is perhaps best illustrated in St. John. The relative increase in industrial capital, average wages, and output in this community significantly surpassed that of Hamilton, the Canadian city whose growth was perhaps most directly attributable to the protective tariff.[2]

Within the Atlantic region the growth of the 1880's was most unequally distributed. It centred not so much on areas or subregions as upon widely scattered communities.[3] These included the traditional Atlantic ports of St. John, Halifax, and Yarmouth; lumbering and ship building towns, notably St. Stephen and New Glasgow; and newer railroad centres, such as Moncton and Amherst. The factors which produced this curious distribution of growth centres were human and historical rather than geographic. The one characteristic shared by them all was the existence in each of a group of entrepreneurs possessing the enterprise and the capital resources necessary to initiate the new industries. Strongly community-oriented, these entrepreneurs attempted, during the course of the 1880's, to create viable manufacturing enterprises in their local areas under the aegis of the protective tariff. Lacking the resources to survive the prolonged economic recessions of the period, and without a strong regional metropolis, they acquiesced in the 1890's to the industrial leadership of the Montreal business community. Only at the century's end, with the expansion of the consolidation movement, did a group of Halifax financiers join their Montreal counterparts in asserting an industrial metropolitanism over the communities of the eastern Maritimes. This paper is a study in that transition.

I

The Maritime business community in the 1870's was dominated by three groups: wholesale shippers, lumber and ship manufacturers, and the small scale manufacturers of a variety of commodities for purely local consumption. As a group they were deeply divided on the question of whether the economic salvation of their various communities was to be found in the maintenance of an Atlantic mercantile system, or in a programme of continentalist-oriented industrial diversification. A wedding of the two alternatives appeared to be the ideal situation. While they had warily examined the proposed tariff of 1879, most leading businessmen accepted its philosophy and seriously attempted to adapt it to their community needs.[4]

For a variety of reasons the tariff held the promise of prosperity for the region's traditional commercial activities and, as well, offered the possibilities for the development of new manufacturing industry. For most Nova Scotian business leaders the West Indies market was vital to the successful functioning of the province's commercial economy. It was a major element in the region's carrying trade and also provided the principal market for the Nova Scotia fishing industry. These, in turn, were the foundations of the provincial shipbuilding industry. The successful prosecution of the West Indies trade, however, depended entirely upon the ability of the Nova Scotia merchants to dispose of the islands' sugar crop. The world depression in the 1870's had resulted in a dramatic decline in the price of refined sugar as French, German, British and American refineries dumped their surplus production on a glutted world market. By 1877 more than nine-tenths of Canadian sugar was obtained from these sources,[5] a fact which threatened the Nova Scotia carrying trade with disaster. A significant tariff on foreign sugar, it was felt, would encourage the development of a Canadian refining industry which would acquire all of its raw sugar from the British West Indies. Through this means, most Nova Scotian wholesalers and shippers saw in the new policy an opportunity both to resuscitate the coastal shipping industry of the province and to restore their primacy in the West Indies.

Of the newer industries which the National Policy offered, the future for the Maritimes seemed to lie in textiles and iron and steel products. The optimism concerning the possibilities of the former appears to have emerged out of a hope of emulating the New England experience. This expectation was fostered by the willingness of British and American cotton mill machinery manufacturers to supply on easy terms the necessary duty-free equipment, and by the feeling of local businessmen that the market provided by the tariff and the low quality labour requirements of such an enterprise would guarantee that a profitable business could be erected and maintained by the efforts of a single community. Behind such reasoning lay the general assumption that, despite major transportation problems, the Maritimes, and notably Nova Scotia, would ultimately become the industrial centre of Canada. The assumption was not unfounded. The region contained the only commercially viable coal and iron deposits in the Dominion, and had the potential, under the tariff, of controlling most of the Montreal fuel sources. Under these circumstances the development of textiles and the expansion of most iron and steel industries in the Atlantic area was perhaps not a surprising project.

TABLE I

INDUSTRIAL DEVELOPMENT IN PRINCIPAL MARITIME CENTRES 1880-1890

	Population	Industrial Capital	Employees	Average Annual Wages	Output	Industry by Output (1891)
Halifax (1880)	39,886	$2,975,000	3,551	$303	$6,128,000	Sugar**
Dartmouth (1890)	43,132	6,346,000	4,654	280	8,235,000	Rope*
						Cotton
						Confectionary
						Paint
						Lamps
St. John (1880)	41,353	2,143,000	2,690	278	4,123,000	Lumber**
(1890)	39,179	4,838,000	5,888	311	8,131,000	Machinery***
						Smelting
						Rope**
						Cottons
						Brass*
						Nails*
						Elect. Light**
New Glasgow (1880)	2,595	160,000	360	255	313,000	Primary Steel*
(1890)	3,777	1,050,000	1,117	355	1,512,000	Rolling Mills**
						Glass
St. Stephen (1880)	4,002	136,000	447	314	573,000	Cottons

Milltown (1890)	4,826	1,702,000	1,197	320	1,494,000	Confectionary / Fish Canning / Soap / Lumber
Moncton (1880)	5,032	530,000	603	418	1,719,000	Sugar
(1890)	8,765	1,134,000	948	333	1,973,000	Cottons / Woolens / Rolling Stock
Fredericton (1880)	7,218[a]	1,090,000[a]	911[a]	221[a]	1,031,000[a]	Cottons
Marysville (1890)	8,394	2,133,000	1,526	300	1,578,000	Lumber / Foundry Product
Yarmouth (1880)	3,485	290,000	211	328	284,000	Cotton Yarn*
(1890)	6,089	783,000	930	312	1,234,000	Fish Canning / Woolens
Amherst (1880)	2,274	81,000	288	281	283,000	Foundry Product / Shoes
(1890)	3,781	457,000	683	293	724,000	Doors

[a] Estimates. Marysville was not an incorporated town in 1880, and totals for that date must be estimated from York County figures.

* Leading Canadian Producer; **second; ***third.

Source: Canada. Census (1891), III, Table I; Ibid., (1901), III, Tables XX, XXI.

Despite a cautious enthusiasm for the possibilities offered by the new federal economic dispensation, there was considerable concern about the organizational and financial problems in creating a new industrial structure. The Maritimes was a region of small family firms with limited capital capabilities. Other than chartered banks, it lacked entirely the financial structure to support any large corporate industrial entity. Like the people of Massachusetts, Maritimers were traditionally given to placing their savings in government savings banks at a guaranteed 4 percent interest than in investments on the open market.[6] Regional insurance, mortgage and loan, and private savings corporations were virtually unknown. The result was to throw the whole financial responsibility for undertaking most manufactories upon the resources of individual entrepreneurs.

Since most enterprises were envisioned as being of general benefit to the community at large, and since few businessmen possessed the necessary capital resources to single-handedly finance such an undertaking, most early industrial development occurred as the result of co-operative efforts by groups of community entrepreneurs. These in turn were drawn from a traditional business elite of wholesalers and lumbermen. In Halifax as early as May, 1879, a committee was formed from among the leading West Indies shippers ''to solicit capital, select a site and get a manufacturing expert'' for the organization of a sugar refinery.[7] Under its leadership $500,000 was raised, in individual subscriptions of $10-20,000 from among members of the Halifax business community. This procedure was repeated during the formation of the Halifax Cotton Company in 1881; more than $300,000 was subscribed in less than two weeks, most of it by thirty-two individuals.[8]

The leadership in the development of these enterprises was taken by young members of traditional mercantile families. The moving spirit in both cases was Thomas Kenny. A graduate of the Jesuit Colleges at Stonyhurst (England) and St. Gervais (Belgium), Kenny had inherited from his father, the Hon. Sir Edward Kenny, M.L.C., one of the largest wholesale shipping firms in the region. In the early 1870's the younger Kenny had invested heavily in shipyards scattered throughout five counties of Nova Scotia, and had even expanded into England with the establishment of a London branch for his firm. Following the opening of the refinery in 1881, he devoted an increasingly large portion of his time to the management of that firm.[9] Kenny was supported in his efforts by a number of leading merchants including the Hon. Robert Boak, Scottish-born president of the Legislative Council, and John F. Stairs, Manager of the Dartmouth Rope Works. Stairs, who had attended Dalhousie University, was a member of the executive council of Nova Scotia, the son of a legislative councillor, and a grandson of the founder of the shipping firm of William Stairs, Son and Morrow Limited.[10]

In contrast to Halifax, St. John had always been much more a manufacturing community and rivalled Ottawa as the principal lumber manufacturing centre in the Dominion. Development in the New Brunswick city occurred as new growth on an existing industrial structure and centred on cotton cloth and iron and steel products. The New Brunswick Cotton Mill had been erected in 1861 by an Ulster-born St. John shipper, William Parks, and his son, John H. Parks. The latter, who had been trained as a civil engineer under the tutelage of the chief engineer of the European and North American Railroad, assumed the sole proprietorship of the mill in 1870.[11] In 1881 he led the movement among the city's dry goods wholesalers to establish a second cotton mill which was incorporated as the St. John Cotton Company.

The principal St. John iron business was the firm of James Harris. Trained as a blacksmith, the Annapolis-born Harris had established a small machine shop in the city in 1828, and had expanded into the foundry business some twenty-three years later. In 1883, in consequence of the new tariff, he determined to develop a completely integrated secondary iron industry including a rolling mill and railway car plant. To provide the resources for the expansion, the firm was reorganized as a joint stock company with a $300,000 capital most of which was raised by St. John businessmen. The New Brunswick Foundry, Rolling Mills and Car Works, with a plant covering some five acres of land, emerged as the largest industrial employer in the Maritimes.[12] The success of the Harris firm induced a group of wholesale hardware manufacturers under the leadership of the Hon. Isaac Burpee, a former member of the Mackenzie Government, to re-establish the Coldbrooke Rolling Mills near the city.

Yet, despite the development of sugar and cotton industries and the expansion of iron and rope manufactories, the participation of the St. John and Halifax business communities in the industrial impulse which characterized the early 1880's can only be described as marginal. Each group played the role of participant within its locality but neither provided any positive leadership to its hinterland area. Even in terms of industrial expansion, the performance of many small town manufacturers was more impressive than that of their city counterparts.

At the little railway centre of Moncton, nearly $1,000,000 was raised under the leadership of John and Christopher Harris, John Humphrey, and Josiah Woods, to permit the construction of a sugar refinery, a cotton mill, a gas light and power plant, and several smaller iron and textile enterprises. The Harris brothers, sons of an Annapolis ship builder of Loyalist extraction, had established a shipbuilding and shipping firm at Moncton in 1856.[13] Under the aegis of their firm they organized the new enterprises with the assistance of their brother-in-law John Humphrey, scion of Yorkshire Methodist settlers of the Tantramar, longtime M.L.A. for Westmorland, and proprietor of the Moncton flour and woolen mills. They were financially assisted in their efforts by Josiah Wood (later Senator) of nearby Sackville. The son of a Loyalist wholesaler, Wood first completed his degrees (B.A., M.A.) at Mount Allison, was later admitted to the New Brunswick bar, and finally entered his father's shipping and private banking business.[14] The leadership of the Moncton group was so effective that the owner of the *Monetary Times*, in a journey through the region in 1882, singled out the community for praise:

> Moncton has industrialized . . . business people only in moderate circumstances but have united their energies . . . persons who have always invested their surplus funds in mortgages are now cheerfully subscribing capital for the Moncton Cotton Co. Unfortunately for industrial progress, there are too many persons [in this region] who are quite content with receiving 5 or 6% for their money so long as they know it is safe, rather than risk it in manufactures, even supposing it yielded double the profit.[15]

At St. Stephen the septuagenarian lumber barons and bankers, James Murchie and Freeman Todd, joined the Annapolis-born ship builder, Zechariah Chipman, who was father-in-law to the Minister of Finance, Sir Leonard Tilley, in promoting an immense cotton concern, the St. Croix, second largest in the Dominion at the time. The son of a local farmer, Murchie, whose holdings included more than 200,000 acres of timber lands — half of it in Quebec — also developed a number of smaller local manufactories.[16] At the same time two young brothers, Gilbert and James Ganong, grandsons of a Loyalist farmer from the St. John Valley, began the expansion of their small confectionery firm,[17] and shortly initiated construction of a soap enterprise in the town.

At Yarmouth a group of ship builders and West Indies merchants led by the Hon. Loran Baker, M.L.C., a shipper and private banker, and John Lovitt, a shipbuilder and member of the Howland Syndicate, succeeded in promoting the Yarmouth Woolen Mill, the Yarmouth Cotton Manufacturing, the Yarmouth Duck Yarn Company, two major foundries, and a furniture enterprise.[18] The development was entirely an internal community effort — virtually all the leading business figures were third generation Nova Scotians of pre-Loyalist American origins. A similar development was discernible in the founding of the Windsor Cotton Company.[19]

A somewhat different pattern emerged at New Glasgow, the centre of the Nova Scotia coal industry. Attempts at the manufacture of primary iron and steel had been made with indifferent results ever since Confederation.[20] In 1872, a New Glasgow blacksmith, Graham Fraser, founded the Hope Iron

Works with an initial capital of $160,000.[21] As the tariff on iron and steel products increased in the 1880's so did the vertical expansion of the firm. In 1889, when it was amalgamated with Fraser's other enterprise, the Nova Scotia Forge Company, more than two-thirds of the $280,000 capital stock of the resulting Nova Scotia Steel and Coal Company was held by the citizens of New Glasgow.[22] Fraser remained as president and managing director of the corporation until 1904,[23] during which time it produced most of the primary steel in the Dominion,[24] and remained one of the largest industrial corporations in the country.[25]

Fraser was seconded in his industrial efforts by James Carmichael of New Glasgow and John F. Stairs of Halifax. Carmichael, son of a prominent New Glasgow merchant and a descendant of the Scottish founders of Pictou, had established one of the largest ship building and shipping firms in the province.[26] Stairs' investment in the New Glasgow iron and steel enterprise represented one of the few examples of inter-community industrial activity in this period.

The most unusual pattern of manufacturing development in the region was that initiated at Fredericton by Alexander Gibson. Gibson's distinctiveness lay in his ability to impose the tradition and structure of an earlier semi-industrial society onto a changing pattern of development. A St. Stephen native and the son of Ulster immigrants, he had begun his career as a sawyer, and later operated a small lumber firm at Lepreau. In 1865 he bought from the Anti-Confederationist government of A.J. Smith extensive timber reserves on the headwaters of the Nashwaak River,[27] and at the mouth of that river, near Fredericton, built his own mill-town of Marysville. Freed from stumpage fees by his fortunate purchase, the "lumber king of New Brunswick" was producing as much as 100,000,000 feet of lumber annually by the 1880's — about one third of the provincial output. His lumber exports at times comprised half the export commerce of the port of St. John.[28]

One of the wealthiest industrial enterpreneurs in the Dominion, Gibson determined in 1883 to undertake the erection of a major cotton enterprise entirely under his own auspices.[29] He erected one of the largest brick-yards in the Dominion and personally supervised the construction of the plant which was opened in 1885.[30] In that same year he employed nearly 2,000 people in his sundry enterprises.[31] By 1888 his sales of cotton cloth totalled nearly $500,000.[32] That same year the Gibson empire, comprising the cotton mill, timber lands, saw mills, lath mills, the town of Marysville, and the Northern and Western Railroad, was formed into a joint stock company, its $3,000,000 capital controlled by Gibson, his brother, sons and son-in-law.

Several common characteristics distinguished the men who initiated the industrial expansion of the 1880's. They were, on the whole, men of substance gained in traditional trades and staples. They sought a substantial, more secure future for themselves within the framework of the traditional community through the instrumentality of the new industrial mercantilism. Averaging fifty-four years of age, they were old men to be embarking upon new careers.[33] Coupled with this factor of age was their ignorance of both the technical skills and the complexities of the financial and marketing structures involved in the new enterprises.

The problem of technical skill was overcome largely by the importation of management and skilled labour, mainly from England and Scotland.[34] The problem of finance was more serious. The resources of the community entrepreneurs were limited; the costs of the proposed industry were almost always far greater than had been anticipated. Moreover, most businessmen had only the vaguest idea of the quantity of capital required to operate a large manufacturing corporation. Promoters generally followed the normal mercantile practice and raised only sufficient capital to construct and equip the physical plant, preferring to finance operating costs through bank loans — a costly and inefficient process. The Halifax Sugar Refinery perhaps best illustrated these problems. When first proposed in 1879 it was to have been capitalized at $300,000. Before its completion in 1881 it was re-capitalized twice to a value of $500,000.[35] Even this figure left no operating capital, and the refinery management was forced to secure these funds by loans from the Merchants Bank of Halifax. At the end of its first year of operation the bank debt of the corporation totalled $460,000,[36] which immediately became a fixed charge on the revenues of the infant industry. Fearing bankruptcy, the stockholders increased their subscriptions and kept the business functioning until 1885 when they attempted a solution to the problem by issuing debenture stock to a value of $350,000 of which the bank was to receive $200,000 in stock and $50,000 cash in settlement of debts still owed to it.[37]

While many industries received their initial financing entirely from local capitalists, some projects proved to be such ambitious undertakings that aid had to be sought from other sources. The St. Croix Cotton Company at St. Stephen, for example, was forced to borrow $300,000 from Rhode Island interests to complete their huge plant.[38] Some industries came to rely so heavily on small community banks for perpetual loans for operating expenses that any general economic crisis toppled both the industries and the banks simultaneously. The financing of James Domville's enterprises, including the Coldbrook Rolling Mills, was a contributing factor in the temporary suspension of the Maritime Bank of St. John in 1880,[38] while such industrial loans ultimately brought down the Bank of Yarmouth in 1905.[40]

II

The problem of industrial finance was intricately tied to a whole crisis of confidence in the new order which began to develop as the first enthusiastic flush of industrial expansion paled in the face of the general business downturn which wracked the Canadian economy in the mid-1880's. At the heart of this problem was a gradual deterioration of the British lumber market, and the continued shift from sea borne to railroad commerce. Under the influence of an increasingly prohibitive tariff and an extended railroad building programme a two cycle inter-regional trading pattern was gradually emerging. The westward cycle, by rail into the St. Lawrence basic, left the region with a heavy trade imbalance as the central Canadians rapidly replaced British and American produce in the Maritime marked with their own flour and manufactured materials.[41] In return, the region shipped to Montreal quantities of primary and primary manufactured products of both local and imported origins. The secretaries of the Montreal and St. John boards of trade estimated the extent of this inter-regional commerce at about $15,711,000 in 1885, more than 70 percent of which represented central Canadian exports to the Maritimes.[42] By contrast the external trade cycle moved in traditional fashion by ship from the principal Maritime ports to Great Britain and the West Indies. Heavily balanced in favour of the Maritimes, it consumed most of the output of the region's resource industries. The two cycles were crucially interdependent; the Maritime business community used the credits earned in the external cycle to meet the gaping deficits incurred in the central Canadian trade. The system worked as long as the equilibrium between the two could be maintained. Unfortunately, as the decade progressed, this balance was seriously threatened by a declining English lumber market.[43]

In the face of this increasingly serious trade imbalance, the Maritime business community became more and more critical of what they regarded as the subversion of the National Policy by central Canadian interests. Their argument was based upon two propositions. If Canadian transportation policy was dedicated to creating an all-Canadian commercial system, then this system should extend not from the Pacific to Montreal, but from the Pacific to the Atlantic. How, in all justice, could the Montreal interests insist on the construction, at a staggering cost, of an all-Canadian route west of that city and then demand the right to export through Portland or Boston rather than using the Maritime route? This argument was implicit in almost every resolution of the Halifax and St. John boards of trade from 1880 onward.[44]

The second proposition maintained that, as vehicles of nationhood, the railways must be considered as a means of promoting national economic integration rather than as commercial institutions. The timing of this doctrine is significant. Before 1885 most Maritime manufacturers were competitive both with Canadian and foreign producers. Nails, confectionery, woolens, leather, glass, steel and machinery manufactured in the Maritimes normally had large markets in both central Canada and the West.[45] The recession of 1885 reached a trough in 1886.[46] Diminishing demand coupled with over-production, particularly in the cotton cloth and sugar industries, resulted in falling prices, and made it increasingly difficult for many Maritime manufacturers to retain their central Canadian markets. The *bête noir* was seen as the relatively high freight rates charged by the Intercolonial Railway. The issue came to a head late in 1885 with the closing of the Moncton and the two Halifax sugar refineries. The response of the Halifax manufacturers was immediate and decisive. Writing to the Minister of Railways, John F. Stairs enunciated the Maritime interpretation of the National Policy:

> Four refineries have been set in operation in the Lower Provinces by the policy of the Government. This was right; but trade having changed so that it is now impossible for them to work prosperously it is the duty of the Government to accommodate its policy to the change. The reduction in freight rates asked for is necessary to this. . . . If in answer to this you plead that you must manage so that no loss occur running the I.C.R., we will reply, we do not, and will not accept this as a valid plea from the Government . . . and to it we say that the people of Nova Scotia, nor should those of Ontario and Quebec, for they are as much interested, even admit it is essential to make both ends meet in the finance of the railreoad, when it can only be done at the expense of interprovincial trade, and the manufactures of Nova Scotia. . . . How can the National Policy succeed in Canada where such great distances exist between the provinces unless the Government who control the National Railway meet the requirements of trade. . .[47]

At stake, as Stairs later pointed out in a confidential memorandum to Macdonald, was the whole West Indies trade of Nova Scotia.[48] Equally as important and also at stake was the entire industrial structure which had been created in the region under the aegis of the National Policy.

The Maritimes by 1885 provided a striking illustration of the success of that policy. With less than one-fifth of the population of the Dominion, the region contained eight of the twenty-three Canadian cotton mills — including seven of the nineteen erected after 1879[49] — three of five sugar refineries, two of seven rope factories, one of three glass works, both of the Canadian steel mills, and six of the nation's twelve rolling mills.

Although Stairs succeeded in his efforts to have the I.C.R. sugar·freight rates reduced,[50] the problem facing the Maritime entrepreneur was not one which could be solved simply by easier access to the larger central Canadian market; its cause was much more complex. In the cotton industry, for example, the Canadian business community had created industrial units with a production potential sufficient to supply the entire national market. In periods of recession many American cloth manufacturers were prepared to cut prices on exports to a level which vitiated the Canadian tariff; this enable them to gain control of a considerable portion of the Canadian market. The problems of the cotton cloth manufacturers could have been solved by a further increase in the tariff — a politically undesirable answer — by control of railway rates, or by a regulated industrial output.

From a Maritime regional viewpoint the second of these alternatives appeared to be the most advantageous; the limitations of the tariff could then be accepted and, having attained geographic equality with Montreal through a regulated freight rate, the more efficient Maritime mills would soon control the Montreal market. Such was the hope; there was little possibility of its realization. Such a general alteration in railway policy would have required subsidization of certain geographic areas — districts constituting political minorities — at the expense of the dominant political areas of the country, a prospect which the business community of Montreal and environs could hardly be expected to view with equanimity. Apart from the political difficulties of the situation, most Maritime manufactories suffered from two major organizational problems: the continued difficulty faced by community corporations in securing financing in the frequent periods of marginal business activity,[51] and the fact that most firms depended upon Montreal wholesale houses to dispose of their extra-regional exports.[52] Short of a major shift in government railway or tariff policy, the only solution to the problem of markets which seemed to have any chance for success appeared to be the regulation of industrial production, a technique which was to bring into the Maritimes the Montreal interests which already controlled the major part of the distributive function in eastern Canada.

III

The entry of Montreal into the Maritime region was not a new phenomenon. With the completion of the Intercolonial Railway and the imposition of coal duties in 1879, Montreal railway entrepreneurs moved to control both the major rail systems of New Brunswick and the Nova Scotia coal fields. A syndicate headed by George Stephen and Donald Smith had purchased the New Brunswick Railroad from Alexander Gibson and the Hon. Isaac Burpee in 1880,[33] with the intention of extending it to Rivière du Loup. This system was expanded two years later by the purchase of the New Brunswick and Canada Railroad with the ultimate view of making St. John the winter port for Montreal.

In the same year, another Montreal group headed by John McDougall, David Morrice and L.-A. Sénécal acquired from fifteen St. John bondholders, four-fifths of the bonds of the Springhill and Parrsboro Railroad and Mining Company,[54] and followed this up in 1883 with the purchase of the Springhill Mining Company, the largest coal producer in Canada.[55] The following year another syndicate acquired the International Mine at Sydney.[56] The coal mine takeovers were designed to control and expand the output of this fuel source, partially in an effort to free the Canadian Pacific Railways from dependence upon the strike-prone American coal industry. By contrast, the entry of Montreal interests into the manufacturing life of the Maritimes aimed to restrict output and limit expansion.

The first serious attempts to regulate production occurred in the cotton industry. Although informal meetings of manufacturers had been held throughout the mid-1880's, the business depression of 1886 and the threatened failure of several mills resulted in the organization of the first formal national trade association. Meeting in Montreal in the summer of 1886, representatives of sixteen mills, including four from the Maritimes, agreed to regulate production and to set standard minimum prices for commodities. The agreement was to be renegotiated yearly and each mill provided a bond as proof of good faith.[57] The arrangement at least stabilized the industry and the agreement was renewed in 1887.

The collapse of the association the following year was precipitated by a standing feud between the two largest Maritime mills, the St. Croix at St. Stephen and the Gibson at Marysville. Alexander Gibson had long been the maverick of the organization, having refused to subscribe to the agreement in 1886 and 1887. During this period he had severely injured his larger St. Stephen competitor in the Maritime market. By the time Gibson agreed to enter the association in 1888, the St. Croix mill, faced with bankruptcy, dropped out and reduced prices in an effort to dispose of its huge inventory. The Gibson mill followed suit. With two of the largest coloured cotton mills in the Dominion selling without regulation, the controlled market system dissolved into chaos, and the association, both coloured and grey sections, disintegrated.[58] The return to an unregulated market in the cotton industry continued for more than two years. A business upswing in 1889 mercifully saved the industry from what many manufacturers feared would be a general financial collapse. Even so, only the mills with the largest production potential, regardless of geographic location, escaped unscathed; most of the smaller plants were forced to close temporarily.

In the summer of 1890 a Montreal group headed by A.F. Gault and David Morrice prepared the second attempt to regulate the cotton market. The technique was to be the corporate monopoly. The Dominion Cotton Mills Company, with a $5,000,000 authorized capital, was to bring all of the grey cotton producers under the control of a single directorate. In January 1891, David Morrice set out on a tour of Maritime cotton centres. On his first stop, at Halifax, he accepted transfer of the Nova Scotia Cotton Mill to the syndicate, the shareholders receiving $101,000 cash and $101,000 in bonds in the new corporation, a return of 25 cents on the dollar of their initial investment.[59] The following day Morrice proceeded to Windsor, "to consummate the transfer of the factory there",[60] and from there moved on to repeat the performance at Moncton. Fearful of total bankruptcy and hopeful that this stronger organization would provide the stability that earlier efforts had failed to achieve, stockholders of the smaller community-oriented mills readily acquiesced to the new order. Although they lost heavily on their original investment, most owners accepted bonds in the new corporation in partial payment for their old stock.

The first determined opposition to the cotton consolidation movement appeared in St. John. Here, John H. Parks, founder and operator of the thirty-year old New Brunswick Cotton Mill, had bought the bankrupt St. John Cotton firm in 1886 and had proceeded to operate both mills. Despite the perennial problem of financing, the Parks Mills represented one of the most efficient industrial operations in the Dominion, one which had won an international reputation for the quality of its product. The company's major markets were found in western Ontario, a fact which made the continued independence of the firm a particular menace to the combination. The firm's major weakness was its financial structure. Dependent upon the Bank of Montreal for his operating capital, Parks had found it necessary to borrow more heavily than usual during the winter of 1889-90. By mid-1890 his debts totalled $122,000.[61]

At this point two events occurred almost simultaneously: Parks refused to consider sale of the St. John Mills to the new corporation, and the Bank of Montreal, having ascertained that the Montreal syndicate would buy the mills from any seller, demanded immediate payment in full of the outstanding debts of the company[62] — a most unusual procedure. Claiming a Montreal conspiracy to seize the company, Parks replied with an open letter to the dry goods merchants of greater St. John.

   . . . I have made arrangements by which the mills of our company will be run to their fullest extent.

   These arrangements have been made in the face of the most determined efforts to have our business stopped, and our property sold out to the Montreal syndicate which is endeavouring to control the Cotton Trade of Canada. . . . I now propose to continue to keep our mills in operation as a St. John industry free from all outside control. I would therefore ask you gentlemen, as far as your power, to support me in this undertaking —

It remains with you to assit the Wholesale Houses in distributing the goods made in St. John in preference to those of outside manufacture so long as the quality and price of the home goods is satisfactory.

The closing of our mills . . . would be a serious calamity to the community, and you, by your support can assist materially in preventing it. I believe you will.[63]

Parks' appeal to community loyalty saved his firm. When the bank foreclosed the mortgage which it held as security for its loans, Mr. Justice A.L. Palmer of the New Brunswick Supreme Court placed the firm in receivership under his control until the case was resolved. Over the stronger objections of the bank, and on one legal pretext after another, the judge kept the mill in receivership for nearly two years.[64] In the meantime he forced the bank to continue the provision of operating capital for the mill's operations, and in conjunction with the receiver, a young Fredericton lawyer, H.H. McLean, proceeded to run an efficient and highly profitable business. When the decision was finally rendered in December 1892, the firm was found to have cleared profits of $150,000 during the period of the receivership. Parks was unable to use the funds to repay the bank debts and the mill continued under local control.[65]

The St. John experience was unique. Gault and Morrice organized the Canadian Coloured Cotton Company, sister consolidation to the Dominion Cotton Mills, in 1891. The St. Croix Mill entered the new organization without protest early in 1892,[66] and even the Gibson Mill, while retaining its separate corporate structure, agreed to market its entire output through the new consolidation. By 1893 only the St. John Mills and the small Yarmouth plant remained in the hands of regional entrepreneurs.

The fate of the Maritime cotton mills was paralleled in the sugar industry. In 1890 a syndicate of Scottish merchants, incorporated under English laws as the Halifax Sugar Refinery Ltd., bought up the English-owned Woodside Refinery of Halifax.[67] The ultimate aim of the Scottish group was to consolidate the sugar industry into a single corporate entity similar to Dominion Cotton. Failing in this effort because of the parliamentary outcry against combines, they turned their efforts to regional consolidation. With the assistance of John F. Stairs, M.P., they were able, in 1894, to secure an act of incorporation as the Acadia Sugar Refineries which was to amalgamate the three Maritime firms. Unlike the Cotton Union, the new consolidation worked in the interests of the regional entrepreneurs, the stock holders of all three refineries receiving full value for their holdings. Equally important, the management of the new concern remained in the hands of Thomas Kenny, M.P.

The consolidation movement of the early 1890's swept most of the other major Maritime manufactories. In some cases local entrepreneurs managed to retain a voice in the direction of the new mergers — John Stairs, for example, played a prominent role on the directorate of the Consumers Cordage Company which swept the Halifax and St. John rope concerns into a new seven-company amalgamation in 1890.[68] On the other hand, the Nova Scotia Glass Company of New Glasgow disappeared entirely in the Diamond Glass consolidation of that same year.[69] On the whole, saving only the iron and steel products, the confectionery and the staple export industries, control of all mass consumption industries in the Maritimes had passed to outside interests by 1895. Thus, in large measure the community manufactory which had dominated the industrial growth of the 1880's ceased to exist in the 1890's. Given the nature of the market of the period, some degree of central control probably was inevitable. The only question at stake was whether it would be a control effected by political or financial means, and if the latter, from which centre it would emanate.

The failure of any Maritime metropolis to achieve this control was partly a result of geography and partly a failure of entrepreneurial leadership. The fear of being left on the fringes of a national marketing system had been amply illustrated by the frenetic efforts of the St. John and Halifax business communities to promise political policies which would link the Canadian marketing system to an Atlantic structure with the Maritime ports serving as the connecting points.[70]

The question of entrepreneurial failure is more difficult to document. In part the great burst of industrial activity which marked the early 1880's was the last flowering of an older generation of lumbermen and wholesale shippers. Having failed to achieve their position as the link between central Canada and Europe, and faced with the dominant marketing and financial apparatus of the Montreal community, they drew back and even participated in the transfer of control. This failure is understandable in the smaller communities; it is more difficult to explain in the larger. In the latter case it may well be attributable to the perennial failure of most Maritime communities to maintain a continuity of industrial elites. The manufacturing experience of most families was limited to a single generation: Thomas Kenny's father was a wholesale merchant, his son a stock broker. John F. Stairs was the son of a merchant and the father of a lawyer. Even in such a distinguished industrial family as that of John Parks, a second generation manufacturer, the son attended the Royal Military College and then entered the Imperial service. Commerce and the professions provided a much more stable milieu, and while many participants in both of these activities were prepared to make the occasional excursion into manufacturing, usually as part of a dual role, few were willing to make a permanent and sole commitment to an industrial vocation.

IV

The lesson brought home to the Maritime entrepreneur by the industrial experience between 1879 and 1895 was that geography would defeat any attempt to compete at parity with a central Canadian enterprise. In response to this lesson, the truncated industrial community of the region turned increasingly to those resource industries in which geography gave them a natural advantage over their central Canadian counterparts. In the 1890's the thrust of Maritime industrial growth was directed toward the processing and manufacturing of primary steel and of iron and steel products. In part, since these enterprises constituted much of the industrial machinery remaining in the hands of regional entrepreneurs, there was little choice in this development. At the same time, Nova Scotia contained most of the active coal and iron deposits in the Dominion and had easy access to the rich iron ore deposits at Belle Isle. In any event, most competition in these industries came from western Ontario rather than Montreal, and the latter was thus a potential market.

Iron and steel development was not new to the region. Efforts at primary steel making had been undertaken successfully at New Glasgow since 1882. Yet production there was limited and would continue so until a more favourable tariff policy guaranteed a stable market for potential output. Such a policy was begun in 1887 with the passage of the "iron" tariff. Generally labeled as a Nova Scotia tariff designed to make that province "the Pennsylvania of Canada"[71] and New Glasgow "the Birmingham of the country",[72] the act provided an effective protection of $3.50 a ton for Canadian-made iron, and imposed heavy duties on a variety of iron and steel products.[73] Protection for the industry was completed in 1894 when the duty on scrap iron, considered a raw material by secondary iron manufacturers, was raised from $2 to $4 a ton, and most rolling mills were forced to use Nova Scotia-made bar iron rather than imported scrap.[74]

The growth of the New Glasgow industries parallelled this tariff development. In 1889 the Nova Scotia Steel Company was united with the Nova Scotia Forge Company to form a corporation capable of manufacturing both primary steel and iron and steel products. In the same year, to provide the community with its own source of pig iron, a group of Nova Scotia Steel shareholders organized the New Glasgow Iron, Coal and Railroad Company with a capital of $1,000,000.[75] Five years later, following the enactment of the scrap iron duty, New Glasgow acquired the rich Wabana iron ore deposits at Belle Isle — some eighty-three acres covered with ore deposits so thick they could be cut from the surface. This was followed the next year by the union of the Nova Scotia Steel and Forge and the New Glasgow Iron companies into a $2,060,000 corporation, the Nova Scotia Steel Company.

Containing its own blast and open hearth furnaces, rolling mills, forges, foundries, and machine shops, the firm represented the most fully integrated industrial complex in the country. The process was completed in 1900 when the company acquired the Sydney Coal Mines on Cape Breton Island, developed new steel mills in that area and reorganized as the Nova Scotia Steel and Coal Company with a $7,000,000 capital.[76]

The development of the Nova Scotia Steel and Coal corporation had begun under the direction of a cabal of Pictou County Scottish Nova Scotians, a group which was later enlarged to include a few prominent Halifax businessmen. Aside from Graham Fraser, its leading members included James D. McGregor, James C. MacGregor, Colonel Thomas Cantley, and John F. Stairs. All four were third generation Nova Scotians, the first three from New Glasgow. Saving only Cantley, all were members of old mercantile families. Senator McGregor, a merchant, was a grandson of the Rev. Dr. James McGregor, one of the founders of the Presbyterian Church in Nova Scotia; MacGregor was a partner in the large shipbuilding concern of Senator J.W. Carmichael, a prominent promoter of Nova Scotian Steel. Cantley was the only member of the group of proletarian origins. Like Graham Fraser, he spent a lifetime in the active service of the company, having entered the newly established Nova Scotia Forge Company in 1873 at the age of sixteen. Promoted to sales manager of the amalgamated Nova Scotia Steel Company in 1885, he had been responsible for the introduction of Wabana ore into England and Germany. In 1902 he succeeded Graham Fraser as general manager of the corporation.[77]

Aside from its value to the New Glasgow area, the Nova Scotia Steel Company was of even greater significance as a supplier of iron and steel to a variety of foundries, car works and machine mills in the region. Because of its unique ability to provide primary, secondary and tertiary steel and iron manufactures, it was supplying most of the Maritime iron and steel needs by 1892.[78] In this respect, the industrial experience of the 1890's differed considerably from that of the previous decade. It was not characterized by the development of new industrial structures, but rather by the expansion of older firms which had served purely local markets for some time and expanded in response to the demand created by the tariff changes of the period.[79]

The centres of the movement were at New Glasgow, Amherst and St. John, all on the main lines of the Intercolonial or Canadian Pacific railroads. At New Glasgow, the forge and foundry facilities of the Nova Scotia Steel Company consumed half the company's iron and steel output. At Amherst, Nathaniel Curry (later Senator) and his brother-in-law, John Rhodes, continued the expansion of the small woodworking firm they had established in 1877, gradually adding a door factory, a rolling mill, a railroad car plant and an axle factory, and in 1893 bought out the Harris Car Works and Foundry of St. John.[80] At the time of its incorporation in 1902, Rhodes, Curry & Company was one of the largest secondary iron manufacturing complexes in the Dominion.[81] Curry's industrial neighbour at Amherst was David Robb. Son of an Amherst foundry owner, Robb had been trained in engineering at the Stevens Institute of New Jersey and then had entered his father's foundry. Specializing in the development of precision machinery, he expanded his activities into Massachusetts in the 1890's and finally merged his firm into the International Engineering Works of South Framingham of which he remained managing director.[82]

If under the aegis of a protective government policy the iron and steel industry of the Maritimes was rapidly becoming a viable proposition for local entrepreneurs, it was also increasingly attracting the interest of both Boston and Montreal business interests. There was a growing feeling that, once a reciprocal coal agreement was made between Canada and the United States, Nova Scotia coal would replace the more expensive Pennsylvania product in the New England market. Added to this inducement was the fact that Nova Scotia provided the major fuel source on the Montreal market — the city actually consumed most of the coal produced in the Cape Breton fields.[83] With its almost unlimited access routes and its strategic water position midway between Boston and Montreal, Nova Scotia seemed an excellent area for investment.

In 1893 a syndicate headed by H.M. Whitney of Boston and composed of Boston, New York and Montreal businessmen, including Donald Smith, W.C. Van Horne and Hugh McLennan, negotiated a 119-year lease with the Nova Scotia government for most of the existing coal fields on Cape Breton Island.[84] The new Dominion Coal Company came into formal being in March of that year, with David MacKeen (later Senator) as director and general manager, and John S. McLennan (later Senator) as director and treasurer. The son of a Scottish-born mine owner and member of the legislative council, MacKeen had been an official and principal stockholder in the Caledonia Coal Company which had been absorbed in the new consolidations.[85] McLennan was the second son of Hugh McLennan of Montreal, a graduate of Trinity College, Cambridge, and one of the very few entrepreneurs who made the inter-regional transfer in this period.[86] The success of the Dominion Coal syndicate and the growing feeling that the Canadian government was determined to create a major Canadian primary steel industry led Whitney in 1899 to organize the Dominion Iron & Steel Company. The date was significant. Less than two years earlier the government had announced its intention to extend bounty payments to steel made from imported ones.[76] The $15,000,000 capital of the new company was easily raised, largely on the Canadian stock market,[88] and by 1902 the company was employing 4,000 men in its four blast and ten steel furnace works.[89] Graham Fraser was induced to leave Nova Scotia Steel to become general manager of the new corporation,[90] and J.H. Plummer, assistant general manager of the Bank of Commerce, was brought from Toronto as president.

The primacy of American interests in both the Dominion Steel and Dominion Coal companies was rapidly replaced by those of Montreal and Toronto after 1900. The sale of stocks added a strong Toronto delegation to the directorate of the steel company in 1901.[91] In that same year James Ross, the Montreal street railway magnate, bought heavily into the coal corporation, re-organized its management and retained control of the firm until 1910.[92]

V

The increasing reliance on the stock market as a technique for promoting and securing the necessary financial support to develop the massive Nova Scotia steel corporations emphasized the growing shift from industrial to financial capitalism. Centred on the Montreal stock market, the new movement brought to the control of industrial corporations men who had neither a communal nor a vocational interest in the concern.

In emulation of, and possibly in reaction to the Montreal experience, a group within the Halifax business and professional communities scrambled to erect the financial structure necessary to this undertaking. The city already possessed some of the elements of this structure. The Halifax stock exchange had existed on an informal basis since before Confederation.[93] The city's four major banking institutions — the Nova Scotia, the Union, The Merchants (which subsequently became the Royal Bank of Canada) and the Peoples — were among the soundest in the Dominion. The development of Halifax as a major centre for industrial finance began in 1894, at the height of the first Montreal-based merger movement, when a syndicate headed by J.F. Stairs founded the Eastern Trust Company.[94] The membership of this group was indicative of the change that was occurring in the Halifax business elite. Although it contained representatives of the older mercantile group, such as Stairs, T.E. Kenny and Adam Burns, it also included manufacturers and coalman, notably J.W. Allison and David McKeen, a stockbroker, J.C. MacKintosh, and lawyers such as Robert L. Borden and Robert E. Harris.

Until his death in 1894, the personification of the new Halifax finance capitalism was John Stairs. It was Stairs who arranged the organization of Acadia Sugar in 1894, who initiated the merger of the Union Bank of Halifax with the Bank of Windsor in 1899, and who led the Halifax business community back into its traditional imerpium in the Caribbean with the organization of the Trinidad Electric and Demerara Electric corporations.[95] After 1900, it was Stairs who demonstrated to this same group the possibilities for industrial finance existing within the Maritimes. With the assistance of his young secretary, Max Aitken, and through the medium of his own holding company, Royal Securities, he undertook the re-organization of a number of firms in the region, most notably the Alexander Gibson Railraod and Manufacturing Company which was re-capitalized at $6,000,000.[96] The scope of his interests, and the changes which had been wrought in the Maritime business community in the previous twenty-five years, were perhaps best illustrated in the six corporation presidencies which Stairs held in his lifetime, five of them at his death in 1904; Consumers Cordage, Nova Scotia Steel, Eastern Trust, Trinidad Electric, Royal Securities, and Dalhousie University.

Yet, while promotion of firms such as Stanfield's Woollens of Truro constituted a fertile field of endeavour,[97] the major industrial interest of the Halifax finance capitalists was the Nova Scotia Steel Company. In its search for additional capital resources after 1900, the entrepreneurial strength of this firm was rapidly broadened from its New Glasgow base. The principal new promoters of the company were Halifaxmen, notably James Allison, George Campbell and Robert Harris. The New Brunswick-born nephew of the founder of Mount Allison University, Allison had entered the chocolate and spice manufactory of John Mott & Company of Halifax in 1871, and had eventually been admitted to a partnership in the firm. He had invested heavily in several Nova Scotia industries and sat on the directorates of Stanfield's Woollens, the Eastern Trust, and the Bank of Nova Scotia in addition to Nova Scotia Steel.[98] George Campbell, the son of a Scottish gentleman, had entered the service of a Halifax steamship agency as a young man and ultimately became its head. Like Allison he was deeply involved in a number of Nova Scotian firms including Stanfield's, the Silliker Car of Amherst, the Eastern Trust and the Bank of Nova Scotia.[99]

By far the most significant figure in the Nova Scotia Steel Corporation after Stairs' death was Mr. Justice Robert Harris. The Annapolis-born scion of a Loyalist family, Harris shared the same antecedents as the Moncton and St. John entrepreneurs of the same name. After reading law with Sir John Thompson, he was called to the Nova Scotia bar in 1882 and rapidly became one of the leading legal figures in the province. In 1892 he moved his practice to Halifax and there became intimately involved in the corporate promotions of the period, ultimately serving on the directorates of thirteen major corporations including the Eastern Trust, Eastern Car, Bank of Nova Scotia, Maritime Telegraph and Telephone. Acadia Sugar, Robb Engineering, Brandram-Henderson Paint, and held the presidencies of Nova Scotia Steel, Eastern Trust, Demerara Electric, and Trinidad Electric.[100]

Despite the continuing need for additional capital, the Nova Scotia Steel Company found little difficulty obtaining most of this support from the Halifax business community.[101] In turn, the corporation remained one of the most efficiently organized industrial firms in the country. In striking contrast to the larger Dominion Steel enterprise, Nova Scotia Steel's financial position remained strong, its performances solid and its earnings continuous. It was generally credited with being the only major steel company which could have maintained its dividend payments without the aid of federal bounties.[102]

As the first decade of the twentieth century wore to a close, the Halifax business elite appeared to have succeeded in establishing a financial hegemony in the industrial life of an area centred in eastern Nova Scotia and extending outward into both southern New Brunswick and peninsular Nova Scotia. Yet, increasingly, that hegemony was being challenged by the burgeoning consolidation movement emanating from Montreal. The most serious threat was posed in 1909 when Max Aitken, with Montreal now as the centre for his Royal Securities Corporation, arranged the amalgamation of the Rhodes, Curry Company of Amherst with the Canada Car, and the Dominion Car and Foundry companies of Montreal to form the Canadian Car and Foundry Company. The union marked a triumph as much for Nathaniel Curry as for Aitken — he emerged with the presidency and with nearly $3,000,000 of the $8,500,000 capital stock of the new corporation.[103] The move was a blow to the Halifax capitalists, however, as it placed the largest car manufactory in the country, an Amherst plant employing 1,300 men and annually producing $5,000,000 in iron and steel products,[104] firmly in the Montreal orbit of the Drummonds and the Dominion Steel and Coal Corporation. Tension was heightened by the feeling that this manoeuvre was a prelude to the creation of a railroad car monopoly. The reaction was swift. To prevent the takeover of the other Amherst car works, the Silliker Company, a Halifax-based syndicate bought up most of the Silliker stock and organized a greatly expanded company, Nova Scotia Car Works, with a $2,625,000 capital.[105] The following year Nova Scotia Steel organized its own $2,000,000 car subsidiary, the Eastern Car Company.

The contest between Montreal and Halifax finance capitalism reached its climax at the annual meeting of the Nova Scotia Steel Company of New Glasgow in April, 1910. Fresh from that triumph of the Dominion Coal and Steel merger, Montreal stockbrokers Rudolphe Forget and Max Aitken determined to extend the union to include the smaller steel firm, a proposal which the Scotia Steel president, Robert Harris, flatly refused to consider.

Arguing that the firm was stagnating and that a more dynamic leadership in a reorganized corporation would yield greater returns, Forget launched a major effort to acquire proxies with a view to taking control from the Nova Scotia directors. Using the facilities of the Montreal Stock Exchange, he bought large quantities of Scotia stock at increasingly higher prices, an example followed by Robert Harris and his associates at Halifax. At the April meeting, Harris offered Forget a minority of the seats on the directorate; Forget refused. In the voting which followed, the Montreal interests were narrowly beaten. The *Monetary Times*, in a masterpiece of distortion, described this victory as the triumph of "the law . . . over the market place",[105] and proclaimed that "New Glasgow prefers coal dust to that of the stock exchange floor."[107] In fact, it marked a victory, albeit a temporary one, for New Glasgow industrial capitalism and Halifax financial capitalism. More important, it marked the high point of a late developing effort on the part of the Halifax business community to create an industrial region structured on that Atlantic metropolis. It was a short-lived triumph. By 1920 the Halifax group made common cause with their Montreal and London counterparts in the organization of the British Empire Steel Corporation, a gigantic consolidation containing both the Dominion and the Nova Scotia Steel companies. This event marked both the final nationalization of the region's major industrial potential and the failure of its entrepreneurs to maintain control of any significant element in the industrial section of the regional economy.

VI

The Maritimes had entered Canada very much as a foreign colony. As the least integrated part of the Canadian economy, it was the region most dependent upon and most influenced by those policies designated to create an integrated national state. The entrepreneurs of the 1880's were capable men, vividly aware of the problems involved in the transition from an Atlantic to a continental economy. The tragedy of the industrial experiment in the Maritimes was that the transportation lines which linked the region to its new metropolis altered the communal arrangement of the entire area; they did not merely establish a new external frame of reference, they re-cast the entire internal structure. The Maritimes had never been a single integrated organic unit; it was, in fact, not a "region" at all, but a number of British communities clustered on the Atlantic fringe, each with its separate lines of communication and its several metropolises — lines that were water-borne, flexible and changing. In this sense the railroad with its implications of organic unity, its inflexibility, and its assumption that there was a metropolitan point at which it could end, provided an experience entirely alien to the Maritime tradition. The magnitude of this problem was demonstrated in the initial attempts at industrialization; they all occurred in traditional communities ideally located for the Atlantic market, but in the most disadvantaged positions possible for a continental one.

Central to the experience was the failure of a viable regional metropolis to arise to provide the financial leadership and market alternative. With its powerful mercantile interests and its impressive banking institutions, Halifax could most easily have adopted to this role, but its merchants preferred, like their Boston counterparts, to invest their large fortunes in banks and American railroad stocks than to venture them on building a new order. Only later, with the advent of regional resource industries, did that city play the role of financial metropolis.

Lacking any strong regional economic centre, the Maritime entrepreneur inevitably sought political solutions to the structural problems created by the National Policy; he consistently looked to the federal government for aid against all external threats and to his local governments for aid against Canadians. Since the regional politician was more able to influence a hostile environment than was the regional businessman, the latter frequently became both. In many respects the National Policy simply represented to the entrepreneur a transfer from a British to a Canadian commercial empire. Inherent in most of his activities was the colonial assumption that he could not really control his own destiny, that, of necessity, he would be manipulated by forces beyond his control. Thus he produced cotton cloth for the central Canadian metropolis in precisely the same manner as he had produced timber and ships for the British. In so doing he demonstrated considerable initiative and considerable courage, for the truly surprising aspect of the whole performance was that he was able, using his limited community resources, to produce such a complex and diversified industrial potential during the last two decades of the nineteenth century. The inability of the Canadian market to consume his output was as much a failure of the system as of the entrepreneur; the spectacle of a metropolis which devoured its own children had been alien to the Maritime colonial experience. Ultimately, perhaps inevitably, the regional entrepreneur lost control to external forces which he could rarely comprehend, much less master.

NOTES:

1. Nova Scotia's industrial output increased 66 percent between 1880 and 1890; that of Ontario and Quebec by 51 percent each. Canada, *Census* (1901), III, pp. 272, 283. Bertram estimates that the per capita value of Nova Scotia's industrial output rose from 57.8 percent to 68.9 percent of the national average during the period. Gordon Bertram, "Historical

Statistics on Growth and Structure of Manufacturing in Canada 1870-1957,'' Canadian Political Science Association Conference on Statistics 1962 and 1963, *Report*, p. 122.

2. Canada, *Census* (1901), III, pp. 326-9. The increase between 1880 and 1890 was as follows:

	St. John	Hamilton
Population	−3%	34%
Industrial Capital	125%	69%
Industrial Workers	118%	48%
Average Annual Wage	12%	2%
Value of Output	98%	71%

3. See Table 1.

4. For a sampling of business opinion on the National Policy see K.P. Burn's reply to Peter Mitchell in the tariff debate of 1883. Canada, House of Commons, *Debates*, 1883, pp. 551-2; the opinion of Josiah Wood, *ibid.*, pp. 446-8; and the view of John F. Stairs, *ibid.*, 1885, pp. 641-9.

5. Quoted by J.F. Stairs in the tariff debate of 1886. Canada, House of Commons, *Debates*, 1886, p. 775.

6. *Monetary Times*, 4 June, 6 September 1886. Forty-five of the fifty savings banks in the Dominion were located in the Maritimes.

7. *Monetary Times*, 16 May 1879.

8. *Monetary Times*, 20 May 1881.

9. George M. Rose, ed., *Cyclopedia of Canadian Biography* (Toronto, 1886-8), II, p. 729-31 (henceforth cited as *CCB*).

10. *Encyclopedia of Canadian Biography* (Montreal, 1904-7), I, p. 86; *CCB*, II, p. 155; W.J. Stairs, *History of Stairs Morrow* (Halifax, 1906), pp. 5-6.

11. *Canadian Biographical Dictionary* (Montreal, 1880-1), II, pp. 684-5 (henceforth cited as *CBD*); Parks Family Papers, F, no. 1, New Brunswick Museum.

12. *CBD*, II, pp. 684-5; *Monetary Times*, 27 April 883, 22 June 1888.

13. *CCB*, II, pp. 186-7, 86.

14. *CCB*, II, pp. 354-5; *CBD*, II, p. 693; Henry J. Morgan, ed., *Canadian Men and Women of the Time* (Toronto, 1898), p. 1000.

15. *Monetary Times*, 16 December 1882.

16. *CCB*, II, pp. 221-2; *CBD*, II, pp. 674-5; Harold David, *An International Community on the St. Croix (1604-1930)* (Orono, 1950), chapter 18; *Monetary Times*, 1 August 1890.

17. Canada, *Sessional Papers*, 1885, no. 37, pp. 174-97.

18. *Monetary Times*, 11 December 1885; *Canadian Journal of Commerce*, 3 June 1881; *CBD*, II, pp. 409-10, 510; *Canadian Men and Women of the Time* (1898), p. 44.

19. *Canadian Journal of Commerce*, 10 June 1881.

20. W.J.A. Donald, *The Canadian Iron and Steel Industry* (Boston, 1915), chapter 3.

21. *Monetary Times*, 28 April 1882.

22. *The Canadian Manufacturer and Industrial World*, 3 May 1889 (henceforth cited as *Canadian Manufacturer*).

23. Henry J. Morgan, ed., *Canadian Men and Women of the Time* (Toronto, 1912), p. 419; C.W. Parker, ed., *Who's Who and Why* (Vancouver, 1916), VI & VII, P. 259 (henceforth cited as *WWW*)

24. *Canadian Manufacturer*, 1 April 1892.

25. *Ibid.*, 7 March 1890.

26. *CBD*, II, pp. 534-5.

27. A.G. Bailey, ''The Basis and Persistence of Opposition to Confederation in New Brunswick'', *Canadian Historical Review*, XXIII (1942), p. 394.

28. *Monetary Times*, 9 January 1885.

29. *Ibid.*, 11 May, 1883.

30. *Our Dominion. Historical and Other Sketches of the Mercantile Interests of Fredericton, Marysville, Woodstock, Moncton, Yarmouth, etc.* (Toronto, 1889), pp. 48-54.

31. Canada, *Sessional Papers*, 1885, no. 37, pp. 174-97.

32. Canada, Royal Commission on the Relations of Labour and Capital (1889), *Evidence*, II, p. 448.

33. American industrial leaders of the same period averaged 45 years. See W.F. Gregory and I.D. New, "The American Industrial Elite in the 1870's: Their Social Origins," in William Miller, ed., *Men in Business* (Cambridge, 1952), p. 197.

34. Canada, Royal Commission of the Relations of Labour and Capital, *Evidence*, II, pp. 256, 458 and III, pp. 78, 238, 249; *Canadian Manufacturer*, 24 August 1883; *Monetary Times*, 17 June 1887.

35. *Monetary Times*, 18 March 1881.

36. *Ibid.*, 17 February 1882.

37. *Ibid.*, 19 March 1886.

38. *Canadian Journal of Commerce*, 26 October 1883.

39. *Monetary Times*, 18 October 1880.

40. *Ibid.*, 10 May 1905.

41. *Ibid.*, 8 January 1886.

42. *Monetary Times*, 30 January 1885. Principal Maritime imports from Central Canada included flour, shoes, clothing, textiles, alcoholic beverages and hardware; exports to Quebec and Ontario centred on sugar, coal, cotton, cloth, iron and fish.

43. Exports of New Brunswick lumber declined from 404,000,000 board feet in 1883 to 250,000,000 feet in 1887. *Monetary Times*, 9 January 1885, and 7 January 1887, 21 January 1898.

44. See particularly, *Proceedings of the Ninth Annual Meeting* of the Dominion Board of Trade (1879), pp. 65-73; *Monetary Times*, 27 January 1882; Minute Book of the St. John Board of Trade (1879-87), 14 October 1887, New Brunswick Museum.

45. Canada, *Sessional Papers*, 1885, no. 34, pp. 86-125.

46. Bertram, p. 131.

47. J.F. Stairs to J.M. Pope, 10 September 1885, Macdonald Papers, 50080-5, Public Archives of Canada.

48. J.F. Stairs to Macdonald, 5 February 1886, *ibid.*, volume 155.

49. *Monetary Times*, 5 October 1888.

50. *Ibid.*, 12 February 1886.

51. See the problems faced by John Parks and the N.B. Cotton Mills, Parks Family Papers, F. New Brunswick Museum.

52. Montreal *Herald*, 15 October 1883.

53. *Monetary Times*, 8 October 1880.

54. *Ibid.*, 15 December 1882.

55. *Ibid.*, 8 June 1883.

56. *Ibid.*, 16 November 1884.

57. *Ibid.*, 13 August 1886; *Canadian Manufacturer*, 20 August 1887.

58. *Canadian Journal of Commerce*, 7 September 1888.

59. Thomas Kenny in Canada, House of Commons, *Debates*, 1893, p. 2522.

60. *Monetary Times*, 16 January 1891.

61. St. John *Globe*, 1 May 1891.

62. E.S. Clouston to Jones, 25 April 1891, Bank of Montreal, General Managers Letterbooks, vol. 8, Public Archives of Canada.

63. 15 December 1890. Parks Papers, Scrapbook 2, New Brunswick Museum.

64. Clouston to Jones, 13, 22 April, 23 May 1891, Bank of Montreal, General Managers Letterbooks, vol. 8, Public Archives of Canada.

65. St. John *Sun*, 28 December 1892.

66. *Monetary Times*, 18 March 1892.

67. *Ibid.*, 24 October 1890.

68. *Canadian Journal of Commerce*, 22 March 1895.

69. *Monetary Times*, 24 October 1890.

70. *Ibid.*, 12 June 1885, 22 April 1887, 22 August 1902; Minutes of the St. John Board of Trade, 1 December 1879, 8 November 1886, New Brunswick Museum.

71. *Monetary Times*, 20 May 1887.

72. *The Canadian Journal of Commerce*, 29 April 1887.

73. Canada, *Statutes*, 50-1 Victoria C. 39.

74. Simon J. MacLean, *The Tariff History of Canada* (Toronto, 1895), p. 37.

75. *Nova Scotia's Industrial Centre: New Glasgow, Stellarton, Westville, Trenton, The Birthplace of Steel in Canada* (n.p. 1916), pp. 45-6.

76. *Monetary Times*, 9 March 1900; *Industrial Canada*, 20 July 1901.

77. *WWW*, VI & VII, pp. 927. 1075-6.

78. R.M. Guy, "Industrial Development and Urbanization of Pictou Co., N.S. to 1900" (unpublished M.A. thesis, Acadian University, 1962), pp. 120-3.

79. *Canadian Manufacturer*, 20 April 1894.

80. *Monetary Times*, 30 June 1893.

81. *Industrial Canada*, March, 1910; *Canadian Men and Women of the Time* (1912), p. 290.

82. *CCB*, II, p. 183; *CBD*, II, pp. 506-7; *WWW*, VI & VII, p. 997; *Canadian Men and Women of the Time* (1912), p. 947.

83. *Monetary Times*, 26 November 1896. The St. Lawrence ports imported 88,000 tons of British and American coal in 1896, and 706,000 tons of Nova Scotia coal. The transport of this commodity provided the basis for the Nova Scotia merchant marine of the period.

84. *Ibid.*, 3 February 1893.

85. *Canadian Men and Women of the Time* (1912), pp. 698-9; *WWW*, VI & VII, p. 1118.

86. *WWW*, VI & VII, p. 1322.

87. Donald, however, argues that Whitney had been determined to go into steel production even if no bounty had been granted. See Donald, *The Canadian Iron and Steel Industry*, p. 203.

88. Partly, the *Canadian Journal of Commerce* (15 March 1901) suggested, on the promise of the promoters that the Company would receive bonuses of $8,000,000 in its first six years of operation.

89. *Industrial Canada*, May, 1902.

90. J.H. Plummer to B.E. Walker, 3 December 1903, Walker Papers, University of Toronto Archives.

91. *Annual Financial Review*, I (1901), p. 92; III (1903), pp. 158-160.

92. *Monetary Times*, 3 August 1907.

93. *Ibid.*, 17 April 1903.

94. *Ibid.*, 23 February 1894.

95. *Annual Financial Review*, XXIII (1923), pp. 682, 736.

96. *Monetary Times*, 5 December 1902.

97. *Ibid.*, 22 April 1911.

98. *Canadian Men and Women of the Time* (1912), p. 19; *WWW*, VI & VII, p. 762; *Annual Financial Review*, III (1903), pp. 174-6.

99. *Canadian Men and Women of the Time* (1912), p. 192; *WWW*, VI & VII, p. 803.

100. *Canadian Men and Women of the Time* (1912), p. 505; *WWW*, VI & VII, p. 1107; *Annual Financial Review*, III (1903), pp. 174-6.

101. Most of the stock in this concern was held by Nova Scotians who also bought up two-thirds of the $1,500,000 bond which the company put out in 1904. L.M. Jones to B.E. Walker, 5 August 1904, Walker Papers; *Monetary Times*, 15 August 1902.

102. *Monetary Times*, 9 March 1907.
103. *Ibid.*, 8 January 1910.
104. *Industrial Canada*, August, 1913.
105. *Monetary Times*, 29 October 1910.
106. *Ibid.*, 2 April 1910.
107. *Ibid.*, 9 April 1910.

The Urban West: The Evolution of Prairie Towns and Cities to 1930

ALAN F.J. ARTIBISE

The urban frontier was one of the vital elements in Canada's western expansion. Towns and cities introduced a dynamic and aggressive element into the prairie West and played a key role in transforming a sparsely settled fur-trading expanse into a settled and well-integrated region. In this process, the interdependent relationship of city and countryside was clearly evident. But the urban centres were the driving force in the massive changes that occurred in the six decades following Confederation.

I

The process of prairie urban development in the years before 1930 can best be outlined by examining it in four distinguishable phases. The first was a pre-urban stage that lasted for almost two centuries, ending only in the early 1870s when a series of political decisions — Confederation, the sale of Rupert's Land by the Hudson's Bay Company to the Canadian government, and the creation of the Province of Manitoba — opened a new era in western Canadian history. Prior to these dramatic events, the prairie West had no urban centres.[1] The economic base of the region was the H.B.C. fur trade and any agriculture that was practised was at the subsistence level. The only commercial centres were scattered H.B.C. posts managed by a few traders, and these could scarcely claim urban stature. In this pre-railway age, settlement was associated with rivers and the various population concentrations were linked only by boat or by the Red River carts which plied the Carleton Trail.

SOURCE: *Prairie Forum*, Vol. 4, No. 2 (1979), pp. 237-262. Reprinted by permission of the author and the editors.

Five settlements dating from this pre-urban age, however, were destined to become towns and cities in the post-1870 period. At the eastern terminus of the Carleton Trail were located the Red River Colony and Fort Garry. The former had been begun by Lord Selkirk in 1811-1812; the latter was established by the H.B.C. in 1835. Neither of these settlements can be regarded as the basis for urban growth, however, for the lack of immigration and efficient linkages with the outside world resulted in very slow development. It was not until the 1860s that developments occurred which soon led to the establishment of a distinct urban centre. During this decade a small commercial centre named Winnipeg emerged near Fort Garry to compete with the Company in servicing incoming plains traders and supplying the needs of the Red River Colony. By 1870, Winnipeg consisted of a few frame structures and some 100 inhabitants, and offered a number of services, several hotels and specialized retail outlets.[2]

Across the Red River from Winnipeg was the St. Boniface mission. It had been established in 1818 by two Quebec priests, and it soon became one of the most urbane communities on the prairies. Catholic missionaries from central Canada erected a chapel and a school in 1818, and by 1827 the latter was well-established and on its way to becoming the College of St. Boniface. By 1870, the population of this settlement was approaching 800, far exceeding that of Winnipeg.[3]

To the west, along the banks of the Assiniboine River, was Portage la Prairie, established as a mission in 1853. A H.B.C. trading post was erected at the site in 1856 but neither mission nor fort attracted a concentration of settlement. Although all trade for the western area passed through Portage, the settlement was in most respects an offshoot of the settlement at Fort Garry.[4]

To the west and north of Portage, another mission and H.B.C. post were located in close proximity; both Prince Albert Mission and Fort Albert were established in 1866. By 1870, there were approximately 100 inhabitants dispersed along the banks of the North Saskatchewan River but no service centre nucleus had yet developed.[5]

At the western terminus of the Carleton Trail and also on the banks of the North Saskatchewan River was Edmonton House, one of the H.B.C.'s most important entrepôts. This fort acted as a collection centre for furs for the Saskatchewan District and as the distribution centre for goods from Winnipeg. The population of Edmonton House was approximately 150 by Confederation, although this small size belied its administrative and distributive importance.[6]

By 1870, then, the prairie West contained only a few settlement nodes. The entire population of the region was about seventy thousand persons, virtually none of whom could be counted as urban dwellers. Change was in the air, however, and during the next three decades the fur trading economy with its few small posts was replaced by a commercial agricultural economy organized by and around numerous villages, towns, and cities.

II

Between 1871 and 1901, the population of the prairies jumped from 70,000 to more than 400,000, and almost 20 per cent lived in urban centres with populations exceeding 1,000 (Table I). By this date the region also had three incorporated cities, twenty-five towns, and fifty-seven villages.[7] More than eighteen of these centres had populations exceeding 1,000, six had populations exceeding 5,000, and one had a population in excess of 40,000 (Tables II, III, IV).

The reasons for this substantial growth in the number of urban centres are complex and cannot be adequately analyzed here.[8] What is readily apparent, however, is that virtually all the centres which sprang up or grew significantly in this second era of development were located on railway lines or along the paths of projected lines (see Map 1). The fact was that the 1870s were the beginning of a new era for the prairies in which subsistence agriculture was replaced by the production of agricultural surplus for export. The development of commercial agriculture — indeed, the mere anticipation of it — brought about the rise of centres of distribution. The reciprocal relationship between town and country was clear.

> The prairie pioneer was no self-sufficient farmer but an agricultural industrialist engaged in commercial trading. He produced a large surplus of grain and was a heavy consumer of manufactured goods. He needed grain shipping depots, farm implements, hardware goods, wagons, harnesses, lumber and other supplies. He needed banking services to finance these investments. He needed consumer goods that he could not produce himself: clothing and staple foodstuffs. As a result, every rural community needed a town, both as a shipping point that gathered surplus grain, and as a distribution point that fanned manufactured goods back into the countryside.[9]

To survive and to grow, incipient service centres needed capital, agricultural hinterlands, and transportation connections. The most important of these essentials for every aspiring metropolis was the railway. "Railways and continually improving transportation were as essential as rain and sun to progressive settlement on the Canadian prairie. Nearness to railways and projected railways was of first importance to the settler."[10]

In the three decades following 1870, approximately 3,600 miles of rail were laid in the prairie West.[11] The most dramatic growth of settlement occurred along the main line and branch lines of the Canadian Pacific

Railway, and among these settlements none grew as rapidly as Winnipeg. The first railway reached Winnipeg in 1878, connecting the community with St. Paul and Chicago. By 1883, the C.P.R. stretched north of the Great Lakes to link Winnipeg with eastern Canada, and two years later the first transcontinental line was complete. Winnipeg was also a nodal point for several branch lines in Manitoba, and together these external and internal linkages contributed to its growth and dominance. By 1881, Winnipeg's population was 8,000; during the next decade it more than tripled. Wholesaling was organized during these years, and with the growing number of towns and service centres in the prairie West Winnipeg merchants were soon establishing branch offices. Financial, retail and merchandising operations also increased in number. In 1881-1882, Winnipeg experienced a tremendous real estate boom; although the boom soon collapsed, real growth did take place, and the initial physical infrastructure of an urban centre — railways, hotels, warehouses, offices, stores — had been acquired. By the early 1880s, Winnipeg was firmly established as the dominant western urban centre.

Elsewhere in Manitoba, new centres appeared and older centres grew, although nowhere was change as substantial as in Winnipeg. St. Boniface was incorporated as a town in 1883 but, given its proximity to Winnipeg, was to remain in that city's shadow in subsequent years. Portage la Prairie grew more rapidly and established itself as a second-order centre. Incorporated as a town in 1880 and situated on the main line of the C.P.R., Portage grew steadily in the early part of that decade and by 1901 was the third largest settlement in Manitoba. The second largest town was Brandon. Established by the C.P.R. in 1880 and incorporated as a city in 1882 (with a population of 3,000), this centre was evidence of the magic of railways.[12] It was known to most westerners that the C.P.R. would establish a divisional point some 100 miles west of Winnipeg. But when speculators attempted to sell a proposed townsite to the C.P.R. for what the company felt was an unreasonable sum, the company simply moved two miles west and created the instant town of Brandon. When other incipient centres tried to compete with the new boom town they were destined to fail, since no-one was going to buy lots in a town where the train did not stop. The C.P.R. thus became a significant builder of prairie towns, and the Brandon story was repeated many times.[13]

Two other Manitoba centres also learned of the power of the railway during these years, but with less pleasant results than Brandon. Emerson (the former site of Pembina) was surveyed in 1874 when it was believed that its intervening location between Winnipeg and out-of-province centres would guarantee its future. Its rail connection with Winnipeg and the anticipation of further branch-line connections led to the incorporation of Emerson as a

TABLE I

RURAL AND URBAN[a] POPULATION GROWTH IN THE NORTH WEST TERRITORIES AND PRAIRIE PROVINCES, 1871–1931

(in thousands)

	Northwest Territories		Manitoba		Total Prairies		
	Rural	Urban	Rural	Urban	Rural	Urban	% Urban
1871	48	—	25	—	73	—	0
1881	56	—	52	10	108	10	8
1891	95	4	111	41	206	45	18

	Alberta		Saskatchewan		Manitoba		Total Prairies		
	Rural	Urban	Rural	Urban	Rural	Urban	Rural	Urban	% Urban
1901	61	12	86	6	192	64	339	81	19.3
1911	264	110	413	80	269	193	946	383	28.8
1921	411	177	630	128	341	269	1,382	574	29.3
1931	504	228	735	187	357	343	1,596	758	32.2

Notes: (a) In 1871, 1881, and 1891, the urban category includes all incorporated villages, towns, and cities, regardless of size. From 1901–1931, urban population includes incorporated cities, towns, and villages of 1,000 and over and incorporated municipalities of this size range surrounding the larger cities which were later defined as parts of the census metropolitan areas.

SOURCES: *Census of Canada, 1931;* and *Census of Canada, 1956*—"Analytical Report: Rural and Urban Population," p. 26.

TABLE II

POPULATION GROWTH IN INCORPORATED VILLAGES, TOWNS, AND CITIES IN MANITOBA, 1871-1931[a]

URBAN CENTRE	DATE OF INCORPORATION			POPULATION										
	Village	Town	City	1871	1881	1886	1891	1901	1906	1911	1916	1921	1926	1931
Beauséjour	1908	1912						—	—	847	879	994	996	1,139
Brandon			1882			2,348	3,778	5,620	10,408	13,839	15,215	15,397	16,443	17,082
Brooklands	1921													2,462
Carman	1899	1905						1,439	1,530	1,271	1,426	1,591	1,385	1,418
Dauphin	1898	1901						1,135	1,670	2,815	3,200	3,885	3,580	3,971
Killarney	1903							585	1,117	1,010	989	871	901	1,003
Minnedosa		1883				549	614	1,052	1,299	1,483	1,833	1,505	1,681	1,680
Morden		1903					1,176	1,522	1,437	1,130	1,261	1,268	1,354	1,416
Neepawa		1883				255	774	1,418	1,895	1,864	1,854	1,887	1,833	1,910
Portage la Prairie		1880	1907	817		2,028	3,363	3,901	5,106	5,892	5,879	6,766	6,513	6,597
St. Boniface		1883	1908			1,449	1,553	2,019	5,119	7,483	11,021	12,821	14,187	16,305
Selkirk		1882			1,283	705	950	2,188	2,701	2,977	3,399	3,726	4,201	4,486
Souris		1903						839	1,413	1,854	1,845	1,710	1,612	1,661
Stonewall	1906	1908						589	1,074	1,005	1,152	1,112	1,043	1,031
Le Pas		1912									1,270	1,858	1,925	4,030
Transcona		1912								—	3,356	4,185	5,218	5,747
Tuxedo		1913									192	1,062	717	1,173
Virden	1890	1904					606	901	1,471	1,550	1,618	1,361	1,380	1,590
Winkler	1906							391	530	458	547	812	971	1,005
Winnipeg			1873	241	7,985	20,238	25,639	42,340	90,153	136,035	163,000	179,087	191,998	218,785

Notes: (a) Includes only those centres with a population exceeding 1,000 in 1931.

SOURCES: Censuses of Canada, 1871-1931; and Censuses of the Prairie Provinces, 1906-1926. Also, various other sources have been used to provide data for the period of 1871-1891. Unfortunately, I have been unable to locate data on all the communities in existence during these years.

TABLE III

POPULATION GROWTH IN INCORPORATED VILLAGES, TOWNS AND CITIES IN SASKATCHEWAN, 1881–1931 [a]

URBAN CENTRE	DATE OF INCORPORATION			POPULATION								
	Village	Town	City	1881–1882	1891	1901	1906	1911	1916	1921	1926	1931
Assiniboia	1912	1913	—	—	—	—	—	—	719	1,006	1,245	1,454
Battleford	1899	1904	—	—	—	609	933	1,335	1,436	1,229	1,018	1,096
Biggar	1909	1911	—	—	—	—	—	315	830	1,535	2,034	2,369
Canora	1905	1910	—	—	—	—	169	435	835	1,230	1,121	1,179
Estevan	1899	1906	—	—	—	141	877	1,981	2,140	2,290	2,336	2,936
Gravelbourg	1912	1916	—	—	—	—	—	—	463	1,106	1,201	1,137
Herbert	1907	1912	—	—	—	—	—	559	950	827	997	1,009
Humboldt	1905	1907	—	—	—	—	279	859	1,435	1,822	1,751	1,899
Indian Head	—	1902	—	—	—	768	1,545	1,285	1,334	1,439	1,313	1,438
Kamsack	1905	1911	—	—	—	—	204	473	1,202	2,002	1,948	2,087
Kindersley	1910	1910	—	—	—	—	—	456	770	1,003	987	1,037
Lloydminster [b]	1903	1907	—	—	—	—	389	441	494	469	847	1,516
Maple Creek	1896	1903	—	—	—	382	687	936	1,140	1,002	930	1,154
Melfort	1903	1907	—	—	—	—	351	599	971	1,746	1,605	1,809
Melville	1908	1909	—	—	—	—	—	1,816	2,100	2,808	3,352	3,891
Moose Jaw	—	1884	1903	c.100	1,200	1,558	6,249	13,823	16,934	19,285	19,039	21,299
Moosomin	—	1887	—	—	—	868	1,152	1,143	1,329	1,099	1,121	1,119
North Battleford	1906	1906	1913	—	—	—	824	2,105	3,154	4,108	4,787	5,986
Prince Albert	—	1885	1904	c.500	1,009	1,785	3,005	6,254	6,436	7,558	7,873	9,905
Radville	1911	1913	—	—	—	—	—	233	621	883	1,082	1,005
Regina	—	1883	1903	c.800	1,681	2,249	6,169	30,213	26,167	34,432	37,329	53,209
Rosetown	1909	1911	—	—	—	—	—	—	731	865	1,142	1,553
Rosthern	1898	1903	—	—	—	413	918	1,172	1,200	1,074	1,273	1,412
Saskatoon	1901	1903	1906	—	—	113	3,001	12,004	21,048	25,739	31,234	43,291
Shaunavon	1913	1914	—	—	—	—	—	—	897	1,146	1,010	1,716
Sutherland	1909	1912	—	—	—	—	—	421	940	961	1,459	1,148
Swift Current	1904	1907	1913	—	—	121	554	1,852	3,181	3,518	4,175	5,296
Tisdale	1905	1920	—	—	—	—	61	250	458	783	846	1,069
Watrous	1908	1909	—	—	—	—	—	781	843	1,101	1,172	1,303
Weyburn	1900	1903	1913	—	—	113	966	2,210	3,050	3,193	4,119	5,002
Wilkie	1908	1910	—	—	—	—	—	537	815	778	1,041	1,222
Wynyard	1908	1911	—	—	—	—	—	515	682	849	833	1,042
Yorkton	1894	1900	1928	—	—	700	1,363	2,309	3,144	5,151	4,458	5,027

Notes: (a) Includes only those centres with a population exceeding 1,000 in 1931.
(b) Until 1930, population is split between Alberta and Saskatchewan. Amalgamated with Alberta in 1930.

SOURCES: See Table II.

TABLE IV

POPULATION GROWTH IN INCORPORATED VILLAGES, TOWNS AND CITIES IN ALBERTA, 1881-1931 [a]

URBAN CENTRE	DATE OF INCORPORATION			POPULATION								
	Village	Town	City	1881	1891	1901	1906	1911	1916	1921	1926	1931
Beverley	—	1914	—	—	—	231	449	1,137	813	1,039	931	1,111
Blairmore	1901	1911	—	—	—	—	—	—	1,219	1,552	1,609	1,629
Calgary	—	1884	1893	100	3,867	4,398	11,967	43,704	56,514	63,305	65,291	83,761
Camrose	1905	1906	—	—	—	—	412	1,586	1,692	1,892	2,002	1,672
Cardston	1898	1901	—	—	—	639	1,001	1,207	1,370	1,612	2,034	1,704
Claresholm	1903	1905	—	—	—	—	680	809	687	963	956	1,156
Coleman	1904	1910	—	—	—	—	915	1,557	1,559	1,590	2,044	2,034
Drumheller	1913	1916	1930	—	—	—	—	—	312	2,499	2,578	2,987
Edmonton	—	1892	1904	263	700	2,626	11,167	31,064	53,846	58,821	65,163	79,187
Edson	1911	1911	—	—	—	—	—	—	—	—	1,493	1,547
Fort Saskatchewan	1899	1904	—	—	—	306	585	497	500	1,138	943	1,001
Grand Prairie	1914	1919	—	—	—	—	—	782	337	982	917	1,464
Hanna	1912	1914	—	—	—	—	—	—	711	1,061	1,400	1,490
High River	1901	1910	—	—	—	153	1,018	1,182	1,182	1,364	1,377	1,459
Innisfail	1899	1903	—	—	—	317	643	602	838	1,198	1,151	1,024
Lacombe	1896	1902	—	—	—	499	1,015	1,029	1,047	1,133	1,202	1,259
Lethbridge	—	1890	1906	—	—	2,072	2,936	9,035	9,436	11,097	10,735	13,489
Macleod	—	1892	—	—	—	796	1,144	1,844	1,811	1,723	1,715	1,447
Magrath	1901	1907	—	—	—	424	884	995	938	1,069	1,202	1,224
Medicine Hat	1894	1898	1906	—	—	1,570	3,020	5,608	9,272	9,634	9,536	10,300
Olds	1896	1905	—	—	—	218	554	917	730	764	1,003	1,056
Pincher Creek	1898	1906	—	—	—	335	589	1,027	1,026	888	1,003	1,024
Raymond	1902	1903	—	—	—	—	1,568	1,465	1,205	1,394	1,799	1,849
Redcliff	1910	1912	—	—	—	—	—	220	1,294	1,137	916	1,192
Red Deer	1894	1901	1913	—	—	323	1,418	2,118	2,203	2,328	2,021	2,344
Stettler	—	1906	—	—	—	—	570	1,444	1,168	1,416	1,127	1,219
Strathcona [b]	—	1899	1907	—	—	1,550	2,921	5,579	—	—	—	—
Taber	1905	1907	—	—	—	—	578	1,400	1,412	1,705	1,342	1,279
Vegreville	1906	1906	—	—	—	—	344	1,029	1,156	1,479	1,721	1,659
Vermilion	1906	1906	—	—	—	—	623	625	929	1,272	1,203	1,270
Wainwright	—	1910	—	—	—	—	—	788	818	975	1,028	1,147
Wetaskiwin	1899	1902	1906	—	—	550	1,652	2,411	2,048	2,061	1,884	2,125

Notes: (a) Includes only those centres with a population exceeding 1,000 in 1931.
(b) Annexed to Edmonton in 1911. The Edmonton total in 1911 includes Strathcona.

SOURCES: See Table II.

town in 1880, and by the spring of 1882 it had a population of 2,500 and was thriving as the supply base of southwestern Manitoba. But when a railway was constructed to Morris and Morden, bypassing Emerson, the town's growth halted and a long period of population decline set in. By 1886 Emerson was a dull place with empty warehouses and stores, and vacant homes. People had simply left to establish businesses in the new towns along the C.P.R.'s Pembina Branch.[14]

Selkirk's early history was similar, although its story is more dramatic since it had hoped to become the hub of railway operations in the West. Until 1880 it was the plan of the C.P.R. to cross the Red River at Selkirk, not at Winnipeg, placing the former community on the main line and excluding the latter. This anticipation caused a surge of growth in Selkirk until the Winnipeg business community marshalled their forces and succeeded in having the decision changed.[15] Thus, when the C.P.R. crossed the Red River at Winnipeg, Selkirk had to be content with remaining the centre of steamboat, lumbering and fishing operations on Lake Winnipeg. It was, at best, a poor second prize. By 1901 Selkirk's population was barely 2,000.

The rise and growth of towns and cities in the remainder of the prairie West in this era were also closely related to railways. The most dramatic growth occurred along the C.P.R. main line where the towns of Regina, Moose Jaw, Swift Current, Medicine Hat, and Calgary suddenly came to life. All except Calgary were creations of the C.P.R.

Few other western urban centres illustrated the power of the C.P.R. so well as Regina. It possessed no natural advantages as a townsite since it was situated on a treeless plain with only the meandering Pile of Bones (Wascana) Creek as a nearby source of water. Furthermore, the site had not previously possessed any commercial importance; until 1882 the nearest settlement was the H.B.C. post on the Qu'Appelle Lakes, thirty-five miles to the northeast. Yet by 1883 Regina was incorporated as a town and by 1888 it claimed a population of 1,400.[16]

The C.P.R.'s ability to control townsite selection and land sales on the prairies was well known. The choice of Regina, however, was not unchallenged. In 1882, Edgar Dewdney, federally appointed Lieutenant-Governor of the North West Territories, was authorized to select a site for a new capital to replace Battleford, the choice for capital in 1876 when the C.P.R. had been projected to follow a northern route along the North Saskatchewan River. Dewdney and several colleagues had earlier purchased several sections of the H.B.C. land adjacent to the route of the C.P.R. Not surprisingly, it was alleged that in selecting the site of the capital he had been influenced by his investments rather than by the merits of the site. The C.P.R., rarely outmanoeuvred in such matters, located its station two miles from the Dewdney property and, since the railway station was always a focal point in a new settlement, its land sales soon outstripped those of its rivals. The Lieutenant-Governor retaliated by pressuring Ottawa to establish all public buildings on his land, but without much success. At the urging of the C.P.R. , the customs office, post office, and dominion land office were all located near the station and it was here that the centre of the new city remained. The C.P.R. also struck back at Dewdney by situating its divisional point forty miles to the west at Moose Jaw. This move ended hopes for early branch line construction out of Regina and dampened its chances for future growth.[17] Some growth did take place, however, since by the end of 1882 Regina had a population of "around 800 or 900." There was little settlement in the vicinity of Regina, though, and the town functioned mostly as an administrative centre and shipping point rather than as a service centre with a local hinterland. By 1901 it was still only a small town with a population of 2,249.[18]

The complicated manoeuvres of Dewdney and the C.P.R. spurred the rise of Moose Jaw which, unlike Regina, possessed some natural advantages. The site on the Moose Jaw Creek had long been used as an Indian camp and it was situated on several well-used trails. Thus, in anticipation of the railway passing through the Moose Jaw region, prospective settlers and speculators located in the area in July, 1881. But it was the actual arrival of the C.P.R. the next year that "changed Moose Jaw within a matter of months from an outpost on a lonely trail to a bustling prairie boom town of tents, shacks, and small stores."[19] By 1884 Moose Jaw was incorporated as a town with a population of about 700. In the next fifteen years, however, the town grew slowly; by 1901 it had a population of but 1,557. Like most other prairie communities, Moose Jaw suffered from the slowness of settlement in the region in these early years, but evidence exists to suggest that the town's citizens themselves did not always do all that they could to promote and develop their own community.[20]

Swift Current and Medicine Hat were also in large part products of the C.P.R.; both were chosen as divisional points by the company, and during the 1880s and 1890s the C.P.R. payroll sustained both hamlets. Swift Current's growth was painfully slow. By 1901, it had a population — according to the federal census — of a mere 121, and it did not obtain village status until 1904.[21] Medicine Hat developed slightly more rapidly; it became a village in 1894 and a town in 1898, and by 1901 had a population of 1,570.[22] At the turn of the century, however, both communities were still waiting for substantial development to take place.

In contrast, the growth of Calgary was remarkable. The site of Fort Calgary, at the junction of the Bow and Elbow Rivers, was chosen by the North West Mounted Police in 1875, and soon H.B.C. and other traders "clustered under the protective wing of the law to form the settlement first known as the Elbow." In the next seven years, the community acted as a focal point linking the fur trade of the North with American distributing centres, and by 1881 it had a population of about 100. In the next two years, however, dramatic growth occurred with the approach and, in August 1883, the arrival of the C.P.R. line. The railroad changed Calgary from a police post to an urban centre, as the power of the C.P.R. was again demonstrated. The company, rather than locating its station on or near the site of the fort, where a nucleus of permanently settled residents existed, chose a spot three quarters of a mile west of the fort. Despite objections, Calgary businessmen soon followed and many even moved their buildings nearer the station. By 1884, incorporation as a town was secured and Calgary's continued survival and growth seemed assured. In the next few years it quickly grew to become the dominant urban centre on the western plains.[23]

The construction of the main line of the C.P.R. also spawned a number of other, smaller communities during these crucial years. But for most settlements off the main line the period was one of stagnation or decline. Only those which received branch lines, or had other sources of growth, experienced progress. South of Calgary, Lethbridge experienced slow but steady growth. Between 1882 and 1890 the various enterprises incorporated by Sir Alexander Galt established several collieries near Lethbridge and constructed two railways, one to the C.P.R. main line near Medicine Hat, the other to the Great Northern railway at Great Falls, Montana. During peak periods the Galt companies employed as many as a thousand workers, creating a transient male-dominant population and a local economy entirely dependent upon the companies. The railways, however, were subsidized by the federal government, with nearly a million acres of land located south of Lethbridge; when this acreage proved too dry for agricultural settlement, elaborate irrigation works were constructed, a project completed by 1900. Once irrigated, the lands attracted a large number of settlers and thereby transformed Lethbridge from a mere dormitory for the mines to a service centre for its agricultural hinterland. By 1901, shortly after the Crowsnest Pass Railway was built, the incorporated town of Lethbridge had a population of 2,072 — the third largest centre in what was soon to become the province of Alberta.[24]

To the north, Edmonton experienced virtually no growth in the 1880s. With the completion of the main line to Calgary, Edmonton lost much of its function as the depot for the northern fur trading posts. Future prospects brightened considerably in July, 1891, however, when the Calgary and Edmonton Railway reached a point across the river from Edmonton.[25] But the C. & E.R. then announced that its northern terminus would remain across the river from Edmonton, a decision which would give rise to the rival community of Strathcona. During the next decade the rivalry between the two incipient urban centres was constant. Although Edmonton's growth continued to surpass that of Strathcona, the prize of northern metropolitan status was still in some doubt by 1901.[26]

Like Edmonton, other pre-railway settlements experienced difficult times in the 1880s and 1890s. In anticipation of being on or close to the main route of the C.P.R., immigrants moved into the northern prairies in considerable numbers until 1881. The re-routing of the line slowed northern growth considerably. Although a townsite was laid out around the Prince Albert Mission in 1882, incorporation as a town did not come until 1885. At the end of that year, with the Riel Rebellion over, Prince Albert settled into a dull existence as a frontier town 200 miles from the nearest railway. There were few signs of progress in the late 1880s although a Board of Trade was established in 1887; more numerous and conspicuous were the signs of decline, including a drop in population. Despair among the citizens of Prince Albert yielded to confidence only in 1885 when the first sod was turned on the Qu'Appelle, Long Lake and Saskatchewan Railroad. The colonization railway, incorporated in 1883, finally reached Prince Albert in September, 1890. In large part as a result of this linkage, Prince Albert was able to experience modest progress during the 1890s.[27]

The construction of the Qu'Appelle, Long Lake and Saskatchewan Railway also had a significant impact on another prairie community. The site of Saskatoon was chosen in 1882 by the Temperance Colonization Society, which acquired a grant of some 500,000 acres in a block traversed by the South Saskatchewan River. By August, 1883, a townsite had been laid out and settlers began to arrive. The provisioning of the settlers was at first carried out from Medicine Hat, via the South Saskatchewan River, but the hopes of the Society to develop a strong and rapidly growing community did not materialize. There were several reasons. Transportation problems existed from the outset; the South Saskatchewan River was difficult to navigate because of its shallow water and numerous shoals and, although railways got closer to the colony, they passed to the south and channeled prospective settlers away from Saskatoon. The colony was saved from probable extinction when the Qu'Appelle, Long Lake and Saskatchewan Railway, building its line from Regina to Prince Albert, passed through Saskatoon. But, though the railway was fundamental to Saskatoon's continued existence, it did not bring about rapid development in the 1890s. By 1901, the settlement still had a population of only about 100.[28]

While Prince Albert and Saskatoon received second prize in the railway stakes of this era — branch lines rather than location on the main line — another community not only received no rail connection, it lost another prize as well. Battleford was established in 1874 as a camp for the survey parties working on the line of the proposed transcontinental railway. In 1875, surveyors and contractors located their permanent headquarters and supply depot near the mouth of the Battle River and threw up "a collection of roughly constructed log huts with mudded walls and thatched roofs."[29] This primitive work camp on the flats acquired status only in October, 1876, when the Canadian government chose it as the capital of the North West Territories.[30] Within a year the lieutenant-governor's mansion, residences for the judiciary and court officials, and barracks for the N.W.M.P. were under construction. Battleford's future seemed assured and land values and construction boomed. The fertile countryside around attracted numerous settlers in the 1870s and 1880s.

Two decisions soon changed this bright future to a bleak one. There was great disappointment when the C.P.R. was built through the southern prairies instead of along the North Saskatchewan River. It was a long cart haul to Battleford from the nearest point on the railway. Further, in order to facilitate governmental administration the capital of the territories was moved to a site on the railway. Although the selection of Regina was not confirmed until March 1883, instructions to ship government house furniture were received by local civil servants in October 1882. Together, these two decisions drastically changed Battleford's immediate future, and for two decades the town merely survived; it did not prosper. Population grew slowly, and village status was not secured until 1899.[31]

By the end of the nineteenth century, the railways had opened the prairie West to settlement and the basic outline of the region's urban pattern had emerged (see Map I). It was an outline that still needed to be filled in; but that process occurred with great rapidity in the years after the turn of the century.

III

The period between 1900 and 1914 stands in sharp contrast with the previous era. The pre-1900 era was, at best, a period of slow progress. The subsequent era was one of dramatic growth and prosperity. After decades of hesitation, the prairie West suddenly began to realize the potential that so many Canadians had long believed it possessed. A number of important events in widely disparate areas occurred which, when taken together, propelled the region forward. The problems of farming in a semi-arid region were, by 1900, largely solved and the future of prairie agriculture at last seemed assured. Under the direction of an expansive new federal government, immigrants poured into the area in record numbers. Railways were built on an extensive scale: almost 7,000 miles of track were laid in the prairie West between 1901 and 1913, increasing the mileage in the region to well over 10,000.[32] In addition to the building of numerous locally and

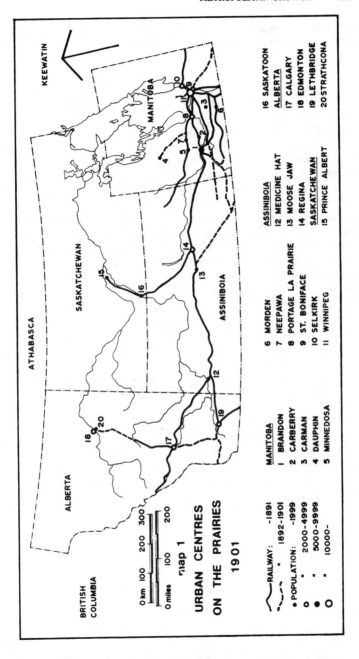

map 1
URBAN CENTRES
ON THE PRAIRIES
1901

0 km 100 200 300
0 miles   100   200

RAILWAY: -1891
1892-1901
-1999
POPULATION: 2000-4999
5000-9999
10000-

BRITISH
COLUMBIA

ALBERTA

ATHABASCA

SASKATCHEWAN

ASSINIBOIA

MANITOBA

KEEWATIN

MANITOBA
1 BRANDON
2 CARBERRY
3 CARMAN
4 DAUPHIN
5 MINNEDOSA
6 MORDEN
7 NEEPAWA
8 PORTAGE LA PRAIRIE
9 ST. BONIFACE
10 SELKIRK
11 WINNIPEG

ASSINIBOIA
12 MEDICINE HAT
13 MOOSE JAW
14 REGINA
SASKATCHEWAN
15 PRINCE ALBERT

16 SASKATOON
ALBERTA
17 CALGARY
18 EDMONTON
19 LETHBRIDGE
20 STRATHCONA

provincially sponsored lines, the C.P.R. constructed branch lines, and two new transcontinental railways — the Canadian Northern and the Grand Trunk Pacific — rapidly found their way across the prairies. Capital for these and other projects was readily available at low interest rates. There were important political changes as well. The North West Territories received responsible government in 1897; in 1905 the provinces of Alberta and Saskatchewan were created; and in 1912 Manitoba's boundaries were extended to 60°N and to Hudson Bay.

The expansion and consolidation of prairie settlement were both aided by and reflected in the growth of villages, towns, and cities. The rapid urban growth of the period was apparent in four significant trends. First, a filling-in process occurred as the prairie region quickly became dotted with hundreds of new urban centres. Most were fairly small service centres, often founded before farmers arrived in the area, or else developing simultaneously with the influx of rural pioneers. These communities usually began with a train station, a grain elevator, and a general store. As soon as settlers moved on to nearby homesteads, attracted both by available land and by the urban centre itself, the general store was duplicated and then supplemented by more specialized businesses such as a lumber yard, hardware store, blacksmith shop, harness and wagon business, an implement dealer, and a bank. Rapid population growth soon led to the construction of a post office, schools and churches; the establishment of a newspaper and a Board of Trade; and, sooner or later, to incorporation as a village, town, or city. Finally, other less essential services appeared; barber shops, hotels and beer parlours, cafés, pool halls, and real estate offices. This pattern of development was repeated over and over. Between the censuses of 1901 and 1916, the number of incorporated cities increased from three to seventeen; incorporated towns from twenty-five to 150; and incorporated villages from fifty-seven to 423.[33]

In addition to the rise of new centres, communities already in existence by 1901 experienced substantial growth in the next decade. Winnipeg strengthened is hold as the chief metropolis of both Manitoba and the prairie region. A medium-sized centre in 1901, it had become the country's third largest city by 1913, with a population of about 150,000 (Table V). Brandon and St. Boniface also more than doubled their population in these years while other Manitoba towns and cities experienced rapid but less spectacular growth (Map 2 and Table II). In Saskatchewan (Map 3), Saskatoon emerged after 1901 to become a focal point for growth in the rich agricultural belt of central Saskatchewan. In rapid succession it was incorporated as a village, town, and city, and by 1911 it was the third largest centre in the province. Regina, as provincial capital, retained its dominant position as the chief city of the province while Moose Jaw, Prince Albert, and Yorkton expanded as regional supply centres (Table III).[34] The changes in Alberta, however, were

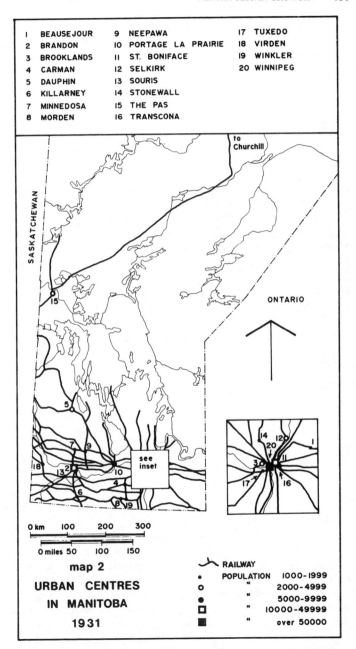

1	BEAUSEJOUR	9	NEEPAWA	17	TUXEDO
2	BRANDON	10	PORTAGE LA PRAIRIE	18	VIRDEN
3	BROOKLANDS	11	ST. BONIFACE	19	WINKLER
4	CARMAN	12	SELKIRK	20	WINNIPEG
5	DAUPHIN	13	SOURIS		
6	KILLARNEY	14	STONEWALL		
7	MINNEDOSA	15	THE PAS		
8	MORDEN	16	TRANSCONA		

SASKATCHEWAN

to Churchill

ONTARIO

see inset

0 km   100   200   300

0 miles 50   100   150

map 2

URBAN CENTRES

IN MANITOBA

1931

RAILWAY

POPULATION   1000-1999
"   2000-4999
"   5000-9999
"   10000-49999
"   over 50000

TABLE V

RANK OF SELECTED CANADIAN CITIES BY SIZE, 1901–1931

RANK	1901	1911	1921	1931
1	Montreal	Montreal	Montreal	Montreal
2	Toronto	Toronto	Toronto	Toronto
3	Québec	WINNIPEG	WINNIPEG	Vancouver
4	Ottawa	Vancouver	Vancouver	WINNIPEG
5	Hamilton	Ottawa	Hamilton	Hamilton
6	WINNIPEG	Hamilton	Ottawa	Québec
7	Halifax	Québec	Québec	Ottawa
8	Saint John	Halifax	CALGARY	CALGARY
9	London	London	London	EDMONTON
10	Vancouver	CALGARY	EDMONTON	London
11	Victoria	Saint John	Halifax	Windsor
12	Kingston	Victoria	Saint John	Verdun
13	Brantford	REGINA	Victoria	Halifax
14	Hull	EDMONTON	Windsor	REGINA
15	Windsor	Brantford	REGINA	Saint John
16	Sherbrooke	Kingston	Brantford	SASKATOON
17	Guelph	Peterborough	SASKATOON	Victoria
—		—	—	—
36	—	SASKATOON	—	—
—		—	—	—
73	CALGARY	—	—	—
—		—	—	—
77	EDMONTON	—	—	—
—		—	—	—
97	REGINA	—	—	—
—		—	—	—
110	SASKATOON	—	—	—

the most dramatic (Map 4). In 1901, Calgary and Edmonton were the most populous places in what was soon to become the province of Alberta, but they were still small service centres, not much different from many others in the western interior. By 1913, however, it was clear that they were to have no competition as the dominant centres of economic activity in the newly formed province.[35] Calgary continued to have an edge over Edmonton, but the latter city's amalgamation of rival Strathcona in 1911 brought the northern metropolis added prominence in the years immediately before the Great War.[36] Between Edmonton and Calgary, only Wetaskiwin and Red

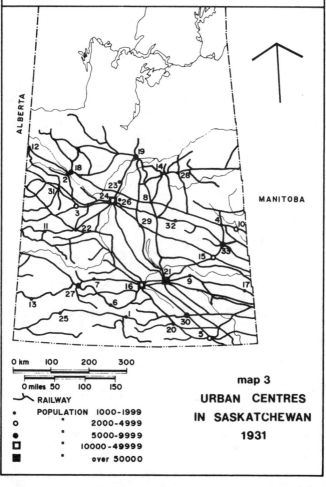

1 ASSINIBOIA	12 LLOYDMINSTER	23 ROSTHERN
2 BATTLEFORD	13 MAPLE CREEK	24 SASKATOON
3 BIGGAR	14 MELFORT	25 SHAUNAVON
4 CANORA	15 MELVILLE	26 SUTHERLAND
5 ESTEVAN	16 MOOSE JAW	27 SWIFT CURRENT
6 GRAVELBOURG	17 MOOSOMIN	28 TISDALE
7 HERBERT	18 NORTH BATTLEFORD	29 WATROUS
8 HUMBOLDT	19 PRINCE ALBERT	30 WEYBURN
9 INDIAN HEAD	20 RADVILLE	31 WILKIE
10 KAMSACK	21 REGINA	32 WYNYARD
11 KINDERSLEY	22 ROSETOWN	33 YORKTON

ALBERTA

MANITOBA

0 km   100   200   300

0 miles 50   100   150

RAILWAY

POPULATION 1000-1999
"   2000-4999
"   5000-9999
"   10000-49999
"   over 50000

map 3
URBAN CENTRES
IN SASKATCHEWAN
1931

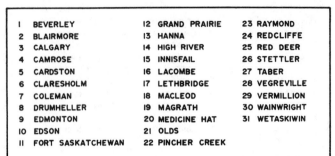

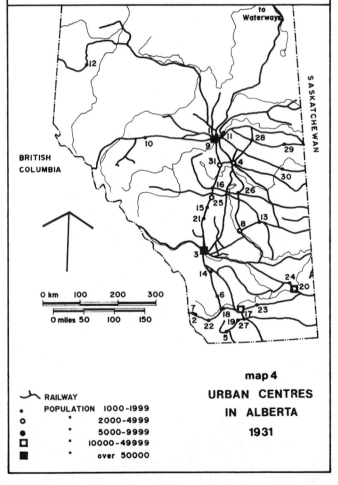

I	BEVERLEY	12	GRAND PRAIRIE	23	RAYMOND
2	BLAIRMORE	13	HANNA	24	REDCLIFFE
3	CALGARY	14	HIGH RIVER	25	RED DEER
4	CAMROSE	15	INNISFAIL	26	STETTLER
5	CARDSTON	16	LACOMBE	27	TABER
6	CLARESHOLM	17	LETHBRIDGE	28	VEGREVILLE
7	COLEMAN	18	MACLEOD	29	VERMILLION
8	DRUMHELLER	19	MAGRATH	30	WAINWRIGHT
9	EDMONTON	20	MEDICINE HAT	31	WETASKIWIN
10	EDSON	21	OLDS		
11	FORT SASKATCHEWAN	22	PINCHER CREEK		

to Waterways

SASKATCHEWAN

BRITISH COLUMBIA

0 km   100   200   300

0 miles 50   100   150

map 4

URBAN CENTRES

IN ALBERTA

1931

RAILWAY
POPULATION 1000-1999
"   2000-4999
"   5000-9999
"   10000-49999
"   over 50000

TABLE VI

POPULATION GROWTH IN SELECTED[a] PRAIRIE CITIES, 1871–1931

CITY	1871	1881	1891	1901	1906	1911	1916	1921	1926	1931
Winnipeg	241	7,985	25,639	42,340	90,153	136,035	163,000	179,087	198,998	218,785
Calgary	—	100	3,867	4,398	11,967	43,704	56,514	63,305	65,291	83,761
Edmonton[b]	—	263	700	4,176	14,088	31,064	53,846	58,821	65,163	79,187
Regina	—	c.800	1,681	2,249	6,169	30,213	26,167	34,432	37,329	53,209
Saskatoon	—	—	—	113	3,001	12,004	21,048	25,739	31,234	43,291
Moose Jaw	—	c.100	1,200	1,558	6,249	13,823	16,934	19,285	19,039	21,299
Brandon	—	—	3,778	5,620	10,408	13,839	15,215	15,397	16,443	17,082
St. Boniface	817	1,283	1,553	2,019	5,119	7,483	11,021	12,821	14,187	16,305
Lethbridge	—	—	—	2,072	2,936	9,035	9,436	11,097	10,735	13,489
Medicine Hat	—	—	1,009	1,570	3,020	5,608	9,272	9,634	9,536	10,300
Prince Albert	—	c.500	—	1,785	3,005	6,254	6,436	7,558	7,873	9,905
Portage la Prairie	—	—	3,363	3,901	5,106	5,892	5,879	6,766	6,513	6,597
North Battleford	—	—	—	—	824	2,105	3,154	4,108	4,787	5,986
Swift Current	—	—	—	121	554	1,852	3,181	3,518	4,175	5,296
Yorkton	—	—	—	700	1,363	2,309	3,144	5,151	4,458	5,027
Weyburn	—	—	—	113	966	2,210	3,050	3,193	4,119	5,002

Notes: (a) Table includes only those centres which were incorporated as cities by 1931 and had a population in excess of 5,000.
(b) Beginning in 1901, figures for Edmonton include Strathcona. See Table IV.

SOURCES: See Table II.

Deer attained city status during these years, but their growth paled in comparison to that of the two major centres.[37] South of Calgary, however, Lethbridge and Medicine Hat expanded their roles as regional service centres (Table IV).

While substantial growth occurred in virtually all prairie centres between 1900 and the Great War, one of the most spectacular developments was the rise of the large prairie city. In 1900, with the exception of Winnipeg, it was not altogether clear which prairie towns would expand to become booming cities. By 1914, Regina, Calgary, Edmonton, and Saskatoon had joined Winnipeg as the region's dominant cities (Table VI). The growth of these metropolitan centres was a response both to massive rural settlement and to the rise of villages and towns, for just as farmers needed service centres, so in turn towns needed cities. Large cities performed a variety of specialized services. They acted as central shipping and distribution points and were the location of such key facilities as railway marshalling yards, roundhouses, locomotive shops, grain terminals, stockyards, warehouses, and wholesale businesses. Cities also provided a complex set of professional and commercial services in the offices of engineers, architects, bankers, insurance and real estate agents, doctors, lawyers, and accountants. The cities were the main repositories of skilled and unskilled labourers, meeting the demands of farmers, railway contractors, bush camp operators, building contractors, and even village and town councils. Manufacturing was also included in the range of city functions. By 1911, Winnipeg was a major centre of manufacturing, and the other large cities were increasing their production of commodities manufactured for the prairie market. Finally, it was in the cities that the region's political and legal institutions (legislatures, court houses, government offices) and educational institutions (universities, trade schools, teacher's colleges) were located. In short, by 1914 the prairies had five fairly large and sophisticated cities. These communities had compressed a century or more of eastern urban growth into a few short years and, together with demographic dominance, displayed considerable power over trade patterns, communications, and development processes in the region, and exercised growing political, social and cultural influence.

The fourth notable trend in this era was the rapid degree of urbanization. No other region of Canada experienced such vigorous urban growth during any one decade as did the prairie provinces between 1901 and 1911 (Table VII). In gross terms, urban residents in the prairie region increased from 19.3 per cent of the total population in 1901 to 28.8 per cent in 1911. While less than 100,000 persons lived in urban centres in 1901, almost 400,000 could be so classified by 1911, a reflection of the facts that the prairie provinces were undergoing a period of massive change and that the area's urban centres were playing an integral part in the development of the region.

IV

1913 was a privotal year in the history of prairie urban development. Before, there had been prosperity and rapid growth; after, there came several decades of relative stagnation and almost continual crisis. Although there were a few short years of prosperity in the 1920s, the period from 1913 to 1930 can be characterized as one of either uncertainty or modest growth for the region's urban centres. This trend was apparent in a number of ways. The prairies switched from being the fastest to the slowest-growing region in the country in terms of urban concentration (Table VII). Between 1911 and 1931, the urban percentage of the prairie population increased by only 3.4 percentage points — far behind the other regions.

TABLE VII

PER CENT OF POPULATION URBAN[a] IN CANADA'S REGIONS, 1901–1931

REGION	1901	1911		1921		1931	
British Columbia	46.4	50.9	(4.5)[b]	56.1	(5.2)	67.3	(11.2)
Prairies	19.3	28.8	(9.5)	29.3	(0.5)	32.2	(2.9)
Ontario	43.6	52.8	(9.2)	60.7	(7.9)	65.3	(4.6)
Quebec	38.2	45.9	(7.7)	52.0	(6.1)	59.7	(7.7)
Maritimes	26.2	32.7	(6.5)	37.9	(5.2)	38.9	(1.0)

Notes: (a) See definition in Table IV, note (a).
(b) Bracketed figures represent increase in percentage points for decade.

SOURCE: *Census of Canada, 1956*—"Analytical Report: Rural and Urban Population," p. 26.

This sharp relative decline took place within the context of general economic difficulties. A severe recession in 1913 was followed by the dislocated of war and a slow recovery, all events which adversely affected the villages, towns, and cities of the prairie region, which were far from booming between 1913 and 1930. The recession immediately preceding the Great War coincided with the slowing down of the great agricultural expansion of the West. The wheat economy — with its commercial and transportation infrastructure and its main institutions — was established and in place. Filling-in and investment in powered farm machinery was carried on in the 1920s, but the scale and rate of expansion was at a much reduced level. As V.C. Fowke notes: "The investment boom which had characterized the early years of the twentieth century had exhausted itself by 1913, and serious economic difficulties faced Canada and the prairie provinces as a result."[38] While the war created an artificial stimulus that temporarily averted the effects of contraction in the growth rate,[39] these effects were felt soon enough. Economic distress characterized the early 1920s, distress caused by inflation, a sharp recession, and a prolonged drought.

In contrast to the early years of the decade, the later 1920s was a period of relative prosperity and expansion. Contemporary observers regarded the developments of these years as a continuation of the conditions that had been interrupted by the recession of 1913 and the war. In terms of urban centres, there were several important developments that received impetus from the comparative prosperity of the period after 1924. The major mechanical revolution that took place on prairie farms, with horse-driven machinery giving way to trucks, tractors, and combine harvesters, increased the dependence of farmers on urban services and skills. It was in these years as well that the road system of the prairies was taking shape, changing dramatically the relation of city and country. Similarly, the aeroplane was beginning to give larger cities additional transportation links. The prairies, it seemed, were apparently again on the road to rapid expansion.

The similarities between the late 1920s and the pre-war boom, however, were more apparent than real. Although many individual activities were much the same as they had been before 1914, their collective significance was vastly different.

> Collectively the economic processes associated with the wheat frontier had been of a magnitude before 1914 sufficient to vitalize and integrate the entire Canadian economy and to diffuse this economic vitality throughout the North Atlantic trading area. In absolute quantities the immigration occupation and improvement of land, and capital formation which were associated with the wheat economy in the latter half of the 1920s were smaller than before the war. In relative terms, however, the diminution was greater still, for other frontiers [in northern Quebec and Ontario and in British Columbia] had meanwhile risen to prominence within the Dominion and the wheat frontier was no longer of unique importance. Possibilities for agricultural settlement in western Canada were no longer adequate to focus attention throughout the Dominion or to serve as the integrating force within the Canadian economy.[40]

The impact of these trends on prairie urban centres was substantial. In general terms, the population of the region's cities grew by only 47.5 per cent between 1916 and 1931 (408,000 to 602,000), compared to an increase of nearly 700 per cent between 1901 and 1916 (52,000 to 408,000). Towns grew by 30.5 per cent (121,000 to 158,000), compared to 278.0 per cent (32,000 to 121,000) in the earlier period. Villages increased by only 64.5 per cent (76,000 to 125,000), compared to an increase of 300 per cent (19,000 to 76,000) between 1901 and 1916.[41] The number of new cities (2), towns (14), and villages (121) incorporated since 1916 was in sharp contrast to the rapid increase in numbers in the earlier era. In terms of the ranking of Canadian cities by size, several larger prairie cities dropped to lower positions, including Winnipeg, Brandon, Portage la Prairie, Regina, Moose Jaw and Yorkton;[42] however, none of the region's cities suffered an absolute loss in population between 1911 and 1931.[43] It was a period in which the larger centres gained population, but only gradually. Some towns and villages, however, actually lost citizens (Tables II, III, IV). Such communities, and others which experienced very slow rates of growth, were those whose prosperity largely depended upon supplying a restricted agricultural hinterland that was floundering. In contrast, the larger prairie cities, and especially Winnipeg, Regina, Calgary, Edmonton, and Saskatoon, had reached the point where their extra-provincial relations coupled with their intra-provincial services ensured slow but steady growth.

The growth of the cities between the end of rapid expansion in 1913 and the major economic crisis of the Depression was thus unremarkable. But there were several important changes in the prairie urban system which deserve notice, even if they were changes of "degree" rather than of "kind." Most important was the decline in Winnipeg's metropolitan position as a result of several events, including the opening of the Panama Canal in 1914 (which allowed Vancouver to penetrate the western prairies); the diffusion of Winnipeg's commercial functions in the wheat economy with the formation of provincial wheat pools in the 1920s (dispersing control and income from Winnipeg head offices of the private grain trade); the erosion of the city's preferential freight-rate structures (resulting in the gradual takeover by other prairie cities of some of the commercial and supply functions formerly centred on the city); and a decline in the importance of grain and an increase in such non-grain products as meat, butter and cheese (areas where Winnipeg's metropolitan position was challenged by other prairie cities).[44] All these changes diminished Winnipeg's financial and commercial hinterland but they did not presage any major alterations in the basic urban system of the prairies. While there was a gradual westward shift in urban population,[45] and while the role of other prairie cities in the region grew considerably, the urban structure in place by 1913 — with Winnipeg at its apex — maintained a high degree of stability through to and beyond 1930.

In spite of this stability, the onset of drought and the Depression in 1929-1930 marked the end of an era for prairie urban development. Although dramatic urban growth in the region had ended as early as 1913, contemporaries had continued to hope — indeed to believe — throughout the 1910s and 1920s that prosperity would soon return. In particular, the short periods of prosperity in the 1920s were seen as the beginning of a new surge of growth. The Depression, however, soon dimmed the hopes of even the most optimistic. By the mid-1930s, prairie urban centres were concentrating, for the first time in their history, not on growth, but on survival.

NOTES:

1. Defining what is meant by "urban" is a complex issue. In this article, I shall use two basic characteristics. First, an urban community consists of a concentration of people organized at a specific site who carry on various functions or services differentiated from the surrounding countryside, functions which may be economic, political, social or cultural in nature and which usually involve some combination of these factors. Second, while it is an arbitrary figure, this article concentrates on those communities which had a population of 1,000 or more. For a succinct discussion of the definition problem see James and Robert Simmons, *Urban Canada*, 2nd ed. rev. (Toronto: Copp Clark, 1974), pp. 8-11.

2. Alan F.J. Artibise, *Winnipeg: A Social History of Urban Growth, 1874-1914* (Montreal: McGill-Queen's University Press, 1975), Chapter 1, "The Origins and Incorporation of Winnipeg."

3. There is no comprehensive history of St. Boniface available. See, however, W.L. Morton, *Manitoba: A History* (Toronto: University of Toronto Press, 1957), *passim*.

4. Margaret J. Bell, "Portage la Prairie to 1907," M.A. Thesis (University of Manitoba, 1926). See also Evelyn Baril, "The Hudson's Bay Company and the Urbanization of the Prairies, 1870-1888," B.A. Thesis (University of Winnipeg, 1978). This excellent thesis contains much detail on prairie urban centres in these early years.

5. Gary Abrams, *Prince Albert: The First Century, 1866-1966* (Saskatoon: Modern Press, 1966), Chapter 1, "A Mission in the Wilderness."

6. B.A. Ockley, "A History of Early Edmonton," M.A. Thesis (University of Alberta, 1932). See also J.G. MacGregor, *Edmonton: A History* (Edmonton: Hurtig, 1967); and Baril, "H.B.C. and the Urbanization of the Prairies."

7. *Census of Population and Agriculture of the Northwest Provinces, 1906*, p. xx.

8. There are a number of good accounts available. See, for example, Paul Voisey, "The Urbanization of the Canadian Prairies, 1871-1916," *Histoire sociale/Social History*, Vol. VIII, No. 15 (May 1975), pp. 77-101; J.M.S. Careless, "Aspects of Urban Life in the West, 1870-1914," in Gilbert A. Stelter and Alan F.J. Artibise, eds., *The Canadian City: Essays in Urban History* (Toronto: McClelland and Stewart, 1977), pp. 125-141; K. Lenz, "Large Urban Places in the Prairie Provinces — Their Development and Location," in R.L. Gentilcore, ed., *Canada's Changing Geography* (Toronto, 1967), pp. 199-211; L.D. McCann, "Urban Growth in Western Canada, 1881-1961," *The Albertan Geographer*, No. 5 (1969), pp. 65-74; and K.H. Norrie, "The Rate of Settlement of the Canadian Prairies, 1870-1911," *Journal of Economic History*, Vol. XXXV (June, 1975), pp. 410-427.

9. Voisey, "Urbanization of the Canadian Prairies," p. 78.

10. W.A. Mackintosh, *Prairie Settlement: The Geographical Setting* (Toronto: Macmillan, 1934), p. 46.

11. This figure is an estimation taken from tables in M.L. Bladen, "Construction of Railways in Canada to the Year 1885," *Contributions to Canadian Economics*, Vol. V (1932), pp. 43-60; and Bladen, "Construction of Railways in Canada from 1885 to 1931," *ibid.*, Vol. VII (1934), pp. 82-107.

12. See G.F. Baker, *Brandon: A City, 1881-1961* (Altona: Friesen, 1977).

13. Voisey, "Urbanization of the Canadian Prairies"; Baril, "H.B.C. and the Urbanization of the Prairies."

14. *Ibid.*; J.M. Richtik, "Manitoba Service Centers in the Early Settlement Period," *Journal of the Minnesota Academy of Science*, Vol. 34, No. 1 (1967), pp. 17-21; and John H. Warkentin, "Western Canada in 1886," *Transactions of the Historical and Scientific Society of Manitoba*, Series III, No. 20 (1963-1964), p. 91.

15. Artibise, *Winnipeg: A Social History*, Chapter 4. See also R.C. Bellan, "Rails Across the Red: Winnipeg or Selkirk," *Transactions of the Historical and Scientific Society of Manitoba*," Series III, No. 18 (1961-1962), pp. 69-77.

16. Two general accounts of Regina's history are available: E.G. Drake, *Regina: A History* (Toronto: McClelland and Stewart, 1955); and J.W. Brennan, ed., *Regina Before Yesterday: A Visaul History, 1882-1945* (Regina: City of Regina, 1978).

17. Some branch lines were built out of Regina in later years, but they were local lines rather than C.P.R. branch lines. See Chester Martin, *"Dominion Lands" Policy* (Toronto: Macmillan, 1938), Chapter V.

18. Brennan, *Regina Before Yesterday*, pp. 3-4. The capital question is discussed in L.H. Thomas, *The Struggle for Responsible Government in the North-West Territories, 1870-97* (Toronto: University of Toronto Press, 1956), p. 107.

19. K.A. Foster, "Moose Jaw: The First Decade, 1882-1892," M.A. Thesis (University of Regina, 1978), p. 22.

20. *Ibid.* See also G.R. Andrews, "The National Policy and the Settlement of Moose Jaw, Saskatchewan 1882-1913," M.A. Thesis (Bemidji State University, 1977).

21. Don C. McGowan, *Grassland Settlers: The Swift Current Region During the Era of the Ranching Frontier* (Regina: Canadian Plains Research Center, 1975), *passim*.

22. J.G. MacGregor, *Alberta: A History* (Edmonton: Hurtig, 1972), pp. 157-158.

23. The best account of Calgary's development is M. Foran, *Calgary: An Illustrated History* (Toronto: Lorimer, 1978). It contains an excellent bibliography.

24. A.A. den Otter, "Lethbridge: Outpost of a Commercial Empire," in Alan F.J. Artibise, ed., *Town and City: Aspects of Western Canadian Urban Development* (Regina: Canadian Plains Research Center, 1981), pp. 177-202.

25. The Calgary and Edmonton Railway also led to the rise of Red Deer. See Wellington Dawe, *History of Red Deer* (Red Deer, 1953). The Calgary and Edmonton Railway is discussed in Martin, *"Dominion Lands" Policy*, p. 323 and *passim*.

26. John F. Gilpin, "The City of Strathcona, 1891-1912," M.A. Thesis (University of Alberta, 1978).

27. Abrams, *Prince Albert*. On the railway, see Martin, *"Dominion Lands" Policy*, p. 296 and *passim*.

28. John H. Archer, "The History of Saskatoon," M.A. Thesis (University of Saskatchewan, 1948); W.P. Delainey and W.A.S. Sarjeant, *Saskatoon: The Growth of a City* (Saskatoon: Saskatoon Environmental Society, 1974).

29. Arlean McPherson, *The Battlefords: A History* (Saskatoon: Modern Press, 1967), p. 35.

30. Thomas, *Struggle for Responsible Government*, p. 80.

31. McPherson, *The Battlefords*.

32. Bladen, "Construction of Railways in Canada from 1885 to 1931."

33. *Census of Prairie Provinces, 1916*, p. xix.

34. Yorkton's early history is discussed in J.W. McCracken, "Yorkton During the Territorial Period, 1882-1905," M.A. Thesis (University of Saskatchewan, Regina, 1972).

35. P.J. Smith and D.B. Johnson, *The Edmonton-Calgary Corridor* (Edmonton: Department of Geography, University of Alberta, 1978), p. 26 and *passim*.

36. John F. Gilpin, "Failed Metropolis: The City of Strathcona, 1891-1911," in Artibise, *Town and City*.

37. The origins and development of these two centres are discussed in Smith and Johnson, *Edmonton-Calgary Corridor*; A. Reynolds, *"Siding 16" An Early History of Wetaskiwin to 1930* (Wetaskiwin: Wetaskiwin Alberta — R.C.M.P. Centennial Committee, 1975); and Dawe, *Red Deer*.

38. V.C. Fowke, *The National Policy and the Wheat Economy* (Toronto: University of Toronto Press, 1957), p. 77 and *passim*.

39. Even the temporary prosperity of the war did not benefit the prairies as it did Canada's other regions. See John Herd Thompson, *The Harvests of War: The Prairie West, 1914-1918* (Toronto: McClelland and Stewart, 1978), Chapter Three.

40. Fowke, *The National Policy and the Wheat Economy*, p. 82.

41. *Census of Prairie Provinces, 1916*; and *Census of Canada, 1931*.

42. *Ibid*. Those included are cities with populations in excess of 5,000.

43. There were, however, short-term losses in population. See Table VI.

44. Paul Phillips, "The Prairie Urban System, 1911-1961: Specialization and Change," in Artibise, *Town and City*.

45. In 1911, Manitoba had 42.7 per cent of the region's urban population. This declined to 35.7 per cent by 1931. Saskatchewan's urban population increased from 28.0 per cent to 32.9 per cent of the regional total, while Alberta's increased from 29.3 per cent to 31.4 per cent. *Census of Canada, 1931*.

IV THE PHYSICAL ENVIRONMENT

One of the most important aspects of urban studies is that it has encouraged many scholars to go beyond their own disciplines in their search for an understanding of the process of urbanization. This is especially true in the examination of the physical environment, for Canadian historians have been encouraged to study this aspect of the city largely because of imaginative work in the fields of geography, planning, and architecture.[1] Historians now recognize that histories of both the process of urbanization and of individual cities cannot be considered complete until the city is studied as a physical entity. This involves not only the study of the visible evidence of the urban environment — architectural styles, landscape design, transportation networks, planning, land use, etc. — but also the process of city building over time.

Approached from the perspective of city building, the city is viewed as a physical container within which complex human and institutional relationships are found.[2] This physical container consists of a structure and a form. The structure is made-up of individuals, groups, institutions, and service facilities distributed spatially across the city in response to certain fundamental living needs and activities. The form is the visually perceptive features of the city which the structure produces. Form includes both the two dimensional and the three dimensional shapes created by surface, spaces and structures. The task of the urban historian in studying the process of city building over time is to describe and analyze the specific decisions by individuals, groups and institutions which influenced urban form and structure and to relate these to the broader social, economic and technological trends which affected the nature of these decisions.

The historian's approach to the study of the physical environment is particularly important since it provides a balance to much of the work already completed in this field. Many social scientists tend to overstress theories of city location and growth with the result that the form and structure of cities are often seen as the creation of complex and impersonal economic and geographic factors that focus in a particular time-space dimension. In terms of this kind of analysis the growth and development of particular cities appears logical and even inevitable. But as historians point out, people also play an important role in the process of city building and the form and structure of one city relative to another is never solely determined by impersonal, external forces. People interact with their environment and shape the city through their beliefs, needs, and actions. The physical environment, in short, develops in a distinctive way as much because of deliberate decisions as because of external forces. The vagaries of time and place, events and personalities, must be taken into account.

Each of the three essays included in this section give some weight to both internal and external, personal and impersonal factors in the process of city building. But besides providing good examples of the balanced work being completed on the subject of the physical environment in a number of disciplines, these essays also provide a solid framework for further work in the field. Through the examination of such varied topics as planning, spatial growth, residential segregation, architecture, housing, suburbanization, and transportation technology, the major changes in the form and structure of several Canadian cities are described and analyzed.[3]

NOTES:

1. Besides the work of Alan Gowans and Deryck Holdsworth reprinted in this section, good examples of studies of the physical environment by non-historians are the following: Alan Gowans, *Building Canada: An Architectural History of Canadian Life* (Toronto, 1966); L.O. Gertler, ed., *Planning the Canadian Environment* (Montreal, 1968); and J.T. Lemon, "Studies of the Urban Past: Approaches by Geographers," in *Occasional Paper No. 13*, Faculty of Environmental Studies, University of Waterloo, 1974. The latter contains an extensive bibliography. Also useful is Deryck Holdsworth, "Built Forms and Social Realities: A Review Essay of Recent Work on Canadian Heritage Structures," *Urban History Review*, Vol. IX (October 1980), pp. 123-138.

2. A useful, concise introduction to this approach is Roy Lubove, "The Urbanization Process: An Approach to Historical Research," in A.B. Callow, ed., *American Urban History* (Toronto, 1969), pp. 642-654. In Canada, there is an increasing amount of work being published that uses the city-building process approach. For a representative sample, see Gilbert A. Stelter and Alan F.J. Aritibise, eds., *Shaping the Canadian Urban Landscape: Aspects of the Canadian City-Building Process* (Ottawa: Carleton Library Series, 1982).

3. Important material in each of these areas is discussed in the final article in this volume. Also, recent work on the history of planning has been collected in Alan F.J. Artibise and Gilbert A. Stelter, eds., *The Usable Urban Past: Planning and Politics in the Modern Canadian City* (Toronto: Carleton Library Series, 1979).

The Fate of City Beautiful Thought in Canada, 1893-1930

WALTER VAN NUS

This paper seeks to summarize and account for the origins of major city beautiful concepts as advanced within the three professions that played the central role in the practice of town planning: architecture, engineering and surveying. It also attempts to explain why, by the end of World War I, almost all advocates of town planning had ceased to urge implementation of those concepts, and emphasized exclusively the need for preventive suburban planning. For the sake of brevity, the term "professionals" will be used to refer to members of the three professions mentioned.

The notion of introducing beauty into the urban environment was, patently, not new to the 1890's and early 1900's, though many laymen and some professionals considered it the essence of city beautiful thought. What its more ambitious professional supporters thought innovative in the city beautiful idea lay in its scope. No longer should beauty be confined to scattered and isolated buildings, its effect more often than not spoiled by an ugly setting. Instead, professionals would plan and regulate the entire city so that people might be surrounded by beauty. Architects who shared in this vision grew impatient with their colleagues' preoccupation with individual commissions. Percy Nobbs, Professor of Architecture at McGill, declared in 1904,

> It would be a great advantage if the idea could be got in the heads of architects that beauty is not a quality to add to a city, but that it is or is not of the structure of it . . . . every street in the city should be made as beautiful as it can be, and every building, as far as possible, should cohere with the general plan; then we will have

SOURCE: Canadian Historical Association, *Historical Papers*, 1975, pp. 191-210. Reprinted by permission of the author and the Canadian Historical Association.

a beautiful city and not otherwise . . . . it is not merely by erecting a fine structure here and there that you will make any great improvement, or even laying out a little bit of park, although that may be an item; the construction of the city throughout should be made as beautiful as it can be.[1]

W. A. Langton, Toronto architect and editor of *The Canadian Architect and Builder* made the same point in criticizing the periodic calls for the beautification of Toronto. "Always an isolated proposition," he complained, "something to be done in one place. But we have never yet heard of any larger scheme which would comprehend the whole of Toronto, which would make . . . a plan of the city as a whole"[2] His journal summarized the aesthetic assumption neatly. "Beauty must be massed to tell, in a city as in any other work of art."[3]

What was the origin of this wider view? For those (relatively few) engineers and surveyors who actively supported city beautiful architects, no general answer seems possible. Many architects had in their training been exposed to pictures of marvellous vistas from Renaissance and modern European cities. Even when in their planning proposals to penurious municipal governments architects avoided any suggestion that the city be remade along such expensive lines, their wish to do so could not always be suppressed: the Ontario Association of Architects' 1909 plan for Toronto was studded with magnificent photos taken in European cities.[4] In later years, when leaders in the Canadian planning movement talked of its beginnings, they often traced the North American planning movement back to the Chicago World's Fair of 1893.[5] Though Canadian engineering and surveying journals show no significant response to the event, the Fair aroused considerable admiration among Canadian architects. Not only did its massed beauty move them, but the planning control exercised by the Fair's team of architects also stirred their envy. This immediate two-fold reaction was evident at the conventions of the Ontario Association of Architects and the Province of Quebec Association of Architects following the Fair. Addressing the Ontario group in early 1894, J. Gemmel gave a detailed and lyrical description of what he had seen; he summarized the vision thus:

. . . the buildings rose in one harmonious whole, with no jarring rivalry of men and styles. [It was] a panorama conceived and carried out as genius only can.[6]

Similarly, A. T. Taylor told his Quebec colleagues in 1893 of "the fair white city on the shores of Lake Michigan." The discussion at both meetings drew the inference of architectural mastery over existing cities. But we must note the tone of resignation, the feeling that no architectural power could ever be wielded over a real city. At the 1984 meeting, OAA President D. B. Dick spoke of how the architects had co-operated in designing the various buildings, determining the main features of the general ground plan, and how they had decided on a uniform architectural style, and on a modulus of height for all the principal buildings. He said nothing, however, of applying such power to a Canadian city.[7] A. T. Taylor's resignation to jumble growth for our cities was explicit:

> It is not often the happy lot of any members of our profession to be called upon to design an ideal city. The average modern city is not planned — like Topsy, it just grows, and we are only allowed to touch with the finger of beauty a spot here and there. One longs for the days of Pericles or Caesar, or even those of the First Empire, when cities were laid out with beauty and effect, and were exquisite settings for noble gems of architecture.[8]

Moreover, Canadian architects mentioned the Fair in print very rarely after 1894, and then in passing. On this evidence one hesitates to view it as a lasting stimulus to city beautiful thinking among Canadian architects. There may, however, have been an ongoing influence on the part of the many American civic centre projects inspired by the Fair between 1893 and 1917.[9] Canadian architects were exposed to this model: in 1905, for instance, the OAA was addressed by Horace McFarland, President of the American Civic Association, who told how the slum area around the new state capital building at Harrisburg had been cleared away after a "reform" administration had taken over the local government.[10]

Probably the most significant stimulus to city beautiful thinking among architects, though, was the contrast between the profession's commitment to the creation of beauty and the ugliness of Canadian cities around the turn of the century. A common self-image among architects was that of "an artist, with the practical knowledge necessary to be able to carry out his dreams on a sound constructional basis."[11] Preoccupation with beauty, abundantly manifest in architectural journals, was never criticized in their pages, unless it were unaccompanied by the engineering technique needed to erect safe and sanitary buildings.[12] In explaining why this professional commitment was extended from the individual building to the city as a whole, Langton suggested a development of community consciousness which refused to accept perfection in occasional buildings and squalor in between.[13] This explanation really begged the question, of course. In any event, a number of architects from the 1890's to the 1930's seemed to assume that an ugly environment did psychological damage to all who beheld it, and that therefore to beautify the city as a whole was socially beneficial. Usually this assumption remained only implicit, but occasionally it was expounded. A painting, J. W. Siddall told the OAA in 1899, would be seen only by a chosen or limited number; a sculpture only by those who sought it; the same applied to music and poetry. ". . . [B]ut architecture, as a decorative art, is seen by all men at all times, and its silent influence, consciously or unconsciously, affects the minds of the cultured and uncultured. The beautiful gives us pleasure; the ugly pain, and we cannot escape the ugly buildings which disfigure our streets.''[14] This argument took for granted that architects' sensitivity to ugliness was more or less universal, if too often only subconscious. Those who believed this could easily justify government expenditure on and/or regulation of urban aethetics. As Philip Turner, President of the PQAA, told a radio audience in 1933, an art that so profoundly affected our daily life, and from whose influence no mind could escape, must be subject to social control.[15]

Certainly downtown areas seemed to be getting uglier by the early 1900's, as to overcrowding became every more acute, as taller buildings began to disturb streetscapes, and as utility poles blemished most streets. The outrage which urban ugliness could arouse in the breasts of architects may be gauged by this outburst from Professor Nobbs:

> The Streets! — the numerous poles which make our main thoroughfares look like a Chinese harbour after a typhoon . . . the water tanks — the sky signs — the horrible advertisements painted in epic scale on the flanks of buildings — the lettering falling like a veil over many a fair piece of architecture — and the boardings bedight with playbills — all these things are without decency and contrary to the expression of any civic spirit or virtue.[16]

That architects' reaction against the local environment might come first, and use of foreign models only subsequently, was suggested by W. A. Langton in explaining the genesis of the OAA's 1905 plan for Toronto:

> When the idea of planning the future development of Toronto first came into our minds, some of us thought that we had got hold of an original idea, but when, having become interested in the matter, our attention was awake to allusions (in professional and other journals) to similar efforts elsewhere, we found that everybody else on the Continent of America seemed possessed by the same idea.[17]

The three chief principles of urban aesthetics which preoccupied city beautiful architects and their professional allies I shall term coherence, visual variety, and civic grandeur. The first of these principles was frequently expressed when architects discussed the appearance of an aggregate of buildings within view of street level, as opposed to the merits of one particular structure. In 1896, for example, OAA President Darling, in closing such a discussion, emphasized that it would be impossible to have architectually satisfying streets until people stopped erecting houses as though theirs was to be the only one on the street. Instead, they should co-operate with their neighbours ''to gain more uniformity along the street.'' Darling and most professional writers on this matter were advocating not rows of identical buildings, but buildings whose basic appearance together was harmonious, with their cornice lines running in accord with those of their neighbours, so that they produced the impression of a unified streetscape.[18] Haphazard mixture along a street of architectural style and of building size was held to create a disturbing effect on the minds of passers-by, while coherence of line among buildings along a street fostered serenity.[19]

Many of those who believed in the principle of coherence agreed that it should be imposed by an appointive municipal architectural control board, including architects, which would approve plans for all new buildings. As early as the 1890s, architects Taylor and Raza of the POAA were arguing that only such a system would ensure that the ruination of whole streets by ill-proportioned buildings did not continue.[20] Behind the proposal was the belief that a trained architect could judge urban aesthetics better than anyone else. In a petition to Montreal City Council requesting the setting up of a Standing Art Committee, the PQAA in 1895 contended that ". . . taste and a wise knowledge of art requires [sic] a special and long training, which it is not in the power of everyone to command."[21] Architects continued the campaign for architectural control in the 1920s,[22] and were supported by the *Journal* of the Town Planning Institute of Canada, which understood and accepted their assumption of superiority: "[t]he architects are of course right in dreading any control of design by untrained and unqualified public opinion. . . ."[23] Their only success in achieving city-wide control occurred in Quebec, which in 1928 authorized the establishment of an architectural jury for its capital city with veto powers over the design, spacing, location, height and general suitability of all new buildings. It was to use architectural harmony with neighbouring buildings as one of its criteria. In late 1929, however, the Town Planning Institute's *Journal* reported indications that commercial pressures were limiting the commission's effectiveness.[24]

On the face of it, planning cities to avoid visual monotony might seem at odds with regulation for similarity of neighbouring architecture. Architects recognized no contradiction here because the beneficiary of visual variety was always assumed to be a person *travelling* along city streets or through a city parks system. The major solution to visual monotony offered in our period attacked slavish adherence to the rectangular street pattern. Professionals associated with prairie cities were particularly vexed on this point, especially in the early years of the century, when large trees had not had time to grow, thus leaving the expanse of dullness exposed throughout the year. In 1912 the Park Superintendent of Regina, Malcolm N. Ross, produced a classic indictment of the grid pattern on aesthetic grounds. Monotony, he argued, was the most damaging feature of any visual environment, and nothing could be more monotonous than the long straight roads in Canada's new cities, due to the prevalent rectangular plan.

We must get away from the idea that interminable paved streets and concrete sidewalks, accompanied by equally interminable grass strips and rows of trees spaced at equal distances from each and other, varied by an occasional open space in which are a few flowers and shrubs will constitute a satisfactory place to live in, they never can; we must have more originality; variety and change, and get away from the present idea of uniformity in every thing, uniformity becomes only another name for monotony when it is carried out far enough and is used as a very convenient catch word for those who wish to avoid too much work and thought, as it is manifestly more trouble to make plans showing constant variety and change than it is to have one or two stock plans that will with few modifications be applied under all conditions.

The architect, he concluded, should be put in charge of the development of public property.[25] Ross' plea was not the isolated call of a self-interested landscape architect. At about the same time, Professor Nobbs was writing at McGill of the same principle. "The effects of City Planning, like those of any art, fall into the categories of contrasts and climaxes, symmetrical repetitions and non-symmetrical groupings of individual character."[26]

Architects and like-minded professionals prescribed two simple forms of relief from the monotony of long, straight streets: the vista and variation in street pattern. Major avenues, opined *The Canadian Architect and Builder*, "should have what would be a great advantage to their beauty and interest — vistas of moderate length terminating with a building."[27] Civil engineers W.R.O. Wynne-Roberts, hired by Regina in 1910 to improve its waterworks, and C.J. Yorath, Civil Commissioner of Saskatoon in the years before World War I, were both willing to accept the engineering heresy of street curves where topography made straight streets more efficient. Long straight avenues with no object to break the horizon should be avoided, wrote Yorath. If no natural scenic effect could be obtained, some architectural feature should be provided to break the skyline and thus "relieve the monotony of long streets."[28] Both curved and diagonal streets were suggested in the effort to vary the street pattern. Curves were of course needed to obviate the beautiful views which were to terminate sections of an avenue. *The Canadian Architect and Builder* also recommended curves for their own sake, since they added little to street length and removed much of the fatigue in traversing a long street.[29] Engineer Wynne-Roberts tried to explain men's nervous irritation with long, straight streets. Nature, he explained, abhorred corners; instead she built up graceful curves. Although man worked with straight lines because they were simpler and perhaps cheaper, they were still unnatural and thus could not afford the visual relief in which men delighted.[30] Other professionals noted the potential for stimulation of diagonal streets. In discussing his proposal for diagonal through roads in Toronto, W. A. Langdon stressed "how much variety will be introduced into our uninteresting street plan when every street north of Queen Street is crossed by one of the diagonals, making pleasant irregularities, striking building sites, small open spaces, places for monuments, fountains, and seats under trees."[31] As in the case of Malcolm Ross, the stress in Langdon's thought was less on grandeur than on surprise and delight — something at every corner "to feed one's imagination on."[32]

When professionals wrote about parks, they usually did so regarding recreation for the family. But for many city beautiful writers, the parks were also to be integrated into a system connected by parkways, which was designed to offer visual delight to vehicular traffic. The architects who drew up the Toronto Civic Guild's plan for the city in 1909 made such a system one of their two key proposals.[33] The PQAA's 1906 sketch plan for Montreal recommended the creation of a number of fine avenues forming uninterrupted circuits connecting the principal parks and open spaces.[34] A few engineers engaged in planning also supported this non-utilitarian proposal. The plan for Ottawa and Hull of 1915 was a joint product of the American landscape architect E. H. Bennett and a Canadian engineering staff headed by A. E. K. Bunnell, with E. L. Cousins of Toronto as consulting engineer. Their report emphasized the principle that the proposed parks system be "continuous and comprehensive," connected by parkways.[35] The Vancouver plan of 1930 was drawn up by the American city plan engineering firm of Harland Bartholomew, whose Resident Engineer and political troubleshooter was a Canadian, Horace L. Seymour. The report of 1930 contained the most sweeping programme of street development for visual pleasure of any plan in our period. "It is time," it declared, "the city considered giving those who find great enjoyment in these leisure-time and holiday tours a special route touching many of the larger parks and having qualities not possessed by ordinary city streets." These wide thoroughfares would be planted with trees, and lead past scenic views and places of outstanding interest. To avoid heavy utilitarian use of these drives, a major street was if possible to lie parallel to every pleasure route. The report aptly summarized the intended aesthetic effect of travelling along such a system, of "just riding, riding for pleausre. There is *fascination in a changing picture* such as one gets from the window of a smooth-running motor car."[36]

The third basic city beautiful principle, that of civic grandeur, usually manifested itself in advocacy of gradiose public buildings set in spacious surroundings — a "civic centre." This idea got more support among architects than other city beautiful principles since it attracted not only those who considered the civic centre as the focal point of overall city design, but also those who still thought of introducing beauty into the city by creating a beautiful building or cluster or buildings. It was partly because of this greater professional support that this expensive component of the city beautiful vision became the best publicized. Like the other aesthetic strategies we have discussed, a monumental civic centre was intended to have an important psychological effect on the citizenry. Alan Gowans has epitomized the Victorian tradition which dominated Canadian architecture from about 1820 to 1930 as the "tendency to look on architecture as a means of communicating ideas, to choose architectural forms for their symbolic implications."[37] The architects and engineers who sympathized with civic centre proposals certainly wished to instil civic pride,[38] if not a feeling of subordination to governmental authority. Common to all government centre designs was the insistence that official buildings not be dwarfed by nearby structures. The plan submitted for Ottawa and Hull in 1915, for example, set out specific elevations above the streets near the Parliament Buildings, over which no building might be raised. The restriction was explained as "preserving the dominating sky-line of the Parliament and Departmental" groups of buildings by preventing the city's commercial buildings from reaching "such a height as to detract from the beauty and importance of its government buildings."[39] Vancouver's plan of 1930, which included an awesomely massive civic centre designed by two local architects, stated as a general rule that wherever possible, government buildings should be grouped on high ground, in order to permit a more imposing plan than would level terrain.[40] Another means advanced to emphasize the importance of government buildings was to construct a magnificent avenue leading to them. The redevelopment plan for downtown Toronto of 1929 advocated a uniform cornice line and other architectural restrictions for University Avenue, so that it might lead northward to the legislative buildings in a "dignified and noble" manner.[41] Similarly, engineer Noulan Cauchon's 1921 plan of a civic centre for Hamilton involved a broad, tree-lined avenue leading to it from an amphitheatre.[42] The language in some of these plans suggests and authoritarian impulse, but it is well to remember that many architects spoke about the proper display of buildings simply in aesthetic terms. As C. H. C. Wright, Professor of Architecture at the University of Toronto, complained in 1901, the effect of good architecture was often spoiled by incongruous buildings crowded around what would otherwise have given delight.[43] Percy Nobbs observed in 1906 that spacious grounds were particularly important for public buildings in the classical style, for they depended on proportion for their effect; if buildings of similar style and height were placed alongside them, they would "simply ruin one another."[44] By 1900, symbolism in public architecture had become something of an automatic cliché, the use of which need not have involved conscious political purpose.

Whatever their motivations, advocates of new civic centres and broad avenues had to concede that such projects would be costly, and this fact encouraged critics to question the proponents' sense of social priorities. The fact that the most grandiose of pre-war civic centre proposals — such as the truly monumental one for Calgary submitted by Thomas Mawson in 1914[45] — seemed to come from foreign planning experts, did not lessen the vehemence of attacks on Canadian city beautiful advocates. The burden of these attacks, which became widespread after 1910 and reached a crescendo during and immediately after World War I, was that the first duty of professionals lay in pressing for suburban regulation which would minimize the cost of providing workers' housing, and that people's identification of planning with costly city beautiful projects impeded public acceptance of the need for suburban planning. The *Canadian Municipal Journal*, one of the chief journalistic vehicles for professional planners, argued in 1911 that providing sanitary housing for the poor was "the real meaning of city planning":

> Magnificent avenues, leading to grand buildings, are desirable. Lovely and artistic parks should be in every city. But the dwellings in which those live who cannot get away from their homes the whole year long, really decide whether any city is to be healthy, moral and progressive. The common people are in the great majority; their proper accommodation is the greatest problem.[46]

By the end of 1915, attacks on city beautiful projects had become qualitatively different; instead of accepting their validity as part of improvement of the urban environment, though pointing out that decent housing had a higher priority, professional critics began to insist that society must choose *either* the city beautiful approach *or* the suburban regulation approach. The term "low planning," argued the *Canadian Engineer*, had been interpreted in two different ways, respectively by "the aesthetical school" and "the practical school." The former "associate the phrase with the beautification of towns and cities by laying out picturesque boulevards, pretty gardens, fine parks, impressive civic centres, and so on." The latter school, which included the magazine, concentrated on "the economic considerations in providing for the future in the matter of health, homes, traffic, etc."[47] Such leading Canadian planners as engineers A. G. Dalzell and Horace Seymour felt it necessary through the whole period 1915 to 1939 to repeat *ad nauseam* that their variety of town planning did not involve grandiose civic projects.[48]

Why did these critics insist, beginning about 1910, that provision of workers' housing must be the first priority in Canadian planning? Why, during World War I, did they start to reject city beautiful projects as part of planning correctly understood? The answer to the first question is that after 1910, the shortage of decent housing became popularly regarded as Canada's greatest social problem, and suburban planning as the principal solution. The rate of population growth in the major centres of central and western Canada in the first decade of the century had been phenomenal,[49] and it did not slacken before 1914. Because this influx of people contained an unusually high concentration of persons of child-rearing age,[50] the consequent demand for family accomodation was even greater than sheer numbers would suggest. Private enterprise proved incapable of providing all of these people with decent housing at prices they could afford. (In speaking of "decent" housing, contemporaries though in particular of two criteria: the individual privacy required to safeguard morality, and sanitary surroundings.) Between 1910 and 1914 rents in Canada increased by 35.9 percent[51], as owners charged all the traffic would bear. Many owners converted their houses into flats, and tenants' financial straits forced many to subdivide their homes and apartments, or to take in lodgers, so that room overcrowding reached distressing intensity.[52] By 1914, many thousands of families occupied only one or two rooms each.[53] The severest cases of overcrowding were truly pitiable. In October, 1909, a Winnipeg health inspector paid a midnight call on a boarding house, and came upon twelve occupants in one room measuring $13 \times 12 \times 7$ feet.[54] Inspector Allison of the Toronto Police discovered no fewer than 565 people in five houses on King Street East.[55] Public health authorities observed a striking correlation between overcrowding and high mortality rates. This they attributed in part to the lack of sunshine and fresh air, and to the absence of adequate sewage facilities, in overcrowded neighbourhoods. The slum, with its damp and filthy houses, was pictured as the breeding-ground "wherein huge cultures of disease are growing, ready when ripe to rise and sweep the city streets."[56]

Many of the socially concerned citizens who were determined to overcome the shortage of low-income housing had by 1914 come to the conclusion that the realistic solution was to erect workers' suburbs. To threaten the owners of unhealthy buildings with demolition of these structures was unrealistic, since the evicted would have nowhere to go. The lower the cost of a decent house in the suburbs, the argument ran, the greater would be the proportion of workingmen's families which could afford to buy one. If enough slum dwellers moved to these suburbs, the surplus population would be drained from overcrowded areas. As the exodus continued, slumlords would be forced to improve their properties because of the competing attraction of cheap and decent suburban housing.

Suburban planning came to be seen as a prerequisite to this process because the system of land development impeded the efficient provisions of housing; in particular, it unnecessarily inflated the cost of servicing lots. That system, in essence, consisted of piecemeal development by speculative subdivision of individual farms into building lots. (Land speculators were numerous, and typically did not buy two or more adjacent farms, but only one.[57]) In the absence of regulation, a developer's desire to extract the maximum number of lots from his farm often led him to ignore the location and/or width of projected or existing streets nearby, if by doing so he could squeeze more lots out of the property. This lack of co-ordination forced expensive road relocation and therefore higher local taxes.[58] The desire for quick and maximum profit also encouraged speculators to instruct surveyors merely to lay out the farm on the familiar grid pattern, regardless of topography. Not only were rectangular lots the cheapest to survey, but they were also the most saleable in the short run, since lots had to be of a standard size and shape to maximize the uncertainty as to the use to which the land would be put; that is, to maximize its *speculative* resale value.

To the extent that the topography was irregular, serious inefficiencies arose when municipalities constructed roads, or pumped water, in the face of unnecessarily steep grades. The problem was significant in most Canadian cities; in British Columbia it reached ludicrous extremes. Thanks to the application of the grid system, some streets in Vancouver were so positioned as to create grades of 16 percent, whereas it had been possible to lay them out with grades of 5 percent. The problem was even worse in other centres in the province.[59] Perhaps the most serious widespread cause of unnecessarily high servicing costs was the scattered nature of subdivision development. As land along street-car routes rapidly appreciated in value, people would settle a little beyond the street-car terminals in order to obtain cheaper building lots. Since terminals often coincided with the city limits, these settlements were not eligible for city sewages and water supply services. Neighbouring municipalities did at first offer lower property taxes and far less stringent — or even non-existent — plumbing and building regulations, so that the suburban pioneer could build a cheap rudimentary house. Unfortunately, one's water supply and waste disposal could be maintained only on an area of half an acre or more, and then only in favourable spots. After most surrounding lots had been occupied, residents were impelled to demand the provision of municipal water and sewerage services to their scattered clusters of homes. In numerous cases, the local municipality did attempt such works programmes, either incurred or foresaw financial disaster, and managed to have itself annexed. With annexation might come street-car service, and another cycle of population dispersion.[60] As well, the years before 1914 witnessed a significant suburbanization of industry near major cities in central and western Canada, as factories were strung further and further along railway lines.[61] The trend was intensified because some suburbs offered location bonuses[62], and because manufacturers located downtown found it too costly to acquire additional properties there for expansion.[63] Some of the employees of a relocated factory would commute from downtown to suburb, but others created little shack-towns near each plant.[64]

These factors help explain why the suburban rate of population growth in Canada could overtake the central city rate in the decade after 1910[65], but the reality of population increase could never have justified the orgy of suburban subdivision which took place before 1913. In Ottawa and Hull, for example, the population had by 1914 reached 123,000 souls, who would have occupied five square miles, given a density of forty per acre. In fact, the subdivided area covered sixty-five square miles, some of which was dotted with scattered shack dwellings, but a great part of which was unused, held by absentee owners in search of speculative profit.[66] By 1914, before either Calgary or Edmonton had a population of 50,000, both cities had subdivided areas equal to the size of Toronto, which by that date had a population approaching 500,000.[67] In the boom years before 1913, municipalities both large and small actually encouraged speculation by servicing lots before they were sold for building purposes. The extent of this error varied from one centre to the next; Toronto, for example, was less irresponsible than Vancouver or Calgary. The latter by 1914 possessed 26,763 vacant lots served with sewers and watermains, enough at two persons per lot for its entire population.[68] The servicing of scattered subdivisions meant the uneconomical extension of pavement and sidewalk, water and sewer pipe, through stretches of unoccupied lots. In a surprising number of cases, promoters ignored the fact that their suburban developments were beyond the natural drainage area of the nearby city. The cost of a new trunk sewer and perhaps also of a new sewage-treatment plant, constituted yet another needless burden on the local taxpayer.[69]

Housing reformers were all the more determined to control subdivision development because the suburban householder, far more than the speculator, paid for road relocation, for the imposition of a grid plan on a hilly site, and for the cost of pushing local improvements through unoccupied areas. To understand why, we must note how local improvements were financed. The proportion of the cost charged to general revenues, as opposed to owners of property immediately benefitted, varied considerably within Canada. Usually, however, the total cost was considered part of the city-debt, with only the sinking fund and interest charged levied directly on the improved properties. In a period of inflating land values, the speculator was willing to pay these charges for a year or two, in order to obtain servicing which increased both the saleability and value of his lots. Many speculators did not own land long enough to find themselves liable for taxes at all: wherever they could, they passed on the liability to purchasers for use.[70]

The lesson which housing reformers drew from the domestic situation was confirmed by the example of Great Britain, where the emphasis on preventive suburban planning had been embodied in the Town Planning Act of 1909. The Governor-General, Lord Grey, had for years been interested in the garden suburb solution to the housing shortage in Britain, and on his urging many leading Canadians visited workers' suburbs while in England. It was Grey who invited the leading housing reformer, Henry Vivian, M.P., to conduct a speaking tour of Canada. In his address during 1910, Vivian contrasted the expense of altering built-up areas with the relative ease of planning healthful new suburbs.[71] In 1912, a large number of business and reform organizations determined to help solve the housing crisis by requesting the Commission of Conservation to secure the services of the Englishman who knew most about the solution in which they believed: the proper planning of workers' suburbs. In July of 1914 Thomas Adams, who had supervised the early implementation of the Act of 1909, was appointed Town Planning Adviser to the Commission[72], and became a major influence for the preventive approach both on public opinion and on provincial planning acts.

Such housing reform organizations as the Greater Montreal Housing and Planning Association helped popularize the phrase "housing and town planning," which by 1914 had come to summarize the new view of planning as oriented essentially to the efficient provision of suburban housing.[73] But the professionals who wished to obtain planning contracts or perhaps a newly-created government planning job[74] did not come to condemn city beautiful thought just because housing reformers were stressing suburban regulation. Rather, they were doing so by 1918 because by war's end their prospective employers, the provincial and local politician, had confined their interest in planning almost exclusively to suburban regulation. It was already evident before World War I that municipal politicians were more sympathetic to preventive regulation than to expensive projects to reshape the downtown. Apart from parks, city beautiful proposals for which no provincial or federal funding was available usually were rejected. Despite support from the prestigious Guild of Civic Art, the OAA's 1905 plan for Toronto was placed on the shelf by Mayor Coatsworth, who noted cagily that without the proposed trunk sewer, which would cost two and a half millions, Toronto's beauty would be largely lost.[75] In Calgary, budget-conscious councilmen seized on the grandiose elements of Mawson's plan of 1914, and were able to have the plan rejected in its entirety.[76] Councils such as Winnipeg's had no sympathy even for plans whose proposals for remaking the downtown were quite efficiency-oriented.[77] As for provincial governments, even before the recession of 1913-1915 they were giving municipalities wider powers to regulate suburban development beyond their boundaries. In 1912, Nova Scotia and New Brunswick passed virtually identical Town Planning Acts based on the British Act of 1909. Their scope was confined largely to the preparation of schemes for land in the course of building development, or which was likely to be developed. Lands already built upon could be included only if necessary for carrying out the scheme.[78] The Ontario City and Suburbs Plans Act of 1912 established a five-mile wide suburban zone around each centre of 50,000 or more, and required that plans for new subdivisions within such cities and their zones be approved by the Railway and Municipal Board.[79] In 1911, Saskatchewan made all new subdivision layouts subject to approval by an Inspector of Townsites.[80]

The determination of towns and cities to end the gross inefficiencies in suburban development was much intensified by the crisis in municipal finance which may be dated roughly from 1913 to 1923. In 1913, the land boom collapsed. Where now was the profit with which speculators could pay property taxes on their lots and, in addition, interest and sinking fund charges on any improvements? The war dashed hopes that heavy immigration would revive real estate actively; soon after the fighting ended came the great deflation of 1920-1923. During this period of low real estate values, municipalities found it increasingly difficult to collect the high taxes which servicing scattered development had necessitated. Moreover, during the war they incurred the new expense of supporting soldiers' families. Because of the war it became more difficult between 1915 and 1918 to float municipal bond issues, and taxes were repeatedly increased.[81] Arrears and tax sales became commonplace in Canada, especially in Western Canada. By the mid-1920's, Calgary had by this means acquired 73,000 lots![82] In the early 1920's, suburban municipalities around Toronto, Winnipeg and Vancouver were approaching financial collapse.[83] Between 1913 and 1918, Nova Scotia, Ontario, Manitoba, Saskatchewan and Alberta strengthened provincial laws concerning suburban regulation, and in 1916 and again in 1917, the Union of British Columbia Municipalities demanded similar action.[84] The tax burden on workingmen's suburban homes was of course not relieved by this tardy provincial action, and indeed reached crushing levels.

The housing shortage became even more desperate during the war. While high taxes put suburban homes further out of the reach of workers' families, private capital to finance homebuilding became difficult to obtain even at higher rates. Material and labour costs rose steeply, so that building a house cost between 30 percent and 60 percent more in 1918 than it had in 1913. Builders expected a post-war deflation that would involve losses to those building under war-time conditions, and by 1918 private capital had deserted the home-building field. In 1918 many were asking along with Thomas Adams, "If we are now short of houses to provide for newleyweds and industrial workers, what will the situation be when great numbers of soldiers return?"[85]

The war-time spirit of sacrifice, the desperate need by 1918 for practical steps to provide low-cost housing for war workers and veterans, and the financial plight of municipalities by war's end all served to discredit costly, non-utilitarian planning. However, many people had in the years before 1913 been introduced by the media to the phrase "town planning" in conjunction with the presentation of a costly city beautiful proposal. The intensity of the attack after 1912 by engineers and surveyors on the city beautiful approach is explicable in part as a desperate attempt by these would-be planners to change their public image in accordance with the nation's sense of social priorities. The city beautiful movement, contended engineer James Ewing in 1920, and undermined public confidence in anything labelled "city planning" or the like. Before the war, he recalled, magnificent plans had at first been greeted with awe and admiration, but people had come to realize that those plans had ignored basic urban problems.[86] Because planning experts had in boom times participated in drawing up such proposals without due regard for a general city plan, admitted engineer A. G. Delzell in 1921, the public now regarded city planning as an "artistic fad."[87] In 1918, Adams bemoaned the same popular misconception and its corollary: "it is still assumed that by many that it [town planning] is only concerned with what is called by the ugly word 'beautification,' and, therefore, is only a scheme for spending the money of the citizens."[88] During the prosperous later 1920's, however, it was Adams who condemned those opposing expenditure of public funds on civic beauty.[89] Engineers like Norman Wilson and Horace Seymour not included city beautiful elements in their planning proposals.[90] These facts suggest that political realities more than their own indifference to aesthetics account for at least some of the professionals' attack on city beautiful thought. One wonders whether the imagination of a second generation of Canadian planners was circumscribed by the mundane priorities during the housing shortage of the 1940's and early 1950's.

While the principle of civic grandeur was condemned by engineers and surveyors after 1912, they did advocate that zoning be used to enforce the principle that a city should have coherent streetscapes. While the chief benefits claimed for zoning were preservation of property values and economic efficiency, its proponents also cited the orderliness it would impose. The stress in city beautiful thought upon symmetry and order — as opposed to visual variety and civic grandeur — was shared by the advocates of zoning and presented as a bonus, a by-product of efficiency. In 1922, for example, James Ewing rejected the current campaign for a programme of embellishment for Montreal. Embellishment, he wrote, "is beginning at the wrong end. If we can plan wisely on useful, economical, orderly and symmetrical lines, the city will naturally embellish itself."[91] Similarly, Adams argued in 1920 that "orderly development" through planning and proper zoning "will produce beauty without seeking beauty as an end in itself."[92] Paul Seurot, Chief Engineer of the Montreal Tramways Commission, aptly summarized the aesthetic benefits such planners envisioned when he told the Montreal Town Planning Convention of 1921 that well-governed cities were characterized by "symmetry," "quiet orderliness," "regularity and harmony."[93]

Most obviously, zoning fostered orderly streetscapes by segregating various economic activities — and the differing sizes and shapes of buildings needed to accommodate them. In a zoned city, ugly laundries and light manufacturing could no longer invade fine residential areas.[94] No longer could developers erect apartment buildings alongside fine homes, and build them up to the street and side lot lines, blocking the view up and down the street, for which sins they were notorious in both Ottawa and Vancouver.[95] Moreover, within each zone minimum standards of front yard depth and side yard width for homes, and set-back provisions for commercial buildings, would lead to a symmetrical arrangement of buildings along the street. This "inevitable by-product" of zoning was welcomed by B. Evan-Parry, Supervising Architect of the federal Department of Health[96], and such regulations were part of the zoning by-laws adopted by Kitchener in 1924 and by Vancouver in 1928.[97] Within each restricted zone there was generally also one narrow range of permissible building heights. The rule of height in a zoning by-law, explained G. H. Ferguson, Chief Engineer of the federal Department of Health, "connotes a human quality. Absence of scale, or being 'out of scale,' means that one building is out of harmony with another, that in each street the general setting is marred by some impertinent and illmannered intrusion."[98]

The narrow view of beauty as orderliness quite ignored that central criterion of city beautiful thinkers: the avoidance of visual monotony. Regarding this failure, we find a lack of actual, as opposed to implicit, debate in the sources. The city beautiful architects had offered relief, at least to the travelling public, by street curves, series of beautiful and varied terminations along lengthy avenues, parkway systems, and grand civic centres. The engineers of order offered none. Yet no debate ensued. In the years of municipal retrenchment after 1912, the architects and their friends may have recognized the orderliness resulting from efficiency as the only part of their vision the taxpayers would support.

NOTES:

The following abbreviations are used:

AOLSP   —Association of Ontario Land Surveyors, *Proceedings*

CA & B —*The Canadian Architect and Builder*
CE —*The Canadian Engineer*
CMJ —*The Canadian Municipal Journal*
C of CR —Canada, Commissions of Conservation, *Annual Report*
MRC —*The Municipal Review of Canada*
OAAP —Ontario Association of Architects, *Proceedings*
RAICJ —Royal Architectural Institute of Canada, *Journal*
TP & CL —*Town Planning and Conservation of Life*
TPICJ —Town Planning Institute of Canada, *Journal*

1. OAAP, 1904, p. 95.
2. *Ibid.*, 1906, p. 49.
3. CA & B, XVIII, 210, June 1905, p. 82.
4. Toronto Guild of Civic Art, *Report on a Comprehensive Plan for Systematic Improvements in Toronto* (1909).
5. J.P. Hynes, "Town Planning Suggestions for Canadian Municipalities," CE, XXL, Sept. 21, 1911, p. 337; J.F.D. Tanqueray, "The Vancouver Civic Centre and English Bay Development Scheme," TPICJ, VIII, 1 Feb. 1929, p. 2.
6. CA & B VIII 2, February 1894, pp. 32-33.
7. CA & B, VI 10, Oct. 1893, p. 104; and VII, 2 Feb. 1894, p. 25.
8. *Ibid.*, VI, 10, Oct. 1893, p. 104.
9. Arthur B. Gallion and Simon Eisner, *The Urban Pattern: City Planning and Design* (Second edition, Toronto: Van Nostrand, 1963), pp. 191-201.
10. OAAP, 1905, p. 47.
11. As one Mr. Doran put it as a P.Q.A.A. "At Home." CA & B, XIV, 5, May 1901, p. 92. The same perception was emphasized by J.W. Siddall before the O.A.A. in 1899. CA & B, XII, 2, Feb. 1899, pp. 28-29.
12. *Ibid.*, IX, 2, Feb. 1896, p. 18.
13. *Ibid.*, XIX, 217, Jan. 1906, p. 3.
14. J.W. Siddall, "The Advancement of Public Taste in Architecture," CA & B, XII, 2, Feb. 1899, p. 28.
15. RAICJ, X, 5, May 1933, pp. 92-93.
16. Percy Nobbs, "City Planning," CMJ, VIII, 4, April 1911, p. 141. See also the savage comments of A.T. Taylor, CA & B, VII, 10, Oct. 1894, p. 130.
17. OAAP, 1906, p. 90.
18. CA & B, 2, Feb. 1896, p. 26. See also Nobb's comments in CE, LIII, Dec. 13, 1927, p. 611.
19. Vancouver Town Planning Commission, *A Plan for the City of Vancouver, British Columbia, including Point Grey and South Vancouver and a General Plan of the Region* (1930), p. 254. See architect John Lyle's comments in RAICJ, XII, 4, April 1935, p. 61.
20. CA & B, VII, 10, Oct. 1894, p. 130; and XI, 11, Nov. 1898, p. 192.
21. CA & B, XIII, 6, June 1895, p. 80.
22. TPICJ, VI, 1, Feb. 1927, p. 67. For an indication of the heated denunciation that might be expected from colleagues by architects opposing the idea, see the reaction to Nobb's opposition related in CA, LV, Sept. 18, 1928, p. 320.
23. TPICJ, VII, 2, April 1920, p. 30.
24. *Ibid.*, VI, 6, Dec. 1927, p. 197; VII, 2, April 1928, p. 29; and VIII, 5, Dec. 1929, p. 99.
25. Malcolm N. Ross, "Landscape Art and City Design," CE, XXII, March 28, 1912, pp. 457-458. The unorthodox punctuation comes from the original.
26. Percy Nobbs, "City Planning," CMJ, VII, 4, April 1911, p. 140.
27. CA & B, XVII, 201, Sept. 1904, p. 145.
28. For Wynne-Roberts' comments, see CE, XXII, March 28, 1912, p. 458; C.J. Yorath, "Town Planning," CMJ, IX, 10, Oct. 1913, p. 434.

29. CA & XVII, 201, Sept. 1904, p. 145.

30. CE, XXII, March 28, 1912, p. 459.

31. Toronto Guild of Civic Art, *Report* . . . p. [16]. (The document is unpaginated.)

32. Langton, "The Plan of Improvements to Toronto," OAAP, 1906, pp. 98-99.

33. Toronto Guild of Civic Art, *Report*. . . . The proposal is most readily comprehended by looking at the map facing the first page.

34. CA & B, XIX, 222, June 1906, p. 88.

35. Canada Federal Plan Commission, *Report on a General Plan for the Cities of Ottawa and Hull* (1915), p. 125.

36. A.E. Foreman, "A Major Street Plan for Vancouver," TPICJ, VI, 4, Aug. 1927, p. 129; *A Plan for the City of Vancouver* . . ., pp. 175-176, 207. Emphasis added.

37. Alan Gowans, *Building Canada: An Architectural History of Canadian Life* (Toronto: Oxford University Press, 1966), p. 86.

38. C.H. Mitchell, "Town Planning and Civic Improvement," CE, XXIII, Dec. 26, 1912, p. 913.

39. Federal Plan Commission, *Report* . . . , pp. 119-120.

40. *A Plan for the City of Vancouver* . . ., p. 239; J.F.D. Tanqueray, "The Vancouver Civic Centre and English Bay Development Scheme," TPICJ, VIII, 1, Feb. 1929, pp. 2-4.

41. Toronto Advisory City Planning Commission, *Report* (1929), pp. 25, 29.

42. CE, XL, Feb. 24, 1921, pp. 251-252.

43. Wright, "Design in Modern Architecture," CA & B, XIV, 2, Feb. 1901, p. 40.

44. Percy Nobbs, "The Official Architecture of European Capitals," OAAP, 1906, p. 85.

45. Thomas H. Mawson and Sons, *Calgary: A Preliminary Scheme for Controlling the Economic Growth of the City* (Calgary: City Planning Commission, 1914), pp. 39-42.

46. CMJ, VII 6, June 1911, p. 213. See also the editorial in CE, XX, April 13, 1911, p. 562.

47. CE, XXIX, Oct. 21, 1915, p. 505.

48. A.G. Dalzell, "Is Town Planning Too Costly?," *ibid.*, LIII, Oct. 26, 1927, p. 481; H.L. Seymour, "Town Planning Reduces City's Taxes," CE, LXXVI, April 25, 1939, p. 4.

49. Some examples are:

	Montreal	Toronto	Winnipeg	Regina
1901	328,172	209,892	42,340	2,249
1911	490,504*	381,833*	136,035	30,212

	Calgary	Edmonton	Vancouver
1901	4,392	4,176	29,432
1911	43,704	31,064	120,847

*Due in part to annexation.

Source: Canada, Dominion Bureau of Statistics, *Census 1921*, Vol. I, Table 12; Canada. Dominion Bureau of Statistics, *Census 1931*, Vol. II, Table 8; Canada. Dominion Bureau of Statistics, *Census 1941*, Vol. II, Table 16. Unless otherwise noted, the figures are based on constant boundaries (those of 1941).

50. L.O. Stone, *Urban Development in Canada* (Ottawa: Queen's Printer, 1967), pp. 63, 147, 149-151.

51. TP & CL, I, 3, Jan. 1915, p. 56.

52. W.J. Burditt, "Civic Efficiency and Social Welfare in Planning of Land," in Canada, Commission of Conservation, Conference on Urban and Rural Development in Canada, Winnipeg, May 28-30, 1917, *Report*, p. 75.

53. J. Frank Beer, "A Plea for City Planning Organization," C of CR, 1914, p. 112; James Roberts, "The Housing Situation, Hamilton," CMJ, VIII 7, July 1912, p. 255; Alan

Artibise, "The Urban Development of Winnipeg, 1874-1914," Ph.D. thesis (University of British Columbia, 1971), p. 233.

54. J.S. Woodsworth, *My Neighbour* (Toronto: University of Toronto Press, 1972), p. 139.

55. CMJ, IX, 5, May 1913, p. 169.

56. See the excellent summary of current findings and interpretations by public health officials concerning housing conditions in Dr. Charles A. Hodgetts, "Unsanitary Housing," C of CR, 1911 pp. 51-54, 61-65. The quotation is found on p. 54.

57. Donald Kerr and Jacob Spelt, *The Changing Face of Toronto — A Study in Urban Geography* (Toronto: University of Toronto Press, 1964), p. 66.

58. *Ibid.*, pp. 66-67, 113; Eric Arthur, *Toronto: No Mean City* (Toronto: University of Toronto Press, 1964), p. 24; Artibise, pp. 243, 250; James and Robert Simmons, *Urban Canada*, (Toronto: Copp Clark, n.d.), pp. 31-32, 68-69; CA & B, I, 6, June 1888, p. 4; XVIII, 208, April 1905, p. 51; TPICJ, VIII, 3, June 1929, p. 163; CMJ, XI, 2, Feb. 1915, p. 52; CE, XLVII, Sept. 16, 1924, p. 334; TPICJ, I, 6, Oct. 1921, pp. 5, 7.

59. Thomas Adams, "Town and Rural Planning in British Columbia," CMJ, XV, 1, Jan. 1919, p . 25; A.G. Dalzell, "A Contrast in City Planning," TP & CL, VII, 1, Jan.-March 1921, pp. 9-10; A.E. Cleveland, "Regional Planning," TPICJ, VI, 4, Aug. 1927, p. 144.

60. CE, XLVIII, May 12, 1925, p. 475; and LX, March 31, 1931, pp. 17-18; Kerr and Spelt, p. 59; P.J. Smith, "Calgary: A Study in Urban Pattern," *Economic Geography*, XXXVIII, 4, Oct. 1962, pp. 315-329; MRC, XXIII, 5, May 1927, p. 198.

61. Kerr and Spelt, pp. 129-130; Smith, pp. 317, 319; John Irwin Cooper, *Montreal: A Brief History* (Montreal, 1969), p. 127; Artibise, pp. 239-240, 354.

62. CMJ, X, 8, Aug. 1914, p. 309.

63. L.B. Duff, "The Town Plan and the Factory," CE, XXXVII, Dec. 18, 1919, p. 544; A.G. Dalzell, "Classification of Land for Industrial Purposes," TP & CL, VI, 2, April-June 1920, p. 28.

64. Dalzell, "Development of Urban Communities," CE, LVI, Feb. 26, 1929, pp. 268-269.

65. Stone, p. 135.

66. Thomas Adams, *Rural Planning and Development; A Study of Rural Conditions and Problems in Canada* (Ottawa: Commission of Conservation, 1917), pp. 109-110.

67. A.G. Dalzell, "The Relation of Housing and Town Planning in Cities Such as Vancouver," MRC, XXIII, 5, May 1927, p. 199; see also AOLSP, 1924, p. 238; W.A. Begg, "Town Planning and Development in Saskatchewan," CE, XL, Feb. 17, 1921, p. 220; Dalzell, "Should Shack-Towns Be Encouraged?," CE, L, March 23, 1926, p. 412.

68. Adams, "Planning and Development of Land," in Conference on Rural and Urban Development, *Report*, p. 81; Adams, *Rural Planning and Development*, p. 118; MRC, XXVII, 2, Feb. 1931, p. 16; AOLSP, 1924, p. 238; *A Plan for the City of Vancouver. . . ,* p. 31; CE, XLVIII, May 12, 1925, p. 477.

69. A.G. Dalzell, "Problems of Sewer Design in Canada," CE, XLVIII, May 12, 1925, p. 475; George R. MacLeod, "The City Engineer's Work in Relation to Town Planning," MRC, XXXIV, 7, July-Aug. 1938, p. 17.

70. C.J. Yorath, "Municipal Finance and Administration," Conference on Urban and Rural Development, *Report*, p. 28; Adams, *Municipal and Real Estate Finance in Canada* (Ottawa: Commission of Conservation, 1921), p. 10.

71. CMJ, VI, 10, Oct. 1910, pp. 401, 403.

72. Among the supporters of the petition were the Canadian Manufacturers' Association, the Canadian Public Health Association, the Order of the Daughters of the Empire, the National Council of Women, the Montreal Parks and Playgrounds Association, the Union Committee of Charitable Organizations, Montreal, the Union of Charities of Toronto, the Hamilton Board

of Trade and "a very large number of the most prominent citizens of Canada." C of CR, 1913, pp. 8-9, 11; see also *ibid.*, 1915, p. 162; and *ibid.*, 1917, p. 25.

73. *Canadian Annual Review*, 1913, pp. 723-724; see also the accounts of the First Canadian Housing and Town Planning Conference, held at Winnipeg in 1912, in CMJ, VIII, 9, Sept. 1912, p. 338, and CE, XXIII, July 25, 1912, p. 235.

74. For revealing evidence of this job-hunger among surveyors, see AOLSP, 1918, pp. 15, 22, 35-42.

75. OAAP, 1906, pp. 56, 61.

76. TPICJ, VI, 6, Dec. 1927, p. 205.

77. Artibise, pp. 408-422; TPICJ, VI, 6, Dec. 1927, p. 190.

78. C of CR, 1913, pp. 206-207, 211-212.

79. CMJ, VIII, 6, June 1912, p. 209.

80. Stewart Young, "Planning Progress in Saskatchewan," TPICJ, X, 1, Feb. 1931, p. 5.

81. CMJ, XI, 2, Feb. 1915, p. 76; *ibid.*, XIV, 1, Jan. 1918, p. 26; *ibid.*, CMJ, XI, 12, Dec. 1915, p. 441; *ibid.*, CMJ, XIII, 12, Dec. 1917, p. 512.

82. CMJ, XVI, 1, Jan. 1920, p. 11; CE, LII, June 21, 1927, p. 618.

83. MRC, XXIII, 5, May 1927, p. 199.

84. CMJ, XII, 12, Dec. 1916, p. 630; *ibid.*, XIII, 12, Dec. 1917, p. 505.

85. Adams, "The Housing Problem and Production," TP & CL, IV, 3, July 1918, pp. 53, 55-56.

86. Ewing, "Town Planning That Pays," CMJ, XVI, 3, March 1920, p. 82.

87. TP & CL, VII, 1, Jan.-March 1920, p. 10.

88. *Ibid.*, IV, 3, July 1918, p. 65.

89. Adams, "The Die-Hard Economist and the Subject of Civic Beauty," MRC, XXIV, 5, May 1928, p. 199.

90. TPICJ, X, 3, June 1931, p. 57; CE, XLVII, July 8, 1924, p. 129.

91. Ewing, "The Montreal Situation with reference to Town Planning," CE, XLIL, March 21, 1922, p. 235.

92. TP & CL, VI, 2, April-June 1920, p. 35.

93. CE, XLII, Jan. 10, 1922, p. 132.

94. J.M. Kitchen, "Preparing Zoning By-laws for the City of Ottawa," TPICJ, III, 3 June 1924, p. 22.

95. TPICJ, VI, 1, Feb. 1926, pp. 19, 25-26.

96. B. Evan-Parry, "Zoning for the Health of the Community," CE, XLIX, July 21, 1925, p. 150.

97. TPICJ, IV, 1, Jan. 1925, pp. 2-4; *A Plan for the City of Vancouver* . . ., pp. 278-288.

98. G.H. Ferguson, "Need for Zoning in Canadian Cities," CE, LI, Oct. 5, 1926, p. 353.

House and Home in Vancouver: Images of West Coast Urbanism, 1886-1929

DERYCK W. HOLDSWORTH

> The realities cannot sometimes be communicated without the appropriate images; they cannot sometimes be perceived because of them. Both the realities and the images are of many different orders and it becomes a matter of discovering just how much of each is revealed by the other, and which is really which.[1]

The city of Vancouver combined people, capital, and ideas from the British Isles with West-Coast American building technology, design, and marketing systems in the development of its residential landscape. English social values and industrial capitalism met; Old World ways intermingled with the materialism and individualism of the North American continent. A study of these forces is illuminating both for the picture of the city it reveals and for the view it gives of wider forces at work beyond the city.

Vancouver's landscape was characterized by detached houses. The individual home ownership rates ran as high as 80 percent.[2] This can be compared with many cities where houses of wealth were blatantly juxtaposed with large numbers of tenements of poverty. The Vancouver case reflects not only a broad availability of inexpensive land and reasonably priced shelter, but also a deep-seated attachment to home and family as a focus for survival in a confusing modern society.

The Vancouver landscape of 1929 was decidedly suburban (see Figure 1). Rather than a dense concentration of workers' housing, as a Pittsburgh or a Hamilton might present, potential Vancouver homeowners had access to a

SOURCE: This an original paper, written expressly for the first edition of this volume. For further work by this author in this area, see "Regional Distinctiveness in an Industrial Age: Some California Influences on British Columbia Housing", *American Review of Canadian Studies*, (Summer, 1982), pp. 64-81.

Figure 1: South Vancouver: Garden Suburb of the West. Forty years of working class settlement in South Vancouver still presented an amazingly low density profile in 1929, in spite of the fact that the CPR's 6000 acre land grant to the west of Ontario St. was still undeveloped in this area, denying land for settlement to all but the most wealthy Vancouverites. Smoke from False Creek sawmills masks downtown Vancouver and most of the North Shore mountains. (*George Allan photo*)

wide range of residential locations all within a thirty minute streetcar ride to central city employment. In South Vancouver, workers in False Creek sawmills and downtown offices were living at the end of Main Street at densities of nine houses per acre.[3] At a time when British experiments with Garden City alternatives to high density working-class housing were in their infancy and eastern Canadian cities were beginning to come to terms with their own inner city housing problems.[4] Houses were for the most part simple wooden cottages and bungalows; the setting was almost rural. To the west, the undeveloped southeastern edge of the CPR's six thousand acre land grant was clearly evident, awaiting development in rational fashion, while even further to the west the middle-class residential suburbs of Point Grey municipality offered a more gentlemanly estate setting for English style houses to complement the working-class rurality of South Vancouver.

The complex web of land speculation and municipal policies that created and perpetuated this social landscape are explained elsewhere.[5] This paper examines two particular building styles — the California Bungalow and the Tudor Cottage. In these two styles are found many of the external connections important in an explanation of Vancouver's distinctive character. To what extent do these homes replicate old ways; to what extent do these homes signify a rejection of the past and the creation of a new identity? Houses have specific meaning in their external styling. They also have internal meaning as homes. The task is to move between style and meaning, from house to home and *vice versa*. In that the newly arrived Vancouver residents built and inhabited emphatically North American houses, it is possible to use landscape statements to infer social aspirations?

OLD HEARTHS

Undoubtedly, the active interest of British capital in land speculation, in the London-based Vancouver streetcar company, and in the British Columbia Electric Railway was one important external connection. Sharing the same building as the British Empire Trust Company, one of the main organizers of colonial portfolios for British investment funds, the streetcar company was often regarded as the barometer for British Columbia's economic stability.[6] Many of the early accounts of Vancouver were pervaded by imperial sentiment,[7] and many speculators dealt in land by boosting the city through confident visions of its broader destiny — the "Liverpool of the Pacific" and "Glasgow of the North West" being two popular slogans to add to the CPR's earlier "Terminal City." Another example was a ringing address Rudyard Kipling made to a prominent Vancouver business circle:

> You have a right to your pride in your city; my pride is in your destiny, because it devolves right upon you here to build up, rivet, and make secure a stable Western

Civilisation facing the Eastern sea (Applause). The head of a great army of peace is scarcely emerging yet through the mountain passes, but in a shorter time than any dare believe, it must come through in full flood. It is you, gentlemen, who must be responsible for handling of that great army . . . men looking for homes for themselves and their women where they might rear up their children.[8]

Direct transfer of distinctively English forms and styles of housing to Vancouver was not to be expected. English urban dwellers were several generations removed from building their own houses, and ubiquitous brick and Welsh slate had eroded nearly all regional distinctivensss. For some, brick was the only appropriate material, as the perceptions of one English bricklayer indicated in a letter home:

The Canadian Pacific Railway are doing their best to make the place a permanent one. Their Hotel Vancouver has taken over a million bricks and an immense quantity of stone to erect it; and they are about to build an Opera House that will require one and a half million bricks in it. But it must be added that every stone, every yard of sand, and every cube of stone have to be imported into this town from a distance. The timber is close to here, and may be said to be almost on the spot, while it is sawn and worked in the town, but the stone, whether for building or for lime has to come from a distance. The sand is brought from the seashore some miles away, the brick still farther, and every barrel of cement has to be brought from England. These facts make me doubtful as to the permanency of Vancouver, or of her ability to maintain her present rate of growth for long.[9]

Such confident logic in the midst of the West Coast rain forest is as revealing as it is amusing.

Industrial landscapes were not necessarily warm and friendly memories to be transferred as vital touchstones in the continuity of the old life in a new setting. The memories and experiences of that brick urban world were more likely to revolve around negative features. The environment of industrial urbanism was all-embracing and predominantly hostile. This is perhaps most powerfully conveyed by Dickens' famous descriptions of Coketown, or in English painter L.S. Lowry's portrayal of industrial Lancashire, in which the factory landscape and rows of mean terraces dominate faceless, stick-like figures.[10] The only time such figures had faces and identity was in ''home,'' where the private world of family life provided mutual aid against all the troubles outside. Roberts' description of his childhood life in the Salford slums, *Home, Sweet, Home*, almost became a second national anthem.[11] In short, in working class life, home had a very special meaning. ''Where almost everything else is ruled from outside, is chancey and likely to knock you down when you least expect it, the home is still yours and real: the warmest welcome is still 'Mek y'self at 'ome'.''[12]

Yet even the home was not sacred space if the landlord could enter to collect rent. As the nineteenth century progressed, many attempted to escape

Figure 2: "Be it ever so humble, there's no place like home." The Daniel McPhalen home, 209 Harris Street (later E. Georgia), 1891. (*Vancouver City Archives photo*)

from such external forces, as the rise of working class buildingf societies indicate.[13] Escape was attempted in a spatial as well as an emotional sense; it often involved re-establishing home life in non-city settings. For the majority, such relocation often had to await the municipal socialism of the 1920's, when council estates were cast in quasi-rural images following on earlier Garden City experiments[14] or in private speculative estates invoking similar images.[15] The direction was clearly pointed out by the middle-classes who had escaped before them; they too had established a controlled private world of family, but through suburban villas and a life managed by the paraphenalia of gentility.[16] As a recent study concludes, the Victorian city was defined in part through fugitive processes: "not only for the middle classes retreating to their laburnum groves but for the masses following behind in workmen's trains or making for emigrant ships instead."[17]

HOUSE-OWNERSHIP EQUALS HOME

At the risk of oversimplification, it can be said that the emigrant ships and trains that arrived in Vancouver brought with them a population that had a deep-rooted sense of home as a haven, and aspired to middle-class suburban house-ownership. Those selling houses to new arrivals were quick to point back to the old life:

> In the big bad cities such as New York and London, the acute issue is the rent question, the tenement house evil. The London County Council is putting up houses for thousands of families — not in London, but outside, in the suburbs, where people can have fresh air, and yards for the kids to play in, and gardens — same as here in Kensington. [A Vancouver suburb][18]

The west coast equivalent to laburnum groves was available. The despairs of high-density living — "living factories called apartments" — were to be shunned, and a detached house was the only form to be tolerated, even if it was only a simple cabin (see Figure 2). A multitude of building companies could offer a wide range of housing styles and prices, from cabins to ornate, turreted structures. Although style was an important selling feature, home-ownership was of prime importance. Under a banner headline, "The Magic Word HOME," and pictures of smiling families in front of simple houses, one advertiser offered the following:

> What a world of fond associations and dear memories is conjured up by those four letters, "H-O-M-E." How it makes us think of domestic joy, a warm fire before the hearth, and warmed hearts to welcome us when day's work is over; better still, how it makes us think of sturdy independence, freedom from care and worry, and increasing prosperity. The house you live in is not "home" if you don't own it. If you are paying rent you are living in someone else's home, not your own home.[19]

Figure 3: Sketch used in National Finance Company mortgage funds advertisement, 1911.

The fireplace, the hearth, and the family sitting around in safe comfort was a theme used in many house advertisements. The National Finance Company, offering mortgage money for Prudential Builders houses, cleverly used the symbolic sketch (see Figure 3) of a house sitting above the mantlepiece clock — the innermost meaning of house-as-hearth and the exterior image of the attractive house intertwined.

Such appeals to home obviously made sense only if the costs made the dream a possibility to large numbers of potential home owners. Those who controlled the money (for land, building and credit were as keen on universal ownership as were the purchasers, and for broader political motives as well as their profit gains. A person who was denied home-ownership was seen as a threat to society, since those who had no stake in society could not be expected to work within the social and economic rules of those that did. Several examples can be drawn from local organizations. In 1911, the Vancouver Board of Trade formed a committee called the Imperial Home

Re-Union Association[20] which acted as a high-risk loan company for existing British settlers in Vancouver to bring over their families, via CPR ships and trains. A happy worker was a better worker. He was less likely to be a radical threat to Vancouver business interest. The scheme, however, was proudly announced as "humanitarian and imperialistic".[21] The more immediate benefit would also include higher home-ownership, and in many cases on land owned by the same West End entrepreneurs and British investment companies that espoused the cause. As was often the case among businessmen, humanitarian goals and profits intersected.[22]

In the 1920's, the Vancouver Real Estate Exchange ran a home-ownership campaign, deciding that home-ownership "teaches thrift and sobriety; it makes better and more contented citizens and eliminates that prey of unrest and radicalism — discontented rent-payers."[23] Appealing to the logic that homeowning must embrace all classes of society, the builders and real-estate industry asked themselves to work to bring homeownership within the reach of all through reasonable land costs and low interest rates:

> No man can feel entirely safe in the possession of his property as long as there are people who have no property at all. The man who has a stake in the country will uphold its laws and defend its institutions, because it is in his vital interests to do so. If owners are to be safe from anarchy and revolution as well as to help build up the country, then as many as possible must be owners. Hence the necessity of encouraging the acquisition of property on the part of poor people. Make it easy for them to get it and easy for them to keep it.[24]

The businessmen who held these views might well have been looking over their shoulders at the radicalism of the coal-mining towns on Vancouver Island. The bitter contrast between mine-owner Dunsmuir's palatial Craigdarroch Castle in Victoria and the mean, rented shacks of Cumberland and Ladysmith[25] might understandably encourage the Vancouver elite to help the workers. Their homes would not be threatened if the working man was happily tending his vegetables in the backyard of his own home.

What were the concrete expressions of these different homes? The scholarly assessment of Vancouver's architectural history is limited,[26] and redevelopment has obliterated much of the city's nineteenth century stock. It is still possible, however, to re-create a picture of a new frontier city that displayed surprisingly sophisticated designs. Italianate, Queen Anne, and Single Style houses[27] reflect San Francisco influences prevalent throughout New York and other eastern American cities were also evident through the work of architects hired by the CPR to distinguish their "Terminal City" from the earlier sawmill town. Complementing this mixture of "imported" styles are the simple frame houses, cabins, and cottages that were the product of local initiative and the output of local sawmills.[28] In this study,

Figure 4: California Bungalow, West 5th Avenue, Kitsilano. This home was built in 1921 for $2500.

Figure 5: Kitsilano in 1929. The abundance of home sites throughout the streetcar suburbs help explain the stumps and vacant lots surrounding the 1912 house to the left of the picture. This area is now infilled and contains lots with smaller houses, while freshly opened streets up the hill to the west offer more suburban locations. (*Vancouver City Archives photo*)

attention is focussed on the dominant styles, and therefore the concern is largely with the housing stock of the city during the two important booms prior to and after World War I, when Vancouver grew from 27,000 in 1901 to over 100,000 in 1911, to almost a quarter of a million on the eve of the depression.[29] Within the streetcar suburbs, the most prevalent form in both booms was undoubtedly the California Bungalow, and this is examined as the first landscape metaphor summarizing Vancouver home images.

THE CALIFORNIA CONNECTION TO HOME

The California Bungalow style has a simplicity and craftsmanship that was an appealing contrast to the fussiness and clutter of turn-of-the-century housing. Paradoxically, these attractions define one of the most mass-produced of all North American housing styles.[30] Its Canadian popularity was not unique to Vancouver. The style was also found in Halifax, Nova Scotia, just as a Spanish Mission adobe could be found in Minneapolis, Minnesota. This was the consequence of the increasingly pervasive influence of mass circulation magazines and journals, both professional and popular. Wherever such plans and designs could be mailed, the style could be found. That aside, the California Bungalow was right at the centre of the ''mood'' of the new west-coast urban lifestyle that united both the Vancouver and Los Angeles experiences. Southern California offered both an easier climate and a simpler, less formal way of life than the Eastern American cities; ''the climate necessarily has brought about a somewhat different mode of life — a life of which the bungalow is in a manner a true expression.''[31] The style featured indoor-outdoor rooms, using deep verandahs and sleeping porches to take advantage of sun and shade, ''porches and patios extended the house until it met surrounding nature.''[32] Pioneered by the sensitive craftsmanship in the designs of Pasadena architects Greene and Greene,[33] the popular translation of the bungalow style emphasized honest construction of all parts — rafter ends and porch supports were exposed, brick piers highlighted material variety and textures, and eave brackets were exaggerated (see Figure 4).

This honesty and openess had a deeper meaning. Inspired by Morris and Ruskin in England, American cities of industrial technology and society popularized magazines that advocated a return to simpler and morally healthier ways of building and living.[34] With less indigenous pre-industrial history to recall than Morris' medievalism, the Americans latched on to the closest version: the early California style. A twentieth century interpretation of this was mission furniture, and in housing, the California or Craftsman Bungalow. For those who moved to Southern California, a bungalow was a testimony to the benefits of the new life. In lauding the qualities of Los Angeles, one commentator wrote:

> William Morris taught it is the business of each of us to build and adorn a house for our own physical and social comfort and joy. In California as nowhere else are found the conditions making this easy of accomplishment. . . . The working man is able to possess a home of his own, and though its walls may be only the thickness of a single board, yet covered with flowers and vines, it equals in comfort an Eastern palace.[35]

A recent examination of the myths about Los Angeles notes that "Migrants to Los Angeles were more urban than those to the classic urban centres of the East."[36] They were seeking the same suburban pre-industrial alternative that motivated the English fugitive from the city. Consequently, although the house-form was North American, and its hearth Californian, the Craftsman Bungalows of Vancouver met the same sympathetic chords with the city's English urban past as they did for Pasedena's American east-coast antecedents. One California pattern book of house plans used in Vancouver had this common appeal:

> There's a little side street at the edge of the town
>   That sloped from the brow of the hill
> Where the shadows lie deep from the sun going down
>   And the harsh city noises are still
> The white wings of peace seem to brood in the air
>   Of this little side street that I know
> And Phyllis so fair is awaiting me there
>   In our own little Bungalow[37]

A detailed documentation of the architectural links connecting California and Vancouver is not feasible here. They can be seen, however, in the works and writing of architects like R. Mackay Fripp[38] who practiced in both Los Angeles and Vancouver, built Greene and Greene style houses, and was also sufficiently *au fait* with the Arts and Crafts movement that he could build either English or Californian variants for his Vancouver clients. At the vernacular level, there are myriad examples of specific plans used from Californian books appearing by blueprint number or design firm in the city's building permit records. One particularly popular pattern book was "Bungalow Specialist" Jud Yoho's *Craftsman Bungalows*, which was extracted and advertised regularly in the Vancouver newspapers, where the education of potential clients in the subtleties of good taste went on incessantly amidst the real estate advertisements: "No attempt should be made to make a smooth or regular-surfaced wall beyond the demands of strength and solidarity. If points stick out, or if the pointing lines, either vertical or horizontal, waver like a snake and if broken-ends show, it is all to the better, from the artistic standpoint."[39] This and other pattern books were used for all shapes and sizes of bungalows, including a two-storey variant called a 'Swiss Chalet' that was regarded as a bungalow, since the abundance of craftsmen detail it contained was in the bungalow spirit.

These plan books and monthly magazines made it possible for anyone to erect a bungalow. Individual owners might build one or small contractors could build clusters of two or three on adjacent lots. For more integrated speculative ventures in building and real estate, not only the style of California but also its marketing practices were imported. The most popular model for success seems to have been that of the Los Angeles Investment Syndicate, which used scale economies in initial land purchases, materials, designs and construction to skilfully manipulate large tracts of land yet keep the appeal of variety. One local imitator, Vancouver Free Homes, promised this same individuality in a bungalow, and reminded shareholders in its prospectus of the moral value of its artistic product: "The better, the more attractive, the more wholesome, the more beautiful and comfortable and inspiring a city's houses, the better, truer, homelier and more virtuous will its citizens be."[40]

For most of the working-class immigrants who helped swell the city during the great pre-World War I boom, and those who followed after the war, such a combination of home-ownership and artistic quality, primed by aggressive real estate speculation, offered a broad choice of land for housing. The result was the extremely low-density suburban character of most of Vancouver (see Figures 1 & 5).

FORMAL HOME AND OVERT ENGLISH LINKS

If the working-class home was an inward retreat towards emotional privacy through family, then the middle-class equivalent was achieved through suburban sameness and a formal code of social relations. Both Sennett's study of middle-class Chicago families[41] and Davidoff's examination of the social rules of Victorian England[42] suggest that the middle class were also alienated by the confusing dynamics of a fluid industrial order. One way to overcome such uncertainty was to be in control of some limited certainty. The social display of suburban villas, the management of the household through a broad set of home standards,[43] and the regulation of social intercourse within a safe group brought a sense of security.

Vancouver's West End, the elite area for the first twenty years of the century, was characterized by a variety of impressive mansions and villas, each with its own flurry of gables, trim, balconies, or turrets, reflecting the latest in high Victorian taste (see Figure 6). Overall, the composite streetscape was one of sameness, in which upper class landmarks of ostentatious wealth and middle income houses tended to blend together

Figure 6: Victorian eclecticism on the English Bay slopes, the West End, 1908. (*Vancouver Public Library photo*)

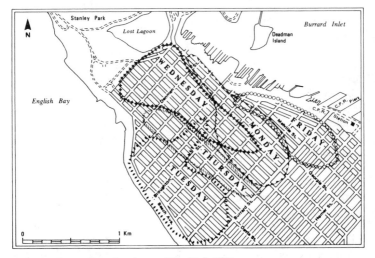

Figure 7: The At Home Landscape, West End, 1908.

architecturally and intermingle spatially. Within this "sameness," a social world of status-equals emerges through an examination of the "rule book" of social etiquette, *The Elite Directory*. Mapping the days on which each family was "At Home," the subworlds within the West End neighbourhood become apparent (see Figure 7). The Friday group, along Melville Street in the north East, was dominated by early West End elite families who had maintained their homes on the bluffs overlooking Coal Harbour. They include many of the CPR executives and key early real estate magnates. South of Davie Street, the Tuesday Group included important industrialists (such as B.T. Rogers, the sugar magnate; John Hendry, president of Vancouver's leading lumber conglomerate; and George Coleman, shipping interests). Other streets had their own social orbits of like members within the elite hierarchy,[44] and there was a surprisingly low overlap between these worlds.

Some sense of the social orbit comes through in a semi-autobiographical novel on Vancouver by Ethel Wilson, in which a Stafford merchant family cross sea and continent, and re-establish their life among transplanted society:

> By this time, the Grandmother and her family were established with At Home days, like all the other people who knew what was what. Aunty delivered a great deal of pleasure from dressing herself with unusual care and paying and returning calls, but most of all she loved the first and third Thursdays. Aunty loved what was being called Society, but she found people who were not designated as in Society equally delightful.[45]

In these images and maps the meaning of the home is vividly clear. A smart exterior is presented to a conforming streetscape, while the house itself was the umbrella for a private world of family life beyond the business of profit and public service with which the whole neighbourhood concerned itself. Such a private world was breached only on strict rules: the home of family friendship became the monitored venue of public friendship, with codified rules for "home" behaviour. Such metropolitan social values instilled in a frontier city parallel the equally external inspirations for the house-styles.

When streetcar suburbs developed in the Point Grey peninsula, the rather anomalous position of an elite adjacent to the docks and an expanding business core became apparent. The West End middle class vacated their turreted houses, and the more distant suburban home became an individual private world set out behind pastoral landscapes. The subdivision Bryn Mawr, "where sunshine and fresh air meet," invited the prospective buyer to "bring your wife along — the home is where she spends most of her life, and it is the centre of her little kingdom."[46] This was not condescending sexism in operation, but rather recognition of the then accepted role of the

Figure 8: The Tulk House, Selkirk Street, Shaughnessy Heights, 1912. The architect was Sam Maclure. (*Vancouver Public Library photo*)

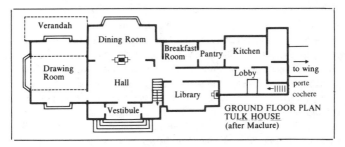

wife in guarding the domestic hearth and providing the relaxed setting for the husband returning to "a home just far enough away from the noise and bustle of the city for peace and contentment."[47]

The ultimate in suburban splendour was provided by the CPR's Shaughnessy Heights subdivisions, an area of crescents, boulevards, large minimum lot sizes, and architectural controls that guaranteed a world apart. The imagery was pastoral, the layout emphatically different from the gridded city, and the house styles chosen by clients matched this imagery. The most popular styles were appeals to English antecedents, by imitating the simple lines of old farm houses or in the emphatic use of half-timbered decoration in expansive Tudor Revival mansions. These houses and their settings created a sense of a stable home environment where generations had grown up and where the present occupant would carry the tradition into the future; such an image became more plausible as the CPR's landscape grew up around these instant "old" houses. One such home is that shown in Figure 8, built in

1912 for a barrister, and designed by perhaps the leading B.C. architect of the day, Samuel Maclure.[48] With several apparent ages of construction — a Jacobean stone archway and smaller wing added to an earlier Elizabethan house — the appearance belied its newness, but provided a sophisticated and "rooted" setting for a family to enjoy its new position in society and the city. The floor plan indicates the important social rituals of such a house, with the "public home" for entertaining taking precedence over family space. The huge entrance hallway and gallery, flanked by dining room and lounge, dominate the plan, with more intimate family space being well separated from such functions.[49]

Although the half-timber motif was certainly popular elsewhere on the continent as one of a set of revivalist styles, its use had a special place on the Vancouver scene as a confirmation of realized aspirations. Paralleling the enthusiasm for the Tudor Revival style was an interest in the simple English farmhouse that had been restated in arts and crafts terms by English architects such as Baillie Scott, Ashbee, and in particular, Voysey.[50] This was a "cosey", "cottagey" architecture, characterized by rough stucco surfaces, buttress-like sloping end-walls, and exaggerated roof lines. Translated into a suburban lot it inevitably lost some of the intended effect (see Figure 9), but even the archways through the end-walls seem to add to the child-like cottage mood that was part of the style's attraction.

Both the Tudor Revival and the Voysey-inspired cottages — summarized on the surrogate label "Tudor-Cottage" to describe these broad Old English inspirations — had a popularity in the middle-class west-side suburbs, mimicing the more elaborate Shaughnessy examples. Like the California Bungalow, they came in all shapes and sizes, some with a token half-timber gable and curved roof edges to resemble thatch, others almost faithful replicas of specific Cotswold or Kent examples. Certainly they offered a subtle and refined image of sociability, and, as the streetscape in Figure 10 suggests, the appeal was to a pastoral, pre-industrial way of life. Here too, the exterior style and form of the house had meaning.

Through the twenties, local newspapers carried regular articles by architects on the "correct" style for a Vancouver home dweller. Designs were presented as a "modern Canadian Home", or an "Ideal House for Vancouver", yet overwhelmingly the styles were English. A "Canadian Home of Charming Character" was described as a "splendid spacious home in Elizabethan half-timbered design which possesses in full measure the comfortable homelike atmosphere of this style".[51] Paradoxically, small houses built as Vancouver homes for Canadian buyers in the twenties were closer in design to English styles than they were to the California bungalow style initially adopted when many of the settlers arrived. In a pioneer analysis of nineteenth century west-coast architecture, one American

Figure 9: "Tudor-Cottages," West 10th Avenue, Point Grey.

Figure 10: The Point Grey pastoral landscape. (*Vancouver Public Library photo*)

architectural historian argues that the California Bungalow marked the coming of age of California. Californians finally rejected a succession of imported styles and gained a sense of being of the place and were eager to explore their roots.[52] The appeal of the English Tudor-Cottage seems to strike a similar chord in west-side Vancouver home purchasers, as it had done in Victoria during its Edwardian heyday. Although post-war Canada had become more aware of its own identity, British Columbia still retained its strong ties with the "Old Country," and seemed confident in adopting English styles as evidence of their vision of themselves.[53] Only recently, as an earlier heritage is recognized in the woodwork of the coast Indians and in the potential of the west coast rain-forest, are cedar siding and shed roof houses beginning to challenge as an alternate regional statement.

CONCLUSION

When the St. Louis firm of Harland Bartholemew was brought in to provide a coherent land-use plan for the city, it recognized some of the city's cultural history. In a section on Civic Art, it reported: "What Vancouver needs is an agreement as to a style of building that is at once aesthetically pleasing and adapted to local climatic conditions. The half-timber house should be studied . . . for it seems to be appropriate to these surroundings."[54] The plan that Bartholemew prepared was for a city that had grown to full metropolitan status. Primed by speculators and accepted by settlers seeking alternative urban structures to those of eastern Canada or Britain, the wider city (after amalgamation with Point Grey and South Vancouver) was undoubtedly a city of homes, and the planning commission recognized the need to protect this heritage:

> The wise foresight which Point Grey has used in planning at an early stage of its growth should provide Vancouver with one of the most desirable residential districts possessed by any city on the continent, and those who have gained their livelihood by manual labour should find in Hastings Townsite, and in a replanned South Vancouver, a place where they can build up modest homes which should differ only in size from that of the more opulent employers. The retention of Vancouver as a city of single family homes has always been close to the heart of those engaged in the preparation of this plan.[55]

This city of single family homes helped define a stable labour force and a good location for new business. The high level of home-ownership provided for a high degree of contentment, in which material possessions across the city's social and spatial spectrum provided ammunition for those who would claim that Vancouver and Canada had a classless society. Such a view could be challenged if the income gradients, the differences in house values, and access to civic power were examined as one moved east from the University of British Columbia to the other end of the city. Only in recent years is the myth of the classless society being eroded locally as a new generation seeking the comforts of ''home'' are denied that goal (even if it is space in a cooperative townhouse or condominium) through the restrictive tactics of influential West-Side home owners.[56] The emotional opposition to higher density renewal of the city is itself a revealing indication of the resilience of the sacrosanct concept of single family homes that several generations have achieved in Vancouver.

This paper has examined the transplant of English urban culture to the Canadian West Coast. It was partly a negative transfer — models of urban life that the immigrant refused to live with, having experienced them in the Old Country. On the positive side, this experience galvanized a strong desire for home-ownership, in an attempt to define a meaningful existence within urban society. The vehicle for these aspirations was predominantly the California Bungalow. Its popularity was partly due to the pervasiveness of tastemakers, and the strong north-south coastal connection. In addition, the Californian image of a simpler, natural life born out of a rejection of forms and modes of the industrial East and mid-West coincided with many of the feelings of the immigrant Vancouverite. In some ways Vancouver is the Canadian Los Angeles.

A second, complimentary trend was the nostalgia for certain images of the past that had strong meaning; these were proudly exaggerated here as statements of accomplishments. The Tudor Cottage was many an Englishman's castle in Spain, and also a popular turn-of-the-century memory of an England prior to the industrial age. In broad terms, the two landscape metaphors presented in this essay can be seen as compartmentalizing the city, both socially and spatially, although there are many instances where fine examples of each image can be found in the same area. With both styles, the transfer of British settlement was tied up with the search for a quasi-rural suburban environment for home life, in which home-ownership of a detached house on a separate lot was central to the immigrant's desires.

NOTES:

1. H.J. Dyos and M. Wolff, *The Victorian City: Images and Realities* (London: Routledge and Kegan Paul, 1973), p. xxviii.

2. Statistics from the Bartholemew Report, *A Plan for the City of Vancouver including Point Grey and South Vancouver* (Vancouver, 1929), suggests 84% homeownership for South Vancouver (p. 311), with 75% of the population housed in single-family dwellings (p. 357); 72% of the City of Vancouver population were housed in single-family dwellings (p. 217). According to the Vancouver Board of Trade, the region boasted 58% owning homes, which contrasted with rates of 39% for Philadelphia and 41% for Minneapolis. See Table of Percentage of Owned and Rented Gomes, *Industrial Survey of Vancouver and its Adjacent Territory* (Vancouver: Vancouver Board of Trade, 1929).

3. The overall South Vancouver density was 8.8 houses per acre; Bartholemew Report, *A Plan*

for the City of Vancouver, p. 357. For one area, Grimmett, a 22-block, 180-acre area bounded by Ontario St., 58th Ave., Prince Edward St., and River Road, 160 dwellings occupied land at a density of less than one per acre; *Vancouver City Directory*, 1913, 1926.

4. P. Rutherford (ed.), *Saving the Canadian City: The First Phase 1880-1920. An Anthology of Early Articles on Urban Reform* (Toronto: University of Toronto Press, 1974).

5. The historical antecedents for current Vancouver growth are discussed in D. Gutstein, *Vancouver Ltd.* (Toronto: James Lorimer, 1975), particularly in chp. 2, "Vancouver: Brought to you courtesy of the Canadian Pacific Railway," pp. 11-18. The impact of contrasting municipal policies are summarized by E.M.W. Gibson, "Loggers, Lotus Eaters and the Vancouver Landscape", in L.J. Evenden and F.F. Cunningham, eds., *Cultural Discord in the Modern World* (Vancouver: B.C. Geographical Series, No. 20), pp. 57-74. The broad outlines of suburban development are discussed by W.G. Hardwick, *Vancouver* (Toronto: Collier-McMillan, 1974), pp. 100-126.

6. P.E. Roy, "The British Columbia Electric Railway, 1897-1928: A British Company in British Columbia" (unpublished Ph.D. dissertation, University of British Columbia, 1970). The streetcar company sold land under the name of St. Nicholas Estate Co., the title inspired by their head office address, "34 St. Nicholas Lane, Lombard St., London." For an excellent overview of foreign speculation in British Columbia, see D.G. Paterson, "European Financial Capital and British Columbia: An Essay on the Role of the Regional Entrepreneur," *B.C. Studies*, No. 21 (Spring, 1974), pp. 33-47.

7. The best of these is D. Sladen, *On the Cars and Off* (London, 1895).

8. R. Kipling, "Imperialism, Canadian Nationalism and Patriotism," *Proceedings of the Vancouver Canadian Club*, Vol. 8, 1907, pp. 98-101, Vancouver City Archives.

9. W. Towler, "Letters From an Emigrant," *Peterborough Telegraph*, August, 1889.

10. Lowry's paintings have a timeless quality, echoing passages from Charles Dickens, *Hard Times* (1854), or George Orwell, *The Road to Wigan Pier* (1937). The most numbing North American parallel could be P.U. Kellogg, *The Pittsburgh Survey* (Russell Sage, 1914), a six-volume appraisal of the quality of life in the town where Carnegie made his millions.

11. R. Roberts, *The Classic Slum: Salford Life in the First Quarter of the Century* (London: Pelican, 1973), p. 53.

12. R. Hoggart, *The Uses of Literacy; Aspects of Working Class Life* (London: Pelican, 1958), p. 34.

13. P.H.J.H. Gosden, *Self-Help: Voluntary Associations in Nineteenth-Century Britain* (London: Batsford, 1974). See also S.D. Chapman and J.N. Bartlett, "The Contribution of Building Clubs and Freehold Land Society to Working Class Housing in Birmingham," in S.D. Chapman, ed., *The History of Working Class Housing* (Newton Abbott: David and Charles, 1971), pp. 221-46.

14. See W.L. Creese, *The Search for Environment: The Garden City, Before and After* (New Haven: Yale University Press, 1966); and J.N. Tarn, *Five Per Cent Philanthropy* (Cambridge: Cambridge University Press, 1973).

15. A.A. Jackson, *Semi Detached London* (London: George Allen and Unwin, 1973).

16. See J.A. Banks, *Prosperity and Parenthood* (London: Routledge and Kegan Paul, 1954), for a profile of middle-class Victorian life; and H.J. Dyos, *Victorian Suburb: A Study of the Growth of Camberwell* (Leicester: Leicester University Press, 1961), for a detailed account of the suburban process in the nineteenth century.

17. H.J. Dyos and M. Wolff, *op. cit.*, p. 904.

18. Advertisement, "Be Independent and Happy — Buy and Build in Kensington," *Vancouver Province*, July 5, 1906, p. 7.

19. Leibly and Blumer Realty, "The Magic Word HOME," *Vancouver Province*, August 29, 1911.

20. Imperial Home Re-Union Association, Vancouver Board of Trade Special Committees, Vol. 142, Add. Mss. 300, Vancouver City Archives.

21. "South Vancouver the Mecca of Emigrants from the Old Country; Imperial Home Re-Union Association Outlines its Work — Humanitarian, Imperialistic and a Great Business Proposition," *The Greater Vancouver Chinook*, South Vancouver, Saturday, August 3, 1912, Vol. 1, No. 12, p. 1.

22. See, for example, M. Bliss, *A Living Profit: Studies in the Social History of Canadian Business, 1883-1911* (Toronto: McClelland and Stewart, 1974).

23. "Housing Shortage Boosts Home Ownership Plan," *British Columbia Record*, April 16, 1920, p. 1.

24. "Necessity for Home Owning Embraces All Classes of Society," *British Columbia Record*, February 23, 1921, p. 2.

25. P.M. Koroscil, "The Dunsmuirs and the Settlements of Vancouver Island, 1860-1910," in B.S. Osborne, ed., *Origins, Transfer and Settlement; Some Themes in the British Settlement of Canada* (Carleton Library Series, forthcoming). See also, P. Phillips, *No Power Greater: A Century of Labour in British Columbia* (Vancouver: Broadway Printers, 1967).

26. See H.D. Kalman, *Exploring Vancouver: Ten Tours of the City and its Buildings* (Vancouver: University of British Columbia Press, 1974); B.C. Palmer, "Development of Domestic Architecture in British Columbia," *Journal of the Royal Architecture Institute of Canada*, Vol. 5 (November, 1928), pp. 405-416; "100 Years of B.C. Living," *Western Homes*, January, 1958, pp. 6-43; and D.W. Holdsworth, "House and Home in Vancouver: the Emergence of a West Coast Urban Landscape," 1981 Ph.D. thesis, University of British Columbia.

27. M. Whiffen, *American Architecture Since 1780: A Guide to the Styles* (Cambridge: M.I.T. Press, 1969), provides a good introduction to these styles.

28. One such local product is documented by E.G. Mills and D.W. Holdsworth, "The B.C. Mills Prefabricated System: The Emergence of Ready-Made Buildings in Western Canada," *Canadian Historic Sites: Occasional Papers in Archeology and History*, No. 14 (Ottawa, 1976), pp. 127-69.

29. The actual year-by-year mix of immigrants and their origins is dealt with succinctly by N. MacDonald, "Population Growth and Change in Seattle and Vancouver, 1890-1960," *Pacific Historical Review*, 39 (August, 1970), pp. 297-321. MacDonald has also investigated the dynamics of one of Vancouver's boom periods. See "A Critical Growth Cycle for Vancouver, 1900-1914," *B.C. Studies*, No. 17 (Spring, 1973), pp. 26-42. (Reprinted in this volume as Chapter 6).

30. C. Lancaster, "The American Bungalow," *Art Bulletin*, Vol. 40 (September, 1958), pp. 239-53; D. Gebhard and H. von Breton, *Architecture in California, 1868-1968* (Santa Barbara: The Art Galleries, 1968), pp. 13-16; R. Lynes, *The Tastemakers* (New York: Grosset & Dunlap, 1949), pp. 186-95.

31. H.R. Saylor, *Bungalows: Their Design, Construction and Furnishings* (New York: McBride, Nast, 1911), p. 21.

32. L.M. Freudenheim and E. Sussman, *Building with Nature: Roots of the San Francisco Bay Region Tradition* (Santa Barbara: Peregrine Smith, 1974), p. 106.

33. R.L. Makinson, "Greene and Greene," in E. McCoy, ed., *Five California Architects* (New York: Praeger, 1975), pp. 103-48. See also R. Winter, "Charles and Henry Greene," in T.J. Anderson, E.M. Moore, and R.W. Winter, eds., *California Design 1910* (Pasedena: California Designs, 1974), pp. 96-109.

34. See, for example, *The House Beautiful, Indoors and Out, Ladies Home Journal*, and *The Craftsman*. For a discussion of the philosophy behind *The Craftsman*, see J. Freeman, *Gustav Stickley, The Forgotten Rebel* (New York: Century Crofts, 1971). For the impact of the

English Arts and Crafts movement on North American design, see J.D. Kornwolf, *Baillie Scott and the Arts and Crafts Movement* (Baltimore: Johns Hopkins, 1972); and for the Arts and Crafts in California, see T.J. Anderson, *op. cit.*, especially "The Arroyo Culture," pp. 10-29.

35. D. Bartlett, *The Better City: A Sociological Study of a Modern City* (Los Angeles: Neuner, 1907), p. 39.

36. S. Thernstrom, "The Growth of Los Angeles in Historical Perspective: Myth and Reality," in W.Z. Hirsch, *Los Angeles: Viability and Prospects for Metropolitan Leadership* (New York: Praeger, 1971), pp. 3-19. The ambivalent attitude towards suburbanization that lies behind the suburban landscape is discussed in R.M. Fogelson, *The Fragmented Metropolis: Los Angeles 1850-1930* (Cambridge: M.I.T. Press, 1967); and R. Banham, *Los Angeles: The Architecture of Four Ecologies* (London: Allen Lane, 1971).

37. Stilwell, *Representative California Homes* (Los Angeles, 1912).

38. Fripp practiced in England, New Zealand, Vancouver, and Los Angeles over a thirty year period. He was an instigator of the Arts, Historical and Scientific Association of Vancouver, lecturing on art and archeology, and publishing essays on Arts and Crafts, Maori artifacts, and regular critiques of the quality of Vancouver architecture. His enthusiasm for the works of Ruskin and Morris, and his first hand knowledge of the work of Greene and Greene, all backed by a strong library of current British and American art journals, are reflected in his designs exeucted during the pre-war boom.

39. Jud Yoho advertisement, *Vancouver Province*, July 27, 1911, p. 9.

40. Vancouver Free Homes Company Limited, "Prospectus," Company Records File 438 (1910), Public Archives of British Columbia. Other leading Vancouver firms operating on similar lines included The Bungalow Construction and Finance Co., Vernon Bros., Prudential Builders, and The Artistic Bungalow Constructors Co.

41. R. Sennett, "Middle Class Families and Violence: the Experience of a Chicago Community," in Thernstrom and Sennett, eds., *Nineteenth-Century Cities: Essays in the New Urban History* (New Haven: Yale University Press, 1969), pp. 386-420.

42. L. Davidoff, *The Best Circles: Etiquette, Society and the Season* (London: Groom Gelm, 1973).

43. The features advocated and cherished in nineteenth century family life, on both sides of the Atlantic, are explored in B. Frankle, "The Genteel Family: High Victorian Conceptions of Domesticity and Good Behaviour," unpublished Ph.D. thesis, University of Wisconsin, 1969. For the American case, see D.P. Handlin, "The Detached House in the Age of the Object and Beyond," in *W.J. Mitchell, ed., Environmental Design: Research and Practise* (U.C.L.A., 1972). For English suburbia, see H.J. Dyos, "A Castle for Everyman," *London Journal*, Vol. 1, No. 1, 1975, pp. 118-34.

44. For a discussion of the West End elite, see A. Robertson, "The Pursuit of Profit, Power and Privacy: A Study of Vancouver's West End Elite, 1886-1926," M.A. thesis, University of British Columbia, 1977.

45. E. Wilson, *The Innocent Traveller* (Toronto: Macmillan, 1944), pp. 129-30.

46. Greater Vancouver Ltd., "Bryn Mawr: Choosing a Wife and Choosing a Home," *Vancouver Province*, October 7, 1912, p. 17.

47. J.A. Paton, "Kerrisdale," *Point Grey Gazette*, Special Progress Edition, 1913.

48. See L.K. Eaton, *The Architecture of Samuel Maclure* (Victoria: Art Gallery, 1971). Maclure published the description of one Victoria house (for A. Martin) in the *Canadian Architect and Builder*, later reprinted in *The Craftsman*, March, 1908, pp. 675-81, which had interior designs by Baillie Scott. The article stated that "a house that is built of local materials and is absolutely suited to its environment, but which yet shows decided evidences of the tastes and traditions of another country" (p. 675).

49. A discussion of the social and spatial logic of floor plans in large country homes can be found in M. Girouard, *The Victorian Country House* (Oxford: Clarendon, 1971).

50. D. Gebhard, *Charles F.A. Voysey, Architect* (Los Angeles: Hennessey Ingalls, 1975). For Baillie Scott, see Kornwolf, *op. cit.*

51. Townley and Matheson, "A Canadian Home of Charming Character," *Vancouver Province*, May 3, 1927.

52. H. Kirker, *California's Architectural Frontier: Style and Tradition in the 19th Century* (Santa Barbara: Peregrine Smith, 1973).

53. This adoption of old English images echoes Laslett's observation that "the English still seem to want to live in the structures of the pre-industrial world, prizing the thatched cottage and the half-timbered house as the proper place for the proper Englishman to dwell." P. Laslett, *The World We Have Lost, England Before the Industrial Age* (New York: Scribners, 1971), p. 26.

54. H. Bartholemew, *op. cit.*, p. 255. For a detailed description of how the American firm of Harland Bartholemew came to plan Vancouver, see J. Bottomley, "The Business Community, Urban Reform and the Establishment of Town Planning in Vancouver, B.C., 1900-1940," 1977 Ph.D. thesis, University of British Columbia.

55. A.G. Smith, "Chairman's Introduction," in Bartholemew, *op. cit.*, p. 26.

56. Their position is well summarized by B. McKee, "Family Homes . . . Our Greatest Asset; A Survey of Zoning Past and Present with Special Reference to Point Grey", North West Point Grey Home Owners Association (Vancouver City Archives; pamphlet collection, c. 1963). See also Bottomley and Holdsworth, "A consideration of attitudes underlying community involvement with civic issues," in D. Ley, ed., *Community Participation and the Spatial Order of the City* (Vancouver, B.C. Geographical Series No. 19, 1974), pp. 59-74.

The Evolution of Architectural Styles in Toronto

ALAN GOWANS

There are at least three valid ways of looking at these photographs of Toronto. You may think of them as documentation — in this case as a visual record of the appearance, especially the architectural appearance, of a particular Canadian city just after the middle of the twentieth century. Or you may admire them as an art form with an aesthetic interest transcending time and place. Or finally, taking documentation and art together, you may read them as the cultural history of a city. More exactly, of three cities, for there are three Torontos depicted here. There is Georgian Toronto — the town founded late the eighteenth century by the same sort of Anglican and Tory patricians who ruled Lower Canada from Montreal and Quebec, the Maritimes from Halifax and Saint John. There is Victorian Toronto, the Protestant and middle-class creation of waves of settlers from the United States and Britain who came into the city from the 1820's through the 1850's, took over control of it from the old Tory families, and remained its dominant element down to the Second World War. And there is the ''new Toronto'' that began to emerge in the 1940's, the modern city that twentieth century technology has been building and twentieth-century warfare has been peopling, whose final shape we can only begin to surmise. To appreciate these photographs fully, I think, we need to see them in all three lights.

First the visual record. That primarily means architecture because the face

SOURCE: This article is a revised version, including a retrospective note, of the introduction for *The Face of Toronto* (Toronto: Oxford University Press, 1960). It is reprinted here by permission of the author and the publisher. The photographs accompanying the article were taken by Ralph Greenhill and are reproduced with his permission.

of a city is determined more by its buildings than by anything else. If we cannot paraphrase "God made the Parks, man made the buildings," still it is true that one river or ravine or clump of trees by the water looks pretty much like another; it is when they build on it that men really put a distinctive hand on the landscape. Architecture is human history made manifest; in architecture the past lives on into the future. Just as in the man's face you can still find traces of the boy's and the child's, so back of the modern face of Toronto is the face of Victorian Toronto, and behind that again the face of an old Georgian town; and there is something of all of them in the photographs presented here.

Of earliest, Georgian Toronto not much is left. Here and there, however, you can still find traces of the distinctive concept of architecture, inherited from the British classical tradition of the eighteenth century, which gave the place its character. Some reminiscence of its concern for the formal beauty of balanced arrangements of solids and voids is preserved in surviving fragments of what was once lower-middle-class housing on the outskirts of the city, now buried deep in the downtown area. Occasionally you can pick out vestiges of the characteristic symmetrical rooflines and dormers of old Georgian city houses above remodelled facades of office buildings and warehouses in the old heart of the city around King, Church, Duke, and Duchess Streets. Something of the elegance of its last, Regency phase may still be sensed in the decoration and proportion of conservative public buildings like the old St. Lawrence Hall. But these vestiges are few and far between. By the 1820's this city is dying. Its kind of architecture, based on the concept of an absolute beauty independent of any particular forms, is coming to seem retardataire, old-fashioned. In place of it appears a new kind of architecture, based on a very different concept, which will characterize Toronto for its next hundred, Victorian, years.

For a variety of reasons — some sociological, some aesthetic, some no more than part of the "trend of the times" — "progressive" people by the time of Toronto's first great spurt of growth in the 1820's are beginning to think of architecture not, in the old phrase, as "the art of building well," but as a kind of symbolic language. They begin to look for "styles" in building — for details borrowed from architecture of past ages that by their historical associations can suggest moods and bring to mind specific ideas and principles. Osgoode Hall and St. James Cathedral are good examples of what results. Both are originally conceived in the 1820's to be symbols of the cultural superiority of Toronto's Tory and Anglican founders over their middle-class rivals. Characteristically, the style is different in each case; it is typical of this early Victorian age that, unlike the eighteenth century, it will favour no one style over another. Osgoode (photograph #1), with proud Roman portico and elegant rows of pedimented windows, imitates the style

Photo 1—Osgoode Hall(1829—1859): home of the Law Society, courts, & law school.

of London club-houses which in turn borrows their forms from the palaces of sixteenth-century Roman nobility; it proclaims a heritage of family and wealth. St. James, as first built (the present structure is a later and more elaborate version of this first concept), makes its point by studious reproduction of the forms of fourteenth-century English cathedrals (its spire was once the most prominent object on the skyline); its archaeological correctness overwhelms with supercilious ease the haphazard collections of pointed windows and buttresses that pass for Gothic among less erudite, less culturally endowed middle-class builders. By the 1840's and 50's architecture is turning into an erudite game indeed; but it is a game people everywhere, high and low, ept and inept, are eager to play. And they will be long tiring of it. In fact, concern for symbolic values, to the subordination of beauty and functional convenience alike, is what will be the common denominator of most architecture built for the next hundred years. But the game will not always have the same rules. In Victorian architecture three quite well-defined phases can be discerned, each ultimately based on symbolism, but with distinct characteristics of its own. By the 1850's the first, early Victorian, phase — the simple use of particular historical styles to suggest more or less well-defined ideas (Gothic for Christian ideals, Roman for civic virtue, Egyptian for permanance, and so on) — is passing away, and the second, High Victorian, phase begins.

University College of the University of Toronto, as seen through the Queen's Park bandstand (see photograph #2), catches the essence of this new age, I think, surviving almost intact into ours. Through a maze of

Photo 2—*Right*. Queens Park: the bandstand.

diverse shapes — squares, oblongs, circles, arches, triangles — you glimpse a vista of what the Victorians liked to call "dreaming spires" hung between sky and snow, most prominent of them the single asymmetrical turret on the chunky tower of University College (certainly the finest building of its age in Toronto, and one of the best examples of the period anywhere). Even now, the total effect is one to evoke nostalgia, reverie; there is something about the everchanging panorama of shapes in High Victorian buildings — which only becomes more variegated, more complex, more visually interesting the closer we approach them — that irresistibly suggests the steady and sure passage of present into past. It is the mood of Turner's late paintings, of poems like *In Memoriam* and *Dover Beach*; and this is the effect that High Victorian architects above all wanted to create. They called it "picturesque."

To achieve the "picturesque," there was no need to stick to any one architectural style — Roman, or Gothic, or whatever. The more you mixed

Photo 3—Scarborough: a farmhouse c. 1880.

styles, indeed, the better: for the more different elements from the past you combined in a building, the more variegated, the more eye-catching, the more evocative of pastness in general your building would be. ''Picturesque eclecticism'' like this was the dominant mode of building in Toronto from the 1850's through the 1880's, and inasmuch as these were years of great growth there is still a good deal of it left, enough to trade its whole history. Its earliest manifestations was the sharp, eye-catching, ''picturesque'' gable form just beginning to interrupt stolid horizontal Georgian symmetry. In a Scarborough farmhouse (photograph #3) there is an intact island of mature High Victorian art in the 1860's and 1870's, still defying the new city swirling around, still a perfect example of the patterned red-and-yellow brickwork so characteristic of Ontario building in this age, and of its new attitude to space — no longer the tightly self-contained unit of Georgian times, the Victorian house moves in and out, back and forth, its outlines projecting here and receding there, blurred by ironwork fringes and lathes pinnacles so that it trails off into space in all directions, just as its forms, suggestive of many bygone eras but distinctive if none, trail back into definite time. By the 1880's and '90's, the style begins to disintegrate, relapsing into simple — though often subtle — variations in the sizes and

Photo 4—*Right*. Yonge and Front Streets: the Bank of Commerce (1930) looms behind the Bank of Montreal (1886)

shapes of doors, windows, steps, and balconies that presage the end of this era and the onset of the succeeding, Late Victorian, style.

Now the light, fanciful imaginiative quality of mid-century Victorian building is gone, and in its place is an architecture of heavy, pompous, ostentatiously archeological forms (photograph #4). This is the characteristic expression of the late Victorian age. Coming in around the 1890's, it will be still in evidence well into the twentieth century. In that symbolism still primarily motivates them, its builders remain good Victorians; but now, with immense stocks of information amassed by a century of scientific scholarship, and photographic archives to draw on, they are much more sophisticated and erudite about it all. They know how to encase the pomp and circumstance of increasingly big business in an appropriated envelope of massive pilasters, ponderous swags, and waddling balusters from Louis XIV's great seventeenth-century Baroque palaces; they know how to gratify the pretensions of classes made newly rich by the prosperous late decades of Victoria's reign and Edward VII's with piles of studious detail from medieval castles and the palaces of Imperial Rome.

The feel something, too, of the stirrings of "creative eclecticism" south

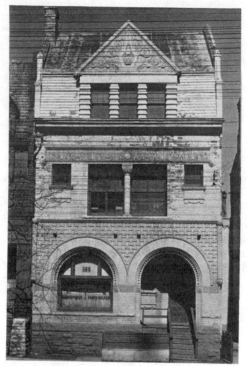

Photo 5—*Right*. Church Street.

of the border. In this era Toronto builds a City Hall in the massive brown sandstone forms of "Richardsonian Romanesque" — so-called after the leading American architect of the late '70's and early '80's; it imports a Buffalo architect to design its Provincial Parliament building in the same style, and dozens of minor architects rush to follow the new suit. The new fashionable residential areas north and south of Bloor Street begin to fill with round-arched, strip-windowed homes in massive brick and stone (photograph #5), sporting patches of lavish decoration in the manner of Richardson's followers in Chicago, Boston, and New York — this is the atmosphere of Reciprocity, of warm winds southward, with Laurier rising to power and Conservatives panicking: "Don't sell the country to the States." They need not worry; of the more advanced movements in this age, Toronto will get only echoes. Of the theories of "organic ornament" advanced by Louis Sullivan in Chicago, some slight reminiscence (badly misunderstood) in decorative details perhaps. Of the trailing, graceful curves of Art Nouveau design in England and France, a suggestion here and there — as, for instance

Photo 6—Scarborough: St. Jude's (Anglican) Church, Wexford (1848).

(of all places) in brackets supporting a waterfront shelter on Ward's Island. And little else. Victorian Toronto dies very hard. Still in the 1920's, indeed, some landmarks (like the Union Station and the CNE Ontario Government Building) are being completed in the full grandiose style of the 1890's, while others (like the Bank of Commerce and the Royal York Hotel) cling only superficially simplified, "modernistic" versions of it. Not until the end of the Second World War does the twentieth century begin to make any great mark on the face of Toronto. But when it does, it comes in with a rush. How it envelopes and obliterates the old city in great gulps and swathes, photograph #6, illustrates perceptively.

Once there was a country church here. Once this was a country churchyard, with a sagging wire fence around it, and a weathered carriage-sled at the back. Once the solid white spire was set off against a backdrop of great spruce and maples, and the lush Ontario fields of timothy and alfalfa stretched away on all sides. But the bulldozers have changed all that. Now the spire stands out against a stark brick cliff punctuated with great glass holes and harsh-angled steel protrusions. The churchyard is shaved to the size of a city lot. Instead of alfalfa fields, that no-man's land of barren, stony, weedy, rubbish-strewn ground which so pitilessly marks the line of advance of modern progress. Soon the church, too, will go: something less naive, more ingenious, more technologically satisfying — no doubt — will replace it. And it is the same everywhere. Downtown, where raw steel cages climb like fabulous mechanized beanstalks, far into the sky. Along the old highroads out of the city, where used-car lots and diners and delicatessens stretch mile after gaudy mile. In the new suburbs, where prosperity is just a payment away. In the mass housing developments, where forests of wire shade the slums of the future.

In all this there is cause for pride. And there is cause for regret, too. Architecturally perhaps the most regrettable thing is that when Toronto finally "goes modern," it goes for the "International Style" of modern architecture, the stark functional building promoted by the severe German theoreticians of the Bauhaus school in the 1920's. From these buildings it is obvious that this tendency to be retardataire, to take inspiration from more remote and artificial sources, rather than those that are close and natural, is not limited to the "new" Toronto; it is a characteristic common to all three Torontos depicted here.

* * * * *

Reviewed after many years, this introduction seems most dated by its lingering implication of architectural history as a parade of "styles" which "reflect" history. This needs to be corrected by more emphasis on social function.

By its nature, architecture is the most inappropriate of all artistic vehicles for personal self-expression; conversely, it is the art most typically created by and for Establishments, which alone command the time and resources required to build on any grand scale. Changing tastes in architecture are therefore most basically to be understood as political history in three dimensions.

"Styles" can be most succinctly defined as distinctive combinations of shapes and voids. As time passes, taste changes and these distinctive combinations change with it. But architectural history would be distorted by any implication that changing taste is the *cause* of changing styles. Neither are they to be explained as reflections of political or social or economic or intellectual life. Styles are shaped by, and manifest, social function. That is, they originate from and are determined by, what buildings *do* in and for society. And what historic architecture traditionally did was to create visual metaphors (by shape, by proportions and materials, and by eclectic forms) of those convictions on which all the institutions of any society must ultimately rest. Architectural design was the art of composing compelling symbols which would transmit from one generation to the next fundamental values; and convictions, so enabling cities, states, and societies to endure.

Thus, so far from reflecting political, social or religious trends, historic architecture should be understood as an instrument for shaping them. We should not rid our minds of any lingering comparisons with a modern avant-garde artist who sits down and muses, "My art must reflect the spirit of the times. Now what is the spirit of our times?. . ." If we must make modern comparisons, then make them with the political cartoonist or the popular/commercial designer, who works primarily to influence the population somehow, and employs artistic devices to further that end. Contemplating historic buildings may give us aesthetic delight; but we should always remember that they were not primarily built for any such purpose — any more than Greek pots or Baroque altarpieces were made to be installed in museums, or stained glass originally intended to be viewed like easel paintings. Historic High Architecture at all times and places was made to promote the convictions and interests of whatever Establishments commissioned them. It follows that what remains when these Establishments have gone the way of all things human is less to be seen as precious objects for connoisseurs, than as old farm machinery whose usefulness has gone, obsolete instruments for shaping history now left to litter odd corners in the fields of time.[1]

NOTES:

1. To develop this theme at any effective length goes far beyond the scope of this essay. For the past two years I have been engaged upon a study of the interrelationships of style and social function in North American architecture, first on a long research trip across North American sponsored by the Social Sciences and Humanities Research Council of Canada, then at the National Gallery of Art in Washington, D.C., on a fellowship from the Centre for Advanced Study in the Visual Arts. The complexities of this subject have been by no means exhausted yet.

V URBAN SOCIETY

The study of Canadian urban society is characterized by a diversity of approaches and topics. No one methodology or conceptual framework has been widely adopted. Still, it is possible to make several important generalizations based on the current state of research in this area.

It must first be noted that Canadian urban historians have not accepted the proposition, so prevalent in the United States, that urban history is a sub-discipline of social history.[1] Rather, Canadians have recognized that urban history is both more and less than social history. It is more in the sense that the history of urban centres — villages, towns, cities — touches on many topics beyond the scope of social history. It is less in the sense that the urban dimension represents only a portion of a total society. As well, Canadian urban historians, refreshingly, have not been unduly distracted by debates about precise definitions of fields and sub-fields, approaching urban history not as a discipline or sub-discipline in any exclusive sense, but rather as a field of knowledge in which many disciplines converge.

Related to this first generalization, and emphasizing the distinction in approaches between Canada and the United States, is the fact that a systematic approach to the study of urban social structure has not become widely adopted in Canada. While most historians recognize the contributions this kind of analysis can make, more conventional topics and approaches have remained more popular.[2] Thus the concepts and methods pioneered by Michael Katz in his path-breaking study of Hamilton remain an almost isolated approach in Canada.[3] There is, however, a growing concern that this kind of approach does deserve more attention, and some work has been done in this area. In addition to Sheva Medjuck's article in this volume, Chad Gaffield's historiographical article does indicate that a few historians have made significant contributions and that more research on such topics as demographic behaviour, transiency, occupational structure and social mobility can be expected.

While systematic analysis of urban social structure may not have "caught on" in Canada, the concept of "urban as process" has recently received a good deal of attention.[4] In this approach, the question is: How did the urban environment affect the people within it? Thus the city is regarded as an independent variable in some way influencing social organization and behaviour. Some of the best clues to understanding urban as process derive from Theodore Hershberg's Philadelphia project. He takes "work and residence as the basic building blocks of the physical and social environment,"[5] and suggests that major changes in these occur as the environments change. A growing body of Canadian urban history adopts, at least in part, this approach. It is represented in this volume by the work of Murray Nicolson and Carl Betke, but other material not included here can also be categorized as urban as process.[6]

Although studies of social structure and urban as process are proceeding slowly, there are many indications that studies of immigrants, women, and labour in an urban setting are proceeding more rapidly. It is apparent that many topics and places still need attention but much progress has been made. In addition to the articles by Robert Harney and Alan Artibise in this volume, Harney and Harold Troper have edited two special journal issues on "Immigrants in the City," and a recent urban bibliography includes numerous entries on immigrants and ethnicity.[7] Studies of women and workers in an urban context are also growing in number and complexity.[8] In many cases, these studies adopt an "urban as setting" approach; that is, the city itself is not the central concern but merely a backdrop or arena within which subjects can be discussed. This observation is not meant to denigrate such studies for they can be of considerable importance to the urban historian. However, it is important to note that urban as setting studies differ substantially from urban as process studies, even though both may deal with the same subject.

The approaches and examples described and listed here provide a loose framework for an understanding of the historical development of urban society. But one should not conclude that subsequent work in this area will fit neatly into any of the patterns outlined here. Indeed, it is to be hoped that students of urban society — while aware of the observations, insights, methods, and conclusions of those who preceded them — will follow the leads of their own evidence.

NOTES:

1. See, for example, several of the interviews in Bruce Stave, *The Making of Urban History:*

Historiography Through Oral History (Beverly Hills: Sage, 1977). See also Bruce Stave, "A Conversation with Gilbert A. Stelter: Urban History in Canada," *Journal of Urban History*, Vol. 6 (1980), pp. 177-210.

2. See Gaffield, "Social Structures and the Urbanization Process," in this volume.

3. Michael B. Katz, *The People of Hamilton, Canada West: Family and Class in the Mid-Nineteenth Century* (Cambridge, Mass.: Harvard University Press, 1975), and Katz, Michael B. Doucet, and Mark J. Stern, *The Social Organization of Early Industrial Capitalism* (Cambridge, Mass.: Harvard University Press, 1982).

4. For a discussion of "urban as process," see the introduction to Alan F.J. Artibise and Gilbert A. Stelter, *Canada's Urban Past: A Bibliography to 1980 and a Guide to Canadian Urban Studies* (Vancouver: University of British Columbia Press, 1981).

5. Theodore Hershberg, "The New Urban History: Toward an Interdisciplinary History of the City," *Journal of Urban History*, Vol. 5 (1978), p. 12.

6. See, for example, Peter Goheen, *Victorian Toronto, 1850-1900: Pattern and Process of Growth* (Chicago: University of Chicago, Research Paper No. 127, 1970).

7. See *Urban History Review*, No. 2-78 (October 1978); and *Canadian Ethnic Studies*, Vol. 9, No. 1 (1977). Also, see entries for immigration and ethnicity in Artibise and Stelter, *Canada's Urban Past: A Bibliography and Guide*.

8. On women, see the Cross article in this volume and several of the articles in M. Stephenson, ed., *Women in Canada* (Toronto: General Publishing, 1977) and S.M. Trofimenkoff and A. Prentice, eds., *The Neglected Majority: Essays in Canadian Women's History* (Toronto: McClelland and Stewart, 1977). On labour, see Bryan D. Palmer, *A Culture in Conflict: Skilled Workers and Industrial Capitalism in Hamilton, Ontario, 1860-1914* (Montreal: McGill-Queen's, 1979), and Gregory S. Kealey, *Toronto Workers Respond to Industrial Capitalism, 1867-1892* (Toronto: University of Toronto Press, 1980).

The People of a Canadian City, 1851-1852*

MICHAEL B. KATZ

On an average day in 1851 about 14,000 people awoke in Hamilton, Ontario. Most of them were quite unremarkable and thoroughly ordinary. In fact, there is no reason why the historian reading books, pamphlets, newspapers, or even diaries and letters should ever encounter more than seven hundred of them. The rest, at least ninety-five out of every hundred, remain invisible. Insofar as most written history is concerned, they might just as well have never lived.

One consequence of their invisibility has been that history, as it is usually written, represents the record of the articulate and prominent. We assume too easily, for example, that the speeches of politicians reflected the feelings and conditions of ordinary people. Another consequence is that we lack a

SOURCE: *Canadian Historical Review*, Vol. LIII, No. 4 (December 1972), pp. 402-426. Reprinted by permission of the author and the University of Toronto Press. A revised version of this paper appears in the author's book, *The People of Hamilton, Canada West: Family and Class in a Mid-Nineteenth Century City* (Cambridge: Harvard University Press, 1975), which contains extensive discussions of the themes touched upon here. For the most complete description of Hamilton's social structure, see Michael B. Katz, Michael J. Doucet, and Mark J. Stern, *The Social Organization of Early Industrial Capitalism* (Cambridge, Mass.: Harvard University Press, 1982).

* The research on which this essay is based has been entirely supported by the Ontario Institute for Studies in Education. The project is official titled "The Study and Teaching of Canadian Social History" (The Canadian Social History Project, for short).

foundation on which to construct historical interpretation. It was, after all, the activities, interactions, and movements of these invisible men and women that formed the very stuff of past societies. Without a knowledge of how they lived, worked, behaved, and arranged themselves in relation to each other our understanding of any place and point in time must be partial, to say the least. A third consequence is that we apply contemporary assumptions to past society. We use our everyday experience of modern social relationships to make models which we apply to the past. We believe, for instance, that we are more sophisticated than our ancestors about sex, marriage, and the spacing of children. As a result, we imagine that they must have married younger than we do today and reproduced as fast as nature would allow. Both of these assumptions, as it happens, are generally quite untrue.

The problem, of course, is evidence. How are we to write with meaning of the life of an ordinary labourer, shoemaker, or clerk in a nineteenth-century city? Or trace the most common patterns between important social features such as occupation, wealth, religion, ethnicity, family size, and school attendance? Those questions may be answered more directly and in a more straightforward manner than we have often imagined, as I hope to make clear in the rest of this essay. My purpose is twofold: first to show the range of questions about ordinary nineteenth-century people that may be asked and answered, and second, to sketch what, at this juncture, I take to be the primary social and demographic patterns within a mid-nineteenth-century Canadian city. The two great themes of nineteenth-century urban history, I shall argue, are transiency and inequality; I shall devote a section of this paper to each and, as well, to the nature of the family and household. For differences in family and household structure reflected, in part, the broad economic distinctions within urban society.

At the beginning two caveats are necessary: the quantitative information presented here is only partial; it is drawn from a great many detailed tables.[1] Second, figures given here are approximate. Such must be the case with all historical data. However, and this is the important point, the magnitudes, the differences between groups, may be taken, I believe, as a fair representation of the situation as it existed.

The manuscript census is the most valuable source of information about people within nineteenth-century cities. Its value is enhanced by its arrangement because it provides a list of features not only for each individual but for each household as well. For individuals the census from 1851 onward lists, among other items, name, age, birthplace, religion, occupation, school attendance, and birth or death within the year. It provides a residential location for each household and a description of the kind of house occupied; it permits the differentiation of relatives from non-relatives and the rough delineation of the relationships of household members to each other. In some cases it provides information about the business of the household head by listing other property, such as a store or shop owned, and number of people employed. Assessment rolls supplement the manuscript census with detailed economic information, usually about each adult member of the workforce. The assessment lists income over a certain level, real property, personal property, and some other economic characteristics. As well, it lists the occupation of each person assessed, the owner of the dwelling, and hence, whether the individual was an owner or renter of property. (In some instances a man who rents one house or store owns another; in other cases individuals own property around the city. These bits of information about individuals may be gathered together to present a more complete economic profile.) Published city directories corroborate the information from other sources and provide, additionally, the exact residential address of people and, in the case of proprietors, the address of their business if outside the home. Directories include, additionally, listings of people in various important political, financial, and voluntary positions within the city. Many other sources which list information about ordinary people supplement the census, assessment, and directory. Newspapers are the richest of these; mined systematically they yield an enormous load of information about the activities of people within the city. There are marriage records, church records, records of voluntary societies and educational institutions, cemetery records, and listings of other sorts as well. Each of these sources may be studied by itself and the patterns it presents analysed and compared with those found in other places. It is most exciting and rewarding, however, to join records together. By finding the same individuals listed in different records it is possible to build up rich and well-documented portraits of the lives of even the most ordinary of people.[2]

The project on which this essay rests uses all of the various records described above. Its most general purpose is to analyze the impact of industrialization on urban social structure and social mobility, using Hamilton, Ontario, as a case study. It deals with the years 1851 through, at the least, 1881; its basis is coded information about all, and not a sample, of the individuals listed in the kinds of sources described above, studied at differing intervals.

This essay discusses, primarily, the early 1850s. Its principal sources are, specifically, the manuscript census of 1851, the assessment roll of 1852 (compiled three months after the census), the city director of 1853 (the first published within the city), the marriage registers of 1842-69, and two local newspapers, one for both 1851 and 1852 and one for 1852.[3] In some instances the analysis rests on one source alone, in others on sources combined.

The sources for Hamilton as well as studies of American cities make clear that the first great theme of a nineteenth-century city is transiency. The most careful students of transiency to date, Stephen Thernstrom and Peter Knights, conclude from their study of Boston that far more people lived within the city in the course of a year than the census taker could find present at any specific time. The census listed the population of Boston as 363,000 in 1880, and as 448,000 in 1890. However, during those ten years the authors estimate that about one and one-half million different people actually lived within the city. Elsewhere Knights has estimated that twice as many artisans in some crafts plied their trade within the city in the course of a year as might be found there at any given moment. Eric Hobsbawm's tramping artisans, quite obviously, were a North American as well as a British phenomenon.[4]

The same transiency characterized the population of Hamilton. At this point it is not possible to provide exact figures or to say more than that transiency was a mass phenomenon. We do so on the following evidence. The assessment roll of 1852 listed 2552 people. Through careful linkage by hand (later replicated by computer) we have been able to join only 1955 of them to people listed on the census, which, as mentioned above, had been taken three months earlier. (There is no reason to assume that the intervening three months were unusual in any way.) Even with a generous allowance for error, large numbers of people could not be found because they had moved into the city during the intervening three months. In the same way a comparable percentage of household heads listed on the census could not be found three months later on the assessment. Most of them had left the city. Similarly, fewer than half the people on census or assessment could be found listed in the city director compiled about a year and a half later, and there were a great many people listed on the directory and not on either census or assessment. Death records point to the same conclusion. Each household head was required to record on the census the name of any person within his household who had died during the preceding year. However, Hamilton cemetery and church records for both 1851 and 1861 reveal that the number of people who actually died within the city far exceeded the number recorded on the census. Only a few can be linked to families resident within the city at the time the census was taken.[5] In most instances the families apparently had left the city. It is difficult to estimate the number of deaths that fall into this category; certainly it is not less than a number half again as large as the number of deaths recorded on the census.

The population, this evidence suggests, contained two major groupings of people. The first consisted of relatively permanent residents who persisted within the city for at least several years. This group comprised between a third and two-fifths of the population. The remainder were transients, people passing through the city, remaining for periods lasting between a few months and a few years.

Many of the transients were heads of households, not, as we might suspect, primarily young men drifting around the countryside. The age distribution among the transient heads of household closely resembled that among the more permanent. If anything, the transients on the average were very slightly older. Nor, as one might expect, were the transients all people of little skill and low status. The percentage of labourers among the transients (15 percent) was only slightly higher than among the more permanent residents. Indeed, there were many people with skilled or entrepreneurial jobs who moved from place to place; the transients included twenty-four merchants, fifty-eight clerks, seven lawyers, fifty-one shoemakers, twenty-eight tailors, and so on.

Although the transients approximated the rest of the population in age and occupation, they differed in one critical respect: wealth. Within every occupational category, the people who remained within the city were wealthier.[6] Thus, it was the *poorer* merchants, shoemakers, lawyers and, even, the poorer labourers who migrated most frequently. All of this points to the coexistence of two social structures within nineteenth-century society: one relatively fixed, consisting of people successful at their work, even if that work was labouring; the other a floating social structure composed of failures, people poorer and less successful at their work, even if that work was professional, drifting from place to place in search of success.[7]

The significance of the existence of transiency as a key feature of social structure in both Boston, Massachusetts, and Hamilton, Ontario, becomes evident from considering the fundamental differences between the two cities. Late nineteenth-century Boston had become an industrial city; mid-century Hamilton remained small, commercial, and pre-industrial. Yet both were filled, in Knights' and Thernstrom's phrase, with "men in motion"; transiency formed an integral and international feature of nineteenth century society and one not immediately altered by industrialization.

The relationship between workplace and residence underscores the pre-industrial nature of Hamilton. The separation of work and residence has been one of the most profound consequences of industrialization; the degree to which they remain united provides a rough guide to the extent of industrial development within a society. Contemporary sociologists contrast the organization of family and workplace by pointing to their basic structural differences in terms of authority relationships, criteria for rewards, and so on. They argue that people must play radically different roles in each setting. It becomes the task of the family and the school to teach the individual to make the transition between home and work and to learn to live with the sorts of internal switching required by a continual shifting from the personal and warm relations to the family to the impersonal, bureaucratic organization of work. This dichotomy in roles is a consequence of modern work organization. It came about as a result of the separation of residence and workplace. Its implication for the psychology of the individual person and for the functions of family and school are what make the shift of such profound significance.[8]

It is almost impossible to state precisely the proportion of men who were self-employed and the proportion who worked at their homes in Hamilton in the 1850s. What follows is a rough estimate of the minimum numbers in each category.[9] In 1851, 1142 male household heads were employees and 957 employers. Adding 1310 male adult boarders, almost all employees, gives a total male workforce of 3409 of which 2452 or 74 percent were not self-employed and 26 percent were. Given the approximate nature of the figures it would be unwise to claim more than that between a quarter and a third of the men within the city worked for themselves. Certainly, this is evidence enough to point to a contrast with contemporary industrial society.

Of those men who were self-employed about 137 (comprising roughly half of the proprietors of businesses and attorneys) worked away from their homes. Interestingly, if the proportion had been based on the number of *businesses*, not the number of proprietors, the proportion uniting work and residence would have been much higher. For many businesses were partnerships in which one member lived at the place of business, the other elsewhere. On the basis of this estimate approximately 14 percent of self-employed men worked away from their place of residence as did 72 percent of all employed males or 60 percent of household heads. Put another way, at least four out of ten households combined the function of place of work and place of residence for some of their members. That figure clearly demonstrates the pre-industrial character of life within the city.

Even though many people had to leave home each day to go to work, few spent their time in large, formal settings. Most people, regardless of where their job was done, worked in small groups. According to the census of 1851 (which is undoubtedly an underenumeration in this respect) there were within the city 282 artisan shops, offices and manufactories. The proprietors of over half of these (52 percent) listed no employees. A further twenty-five listed one and an additional sixty, between two and five employees. Only thirty places had between six and ten employees and but a handful had more than ten. This picture of smallness and informality is completed by the city government, which employed approximately fifteen people full-time, a few others part-time, and spent annually only about £18-20,000.[10]

The preceding discussion has described features of a nineteenth-century city that might be located almost anywhere in North America or Great Britain. There was, however, one feature of Hamilton that marked it as distinctively Canadian and, at the same time, adds more evidence to the theme of transiency; this was the birthplaces of its residents. Only about 9 percent of Hamilton's workforce had been born in Canada West. The rest were immigrants, about 29 percent from England and Wales, 18 percent from Scotland, 32 percent from Ireland, 8 percent from the United States, and the rest from elsewhere. Hamilton in 1851 was an immigrant city and so it remained for at least a decade, as the figures for the birthplace of household heads in 1861 reveal. It was, thus, in a double sense that the people of Hamilton were "men in motion." At a very basic level, the origins of their people, early Canadian cities differed fundamentally from ones in the United States and Great Britain. The consequences of this demographic difference might provide a fruitful perspective from which to begin the comparative study of national development and of national character.

The immigrants to Hamilton did not gather themselves into ghettos. On the basis of indexes of segregation used by both sociologists and historians, the degree of residential clustering by ethnicity, religion, and wealth appears slight, a feature apparently characteristic of Philadelphia and Boston in the same period as well. Nonetheless, there were some broad economic differences between regions of the city. It is possible to distinguish three zones: a core district, a district surrounding the core, and an outer district. The core zone had disproportionately few poor, 9 percent, and disproportionately many well-to-do people, 45 percent. In the outer district that situation was reversed: 32 percent of the people there were poor and 24 percent well-to-do. In the middle district over half the people were of average wealth and 18 percent poor. This pattern reflects what other scholars have described as the typical residential patterns within a nineteenth-century city before the coming of urban transport systems, a pattern that changed when the well-to-do were able to move to the suburbs and the poor clustered in downtown ghettos.[11]

Despite these trends, people of all degrees of wealth lived in close proximity to each other, the poor and the affluent intermingling on the same streets far more, probably, than they do at present. Indeed, it is clear already the extent to which the nineteenth-century city differed from the urban environment which we know today. The transiency, the newness, and the intermingling of its population, the small scale of its enterprise, the high degree of self-employment, and the continued unity of work and residence: all define a situation which our own experience of urban life prepares us poorly to comprehend, but which, as historians, we must try to recapture.

In fact, it is easy to be nostalgic about small pre-industrial cities. The absence of large-scale industry, the informality of government, and the lack of bureaucratic forms suggest an urban style both more cohesive and personal than that which we know today. We can imagine them, without too much difficulty, as filled with less tension and more warmth than contemporary cities, as stable, neighbourly, and easy places in which to live, as communities in a sense in which urban places have ceased to be. Unfortunately, the image just emerging from close, empirical study of nineteenth-century cities does not support the nostalgic vision. From one perspective it is partly contradicted by the facts of transiency, which we have already observed. The continual circulation of population prevented the formation of stable and closely integrated communities within nineteenth-century cities. At the same time, sharp inequalities in wealth and power reinforced the pressures of population mobility against cohesion and integration; together they made the nineteenth-century city, even before industrialization, a place at least as harsh, as insecure, and as overwhelming as urban environments today.

It is scarcely novel to assert that sharp inequalities existed within nineteenth-century cities or to posit a sharply graduated rank ordering of people. What should be stressed about that inequality is this: first, it may have been greater even than we have imagined; second, it underlay other social differences between people, such as household size and attitudes toward education; third, it shaped political patterns and processes. In short, the division of people on most social measures corresponded to the economic differences between them. Social, political, and economic power overlapped and interlocked, creating a sharply divided society in which a small percentage of the people retained a near monopoly on all the resources necessary to the well-being of the rest.

There are various ways with which to measure the division of wealth within a community, and each one, each scale that is adopted, yields a different result.[12] One division is property ownership: about one quarter of the population owned all the real property within the city. Roughly three-quarters of the people rented their living accommodations and owned no other real property whatsoever. The most affluent 10 percent of the population held about 88 percent of the wealth represented by the possession of property. From a slightly different perspective, people in the top 10 *income* percentiles (as reported on the assessment) earned nearly half the income within the city, and this figure, for a variety of reasons, is undoubtedly greatly understated. At the other extreme the poorest 40 percent earned a little over 1 percent of the income. Measured on a third scale, one designed to show economic ranking, the pattern of inequality is similar. On this scale "wealth" is a construct of different items and does not correspond exactly to either total income or assessed property; it is, however, the best available indicator of economic rank. On the basis of this measure, the wealthiest tenth of the people controlled about 60 percent of the wealth within the city and the poorest two-fifths about 6 percent.

The scale of economic ranking also reveals differences between the wealth of the various sectors of the city's economy. The people engaged in building, about 14 percent of the workforce (indicating the rapid expansion of the city), held only about 7 percent of the city's wealth; similarly, those engaged in some form of manufacturing (primarily artisans), about one-quarter of the workforce, had only 15 percent of the wealth. Likewise, as might be expected, the unskilled and semi-skilled labourers, about 22 percent of the workforce, had less than 5 percent of the wealth. At the other extreme those engaged in professions, about 4 percent of the workforce, held over 7 percent of the wealth, and the men in commerce, about a quarter of the workforce, controlled nearly 59 percent of the wealth, a figure which underscores the clear commerical basis of the city.

Religious and ethnic groups, like the various sectors of the economy, shared unequally in the city's wealth. Of the various immigrant and religious groups, the Irish and the Catholics fared worst. It is fair, I have argued elsewhere, to consider as poor the people in the lowest forty economic ranks. Using this criterion, 47 percent of the working population born in Ireland were poor as were 54 percent those who were Catholic. This, of course, is not a surprising finding. On the other hand it might be supposed that the English and the Anglicans were disproportionately wealthy, but this was not the case. Both groups formed a microcosm of the larger social structure, distributed quite normally among different economic categories.[13] The Free Church Presbyterians did rather better but the most affluent group, considering both numbers who were poor and numbers who were well-to-do, were the Wesleyan Methodists.[14] In terms of birthplace, the native Canadians and Americans fared best, a prosperity no doubt reflecting the problems of trans-Atlantic migration rather than inherent ethnic capacity or style. Of the Canadians 32 percent were well-to-do as were 31 percent of the Americans.[15]

It is difficult to associate economic rank with standard of living and to demarcate with precision the line separating the poor from the comfortable. To say that the fortieth economic rank marks the spot at which people ceased being poor means that it was the point at which they probably no longer had to struggle for and occasionally do without the necessities of life. Poverty in nineteenth-century cities did not mean the absence of luxuries, simple spartan living with good home grown food and sturdy home-sewn clothes. Poverty meant absolute deprivation: hunger, cold, sickness, and misery, with almost no place to turn for relief. The poor within Hamilton, it is important to remember, remained quite at the mercy of the well-to-do, who controlled not only employment opportunity but dispensed what little welfare there was as a gift, not as a right. The Ladies Benevolent Society, a voluntary and paternalistic body, formed in effect the city welfare department. Financed by charitable donations and grants from the City Council, it assigned teams of gracious ladies to roam the streets, locate the worthy poor, and dispense loaves of bread, sometimes coal and groceries, even occasionally rent. The City Council coped with massive numbers of immigrants overcrowding the combination hospital and poorhouse by transporting newly arrived Irish people in wagonloads to country towns where they were summarily left. Clearly, they believed such widespread poverty was only a temporary problem which could be solved by simple expedients that did not require the permanent and institutionalized extension of public responsibility for individual welfare.[16]

Aside from economic hardship, poverty in Hamilton meant powerlessness and invisibility. The lack of public provision for welfare reveals part of the powerlessness: the poor had no assistance on which they could draw as a right. Nor could they make their wants heard in any legal way, as the suffrage restrictions show. Less than half of the adult males in Hamilton owned or rented enough property to vote; 53 percent of all adult men, or 43 percent of household heads, could not meet the economic requirements for suffrage. Neither could 80 percent of the labourers, 56 percent of the artisans, or 59 percent of the business employees (primarily clerks). No working class political protest could be expressed through the ballot in Hamilton; most of the working class simply lacked the vote. The invisibility that accompanied powerlessness is harder to demonstrate; its existence has come to light by comparing the records of the Ladies Benevolent Society with the manuscript census. The former contain a month by month listing of the recipients of welfare. Early checking to find these names on the census, even for the very month in which the census had been taken, located very few of them. Perhaps they were simply passed by, a blot on the city it was as well, if possible, to ignore.

Even within a relatively simple society like Hamilton's, the affluent had tangible means of demonstrating their degree of success. One was the employment of servants. It was at the 80th economic rank that a family became more likely than not to employ domestic help, and the likelihood increased with each higher rank on the scale. Overall, about one-quarter of the families in Hamilton had a servant living with them. If Hobsbawm's assertion that the possession of a servant defined middle-class status applies to Canada as well as England, then the percentage of households without servants indicates, again, the magnitude of the working class in Hamilton.[17] Most of the servants, 60 percent, had been born in Ireland and 47 percent were Catholic. They were by and large young girls: slightly more than half were under twenty years old, and three-quarters were under twenty-five. Nearly nine out of ten servants were females, 93 percent unmarried, although some of the latter had children of their own. Families that employed servants were likely to live in a brick or stone house with two or more stories surrounded by an extra-large plot of land. The first two became, like the employment of servants, more likely than not at the 80th economic rank, the latter, size of plot attached to dwelling, increased most often at the 90th.

Household size also increased quite directly with wealth: to take one example, 15 percent of the households in the 20-40th ranks were large (eight or more members), compared to 30 percent of those in the 60-80th and 61 percent of those in the top 1 percent. There was, however, little relationship between wealth and number of children. Consequently, the presence of servants, boarders, and relatives accounted for the larger household size of the wealthy. In fact, servants, boarders, and relatives all lived more frequently with affluent than with poor families. School attendance also varied directly with economic standing. Families with no servants sent only slightly more than a third of their school age children to school; families with one servant sent just over half; families with more than one servant sent still larger proportions. Wealthier people also kept their children in school longer. Twenty-two percent of the fourteen-year-old children from families with no servants had attended school compared to 42 percent of those from families with one servant and 82 percent of those from families with two servants. The employment of servants, the occupancy of a large brick or stone house, a spacious plot of land, a large household, the steady and prolonged attendance of one's children at school: these, then, were the principal means through which the affluent demonstrated their success to their neighbours.

The affluent of the city solidified their economic control with political power. First of all, as we have already observed, property qualifications excluded most of the poor from voting. Moreover, the wealthy monopolized local political offices. Despite the fact that nearly 30 percent of elected city officials called themselves by an artisan title, most were wealthy. They were by no means workingmen as we usually employ that term. Of the elected officials, nearly 70 percent were in the top ten economic ranks; 83 percent were in the top twenty. In the two years 1851-2, 42 percent of the wealthiest 1 percent of the workforce held political office.

To understand the exercise of power within the city it is necessary to grasp the extent of overlap between membership in elite positions. Measured grossly from listings in the newspaper, the overlap between membership in three elites — people elected to city political offices, business officials, and officers of voluntary societies — is striking and, beyond question, statistically significant.[18] Of the forty-eight elected city officials, for instance, fifteen were business officials, twenty-one officers of voluntary societies, and eight jurors. Of the 130 business officials, fifteen were elected city officials, forty-one officers of voluntary societies, thirty-six petitions (asking the city for favours), and twelve jurors. Among 196 officers of voluntary societies (a very high figure suggesting an extraordinarily important role for voluntary activity with this society), twenty-one were elected city officials, forty-one business officials, eight appointed city officials, six school trustees, and eighteen jurors. Of the seventy-four jurors who served during 1851 and 1852, eight were elected city officials, twelve were business officials, and one was an elected city official. Ten people were elected city officials, business officials, and officers of voluntary societies simultaneously.

Measures designed to test statistical significance — to see whether or not the results described above could have occurred by change — tell the same story. The relationships were strong and real. The unmistakable overlap between elites underlines the interconnections between economic, political, and social power within this nineteenth-century city. More than that, the relation of people in elite positions with petitioners and jurors is revealing. A poor or unimportant man in Hamilton, it is quite clear, lacked the temerity to ask the city for favours, and, in fact, if he incurred its displeasure he was not even tried by a jury of his peers.[19]

Just as poverty and powerlessness brought invisibility, so did affluence and power make a man visible. On the basis of their mention in local newspapers it is possible to divide the people of the city into three groups according to their "visibility": those "invisible" (not mentioned in the newspapers at all) or about 94 percent of the population in 1851; those moderately "visible" (mentioned once or twice); and those highly "visible," mentioned five or more times, about 1 percent of the population. Who then were the highly visible people? They were, as might be expected from the foregoing analysis, the members of the interlocking elites. Highly visible people comprised more than half of the following categories: city and county officials, appointed city and county officials, business officials, officers of voluntary societies, school trustees, petitioners, jurors, advertisers, union members (only six were mentioned in the newspapers at all), political committee members, and people publicly honoured. Interestingly, as with the case of overlap between various sorts of officeholders, jurors and petitioners interconnect with the most powerful men within the city.[20]

These interconnections between kinds of power within Hamilton pose important comparative questions. Did economic, social, and political power exist in a closer relationship at that time than they do at present? What impact did industrialization have upon their relationship to each other? Is the curve of inequality steady over time, or, did it widen in the initial stages of industrialization and then diminish in the twentieth century? Whatever the answers to these questions turn out to be, the detailed examination of the distribution of income and power should help dispel any lingering nostalgia about the existence of equality and community in nineteenth-century cities.

Detailed examination of actual cases also dispels a number of common notions about families in pre-industrial society. It is often thought that the nuclear family emerged as a consequence of industrialization, that in early times people married at very young ages, and that the poor, especially, had very large families. None of these propositions are true. There were clear relations between transiency and inequality, the two great themes of the nineteenth-century city, and the domestic arrangements of its people. However, to some extent the family and household exhibited characteristics partially independent of wealth and related rather (sometimes at this stage of research inexplicably) to other measures. Thus, it is important to consider family and household structure by themselves.

We may begin with the formation of the family through marraige. The statistics are based upon the marriage registers for Wentworth County for the years 1842-69.[21] Marriage patterns within Wentworth County were endogamous. Of 5327 brides, 4443 resided in Wentworth County as did 4026 of the same number of grooms. It is to be expected that most brides would be from Wentworth County, since marriage customarily takes place at the bride's residence. What is more notable is the small proportion of local girls who married men from outside the county. Nevertheless, the majority of marriages throughout the period involved people who had both been born outside of Ontario and, indeed, outside of Canada.

For the most part the figures for age of marriage contradict our stereotypes of early marriage among the people of pre-industrial society. The mean age of marriage for men was 27.7, the median 25.7; 61 percent of grooms were twenty-five years old or over; 25 percent were over 30. Brides were considerably younger, about four years on the average. Their mean marriage age was 23.2 and the median 21.8. Just over one-quarter of the girls married before they were twenty and 72 percent had married by the time they were twenty-five.[22] Both religion and birthplace influence marriage age, though of the two birthplace appeared strongest. Younger marriages were slightly more common among Baptists and 'Protestants' and later marriages more common among Presbyterians. Similarly, the Scottish people married notably later than other groups.[23] People born in Canada West married youngest by far, and there were no unusual distributions of age among brides and grooms born in England, the United States, or, contrary to what might be expected, Ireland.[24]

Figures for births, like those for marriage, do not support common notions about Catholic families. From what we can tell at this point, the birth-rate among Catholics or Irish born people was no higher than among the population as a whole. What appears striking from an analysis of the births listed in the 1851 manuscript census is the congruence between the percentage of total births in the city occurring among a particular group and that group's percentage of the total population. Thus, Catholics aged 20-29 formed 18 percent of the household heads of that age group within the city; to them occurred 18 percent of the births among that age group. The poor form 26 percent of the household heads; they had 27 percent of the births. It would be tedious to continue to present these figures; with one exception they remain the same for ethnicity, religion, and wealth. That exception, and an interesting one, is the people born in French Canada, who formed a tiny 0.4 percent of the 20-29-year-olds but accounted for 2 percent of the births, a disproportion consistent with trends in French-Canadian demography.[25]

This initial survey of Hamilton's demography would be incomplete without some mention of death and death rates. At this juncture it is not possible to discuss the relations between death rate, age at death, and other social variables, such as religion, ethnicity, and wealth. We do know that the infant mortality rate was staggeringly high. Of 210 people recorded as having died on the census, 106 or 51 percent were five years old or younger; all but twenty-one, or 10 percent, were under the age of fifty.

Figures for the number of children within a household are generally, though not completely, consistent with the statistics of marriage and birth. Amongf the heads of households as a whole 55 percent had small families (0-2 children); 36 percent had medium sized families (3-5 children), and 10 percent had large families (6 or more children). Any discussion of family size is affected by the age distribution of the population. In order that we may have a fair basis of comparison I shall restrict the following discussion to heads of household aged 40-49, those whose families were both complete and, to the largest extent, still living together. Of the 40-49-year-old household heads, 37 percent had small families, 44 percent medium sized ones, and 18 percent larger numbers of children.

First of all, as with births, family size among the 40-49-year-olds shows little relation to wealth.[26] The poor did not breed more quickly than the rest of the population. In fact the only discernible relation between wealth and number of children works in the other direction. Among the heads of household as a whole 0.3 percent of the very poorest people, those in the bottom twenty economic percentiles, had a large number of children compared to 15 percent of those in the 95-99th percentiles. Among the 40-49-year-old household heads the poorest men had no children about twice as often as most other groups; they had the smallest percentage of medium-sized families of any group. Considering all ages together, the mean number of children among the poorest 20 percent of household heads was 0.54 and, among the wealthiest 1 percent, 3.32. In between, however, scores are quite similar. One other difference, which relates to economic standing, shows the same trend. Transients, who were poorer than those people we consider more permanent residents, had a slightly lower mean number of children despite their similarity in age.

An examination of the mean number of children among 40-49-year-old household heads highlights some ethnic and religious distinctions generally unrelated to wealth. North Americans, natives of Canada West and the United States, had small families. The lowest mean score, 2.40, was that of the Americans, followed by the Canadians, the English, the Irish, and the Scottish in that order.[27] These figures reflect the late marriage age of Scottish people, which we observed earlier.[28] Among religious groups those with heavily Scottish membership rank high in mean number of children among 40-49-year-olds.[29] At the other end of the scale, the denomination with the smallest mean family size, the Baptist, is heavily American in origin.[30] The mean size for the Catholics, it might be pointed out, was quite average for the 40-49-year-olds, although their mean for the 20-29 year olds was the highest in that cohort, which indicates that Catholics had more of their children when they were younger, not, as is often thought, that they had a great number in all than did other groups.[31]

The mean family size of different occupational groups reveals more systematic differences. The means for all merchants and clerks were 1.78 and 1.91. For bakers, blacksmiths, carpenters, shoemakers, tinsmiths, and labourers the means were 2.69, 2.96, 2.78, 2.34, 2.89, and 2.89 respectively. Quite clearly, the entrepreneurial white collar groups had fewer children than men who worked with their hands. In this respect it is the line separating the people engaged in commerce from those following the trades that counts most. Distinctions between skilled and unskilled workers appear to matter but little. More than that, the difference in number of children appears more related to kind of work performed that it does to wealth. The mean number of children, as we have observed, varied but little with economic rank, and the relations between occupation and wealth were not as tidy as we might expect, as we have noticed in the case of elected city officials. In fact, there was usually a great variation in wealth between individuals in the same trades. Thus, on the basis of the evidence at hand, it is entirely reasonable to suppose that the aspiring business classes had begun to practice some form of family limitation.[32]

There were distinctions, it is critical to note, between the family size of people engaged in commerce and other non-manual workers. Relatively small family size remained more a hallmark of men with an entrepreneurial outlook than a badge separating white and blue collar workers in our modern sense. This becomes apparent from the mean family size of other, non-entrepreneurial and non-manual groups: the mean family size of teachers, for instance, 3.71, was the highest of any group; the mean for gentlemen was 2.89, the same as for labourers and tinsmiths; and the mean for lawyers fluctuated strangely with age. For lawyers in their forties it was 6.00. All of this suggests that limiting the number of his offspring had become linked in the mind of the aspiring entrepreneur with increasing his wealth. The source of that idea is particularly important to lcoate. For, if the facts that I have presented here are correct, he would not have learned it from the world around him where, in fact, the most successful men did not have small families.

As we have observed already, the mark of a wealthy man was the size of his household, not the number of his children. That household was composed of boarders, servants, relatives, and visitors in addition to husband, wife, and children. There were fewer extended families in this pre-industrial city than we might have expected; relatives other than husband, wife, and children lived in only 15 percent of the households. Like the families Peter Laslett and his associates have studied in England over a period of four hundred years, the ones in Hamilton were overwhelmingly nuclear. As with servants, relatives lived most frequently in the households of the well-to-do; they were present in 4 percent of the poorest 20 percent of the households and in 24 percent of those in the 95-99th economic ranks.[33]

The same is true of boarders, who were found in 28 percent of the households. They lived, however, with 8 percent and 15 percent respectively of the families in the 0-20th and 20-40th economic ranks and with 46 percent of those in the 90-95th. There were boarders, in fact, in more than four out of ten households in each group above the 80th economic rank. This finding is somewhat surprising. We might suppose, offhand, that boarders would be most likely to live with poorer families, who needed the extra income they could provide. But this was not the case. It prompts us to look closely at exactly who boarders were and at their place within the household.

The presence of boarders in so many households reflects an important characteristic of social life: it was extremely unusual for people to live alone; everyone was expected to live within a family grouping. Not much more than 1 percent of the workforce lived by themselves. Large numbers of young unmarried people living alone is clearly a modern development. This pattern of residence, moreover, constituted an informal system of social control. For young men a close supervision and a constant scrutiny of their behaviour constituted the other side of the warmth of living in a family grouping. Boarding the young men of the town provided the affluent with a convenient means of keeping a close check on their behaviour.

Most of the boarders, 71 percent, were men; 14 percent were married. This accounts in large part for the women and children who were listed as boarders. Like the servants, boarders were young, though not quite so young: 34 percent were under twenty and a further 52 percent between twenty and twenty-four years old; 84 percent were under thirty. They came more often from Ireland than from elsewhere, in 43 percent of the cases, but many, 19 percent, had been born in Canada West, a disproportionately large number considering that men from Canada West made up only a bit more than 9 percent of the workforce. These boarders were, perhaps, young migrants to the city from rural areas. A little over one-third of the boarders were Catholic, the largest single figure for any denomination, and the rest were scattered among other religious groups. Boarders followed a staggering variety of occupations. Many of them, about 54 percent, were craftsmen of one sort or another; of the remainder, about 13 percent were labourers and 8 percent clerks. Spinsters, widows, and women following domestic occupations like dressmaking frequently boarded as did some young professionals, nine lawyers and seven physicians probably establishing themselves in practice.

It appeared likely, from these figures, that many boarders were young men living with their employers in households that combined work and residence. However, a close comparison of the occupations of boarders and their landlords demolished that hypothesis. It is extremely difficult to determine if a boarder and a household head might have worked together. Occupational terminology is vague and sometimes misleading. But in most cases it was clear that no reasonable connection could be made. Not only occupation but class seemed to make little difference. Labourers lived with judges, physicians, attorneys, and gentlemen, as well as with fellow labourers, moulders, and widows. Widows, in fact, took in many boarders, obviously a way to make a little money. Other than that, there seems little pattern in the distribution of boarders by occupation. Over all, slightly over 9 percent of the boarders might have been living with their employers.

Other obvious principles on which boarders might have selected their residence are religion and ethnicity. Perhaps young men coming to the city looked for families of similar ethnic and religious backgrounds with whom to live, whatever their occupation might be. In most cases this did not happen. There was some tendency for Irish and for Catholic boarders to choose landlords of the same background, and a very slight tendency for the English and the Anglicans to do the same. But in no instance did those living with people of similar religious or ethnic backgrounds constitute a majority.

In short, it appears that other factors were more important in the choice of a lodging, probably convenience, price, and the presence of some friends already living there or nearby. The population of Hamilton, we must not forget, was expanding rapidly. The estimated growth between 1850 and 1852 was from ten to fourteen thousand. The practical implication of this must have been a severe strain on housing facilities. Perhaps rooms were in such short supply that people took whatever they could find. Perhaps, too, there was great pressure on anyone with a spare bed to take someone in. This is why so many of the more affluent, with larger houses, had boarders.

It is as important to discover the behavioural patterns associated with types of families and households as it is to determine their size and structure. There are, however, fewer indexes of behaviour than of structure on which to base systematic observations. One of the most readily available, and most interesting, is school attendance. The analysis of school attendance links parental attitudes to social, demographic, and economic measures and, as our data reveal, to family size as well. It thus provides a way of joining the family and household to the large social context in which they are embedded.[34]

Of all the children in the city aged 5-16 in 1851, 50 percent attended school at some point during the year. Rather more boys than girls attended at each age level. Very few children entered school before the age of six. At the age of six a third began to attend, but the ages from 7-13 were the period of heaviest school attendance, the proportion attending exceeding 40 percent only in each of those years. The peaks were reached between the ages of nine and eleven, the only time when more than half of the age group attended school.

Part of the variation in school attendance can be explained by family size. It is often thought that small families provide settings conducive to education. Indeed, twentieth-century studies have shown an inverse relation between school achievement, scores on intelligence tests, and family size. If our data have anything to contribute on this point, it is that the contemporary relationship did not hold within the nineteenth century. The percentage of school-age children attending school generally increased with the number of children in the family.[35] This relationship held even for the youngest and eldest children attending school: 3 percent of children aged 3-5 from families with two children attended school compared to 10 percent from families with five children; 18 percent of 15-16-year-old children from families with two children attended school compared to 23 percent from families with five children.

The birth-place of the head of household also affected school attendance. Irish fathers were least likely to send their children to school. The percentage of Irish children aged 5-16 attending school was under one-third. For two groups, however, it was over one-half; these were the Scottish and the native Canadians. The relations between religion and attendance reinforce these findings: fewer than 30 percent of Catholic children attended schools, compared to over 50 percent for Church of Scotland and Wesleyan Methodist and over 60 percent for Free Church Presbyterians. Scottish

Presbyterianism should obviously be added to family size as an important factor promoting school attendance.

So should wealth, as we observed earlier. Measuring wealth by the possession of servants, the relation with school attendance was striking. That relation supports the observations of school-promoters who perceived their problem as persuading poor families to school their children. Insofar as educational reform took its impetus from a perception of idle, vagrant children from poor homes wandering the streets, it was based on a very real situation.

The relations between occupation and school attendance spoil the neatness of the foregoing analysis, for they fail to adhere completely to the boundaries set by wealth, ethnicity, and relgion. Lawyers, for instance, sent few of their children to school. It is entirely possible that they hired private tutors. Tinsmiths, on the other hand, were exceptionally conscious of schooling; 85 percent of their school-age children attended school during 1851, a figure exceeded only by the children of teachers, 92 percent of whom had attended. Labourers, as could be expected, were at the bottom; less than one-quarter of their school-age children went to school in 1851, compared, for instance, to 46 percent of the children of merchants and 58 percent of the children of physicians. Differences between artisan groups parallel those between professionals; 38 percent of shoemakers' school-age children attended school, for instance, as did 54 percent of the children of cabinet-makers. There are at present no explanations for most of these differences.

Although school attendance often followed economic lines, it is clear that cultural and social factors intervened to make the pattern that finally emerged quite complex. Two of these factors are noteworthy: North Americans kept their children in school somewhat longer than other groups, and the relationship between wealth, Catholicism, Irish origin, and low school attendance did *not* hold among the very youngest age groups. Perhaps school served as baby-sitting agencies for large, poor families, relieving the parents of pressure at home and permitting the mother to work. At the same time affluent parents of large families may have realized that they were unable to teach at home certain basic skills, which it was traditional for children to learn before they started school at age seven. They may have used the school to remedy what, given the size of their families, would have had to be accomplished by a private tutor if their children were not to lag educationally.

But all conclusions must remain tentative at best. The most we can say is this: the people who most frequently sent children to school were well-to-do, had larger than average families, and had been born in Scotland or North America. Those sending fewest were poor, Irish Catholic, and labourers.

The same groups generally kept the most and the fewest children in school past the usual school leaving age. But the figures for early school attendance revealed slightly different rankings, which indicates that early schooling served important economic functions for some poor families and important psychological ones for large families. The relations between occupation and schooling are unclear, aside from the figures for labourers. Why did the lawyers send so few children? Why did the tinsmiths send so many? We cannot answer these questions at present; like so many of the findings discussed in this essay they remain beginnings, as much questions to be answered as conclusions.

Clearly family and household patterns in Hamilton were complex; they defy simple general descriptions. Equally clearly, they contradict many commonly held assumptions about pre-industrial families. Men and women married relatively late, later probably than most people do today. In the vast majority of instances they formed nuclear families, the more wealthy adding a servant, a boarder, or, in comparatively few instances, a relative. Almost everybody lived in a family, whether they were married or not, young or old. Within families there was relatively little difference in the number of children born to parents of different economic conditions. Ethnicity and religion, in fact, were more influential than wealth in determining age of marriage and number of children. The traditional image of the frugal, self-denying, and ambitious Scot emerges intact; the picture of the indulgent, overbreeding Irish Catholic is shattered. In fact, there were at least two types of households within the city. At one extreme was the Irish Catholic labourer living with his wife and two or three children in a one and a half story frame house. At the other extreme, but perhaps on the same street, was the prosperous merchant living with his wife, two or three children, a servant, and a boarder in a three story stone house surrounded by a spacious plot of land. Most other families fell somewhere in between. It will take a good deal more analysis to isolate other widespread family types, and a good deal of imaginative research into other sorts of sources to explain the results that emerge; to answer, that is, questions such as why did American Baptists have small families?

It is also important to ask if the relations between family size and ethnicity that existed in Hamilton were present in other Canadian cities as well. That, in turn, is part of the larger issue of representativeness. How can one know that the findings from Hamilton have meaning for any other place? From one viewpoint the question is irrelevant. Every city's history is both unique and at the same time representative of larger trends and forces. More than that, the relationships we wish to study can be investigated only on the local level. Even if Hamilton turns out to be less "representative" than one might wish, the study is important because it provides a datum with which to begin an analysis of what is special and what is general within nineteenth-century cities in Canada and elsewhere.

Hamilton was not representative of some things, quite obviously; for instance, it was not like villages and rural areas. On the other hand, it should have had a number of similarities to pre-industrial cities in nineteenth-century Britain and the United States. Most of all, it was not too unlike other cities in Canada West. That is clear from studying published census figures for a number of Canadian cities. It is striking to observe the extent of similarity between Kingston, London, Toronto, and Hamilton with respect to the birthplace and religion of their residents; their age structures and sex ratios; their birth and death rates; and, even, their occupational structures. On the basis of these similarities it is obvious that Hamilton was structurally similar to other cities in Canada West. On that basis we may conclude with some general observations about the nature of a pre-industrial Canadian city.[36]

First, even in the mid-nineteenth century a relatively small commercial city was an enormously complex place. Simple general statements about its society, families, or households are inadequate to the richness of its structural patterns. Economically, even before industrialization, Canadian cities were highly differentiated. Socially, they were highly stratified.

Second, the pre-industrial family was more a rational and "modern" organization than we have often suspected. Even at this early date people clearly related decisions about marriage and often about the size of their families to other, undoubtedly economic, considerations. The difference between the pre-industrial and modern family does not rest in structure; both are nuclear. It lies, rather, in the number of children born to the average couple and in the structure of the household, which in terms of size has lost its clear relation to affluence.

Third, in no sense can we think of pre-industrial cities as communities defined by stability, integration, and egalitarianism. The problem of inequality we have touched on above; the facts of transiency destroy any further illusions about community. The population simply changed too rapidly.

Fourth, the articulation of various structures with each other produced a powerful concentration of interlocking forms of power in the hands of a very small group of people. Household structure, political power, school attendance — the privileges that this society has to offer — all related to wealth. The distribution of men by economic rank corresponded to their division on most other social measures. Looked at another way, the business elite, the political elite, and the voluntary elite overlapped to a striking and significant extent. We know already that the political elite overlapped with the top rungs of the scale of economic rank. There is every reason to believe that the others did so as well.

The group that controlled economic, political, and social power within Hamilton contained at most 10 percent of the household heads. People within elite positions formed slightly more than 8 percent of men aged twenty and older. This figure is quite close to the 10 percent estimated elsewhere as wealthy. It is close, in fact, to the approximately 75 percent of elected city officials who we know to have been within the top ten income percentiles. Hence we can conclude that about 8 or 10 percent of the adult men, at the very maximum, controlled virtually all the resources necessary to the health, well-being, and prosperity of the rest.

In Hamilton the rulers, the owners, and the rich were by and large the same people. They clearly headed the stratification system. At the bottom the grouping was likewise clear: poor, propertyless, powerless men made up about 40 percent of the workforce or between a fifth and a quarter of the household heads. In between fell the rest. About 40 percent were marginal; they owned no property, they possessed no power, but they were prosperous enough to differentiate themselves from the poorest families. Their margin seems so slim and the consequences of falling so appalling, however, that these people must have lived always with great tension and great fear. Between them and the wealthy, comprising about a fifth of the families, was a qualitatively more affluent group. Most of them employed a servant and lived in a brick house, which they owned. They were likely to vote but still not very likely to hold political office.

These four groups existed within Hamilton in the middle of the nineteenth century. Using wealth, power, and ownership as dimensions on which to rank people, they form somewhat overlapping but nonetheless distinguishable clusters of people holding a similar position on each scale. Were they classes? That depends on the definition of class, which is a subject beyond the scope of this essay. Clearly, however, by whatever definition is followed it would seem difficult to deny that class was a fundamental fact of life in mid-nineteenth-century urban Canada.[37]

NOTES:

1. For detailed quantitative information see the first two interim reports of the project as well as subsequent working papers, all of which are available from the Department of History and Philosophy of Education of the Ontario Institute for Studies in Education. See also my essay, "Social Structure in Hamilton, Ontario" in Stephen Thernstrom and Richard Sennett, eds., *Nineteenth-Century Cities: Essays in the New Urban History* (New Haven and London, 1969), pp. 209-44. I have rounded all percentages in this essay to whole numbers. Considering the inexactness of historical data, this seems quite appropriate, especially when it increases ease of reading.

2. Record-linkage is one of the central technical problems of all studies similar to the one described here. For a discussion of the problem, and of our approach to it, see Ian Winchester, "The Linkage of Historical Records by Man and Computer: Techniques and Problems," *Journal of Interdisciplinary History*, I, 1, autumn 1970, pp. 107-24. The hand-linkage of the 1850 census, 1852 assessment, and 1853 directory was done by Mr. John Tiller, who also has done most of the coding of the 1851 census and assessment. I should like to acknowledge Mr. Tiller's continued and invaluable participation in this project.

3. The *Spectator* and the *Gazette*.

4. Stephen Thernstrom and Peter Knights, "Men in Motion: Some Data and Speculations about Urban Population Mobility in Nineteenth Century America," in Tamark K. Hareven, ed., *Anonymous Americans, Explorations in Nineteenth Century Social History* (Englewood Cliffs, N.J., 1971), pp. 17-47; Peter R. Knights, "Population Turnover, Persistence, and Residential Mobility in Boston, 1830-1860," in Thernstrom and Sennett, *Nineteenth-Century Cities*, pp. 258-74; E.J. Hobsbawm, "The Tramping Artisan" in his *Laboring Men: Studies in the History of Labour* (London, 1964), pp. 34-63.

5. Unpublished papers by Mrs. Judy Cooke and Mr. Dan Brock, OISE.

6. The mean assessed wealth of all the people engaged in commerce was £96; of the transients in commerce, £63; of resident professionals, £71; of transient ones, £21; of resident artisans, £25; of migrants, £13; of resident labourers, £9; of migrant ones, £7.

7. The existence of a similar phenomenon (a division of success within trades) is clearly revealed by Henry Mayhew's description of the organization of various trades in London in the middle of the nineteenth century. An example is the distinction between the "honorable" and "dishonorable" parts of the tailoring trade. See, E.P. Thompson and Eileen Yeo, *The Unknown Mayhew* (London, 1971), pp. 181-277, on tailors.

8. Robert Dreeben, *On What is Learned in Schools* (Reading, Mass. 1968), p. 95, provides an example of this point. See also Talcott Parsons and Robert F. Bales, *Family, Socialization and Interaction Processes* (Glencoe, Ill., 1955).

9. Not all employed men necessarily worked away from their homes. As Thompson and Yeo, *The Unknown Mayhew*, points out, it was common for manufacturers of various sorts to give work to craftsmen to perform in their own homes.

10. See, for example, Proceedings of the Council of the City of Hamilton, 22 Jan. 1851, pp. 398-9; 19 Jan. 1850, pp. 128-9, available on microfilm in the Public Archives of Ontario.

11. For a discussion of calculating the Index of Segregation see Karl E. Taeuber and Alma F. Taeuber, *Negroes in Cities: Residential Segregation and Neighbourhood Change* (Chicago, 1965), pp. 195-245; for the application of the index, see Leo F. Schmore and Peter R. Knights, "Residence and Social Structure: Boston in the Ante-Bellum Period," in Thernstrom and Sennett, *Nineteenth-Century Cities*, pp. 247-57, and Sam Bass Warner, Jr., *The Private City: Philadelphia in Three Periods of its Growth* (Philadelphia, 1968), p. 13. For studies of residential patterns in nineteenth-century cities, see also two recent monographs, David Ward, *Cities and Immigrants: A Geography of Change in Nineteenth Century America* (New York, 1971), and Peter Goheen, *Victorian Toronto* (Chicago, 1970).

12. I have discussed the construction of these scales in working paper no. 21, "The Measurements of Economic Inequality."

13. Fifty-one percent of the working population born in England and Wales were in the middle (40-80th) economic ranks as were 46 percent of the Anglicans.

14. Of the Free Church Presbyterians 26 percent were poor, compared to 16 percent of the Wesleyan Methodists. At the same time 31 percent of the Free Church Presbyterians were well-to-do (80-100th economic ranks) as were 29 percent of the Wesleyan Methodists.

15. Of the other major ethnic and religious groups, briefly: The Scottish-born were predominantly middle-income, much like the English; the adherents of the Church of Scotland, and those who called themselves simply Presbyterians, were likewise middling in terms of wealth,

except that the former had few wealthy adherents. The figures for Methodists were much like those for Presbyterians; and for Baptists, much like members of the Church of Scotland.

16. The records of the Ladies Benevolent Society are available in manuscript at the Hamilton Public Library. For the actions of the City Council with respect to immigrants see, eg, Proceedings of the Council, 20 Aug. 1849, p. 31; 10 Sept. 1849, pp. 149-50. On the institutionalization of poverty in the United States see the recent, provocative book by David Rothman, *The Discovery of the Asylum* (Boston, 1971).

17. E.J. Hobsbawm, *Industry and Empire* (London, 1969), p. 157.

18. Mrs. Anne-Marie Hodes coded the 1851 and 1852 newspapers for the project.

19. Only the top three-quarters of the assessed population were eligible to serve on the jury. I suspect that those actually chosen did not represent a cross-section of that group.

20. For the idea of constructing a scale of visibility I am indebted to the work of Professor Walter Glazer of Cincinnati.

21. The marriage registers were coded by Mrs. Margaret Zieman.

22. The figures are supported by those found for European countries. See, eg, Peter Laslett, "Size and Structure of the Household in England Over Three Centuries," *Population Studies*, XXIII, 2, July 1969, pp. 199-223.

23. Only 20 percent of Scottish grooms were less than twenty-five years old compared to 39 percent of all grooms, while 30 percent of Scottish grooms were in their 30s compared to 18 percent of all grooms.

24. Among people born in Canada West, 51 percent of the grooms, compared to 39 percent of all grooms, had been married before the age of twenty-five; of the brides, 82 percent, compared to 75 percent of all brides, had been married before they were twenty-seven years old.

25. For an overview of Canadian population history that makes this point, see *Census of Canada*, 1931, Chapters 2 and 3 of the excellent monograph on the family.

26. Of the poor, 18 percent had a large family; so did 20 percent of the middle-income and 21 percent of the well-to-do. Similarly 38 percent of the poor had a small number of children, as did 35 percent of the middle-rank and 38 percent of the well-to-do.

27. The means are as follows: US born, 2.40; Canadian, 3.18; English, 3.35; Irish, 3.52; Scottish, 4.01.

28. The Scottish rank third in mean number of children among 20-29-year-olds, fifth among 30-39, and first among the 40-49-year-old group.

29. Thus the mean for members of the Church of Scotland is 4.39 and for Free Church Presbyterians, 4.62.

30. The Baptist score is 2.17.

31. In fairness to traditional ideas it should be pointed out that very preliminary inspection of the 1861 results indicates a larger than average family size for Catholics and Irish. At this point the change is inexplicable.

32. For comparative figures on class and birth-control, see E.A. Wrigley's excellent book, *Population and History* (New York, 1969), pp. 186-7. On the method of studying birth-control in past societies, see E.A. Wrigley, "Family Limitation in Pre-Industrial England," *Economic History Review*, Second Series, XIX, I, 1966, 82-109. For more on the relation between status and birth control in the nineteenth century, see J.A. Banks, *Prosperity and Parenthood: A Study of Family Planning Among the Victorian Middle Classes* (London, 1954) and D.E.C. Eversley, *Social Theories of Fertility and the Malthusian Debate* (Oxford, 1959).

33. On general patterns of household size in England over four hundred years, see Laslett, "Size and Structure of the Household."

34. There has been amazingly little written on the history of school attendance. The only monograph in English that I know to be specifically devoted to the topic is David Rubenstein,

School Attendance in London 1870-1904: A Social History (Hull, 1969). See also my article, "Who went to School," *History of Education Quarterly*, XII, 3, fall 1972.

35. For families with two children it was, for instance, 42 percent; for families with five children, 61 percent. Similarly, the percentage of families which sent more than half their school-age children to school rose from 24 percent for families with one child to 35 percent for families with two, to 58 percent for families with five children, and 67 percent for families of seven.

36. Tables comparing these cities are in the project working paper no. 23.

37. I want to include a plea that more Canadian historians undertake empirical analyses of past social structures. Those who are interested but hesitant should gain some knowledge of how to proceed from two recent books: Edward Shorter, *The Historian and the Computer: A Practical Guide* (Englewood Cliffs, N.J. 1971), and Charles M. Dollar and Richard J. Jensen, *Historian's Guide to Statistics, Quantitative Analysis and Historical Research* (New York, 1971). Our team is continually developing a store of practical lore which we should be delighted to share with anyone venturing into related studies.

Family and Household Composition in the Nineteenth Century: The Case of Moncton, New Brunswick, 1851-1871.

SHEVA MEDJUCK

In recent years social historians have provided students of society with many new, and sometimes startling, insights into the conditions of people's lives in the nineteenth century. This study aims at adding to this reconstruction of the past by a case study of Moncton, New Brunswick from 1851 to 1871. Specifically, household and family structure in Moncton is examined in order to determine the validity of various theories about the effects of industrialization on household structure. In the first part of this paper, a review of major theoretical formulations is provided. This is followed by an examination of these formulations in light of empirical data from Moncton.

THEORIES OF THE DEVELOPMENT OF HOUSEHOLD AND FAMILY STRUCTURE

Sociologists have long recognized the significance of the family as a critical social organization for the transmission of societal values. The family, however, has boundaries that are highly malleable. As Anderson notes, the family can be seen as a recruitment base, selecting new members on the basis of blood or marriage ties, and having a limitless potential for expansion.[1] It is, of course, obvious that families do not expand to this theoretically limitless possibility, but rather restrict their membership. The rationale behind this selective recruitment of family members has long occupied the attention of sociologists. It has recently been reformulated by social historians into a question of determining the boundaries of the family. More

SOURCE: This article is a revised version of a paper first published in the *Canadian Journal of Sociology*, Vol. 4, No. 3 (1979), pp. 275-286. Reprinted by permission of the author and the editors of the *CJS*.

specifically, social historians have addressed the question of the effects of industrialization upon the structure of the family.

The major position advanced by much sociological theory in the last decades uncritically accepted the premise that the preindustrial family was extended. This position suggested that it was the advent of industrialization that was responsible for the nuclearization of the family. This argument is most strongly supported by the functional theorists.[2] Functionalists work within a paradigm that sees societies as wholes which can maintain themselves only if certain functional pre-requisites are met. In order to meet these needs and thus ensure the predictability and stability of the system, a series of structures must exist within every society that support these needs. These structures are presumed to be interrelated and each performs a function for the system as a whole.

Within this framework it is argued that the family before industrialization performed seven functions: (1) it served as the basic economic unit of society; (2) it was the principal agent for the conferring of status upon members of the community; it provided the (3) protectional, (4) educational, (5) religious and (6) recreational needs of the family; and, finally (7) it fulfilled the emotive needs of its members.[3] The Industrial Revolution brought major technological changes. These innovations required a structural differentiation of the family to meet the needs of this new industrial system. For example, the factory system required greater differentiation of the economic roles of the family. The economic role of the head became more specialized insofar as the role no longer implied co-operation with, training of, and authority over other family members.

Similarly, as child labour became more common, a differentiation occurred between the family and the educational, recreational and moral training of its children. As a consequence of these changes, the family was no longer the economic unit and no longer controlled education.[4] This transformation of the functions of the family, it is argued, brought with it a concomitant transformation of the family's structure. The function of the family during industrialization was to provide support for its members against this new social order, a system based on rational, impersonal and universalistic criteria. The individual could escape from this world within the sanctuary of the family, and the nuclear family could best provide this haven. In addition, the nuclear family was better able to provide the particular form of socialization necessary to promote the values of this new, rational, industrial society — affective neutrality, achievement and, above all, individualism. The extended family, therefore, being no longer functional, disintegrated.[5]

This theoretical formulation about the progressive nuclearization of the family has aroused the interests of many social historians who have addressed themselves to the question of whether or not industrialism undermined the extended family. This analysis of the family is central to the study of Moncton and thus a brief review of major positions is necessary. Michael Anderson, on the basis of his data on Lancashire, suggests that industrialization and urbanization did *not* affect the structure of the family; the relationship between kind was not destroyed by industrialism. In nineteenth century Lancashire the nuclear family-based residence was the normal pattern. However, there was a great deal of variation to this pattern.[6] Kin frequently resided with other kin.

Anderson's theoretical position is borrowed largely from exchange theory, which emphasizes that people enter into social relationships principally in order to attain personal goals. Individuals judge these relationships on the basis of their "profitability". Based on this formulation, Anderson suggests that in rural areas family ties were solidified by normative considerations justified principally by tradition and by religion. In the city, these normative considerations indeed began to break down, but they were often replaced by another set of considerations; "calculative considerations" based on short-term reciprocity. Ties with parents, children, and kin might be useful for the attainment of certain goals.

> Although they [Lancashire Victorian working class people] were largely free from the economic and normative constraints which, in the rural areas, made terminating relationships with family and kin such a precarious and consequently rare business, yet, because they faced the problems of social welfare, and for migrants, of accommodation and information, they could not exist for long at an optimum level of satisfaction without some kind of assistance from others. Kin were the major source of assistance.[7]

Anderson thus concludes that in certain life-crises situations, kin might go live with other kin. This allows for the introduction of the concept of a "life-cycle" approach to the family. The utility of this construct is that it conceives of the family in terms of a dynamic process, rather than as static. It is therefore possible to think of the history of the family changing dramatically in the course of its life. Instead of examining a family or a household at one particular time, this construct makes the need to trace the family through time necessary.

Anderson's main thesis, however, seems somewhat less useful. His argument is based on uncovering the underlying motives of people who lived in the nineteenth-century without any clear evidence that they motives existed, either in the country or the city. His argument for their existence appears, at this point, highly speculative. Because his data shows similarities in the family structure from country to city despite the changing society, he postulates that there are different motivations in the city and the country. It is, however, difficult to evaluate psychological rationales attributed to people long since dead.

A second major, non-functionalist position on preindustrial family and household structure is advanced by Peter Laslett.[8] Laslett attacks not only the thesis that industrialization totally undermined the extended family, but also the view that the extended family survived industrialization. Although Laslett's later work with the Cambridge Group speaks more specifically to this issue (1972), his earlier book, *The World We Have Lost* (1965), provides an introduction to his concern with the question of nuclearization and thus warrants a brief discussion here.

Laslett provides evidence in *The World We Have Lost* suggesting that the extended family was no more a part of traditional society than of industrial society. Evidence from England in general suggests that average size of households was small — 4.75 persons — at all times from the late sixteenth until the early twentieth century.[9] The composition of the family, Laslett concludes, was based on the rule that no two married couples or more constituted a family. When they were ready to marry, children would leave their family of origin to start their own families. If they could not do so, they would not marry. In this way, the nuclear structure of the family was maintained.

While these conclusions, based on data from England, provide useful insights into family composition, it is Laslett's more general comparisons that must be challenged. Preindustrial society on the whole was, he submits, patriarchal and politically stable, with the family being the pivot about which all life revolved. The fundamental characteristic of traditional society was the scene of labour, which was in the home. While the structure of the family was nuclear both before and after this world was lost, industrialization nevertheless causes profound transformations in the family. As the work place moved outside the home, the family ceased to be patriarchal, and life which before had centred around the family now consisted of a mass, alienated, individualistic society. While Laslett's original attempt is to discredit the myth of the large extended family as a romantic ideal, he substitutes in its place another romanticization of the past:

> Time was when the whole of life went forward in a family, in a circle of loved, familiar faces, known and fondled objects, all to human size. That time has gone forever. It makes us very different from our ancestors.[10]

This general conclusion introduces into Laslett's work the distinction between *Gemeinschaft* and *Gesellschaft*,[11] with the critical difference between the two stages of development being industrialization. He quickly dismisses as distortions explanations based on "capitalism, the rise of the bourgeoisie, and so on" as causal agents, opting instead for a simpler way of dividing the past — a division between preindustrialization and postindustrialization. As Lasch points out,

> Laslett restates, as if it were the latest historical discovery, the ancient sociological tradition that subsitutes his historical analysis distinctions between Gemeinschaft and Gesellschasft, status and contract, tradition and modernity — mummified abstractions into which social historians now attempt to breathe life with the aid of yet another lifeless abstraction "patriarchal society".[12]

The work of Lutz K. Berkner provides a somewhat different formulation.[13] Berkner uses the concept of life cycle to criticize Laslett's work. Using data from his study of Austrian peasants, Berkner argues that the family expands and contracts depending on the particular stage in its life cycle. Early in their married life an eldest son, his wife, and their children might for a while reside with his parents. The structure would be nuclear again when the parents die or when the young couple move out. Although at any time the majority of households would be nuclear, Berkner's argument suggests that most people have at one time or another lived in extended families. Although Berkner's conclusions are far more conservative, his appreciation of the life-cycle concept is in agreement with the work of Anderson discussed earlier.

Michael Katz, in his work on Hamilton, Ontario, also suggests that Laslett's scheme ignores the possibility of a life-cycle approach to household composition.[14] Nevertheless, he brings evidence to bear which suggests that at least for Hamilton the simple-family household was most common. Simple-family households represented from 79 to 80 percent of household types from 1851 to 1861 in Hamilton. Nevertheless, despite this remarkable stability, Katz finds evidence to suggest that the dynamic model is the most appropriate for examining household composition. Although the simple household is most common, the composition of households varies over time. Most households had a boarder or a relative living with them at some time, although when this might occur appears to have little relationship to the life-cycle of the household. Most young people, Katz concludes, had the experience of living in a household which at one time contained an individual who was not a member of the simple family.

THE CASE OF MONCTON, NEW BRUNSWICK 1851 to 1871

This brief overview presents the dominant arguments concerning the history of family and household structure. In the subsequent analysis, some of the issues raised in this literature will be discussed in the context of a particular case: the Parish of Moncton, New Brunswick. Moncton was a rapidly growing and industrializing community in the late 1840s and early 1850s.

Shipbuilding was a major industry employing over a thousand men. Yet, the economic viability of the shipbuilding industry was totally destroyed by the late 1850s and early 1860s. This boom and bust cycle had important implications for the analysis of household structure.

One of the most surprising findings from the data on Moncton[15] is the very high and unstable household size. The extraordinary mean household size of 8.49 in 1851 shrank to 5.95 in 1861, and grew very slightly again to a mean of 6.07 in 1871. These results are in sharp contrast to Laslett's finding that household size was stable at about 4.75 in England. What accounts for the variation between the three decades? In order to answer this question, it is necessary to move to an analysis that sees structure as crucial.

As noted, the mean household size in 1851 was considerably larger than in 1861 and 1871. A major difference among these three years is that in 1851 there were many households that contained more than one family (Table 1). These multiple-family households no longer existed by 1861 and, with the exception of three households (six families), did not re-emerge in 1871. It is precisely because almost 40 percent of the population lived in multiple-family households in 1851 that the mean household size was so large.

TABLE I

TYPE OF HOUSEHOLD IN MONCTON, 1851–1871

Type	YEAR		
	1851	1861	1871
Simple and extended	75.6%	100.0%	99.5%
Multiple-family	24.3	0.0	0.5
Total percent	99.9	100.0	100.0
N	313	699	796

A comparison with Hamilton, Ontario during the same period illustrates how unusual this phenomenon is. While 24.3 percent of all households were multiple in Moncton in 1851, only 1.7 percent and 2.5 percent were multiple in Hamilton in 1851 and 1861, respectively.

The question that must be addressed is why this phenomenon occurred in 1851. If the type of household (single- or multiple-family type) is examined by the characteristics of the family heads, a clear distinction can be made. Young family heads (under thirty-five years of age) were more likely to be in multiple-family households than older family heads (only slightly more than 40 percent of the under thirty-five year olds lived in single-family households, compared to almost 65 percent of those between thirty-five and sixty-five). This pattern, however, reversed itself for those sixty-five years of age and over. The aged also lived in multiple-family households (Table II). In addition, native-born family heads were far more likely to be in single-family households than foreign-born family heads (Table III).

TABLE II

AGE OF FAMILY HEAD BY NUMBER OF FAMILIES IN THE HOUSEHOLD, 1851

		AGE	
Number of Families	**20-34**	**35-64**	**65+**
One	40.3%	64.7%	45.2%
Two or more	59.7	35.3	54.9
Total percent	100.0	100.0	100.1
N	119	266	31

TABLE III

NATIVITY BY NUMBER OF FAMILIES IN HOUSEHOLD, 1851

	NATIVITY	
Number of Families	**Native**	**Foreign**
One	61.2%	48.8%
Two	38.8	51.2
Total percent	100.0	100.0
N	250	166

Most importantly, the single- and multiple-family households differed in terms of the economic sector of the family head. Farmers were overwhelmingly to be found in single-family households, while builders and manufacturers were found in multiple-family households (Table IV). It is apparent from this evidence that there were important distinctions between single- and multiple-family households in terms of the heads of families that composed them. In multiple-family households, the family heads were younger, more likely to be immigrants (particularly recent immigrants), and more likely to be employed in the industrial rather than the farming sector.

These differences explain why multiple-family households were so predominant in 1851. These families were those who were attracted to Moncton to work for the growing shipbuilding industry. Migrating to Moncton in the dawning years of shipbuilding, these young adventurous families had not yet established their households. Coming to this new colony, undoubtedly with little money, they found it in their interests to share quarters with others in similar circumstances.

This conclusion, however, in no way provides evidence supporting the existence of the extended family in Moncton Parish in 1851. In fact, a close examination of extended households indicates that they comprised only 11.5 percent of the total in Moncton Parish in 1851 (Table V), a figure which is similar to Katz's finding for Hamilton in 1851 (11.3 percent). It is quite evident, therefore, that the distinction between Moncton Parish and other studies was not in terms of the preponderance of extended families but rather in terms of the extraordinary number of multiple-family households. The distinctiveness of Moncton lies in the tendency of families to cohabitate with other families and not with kin.

TABLE IV

INDUSTRIAL SECTOR OF FAMILY HEAD BY NUMBER OF FAMILIES IN HOUSEHOLD, 1851

Industrial Sector	Number of Families				
	One	Two	Three or More	Total Percent	N
Farming	75.9%	18.9%	5.3%	100.1	228
Building	39.5	31.6	28.9	100.0	38
Manufacturing	28.6	41.1	30.4	100.1	56
Transportation	33.3	33.3	33.3	99.9	3
Dealing	63.6	31.8	4.5	99.9	22
Banks, Government & Public Service	23.1	30.8	46.2	100.1	13
Domestic & Personal	0.0	100.0	0.0	100.0	1

Unlike Katz's conclusion about Hamilton — that household structure remained stable across the decade — the findings here suggest the considerable malleability of household structure. The evidence presented above recommends the view that household structure was able to expand to accommodate a second or even a third family when the economic situation demanded it, and return to the more common model (as found by Katz and others) when the situation changed. Thus in Moncton in 1851, 64 percent of all households were simple while 24 percent of all households were multiple. In 1861, when industry declined, 82 percent were simple-family households. Again, unlike Hamilton in the nineteenth century, the dominant form of this complex household in 1851 was not the extended household but the multiple-family household. The overall portrayal of stability of household structure that Katz presents for Hamilton differs from the volatile situation in Moncton in the 1850s. It can be concluded that the stability of household structure was markedly affected by rapid economic growth. The precise economic conditions of the community are an extremely important determinant of household structure.

TABLE V

TYPE OF HOUSEHOLD IN MONCTON, 1851 and 1861

Type	1851	1861
Solitary	**1.0%**	**.4%**
Simple		
(Nuclear family only)	43.5	66.4
Nuclear family and boarder	19.8	4.9
Nuclear family and servant (no boarder)	0.0	11.1
Total Simple	63.3	82.4
Extended		
(Nuclear family and additional kin only)	8.3	10.3
Nuclear family, additional kin & boarder (includes families with boarder & servants)	3.2	3.2
Nuclear family, additional kin & servants (no boarders)	0.0	1.7
Total	11.5	15.2
Multiple		
(Two or more couples only)	10.5	—
Two or more couples with kin	1.6	—
Two or more couples with kin and boarder	1.6	—
Two or more couples with boarders (includes boarders and servants)	10.5	—
Two or more couples with servants	0.0	—
Total percent	100.0	100.0
N	313	699

Also dwelling under the same roof in nineteenth-century households were boarders and lodgers. In Hamilton, boarders dwelt in 29 percent of households in 1851 compared to 20 percent in 1861.[16] In Moncton, on the other hand, 35.1 percent of households had boarders in 1851, a figure that declined to only 8.1 percent in 1861 (Table V). Katz's data on Hamilton indiciates a decline as well, albeit less drastic, as a result of the outmigration of young men. This decrease in Moncton was probably a result of economic difficulties. The actual number of boarders in the population declined from 12.5 percent of the population to only 2.7 percent. If a demographic profile of persons who were boarders in 1851 and 1861 is examined, it is apparent that they were predominantly male, were greatly overrepresented in the twenty to twenty-nine age group, and were primarily foreign born. These data are consistent with the thesis that the economic boom of the late 1840s and early 1850s attracted young, single men from overseas to Moncton. Like the families migrating at the same time, they did not establish their own households but rather lived in already established households. The decline in boarders from 12.5 percent to 2.7 percent of the population is further indication that these young men were unable to sustain the economic impact of the late 1850s.

What accounts for the enormous variation between the size of the household in 1851 and in 1861? As noted, the compositional variation of households, that is, the number of multiple-family households in 1851, was a partial factor in explaining this difference. A second important structure component — the number of boarders in the household — may now be introduced. In 1851 households were larger not only because of the extraordinary number of multiple-family households, but also because of the number of boarders dwelling within the household.[17]

CONCLUSIONS

Several conclusions can be drawn from this examination of Moncton Parish evidence. Anderson's thesis suggests that urbanization and industrialization did not destroy already strong family ties, but rather changed the basic motivations for maintaining these ties. In Moncton in 1851 with the growth of industry, no strengthening of family ties is apparent. Rather, it was not family members who came to live within these complex households, but total strangers. On the other hand, as the degree of industrialization and urbanization declined in the late 1850s, relatives began to replace boarders in the household. There is no reason to assume that the benefits that could be obtained (calculative considerations) through the maintaining of strong kin ties could not be as easily obtained by boarding in others' households (especially in time of boom).[18]

Laslett's conclusion — that since children leave to start new families there is a preponderance of simple-family households — appears only partially accurate. What Laslett does not envisage, however, is the possibility that families who are not related would, in certain situations, dwell within the same household. If one were to examine only 1861 and 1871 data for Moncton, one would have to agree with Laslett (and also with Katz) that the simple-family household was by far the most common. In Moncton, however, given certain circumstances — in this case an influx of families and young men from outside the colony who participated in the economic boom — the model breaks down. If Laslett's model can be considered the norm, then as the boom turns into a decline, the household structure quickly changes to resemble the simple-household model. While it is impossible to posit all instances where particular circumstances would revolutionize the household, it is possible to conclude that very rapid economic growth appears to have a dramatic effect on household structure and, consequently, on household size. Laslett's model must at least be modified in order to account for these 1851 findings.

The notion of life cycle as introduced by Anderson and Berkner proves valuable. In 1851, the family heads of multiple families were young, recent immigrants. Older immigrants were more likely to head their own households. Thus, these families, at the beginning of their life cycle in terms of both their age and their recent immigration, formed unique household structures. The native born and the older immigrant were more likely to fit the more typical pattern — the simple-family household.

This finding in the 1851 census of Moncton Parish suggests the need for an "economic cycle" as well as a life cycle approach to household structure. It is clear that it is important to consider the historical context. The household is flexible enough to respond to changes in the larger economic structure of the community. The particular set of historical events in Moncton intersect with the whole complex of household and family development. The household, it appears, is very malleable. In nineteenth-century Moncton, it served as an institutional interface between economic conditions and individual well-being, providing many new immigrants, as well as the community at large, a mechanism for adapting to the rapidly changing economic conditions of the nineteenth century.

Finally, it may be concluded that the household in Moncton Parish, particularly in 1851, was not like the household in nineteenth-century Hamilton in that there were so many multiple-family households in Moncton. In 1861 and 1871 there were greater similarities between household structures in the two cities.

To be a resident of Moncton Parish in the mid-nineteenth century thus meant not only living in an economically volatile climate but also in a volatile household structure: the problems that occurred in the economic structure of Moncton were felt in one of the most basic of social institutions — the family.

NOTES:

1. Michael Anderson, *Family Structure in Nineteenth Century Lancashire* (Cambridge: Cambridge University Press, 1971), p. 10.
2. See, for example, William F. Ogburn, "The Changing Functions of the Family," in Robert F. Winch and Louis Wolf Goodman, eds., *Selected Studies in Marriage and the Family* (New York: Holt, Rinehart and Winston, 1968), pp. 58-63; Talcott Parsons and Robert F. Bales, *Family, Socialization and the Interaction Process* (Glencoe, Illinois: The Free Press, 1965); and Ernest W. Burgess and Harvey J. Locke, *The Family: From Institution to Companionship* (New York: American Book Company, 1945).
3. Ogburn, "The Changing Functions of the Family."
4. Neil Smelser, *Social Change in the Industrial Revolution* (Chicago: Chicago University Press, 1957), Chapters 10, 11, and 15.
5. Parsons and Bales, *Family, Socialization and the Interaction Process*.
6. Anderson, *Family Structure in Nineteenth Century Lancashire*, p. 56.
7. *Ibid.*, p. 161.
8. Peter Laslett, *The World We Have Lost* (London: Methuen, 1965); Peter Laslett and Richard Wall, eds., *Household and Family in Past Time* (London: Cambridge University Press, 1972).
9. Laslett, *World We Have Lost*, p. 93.
10. *Ibid.*, p. 22.
11. Christopher Lasch, "The Family and History," *New York Review of Books* (November 13, 1975), pp. 33-38.
12. *Ibid.*, p. 38. The theme that the nuclear family predates industrialism is reiterated in Laslett and Wall, *Household and Family in Past Time*. Laslett has in the introduction to this work been far more cautious, abandoning his romantic reformulations of the past. Here he proposes the null hypothesis: the history of the family forces us to assume that the organization of the family was always and invariably nuclear, unless the contrary can be proven.
13. Lutz K. Berner, "The Stem Family and the Developmental Cycle of the Peasant Household: An Eighteenth-Century Austrian Example," *American Historical Review*, Vol. 77 (1972), pp. 308-418.
14. Michael Katz, *The People of Hamilton, Canada West: Family and Class in a Mid-Nineteenth Century City* (Cambridge, Mass.: Harvard University Press, 1975).
15. The source for the data is the microfilm reels of the census records for the Parish of Moncton in the County of Westmoreland, New Brunswick, for the census years 1851, 1861, and 1871.
16. Katz, *Hamilton*, p. 222.
17. The exact status of boarders in the household is one that has recently been addressed by several social historians. Katz argues that boarders and co-residing kin occupied similar positions. I suggest that this conclusion is neither substantiated by Katz's data on Hamilton nor by my data on Moncton. There is no evidence to suggest that the family provided a "family surrogate" for boarders. Rather the distinction between boarders and co-residing kin is important. See John Modell and Tamara K. Hareven, "Urbanization and the Malleable Household: An Examination of Boarding and Lodging in American Families," *Journal of Marriage and the Family*, Vol. 35 (1973), pp. 467-478; and Sheva Medjuck, "The

Importance of Boarding for the Structure of the Household in the Nineteenth Century: Moncton, New Brunswick and Hamilton, Canada West," *Histoire sociale/Social History*, Vol. 13 (1980), pp. 207-214.

18. While I appreciate that domestic arrangements are only one indication of extended kin ties, I believe that these arrangements can serve as an example of the strength of kin ties.

Social Structure and the Urbanization Process: Perspectives on Nineteenth Century Research

CHAD GAFFIELD

During the early 1970s, social structural analysis and urban history developed a close relationship in North America. Most major projects which examined social structure focussed on the experience of cities. In Canada, Michael Katz challenged traditional historiography by rigorously describing the lives of both famous and anonymous residents in Hamilton, Canada West during the mid-nineteenth century.[1] This work was the inspiration for the Philadelphia Social History Project under the leadership of Theodore Hershberg. Over the decade, Hershberg attracted a multidisciplinary group of scholars to examine a massive data base and thereby to work toward a synthetic re-interpretation of nineteenth century Philadelphia.[2] Taken together, the Hamilton and Philadelphia projects had an enormous impact on the discipline of history generally but especially on the field of urban history. Their work helped scholars re-think the nature of urban development and re-evaluate the traditional approaches to city growth.

In the late 1970s, the association of urban history and social structural analysis weakened considerably in both the United States and Canada. However, this weakening has occurred for different reasons in the two countries. In the United States, historians who are interested in social structure are now becoming reluctant to call themselves urban historians even though their work focusses on the city experience. They see the term "urban history" as an inappropriate delimiter of historical attention given the general nature of large-scale social change throughout the landscape. Samuel P. Hays, for example, has recently emphasized that historians should recognize that cities were affected by processes that obtained "throughout the whole society." His own approach is now "first to talk about these

SOURCE: This is an original paper, prepared especially for this volume.

processes generally and then to have a series of different geographical contexts where they are worked out in more detail: the community, the city, the region, the nation.''[3] Stephan Thernstrom has completely abandoned the term ''urban history'' since it has gained an ''unfortunate implication . . . that one isn't interested in rural social processes.'' He now defines himself simply as a social historian, a reflection of his general interest in social change both within and outside cities.[4]

In Canada, there has been no retreat from the label ''urban historian.'' Since the time the Hamilton Project published the first project reports, the field of urban history has developed into a central component of the discipline of Canada. One index of this development is the emergence of the *Urban History Review* as a major scholarly journal. The *U.H.R.* has benefitted from a rapid increase in the number of researchers focussing on the urban experience. Gilbert Stelter reported in 1980 that urban history in Canada was ''thriving'' with more than 300 researchers actively studying the development of particular cities. Although Stelter observed that about half of these researchers were working in Ontario, he also noted that urban history was underway throughout Canada. The largest component of this activity involved social history, including ''everything from institutions such as schools, churches and unions in an urban setting, to systematic analyses of society.''[5]

The 1970s witnessed the maturing of social structural analysis in Canada[6] but developments in urban history have occurred far more rapidly with respect to other approaches. The study of social structure is now a small component of urban history as a field of research. Unlike the United States where historians of ''society'' have become dominant within both urban and rural research, Canada's major contributions have emphasized other aspects of cities as historical phenomena.[7] Although Stelter's broad definition of social history captured the largest proportion of urban study, this proportion included only one-third of research activity and ''systematic analyses of society'' were an even smaller proportion therein.

Analysis of urban social structure has not become widespread in Canada. While scholars remark upon the importance of such analysis, they generally choose more conventional topics and approaches for their own work. Neither the concepts nor methods of the major projects have gained much popularity. For example, Katz' major argument concerning the ongoing social inequality of mid-nineteenth century Hamilton remains an almost isolated finding in the Canadian literature. The central theme of *The People of Hamilton* was the apparent paradox of rapid population turnover and steady structural configuration; the names and faces changed constantly but the city evolved very slowly.[8] This theme has numerous implications for the ways in which historians view the urban past. Civic leaders become important as a social group rather than as specific personalities. Urban development is associated with increasing social inequality and, thereby, class consciousness rather than community spirit. A "sense of place" gives way to a hope that economic opportunity is better somewhere else. These redefinitions of city life emerged from historical evidence which previous scholars had considered unimportant or unmanageable. The backbone of the Hamilton Project was the 1851-1871 manuscript census returns and other routinely-generated sources such as assessment rolls. This evidence went beyond the attitudes and perceptions of a small elite to the social experience of the vast majority.

This approach has been less important among urban historians in Canada than the study of municipal policy and major civic leaders. Urban historians have argued that Canadian cities must first be treated as unique places created by specific city-builders. Each city represents a particular convergence of individuals and environment and thus historical analysis must begin at the level of character and circumstances. Alan F.J. Artibise promoted this perspective in his study of Winnipeg, a major contribution to Canadian urban history during the 1970s. He argued forcefully that Winnipeg should be approached "as a special kind of social environment, set in a particular place and time, and with unique internal patterns and organizations." While admitting that variables such as population and technology required consideration, Artibise stressed that Winnipeg was largely the result of the "human and accidental, the contingencies of events and personalities."[9] The study, itself, pointed out similarities and differences between Winnipeg's experience and developments elsewhere and, in so doing, suggested that the differences outweighed the similarities. Winnipeg was simply Winnipeg and not a representation of a widespread city-building phenomenon. From this perspective, Artibise selected munici-pal documents such as council minutes and reports as the foundation of his evidence. These documents allowed Artibise to analyse the thoughts and action of the "Big Men" in Winnipeg and thereby to detail the city's development.[10]

In his later work on general prairie urban development, Artibise has qualified this perspective by emphasizing that historical period and geographic context are two variables which define the possibilities of individual agency. He argues that individual and group decisions become less important as urban development progresses and that a town or city growing in the 1840s, for example, will face different challenges than one growing in the 1880s. In this sense, the importance of agency is related to the historical moment of the urban process. Similarly, Artibise stresses that regional differences necessitate analytical adjustment. Generalizations about the prairies do not necessarily hold for central Canada just as concepts of urban industrial development would not apply to Winnipeg or Saskatoon.[11] Nonetheless, the emphasis on individual agency and the decision-making of elites within urban development has become the dominant approach of urban historians in Canada. Studies have now portrayed the attitudes and behaviour of civic officials in numerous Canadian cities and municipal documents have become the staple source of research strategies.

A second approach to urban history is represented by a group of scholars who look at cities as parts of urban systems. These scholars eschew case studies as well as reference to specific individuals or leadership groups. For example, James W. Simmons analyses cities as spatially interdependent elements.[12] He suggests that in Canada the productive power of the surrounding hinterlands often determines urban status since the economy is largely dependent on primary products. The importance of "site resource base" is especially crucial to smaller urban centers which can quickly appear or disappear on the basis of commodities such as grain, wood, pulp or nickel. Simmons argues that specific businessmen and politicians cannot be held responsible for the pace or nature or urban development. He concludes that "It is not industry or entrepreneurial skill but the ability of the hinterland to generate wealth which is essential" in the Canadian context. Cities rise and fall as part of urban systems without regard for the leadership of local elites.[13]

The dependent character of Canadian cities is also stressed by John McCallum who has examined the economic development of Quebec and Ontario during the mid-nineteenth century.[14] McCallum argues that rural development in the two provinces had a determining influence on the nature of urban expansion. The crucial rural-urban link was the extent to which agriculture facilitated capital accumulation. McCallum suggests that since Quebec agriculture was in difficulty throughout the decades before the 1860s, industrial development was seriously hindered. In contrast, Ontario's prosperous wheat economy provided a foundation for rapid industrial expansion.

> Ontario industry developed on classic lines as the agriculture-based economy grew. The enterprising blacksmith became a founder, the successful tailor began to employ outside labour, and the printer expanded his operation as local demand for newspapers rose. Markets, capital, materials, and labour were overwhelmingly local. Meanwhile, industrial growth in Quebec was based mainly on elements external to the province. Montreal's commercial base was founded on the production and consumption of other regions, while the city's industry depended on external markets and often external raw materials. The same was true of the few large enterprises outside Montreal which emerged alongside the weak local industry. Owned by outsiders, such enterprises operated large-scale plants importing raw materials to produce a product that was sent to external markets on

railways that happened to pass through rural Quebec on their way to the eastern seaboard.[15]

McCallum suggests that this situation explains why the focus of economic activity shifted from Montreal to cities such as Toronto and Hamilton by the late 19th century and why urban development progressed differently in Quebec and Ontario. McCallum concludes that

"outside Montreal and Quebec City, little occurred. In contrast to the proliferation of Ontario towns competing with each other by means of roads and railways for the prosperous agricultural hinterland, Quebec towns were few in number, with neither the incentive nor the resources for local transportation developments. Such meagre industrial development as occurred outside the two main cities was of very low productivity, and Quebec's unproductive agriculture offered an unlimited supply of labour at wage rates well below the levels experienced in rural Ontario."[16]

In many ways, this argument is a revitilization of the staples approach which for so long dominated Canadian historiography. Unfortunately, most of the claims remain speculative. McCallum represents very little new evidence and he does not attempt to specify the precise ways and extent to which capital was accumulated and invested in industry. The data are generally aggregate and the evidence is circumstantial. However, the emphasis on environmental factors undermines several notions of human agency including those which assume fundamental cultural differences between Anglo-Canadian and French-Canadian economic behaviour. In the end, McCallum bluntly concludes that "nineteenth century Quebec developed along the lines that were beyond the control of merchant and habitant alike."[17]

Despite differences among scholars of social structure, "Big Men," and urban systems, their approaches have two important similarities: they support a developmental approach to urban development and they encourage comparative studies of different cities. Michael Katz thought that an industrial city was under study when the Hamilton project began. When the data were examined, however, it became clear that, in the 1851-1861 period, Hamilton was still a commercial centre. By implication, Katz' study suggested a commercial-to-industrial process of urban development in the nineteenth century that could be tested as a general model. Katz employed some specific comparisons of social structure with communities elsewhere but did not attempt a full comparative analysis.[18] Nonetheless, the ultimate ambition of an overall theory was foremost in the study.

Alan Artibise would not pursue the notion that a particular developmental process characterized city growth in the nineteenth century but he strongly encourages a change-over-time perspective. In his urban biography, Artibise endeavoured "to identify and describe the events, personages, trends, and movements which have played a key role in the development of Winnipeg."[19] This longitudinal perspective did not imply identifiable developmental stages in Winnipeg but rather general periods of urban growth leading to "urban maturity" by World War I. Artibise described the path of development in terms of the goals of civic leaders, and a major question posed in the book concerned the extent to which these goals were shared in other cities. Thus Artibise promoted comparative history and hoped that similar studies would be carried out in different urban areas. However, human agency remained the crucial variable in the urban development process and in this regard, Artibise's perspective differs markedly from the Katz approach. In Artibise's study, Winnipeg's destiny was determined by the energy, competency, and goals of its leaders. With changes in leadership, Winnipeg's development might have been quite different.

Recent emphasis on urban development either in terms of economic stages or "boosterism" raises two specific problems in terms of nineteenth century society. To begin with, the developmental approach has certain pathological underpinnings. Small towns became, by implication at least, failures. Places that do not grow or commercial centers which do not become industrial invite urban analysis in terms of etiology. At one level, such diagnosis would be valid. Stephen Leacock's *Sunshine Sketches* captured a mood of great anticipation common to many emerging centers in the nineteenth century. The people of "Mariposa" were convinced that they were on their way to great urban heights despite outside opinion to the contrary.

> In point of population, if one must come down to figures the Canadian census puts the numbers every time at something around five thousand. But it is very generally understood in Mariposa that the census is largely the outcome of malicious jealousy. It is usual that after the census the editor of the Mariposa *Newspacket* makes a careful re-estimate (based on the data of relative non-payment of subscriptions), and brings the population up to 6,000. After that the Mariposa Times-Herald makes an estimate that runs the figures up to 6,500. Then Mr. Gingham, the undertaker, who collects the vital statistics for the provincial government, makes an estimate from the number of what he calls the "demised" as compared with the less interesting persons who are still alive, and brings the population to 7,000. After that somebody else works it out that it's 7,500; then the man behind the bar of the Mariposa House offers to bet the whole room that there are 9,000 people in Mariposa. That settles it, and the population is well on the way to 10,000, when down swoops the federal census taker on his next round and the town has to begin all over again.[20]

As it turned out, of course, "Mariposa" never grew dramatically and the great expectations went largely unfulfilled. Orillia lost to Barrie in the battle for predominance in Simcoe County, and reconciled itself to status as a tourist attraction.[21] In this sense, Orillia is an urban failure. Katz might suggest causes such as the failure of economic development to move Orillia beyond its service center function while Artibise would probably compare the personalities of the civic leaders in Orillia and Barrie with reference to their ability to attract immigrants and industry.

Theoretically, however, these analyses imply a particular path of urban development on which specific cases can be located at various points in time. A linear rural-to-urban continuum lurks in the background of their studies. Just as Leacock claimed, Mariposa had no real identity of its own; "if you know Canada at all, you are probably well acquainted with a dozen towns just like it."[22] Similarly, the studies of Hamilton and Winnipeg imply that, within certain limits, specific cities might have progressed to different points on the path of urban development from those actually attained. Hamilton might have been Toronto and Winnipeg might have been Dauphin. It should be noted that the urban systems approach avoids this kind of analysis by differentiating among various types of Canadian cities on the basis of their hinterlands and their linkages to other urban centers. Thus, a small town is not a failure but rather a necessary link between rural areas and major cities. The researcher's object is to identify and explain this link rather than to interpet unfulfilled ambition. Still, questions remain concerning the nature of the urban system as a whole. Why do primary resources continue to determine the Canadian urban system? Is entrepreneurial skill a determining influence at this level? Is transiency or structural rigidity a factor?

One way of addressing these issues is to confront systematically the need for a "scheme of conceptualization" relating to the urban experience. Recently, Theodore Hershberg has taken up this task by promoting the view that urban history must be approached as a dynamic and complex interconnection of three fundamental forces. "*Urban as process* should be thought of as the dynamic modeling of the interrelationships among environment, behaviour, and group experience — three basic components in the larger urban system." Significantly, Hershberg's perspective includes attention to social structure, city elites, and urban systems; he suggests that we need to understand the "interplay of personalities, political decisions, major events, institutional behaviour, and impersonal, large-scale, socio-economic and demographic forces." In this way, Hershberg promotes a far more integrated approach to urban history than is apparent in the Canadian context thus far. This approach may be far easier to recommend than to implement. Hershberg suggests three research topics: "First, how the urban environment changed over time. Second, what social experience was correlated with different aspects of urban settings; neither relatively simple behaviours such as intermarriage nor complex processes such as assimilation occurred in a vacuum. Finally, what were the mechanisms through which environmental and social change were effected."[23]

These research topics may be legitimate (in fact, research is already well underway on these fronts) but they do not respond to the most important weakness of urban history during the last decade; specifically, that the urban experience has not been addressed within a larger social and environmental context. Hershberg's own project on Philadelphia has examined the city without systematic reference to a regional or national setting.[24] Clearly, the work of the project implies that, once Philadelphia is studied, its history can then be placed in a larger context but this approach sidesteps questions about the specific nature of "urban as process." The basic question is whether scholars interested in urban history should only study urban centers. Obviously, each piece of research must drawn the boundaries somewhere, but can we understand urban development in particular cities without a more geographically-integrated framework?

The recent work of David Gagan illustrates some of the benefits of approaching the history of urban social structure as a regional phenomenon. Gagan studied the emergence of Brampton as an urban center in Peel County, Ontario. This development is analysed in the context of decades of regional rural history and of general urban growth in south-central Ontario.

> In 1851 Peel contained no incorporated places. Its principal hamlets, Brampton, Streetsville, and Port Credit, counted among them fewer than 2,000 inhabitants associated with the primary functions of each place, the grain trade in Brampton, fishing and shipping in Port Credit, and the cloth industry in Streetsville. Twenty years later Streetsville and Port Credit were still hamlets, in fact, declining villages. But Brampton had become an urban centre with all the trappings of mid-Victorian urbanism: the railway, proto-industrialization, vigorous commercial development, high rates of transience, and a rigid, indeed restrictive, social structure. And Brampton's 2,000 inhabitants were urban people, but not merely because they were smugly imperious toward their rural neighbours. After less than a dozen years of separate development the two populations had quite distinct demographic characteristics which set them worlds apart.[25]

Gagan's study of this Canadian "urban frontier" is selective and many questions remain unanswered about the distinctiveness of the rural and urban "worlds" of Peel County. Nonetheless, his comparative approach permits some specification of the process of urbanization itself and includes treatment of the city as both an independent and dependent variable. Gagan does address the question of how Brampton grew and why more and more people were attracted to the community. More importantly, Gagan attempts to indicate what it meant to be "urban" rather than "rural" in Peel County, and thus to consider urbanization as an independent force within his overall analysis. Gagan compares fertility ratios, age-at-marriage, and persistence rates for Brampton and rural Peel County, and concludes that rural-urban differences were important. "What is significant about the town and its population is that they embodied a demonstrable departure from the forms, structures, and rhythms of life and of individual experience in the countryside."[26]

A regional approach to analysing the process of urbanization has the advantage of placing specific city development into a context where the meaning of "urban" can be assessed systematically. Recent research suggests that four aspects of social structure would provide an excellent point of departure for this type of assessment: demographic behaviour, transiency, occupational structure, and social mobility. Studies of these topics have been quite numerous, especially during the past decade, and a selective survey of their findings suggests the potential value of undertaking the history of urban social structure in a regional context. No single answer becomes apparent but better questions certainly emerge.

To begin with, research on demographic behaviour in the nineteenth century has strongly challenged traditional assumptions about the meaning of urbanization. The most forceful challenge has focussed on the relationship between declining fertility and urban growth. Conventional wisdom argued that urbanization was the engine of the nineteenth century fertility decline and that rural areas maintained larger families throughout this period. This view was then attacked by scholars such as Y. Yasuba who maintained that rural fertility was also in decline by the first half of the nineteenth century.[27] Subsequent studies have pursued the argument that diminishing available farmland inspired rural parents to control their family size in rational response to their changing material environment. This argument considers children as contributors to family economies and assesses their importance in relationship to household requirements. This importance is assumed to decrease as settlements mature and cities grow. In land abundant areas, economic opportunity and labour-intensive production combine to make children valuable contributors to family security and thus fertility rates remain high. Children are less needed in established farm communities, however, and their relative cost inspires parents to begin limiting family size. This process is further advanced in cities where the few productive opportunities for children make parents even more determined to prevent the burden of extensive child care.[28]

In Canada, R.M. McInnis has examined this perspective by studying census data from mid-nineteenth century Ontario. He found an aggregate relationship at the county level between land availability and fertility but a subsequent household-level analysis failed to support a coherent model of demographic behaviour based on "old" and "new" agricultural areas. However, McInnis' conclusions included a tantalizing suggestion about the interrelationships of rural and urban centers.

> As was expected, an abundance of nearby, uncultivated land affects the probability of there being young children in the household. However, the magnitude of its influence is small and it does not consistently affect other childbearing variables in the same way. The strongest result obtained is that fertility falls as larger cities develop sufficiently close by for there to be a real influence of urban life and culture. The behavioral basis for that remains insufficiently explored, however.[29]

The suggestion that "urban life and culture" may have been responsible for the general fertility decline of the nineteenth century indicates that a single theory may explain both rural and urban experience. Thus, research should perhaps focus on the changing *mentalité* of urban residents as the crucial independent variable of nineteenth century patterns. This approach joins a larger challenge to earlier studies which had implied that distinct economic explanations are required to account for urban and non-urban demographic behaviour. In cities, changing modes of production related to industrialization were said to have engendered new perspectives on children and their role in family security. In the countryside, declining land availability, a phenomenon unrelated to industrialization, was claimed to have changed family calculations about labour requirements and therefore to have inspired birth control. In recent years, however, scholars have not been content with the notion of two distinct explanations for a phenomenon which obtained at about the same time in both rural and urban areas. Maris Vinovskis, in particular, has looked for a general social change which influenced fertility in various geographic environments.[30] This search has led to revitalization of the old concept of "modernization," which had been largely abandoned after careless use by sociologists during the 1950s and 1960s. Problems of definition and ideological bias are still evident but an increasing number of scholars now suggest that modernization can serve as a general explanation for demographic patterns in both rural and urban areas.[31] In this perspective, the process of urbanization becomes one aspect of a larger social change which affected residents in both cities and the countryside.

An alternative perspective on parallel rural-urban demographic developments has emerged from the work of Mark J. Stern on fertility in Erie County, New York during the mid-nineteenth century. Stern has examined nominal level data for rural and urban areas and applies a single conceptual framework to explain differentials within and between each context. Stern argues that the crucial independent variable is the "class position of individual families and the economic position associated with that position."

This perspective goes beyond social and economic considerations. Stern claims that class influences "were mediated through a set of cultural perceptions associated with ethnicity which also had an immense effect on the family planning strategies of urban and rural families."[32]

In applying this concept to Erie County, Stern perceives class in terms of a two-tiered social structure which obtained in both the city and countryside. Class is defined as a relationship determined by the position of individuals with respect to the means of production. This definition entails different considerations in rural and urban areas but in each setting produces a two-class social structure. In the agricultural context, property represented the basis of production and thus property-ownership divided the population into two classes, owners and tenants. Stern finds a significant different in fertility between these two classes and explains the difference in terms of rational family strategies. Tenants exhibited a fertility ratio twelve percent higher than that of owners. Although land owners were more materially secure than tenants, they were also more concerned about inheritance possibilities. "Land owners could keep the full reward from their work, but they also had to worry about the disposal of their land and its division among their children. Tenants on the other hand had to pass part of their product to the landlord, but with no land to pass on they may have been less concerned with the partibility of their estate." Thus, owners generally limited their fertility while tenants continued the traditional pattern.[33]

Stern's argument is speculative since he does not systematically link inheritance strategies to land-ownership patterns but his perspective has two important implications for research on rural-urban change. The Erie County study suggests that rural and urban experiences can be approached from a unified conceptual framework and that the most appropriate framework is built on class analysis. Thus, researchers should not simply compare rural and urban centers vertically but rather should examine the behaviour of social classes within these centers. Stern's work suggests that scholars must examine the specific interaction of various social groups with various environments. By implication, his study undermines any sense of urbanization as a monolithic phenomenon producing consistent changes throughout the population. Rather, class position remains the crucial determinant of life experience during both rural and urban development.

The theoretical questions about "urban as process" which are raised by research on demographic behaviour have been less directly considered in studies on transiency. Ever since systematic research first undermined traditional assumptions about a geographically stable past, scholars have focussed more on measurement than on motivation.[34] We know a great deal about how frequently individuals moved in different environments but much less about why some stayed and others left. Wherever researchers have looked in the nineteenth century, they have found astounding rates of population turnover. Studies of urban centers gained momentum with the finds of Stephen Thernstrom and Peter Knights who examined mid-nineteenth century Boston.[35] Their discovery of rapid population turnover has subsequently been confirmed by numerous studies of other cities. A general conclusion is that new residents replaced about half to three-quarters of urban populations during the course of any ten year period.[36]

In some ways, the discovery of such high transiency in cities is not surprising. A variety of urban circumstances clearly worked against long-term settlement during the emergence of a wage-labour economy. Seasonal job opportunities, residential insecurity, and the dream of something better are only some of the forces which undoubtedly inspired or forced city dwellers to move on. However, studies have now shown than population turnover is just as apparent in the countryside as in the city during the nineteenth century. These studies challenge the concept that urbanization undermined rural stability and produced a modern mobile population. Rather, they show that rural communities were also in a constant state of flux.[37] Gagan found that rural Peel County was in "perpetual motion." The vast majority of mid-nineteenth century residents were only passing through the county. Seventy percent were enumerated in the census just once. Not surprisingly, those who left were often agricultural tenants or unskilled labourers. However, farm ownership was certainly no guarantee of ongoing residence. In fact, Gagan argues that out-migration can sometimes be considered as a family inheritance strageey. He quotes one explanation offered for Ontario in the 1870s. "The farmer whose farm of one hundred acres was at one time sufficient to yield a comfortable living for himself and family now finds himself surrounded by grown up sons for whom he feels it incumbent upon himself to provide. . . and proceeds to Michigan, or some other western state or territory . . . to buy land sufficient for himself and his boys.' " In this way, established farm families contributed to the perpetual motion of nineteenth century society.[38]

Gérard Bouchard has applied a similar argument to the Saguenay Valley during the late nineteenth and early twentieth centuries. As elsewhere, the small village of Notre-Dame le Laterrière exhibited high rates of transiency and, in order to explain this phenomenon, Bouchard introduces the concept of family strategies. This approach goes beyond a simple model of rational economic behaviour. The strength of the family unit looms especially large. The prospect of material difficulty in the future caused economically secure families to emigrate in order to preserve their own cohesion. As in Peel County, immediate economic crisis was not necessary. "In this perspective, we think that a spirit of caution and sensible foresight, rather than atavistic carelessness, led to the emigration of families which, however well-established, had many sons to provide land for."[39]

Taken together, rural and urban studies of transiency further support the need for a geographically-integrated view of urban development. Just as in the case of fertility, the similar rural and urban patterns suggest than an encompassing dynamic was at work. One question concerns the extent to which nineteenth century individuals saw themselves as city or countryside people. Did a rural-urban distinction have meaning with respect to individual residential patterns. The well-known case of Wilson Benson suggests clearly that individuals' lives were not necessarily associated with exclusive rural or urban existence. Benson moved from place to place with steady frequency and without consistent regard for type of environment. Benson's life was spent in major cities such as Kingston and Toronto, frontier areas such as Artemsia Township, and small villages such as Markdale. During his early years in Canada West, his lack of agricultural experience caused him to lose a job as a farm labourer and thereafter to seek employment in a trade. However, learning a trade was not easy and Benson does end up on a farm "scratching out a living." It was only after a near-fatal accident with a threshing machine that he returned to a village for his remaining days.[40]

The representativeness of life histories such as Wilson Benson's can only be assessed through the kind of meticulous research currently being completed by Peter Knights. As an advance on his transiency study of Boston, Knights has attempted to follow out-migrants in order to achieve a sense of the actual migration process. His search has discovered emigrants in all parts of the United States and, in fact, many parts of the world. Although he has not yet published his findings, this approach promises to force re-evaluation of the extent to which nineteenth century individuals viewed themselves as either "rural" or "urban."[41] Just as in the case of Wilson Benson, these out-migrants appear to have viewed the nineteenth century environment as a totality in which survival and security had to be pursued wherever it was perceived.

The Benson example also questions the extent to which nineteenth century city growth should be considered a straightforward result of rural to urban migration. Such movement certainly obtained at an aggregate level but, for individuals, the process may have been far more complicated involving at least several treks between country and city. In this regard, it is important to remember that throughout the nineteenth century land hunger was a compelling force of human activity. By and large, families did not want to be in cities. The ideal of a rural homestead loomed large despite the hype of urban boosters. Urban life was the antithesis of the common aspiration. "Cities, many feared, were serpents in Eden, ensnaring, enfeebling, and corrupting their inhabitants. They pinned a man down and drained him of the vital energies that he needed to pull up stakes and move on to the greener pastures that lay ahead.''[42] The insecurity and marginal existence offered by a wage labour economy nourished the dream of pastoral autonomy. Although many individuals learned that this dream was not easily fulfilled, research has yet to demonstrate that a willing attachment to urban life paralleled actual city growth in nineteenth century society. City residence may not have engendered "urban" as a state of mind.

A general conclusion, therefore, is that a rural-urban conceptulization does not adequately reflect the reality of nineteenth century society. These systematic studies suggest continuity rather than dichotomy in individual experience. It should be recognized that this finding directly challenges those studies which suggest that "urban" has significant cultural meaning in terms of norms, values and attitudes. Basic questions concern the ways in which individuals actually become "urban." What was the process? How long did it take? Was it inevitable? What proportion of nineteenth century city dwellers can actually be considered psychologically "urban" at different points in time?

These questions become even more complex if evidence from small towns is brought into the discussion. Similarities in fertility and transiency between rural and urban areas are matched in the case of small towns by remarkable consistency in occupational structure. Katz' study of Hamilton argued that one of the principal distinguishing characteristics of that mid-nineteenth century city was an occupational structure which remained stable despite rapid population turnover. Katz and other scholars joined together to produce a system of occupational classification based on five categories; professional/large proprietor; commercial/small proprietor; skilled; semi-skilled; and unskilled. Between 1851 and 1861, the relative importance of each of these categories remained quite constant. Katz finds that "in each year about one quarter of the adult men worked in commercial occupations, another quarter in laboring jobs, a third quarter in skilled trades, about 15 percent in construction, just under 5 percent in the professions, and the rest in a variety of different capacities." This distribution also obtained in other cities such as Buffalo and Philadelphia and Katz suggests the division of labor in Hamilton may represent the common pattern in nineteenth century commercial cities.[43]

However, the occupational structure of urban Hamilton was also quite similar to certain rural hamlets. For example, Orillia in 1861 had a distribution of male occupations as follows: professional/proprietor, 14%; commercial/small proprietor, 26.1%; skilled, 29.9%; semi-skilled, 11.5%; and unskilled, 18.5%. These proportions shifted significantly as Orillia developed as a commercial service-center during the 1860s. In particular, the skilled category enlarged to encompass 46.6% of male workers as demand increased for artisanal activity. It is noteworthy that this development made Orillia's occupational structure look less like urban Hamilton than when the village was a small hamlet.[44] An important question, then, concerns the relationship of occupational structure to community growth before status as a city is achieved. If urbanization has no direct effect on occupational structure in major commercial centers, what is the impact of rapid population growth on the dimension of labour in smaller communities?

Similar questions are raised by a systematic examination of a small city in Wisconsin during the nineteenth century. William Crozier has examined manuscript census returns for the 1860-1880 period in Winona and he finds important changes in occupational distribution between 1860 and 1870 but not thereafter. In these decades, Winona experienced substantial population increase and the emergence of industrial activity. These developments re-distributed occupational importance during the 1860s but further development in the 1870s had no real effect on the relative proportions of different categories.

> In 1860, over a third of the occupations fall within the white collar class; over a quarter of the work force are skilled workers; and slightly over a third are unskilled occupations. The social structure reflects a society with education, skills, or capital that has established itself in a new city where there was opportunity for growth and profit. Almost two-thirds of the work force were in occupations that provided services or skills needed during the early stages of the city. Clerks, carpenters, merchants, teachers, and lawyers dominated the upper three classes of the social structure when the major activities of the city centered on commerce, commissions, and services. Almost half of the unskilled workers were domestics. Industry was in its infancy and the need for a large unskilled labor force did not surface until the transition to an industrial economy began to take place.[45]

This transition began in the 1860s and was evident by 1870 when white collar occupations declined in importance and the unskilled rose to almost one-half of the labour force. Industrial development continued during the 1870s but, surprisingly, Winona's occupational structure remained largely unchanged; only slight shifts are apparent in the 1880 enumeration. Viewed in the context of Katz' study of Hamilton, this pattern suggests that urbanization can be associated with structural rigidity only after a certain point of development has been achieved. Exactly where that point is remains vague but further systematic studies of transitional communities should help clarify this component of the urbanization process.

The importance of systematically studying towns and small cities is similarly suggested by research on social mobility. The central hypothesis which emerged from the early studies of Boston and Hamilton indicated that nineteenth century urbanization engendered a rigid social structure which only tolerated a small amount of vertical movement. This mobility, both downward and upward, occurred "within three relatively large and stable, hierarchically ordered groups, separated by unstable, transitional strata."[46] These three groups composed the class structure of mid-nineteenth century Hamilton: entrepreneurs, artisans, and labourers. Mobility between these classes was unlikely and, over time, became even less probable as social inquality increased. Katz concludes that Hamilton supports the possibility that "within nineteenth century North America, industrialization, urban growth, and complexity may have increased the already unequal distribution of wealth."[47]

To what extent was this level of social rigidity limited to urban centers? Were small towns more fluid? A preliminary look at Orillia revealed that as a tiny community in 1861, individual maturity was associated with improved occupational status. The professionals and large proprietors of Orillia were mature men in 1861 with an average age of 45.3 years. In contrast, semi-skilled and unskilled workers represented a younger generation with average ages in their late twenties. After a decade of rapid immigration, however, the age structure of the now established village's occupational structure approximated the pattern of urban Hamilton. Young men no longer dominated the lower status jobs. Rather, an average age in the thirties characterized all occupational categories in 1871. One hypothesis is that social rigidity had come to Orillia much in the way Katz theorized about Hamilton.

> This finding is somewhat ironic in light of the early aspiration that Orillia would someday rival southern Ontario's established centers. During the mid-nineteenth century civic leaders enthusiastically welcomed their town's economic growth and development. They expected that the arrival of the railroad would further facilitate population growth and enhance Orillia's strategic position as a service center for northwest Simcoe County. If we are justified in applying Katz' theory, the partial fulfillment of this expectation may have brought a general rise in the standard of living but it also led to more clearly-defined social boundaries and to an increasingly uneven distribution of wealth.[48]

Although this evidence is fragmentary, the potential implications should stimulate further research. The process of class formation is at the heart of the issue. Although recent studies in working-class history have questioned the traditional connection of urbanization and class action, the focus of research has remained on the large cities especially in recent major studies. Bryan Palmer has examined the emergence of industrial capitalism in Hamilton during the late nineteenth century while Gregory Kealey has analysed the experience of Toronto in the same period.[49] Recent work has begun to uncover the parallel histories of towns and small cities but the evolution of urban centers remains far more familiar. Similarly, class formation is generally viewed only in manufacturing and industrial contexts.

For example, scholars have carefully examined the ways in which technology diluted artisanal skills and thereby proletarianized an educated and articulate group. It was this group that became the leadership of the labour movement in the major cities of Ontario as well as elsewhere.[50] But what happened in small towns where productive activity was increasingly limited to service center functions? Was there less class conflict? Or has an urban research focus simply distorted the true generality of this phenomenon?

In sum, the writing of urban history during the 1970s has left unresolved a series of issues related to both theory and method. Conceptual headway appears most promising in the direction of a regional approach which could incorporate the strengths of the established perspectives on urban social structure, city elites and urban systems. Scholars who wish to understand "urban as process" cannot focus exclusively on the urban experience. The rural and small town context of city development must also be appreciated if "urban" is to be recognized and studied. Researchers must view urbanization not only in terms of residence but, more importantly, with reference to behaviour and *mentalité*. The central questions surround the impact of urban development on the experiences and thoughts of nineteenth century individuals. A comparative and geographically-integrated perspective promises to advance understanding of this impact.

Recent research suggests that four specific topics remain at the heart of the history of urban social structure: demographic behaviour, transiency, occupational structure, and social mobility. Although other concerns remain important, further pursuit of these topics promises to add significantly to an understanding of the process of urbanization. The available findings indicate that urban case studies will not be sufficient to reach this understanding. Rather, researchers must examine social structure in the broad geographic context which characterized nineteenth century experience. This strategy will produce a richer appreciation of "urban" as an historical process which may have been as much a state of mind as a sense of place.

NOTES:

1. The Hamilton Project has produced a long list of publications including two major books: Michael B. Katz, *The People of Hamilton, Canada West: Family and Class in the Mid-Nineteenth Century* (Cambridge, Mass.: Harvard University Press, 1975), and Michael B. Katz, Michael B. Doucet, and Mark J. Stern, *The Social Organization of Early Industrial Capitalism* (Cambridge, Mass.: Harvard University Press, 1982).

2. The major work of the Philadelphia Social History Project is Theodore Hershberg, ed., *Philadelphia: Work, Space, Family, and Group Experience in the Nineteenth Century. Essays Toward an Interdisciplinary History of the City* (Oxford and New York: Oxford University Press, 1981).

3. "Conversation with Samuel P. Hays," in Bruce M. Stave, *The Making of Urban History: Historiography Through Oral History* (Beverly Hills and London: Sage, 1977), p. 302.

4. "Conversation with Stephen Thernstrom," in *ibid.*, p. 230.

5. Gilbert A. Stelter, "Current Research in Canadian Urban History," *Urban History Review*, Vol. IX (June 1980), p. 112.

6. Two examples of this maturity are the rapid development of the journal *Histoire sociale/Social History*, and the types of articles that have recently been selected for the annual volume of the Canadian Historical Association's *Historical Papers*.

7. For an indication of the interests of Canadian urban historians, see two volumes edited by Alan F.J. Artibise and Gilbert A. Stelter: *The Usable Urban Past: Planning and Politics in the Modern Canadian City* (Toronto: Macmillan, 1979) and *Shaping the Canadian Urban Landscape: Essays on the City-Building Process, 1821-1921* (Ottawa: Carleton University Press, 1982). Also useful is the introductory essay in Artibise and Stelter, *Canada's Urban Past: A Bibliography to 1980 and Guide to Canadian Urban Studies* (Vancouver: University of British Columbia Press, 1980), pp. xiii-xxxii.

8. Katz, *The People of Hamilton*, "Introduction."

9. Alan F.J. Artibise, *Winnipeg: A Social History of Urban Growth, 1874-1914* (Montreal: McGill-Queen's, 1975), p. 1.

10. The title of Part Two of Artibise, *Winnipeg*, is "Big Men, Come Together with a Big Purpose."

11. See, for example, "Continuity and Change: Elites and Prairie Urban Development, 1914-1950," in Alan F.J. Artibise and Gilbert A. Stelter, eds., *The Usable Urban Past: Planning and Politics in the Modern Canadian City* (Toronto: Macmillan, 1979), pp. 130-154; "The Urban West: The Evolution of Prairie Towns and Cities to 1930," *Prairie Forum*, Vol. 4 (1979), pp. 237-262; "Boosterism and the Development of Prairie Cities, 1871-1913," in Alan F.J. Artibise, ed., *Town and City: Aspects of Western Canadian Urban Development* (Regina: Canadian Plains Research Center, 1981), pp. 209-235.

12. James W. Simmons, "The Evolution of the Canadian Urban System," in Artibise and Stelter, eds., *The Usable Urban Past*, pp. 9-33.

13. For other examples of this approach, see Paul Phillips, "The Prairie Urban System, 1911-1961: Specialization and Change," in Artibise, ed., *Town and City*, pp. 7-30; and Derek Hum and Paul Phillips, "Growth, Trade and Urban Development of Staple Regions," *Urban History Review*, Vol. X (October 1981), pp. 13-24.

14. John McCallum, *Unequal Beginnings: Agriculture and Economic Development in Quebec and Ontario until 1870* (Toronto: University of Toronto Press, 1980).

15. *Ibid.*, pp. 6-7.

16. *Ibid.*, p. 6.

17. *Ibid.*, p. 122.

18. In several instances, Katz compared his Hamilton data with the findings of Michael Anderson in *Family Structure in Nineteenth Century Lancashire* (Cambridge, Eng.: Cambridge University Press, 1971), and Bernard Farber in *Guardians of Virtue: Salen Families in 1800* (New York: Basic Books 1972). A systematic comparison of occupational structure was offered by Stuart Blumin, Laurence Glasco, Clyde Griffen, Theodore Hershberg, and Michael Katz, "Occupation and Ethnicity in Five Nineteenth Century Cities: A Collaborative Inquiry" *Historical Methods Newsletter*, Vol. 7 (June 1974), pp. 174-216.

19. Artibise, *Winnipeg*, p. 1.

20. Stephen Leacock, *Sunshine Sketches of a Little Town* (Toronto: McClelland & Stewart, 1948), pp. 7-8.

21. E.J. Noble, "Entrepreneurship and Nineteenth Century Urban Growth: A Case Study of Orillia, Ontario, 1867-1898," *Urban History Review*, Vol. IX (June 1980), pp. 64-89.

22. Leacock, *Sunshine Sketches*, p. 3.

23. Theodore Hershberg, "The New Urban History: Toward an Interdisciplinary History of the City," *Journal of Urban History*, Vol. 5 (November 1978), pp. 3-40.

24. For a listing of completed research at the Philadelphia Social History Project, see Appendix I in Hershberg, ed., *Philadelphia*, pp. 496-502.

25. David Gagan, *Hopeful Travellers: Families, Land, and Social Change in Mid-Victorian Peel County, Canada West* (Toronto: University of Toronto Press, 1981), p. 126.

26. *Ibid.*, pp. 141-142.

27. Y. Yasuba, *Birth Rates of the White Population in the United States, 1800-1860: An Economic Study* (Baltimore: John Hopkins University Press, 1961).

28. The major promoter of the economic theory of fertility has been R.R. Easterlin who offers his theoretical perspective in "Does Human Fertility Adjust to the Environment?" *The American Economic Review*, Vol. LXI, pp. 399-407. For examples of recent work in historical demography, see Maris A. Vinovskis, ed., *Studies in American Historical Demography* (New York: Academic Press, 1979); Ronald Demos Lee, ed., *Population Patterns in the Past* (New York: Academic Press, 1977); and Charles Tilly, ed., *Historical Studies of Changing Fertility* (Princeton, N.J.: Princeton University Press, 1978).

29. R.M. McInnis, "Childbearing and Land Availability: Some Evidence from Individual Household Data," in Lee, ed., *Population Patterns*, pp. 201-227.

30. Maris Vinovskis, "Recent Trends in American Historical Demography: Some Methodological and Conceptual Considerations," *Annual Reviews in Sociology*, Vol. 4, pp. 603-627.

31. Vinovskis, himself, is the strongest supporter of the usefulness of modernization as an explanatory concept. His major work is *Fertility Decline in Antebellum, Massachussets* (New York: Academic Press, 1981).

32. Mark J. Stern, "Differential Fertility in Rural Erie County, New York, 1855," mimeo. This paper is based on Stern's dissertation, "The Demography of Capitalism: Industry, Class, and Fertility in Erie County, New York, 1855-1915," Ph.D. Thesis, York University, 1979.

33. Stern, "Differential Fertility," p. 25.

34. Important exceptions to this generalization include the recent articles by Michael Katz, Michael J. Doucet and Mark J. Stern, "Migration and Social Order in Erie County, N.Y.: 1855," *Journal of Interdisciplinary History*, Vol. 8, pp. 669-702; and A. Gordon Darroch, "Migrants in the Nineteenth Century: Fugitives or Families in Motion?" *Journal of Family History*, Vol. 6 (Fall 1981), pp. 257-277.

35. Stephen Thernstrom and Peter R. Knights, "Men in Motion: Some Data and Speculations about Urban Population Mobility in Nineteenth-Century America," *Journal of Interdisciplinary History*, Vol. I (1970).

36. An example of recent work is Lawrence Glasco, "Migration and Adjustment in the Nineteenth-Century City: Occupation, Property and Household Structure of Native-born Whites, Buffalo, New York, 1855," in Tamara K. Hareven and Maris A. Vinovskis, eds., *Family and Population in Nineteenth-Century America* (Princeton, N.J.: Princeton University Press, 1978), pp. 154-178.

37. One of the first studies to emphasize this point was Anders Norberg and Sune Åkerman, "Migration and the Building of Families: Studies on the Rise of the Lumber Industry in Sweden," in Kurt Agren, David Gaunt, Ingrid Eriksson, John Rogers, Anders Norberg, and Sune Åkerman, *Aristocrats, Farmers, Proletarians: Essays in Swedish Demographic History* (Uppsala: Studia Historica Upasliensia, 1973).

38. United States Department of State, Consular Reports, RG 59, Reel T488-2, Trade and Commerce Report for Sarnia, 17 July 1879, as quoted in David Gagan, "Land, Population, and Social Change: The 'Critical Years' in Rural Canada West," *Canadian Historical Review*, Vol. LIX (September 1978), p. 315.

39. Gérard Bouchard, "Family Structures and Geographic Mobility at Laterrière, 1851-1935," *Journal of Family History*, Vol. 2 (Winter 1977), p. 367. Bouchard's project has now

published numerous articles concerning both methodology and preliminary conclusions. These articles include Gérard Bouchard, "Introduction à l'étude de la société Saguenayenne aux XIXe et XXe siècles," *Revue d'Histoire de l'Amerique française*, Vol. 31 (juin 1977); and "Démographie et société rurale an Saguenay, 1851-1935," *Recherches Sociographiques*, Vol. XIX (Jan.-Aug. 1978).

40. Wilson Benson, *Life and Adventures of Wilson Benson, Written by Himself* (Toronto, 1876). This autobiography was used extensively by Michael Katz in *The People of Hamilton*, Chapter 3.

41. Some initial conclusions are presented in Peter Knights, "The Facts of Lives, or Whatever Happened to 2808 Nineteenth-Century Bostonians?" Paper presented to the Canadian Historical Association, June 1982.

42. Thernstrom and Knights, "Men in Motion," pp. 17-18.

43. Katz, *The People of Hamilton*, pp. 52-53.

44. Chad M. Gaffield and David Levine, "Dependency and Adolescence on the Canadian Frontier: Orillia, Ontario in the Nineteenth Century," *History of Education Quarterly*, Vol. 18 (Spring 1978).

45. William L. Crozier and Chad Gaffield, "Small Towns, Cities, and the Urbanization Process in North America: Orillia, Ontario and Winona, Minnesota." Paper presented at the Northern Great Plains History Conference, University of Minnesota, Duluth, 1980, p. 7.

46. Katz, *The People of Hamilton*, p. 208.

47. *Ibid.*, p. 30. For a more recent view, see Michael B. Katz, "Social Class in North American Urban History," *The Journal of Interdisciplinary History*, Vol. XI (Spring 1981), pp. 579-605.

48. Gaffield and Levine, "Orillia," p. 44.

49. Bryan D. Palmer, *A Culture in Conflict: Skilled Workers and Industrial Capitalism in Hamilton, Ontario, 1860-1914* (Montreal: McGill-Queen's University Press, 1979), and Gregory S. Kealey, *Toronto Workers Respond to Industrial Capitalism, 1867-1892* (Toronto: University of Toronto Press, 1980).

50. For an excellent sampling of recent works in the field, see the journal *Labour/Le Travailleur* which has quickly emerged as a leading publication in Canadian History.

Boarding and Belonging: Thoughts on Sojourner Institutions

ROBERT F. HARNEY

The gap between the subject matter of migration studies and that of North American urban and ethnic history has narrowed in recent years. Historians of migration now study in detail the precise local causes of the movement from old world locations and the pattern of the consequent diaspora. At the same time, those who study major American cities and small industrial towns have begun to show some appreciation of the relationship between migration causes and settlement. In most studies, however, there remains a lacuna between accounts and explanations of the crossing and the history of ethnic institutional and neighbourhood life on the North American side. Although we have moved from Oscar Handlin's compelling, if often incorrect, metaphors of ''uprootedness'' and ''in fellow-felling'' to explain the processes of migrating, ghettoizing, and acculturating, we continue to depend too much on mono-causal agents of settlement such as family chain migration or the padrone system.[1] Using these ideas to carry them over the rough spots in narration, historians lose sight of the important mental transition from sojourner to settler among newcomers, and of the formative period in ethnic settlement when male sojourners predominated. Even if it is a proper reflection of the sojourner's ambivalence as a man neither in his home place nor reconciled to his new place, this lack of study destroys our chance to discover the stages of cultural and institutional transition from migration to sojourning and settlement.

Abrupt transition from the locus of emigration to full-fledged ethnic settlement and the use of padronism or extended family as *deus ex machina*

SOURCE: *Urban History Review*, No. 2-78 (October, 1978), pp. 8-37. Reprinted by permission of the author and the editors of the *Urban History Review*.

to turn migrants into urban North Americans can be found in even the best recent studies of immigrants in cities, as, for example, in H. Nelli's *Italians in Chicago* and J. Barton's *Peasants and Strangers: Italians, Rumanians and Slovaks in an American City*.[2] Nelli, building a model of padronism and an indistinguishable mass of the exploited for whom the generic "southerner" provides both a class and ethnic identity, must wait until the newcomers have broken the sojourning thrall enough to be on Chicago's registered voter rolls or in commercial directories before he is able to study geographical and occupational mobility. For the sojourning period, he offers nothing but the stock characters, padrone and southerner, and a few biographies of exceptional immigrants. There is, in his account, neither a history and analysis of sojourner institutions nor a guide to the changing sentiments, intentions, and ethnic identity of the newcomers.

Barton makes more effort to explain the pattern of settlement in North America in terms of old world causes such as family and *paese* (home town) loyalties and the larger push factors that existed in specific European areas. There is, however, no "interior" history of the migrants. We do not know their frame of mind, their levels of expectation, nor how long they intended to stay. Nor is any thought given to whether knowing these things would enable us to understand better the pace of acculturation or the intensity of ethnic persistence in Cleveland. So, although Barton implements the best ideas of Handlin about the migrant as a villager and of Vecoli about family and *paese* reconstitution in the city, his chapters on the Old World remain strangely disjoined from those which deal with the new ethnic institutions of the city such as benevolent societies, visible ethnic business enterprises, and parishes. By failing to appreciate and study the informal, often amoebic, institutions of the sojourning period and by maintaining stock characters like the padrone and the "southerner," the historian fails the immigrant in his continuous, if tortuous, journey from migrant to "ethnic" and retrospectively confirms the stereotyping of male sojourners as Wops, Bohunks, birds of passage, *cafoni* — the faceless guestworkers of North America at the turn of the century.[3]

It is my belief that a chrysalis of the ethnic settlement of the North American ethnic group itself, its boundaries and its content, can be found in those first years of urban migrant life, now shrouded in creation myths and filio-pieties. Careful study of the sojourner, his frame of mind, his needs, his amoebic institutions, and the impact of the sojourn on his identity will demonstrate this. Such study will require the use of oral testimony as well as a change in approach. In fact, North American historians have ceased to view immigration, the ethnic colony, and acculturation as an obvious continuum, and, in the face of startling ethnic persistence, more time has been spent rethinking the relationship between the last two pictures in the triptych than between the first two. The distinctions between migrants and immigrants, sojourners and settlers[4] is not always made and the result is that family settlement is very often seen as the first stage of ethnic neighbourhood life.

Now, when so many excellent local studies of specific ethnic groups and their settlement are appearing, it seems the right time to reassert the need for thorough comparative studies of the migration, sojourning, and settlement patterns of each ethnic group. Stock characters such as steamship agents, immigrant bankers, foraging foremen sent to Europe to recruit, and labour brokers need to be studied as part of an economic structure rather than simply appearing on the stage in the immigrant drama. Households with boarders, extended families, boarding-houses, padrone-run bunkhouses and commissaries, informal *paese* clubs, mutual aid and burial societies — all elements in the sojourner's world — require analysis as institutions.[5] If we are to understand the transition from sojourning to settling to ethnicity in terms worthy of historians rather than those of latter day restrictionists or settlement house workers.[6]

I will look at the institution of boarding from the perspective of the sojourner and the settler. We must first remove some of the confusion that surrounds the practice of boarding among newcomers, and then we can see it as a form of entrepreneurship for some settlers, as a social institution fulfilling most needs for sojourners, and finally, as a frame within which aspects of North American ethnicity were defined. Two points need to be made at the outset. In attempting to show the entrepreneurial and institutional nature of boarding, I am not denying the important contribution made to the subject from the perspective of household and family studies. For example, Modell and Hareven's excellent study, "Urbanization and the Malleable Household: An Examination of Boarding and Lodging in American Families," although it does not pay attention to sojourning as a concept, informs most of my thinking on the places of households in the study of boarding.[7] Also, I am aware that much damage is done to separate ethnic traditions and patterns of boarding by my cross-cultural approach. I wish only to show in this paper that the condition of being a sojourner, which was shared by most male migrants of the so-called "new migration" of the 20th century, encouraged similar institutions among all groups.[8]

Questions of morality and definition linger from then, and, before we can discuss the role of boarding in the sojourner economy and society, some confusions need to be sorted out. The Dillingham Commission, despite its misuse of the statistics on boarding, offered in 1911 a sensible classification of varieties of the boarding phenomenon among newcomers. The three general categories listed were: households consisting of two or more families living together; households consisting of one or more families with boarders and lodgers; and "scattering households" in which no family is present and called for this reason "group households." This last category divides into "either . . . a group of men who share all expenses or . . . a 'boarding house' usually [run by] a man without a family, and boarders and lodgers."[9]

Two subspecies of the first and last classifications have received most attention from historians. The household of an extended family has been the focus of chain migration studies, and the boarding house/inn as an adjunct of padronism has interested those who view migration a strict relationship of labour, flowing through brokers, to capitalist demand. The phenomenon of several families, related or from the same old country locale, living as a single household was not uncommon, especially for short periods of time while people inserted themselves into the North American economy. However, one or more families living with relatives or fellow countrymen as boarders was far more than a "malleable household"; it was also a complex network of informal trust, written contract, and cash exchange. Oral testimony shows that there was almost always exchange of money, precision about services rendered and terms of *modus vivendi*, as well as careful accounting of food and other costs. Analysis of boarding among sojourners then as simply family or household history does fall short of the cash nexus that existed and animated the institution at least as much as "in fellow-felling" did. The other subspecies, which skews our understanding of boarding much more than a too simple view of family and paesanism, is the extreme form of exploitation found in padroni inns and isolated work camps.

Confusing the traits of remote work camps with boarding itself is the same as identifying private enterprise with monopoly capitalism. Indeed, it was monopoly — through cultural or geographical isolation — of lodging, transport, job opportunity, and food supply which produced the extreme forms of exploitation. In both Canada and the United States, work camps on the railways, shanties near coal patches, isolated barge canal camp sites, and lumber camps led to virtual enslavement . . . a condition which was luridly detailed by social reformers and immigration, industrial, and royal commissions. This spectre of the padrone-run commissary and bunkhouse or of the overcrowed inn near train stations and harbours created the aura of depravity and criminality which surrounds all of the Dillingham Commission's third category, "group households."[10]

In the case of Sicilians in the southern United States and the Chinese along the entire west coast of the Americas, insertion into the North American economy, often to replace black slave labour, was so reminiscent of negro servitude that the housing of the newcomers was naturally compared to slave quarters.[11] In 1930, an exposé of padrone and company-run camps in West Virginia showed that Italian migrant labour was often shanghaied, threatened with physical violence, and that camp security was maintained by armed

Boarding house on York Street, winter, 1910. (*City of Toronto Archives*)

guards and, in one case, a gatling gun.[12] Thus, the housing of foreign sojourners and the image of slavery ran together in the public mind. In the cities, immigrant entrepreneurs sometimes kept their employees in crowded lodgings near their shops. Especially in cases when those employees were immigrant minors, such as Greek or Basilicatan bootblacks or Syrian and Lebanese confectioners and pedlars, boarding became associated with white slavery and child abuse.[13]

Boarding in the city was rarely seen as the product of rapid population growth and poor urban planning or, conversely, as the sojourner's choice. For Nelli's Chicago, it was the padrone control of lodging itself which served as the mechanism by which target migrants were trapped and sojourners transformed into settlers.

> Unemployed workers who remained in Chicago had no problems in obtaining food or lodgings, for padroni and Italian bankers saved and operated tenement houses where they encouraged guests to indulge in extravagance in order to place them more completely in debt.[14]

Turn-of-the-century eyewitnesses noted the geographical proximity of "employment agencies, saloons, cheap lodging houses, lunchrooms, and cheap or second-hand clothing stores."[15] Amy Bernardy saw the same link between boarding and labour exploitation in Boston's North End:

> The problem of capital and labour shines through between the lines in the notice

outside the banchista's office: 'need 300 men for work on the railroad.' The horror of the unsanitary and degrading accommodations shows itself beneath the laconic sign: 'bordo' or 'we take in boarders'.[16]

In Toronto, a cluster of bankers, travel agencies, and hotels existed in the heart of the first 'Little Italy' in the St. John's Ward; the Venzia Hotel, a steamship agency, an "immigrant bank," and a working class hotel dominated b the main intersection of the second neighbourhood around St. Francis (St. Agnes) Parish. The Royal Commission which dealt with fraudulent labour practices surrounding the importation of Italian labour to Montreal demonstrated the close ties between the Canadian Pacific's recruiters, the padrone, Antonio Cordasco, and a number of boarding houses.[17] Inevitably the boarding of alien migrant males became almost synonymous in Canadian cities, as it already was in the rural work camps, with exploitation and monopoly of services. In fact, any sense that sojourners might prefer such a boarding system was lost in a haze of moral outrage. The very place of boarding as an aspect of the commerce of migration rather than an exploitative end in itself became lost. The United States Industrial Commission of 1901 heard this testimony: "However, I have called the attention of the commission to many cases of Italian hotel keepers who have tried to get hold of the Italian immigrants in order to speculate upon them." And boarding was identified with outright violent crime as well. "Others have told me," wrote the director of Ellis Island, "how they were led to boarding houses where they were beaten and robbed or shanghaied to some far off mine, quarry, or construction site."[18]

If boarding came into the cities from the remote work camps with a criminal record, in the city, the sojourners and their lodging system were immediately caught in yet another vortex of moral and sociological confusion. Boarding was associated with overcrowding, tenement conditions, and the dangers of the "lodger evil." All of those masks of social distintegration intensified when the "pipeline to the cesspools of Europe" was attached. The lodger evil itself, of course, had emerged as a moral issue only when the majority of boarders in the city ceased to be middle class and were replaced by rural, lower class migrants and foreigners.[19] In that sense, ethnic and cultural disparities were merely a convenient rallying cry for the city reformers and social gospellers, but reform, inspired by the social gospel or not, and prejudice fed on each other. J.S. Woodsworth, describing immigrants in Winnipeg and Toronto, could not comprehend why Galicians would live "twenty-four in one room where only seven should have been. Fancy such conditions," he added, "with illimitable prairies stretching to the north and west."[20] Thus, someone like Woodsworth could see boarding as an aspect of clannishness, a failure to acculturate, and a judgmental category which served to portray the sojourners (not incorrectly, only maliciously) as being like Emily Dickinson's rats, "the concisest tenants of the Earth," providing unfair competition for native stock. By living and surviving in the bestial nests of the boarding house, sojourners not only lowered standards, but also threatened to succeed. In Toronto, the muckraking newspaper *Jack Canuck* clearly expressed the danger that the sojourner might prove to be the fittest breed in the industrial city: "Not so the Italian. He is content to 'pig-in' with a crowd of others and live under conditions which an Anglo-Saxon would be ashamed of."[21]

The Report of the Toronto Medical Health Officer Dealing with the Recent Investigation of Slum Conditions in Toronto, Embodying Recommendations for the Amelioration of the Same, prepared for the city by Dr. Hastings in 1911, contained a typical interplay of hostility toward boarding, foreigners, and the burgeoning industrial city itself. Charts of overcrowed rooms, dark rooms, rear houses, tenement houses, common lodging houses, cellar dwellings, and one-roomed dwellings — all obviously employed as indices of squalor and social disintegration — were juxtaposed page on page with lists of ethnic households in the neighbourhoods studied in the report.[22] Boarding then, rather than being approached as a possible variation on the "malleable household," a sign of the resilience and initiative of migrant networks, was treated as urban pathology.[23]

If we can pass from the moralizing and emotion that surrounds turn-of-the-century boarding to its social reality, a different set of questions can be asked about the institution itself: questions about the uses of family and household to cope with a new North American situation, about boarding as a form of ethnic entrepreneurship and proprietorship — one of the earliest such forms — and as a community institution and a force shaping the boundaries of ethnicity itself. Further questions about the role of boarding in establishing the *ambiente* and density necessary for an ethnic settlement, and indeed, in moving the sojourner into the position and attitudes of a settler need answering as well. A new perspective, informed by much oral testimony and by the concept of sojourning, when combined with an understanding of different ethnic household traditions, should enable us to see boarding as one of those key institutions now lost in the mists between migration and permanent settlement.

Whether we are dealing with a family with boarders or a "group household," no amount of rhetoric about paesanism and kinship ties should draw us away from the economic matrix of the institution as it was understood and used by both the boarder and the keeper of boarders. For the boarders, the nature of the arrangement satisfied the needs of their sojourning frame of mind. That frame of mind (*mentalitá*) called for maximizing savings, minimizing potentially costly encounters with the host society, and, as much as circumstances permitted, recreating or remaining in the *ambiente* of the home country.[24] Considered in these terms, one can see that the family-run boarding system was not so much a different institution from the "group household" as it was a felicitous and highly efficient form of it. Enterprise, a labour intensive and administrative organization around a working wife and serving children, was not only a traditional aspect of the European rural family but was also an efficient adaptation of that tradition to the city. The study of boarding benefits enormously from recent interpretations of the role of women in the work force and reassertions of older ones about the family as a single economic unit.[25]

Boarding then was a practical use of family and village ties as well as of certain qualities within the pre-industrial family itself. Historians have rarely felt that they could penetrate the complex nucleus of fellow-feeling and entrepreneurship in the relationship of relatives and fellow villagers who lodged together in North America.[26] In 1941, Oscar Handlin's eloquence could not hide the fact that he had thrown in the towel with the remark that, among the Boston Irish, "no matter how cramped the quarters of those already settled, there was always room *for the sake of rent, charity or kinship*."[27] Even in Vecoli's articulate critique of Handlin's *Uprooted*, the sojourner's family and "belongingness with his fellow townsmen" are contrasted with padronism, as if the former had no cash nexus.[28] Since then, perhaps because of the heritage of padronism or the image of sex roles, the study of boarding among Italian migrants remains too dichotomized. Certainly Slavic and Hungarian studies have no trouble in dealing with the family with boarders and the "missus" of the establishment as both a household and a well-organized business enterprise.[29]

Thomas Kessner's recent study of Jewish and Italian social mobility in New York City concludes that "lodgers represented the closest of neighbours and immigrants were careful to choose those of similar ethnic origin and religious background. These boarders became part of the immigrant household." Kessner notes in passing that in 1880 most Italian *bordanti* in the city were unrelated to the family with whom they formed a household, and that even by 1905, by which time chain migration could presumably have done its work, over 62% of *bordanti* were unrelated to the household in which they lived.[30] All this suggests more family enterprise than chain migration and kinship.

Among Italian lodgers, words like *bossa* for the keeper of the house, *bordo* for their arrangement, and *bordante* to describe themselves were borrowed and the Italian expression *covivenza* was rarely used. Perhaps an ethno-linguist could explain what qualities in the Italian North American household were sufficiently alien to require such borrowing. That boarding confused the newcomers themselves can also be seen in the attempt to force an ascriptive setting. Older boarders were called uncle by the young women who, after marriage to a boarding-boss, found themselves wives and keepers of boarders. Younger lodgers called the lady of the house auntie or *nonna* (grandmother), and *la padrona* when they referred to her with third parties. Hungarians usually referred to the boarding-boss's wife as the "miszisz."[31] Many of these terms were obviously used to impose vigorous sexual controls on the boarding house, but they also reflect the attempt to make the institution fit either household or family situations which could be understood from the old world experience.

The use of terms of respect or of familial designations between boarder and the boarding-boss's wife cannot obscure either the menial labour status of the woman who ran the boarding establishment or the precise business arrangements which existed between boarder and keeper. Although oral testimony invariably emphasizes the atmosphere of trust, family values, and sense of shared fate in early Italian Canadian boarding, further questioning always brings out descriptions of highly structured arrangements about services rendered, payment for services, controls on boarder behaviour, and on the organization of boarding itself. These latter aspects are clearer in the "group household" than in the family with boarders or the boarding-boss variations, but they are present in all forms of immigrant boarding.

A Methodist colporteur in Toronto complained that Sicilian women in the 1900s were so busy tending to boarders that they could not come to church gatherings; he did not understand that caring for a group of *bordanti*, or a boardinghouse, was an occupation for the whole family and a profession for the wife of the household: "Thus the rooming house is lucrative because it utilizes almost completely the family spare time labour. Similar is the case with lunch bars, grocery stores, etc."[32] Whether we can find sufficient material in traditional sources, such as assessment rolls, income statistics, and city directories, to measure how lucrative keeping boarders was as an ethnic enterprise, the psychic saving involved in keeping the mother and wife at home to work and in maintaining the family as a single economic unit was clearly supplemented by much real profit from taking in sojourners.[33]

Fortunate the settler who could turn his household and his dependents into a source of income while still working outside the home himself. He was like the rich *contadino* of the old country who owned a draft animal which could be rented out for extra income. A wife as a beast of burden in the boarding business was certainly the equivalent of a mule in southern Italy or Macedonia, and small children were as valuable an asset as healthy sons had been on the land.[34] The profit margin for the family with boarders was potentially great, limited only by the energy of the family, the size of the house, the satisfaction of the clientele, and, very occasionally, public inspection and intervention. For example, in Toronto in 1911, at a time when an Italian unskilled sojourner could earn about $2 a day as a labourer, a

Toronto Italian family collected $3 a month from each of thirty boarders. The house they used rented for $28 a month. Depending on food arrangements, clear profit as well as free shelter accrued to the entrepreneurial family, and the husband was able to work full time outside of the home. In other instances, men paid $1.25 a week or the equivalent of a day's wages on board. The Hastings Report remarked darkly that there was "some evidence that certain small hotels and old rooming houses are about to undergo the dangerous transformation into foreign lodging houses."[35] If the Report saw such changes as heralding the spread of slum conditions, we should see it as proof of a successful entrepreneurial form and evidence of the existence of a satisfied clientele. Egisto Rossi, a special commissioner for the Italian government, calculated the sojourner's reasons for supporting a boarding system:

> Accepting my conclusions about the second and third points, it should be noted that the cost of food and lodging in Canada does not differ much from that of the United States. With 3 or 4 dollars a week, a manual labourer can live well enough in both countries. Certainly, our labourers do not spend on average more than 15 dollars a month, and that, when you consider that they early usually about $1.25 to $1.75 a day, enables them to save and to return to Italy at the end of a season with some *gruzzolo di denaro* (nest-egg).

Thus, there is every reason to believe that groups of sojourners would have created boarding institutions if entrepreneurial families and boarding-bosses had not done so.[36] That is, after all, what the existence of so many "group" or "scattering households," as described by the Dillingham Commission and many other contemporaries, signifies.

Despite the camaraderie and intra-ethnic warmth that emerges from much of the oral testimony, boarding was a business. In an oral history of Pennsylvania immigrants, the authors describe a boarder in a South Slav establishment who found his "plate [turned] upside down at the boarding house when he did not have work." Moreover, the definitions of services to be rendered between keeper and boarder, regardless of kinship or paesanism, were so precise and so quickly surrounded by local custom that it very soon did not depend on the ritual of affecting kinship described earlier. Whether the mistress of such a "malleable household" was called la padrona, auntie, or the missus, if she took money for bed and board, she accepted a more rigorous set of commitments for service than any boarding house boss.[37] The woman was responsible for serving the boarders in a way that closely resembled the duties of a peasant wife to her husband. (Perhaps that is why, in the Hungarian case, the missus was assumed by many boarders also to share sexual favours with them, and why Italian feminists like Amy Bernardy railed against boarding as a source of adultery.)[38]

Giovanni Verga, in one of his short stories about Sicilian life, describes the obligations of a good peasant wife thus: "She made sure that he found a fresh sheet on the bed, the macaroni made, and the bread for the following week already leavening."[39] The female boarding house keeper, and this varied considerably from ethic group to ethnic group, washed the workers soiled work clothes, bedding and dirty underclothes, and sometimes even the back and legs of the boarders themselves when they came in from mines and factories. The services rendered require much more study, for the status of women and the sexual mores of each country of emigration must have affected services offered in North American boarding arrangements.

Contractual arrangements revolved around the food supply, clothing, and bedding, but it was the first of these that seems almost to have been a preoccupation. A Roumanian account indicates that groups of boarders sometimes moved in search of better food.[40] For historians and social scientists who fear that contemporary emphasis on varieties of ethnic cuisine may trivialize ethnicity, the study of the place of food in boarding is instructive. The food supply was the most flexible of the sojourner's costs, and its preparation, along with language and daily contact with boarders of the same origin, was the most salient aspect of the sojourner's struggle to insulate himself from cultural change. The boarder balanced his concern to maximize savings with his need for ample and hearty food in labour intensive job situations. He refused usually to sacrifice fully his *ambiente* and culture by eating food prepared in an "English" or North American style every day of the week.

The boarding-boss or the housewife with boarders wished to maximize profits while not alienating clientele. Again, it is obvious that excesses occurred where isolation and company indifference gave the commissary or those in charge of the food supply a virtual monopoly. For example, since most foremen and section bosses of Italian work gangs on the Canadian Pacific Railroad depended on Montreal padroni for their supply of Italian food, the railroad navvies in isolated camps paid as much as five times the going city rate for mouldy bread and tainted sardines (anchovies). In the city, competition between forms of lodging and perhaps greater "fellow-feeling" caused more balance between the profit motive and the workers' tastes and requirements. On the other hand, taste in food did maintain ethnic boundaries. Certainly sojourners saw it as an important difference between themselves and other groups, and it was used as a reason for maintaining ethnically homogeneous bunkhouses at many work sties. "All Japanese stay in same bunkhouse. The Canadians live in a separate bunkhouse and of course didn't like to eat Japanese food from our Japanese cook." What was true of isolated camp sites was equally true of the city, and *Jack Canuck*, lamenting the clannishness of Italians and the fact that they received work from the city through subcontracts, remarked: "It is said that the Italian employed by the city of Toronto refuse to buy any other than Italian macaroni. That they live in gangs of from 6 to 9 in one room. . . ."[41] The newspaper's bitter comment tells us something about the place of boarding in the creation of ethnic density, of making other ethnic enterprises such as food importation possible, and the importance of food in defining ethnic boundaries and choice of housing.

Although carefully arrived at agreements between a boarding-boss and his boarders or in a "group household" might be expected, the degree of organization in the arrangement of meals in the household with boarders is a bit startling. Even in warm, family-based, and *paesani* (fellow townsmen) boarding circumstances, the question of food supply was matter for careful accounting and individual, if usually unwritten, contracts. In one household, a hurdy gurdy man and his wife kept three or four younger boarders, often men from their *paese*. In the kitchen was a great black stove with separate pots of food prepared by each lodger for himself. An affluent or prodigal man might be preparing veal while a boarder more concerned about the cost of prepaid steamship tickets limited himself to the same meatless minestra or pasta every day. Yet another had made a full board arrangement with the family and ate their prepared meal with them. Everyone took his food from the stove and sat down to eat at the kitchen table together.[42]

A Slovak migrant in the Niagara peninsula described his boarding arrangement thus:

> The rooming house . . . see we paid the lady a dollar a month for cooking. You paid a dollar and we paid the room extra. And every week she bought what she need in the grocery store. She was purchaser. She chose — sometimes she says well tomorrow we're going to have real meat or something like that — or breaded veal or pork chops. Okay everybody agree. And then, end of the week — Sunday usually — they calculate everything — how much she spent — and then she spread the expenses amongst all of us. We pay a dollar and she had a free board. And her husband had to pay same as we do.[43]

The ethos of this arrangement hovers between family, trust, and good business, and the possible mutations of the boarding arrangement seem endless. Without a much larger sample, and some attempt at controlling that sample by time, place, and ethnic group, it is difficult to tell how much old world traditions affected the nature of the arrangement, but it should be clear that the simple line between family and enterprise is quite useless. For example, a Donau-Schwaben (German from Hungary) boarding house in Welland, Ontario had only lodgers who were related to one another and the owner. The lady of the household cooked for all the men, but

> We paid so much a week and she cooked. She cooked for us and we could buy our

own food and take it to her and she cooks it or sometimes — the butcher came to the house. Butcher send young fellow and he notes down what you want and the next day they delivered it.[44]

The boarding system was further complicated by whether the household was responsible for preparing the lunch pail for each worker/boarder as well. In that instance, the matter could range from a commitment to so many sandwiches or cold sausage per day to no agreement. (In Toronto, for example, many Polish and Lithuanian boarders in the Niagara-Queen Street factory district found it easier to save by buying monthly lunch tickets from local Chinese and Macedonian restaurants who had packed lunches waiting for them each monring as they passed by.)

The sojourners' preoccupation with their meal arrangements grew from two different sources. First, as the most variable of their expenses, it bore constant and close scrutiny by men committed to saving. However, we must not deny the centrality of familiar cuisine to their maintenance of popular culture while away from the homeland. Moreover, it seems likely that boarding as an important and pioneering form of enterprise in immigrant neighbourhoods would not have existed if those who maintained boarders could not meet their dietary and culinary demands. Those Roumanian boarders in Cleveland expected a Sunday noon meal of noodle soup, pork meat, and dumplings. They demanded sauerkraut, sausage, and pureed white beans a certain number of times a week.[45] Like the Italian labourers who would only eat imported pasta, the Roumanians were practicing a primitive but determined consumer power. Their existence made possible small entrepreneurial successes for those who imported pasta and tomatoes or made sauerkraut to some old country formula. Storefronts, *ambiente*, and ethnic settlement followed.

Concern over the cost, quality, and ethnicity of food existed in the "group households" as much as in the family with boarders where instead of agreements with *la padrona*, the boarders had to evolve a regime as a group. The organization of a cooking roster, rent payments, a budget of shared costs for food and drink, and even the laying out of rules for behaviour between boarders took time and consensus. Sometimes one would be hard put to tell the difference between a commercial boarding-boss and the sort of authoritarian leader who emerged to dominate such households. Usually the latter was an older member of an extended family of males involved in the boarding establishment, or a village man whose reputation had been great in the old country as well. He might differ from a boarding-boss only in so far that his power lay in his influence rather than in proprietorship over the location.[46] In other cases, remarkable democracy prevailed. More oral testimony, especially about weekly budget meetings and arrangement of a roster, will certainly show that "group boarding" nurtured the more formal institutions of the later community, such as burial societies, mutual aid organizations, and *paese* clubs. Some boarding establishments sounded more like settlement houses or fraternal organizations than households anyway. Peter Roberts described what he, as a social gospeller, had found to be an ideal "group household" of Japanese in Omaha:

> One of the best samples of housekeeping I have ever seen was done by the 140 Japanese who lived in the House of the Good Shepherd in South Omaha. A board of managers had charge of the affairs of the group. The secretary of the board kept all records, accounts, and transacted all business with outsiders; the commissary had charge of the feeding of the group; the cooking, washing, and scrubbing were systematized, and each member was bound by a set of rules that secured peace and order.[47]

As we turn to the role of boarding the dynamic of changing ethnic identities in North America, we should observe that for the true sojourner, the boarding place, whether under a padrone system, with a family, or in a "group household," provided a means of living with one's own on a scale larger than the family, and yet, smaller than the host society or even of that North American invention, the ethnic group. The lodging place served as the focus of "fellow-feeling," of gossip about townsmen and countrymen who were mavericks, philanderers, or drunks, of the news' network coming from the home village, of intelligence about job opportunities, of the arranging of marriages and the travel of other family members, and finally, of who were reliable merchants, money-lenders, and go-betweens. It was the place to play old world card games and spend leisure time. In that sense, the boarding house, especially if one includes the saloons and ancillary enterprises often in its immediate environs, had for the sojourner a variety of the ethnic "completeness of institutions"[48] that Raymond Breton had described as necessary to a later stage of ethnic development.

In its informal and amoebic way, boarding provided for all the needs of the sojourners. If we could keep that in mind, the early period of ethnic settlement, dominated by male migrants and boarding arrangements, could be understood not in terms of the failure of acculturation or the pathology of marginality, but as a period when the sojourners' needs were met and when those entrepreneurs who drew their income from serving and exploiting the sojourners began the formation of permanent settlement and, indeed, of an ethnic bourgeoisie. One need only think of the sojourner's agenda to predict those institutions which would grow up in his presence and those which would be retarded.[49] Institutions of acculturation or culture mattered little. There were no children to educate in the new ways or to make steadfast in the old. For most of the groups involved, the presence of women was required to make ethnic parishes necessary. On the other hand, the sojourners did require ethnic food, rough leisure in the form of saloons, coffee-houses, and billiard rooms, steamship agencies, banks, employment bureaux, and some form of mutual aid or burial insurance. Just as oral testimony can show the presence of successful immigrant enterprise before city directory or tax roll evidence existed,[50] interviews also confirm that early community business notables and leaders of *paese* clubs or benevolent societies began as heads of group households or as boarding house bosses. Dr. Juliana Puskas of the Hungarian Academy of Sciences has pointed out that in those groups, such as the South Slav and the Hungarian, where the "miszusz" had a special role in running the boarding establishment, many such women were the moving spirits and first officers of parish and benevolent society committees.[51]

One suspects that the study of boarding and especially of the "group household" could bring us to the very heart of the relationship between ethnic identity and socio-economic reality, as well as providing a means of understanding the shifting boundaries of that identity. At a simple level, boarding often provided a neighbourhood with the density and concentration of people necessary to attract or create institutions which more overtly nurtured a separate ethnic existence. At a more important level, boarding as a form of clustering people from the same homeland began the process of breaking down extreme localism, even when each household seemed to represent only one local origin, and thus, led to what Helen Lopata has described as the "gradually emerging fabric" of North American ethnicity.[52]

If we look closely at the place and scale of "fellow-felling" in boarding, we can begin to grasp the way in which localism and ethnicity among the sojourners existed as both a continuum of identities and as conflicting loyalties or, at least, loyalties of different intensities. For example, when in Upton Sinclair's *The Jungle*, Jurgis Rudkus and his Lithuanian group reach the Chicago stockyard area, they find housing that seems to reflect both their Lithuanian ethnicity and the melting pot:

> There were four such flats in each building, and each of the four was a "boarding house" for the occupancy of foreigners — the Lithuanians, Poles, Slovaks, or Bohemians. Some of these places were kept by private persons, some were co-operatives.[53]

Rudkus, however, did not end up in that boarding-house because he was a Lithuanian, he was led to it by a man from his own village: "The two families literally fell upon each others' necks — *for it had been years since Jokubas Szedvilas had met a man from his part of Lithuania*." In almost every account of boarding, what appears to be camaraderie based on large ethnic definitions recedes upon closer examination, and one finds people from one village, town, or district clustering together. Optimum size for "group households" and families with boarders tended to stay within such parochial definitions of their group. In such instances, at least within the boarding establishment, ethnicity did not extend beyond the *paese* or local area of emigration. Yet boarding was an expedient and a functional institution for sojourners, allowing them to adapt their sense of "fellow-feeling" to the scale of ethnicity imposed upon them by the nature of their migration, their jobs, or their lodgings.

A look at a single sojourner's experience can demonstrate this point. Paul Bertoia, an immigrant from near Udine in Friuli, the northeast of Italy, arrived alone in Toronto after World War I. In seach of work and relatives, he went on to Edmonton. There he stayed in boarding house/inn known to its residents as the Roma Hotel. One floor was occupied completely by Friulan sojourners, and the next floor by Trevisans from a neighbouring region of Italy. Each floor had its own cooking, dialect, card games, and camaraderie, even though the inn was named for Italy's capital and the native Edmontonians considered everyone in the building an Italian migrant. When Mr. Bertoia boarded with kinfolk in Drumheller, he associated chiefly with people from his home town near Udine, and later, when he came to Toronto, became involved in benevolent organizations like the Fratellanza which took in members from all over the Italian peninsula.[54] His ethnic reference group changed according to his setting.

Men who found themselves in more remote work situations with few *paesani* with them seem to have developed a sense of belonging to a larger Italian or Italian Canadian ethnic group more quickly than those who were able to lodge with *paesani*:

Question: Were there a lot of people working on that job from your home town in Calabria?

Answer: No. They were mostly from other provinces. Was mixed you know. Mostly from southern Italy. In this gang we passed the winter in this converted horse stable — we were all Italian.[55]

Mr. Carnovale, the man who answered the above query, had three possible reference groups other than acculturation to Canadian ways: his *paese*, his region defined either as Calabria or the Italian south (Mezzo giorno), or the nation state of Italy. It is impossible to doubt that the background of the men with whom he sojourned and boarded did not affect his commitment to one identity or another, or at least his pace along a continuum from *campanilismo* to an Italian Canadian ethnic sense. In that way, detailed study of the social setting of the migrants might begin to yield answers about the historical process of ethnicity.

In an account of a Macedonian "group household" in Toronto in 1920, we can see how the smallest details of the boarding organization could cement village ties or break them down either in favour of a larger Macedonian identity or of acculturation. A father defends his son who has burnt the daily stew prepared for other boarders. There is an angry exchange of words, and, despite the fact that they are all fellow villagers, no turning back. Some moved and found new households; they passed either into the so-called "English" boarding houses or found another Macedonian "group household." In either case, the real conditions of their sojourn caused them to move away from their village loyalties and identity.[56]

If a burnt stew could threaten "fellow-feeling," it should also show that boarding in a "group household," even of fellow townsmen, was no idyll. All the tensions of inter-family jealousies and of life without womenfolk existed. For those families who left after such a contretemps, the "group household" and the village or *paese* that is served in the diaspora lost meaning in that sense which Harold Isaacs, quoting Robert Forst, felt was at the core of ethnicity: as "the place where, when you've got to go there, they've got to take you in."[58] For the many ethnic identities in flux at the turn of the century, boundaries moved, not just because of the broad categories of prejudice used by the North American host society, but also because of the vicissitudes of the sojourning community. Boarding situations, length of sojourn, and neighbourhood density meant that local identities brought from the Old World gave way, although never for various ascriptive purposes disappearing, in favour of North American ethnicity. Toronto's Italians appeared out of a skein of earlier relationships in which Calabrese generally boarded with Calabrese, and Abruzzese with Abruzzese. (Sicilians and Friulians did not mix at all with the mainland Southern Italians.) Even people from regions living together represented a change from localism. At the turn of the century people from the original towns of settlement like Laurenzana and Pisticci had formed their own boarding households and institutions. The Dillingham Commission had counted Brava (Cape Verdean coloured Portuguese) as a separate ethnic group and had listed their boarding houses separately. Ruthenes, Galicians, and Bukovinians found their larger identity as Ukrainian only slowly.

In a sense, not only were ethnic institutions born in the sojourning years, so was North American ethnicity itself. Historians who wish to understand the relationship between the social and geographical processes of migration and the growth of ethnic identity would do well to look more closely at those first years of sojourning and at the institutions adapted to cope with North America. The sojourners themselves knew that it was an important social and cultural formative period. The Appalachian saying of our time sums it up nicely: "We ain't what we want to be and we ain't what we're going to be, but we ain't what we were."[59]

NOTES:

1. O. Handlin, *The Uprooted* (Boston, 1951); R. Vecoli, "Contadini in Chicago: A Critique of the Uprooted," *Journal of American History*, Vol. LI (December 1964), pp. 404-417.

2. H. Nelli, *Italians in Chicago, 1880-1930: A Study in Ethnic Mobility* (Oxford, 1970), offers a detailed chapter on geographical settlement with no analysis of institutions before 1920. A later chapter uses the padrone system to explain occupational patterns. See also, J. Barton, *Peasants and Strangers: Italians, Rumanians and Slovaks in an American City, 1890-1950* (Harvard, 1975). Chapter II uses chain migration to make the leap from a statistical analysis of old world emigration to a skimpy and anecdotal knowledge of sojourning communities. Moreover, there is some disjuncture between emigration locations and origins of Cleveland migrants.

3. R. Juliani, "American Voices, Italian Accents: The Perception of Social Conditions and Personal Motives by Immigrants," *Italian Americana*, Vol. 1, No. 1 (Autumn 1974), pp. 1-25; and "The Origin and Development of the Italian Community in Philadelphia," in J. Bodnar, ed., *The Ethnic Experience in Pennsylvania* (Lewisburg, 1973), pp. 233-261. Juliani's use of oral testimony and background in sociology allow him to say more about the mind set of first arrivals, their institutions and "paesani services."

4. P. Siu, "The Sojourner," *American Journal of Sociology*, Vol. 58 (July 1952), pp. 34-44. Siu describes the sojourner as, not a "marginal man," but one committed to maintaining himself in a manner which will enable him to re-insert himself easily in his country of origin.

5. Of the institutions mentioned, probably the padrone system has received most systematic attention from historians. See L. Iorizzo, "The Padrone and Immigrant Distribution," in S.M. Tomasi and M.H. Engel, eds., *The Italian Experience in the United States* (Staten Island, 1970), pp. 43-75; R.F. Harney, "The Padrone and the Immigrant," *The Canadian Review of American Studies*, Vol. 2 (Fall, 1974), pp. 101-118; H.B. Nelli, "The Italian Padrone System in the United States," *Labor History*, Vol. 5, No. 2 (Spring 1964), pp. 153-167.

6. There were of course many excellent studies of specific institutions by contemporary social scientists. Two which deal with the sojourners well are G. Abbott, "The Chicago Employment Agency and the Immigrant Worker," *American Journal of Sociology*, Vol. XIV, No. 3 (November 1908); and E. Bradwin, *The Bunkhouse Man* (New York 1928). I am using institution in the simplest sense — a relationship or behavioural pattern of importance in the life of a community or society.

7. John Modell and Tamara Hareven, "Urbanization and the Malleable Household: An Examination of Boarding and Lodging in American Families," *Journal of Marriage and Family*, Vol. 35 (August 1973), pp. 467-78.

8. The only detailed study of an ethnic boarding house that I am aware of is A. Vazsonyi, "The Star Boarder: Traces of Cicisbeism in an Immigrant Community," in *Tractata Altaica* (Wiesbaden, 1976), pp. 695-713. This is an ethnological romp through the mores and arrangements of mid-American Hungarian boarders.

9. *U.S. Immigration Commission, 1907-1910 Reports* (henceforth cited as *Dillingham Commission*), Vol. I, *Abstracts*, pp. 422-438. For agreement with Modell and Hareven that the semantic distinction between boarding and lodging was irrelevant, see *Dillingham Commission*, Vol. 26, pp. 79-80. Although padronism and so-called immigrant hotels fall under the last classification, group household, it is clear that many inns and hotels that ran in traditional commercial terms also were essentially ethnic institutions. See D. Esslinger, *Immigrants and the City: Ethnicity and Mobility in a 19th Century Midwestern Community* (Port Washington, 1975), p. 45, has an interesting account of German hotels in downtown South Bend but does not seem to see the phenomenon as an aspect of ethnic enterprise or of the changing Polish and German ethnic boundaries of the roomers.

10. See *Reports of the Industrial Commission* (Washington, 1910) Vol. XV, pp. x-xii; and *Royal Commission appointed to inquire into the Immigration of Italian Labourers to Montreal and the Alleged Fraudulent Practices of Employment Agencies* (Ottawa, 1905). *Dillingham Commission*, II, p. 427.

11. J. Scarpaci, "Immigrants in the New South: Italians in Louisiana's Sugar Parishes, 1880-1910," in F. Assante, *Il Movimento migratorio italiano dall' unita nazionale ai giorni nostri* (Naples, 1976), pp. 206-209. In the Chinese case, the steamship agents' "holding pens" for migrants at Macao bound for America were called barracoons, the word for slave quarters in most of the Iberian world. See John Foster, *American Diplomacy in the Orient* (Boston, 1903), p. 280.

12. "Forced Labor in West Virgina," *The Outlook*, June 13, 1903.

13. T. Saloutos, *The Greeks in the United States* (Cambridge, 1964), pp. 52-53; *Dillingham Commission*, Vol. 2, pp. 401 & 405.

14. H. Nelli, *Italians in Chicago*, p. 60; for the concept of the target migrant, see J.M. Nelson, *Temporary versus Permanent Cityward Migration: Causes and Consequences* (MIT, 1976).

15. G. Abbott, "The Chicago Employment Agency," p. 294.

16. A Bernardy, *America Vissuta* (Torino, 1911), p. 316.

17. See *Royal Commission (Italians)*; and R.F. Harney, "Chiaroscuro: Italians in Toronto, 1885-1915," *Italian Americans*, Vol. 1, No. 2 (Spring 1975), pp. 143-167.

18. *Industrial Commission*, Vol. XV, p. 157; B. Brandenburg, *Imported Americans* (New York, 1903) described all the frauds and violence visited on migrants in process; E. Corsi, *In the Shadow of Liberty* (New York, 1937), p. 38.

19. Modell and Hareven, "Urbanization and the Malleable Household," p. 470. The 'lodger evil' among immigrants also was subject to confusion about extended families and about how kinship might make household proximity more respectable no matter how remote. For example, the Dillingham Commission remarked that "many persons in few rooms is not so serious a matter when all are members of the family as when strangers are included in the household." *Dillingham Commission*, Vol. I, p. 748. So it was not the quality of life, the health hazard, but really the "moral climate" that mattered to the authorities.

20. J.S. Woodsworth, *Strangers Within Our Gates* (Toronto, 1909), pp. 217-220.

21. *Jack Canuck*, January 1, 1912, p. 14. *Saturday Night* at least sensed the relationship of this condition to sojourning (January 20, 1912), p. 2, "He is probably counting the hours to that longed for day when he too shall appear at Salerno and jingle money in his pockets."

22. *Hastings Report*, pp. 17-17. The list of families by nationalities included all groups but Anglo-Celts. The three districts chosen for analysis were St. John's Ward, the Eastern Avenue area, and the Niagara Street district. All were heavily immigrant, commercial, and the last two were industrial as well. They were not however the most squalid in the city. The juxtaposition of ethnicity with social problems was quite misleading since British lower class and Canadian pathological slum neighbourhoods were not included in the study.

23. V. Greene, "The Polish American Worker to 1930: The Hunky Image in Transition," *The Polish Review*, Vol. XXI (1976), pp. 63-78. On page 65 it is pointed out that even sympathetic observers of Slavic group households left the impression that "the workers still required non-group leadership to effect the necessary reforms" in immigrant life including housing. This same view persists among students of European guestworker systems who feel that boarding or hotel accommodations "lead to a ghetto-like life and prevent any contact with the local community . . . (and thus) retard a positive process of learning." W.R. Bohning, "The Social and Occupational Apprenticeship of Mediterranean Migrant Workers in West Germany" in M. Livi-Bacci, ed., *The Demographic and Social Pattern of Emigration from the Southern European Countries* (Florence, 1972), p. 226. This view like that of the turn-of-the-century Toronto assumes that integration is the only proper course for sojourners.

24. See P. Siu, "The Sojourner"; V.G. Nee and B. de B. Nee, *Longtime Californ': A*

Documentary Study of an American Chinatown (New York, 1973) Chap. II "The Bachelor Society"; R.F. Harney, "Men Without Women: Italian Migrants in Canada, 1885-1930," a paper presented to the AIHA-CIHA Joint Sessions (Toronto, Oct. 28, 1977).

25. Traditions among South Slavs like the *zadruga* and *drustvo* and the role of wives in running *czarda* in Hungary obviously made adaptation to being a boarding house mistress easier for female immigrants from those groups. For the Italians, M.H. Ets, *Rosa: The Life of an Italian Immigrant* (Minnesota, 1970); and the story of Rosa Mondavi in A. Pellegrini's *Americans by Choice* (New York, 1956), pp. 138-147, demonstrate the almost involuntary economic performance of immigrant wives. See J. Scott and L. Tilly, "Women's Work and the Family in 19th Century Europe," *Comparative Studies in Society and History* (Jan. 17, 1975); C. Golab, "The Impact of the Industrial Experience on the Immigrant Family: The Huddled Masses Reconsidered," *Immigrants in Industrial America 1850-1920*, Richard Erlich, ed., (University Press of Virginia: September 1977); and V.Y. McLaughlin, *Family and Community: Italian Immigrants in Buffalo 1880-1930* (Cornell University Press, 1977).

26. The study of ethnicity would profit from more awareness of issues in the study of the formation of nationality and growth of national feeling. For example, see A. Smith, *Theories of Nationalism* (London, 1971); and K. Deutsch, *Nationalism and Social Communication* (MIT, 1953). Both suggest that the scale of fellow-feeling is a function of the economic and social network which proves most useful.

27. Oscar Handlin, *Boston's Immigrants* (Harvard, 1941), p. 101.

28. Rudolph Vecoli, "Contadini in Chicago," pp. 408-411.

29. See for example, G. Prpic, *The Croatian Immigrants in America* (New York, 1971); M. Byington, *Homestead: The Households of a Mill Town* (Pittsburgh, 1910); T. Bell, *Out of This Furnace* (Pittsburgh, 1976); L. Adamic, *From Many Lands* (New York, 1939); and Vazsonyi, "The Star Boarders."

30. T. Kessner, *The Golden Door. Italian and Jewish Immigrant Mobility in New York City, 1880-1915* (New York, 1976), p. 100.

31. For the uses of "miszisz," see Vazsonyi "The Star Boarder"; C. Panunzio, *The Soul of the Immigrant*, shows the typical Italian use of "padrone" to describe the head of the establishment; "Bordo" and "bordante" ("bordisti") are terms discussed by Amy Bernardy in *Italia randagia attraverso gli Stati Uniti* (Turin, 1914), pp. 88-122. Louise Tilly's thesis on the formation of the Milan working class, 1881-1911, shows the use of the proper Italian *covivenza* to describe urban boarding of newcomers there (Toronto: History Department, 1972), R.F. Harney, Director, p. 291. The uses of family terms like auntie, nonna, uncle, and daughter to reduce tension and define roles is mentioned in most oral testimony.

32. John Kosa, *Land of Choice: The Hungarians in Canada* (Toronto, 1957), p. 31.

33. J. MacDonald and L. MacDonald, "Chian Migration, Ethnic Neighbourhood Formation and Social Networks," in C. Tilly, ed., *An Urban World* (Boston, 1974), p. 231. This, like most sources, concentrates on the importance of sheltered work for Latin immigrant women rather than on the entrepreneurial role of family.

34. J. Marlyn, *Under the Ribs of Death* (Toronto, 1971), pp. 19-22, presents a convincing picture of the ambivalence of the children of boarding house keepers toward their role in the extended household. Lithuanian and Polish landlords in Chicago often rented out the better units to tenants but lived in the worst rooms themselves to minimize costs: see Victor Greene, *For God and Country: The Rise of the Polish and Lithuanian Ethnic Consciousness in America, 1860-1910* (Madison, 1975), p. 53.

35. *Hastings Report*, pp. 8 and 14.

36. E. Rossi, "Delle Condizioni del Canada respetto all' immigrazione italiana," *Bollettino dell' Emigrazione #4*, Anno 1903. Although the economics of boarding usually is described in terms of the boarding-boss or family with boarders profit, it must be remembered that the sojourner clientele made the system work. It was they, maximizing their savings to meet old

world needs, who accepted crowded conditions and minimal service. A convincing local example can be found in R. Wilson, *A Retrospective: A Short Review of the Steps taken in Sanitation to transform the Town of Muddy York into the Queen City of the West* (Toronto, 1934), p. 32, which describes a three-room cottage with twenty Italian boarders thus: "They were all jolly good natured fellows and were highly amused at the visit of the health inspector and his inquiries as translated by the boss . . ." — hardly the atmosphere of white slavery and padronism. In the Canadian case, a special service offered by the ethnic boarding system was credit for room and board over the long winter months of unemployment. Nick Lombardi speaks from the perspective of the boarding house keeper: "We had a couple, not because we needed them, but because they were good friends and they wanted to stay with us. We all used to eat together. And if they didn't have the money, daddy and mom never used to worry. They knew they'd pay off the debt in the summer." (Taped Interview, The Multicultural History Society of Ontario, June 1, 1976). His friend, Paul Lorenzo, remembers the situation from the sojourner's view: "We used to live over where they put the new Mount Sinai Hospital, near Mt. Carmel church on McCaul Street, in an Italian boarding house — $2.50 a month. There were about 8 or 10 boarders in the house. In the winter time, we can't pay the rent — we have no money. You must wait for summer to return so you can go out and work again and pay your debts . . . And when you'd go to the store you had to sign a book since you had no money. And my father kept his own book too, so that he would never be cheated." (Taped Interview, The Multicultural History Society of Ontario.)

37. This story was gathered by John Bodnar and Carl Oblinger of the Pennsylvania Museum of Man and will appear in a forthcoming oral history volume. P. Roberts, *The New Immigration* (New York, 1914), p. 131. The sick, wounded, and unemployed threw off the three shift bed rotation and were often evicted. Gina Petroff (Taped Interview, Oct. 12, 1976) tells the story of a man known as Nick Coca Cola. "Anyway he been sleeping on the third floor. Not working. He never get up two days, just sleep and stay there day and night, and the name is Nick . . . There's Depression and nobody give work to you. So anyway they kept him for a little while over . . . and then they kicked him out." (Unless otherwise cited, all oral testimony is from the collection of the Multicultural History Society of Ontario. A computerized guide to that collection is in process.)

38. See Vazsony, "Traces of Cicisbeism"; and A. Bernardy "Da un relazione de Amy Bernardy su l' emigrazione delle donne e fanciullo italiane nelle Stati Uniti," *Bollettino del' Emigrazione* (1909).

39. "Nanni Volpe," in G. Verga, *The She Wolf and Other Stories* (Berkeley, 1958), p. 160.

40. "The Boarding House," from *The New Pioneer* in V. Wertsman, *The Romanians in America, 1748-1974* (Dobbs Ferry, 1975), p. 62.

41. *Jack Canuck*, Vol. 1, No. 14 (January, 1912); T. Hiramatso (Taped interview).

42. Mary Caruso (Taped Interview, Dec. 7, 1976). Her grandfather, a hurdy-gurdy man, left the boarding enterprise completely to his wife.

43. Michael Guzei (Taped Interview (Slovak Barr)).

44. John Krar (Taped Interview Donau-Schwaben #260 Frei) *Dillingham Commission*, Abstracts, Vol. I, pp. 422-552. "Many variations upon this arrangement are met with but some form of it constitutes the method of living usually followed by *recent immigrant households* (read, sojourners.)

45. V. Wertsman, *The Romanians*, p. 63.

46. Stoyan Christowe, *This Is My Country* (New York, 1938). The leader of a "group household" although he depended on a coterie of elders or kin, exercised control.

47. P. Roberts, *The New Immigration*, p. 124.

48. R. Breton, "Institutional Completeness of Ethnic Communities and the Personal Relations of Immigrants," *American Journal of Sociology*, Vol. 70 (September, 1964), pp. 193-205. Anna Kaprielian (Jan. 24, 1978, Armenian) — same sense of the completeness of a

sojourning institution comes out of this conversation. "He had a house. The first floor was a coffee shop and library. People would go there and play backgammon, cards, read books (whoever could read). Armenians would congregate there. Everyone would tell his story, talk about his family. They'd write letters. . . ."

49. For those who believe that the sojourning attitude shapes a migrant's relations with North America, studies about occupational mobility and acculturation should reflect the intensity of the migrant's desire to insert himself as much as it does North American conditions. The contrasting of Jewish settlers and Italian sojourners as to rates of occupational mobility without reference to their frame of mind and attitude about staying in the United States becomes silly. See Betty B. Caroli, "Italian Settlement in American Cities," in H.S. Nelli, ed., *The U.S. and Italy: Proceedings of the 9th Annual Conference of the AIHA* (Washington, 1976), pp. 156-158.

50. For example where would a man who sold balloons at Toronto parades who also was chief money lender in the Italian community, a man who lost his arm in an abattoir accident but made a comfortable living escorting brides back and forth from Macedonia, and all the informal keepers of boarding establishments fit in the gross measures of mobility and status such as S. Thernstrom's *The Other Bostonians* (Cambridge, 1973). Some synthesis of oral testimony and quantitative methods would greatly enhance the value of urban studies.

51. Conversation with Dr. Juliana Puskas, Toronto, January 25, 1978. Dr. Puskas has spent the last year visiting Hungarian committees in the U.S. and Canada.

52. H. Lopata, *Polish American Status Competition in an Ethnic Community* (New York, 1976), pp. 608 and 19-20 gives a clear sociological view of ethnicity as a historical process, in which the *okolica*, the physical and psychic unit of group identity, changes in North America.

53. Upton Sinclair *The Jungle* (New York, 1965), first edition 1906, p. 32.

54. P. Bertoia (Taped Interview Friulian, March 1, 1978). Ethnic identities among sojourners were nowhere near as hard-edged as prejudice and the ethnic groups own retospective falsification now make them appear. Finns, Swedes, and Finn Swedes who lived near quarries on Cape Ann in Massachusetts changed ethnic loyalty with boarding houses. See P. Parsons & P. Anastas, *When Gloucester Was Gloucester: Toward an Oral History of the City* (Gloucester, 1973), p. 21.

55. John Carnovale (Taped Interview, Italian, The Multicultural History Society of Ontario.)

56. F. Tomev (Taped Interview, Macedonian, December, 1977). In a given boarding house, there would be all "pro-Bulgarian" or all patriarchist Macedonians and men from the same village would not board together if their politics differed. The sources of this rising ethnic consciousness lay in local, neighbourhood developments which affect all immigrants, even the most articulate. See Victor Greene, *For God and Country: The Rise of Polish and Lithuanian Ethnic Consciousness in America, 1860-1910*, p. 5.

57. H.N. Brailsford, *Macedonia — Its Races and Their Future* (London, 1906), p. 102. "Is your village Greek, I asked him, or Bulgarian. Well, he replied, it is Bulgarian now but four years ago it was Greek. . . . The Bulgarians heard of this and they came and made us an offer. They said they would give us a priest who would live in the village, and a teacher to whom we need pay nothing. Well sir, ours is a poor village, and so of course we became Bulgarian." For all peasant migrant groups, ethnicity was far more local and malleable than we have assumed.

58. LH. Isaacs, *Idols of the Tribe* (New York, 1975), p. 43.

59. M. Pei, *What's In a Word* (New York, 1968), p. 52.

The Neglected Majority: The Changing Role of Women in Nineteenth-Century Montreal*

D. SUZANNE CROSS

In recent years, historians have responded to the preoccupations of contemporary society by greatly increasing their activity in the fields of social and urban history. Studies on poverty, the working classes, conditions of labour and minority groups have proliferated, but few devote more than a page or two to the female population. It is impossible to say whether this cursory treatment of women in society is due to the scarcity of sources, or whether it reflects attitudes, often unconscious, on the part of historians who conceived of women as another "minority" group, which, lacking political power, is assumed to be devoid of social and economic significance. No doubt both factors operate, one re-enforcing the other. As a result, disproportionate emphasis is placed on some aspects of society to the virtual exclusion of others, thereby distorting our understanding of the whole. This paper by its very title is open to just this criticism, but it has been undertaken in an attempt to restore the balance, and to indicate some of the sources which are available, although not widely known, for the study of women.

The nineteenth century was generally speaking a period of rapid urban growth characterized by large-scale migrations of men and women into the towns from the surrounding countryside. Immigration from the British Isles also contributed to the increasing population of cities, although the evidence suggests that it was of much less importance in Montreal than in some North

* The helpful comments of Professors J.T. Copp and Micheline Dumont Johnson are gratefully acknowledged.

SOURCE: *Histoire sociale/Social History*, Volume VI, No. 12 (November, 1973), pp. 202-233. Reprinted by permission of the author and the University of Ottawa Press.

Graph I: Sex Ratios for Montreal, Quebec City and the Province of Quebec, 1844-1901

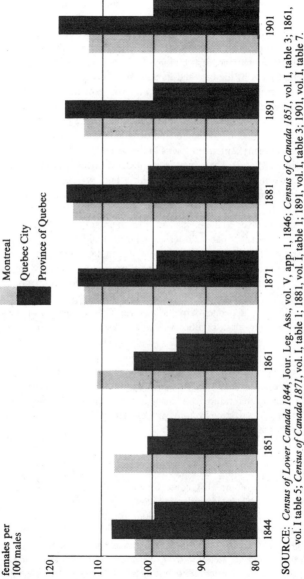

females per
100 males

Montreal

Quebec City

Province of Quebec

SOURCE: *Census of Lower Canada 1844,* Jour. Leg. Ass., vol. V, app. 1, 1846; *Census of Canada 1851,* vol. I, table 3; 1861, vol. I table 5; *Census of Canada 1871,* vol. I, table 1; 1881, vol. I, table 1; 1891, vol. I, table 3; 1901, vol. I, table 7.

American towns. Periodically, as in the early twenties, the thirties, the late forties and again in the early eighties, the stream of immigrants to Montreal turned to a flood, yet comparatively few remained to make the city their home, and the majority passed on to Canada West or the United States.

The first part of this paper examines the growth of the female population in Montreal and the distribution of women by age and location in the different parts of the city and its suburbs. As the countryside offered even less opportunity for young girls than for young men, women participated in the movement from over-populated rural areas to the towns of Quebec and New England, thereby greatly increasing the female proportion of the urban population. This trend was no peculiar to Quebec. The predominance of women in many American towns in the second half of the century has been noted elsewhere.[1] There was a great demand for servants in Brookline, Pasadena and Newton, all towns with a high *per capita* income, and the textiles towns of Lowell, New Bedford and Fall River offered employment in the mills.

Women moved to the towns and cities in order to earn their living, and the second part of this paper discusses the opportunities for employment which Montreal afforded. The establishment of manufacturing on a relatively large scale created employment, and women became the mainstay of the labour force in at least one industry and formed an important sector in several others. Women, many of them married, worked out of necessity in order that they and their dependents might survive. The seriousness of the plight of many working class families was recognized by the religious orders who established a number of day care centres thus enabling many women with children to supplement the family income by working outside the home. It will be shown that Protestant and Catholic women did not share the same experiences, as several of the roads open to the former were closed to the latter. Occasional reference is made to the women's religious orders and the charitable organizations run by women, but only within the context of their effect on the employment scene.

II

Sex ratios indicating the number of females per hundred males have been computed for Montreal, Quebec City and the Province of Quebec, and are given in Graph I. In a population with an equal number of males and females the ratio is 100; when females predominate the figure is above 100; where males are in the majority the ratio drops below 100. Throughout the period women outnumbered men in Montreal and Quebec, and the proportion of women increased steadily from 1851 to 1881. In 1891 and 1901 the proportion of women continued to increase in Quebec, whereas there was a slight decrease in Montreal. The ratios for the cities contrasted with those for the Province as a whole: at mid-century there were fewer women than men in the Province, but from 1871 to the end of the century, the ratios remained stable.

TABLE I

SEX RATIOS (NUMBER OF FEMALES PER 100 MALES) BY AGE GROUP FOR MONTREAL, 1844-1901

	Under 15	15-19	20-29	Over 30
1844	98.5	128.2	106.6	95.7
1851	101.3	126.4	134.0	95.5
1861	97.5	114.6	126.5	101.9
1871	100.6	138.8	132.8	111.8
1881	100.0	127.6	136.2	115.2
1891	102.9	119.6	122.4	112.2
1901	102.3	116.8	120.2	112.6
X^2	.24	46.39*	51.99*	7.20

Source: *Census of Lower Canada*, 1844; *Census of Canadas*, 1851, vol. I, table 3; 1861, vol. I, table 5; *Census of Canada*, 1871, vol. II, table 7; 1881, vol. II, table 8; 1891, vol. II, table 1; 1901, vol. I, table 7.
* Significant at or beyond the .05 level of confidence.

The sex ratios for the different age groups in Montreal are shown in Table I. The ratios were calculated for four groups: children under the age of 15; girls between 15 and 19; young women from 20 to 29 and mature women over 30. The most striking feature was the high proportion of girls and young women. The ratios in the children's group were all very close to 100, whereas the ratios for the girls and young women's groups were well above 100. In these two age groups women outnumbered men for every year studied. The high ratios among the girls could not be attributable to a carry-over effect from the children's group in the previous decade, as there were almost equal numbers of males and females in the children's group. The arrival of large numbers of young girls in Montreal was the cause of the high ratios in that group. The ratios for the young and mature women's groups were, at least in part, due to the carry-over effects from the girl's group for the previous decade. The ratios for the mature women's groups were noticeably higher from 1871 onwards, but did not equal those of the girls and young women, and it seems likely that they were due to the carry-over effects already mentioned rather than to large scale migrations of older women. As early as 1844 there were already a large number of young girls in the city, and it seems safe to assume that the majority of women who continued to come to Montreal throughout the century were, upon arrival, in their mid and late teens or early twenties.

TABLE II

SEX RATIOS (NUMBER OF FEMALES PER 100 MALES) FOR THE WARDS OF MONTREAL, 1861-1901

	1861	*1871*	*1881*	*1891*	*1901*
East	82.5	105.5	107.0	105.7	61.0
Centre	98.0	141.8	100.7	128.8	186.3
West	100.0	149.0	98.1	95.5	95.1
St. Anne	98.7	101.5	103.1	98.5	97.9
St. Antoine	113.2	114.3	124.3	118.6	120.5
St. Lawrence	110.4	118.0	120.7	115.5	111.7
St. Louis	110.7	120.5	117.0	118.6	113.1
St. James	102.1	118.6	118.8	115.7	114.1
St. Mary	103.1	108.6	108.9	104.9	108.2

Source: *Census of Canadas*, 1861, vol. I, table 5; *Census of Canada,* 1871, vol. I, table 1; 1881, vol. I, table 4; 1891, vol. I, table 1; 1901, vol. I, table 7.

The male and female population were distributed unevenly throughout the city, as can be seen by the sex ratios for the wards shown in Table II. Women greatly outnumbered men in St. Antoine, St. Lawrence, St. Louis and St. James throughout the second half of the century. St. Antoine was essentially a middle- and upper-class residential area, although labourers and artisans resided in the lower part of the ward. Industrial establishments were restricted to the extreme south-east corner. Large numbers of domestic servants were employed in the wealthy Protestant homes along St. Antoine street. In 1871, 66 percent of the total number of servants for the whole city were employed in Montreal West.[2] A cursory examination of the census returns for 1861 and 1871 revealed that most of these servants were young Irish Catholic girls. The location of a number of factories employing women which were within walking distance of the central area largely explained the high proportion of women in St. Lawrence, St. Louis and even St. James (see map). It was important for women to live close to their jobs, because .05¢ car fares were a major item for the worker who earned only .50¢ to .75¢ a day. Tickets were available at six for .25¢ and twenty-five for $1.00, but these sums represented a large outlay for the poor. Special workingmen's tickets for use in the early morning and evening were not introduced until 1892. Even the new rate of eight tickets for .25¢ was beyond the means of most working women.

Graph II: Proportion of Women in Industrial Occupations

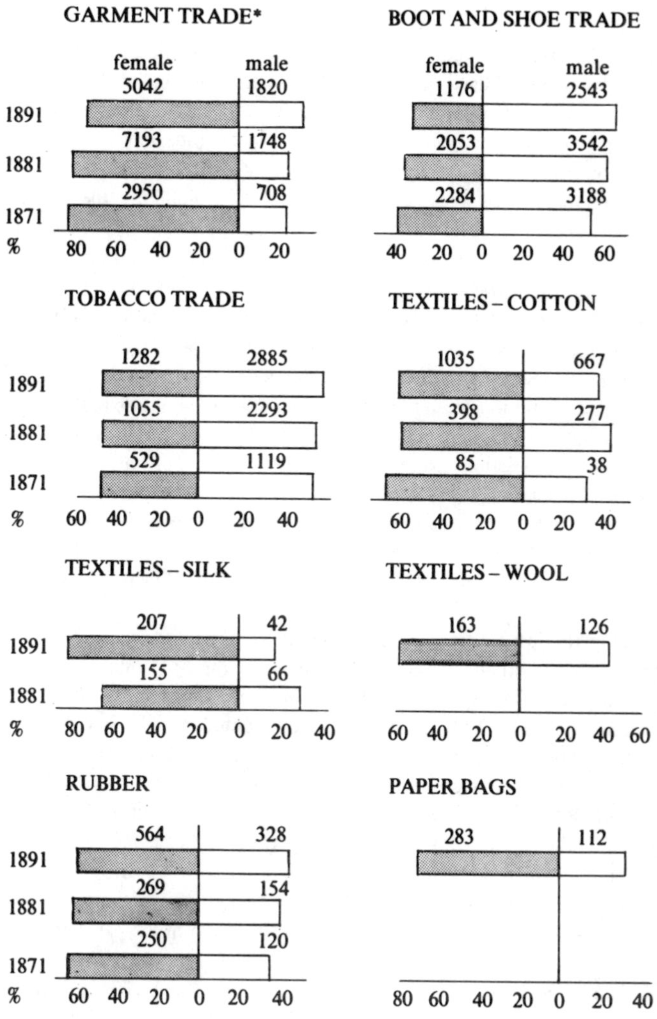

GARMENT TRADE*

	female	male
1891	5042	1820
1881	7193	1748
1871	2950	708

% 80 60 40 20 0 20

BOOT AND SHOE TRADE

	female	male
1891	1176	2543
1881	2053	3542
1871	2284	3188

40 20 0 20 40 60

TOBACCO TRADE

1891	1282	2885
1881	1055	2293
1871	529	1119

% 60 40 20 0 20 40

TEXTILES – COTTON

1891	1035	667
1881	398	277
1871	85	38

60 40 20 0 20 40

TEXTILES – SILK

1891	207	42
1881	155	66

% 80 60 40 20 0 20 40

TEXTILES – WOOL

	163	126

60 40 20 0 20 40 60

RUBBER

1891	564	328
1881	269	154
1871	250	120

% 60 40 20 0 20 40

PAPER BAGS

	283	112

80 60 40 20 0 20 40

SOURCE: Industrial schedules, *Census of Canada,* 1871, 1881 and 1891. *Composite figures for related occupations.

The proportion of women in St. Anne's and St. Mary's wards was lower than in the wards already mentioned. St. Mary's in the east end was an area of rapid population growth and appeared to share the characteristics of the new suburbs which are discussed below. The situation of St. Anne, a well-established and predominantly Irish Catholic ward, was different. The ward was close to the Lachine Canal, the harbour and the Grand Trunk Railway yards, all of which attracted male labour. There were some local factories employing women, but many daughters from homes in St. Anne's went into domestic service in neighbouring St. Antoine.

The population of West and Centre wards, which, together with East ward, formed the core of old Montreal, declined steadily in the second half of the century. These wards constituted the commercial and retail centre of the city, but there was also a concentration of garment and shoe factories in West and Centre. In the 1850's merchants and their male clerks lived over the business premises, but when the Montreal City Passenger Railway began operations in 1860, many left the area to reside away from the centre of the city. It is difficult to account for the fluctuations in the ratios in these wards, but it should be pointed out that the differences very not very important because the populations were small. A majority of only a few hundred of either sex in a small population can produce extreme ratios, but would be of little significance in a larger population. The small proportion of women in East ward in 1861 was due to the presence of the garrison at the Quebec Gate Barracks, but satisfactory explanations for the other fluctuations have not been found.

During the last thirty years of the century, population growth was more rapid in the suburban villages of Hochelaga, Côte St. Louis, St. Louis de Mile End, St. Jean Baptiste, Ste. Cunégonde, St. Henri and St. Gabriel than in Montreal itself. With the exception of Hochelaga, the sex ratios were similar to those in St. Mary's ward falling between 102 and 108, although in a few instances there were as low as 98. The ratio for Hochelaga village was 130.2 in 1871 and 115.7 a decade later. The Hudson Cotton Company and the W.C. MacDonald Tobacco Company were both located in Hochelaga, and many women were employed in their factories. During the 1880's, however, the Canadian Pacific Railway attracted over a thousand men to work in its shops and yards which were constructed in the east end. Part of the area was annexed to Montreal in 1883 and the ratio for Hochelaga ward was 105.7 in 1891 and 103.9 in 1901. There were few employment opportunities for women in St. Louis de Mile End. Côte St. Louis, St. Jean Baptiste and St. Gabriel. The stone quarries in Côte St. Louis attracted men to those suburbs and industry on the Lachine Canal and the nearly Grand Trunk shops provided plenty of employment for men in St. Gabriel. Ste. Cunégonde and St. Henri were industrial suburbs: the Belding Paul Silk mill, the Merchants Cotton Company, the Montreal Woollen Mill and several establishments manufacturing food employed considerable numbers of females, but many were married women which tended to maintain an even sex ratio. These opportunities for women were also counter-balanced by the numerous industries along the Lachine Canal which created work for men. Although a few wealthy citizens employed servants in their suburban homes, the demand for domestics was small in the lower middle- and working-class districts.

Women came to Montreal to earn their living and also to find husbands. With women outnumbering men the competition for husbands was keen, but the chances of success were more favourable than in rural areas where few of the sons of farmers had any hope of acquiring enough land to support a family. As most of the young men and women who came to the city had little or no money with which to set up a home, early marriage was uncommon. In 1891 only 1.5 percent of married women and .2 percent of married men were below the age of 20. Women were generally younger than men at the time of marriage. The incidence of marriage in both the male and female population increased as the century progressed. In 1861, only 32 percent of women and 32 percent of men were married, but these percentages rose to 41 and 43 percent respectively in 1891.[3] By 1891 many of the single men and women who had flocked into Montreal in the previous decades had married. Marriage had to be postponed until such time as a couple had saved for the necessities of a home, and the husband could support a family. It became, however, increasingly common for French Canadian married women to go out to work. This practice may have encouraged couples to marry earlier and live on their combined earnings rather than wait until the husband could support a family on a single wage.

III

Information on the employment of women in the 19th century is fragmentary, and for the early years almost non-existent. Prior to the establishment of factories, working class women had to rely on domestic service, cleaning, washing, sewing and caring for children. According to the 1861 Census, two percent of women were engaged in sewing as seamstresses or dressmakers. Domestic service was the major source of employment as indicated by Table III. No explanation has been found for the great drop in the number of servants between 1844 and 1851, and bearing in mind the arrival of thousands of Irish immigrants in the late 1840's, an increase rather than a decrease in the number of servants would have been expected. Some women were already moving into factory work, but it is doubtful if this adequately explains the decline in the number of servants between 1844 and

1851. It is unwise to place too much confidence in the early census, and it is possible that the number of servants given for 1844 is too high or that for 1851 is too low. The number of servants had increased by 1871 but so had the population, and contemporaries commented on the shortage of servants.[4] Throughout the 1870's the "servant problem" agited the ladies of Montreal, and there was probably truth in the complaint that girls preferred working in the factories.[5] Hours of work were extremely long and conditions bad in the factories, but at the end of the day a girl was her own mistress which was far from the case with the servant who was subject to the rules of the household at all times. At least one editor thought that the ladies were to blame for the reluctance of young girls to enter domestic service. Servants, he said, were badly paid, over-worked, given little or no time off, inadequately housed and fed and subjected at all hours to the capricious demands of the mistress. From the point of view of the employers, matters had improved slightly by 1881, and there was one servant per 4.8 families as compared with one per 5.8 families in 1861.[6]

Domestic service created employment for some women and at the same time released others from devoting all their time to the cares of the household. Increasing numbers of middle- and upper-class women had leisure to devote to social and recreational activities and also to charitable organizations and higher education as witnessed by the foundation of the Montreal Ladies Educational Association in 1871. The shortage of servants was a matter of real concern to the ladies of the upper classes. Various attempts were made to alleviate the problem, but even so supply could not keep up with the demand. The Misses Rye and McPherson, who ran one of several servant registry offices, periodically arranged for young girls to come from England to take up domestic work in Montreal. In 1871, J.E. Pell of the St. George Society suggested that he be given financial assistance in order to tour the villages of England and persuade girls to come to Montreal.[7] Several charitable organizations concerned themselves with finding employment, particularly in domestic service, for women. The Protestant House of Industry and Refuge established a servants' register in 1867[8] and the Y.W.C.A., which began its work in Montreal in 1874, immediately set up a committee for domestic servants.[9] The Women's Protective Immigration Society also tried to channel immigrants in this direction and occasionally advanced passage money to suitable girls.[10] The Montreal Day Nursery functioned as an informal employment office by the end of the century. Anyone wanting charwomen on a daily basis informed the Nursery, and when mothers brought their children in, they were directed to the available work.

The shortage of servants was only one aspect of the problem. Most girls entering service lacked any experience, and few employers wanted to invest

TABLE III

THE NUMBER AND PERCENTAGE OF FEMALE SERVANTS IN MONTREAL

	No. of servants	% of female population
1844	3,013	9.2
1851	915	3.1
1861	2,770	6.0
1871	3,657	6.4
1881	5,898	7.9

Source: *Census of Lower Canada*, 1844; *Census of Canadas*, 1851, vol. I, table 4; 1861, vol. I, table 7; *Census of Canada*, 1871, vol. II, table 8; 1881, vol. II, table 14.

the time and effort in training them. Attempts to provide some preliminary training were made periodically, but it is doubtful that these efforts were very satisfactory. In 1860 the Home and School of Industry made the training of young girls for domestic service one of their principal objectives.[11] Later they instituted a special class for girls of eight years and up in order to train them in housework.[12] Kitchen Garden classes were organized for little girls below the age of seven, and the class at the Day Nursery was reported to be one of several operating in the city. Kitchen Gardens originated in the United States and the idea was introduced to Montreal by a Miss Huntingdon of New York.[13]

IV

A separate listing for men and women in industrial occupations was first introduced in the Census of 1871. Although the number of servants in Montreal declined between 1844 and 1861 and did not reach the 1844 level until 1871, the female population rose from just under 33,000 to over 57,000. It can be seen from Graph II that by 1871 women played an important role in a number of industries, and we can infer that they had been doing so for some time. Many of the industrial establishments employing women were founded in the 1850's and 1860's, and some even earlier. J. & T. Bell began manufacturing boots and shoes in 1819, and the business was still flourishing in 1894.[14] Brown and Childs employed some 800 hands in the boot trade by 1856.[15] During the 1850's, at least six more sizeable factories were established, and another four in the 1860's.[16] The location of these and most of the factories mentioned below can be seen on the map.

Several garment factories, some of which were very large, were in operation in the mid-century. Messrs. Moss and Brothers dated from 1836, the shirt manufacturer John Aitken and Co. from 1851 and the clothing firm of Messrs. McMillan and Carson from 1854.[17] H. Shorey and Co., which later became one of Montreal's largest clothing factories was established in 1865.[18] Two textile mills, one for woollen and the other for cotton cloth, began manufacturing in 1852 and 1853 respectively in the vicinity of St. Gabriel's Locks.[19] The tobacco factory of the W.C. MacDonald Co.,[20] the "Stonewall Jackson" Cigar factory[21] and S. Davis and Sons[22] were all in operation before 1860. It is reasonable to suppose that increasing numbers of women were employed in these factories from the 1850's or possibly earlier. Manufacturers knew that women and children could do this work just as well as men and would accept less pay.

Most industrial work was located in factories, but this was not the case in the garment trade where diverse conditions existed. There were many small dressmakers', milliners' and tailors' shops, and seamstresses and dressmakers worked in private homes on a daily basis. In the manufacture of men's clothing, although some work was done in the factory, more was farmed out to women working in their own homes on machines that were either rented or supplied by the manufacturer.[23] In 1892 the J.W. Mackedie Company had 900 hands on their outside payroll, and the H. Shorey Company, 1,400 in addition to 130 employed in the factory.[24]

Graph II indicates those industries in Montreal which relied extensively on female labour. Several occupations, which are listed separately in the industrial schedules of the census, have been combined to form the garment trade.[25] The number of women declined in this trade between 1881 and 1891: most of the sub-groups remained unchanged, but tailoresses gave place to tailors. There was also a reduction in the number of men and women in the boot and shoes factories. This industry was experiencing difficulties in the late eighties, and by 1891 the value of products was down by close to $2 million and salaries by a quarter of a million. There were 129 establishments compared with 171 in 1881. Many factories were established in response to the "National Policy," but limited Canadian markets restricted growth, and it is clear from accounts of the individual factories that few were able to produce at their full capacity.[26] In the tobacco, cotton, silk and rubber industries there was a steady increase in the number of females employed, but the garment trade remained the major source of work.

Only industries which employed more than 100 women were included in Graph II, but smaller numbers worked in other industries. In 1871, just under 23,000 men, women and children were classified as industrial workers in Montreal and Hochelaga. Of this number over 7,000 or approximately 33 percent of the work force were women and girls. There were over 42,000 employed in industry in 1891 of whom approximately 12,000 were woman and girls. The number of men in industry had doubled, whereas there were

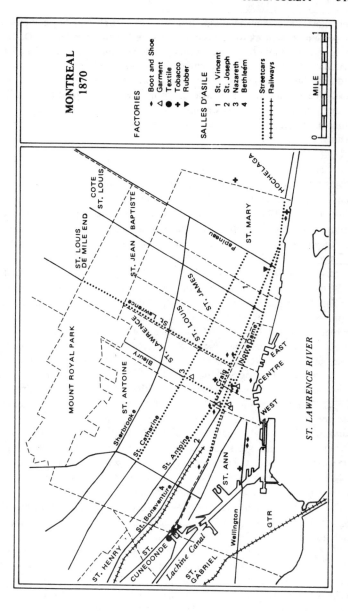

MONTREAL
1870

FACTORIES
- ◆ Boot and Shoe
- △ Garment
- ● Textile
- ✦ Tobacco
- ▶ Rubber

SALLES D'ASILE
1 St. Vincent
2 St. Joseph
3 Nazareth
4 Bethleém

···· Streetcars
┼┼┼┼ Railways

0   MILE   1

only 4,500 more women working in 1891 than in 1871, and they comprised 28 percent of the work force as compared with 33 percent in 1871.[27] During these years new jobs for women were opening up more slowly than for men. The above figures indicate the number of women working on census day, and probably under-represent the number who worked during part of the year. There is no way of estimating the number who worked temporarily when the main bread winner was unemployed or ill. The wage books for the Modern Brewery showed a rapid turnover among the girls in the bottling factory.[28]

V

There is strong evidence that, as early as the 1850's, it was increasingly common for French Canadian married women to go out to work. As an illustration, in 1855 the Sisters of Providence began caring for young children who had been refused admission to schools in the Quebec suburbs, and they established a separate *salle d'asile* in connection with the Hospice St. Joseph in 1860.[29] Children between the ages of two and seven were left by their parents early in the morning and picked up in the late afternoon. In 1858 the Grey Nuns opened the first of five similar centres — the *salle d'asile* St. Joseph. The response on the part of parents was immediate, and *l'asile* Nazareth followed in 1861, *l'asile*-Bethléem in 1868, *l'asile* St. Henri in 1885 and finally *l'asile* Ste. Cunégonde in 1889. As might be expected, *l'asile* St. Vincent de Paul, *l'asile* St. Joseph and *l'asile* Ste. Cunégonde were located in working-class districts. In contrast *l'asile* Nazareth and *l'asile* Bethléem were on St. Catharine Street and Richmond Square, both of which were prestigious addresses. St. Catherine Street was moderately convenient for women in the lower parts of St. Lawrence and St. Louis and also for those who walked in from the village of St. Jean Baptiste to the north. The Richmond Square site was made available by the Hon. C.S. Rodier, and was no great distance from St. Joseph and St. Bonaventure streets. The decline in the number of children at *l'asile* Bethléem after 1887 suggests that a number came from the parishes of St. Cunégonde and St. Henri and later attended the local *salles d'asile*.

The number of children who were registered at the *salles d'asile* run by the Grey Nuns can be seen in Table IV, and Table V gives the totals who attended during five-year periods. A glance shows that considerable numbers of young children frequented *salles d'asile*. It must, however, be asked whether these were children of widowed mothers or of parents who were both living. The registers for *l'asile* St. Joseph for 1858 to 1869 and for *l'asile* St. Cunégonde for 1889 to 1891 have been preserved.[30] The name and age of each child was inscribed together with the address and occupation of the parent. Very few widows registered their children. It appears certain that

TABLE IV

NUMBER OF CHILDREN ATTENDING THE "SALLES D'ASILE" RUN BY THE GREY NUNS

	L'asile St. Joseph	L'asile Nazareth	L'asile Bethléem	L'asile St. Henri	L'asile Ste. Cunégonde
1863	408	334			
1868	604	795	33		
1872	512	500	100		
1877	484	220	360		
1882	348	400	280		
1887	429	187	324	450	
1892	110	387	312	542	352
1897	130	314	256	604	550
1902	*	298	246	404	380

Source: "Les Rapports des Chapitres Généraux," vol. II, Archives des Soeurs Grises.
*Figures missing.

many families in which both parents were employed sent their children to the *salles d'asile*. In 1878 the Grey Nuns stated that "Le but principal de cette oeuvre [*les salles d'asile*] est de donner aux parents de la classe peu aisée, la libre disposition de leurs journées afin qu'ils puissent se livrer à un travail fructueux pour la famille. . . ."[31] At the opening of *l'asile* St. Henri, the curé M. Remi-Clotaire Decary remarked that "Les parents pauvres qui travaillent en dehors de leur maison ont le privilège d'aller placer leurs enfants sous la protection bienveillante des Soeurs de l'asile Saint-Henri."[32] The registers of St. Joseph and Ste. Cunégonde show that almost without exception the children were French Canadian: the Irish and English did not send their children to these particular institutions. The Grey Nuns did not make a regular charge for the care of children, but some parents were able to contribute. For revenue the Sisters depended on donations, bazaars and a small subsidy which amounted to approximately 25 cents per child per year from the Provincial Legislature.[33]

The role of the *salles d'asile* in enabling married women with children to go to work needs further consideration. Children below the age of two were not admitted, and the registers show that most of those attending were over the age of three. Although the evidence is not conclusive, it does not appear that the presence of an infant in the family prevented the mother from working. According to contemporary accounts, French Canadian mothers frequently resorted to artificial feeding instead of breast feeding which made possible an early return to work after childbirth provided that some care could be provided.[34] It is suggested that children between the ages of 10 and 13 were used to look after the children who were too young to attend the *salles d'asile*. The registers of the parish school of St. Joseph which was run by the Sisters of the Congregation of Notre Dame show that the majority of children left after the third grade, but at this age, probably 10 or 11, very few went out to work.[35] There were certainly considerable numbers of children available who could function as baby sitters in their own families or possibly for neighbours, thus releasing the mother for work outside the home.

TABLE V

TOTAL NUMBER OF CHILDREN ATTENDING THE "SALLES D'ASILE" DURING 5-YEAR PERIODS

1858-63	1,704
1864-68	3,408
1869-72*	2,848
1873-77	2,959**
1878-82	6,401
1883-87	5,387
1888-92	7,907
1893-97	9,608
1898-1902	10,126

Source: "Les Rapports des Chapitres Généraux, vol. II.
 * 4-year period.
 ** Figures missing for *L'asile Bethléem.*

There were few day care centres for pre-school children in the English-speaking community, lending substance to the claim that only French Canadian mothers went out to work. In 1886 a group of ladies approached the Y.W.C.A. and asked for their support in setting up a day nursery. A building was rented on Fortification Lane, and two years later the Day Nursery moved to larger premises on Mountain Street. A comparatively small number of children frequented the nursery: in 1899 attendance averaged twenty-five daily,[36] although earlier in the decade it had been as high as forty.[37] The charge of ten cents a day per child and fifty cents a week may have kept mothers away. From the annual reports, it appears that the nursery was used by women who were the sole bread winners of the family.[38] It is possible that some of the other Protestant charitable organizations took in a few children while their mothers worked, but the facilities did not compare in size or number with those of the Grey Nuns.

VI

Other avenues of employment were open to women who had some capital or had the benefit of a sound basic education. The Montreal Street Directories show many women running boarding houses, grocery stores and other small businesses. Other women worked as clerks in retail stores or offices. The typewriter and the telephone were coming into use in the 1880's and 1890's, but were still by no means common. It does not seem likely that many women depended on the typewriter and telephone before 1900.

The care of people, particularly the sick, the destitute and the orphaned, has traditionally been the work of women. The Grey Nuns and the Hospital Sisters of St. Joseph had long undertaken this work in Montreal, and the Congregation of Notre Dame had been involved in education from the earliest days. These orders expanded their work in an attempt to keep up with the rapidly growing city, but the need for additional services became apparent. The 1840's and the 1850's saw many new communities emerge under the direction of Bishop Bourget, and the Catholic charitable organizations became institutionalized by the Church. It is not within the scope of this paper to examine the role of the religious orders, but it should be pointed out that during the 1830's Catholic lay women as well as Protestants were involved in charitable work. The Catholic Orphanage, which was established by the Sulpicians in 1832, was confided to the care of the *Société des Dames de Charité*.[39] During the lifetime of the foundresses, the lay administration was vigorous in meeting the needs of the orphanage, but their successors were confronted with serious financial problems in the 1880's and considered disbanding. Assistance from the Suplicians enabled them to carry on, but in 1889 M[lle] Morin, who had run the orphanage for many years, retired, and the Grey Nuns were invited to assume charge of the children.[40] In 1847 the Suplicians founded a second institution known in its first days as "The House", which was the forerunner of the St. Patrick's Orphan Asylum.[41] The Irish Ladies of Charity were interested in this work from its inception, and during the first years lay women cared for the orphans. The Grey Nuns took over at an early date, but the Irish Ladies of Charity maintained their patronage for many years. *Le Refuge de la Passion*, also established by the Sulpicians in 1861, was directed by the Misses Pratt and Cassant until 1866. It was then taken over by les *Petites Servantes des Pauvres*, and after several changes in management it came under the care of the Grey Nuns who renamed it *Le Patrongage d'Youville* in 1895.[42]

In the 1820's and 1830's Catholic lay women were obviously willing to respond to the needs of society. Bishop Bourget, however, intended all social institutions in the Catholic Community to be controlled by the Church, and "lélan de piété imprimé à tous les fidèles de son diocèse par l'Evêque de

Montréal a fait surgir des nouvelles communautés."[43] A group of ladies led by Mme Gamelin had been caring for sick and destitute women since 1828. The Bishop invited *les Soeurs de la Charité de la Providence* to send members of their order from France to undertake this work. When the order was unable to accede to his request, he established a local order, and six ladies already involved in the work placed themselves under the direction of Mme Gamelin.[44] In 1844 *l'Institut des Soeurs de Charité de la Providence* was established canonically in Montreal. The lay apostolate of Mme Marie Rosalie Cadron and her companions was of shorter duration. In 1845 she left her family, and set up *le refuge Ste. Pélagie* for unmarried mothers. She and Sophie Desmarêts took in eleven girls the first year, but the work grew rapidly and nearly four hundred infants were born at the refuge during the first six years. The Bishop instituted a rule for the ladies in 1846, and the novitiate of *les Soeurs de la Miséricorde* accepted six of those who were already engaged in the work.[45] One can but speculate on what might have happened had the Bishop been a man of less drive and determination. It is possible that much of the charitable work would have continued in the hands of Catholic lay women working alongside the existing religious orders. As it turned out, the religious communities took over the care of the orphans, the old and destitute, the mentally and physically sick, the blind, deaf and mute, the unmarried mothers and the female prisoners, and Catholic lay women were gradually excluded, from all but a supporting role.

In the Protestant community, women were involved in numerous charitable institutions.[46] The role of women in these societies varied considerably. In the larger organizations such as the House of Industry and Refuge, there was a board of directors usually composed of prominent businessmen who looked after the financial and legal matters. Various women's committees set the policy and generally directed different aspects of the work. These ladies were usually from the upper classes and gave of their services freely. Finally a respectable older woman was employed as matron to take charge of the daily running of the institution, possible with the assistance of two or three general servants. Smaller societies like the Y.W.C.A., the Women's Protective Immigration Society and the Women's Christian Temperance Union were run exclusively by women.

XII

The greatest progress made by Protestant women in Montreal was in the field of education and nursing. *Ecole Jacques Cartier*, the Catholic normal school in Montreal, did not admit female students until a women's annex was added in 1899.[47] In 1869 Mme Médéric Marchand opened a private school which later received a subsidy from the Catholic School Commission. This school made an attempt to prepare girls for careers in teaching and office work. Between 1881 and 1901 nearly a thousand girls gained their *brevet d'enseignement* for elementary, model or academic teaching.[48] It is not known how many of these girls taught, but it does not seem likely that they had much impact on the teaching profession, as lay teachers were in the minority. In 1893 there were 142 teaching sisters and 43 women teachers in the schools controlled by the Commission, and another 400 sisters were engaged in independent schools.[49] The McGill Normal School opened its doors to student teachers of both sexes in 1857. Women always greatly outnumbered men, although this had not originally been anticipated. The lower salaries paid to teachers failed to attract men. The school had some unusual features: tuition was free and financial assistance in the form of small bursaries was given for living expenses. Students whose homes were more than ninety miles from Montreal also received a travel allowance. Male students who had a good academic standing in the school were admitted to McGill College, but this privilege did not extend to women. The aim of the school was first and foremost to produce teachers: students had to sign a pledge that committed them to teaching for three years after graduation.[50] The original prospectus was not clear on this point: students were required to promise to comply with Regulation 23, but the meaning of the regulation was not explained. At least one students in the first class did not understand this obligation, and Principal William Dawson received a request from a parent that his daughter should be released from teaching for three years.[51] Dawson's reply has not been found, but an application form used at a later date made the rules of the school more explicit. The applicant promised to pay £10 to the Principal of the Normal School if he or she failed to comply with the regulations which were spelled out and included the three-year pledge to teach.[52]

The financial assistance to normal school students varied from year to year. In 1857 the sum of £8 or £9 was offered.[53] The prospectus for 1867 refers to a sum of $36 for students in the elementary and model course and $80 to those in the academy class.[54] The following year nineteen female students received $24 each.[55]

During the nineteenth century, 1,664 women obtained the elementary diploma, 978 the model, and 160 the academic diploma from the McGill Normal School.[56] The classes steadily increased in size from an initial group of eleven girls, six of whom came from Montreal, to one of 149 in the 1889-99 session.[57] Free tuition and the modest bursaries opened a career to many girls who otherwise could not have afforded a college education. Although the pay for teachers was extremely poor, teaching was considered a socially acceptable occupation for respectable girls. It remains a mystery

how they managed to maintain their social position on salaries of less than
$100 a year. Teaching was the only career open to women that led to a
pension. The average salary for women with diplomas was $99 in 1899,[58]
but as some teachers at the Montreal High School for Girls received salaries
ranging from $350 to $600 a year,[59] many salaries must have been well
below the average. Pensions were even more modest than salaries. In 1900
there were twenty-three women in Montreal receiving pensions which
averaged $67.34 for an average of twenty-three years' service. The lowest
pension was $21.87 a year after twenty years of teaching and the highest
$218.77, also after the same length of service.[60]

Before 1871, the McGill Normal School was the only institution
concerned with the higher education of women, but in 1884 McGill College
opened its doors to women on a regular basis. This enabled graduates of the
Normal School, the Montreal High School for Girls and also ladies who
attended courses organized by the Montreal Ladies Educational Association
to continue their education. A degree from McGill did not, however,
immediately open the doors of opportunity to women. As one editor pointed
out in 1875, there was no demand for highly educated women outside the
teaching profession.[61] The admission of women to McGill had important
consequences for the twentieth rather than the nineteenth century.[62] Only a
very small number of women attended McGill College particularly in
comparison with the Normal School. The faculties of medicine and law
refused to accept women and those who wished to study medicine went to
the medical school of Bishop's College which was located in Montreal. This
insitution accepted women after 1890 and ten completed their training before
the school merged with the McGill medical school in 1905.[63]

The Montreal School of Nursing had greater impact in creating
opportunities for women in the medical field. By mid-century Florence
Nightingale had largely succeeded in establishing nursing as a career for
respectable women, although the term nurse was still used synonymously
with that of servant in Montreal. As the advantages of trained nurses became
increasingly apparent, the medical staff and management committee of the
Montreal General Hospital began to examine ways of training nurses and in
1874 the committee corresponded with Miss Maria Machin one of the
Nightingale nurses at St. Thomas' Hospital, London. The following year
Miss Machin arrived in Montreal for the purpose of establishing a school at
the General. She was later joined by several trained nurses.[64] Financial
difficulties prevented the foundation of a school at that time, and several of
the trained nurses left. The Y.M.C.A. proposed a course for nurses in 1877.
But the hospital was unable to co-operate, and the project was abandoned.[65]
Miss Anna Caroline Maxwell, a graduate of the Boston City Hospital, was
engaged in 1879. A circular was prepared announcing that a school offering

a two-year course would open in 1880, but it also failed to materialize.[66] Miss Rimmer, who was in charge of the hospital during the 1880's, had no formal training in nursing, but was a lady of good sense and organizing ability and she improved conditions and attracted a better class of woman to hospital work.[67]

In 1889 the hospital management committee again resolved on the necessity of a training school, and advertisements were placed in the local papers and in American medical journals. Miss Gertrude Elizabeth Livingstone, who had graduated from the New York Hospital's Training School for Nurses, was appointed, together with two trained assistants. In April 1890 the school opened. Nursing as a career immediately attracted women in Montreal: in the first year, one hundred and sixty applications were received. Eighty candidates were admitted on probation and forty-two were finally accepted.[68] The two-year programme placed emphasis on practical experience, and the curriculum contained only twenty-two hours of lectures. Students were rotated through the different wards and departments, spending a few months in each.[69] In spite of the large enrolment only six nurses graduated from the first class.

VIII

By 1900 Montreal was the home of thousands of women whose place of birth was in rural Quebec or the British Isles. The demand for female labour had drawn them to the city, and they had made the transition to a totally new environment. Girls who grew up on the farm surrounded by the warmth and affection of a large family had adapted to working in a factory and living in a cramped room or a shack euphemistically called a rear dwelling. Young Irish girls, some newly arrived from Ireland and others the daughters of Irish settlers in the counties north and south of Montreal, had learned to conform to the demands of wealthy Protestant families. These women left no testimony of their loneliness, discouragement and homesickness, but there is no reason to believe they escaped such feelings.

One of the most striking features of the period was the emergence of the French Canadian working mother. We do not know what effect this development had on the relationship within the family, but it was probably considerable. The influence of the religious orders in the moral and religious development of French Canadian children was more important than has previously been recognized, as it is now clear that large numbers of very young children passed their formative years in the care of the sisters whose first concern was to instil a set of standards rooted in the Catholicism of nineteenth century Quebec. Prayers and catechism were part of the daily fare of the *salles d'asile*, and the importance of this in the formation of religious, moral and social attitudes should not be underestimated.

In a sense this paper raises more questions than it attempts to answer. One of the most interesting relates to the reasons why French Canadian mothers worked, when apparently those of English, Scottish and Irish origin did not. Was poverty generally more prevalent among French Canadians, or did the large family make it necessary to have a second wage earner? Alternatively, were some French Canadian artisans buying homes in the suburbs as suggested by the rhetoric in the newspapers? The picture tends to confirm the writer's earlier contention that the Irish made a satisfactory adjustment in Montreal, and were no longer at the bottom of the economic ladder in the post-Confederation years.[70]

As the religious orders proliferated, Catholic lay women were increasingly excluded from a variety of occupations. Within the religious community, however, it was possible for women to rise to positions of great authority and responsibility that had no counterpart in the Protestant community. A high degree of administrative ability and business acumen was required to meet the temporal as well as the spiritual needs of a community. The necessity of accommodating the wishes of the bishop, the chaplain and the sisters while conforming to the civil code, called for diplomacy of a high order on the part of the superior.

Industrial expansion created jobs for women and lessened their dependence on domestic service. At the same time, the existence of a pool of cheap female labour encouraged the growth of the garment, boot and shoe, textile and tobacco trades. The number of women employed in industry reached a peak in 1881, when nearly 16 percent of the female population were employed in manufacturing as compared with 8 percent in domestic service. By 1891 just under 11 percent of the female population was employed in industry.[71] These figures probably underestimate the total number of women involved in manufacturing over a given period, because it is likely that marriage, childbirth and family responsibilities produced a mobile work force in which women moved frequently between the factory and the home.

No attempt has been made to examine the wages and working conditions of women. The lack of reliable statistical series of wages, prices and costs of living in the nineteenth century makes research in this area difficult, particularly in relation to women. *The Report of the Royal Commission on the Relations between Capital and Labour*, however, contains much information on conditions in the factories of Montreal.

There is room for research in many other areas. The archives of the religious communities contain a wealth of material of interest to the social historian. One would like to know more about the socio-economic background of the nuns. It is postulated that the majority came from a modestly prosperous rural agricultural setting, but research may well modify this view. Fresh interpretations of the orders themselves are greatly needed, but it may be some time before such work becomes possible.

Newspapers are a fruitful source of material on women in the later years of the century, when women's columns and pages became regular features. It may be possible to reconstruct a clear picture of the role of the woman in the family, and to define stereotypes of ideal women with whom young girls identified. Work based on the French Canadian, English Protestant and English Catholic press might reveal distinct stereotypes for the different religious and ethnic groups.

In conclusion it can be said that during the nineteenth century the role of women in Montreal underwent considerable change. At the end of the period they constituted an important but docile element in the labour force. In the unlikely event of a general strike of women, one suspects that the extent of disruption would have astonished Montrealers. As it was, women raised no voice against the undoubted hardships of their existence, and few spoke on their behalf.

NOTES:

1. Warren S. Thompson and P.K. Whelpton, *Population Trends in the United States*, Demographic Monographs, vol. IX (New York: Gordon and Beach, 1969), p. 192.
2. *Census of Canada*, 1871, vol. II, table 3.
3. Computed from the *Census of Canada*, 1861, vol. I, table 5; 1891, vol. II, table 9.
4. Montreal *Herald*, 10.7.1871, 7.9.1871, 19.11.1872, 21.11.1872, 5.2.1873.
5. *Herald*, 7.9,1871; *Post*, 4.3.1882.
6. Computed from the *Census of Canadas*, 1861, vol. II, table 16, *Census of Canada*, 1881, vol. I, table 2.
7. *Herald*, 7.9.71.
8. *Report of the 4th Annual Meeting of the Protestant House of Industry and Refuge*, p. 7.
9. Mary Quayle Innis, *Unfold the Years* (Toronto: McClelland and Stewart, 1949), p. 21.
10. *Herald*, 22.11.1881.
11. *12th Ann. Rep. of Home and School of Industry*, 1860, p. 3.
12. *21st Ann. Rep. of Home and School of Industry*, 1869, p. 4.
13. *Ann. Rep. of the Montreal Day Nursery*, 1889, p. 8.
14. *Montreal Illustrated, 1884: its Growth, Resources, Commerce, Manufacturing Interests, Financial Institutions, Educational Advantages, and Prospects; Also Sketches of the Leading Business Concerns which Contribute to the City's Progress and Prosperity* (Montreal: Consolidated Illustrating Co., 1894), p. 298.
15. *Montreal in 1856. A Sketch Prepared for the Celebration of the Opening of the Grand Trunk Railway in Canada* (Montreal: Lovell, 1865), p. 45.
16. The factories were: A.Z. Lapierre & Son, 1854 (*Montreal Illustrated, . . . op. cit.*, p. 146); Ames-Holden Co., 1853 (*ibid.*, p. 113); James Linton and Co., 1859 (*Industries of Canada. City of Montreal Historical and Descriptive Review*, Montreal: Gazette Printing Co., 1886, p. 114); J.I. Pellerin & Sons, 1859 (*Montreal Illustrated, . . . op cit.*, p. 195); James

Whithem & Co., exact date unknown (K.G.C. Huttermayer, *Les intérêts commerciaux de Montréal et Québec et leur manufactures*, Montreal: Gazette Printing Co., 1891, p. 169); G. Boivin & Co., 1859 (*Montreal Illustrated 1894, . . . op. cit.*, p. 204); George T. Slater & Sons, *circa* 1864 (*Montreal Illustrated 1894, . . . op. cit.*, p. 140); William McLaren & Co., *circa* 1860's (Chisholm & Dodd, *Commercial Sketch of Montreal and its Superiority as a Wholesale Market*, Montreal 1868, p. 50); B.J. Pettener, 1866 (*Montreal Illustrated 1894, . . . op. cit.*, p. 236); Robert & James McCready (Montreal *Post*, Jan. 3, 1885, *True Witness*, Oct. 15, 1890). Thirty boot and shoe manufacturers existed between 1845 and 1853 according to the Montreal Street Directories (1854-6, pp. 224-228, 1852, pp. 270-1) but most were probably very small concerns which did not employ women.

17. *Montreal in 1856, . . . op. cit.*, p. 46.

18. *Herald*, 6.9.92.

19. *Montreal in 1856, . . . op. cit.*, p. 40.

20. John F. Snell, *MacDonald College* (Montreal: McGill University Press, 1963), pp. 9-10.

21. *Montreal Illustrated 1894, . . . op. cit.*, pp. 138-139.

22. *Ibid.*, p. 292.

23. *Ibid.*, pp. 266, 294, 296.

24. *Herald*, 6.9.1892.

25. Dressmakers, milliners, seamstresses, furriers, hatters, corsetmakers, shirtmakers, glovers, tailors and tailoresses.

26. *Industries of Canada, . . . op. cit.*, p. 114; J. Kane, *Le Commerce de Montréal et de Québec et leurs industries en 1889*, p. 76; *Montreal Illustrated, 1894, . . . op. cit.*, pp. 146, 204.

27. *Census of Canada*, Industrial Schedules, 1871, 1891.

28. 19th century wage books, Molson's Archives.

29. *Le Diocèse de Montréal à la fin du 19e siècle* (Montréal: Eusebe Sénécal, 1900), p. 299.

30. *Salle d'asile* St. Joseph pour l'enfance, Registre d'Inscription 1859-1869, m.s.; *Salle d'asile* Sainte Gunégonde, Registre d'Inscription, 1889-1891, m.s. Archives des Soeurs Grises de Montréal.

31. *Salles d'Asile Tenues par les Soeurs de la Charité de Montréal*, Montréal: 1878, p. 2, Archives des Soeurs Grises.

32. *1747 Souvenir 1897: Descriptions et Notes historiques sur la Maison des Soeurs Grises à Montréal*, 1897, N.P., p. 3.

33. *Salles d'Asile., . . . Montréal, op. cit.*, p. 2.

34. *Herald*, 21.9.1874; S. Lachapelle, *La Santé Pour Tous*, Montréal: 1880, pp. 122-144; Lachapelle, *Femme et Nurse*, Montréal: 1901, p. 43.

35. Registre: Ecole St. Joseph, 309-700/11, archives de la Congrégation de Notre-Dame.

36. *11th Ann. Rep. of the Day Nursery*, 1899, p. 2.

37. *2nd Ann. Rep. of the Day Nursery*, 1890, p. 3.

38. *1st Ann. Rep. of the Day Nursery*, 1889, pp. 3-4.

39. Marie-Claire Daveluy, *L'Orphelina Catholique de Montréal* (Montreal, 1918), p. 14.

40. *Ibid.*, pp. 41-44.

41. J.J. Curran, *St. Patricks Orphan Asylum* (Montreal, 1902), p. 23.

42. *Le Diocèse, . . . op. cit.*, p. 281.

43. C. de Laroche-Héron, *Les Servantes de Dieu en Canada* (Montreal: Lovell, 1855), p. 78.

44. *Le Diocèse, . . . op. cit.*, pp. 261-262.

45. E.-J. Auclair, *Histoire des Soeurs de Miséricorde de Montréal* (Montréal, 1928), pp. 14-16, 40, 46.

46. The most important included the Female Benevolent Society, The Hervey Institute, The House of Industry and Refuge, the Home, the Y.W.C.A., the Women's Protective Immigration Society, and the Women's Christian Temperance Union.

47. Adélard Desrosiers, *Les Ecoles normales primaires de la Province de Québec* (Montréal: Arbour & Dupont, 1909), p. 182.

48. *Nos Ecoles Laïques*, 1846-1946, Album Souvenir d'un siècle d'apostolat (Montréal: Imprimerie de Lamirande, 1947), pp. 57-58.

49. *An Account of the Schools, Controlled by the Roman Catholic Board of School Commissioners*, 1893, pp. 12-13.

50. "Prospectus of the McGill Normal School, 1857", Dawson Papers, acc. 927-I-4, McGill Archives.

51. W. Brethone to J.W. Dawson, 26.2.57, Dawson Papers, acc. 927-4-26.

52. Dawson Papers, acc. 927-20-34A.

53. *Ibid.*, acc. 927-3.

54. *Ibid.*, acc. 927-19-8.

55. *Ibid.*, acc. 927-20-8.

56. *Sess. Pap. Que.*, 63 Vict. 1899-1900, vol. 2, app. VIII, Table G, p. 308.

57. Dawson Papers, acc. 927-3. McGill Archives.

58. *Sess. Pap. Que.*, 63 Vict. 1899-1900, vol. 2, app. VI.

59. Gillian M. Burdell, "The High School for Girls, Montreal, 1875-1914," (unpublished M.A. thesis, McGill, 1963), p. 41.

60. *Sess. Pap. Que.*, 63 Vict. 1899-1900, vol. 2, app. VIII, Table I.

61. *Herald*, 13.4.75.

62. Cleverdon pointed out that all eight graduates of the first class became "unwavering advocates of women's suffrage" at a later date. Catherine Lyle Cleverdon, *The Woman Suffrage Movement in Canada* (Toronto: University of Toronto Press, 1950), p. 217.

63. Maude E. Abbott, *History of Medicine in the Province of Quebec* (Montreal: McGill University Press, 1931), p. 67.

64. H.E. MacDermot, *History of the School for Nurses of the Montreal General Hospital*, Alumnae Assoc. (Montreal, 1944), pp. 17-18.

65. *Herald*, 6.4.1877.

66. MacDermot, *op. cit.*, pp. 28-30.

67. *Ibid.*, p. 32.

68. *Ibid.*, p. 43.

69. *Ibid.*, p. 53.

70. D.S. Cross, "The Irish in Montreal, 1867-1896" (unpublished M.A. thesis, McGill University, 1969), pp. 261-2.

The Other Toronto: Irish Catholics in a Victorian City, 1850-1900

MURRAY W. NICOLSON

The study of the Irish Catholic experience between 1850 and 1900 in Toronto provides insight into another side of that Victorian city. Set apart from the Protestant majority because of their religion and ethnic background, the Irish Catholics also had different cultural adaptations that caused social problems. Although generally considered misfits by the charter population, they refused to accept the predetermined cultural mould dictated by an unsympathetic urban majority as an answer to their social dilemma. Instead, the Irish Catholics were able to retain their ethno-religious identity and to develop a distinctive alternative to assimilation.

The Irish Catholics who arrived in Toronto following the Famine of 1847 were an urban-dwelling peasantry whose struggles formed a vital part of urban history. They were the generational product of an English Celtic Frontier where the peasantry had been under persistent pressure to assimilate. But, despite the harshness of penal laws, a particularistic peasant culture had survived. And in the Post-Famine period, some social mechanism or, for lack of a better term, some Hartzian proclivity allowed for the transfer of that *gehmienschaft* culture and an Irish *weltanschauung* or *dearcadh* to Victorian Toronto where it evolved into a new, urban cultural identity.

The new urban cultural identity was a syncretic vehicle. It could be labelled Irish Tridentine Catholicism because it was formed from the adoption, reinterpretation and fusion of various elements in Irish peasant culture with the standard Tridentine Catholicism of the age. The old attachment to pageantry, pilgrimages and celebrations surrounding weddings and wakes complemented a growing devotional system which was spread through adherence to the positive peasant elements of love of associations, a

SOURCE: This is an original paper, prepared especially for this volume.

sense of community and group voluntarism. The mixture of sacred and profane penetrated Irish social life with a puritanical religious philosophy which allowed for the creation of an Irish sense of the holy. That social mechanism assisted the Irish in the evasion of social pressures which were constant factors in the urban milieu. Irish Tridentine Catholicism supported a sense of exclusiveness and national pride, expressed through a reverence for Irish history which emphasized the unity of people and Church. And that relationship fostered the belief that those in the Irish diaspora were called upon to perform an historic task — the conversion of the English-speaking work.

Following a period of gestation in Cabbagetown and the other core areas of Irish Catholic concentration in Toronto, the urban-born, ethno-religious culture was transmitted to other cities and their controllable hinterlands in Ontario through the Church's metropolitan communication system, the Irish press and extensive Irish kinship patterns. Regardless of the fact that the majority of Ontario's Irish Catholic population was rural-dwelling, group identity was perpetuated through the transfer of new cultural adaptations worked out by an urban-dwelling peasantry.[1]

Even though the experience of Toronto Irish Catholics between 1850 and 1900 was distinctive, it can only be examined as a fragment of the total Irish experience in the broader New World Irish diaspora. Toronto cannot be viewed as an incidental location wherein the Irish experience was so generalized as to be considered standard Irish social process. For if this were done, specific and contextual differentiations would be lost in generalities, and their experience would be denuded of its distinctiveness. Similarly, one must avoid the conception of the Irish experience as only a component of numerous independent variables that shaped Toronto; for then their experiences would be lost among the multiple forces which created or controlled the environment. However, if the Toronto Irish are examined as a product acted upon by urban forces, one can discern clearly the differentiated response of this group to the environmental container in which they lived.[2]

I

Within the last decade interest in Irish studies has been productive of many works. Canadian and American studies have examined the problems and adjustments of the Irish as a part of the urban experience, and elements within this growing literature allow for some comparison with what occurred in Toronto. Factors common to the Irish in Canadian and American cities include: the universal importance of the institutional Church as an agency of social control; the persistence within their population of transiency, drunkenness, violence, poverty and disease; the positive trait of voluntarism; and a growing anti-Irish sentiment within the Protestant segment.[3] However, within the realm of education, labour and politics, the Toronto Irish experience differed from that in American cities.

In the United States, parochial education was supported voluntarily and was multi-ethnic in approach. Toronto Separate Schools were publicly funded by legislation, staffed by Irish teachers and composed of an Irish student body because the Catholics were almost exclusively Irish in that Victorian city. The disruptive problems of separate school educational issues never entered the arena of American politics, as they had in Ontario.[4] While most of the American Irish could vote, a restricted franchise kept the Toronto Irish out of ward politics, limiting their urban voice.[5] However, it should be noted that the Toronto parochial school system, like the American counterpart, was a valuable socializing agency.[6]

An examination of Irish American studies shows that the Irish urban experience was similar in most American cities. Some minor urban and regional variations existed because of varied proportionate mixtures within the Catholic ethnic population. For this reason conclusions drawn from the American milieu are not totally comparable to what occurred in Toronto and other Canadian cities. The Canadian Irish experience was modified by two factors. In most circumstances the Irish numerically dominated urban Catholic populations, associating amiably with other English-speaking Catholics. When the Irish shared urban space with non-English-speaking Catholics it was with French Canadians, who had support from a charter group in Quebec. This ethnic mix was quite different from that in American cities where there was only one charter group, the Protestant Anglo-Saxon. Furthermore, in the United States the Irish Catholics were dominantly urban dwellers and outnumbered Irish Protestants in the cities, whereas the Irish Catholics in Ontario were dominantly rural dwellers and, in Toronto, were outnumbered by the Irish Protestants.[7]

Irish urban cultural experiences were similar in Toronto, Hamilton and London, Ontario. From 1842 to 1856 the three centres were directed from Toronto as parts of a Diocesan See, and from 1870 onward as independent Dioceses subject to a Metropolitan in Toronto. The communication network attached to the ecclesiastical metropolitan structure allowed for the transfer of similar cultural elements among the three major urban areas and their hinterlands.[8] Similarly, Peterborough and Kingston, though slightly modified by small French and Scottish Catholic minorities, became Irish Sees because of the dominance of Irish population and for a period of time were under the direction of an Irish metropolitan in Toronto.[9] The persistence of French ethnic individuality in the Windsor and Penetanguishene areas made the Irish experience there more complicated. In those centres, the French experience was comparable to that of other Catholic ethnic minorities in American cities, perpetually seeking ethnic survival in opposition to Irish dominance.[10] Ottawa, however, showed a more polarized position. After many disputes and attempts at French dominance, French and Irish Catholics were able to establish two equal societies, with separate ethnic parishes and institutions.[11]

In Quebec and Montreal, the Irish response to French dominance seemed to parallel Polish or Italian reaction to Irish dominance which, in American cities, demanded conformity and assimilation.[12] What occurred in the Maritimes was differentiated from central Canada because separate schools were denied to the Catholics there at Confederation or shortly afterwards. Therefore the politics surrounding the separate school question was nonexistant, and for that reason the Maritime experience can be more readily compared to the American one. Similarly, the existence of Scottish, Irish and Acadian Catholics in the Maritimes tends to duplicate the American experience.[13] Multiple Catholic ethnic groups created multiple or mixed ethnic-religious institutions, clergy and religious orders in both the Maritimes and the United States, whereas in Toronto all orders and institutions either were or became Irish.[14] Newfoundland resolved the religious, ethnic and educational question by granting denominational schools to all religions.[15] The development of the Canadian West and British Columbia fall beyond the scope of Irish studies in the Victorian era. In that geographic area, Irish Catholics were few and ethnic conflict began between the two charter groups, English Protestants and French Catholics, to be replaced by the Canadian ethnic mosaic in the late nineteenth century.[16] What makes the Irish Catholic experience in Toronto distinctive is that they were the first large ethnic minority in the city and remained the dominant group within the Catholic Church in the Victorian age.

II

The Catholic peasantry of Ireland who migrated to Toronto and other North American urban centres prior to and after the Famine of 1847, had been a subject people for generations. The centuries-long English occupation had been brutal, for it had been English policy to replace slowly the native Irish with a more docile Protestant population from England and Scotland. Once established, that alien group was pitted by the English against the Irish in a constant attempt to divide and rule.

The defeat of the last Stuart King, in 1688, by the House of Orange ended any hope of Catholic social or political equality with the Protestant population, for it ushered in the Penal Laws, enacted between 1702 and

1715. Those laws were intended to disarm, disinherit, if not exterminate, the Catholic peasantry, to make them poor and to keep them poor. In addition, the laws were enacted to destroy the Catholic aristocracy and middle class, and the Catholic Church. A million acres of land had been siezed; 10,000 officers and soldiers of James' Jacobite army had left Ireland with their retainers to fight in the Irish Brigades of France, Spain, Portugal, Austria and Russia. The departure of those "Wild Geese", followed by the enterprising who could no longer find any mobility in Ireland, decapitated Irish Catholic society. Catholic bishops were forbidden to remain in Ireland and all religious orders were banished. The diocesan clergy were required to register and to pledge loyal and obedient behaviour.[17]

Under that prescribed system, Catholic peasants could not purchase land, hold public office, attend university, teach in or keep a schoool, sit on bench or bar, or vote. Under the Protestant ascendency the children of "Cáitlin Ni Houlihan" were to vanish. They had to support the established Church of Ireland; they had to face the evangelizing and open Souperism of a Protestant Crusade against their religion which lasted from 1800 to 1870 and ended only with the disestablishment of the Church of Ireland and the reforms of Cardinal Paul Cullen.[18]

Defenceless, landless and virtually leaderless, the Irish peasants readapted their *gemienschaft* culture as a defence mechanism for group survival. Denied legal protection or access to the law, they compensated by forming numerous secret societies through which they dispensed their own type of justice. Denied an education or entrance into skilled trades, they developed hedge schools with transient teachers. The economic difficulties encountered in trying to support families created a large group of transient workers, Spalpeens or Navvies, who migrated back and forth to England where they were employed in public construction and harvesting. Abandoned by their leaders, Irish peasant loyalties became parochial or regional with parallel, positive traits of increased kinship relationships and local voluntarism. Adversely, however, parochialism bred factionalism which erupted into violent faction fighting between families, parishes and regions that was tolerated by the English as a method of curtailing ethnic unity. The distilling of illicit spirits and excessive drinking became common and served as an escape from an harsh environment.

The denial of religious freedom in Ireland made Catholicism a fugitive faith. In the most repressive periods, the peasants met at the Scaithlan, or outdoor chapel in the hills, where priests who had refused to take any oath other than to the Church said the Mass from a 'Mass rock'. But the lack of priests and the Gallican nature, superstition and corruption of many allowed for the return to or retention of some pre-Christian beliefs and practices which made Irish Catholicism a syncretic vehicle at best. It was not until after the reforms of Cardinal Cullen in 1870 that 'Holy Ireland' would again exist.[19]

From that abused peasant population came the Irish immigrants to Toronto and the major cities of North America. It is uncertain as to how many died as the result of starvation and disease in the Potato Famines of 1845 to 1846, and 1846 to 1847. Estimates range from 500,000 to 1,000,000. But, by 1851, 1,500,000 had been driven out of Ireland and were followed by 5,000,000 more by 1914.[20]

III

Not only did the Irish immigrants have to carry the burden of their past and the disasterous consequences of the Famine, they also had to bear the effects of a stereotype which victimized them further. The stereotype was one that was generally accepted in the Victorian period and adopted by the Charter population of Toronto as normative in its application to what it considered an uncivilized, almost sub-human, alien group. John J. Appel concluded:

> Behind the stereotype of the Irish there was a kernel of reality along with a highly selective ascription of traits, some based on fancy and malice aforethought, typical of all stereotyping.[21]

Although the physical attributes which supposedly identified a person as Irish were found in a minority of the population only, they were the characteristics that formed part of an image. They were common among a small minority of West County Irish peasants who were tall, broad shouldered, large chested, with big heads, pronounced browridges and broad high foreheads. This particular West County face, often described as stamped with the map of Ireland, had a wide jaw and upturned nose; generally, hair was curly brown or rufus, skin was fair and freckled, and eyes were blue. That appearance, accompanied by the costume of the age and a clay pipe, became the subject for Irish caricature.[22]

In addition, the speech of the Irish immigrants was foreign for they spoke either Gaelic or an Irish brogue filled with Gaelic words. Therefore, coupled with their general appearance of poverty and their religion, language as well placed the Irish at a disadvantage, because English, like the Protestant religion, was the key to acceptance and elitesmanship in English Toronto.[23] All those factors with the inclusion of their social customs, so different from accepted practice among the majority, contributed to the development of the stereotype.

The stereotype produced differential treatment and prejudice. Even two decades before the Famine, Irish immigrants to Upper Canada felt the rejection of the charter population. Father W. P. Macdonald, a Scottish priest who served the Irish of Toronto and in other parts of Upper Canada,

wrote of the prejudice towards his Irish flock. On their behalf, he published a
poem as a plea for understanding:

> Come talk of your Catholic brethern with candour,
> Nor pelt us thus ever with obsolete slander,
> In falsehood's dark devious path would yon wander
> So wilfully headlong, cries Paddy O'Rafferty.
> Don't you see, I'm in all things your poor fellow creature
> In intellect, colour, in size, shape and feature.[24]

But the stereotype stuck and was more viciously applied following the
Famine migration. George Brown, editor of *The Glòbe* in Toronto, made no
attempt at understanding the problems of the Irish and spread a derogatory
picture of Irish character:

> Irish beggars are to be met everywhere, and they are as ignorant and vicious as
> they are poor. They are lazy, improvident and unthankful; they fill our poorhouses
> and our prisons, and are as brutish in their superstition as Hindoos.[25]

There can be little doubt that George Brown and his *Globe*, with its
metropolitan coverage, the Orange Lodge, and some of the Protestant
churches were responsible for fueling the Protestant Crusade against the Irish
Catholics, which lasted from 1850 to 1900. The effects of that crusade were
most strongly felt by the Irish in Toronto where the Protestants controlled
social institutions, civic positions and the workplace. Typical of Presbyterian
sermon literature which contributed to the treatment the Irish were subjected
to was:

> O Lord we approach thee this morning in an attitude of prayer and likewise of
> complaint. When we came to Canada we expected to find a land flowing with milk
> and honey but instead we find a land peopled by the ungodly Irish. O Lord, in thy
> mercy drive them to the uttermost parts of Canada, make them hewers of wood and
> drawers of water, give them no place as magistrates, policemen or rulers among
> thy people. If ye have any favours to bestow or any good land to give away, give it
> to thine own peculiar people the Scots. Make them members of Parliament and
> rulers among thy people but as for the ungodly Irish take them by the heels and
> shake them over the pit of hell. But O Lord don't let them fall in and the glory shall
> be thine for ever and ever Amen.[26]

The social problems that stigmatized the Irish Catholic Famine immigrants
to Toronto stemmed from the fact that they attempted to retain their
rural-born *gemienschaft* culture in an urban setting that displayed an
evergrowing *gesellschaft* structure. Their response to the alien, urban
container seemed only to heighten the cultural differences and caused culture
shock in the Protestant majority who controlled the city.[27]

The social traits which had sustained the Irish through penal times and
during the Famine were unacceptable by majority standards in Toronto and

isolated them from the general population. Voluntarism, which had been a positive factor among the Irish Catholics, had lost much of its vitality because the Famine migration had disrupted the former regional and extended kinship patterns.[28] That voluntarism which had created communal societies was reinterpreted in Toronto and its social thrust was replaced by anarchistic proclivities within the confines of secret societies. The Toronto-based Irish societies existed for purely nationalistic sentiment and a hatred of the English legal system and, therefore, were productive of violence.[29] In the face of an even harsher urban environment, drunkenness which had been endemic became almost genetic, spawning an illicit saloon or Irish shebeen society in the city that aggravated further the problems of a group under considerable stress.[30] Drunkenness and violence placed the Irish at the mercy of the Courts where their religion placed them at a greater disadvantage.

Except for the few who had a hedge education, the Irish immigrants were generally an illiterate group. Lacking skills, they were forced from their Toronto base into manual labour or seasonal employment in public works, the railways and the canals. In the rising industrial city, with the work place under the watchful eye of the Orange leadhand or supervisor, Irish Catholics were second choice, employed only if Protestants were not available to do the work. Where, in the past, transiency had been a mode of life adopted to support families, in Toronto it became generational and the often futile search for work was responsible for numerous 'Irish widows' or abandoned women and children who believed their providers were 'gone with the fairies'.[31]

Their lack of funds dictated housing of a substandard nature but which was at least as adequate as what they had had in Ireland. A number of factors contributed to the overcrowding in the shacks, tenements and boarding houses in the city. It was necessary for multiple family units to group together to pay the rent; widows needed a source of income and took in a number of boarders who sought cheap lodgings; kinship patterns and old parish friendships dictated hospitality and those without shelter were harboured. Furthermore, there was a need to congregate among their own people and to gain the confidence of numbers in working class areas where they were never the majority. But the overcrowded habitations, often shared with chickens and pigs, were conducive to a number of social ills.[32]

Poverty-stricken and disease-ridden on arrival in Toronto, the unsanitary conditions, poor diet, contaminated water supply and filthy habits of waste disposal enhanced the spread of disease and contributed to a high death rate among the Irish immigrants. Fear of eviction caused the urban peasantry to hide knowledge of diseases from city authorities which only augmented the consequences. The lack of privacy, habitual drunkenness and despair were responsible for causal relationships or hand-fast unions. The relationships were usually limited in duration but were productive of numerous neglected children among whom the mortality rate was high. The tendency to maintain tightknit kinship associations was responsible for close inter-breeding which resulted in infantile genetic anomalies, like cluricaunes or ugly dwarfs, clinically identified as Leprechaunism. Many of those children were disposed of quickly and buried in the cabbage patches of Cabbagetown. Folk tales substantiate the belief that weak or deformed children were not considered human but, instead, were changelings left by the sidhe or fairies; and the practice of guiltlessly neglecting or destroying them still took place in Ireland in the early part of this century.[33]

Like the Tinkers and Travellers in contemporary Ireland whose living conditions have forced them to live "on the margins of Irish society for generations,"[34] so, too, the Toronto Famine Irish lived on the margin of English Canadian Society. Having survived the penal laws[35] and a Protestant Crusade in Ireland,[36] the Irish believed in "a law of their own, based upon the will of the peasant community."[37] And this transplanted peasantry, with all its faults, was attempting to retain an agrarian society in an urban setting.[38] Politics and the press became arbitrary elements to the Irish immigrants who were locked out of political life and employment by an Orange city. That conservative peasantry, which sought social adjustment through reform politics, wasted its limited enfranchisement by voting for individual candidates of both parties, who promised much but despised this alien electorate.[39] The Famine Irish were a minority in Toronto, their culture was in decay and they needed a focus to preserve their ethnic identity. They would find it in a reinterpreted Catholicism.

V

The religious practices of the immigrant Family Irish were not those of orthodox Catholicism. In the period prior to the penal laws and the Famine, the Irish showed an attachment to traditional Catholicism with a local interest in holy wells and group pilgrimages. Their belief patterns demonstrated a harmony with nature, little distinction between the material and spiritual worlds and a bond of unity between the living and the dead. But, under the burden of English occupation and the penal laws, the people became isolated from their Church and its teachings. With the destruction of Irish ecclesiastic metropolitanism, they lapsed into ignorance and moral decay.[40] Denial of traditional Catholicism precipitated the retention of partly Christianized customs with a re-emergent, pre-Christian belief in an unseen world.[41] This syncretic or parallel religious vehicle[42] was central to the rites of passage, particularly wakes, but in practice did not perform any Christian function.[43]

The Irish wake as practiced in Toronto by the Famine immigrants was viewed with shock and disgust not only by Protestant observers but also by the hierarchy of the Catholic Church. To the Irish, however, it was an emotional catharsis in which the loss of a community member was resolved. Death was just a continuation of life in Tir Na N'Og, the Celtic rather than the Christian heaven; and the wake encapsulated elements which showed both fear of and respect for the dead. At death, the clock was stopped. The corpse was laid out on a table or in a coffin, with a candle at head and feet, and never left unattended. In some cases, the body was propped upright and, in winter, frozen in a position to allow it to be seated on the stairs or in a chair to view the festivities. Friends and relatives keened the dead with long laments. Dances and lewd games were organized for fun and to entertain and show respect to the dead. Tobacco, food and home-brewed poteen were served to the guests and offered to the corpse. Fighting among the mourners was a common, if not anticipated, occurrence.

In the early years, the casket was carried to the graveside by friends of the deceased where the funeral rites took place. It was a commonly held belief that the last person to be interred was required to serve all the dead in the cemetery until the time of the next committal. Therefore, when two funeral processions approached St. Paul's graveyard at the same time, there was a mad dash to be first in, usually with an ensuing fight among the mourners. Those who died unrepentant by Church standards were buried in unconsecrated ground. But family members would disinter the body by night and bury it in consecrated ground and raise a grand monument over it. Undertaking became a lucrative business venture for a number of Irish immigrants. The respect for and fear of the dead entailed costly funerals, with rental of mourning clothes, hearse and horses decorated with plumes, and the erection of expensive monuments. The culturally expected practices impoverished an already impoverished group and made them appear superstitious in the eyes of the general public.[44]

VI

Although the arrival of the Famine Irish produced culture shock which resulted in some differential treatment, it was the evolutionary growth of the Catholic Church and its fusion of purpose with the Irish population that most concerned the Protestant population of the city. As a result, pressure was exerted on the Irish to assimilate to majority cultural standards. Yet strangely enough, the Church that received the Irish in 1847 was an inappropriate instrument to effect social change. It was the product of a frontier era, a mission entity, bereft of institutions, schools, or priests, with but a single church and an uncompleted Cathedral in Toronto.[45]

From 1819 to 1840, Toronto's Catholic population had been directed by the Scottish Bishop, Alexander Macdonell, from his See in Kingston. Believing that the Rideau Canal system held the promise of future urban development, he failed to envision Toronto as the commercial metropolis of Upper Canada. Macdonell, a Tory Compact member himself, relied upon an influential Catholic section of the Family Compact to further the economic, social and political position of his Church. In Toronto he was supported by a select group of Tories, members of the Councils, military or governmental placemen. Included were the Catholic families — the Babys, the Macdonells, the Kings, and the Elmsleys — and various family members of mixed Protestant and Catholic marriages — the Sherwoods, the Boultons, the Crawfords and the MacNabs. With few priests to serve his Diocese, Bishop Macdonell delegated authority for the administration of St. Paul's Church in Toronto to James Baby, and subsequently to John Elmsley, who served in the capacity of lay-vicars. Those arrangements met with the approval of the governmental and military establishments, the Protestant elite and, at times, the Orange Lodge. In their eyes, Macdonell's methods were a means to keep the Irish as loyal subjects and tended to neutralize the effectiveness of the Church, which allowed for the slow absorption of the Catholic laity into the general population.[46]

Bishop Macdonell's methods, however, did not satisfy the reform-minded Irish laity in Toronto. As early as 1830, the Irish began to organize in an attempt to end Compact control of their Church and of the colony. They were led first by the outspoken journalist, Francis Collins, who was jailed for libel because of his attacks on Compact members. Their stand was taken up subsequently by the lawyer James King and his journalistic partner, Father William O'Grady, antagonists of Francis Collins. Because of his position as parish priest, Father O'Grady became the leader of the slowly-growing Irish Catholic, dissident, working-class population in Toronto and its hinterland.

William O'Grady, an immigrant Irish priest, arrived in Toronto in 1829 from Brazil, and was appointed by Bishop Macdonell to undertake the administration of St. Paul's Church. Initially, O'Grady supported Macdonell and believed it was essential to find some mechanism to control a laity disobedient to any sign of authority. He suggested that Macdonell strengthen the episcopacy in York, organize synods and meetings for closer supervision of an independent-minded, transient Irish clergy, and concentrate effort on the development of schools and institutions to aid the people. There was little sign of any devotionalism among those attending the unadorned church, but there was sufficient evidence to show that the Church was utilized as a stage for inter-class conflict. On the one side was the non-Irish Compact leaders of the Church, who joined the forbidden Masonic Order, were married before more socially acceptable Anglican ministers, raised daughters Catholic and sons Protestant in mixed unions, and resented O'Grady's criticism of what they considered standard religious practice. On the other side was the majority Irish laity who, with little knowledge of religion, emulated the practices of this fast assimilating elite but, as well, demanded a voice in the Church.

Convinced that Tory politics were of no benefit to his Irish laity, O'Grady took a stand with the reform movement and lost the support of Bishop Macdonell and the elite. O'Grady's Irish followers seized St. Paul's Church and Bishop Macdonell reacted by placing it under interdict, excommunicating O'Grady and all those involved. That ended O'Grady's career as a priest. He allied himself to William Lyon Mackenzie but opposed violent action as a means to obtain results. It was the influence of the urban based, former priest, O'Grady, and not that of the absent bishop, Macdonell, that kept the Irish out of the Rebellion of 1837.[47]

With the Union of the Canadas, the Church's political influence diminished with that of the Catholic Compact. Although Toronto became a Diocese in 1842, there was little change in the people or the institutional Church during the tenure of its first bishop, Michael Power, a native born Canadian from the Maritimes. The thrust for social change among Catholics in the city was lost in the building of St. Michael's Cathedral and Bishop's Palace. Furthermore, Power had stamped his approval on an assimilative public school system by accepting the Chairmanship of the Board of Education for Upper Canada. Granted, Power had initiated the traditional metropolitan system by dividing his Diocese into Deaneries for more effective administration and by holding clerical retreats to attempt to discipline the Gallican Irish clergy. But those measures did not pose any threat to the community at large who still considered the Church a sect-like institution. The picture changed, however, with the impact of the Famine migration and the death of the benign Bishop Power ministering to the Irish in the fever sheds of Toronto.[48]

After a leaderless, three year period of interregnum, there arrived in Toronto in 1850, Bishop Armand Charbonnel, the enemy of assimilation and urban conformity. Charbonnel, a French aristocrat, was a Suplician monk who had adopted the life style of a beggar. His past experience in working with the Famine Irish in Montreal suited him for his appointment to Toronto. He began to organize his Diocese to confront both the urban and hinterland environment which imperiled the existence of the institutional Church and its people and to consolidate the laity sufficiently to respond to urban pressure. Building upon Power's diocesan framework, by 1856 Charbonnel succeeded in having the larger Diocese divided into three units, centred around the urban nuclei of Toronto, Hamilton and London. That act of decentralization allowed three bishops to become involved with the particularistic problems of three different areas and laid the groundwork for the establishment of an ecclesiastic province in Canada West, wherein Toronto would become the Archiepiscopal city.[49]

VII

When Charbonnel arrived in Toronto he drew upon the external framework of the Universal Church to obtain money, ideas and personnel to expand the internal communication system of the Diocese. He introduced a number of religious orders to serve the people. With their help, Charbonnel was able to open St. Michael's College to train priests, schools to educate the Irish children, and the House of Providence to care for the orphans, infirm, aged and destitute of the city. He obtained additional secular clergy to provide spiritual guidance for the laity of the city and the hinterland. Control of the priesthood was established by measures of enforced spiritual retreats and strict fiscal accountability to ensure the utilization of parish funds for social and institutional purposes, not personal aggrandizement. Under his auspices, the St. Vincent de Paul Society was organized to assist the poor of the city. In addition, he was responsible for the establishment of the Toronto Savings Bank and for the proposal of a building society to encourage the Irish in thrifty habits, and thereby more independence. However, that vigorous institutional and social activity, coupled with an incessant demand for separate schools, pitted Charbonnel and his laity against the city.[50]

It would be naive to conclude that Charbonnel's arrival immediately caused the fusion of Irish ethnic characteristics with Tridentine Catholicism to produce a new, definable ethnic unit. The process was an evolutionary one, growing out of action and reaction between Church and Irish laity as they responded to environmental pressures. The city and the Church were aware of the positive behavioural trait of voluntarism among the pre-Famine Irish when they provided manual labour and what monetary contributions they could to help build St. Michael's Cathedral.[51] The Famine Irish recognized the concern the Church held for them when Bishop Power, five priests from Canada West and one Catholic layman, John Elmsley, ministered to their needs in the Fever sheds as the city was crippled in fear of the contagion they brought. The accusation by some narrow, bigoted people that what the Irish suffered was the penalty for their race and religion only served to strengthen the ethno-religious identity of this nominally Catholic group. And in the process they accepted the burden of a merged stereotype — that of Papist and Irish.[52]

Prior to 1850, the derogatory stereotype of an ignorant Irish peasant had been applied to both Catholic and Protestant alike. Up to that point, both groups in Toronto participated in a single St. Patrick's society from a purely nationalistic point of view. However, with the inundation of Famine migrants to the city, the Irish Protestants wanted to avoid identification with the negative stereotype. To do so, they relinquished their national identity and acculturated into the urban community as Orange Protestants. As a result, to be Irish was synonymous with being Catholic in Toronto for 'Paddyism and Poperyism' were fused. It was not until the latter decades of the nineteenth century, with the rising concept of Home Rule in Ireland, that Irish Protestants again assumed some ethnic identity. To show that Irish Protestants were loyal to the British Crown, they formed a number of organizations in Toronto, closely identified with the Orange Order. Among them was the Irish Protestant Benevolent Society. That particular organization was formed to counteract the social impact of the St. Vincent de Paul Society that gave aid to all regardless of creed. The Irish Protestant Benevolent Society gave assistance to Irish Protestants or to those Catholics who had abandoned or might abandon their religion.[53]

VIII

The Irish Catholics in Toronto differed from their counterparts in American cities in that they did not have to share their Church with other Catholic immigrant groups. In Toronto, tensions arose from within the national Irish group and were of an ethno-religious nature. Irish Protestants drew upon the support of the English and Scottish groups with whom they shared church, school and lodge. However, the Irish were the dominant element in the Catholic population of the city throughout the period of 1850 to 1900.

The Irish formed over ninety-five per cent of Toronto's Catholic population until 1880 when Germans, French and a few Italians and Syrians reduced their proportion to eighty per cent by 1900. Although Catholics grew in number from 7,940 in 1851 to 28,994 by 1901, their percentage proportion of the city's population fell from a high of twenty-five per cent to fourteen per cent in the same period (see Table I).[54] German Catholics shared St. Patrick's parish with the Irish and joined Irish Catholic benevolent associations. The small group of French Canadians in the city were given a church by the Irish. But they showed signs of absorption and their major concern was for group survival. Therefore, ethnic relations of the conflict model developed in the city as a result of the growth of Irish Catholic institutional activity in the face of a Protestant English, Irish and Scottish population growth of seventy-four per cent in 1851 to eighty-six per cent by 1901.

TABLE I

CATHOLICS AND PROTESTANTS IN TORONTO,
1850-1900

Years	CATHOLICS		PROTESTANTS		
	No.	% of Total Pop'n	No.	% of Total Pop'n.	Total Population
1851	7,940	25.8	22,835	74.2	30,775
1860	12,135	27.1	32,686	72.9	44,801
1870	11,881	21.2	44,211	78.8	56,092
1880	15,716	18.2	70,699	81.8	86,415
1890	21,830	15.2	122,193	84.8	144,023
1901	28,994	13.9	179,046	86.1	208,040

SOURCES: *Censuses of Canada, 1851-1901.*

TABLE II

ETHNIC ORIGINS OF THE POPULATION
OF TORONTO, 1851–1901

Ethnic Group	1851		1880		1901	
	No.	%	No.	%	No.	%
Irish	11,305	36.7	32,177	37.2	61,527	29.6
Scot	2,169	7.4	13,754	15.9	34,543	16.6
English	4,958	16.1	34,608	40.1	94,806	45.6
French	467	1.5	1,230	1.4	3,015	1.4
German & Dutch	3	—	2,049	2.4	6,028	2.9
Others	11,738	38.2	2,597	3.0	8,121	3.9
Total Pop'n.	30,775	100%	86,415	100%	208,040	100%

SOURCES: *Censuses of Canada, 1851-1901.*

The Irish Catholics who came to the Toronto area prior to the Famine were unable to afford city residence. They settled along the waterfront and in the liberty adjacent to the city, particularly in the Don Basin, where the Irish clusters were called Slab Town, Paddy Town or Cork Town. From those early small concentrations developed Cabbagetown. After 1850, more pronounced Irish clusters appeared in Cabbagetown and on the waterfront, extending well into St. George and St. Lawrence Wards, and in an area around Bathurst and Queen Streets which became known as Claretown. From 1880 to 1890, the junction area of West Toronto became one of Irish Catholic concentration. In addition, there were at least a dozen other minor areas of Irish Catholic concentration in the city which were labelled 'Irish Town'.

Throughout the whole period under study, there were no solidly Irish Catholic ghettos in the city because poverty forced the Irish to share the rundown areas of substandard housing and tenements with other, working-class Protestant poor. The Irish Catholics were never a majority in any ward of the city and therefore never segregated by ethnicity or religion, only by class. Area selection was dictated by affordable housing and proximity to work. Confidence arose when numbers increased sufficiently in areas of Irish concentration where the quasi-secret Irish brotherhood could operate against open attacks on Irish labourers during their journey to work. Retribution was quick and took place under cover of night. Insult and injury were in direct proportion to the distance from the place of employment. A worker's confidence grew as the distance lessened and his journey converged with that of his friends' (see Map).

Generally, residence within a specific location of Irish concentration was of limited duration. In their search for employment opportunities and housing suitable to accommodate their growing families, the Irish moved from one area to another. That constant movement within the city, between cities, from urban to rural areas and back tended to increase, strengthen and expand the positive elements of the Irish Catholic urban, cultural and social experience. It was within those enclaves that Irish family reformation occurred and a sense of security evolved. But, as the areas changed and were shared with other members of the working class, the tight knit pattern of multiple Irish family units, friends and relatives allowed for a detachment from the physical environment and a development of a ghetto of the mind. As they had learned to ignore abuse, so too could they ignore the abusers and the dismal surroundings. The departures from and return to the areas of concentration by friends and relatives created an Irish communication network within and beyond the city. Within the framework of their own society the Irish were tightly bound by family ties, Church association, accepted mores, religious organizations and an Irish Catholic press. That structure placed them beyond the assimilative reach of the dominant urban society.[55]

IX

Although the Irish were identified as the Catholics in Toronto, generally they were not an obediant laity. In order for the Church to gain control over that laity and to become an urban actor, it had to be able to exert a real influence. Therefore, the Church expanded with the Irish throughout the city, forming parish units to serve the religious, educational, cultural and social needs of their people and became the focus for group identification.

From 1822 to 1848, the Toronto Irish Catholics had been served by a single church, St. Paul's in Cabbagetown. St. Michael's Cathedral, consecrated in 1848, had been built on the periphery of settlement. Its location was determined by the availability of cheap land, not by the needs of the people. As an administrative centre, it represented the beginning of Diocesan organization, and its construction assisted the advance of the Irish population. Similarly, St. Basil's Church, opened in 1856 in the Clover Hill district, just south of Bloor Street, preceded the Irish population. It was built on the site of a gift of land from John Elmsley to the Basilian Fathers who operated St. Michael's College. But, between 1850 and 1914, fourteen churches were constructed in the city, in each case to serve the needs of growing areas of Irish Catholic concentration (see Map).

As each church was built, priests were dispatched from it into the newer areas of Irish settlement where services were conducted in homes and halls. In that way, the city was linked by a parish network; and urban parishes sent priests to assist the clergy in the country which eventually bound metropolis and hinterland into an interacting unit. The parish church became the nerve centre of an Irish nucleus with its priests' house, school, nearby convent, hall, and religious and social organizations attached. Consequently, it measured for children the journey to school and for Irish families the journey to church. As well this centre of Irish activity measured the priest's journey to the homes of the parishioners to give advice, reprimands, or the last rights to the sick. However, for all Catholics it finally measured the journey to the grave.

X

Before that urban parish system could function, the Church hierarchy and its local representatives, the priests, had to devise some methodology to retain the Irish in an urban container that was hardly congenial to the institution or its people. Ideally, the Church upheld the concept of an universal Catholic society as proposed by St. Augustine in *De Civitate Dei* but, realistically, acknowledged that the Irish must work in the 'City of Man', a Protestant metropolis. In the Church's view, the Irish could only survive if they lived in

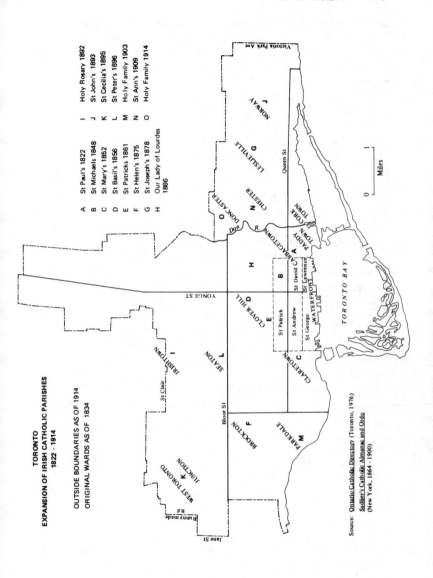

TORONTO
EXPANSION OF IRISH CATHOLIC PARISHES
1822 - 1914

OUTSIDE BOUNDARIES AS OF 1914
ORIGINAL WARDS AS OF 1834

A   St Paul's 1822
B   St Michaels 1848
C   St Mary's 1852
D   St Basil's 1856
E   St Patricks 1861
F   St Helen's 1875
G   St Joseph's 1878
H   Our Lady of Lourdes 1886
I   Holy Rosary 1892
J   St John's 1893
K   St Cecilia's 1895
L   St Peter's 1896
M   Holy Family 1903
N   St Ann's 1909
O   Holy Family 1914

Source: Ontario Catholic Directory (Toronto, 1976)
         Sadlier's Catholic Almanac and Ordo
         (New York, 1864 - 1900)

Miles

the 'City of God', an Irish Catholic city of the mind, a mental ghetto. In that realm, insulated from the assaults of the secular society, they would receive an alternative philosophy of life, faith that their suffering and existence was not in vain. It could be looked upon as a view from eternity, 'sub specie aeternitati'.[56]

The complex, psychological assault embodied a sense of the holy, 'the Irish Holy', a sense of other worldliness, awe, reverence, consolation, acceptance and dependence which gave the Irish a focus for their lives. It incorporated renewed devotional systems which enabled them to carry that sense of the holy from the church into their homes. Within the confines of the constantly accessible churches, men, women and children found a place of comfort and solace, an escape from the insults, abuse and differential treatment so difficult to face in the real world. There they did not feel alone but, rather, that something eternal was on their side, supporting them in their predicament, and from it they drew strength for their seemingly endless struggle with urban pressures. In this way the Church expanded the ghetto of the mind whereby the unacceptable could be blocked out.[57]

To foster that sense of the Holy, one program the Church introduced was intended to contain the fervour of Irish nationalism which was productive of violence. Charbonnel and his religious had set the example for behaviour by suffering public insult and injury in the streets of Toronto. Christian forebearance was demanded of the Irish in the face of insult and bigotry. To limit the violence, Charbonnel and his successors made various attempts at directing the Irish press and the public celebrations surrounding St. Patrick's day, frequently the source of conflict. Eventually, the Church succeeded in exercising some influence over the celebration of St. Patrick's day by emphasizing the religious rather than national nature of the holiday. However it was not until the 1880's that the Church was successful in gaining a newspaper which espoused an ethno-religious approach rather than a nationalistic one.[58]

To replace narrow Irish nationalism the Church began to educate the laity in their religion and its relationship to their ancestral homeland. Sermons and a profusion of Irish Catholic literature identified Irish history and culture with the Church. The beautification of church buildings and ceremonies filled the people with a pride in accomplishment. Missions and pilgrimages were the means to instil a renewed morality.[59] And slowly what evolved from the mixture of Irish practice, Irish nationalism and literature with traditional Catholicism was a laity indoctrinated in a new ethno-religious culture, Irish Tridentine Catholicism, an urban weapon for group survival.

One religious phenomenon that grew out of Irish response to urban pressure and aided the Church's ethno-religious thrust could be called an 'Irish New World Millenium'. The universal concept of transforming an existing imperfect society into a perfect utopia has always had a powerful appeal. Both peasants and urban dwellers, faced with disasters or rapid change, tend to follow the direction of a messianic figure to usher in a new social existence for their group. Michael Barkin has made the statement that, "Ireland, one place where we would most expect millenarian activity, offers in fact an unusually wide range of possible explanations for its absence."[60] In Barkin's evaluation, Ireland emptied quickly during the Famine, leaving it void of leadership. He suggests that the Catholic Church had sufficient strength to explain the disaster, thereby aborting any millenarian activity.[61] But one can question some of his conclusions because the Church in Ireland was a weak institution until 1870.[62]

The Irish were ready for a millenium; it was just suspended in time. According to Barkin, a number of variables are needed to produce millenarian activity: an agrarian peasantry versus an urban society, multiple problems or disasters, the availability of millenarian doctrine, and the presence of a potential leader. These elements were all supplied in Toronto, for there a peasant society confronted an urban one and was faced with numerous problems that seemed insurmountable. The doctrine arose from the Church in its reiteration of the need for the Irish to fulfil a messianic mission, that of converting North America to Catholicism, thereby achieving the millenium. The peasant leader, or 'messiah', was John Lynch, the Irish-born third Bishop of the Diocese of Toronto.[63] The whole messianic thrust commissioned by Lynch was perpetuated through sermons and a specific Irish literature which dictated pride in a past golden age when the people of Ireland were responsible for the conversion of much of Europe. Their suffering and urban rejection were to be considered a sign that they were chosen for an historic task.[64]

When the whole ethno-religious movement was perfected and applied at the parish level, it provided a sense of purpose and direction. Church attendance increased as the devotional system permeated their lives. Other than the priests wearing green vestments at the celebration of Mass on St. Patrick's day, the Irish could not alter the central service, the standard Tridentine Mass, to suit their own ethnic proclivities. Nonetheless, it held a meaning for a people who awaited their historic task. The prayer said by the priest at the foot of the altar seemed specifically applicable to them:

> Judica me, Deus, et discerne causam meam de gente non sancta: ab homine iniquo et doloso erue me. [Judge me, O God, and distinguish my cause from the nation that is not holy: from the unjust and deceitful man deliver me.][65]

XI

The Church and laity recognized mutual needs and obligations for survival in an unfriendly milieu. Therefore, after 1850, various forms of voluntary, church-oriented, social action developed. The pioneer organization for Catholic men in voluntary charitable work in the city was the St. Vincent de Paul Society. Although initially formed and led by a group of elite Catholic laymen, it soon became an Irish working-class association. With the concept that poverty was not a sin and that they were not social observers, the members set about to aid the poor of the city, regardless of race or religion. Beginning with a simple program of outdoor relief, they fed and clothed the needy, found accommodation and provided household necessities for families, supplied medical and nursing care and obtained placement in hospital for the sick, promoted temperance and buried the dead. They visited homes, hospitals and jails. They served as truant officers in the schools, ran night schools for immigrants, youths and prisoners, and encouraged good reading habits by distributing books to homes and establishing lending libraries.[66]

As the work of the St. Vincent de Paul Society expanded, fuel co-operatives and an employment agency were organized and attempts made to form a housing corporation. With the Bishops, the members were responsible for founding the Toronto Savings Bank and the Catholic Children's Aid Society of St. Vincent de Paul. They also initiated the formation of the Bona Mors Society which was intended to stop the practice of excessive cost for funerals. Patterned after the St. Vincent de Paul Society were a number of Irish Catholic benevolent societies which offered insurance benefits to injured workmen and protection to families on the death of a breadwinner. Temperance was mandatory for membership in those benevolent associations. The cumulative effect of those organizations and the St. Vincent de Paul Society brought an end to the shadowy existence of the Irish Brotherhood, which was a secret organization that operated from within the Shebeen society of the city. The Brotherhood, in a ruthless and violent way, had exercised methods to control drunken fathers who maltreated wives and children.[67]

Catholic laywomen began charitable work as a group in the city before the men did. From 1849 to 1851 the Catholic Ladies were responsible for founding and provisioning an orphanage and shelter for Irish children and unemployed servant girls. Their work ended when the Sisters of St. Joseph took over the responsibility. But the wives and daughters of St. Vincent de Paul Society members organized various groups to perform charitable work. Food, clothing and shoes were given to school children; homes were visited to teach sanitary habits; and Sunday schools set up to teach catechism. Funded by the St. Vincent de Paul Society, Catholic women visited the hospital and jails and found accommodation and work for released female prisoners.[68]

All the Catholic charitable organizations operated on a voluntary basis, utilizing donations, bazaars, picnics and raffles to collect funds for Irish ethnic improvement. But what began as programs of simple outdoor relief in 1850 moved to the foundation of lasting institutions by the end of the century supported, in part, by voluntarism.

XII

The concern and commendable efforts of the lay organizations of men and women were not enough to solve the dilemma of the Famine Irish immigrants in Toronto. Bishop Charbonnel believed that religious orders of men and women were required to improve the religious, social and educational needs of the Irish poor. He hoped to strengthen his Diocese by producing institutions to aid the Irish laity and to end the abuse and proselytizing tactics the immigrants were subjected to in public instutitions like the hospital, House of Industry, and schools.

In choosing models to fulfil those purposes Charbonnel selected specific orders from France whose work was known to him. The religious orders were the products of a new philosophy which encompassed the ideals of a devotional renewal, as inspired by Alphonsus de Liguori, and of social work among the poor, as instigated by St. Vincent de Paul. Adopting those principles, the new orders of women, though still leading partly cloistered lives in convents, were allowed to provide service in the secular city.[69]

When Charbonnel arrived in Toronto, there was only one small group of the Sisters of Loretto who had been invited by Bishop Power in 1847. To complement the work of that teaching order, Charbonnel brought out the Christian Brothers, in 1851, who founded St. Michael's College for boys and taught in the parish schools of the city. At Charbonnel's request, the Basilian Fathers, who came to Toronto to assist with pastoral work, took over St. Michael's College and established it as a seminary school to train priests and to provide for the higher education of the future leaders of the Irish community. The Sisters of St. Joseph were selected by Charbonnel to administer the orphanage for Irish Catholic children. However, that versatile group of women, living in great hardship themselves, soon began a program of outdoor relief, visited and counselled the poor, and shared teaching responsibilities among the girls in the parish schools.[70]

Charbonnel had perceived that the best weapon to guard the Irish against secularism and assimilation was a separate system of education. And in fighting to uphold that principle, Charbonnel was pitted against Egerton Ryerson and the full force of the city and the province, for public schools were the vehicles of the Protestant churches to standardize the population. But pressure against the separate system met with Irish response to retain it.

However, it was not until 1867, when the School Question was settled, that Irish Catholic rights were guaranteed.

By that time, the religious orders Charbonnel had invited to Toronto were more Irish in composition, having drawn postulants from the Irish community. Therefore the separate schools of Toronto, under the control of the Church, had an Irish student body who were instructed by Irish teachers. Within that cohesive institution many functions were performed simultaneously. The normal academic program of the age was offered, but it was interspersed with catechism and preparation for the sacraments of the Church. In addition, moral values and the role of the child in the family and the community were stressed to perpetuate social control. Irish history was emphasized, often becoming the topic for essays and debates, in order to develop a sense of pride. A literature sympathetic to the Church was presented to promote a peculiar sense of the holy and an Irish Tridentine devotionalism. Award nights were staged to produce pride in accomplishment and the programs for these gatherings included a mixture of religious and ethnic music, poetry and speeches presented for an audience of teachers, priests, parents and relatives. The separate schools allowed for an adequate alternative to public education, but their strength lay in the fact that they served as a vehicle for socialization of the Irish children in a protected environment.[71]

The religious orders were sufficiently established to expand education beyond the elementary level. The Christian Brothers established De La Salle as a secondary and commercial school which complemented the convent schools of the Sisters of Loretto and of St. Joseph. The Basilian Fathers were instrumental in achieving university status for St. Michael's College which, through the efforts of the Sisters of Loretto and St. Joseph, became co-educational in the early decades of the 20th century.[72]

Under Bishop Charbonnel's patronage, the Sisters of St. Joseph opened the House of Providence in 1858. Its purpose was to provide shelter for the aged, the orphaned, the destitute, the deaf, the dumb and the infirm. From that beginning the Sisters expanded their work to set up three orphanages. In addition, they established Notre Dame des Anges, a boarding home for women, and administered St. Nicholas Hotel, a home for newsboys and apprentices.

In the 1870's, Bishop Lynch invited additional orders to the city to fill more specific requirements. Disturbed by the number of Irish Catholics in trouble with the law, Lynch asked for the services of the Sisters of the Charity of St. Vincent de Paul, who were to be succeeded by the Sisters of the Good Shepherd. Both orders were renowned for work with women and under their direction an industrial school for girls was founded and a refuge set up for indigent and troubled women.[73]

As a preventative measure Bishop Lynch, assisted by a group of Irish laymen and Father Eugene O'Reilly, established an Agricultural and Industrial School in the Gore for wayward boys. The educational program of that school was incorporated into the St. Nicholas Hotel which was urban based and administered by the Sisters of St. Joseph. To guard against proselytism in public institutions and to guarantee the rights of Catholics in them, Lynch succeeded in penetrating the jails, penetentiaries, and institutes for the insane, the blind, and the deaf and dumb with priests and Catholic teachers. Assisted by Archbishop John Walsh, the Christian Brothers opened St. John's Training School for boys in 1893, which became a model for juvenile rehabilitation. [74]

The Sisters of St. Joseph had gained considerable nursing experience in the House of Providence. When the debt-ridden Toronto General Hospital was forced to close its doors, Lynch offered to maintain it under the supervision of the nuns. But the city declined the offer, preferring the hospital to maintain a secular rather than religious identity. With the support of the Irish Catholic laity, the Sisters of St. Joseph opened St. Michael's Hospital in the last decade of the nineteenth century, and followed, early in the twentieth century, with St. Joseph's and Our Lady of Mercy Hospitals. [75]

The various institutions which had developed under the auspices of the Church were supported by the Irish laity. In them, the Irish had found the empathy they needed and the aid they required without the bias they faced in the institutions under secular control.

XIII

One of the Church's goals in the restructuring process of its urban Irish laity was to obtain control over the primary unit, the family. In the Church's view, only stable family relationships could withstand the assimilative assault and, therefore, were paramount for group cohesion and the survival of Irish Catholics. To standardize the family unit, the Church exercised its authority through the use of persuasive and coercive methods. Ultimately, the Irish laity accepted the Church's standards as normative. Each family member assumed a role, and the roles were regulated by societal control from within the group.

Both Charbonnel and Lynch attacked loose family ties and marriages of consanguinity and mixed religions. To correct those practices, they demanded obedience to Church law; noncompliance to the rules bore the censure of excommunication from the Church. And excommunication from the Church brought with it ostracism from the Irish community. In addition, the Church assumed control over the other rites of passage, always emphasizing the religious, familial and communal aspects of the rites. Some of the superstitious practices and excessive use of alcohol at Irish weddings and wakes were replaced with more acceptable Christian behaviour. By organizing bazaars, picnics, outings, pilgrimages and concerts, the Church became the centre of family social activity. Through sermons, retreats and confession, reinforced by teaching in the schools, members of families were made aware of their specific roles and how they related to others. Religion penetrated the homes with family prayers, the rosary, angelus and grace becoming acceptable practice. The promotion of ethno-religious Irish literature and censored reading material encouraged pride in race and devotion to a moral life. In this way, the Church gained standard behavioural responses to the authority that emanated from Bishop to priests, to parents and to children.[76]

One cannot say that the Church succeeded in destroying all the faults that contributed to instability in Irish Catholic family life. Although mixed marriages and those of consanguinity were curtailed Irish still preferred to marry Irish, often waiting for a partner from the same ancestoral county or with a specific family name. Because of poverty, women entered the work force early and marriage age was late — 23 years for women and 26 years for men. As a result, the average Irish family had only three or four children. The preaching of temperance and the practice of having youths pledge abstinence from alcohol until age twenty-one reduced much of the family instability related to drunkenness; but the Church never defeated the Shebeen society, it just moved into public hotels. The Irish love of dancing, many of its forms considered sinful by the Church, was never subdued but it was modified through the acceptance of chaperones. Some superstitious beliefs became syncretic and others, like that in faeries, banshees and changelings, disappeared in the urban milieu. But the telling of ghost tales and an acceptance of miracle workers, like Father McSpirrit, were part of Irish Catholic culture. The fear of the dead was contained in more moderate wakes, which became part of a wider Canadian culture, but with a preference for grand monuments of cost often beyond the means of the Irish.[77]

By the effective use of persuasive and coercive control, the Church was able to mould and standardize the Irish family between 1850 and 1900. Reinforced role identity produced a classic, Irish Catholic family model. Directed by simple rules, the family unit was bound to the Church from the cradle to the grave and remained constant, changing only slightly with the impetus of outside influences.

XIV

The Irish Catholics of Toronto were a working class people and, therefore, the Church could not isolate itself from their problems in the fields of labour and politics. The Church could not enter the work places of the city, but the philosophy of Irish Tridentinism entered them with the Catholic workers. And that tenacity of belief may have been an element in their rejection of early unionism wherein membership in those original quasi-secret societies demanded assimilation.

Generally, the Irish in the city were untrained, unskilled day labourers, kept poor through a practice of continually sending remittance funds to Ireland to support family members or to pay for their immigration to Canada. The construction of St. Michael's Cathedral in the 1840's under the direction of the Catholic architect, William Thomas, had provided many Irish labourers with an opportunity to develop skills in building and contracting.[78] The growth in Church institutions in the early 1850's gave rise to a middle sector of the population from that select group. In addition, that progress supported a group of Irish entrepreneurs who entered the mercantile trade to supply goods first to the Church and Cathedral and then to the quickly growing Irish population of the city and its environs. But the majority of the Irish, both Pre-and Post-Famine, were labourers, often meeting with an early death because of their debilitated physical condition, the hazards of weather in seasonal employment, and the dangerous occupations in which they worked.

Job competition was keen between other unskilled workers and those of Irish origin who flooded the labour market. The Irish had been a burden to the city's few social welfare agencies, draining financial resources. What was essentially an economic problem was reflected in the social attitude of the majority who vocalized their dissatisfaction through application of the dictum 'No Irish Need Apply'. Transiency, with all its social ramifications, was common among the Irish who were locked out of city employment by a militant, anti-Catholic Orange Lodge. For decades the Irish press brought their plight before the public, particularly emphasizing that of Irish Catholic children who suffered most brutally at the hands of Protestant factory and mill owners. The Church was powerless to obtain employment for Irishmen in the municipal sphere of Toronto but, utilizing the threat of a block Irish vote, was persuasive enough to open up opportunities for talented Irish Catholics in the provincial and federal bureaucracy.[79]

The Church did not forbid Irish membership in organizations that were religiously neutral. Therefore it was not difficult for Bishop Lynch to come to terms with the Iron Moulders International and the Locomotive Engineers. But because of skills involved, Irish membership in those organizations was minimal. However, in 1886, under the influence of Daniel O'Donaghue, the Irish Catholic labour leader, and the rise of the Knights of Labor, Irish workers became involved with organized unionsm. The Knights of Labor was an international, non-sectarian association which enrolled both skilled and unskilled men, women and children and, therefore, appealed to the Irish. Bishop Lynch recognized the rights of the Knights of Labor on behalf of his people in defiance of Cardinal E. Taschereau, who had banned it in Quebec, and the antagonism of the influential Irish Catholic industrialist, Frank Smith. It was Lynch's stand in Toronto that added strength to Cardinal H. Manning's, of Great Britain, and Cardinal J. Gibbon's, of the United States, appeal to the Pope to have Taschereau's bann removed. Although the plight of Irish labourers in Toronto did not change significantly, by the end of the nineteenth century they became part of the total work force, not a portion segregated by religion.[80]

In a similar manner, Irish Tridentinism tended to isolate the urban minority politically until some form of accommodation could be made. The Protestant majority of Toronto was frustrated by the resistance of the minority Irish Catholic group to the assimilative tactics used. Denial of municipal employment and attempted reduction of their numbers through proselytism in public institutions only seemed to promote Irish group cohesion and solidarity with their Church. Visible evidence of that bond was the growth and expansion of Church-related religious and social institutions which provided aid to both the Protestants and Catholics of the city. And it was the continued growth which caused a blind rage within the Irish Protestant working-class segment of the city's population whose economic position had not improved. Having abandoned their Irish identity, they were continually manipulated by a mercantile and industrial elite to hate and to discriminate against Irish Catholics. The schoolroom, the Orange Lodge, the press and some churches were utilized to keep ethnic hatred alive. Hatred as a class weapon in a quickly secularizing Protestant population was almost a necessity in the view of the prosperous, for profits would suffer if the working-class united. And, under elite patronage and direction, the Orange Lodge, the Masonic Order and the Oddfellows controlled the municipal council, the work place and the public schools. The Irish, a minority in all wards of the city, could win seats only when there were multiple candidates, and that occurred very rarely.

Locked out of city politics, Irish Catholics failed to realize the strength of their block vote in the provincial or federal sphere until late in the century. Bishop Macdonell's early allegiance to Tory politics drove them into the ranks of the reform party, but George Brown's anti-Catholic sentiments drove them out; and Orange Lodge support of the Conservative party left them isolated. Although Bishop Charbonnel and the Irish Catholic politician, Thomas D'Arcy McGee, assured them the balance of power was theirs, the Irish persisted in voting for local candidates who promised much and did little. It was only through the ingenuity and negotiating tactics of Charbonnel and the early Catholic Institute that separate schools were guaranteed.[81]

After Confederation, however, the formation and potential of the Catholic League, in Toronto, worried the Conservative Federal Government of John A. Macdonald and the Liberal Provincial Government of Oliver Mowat. Because of its existence and determination to use the Irish block vote, working arrangements for patronage were made with federal and provincial administrators. In the latter decades of the century, Irish solidarity in Toronto enabled the group to survive the assault of a second Protestant Crusade, which included the Orange Lodge, Equal Rights Movement and the Protestant Protective Association. By the turn of the century, federal politics was less a factor in Irish Catholic urban survival. At the provincial level, the Liberal government clung to power dependent upon the Irish vote and promoted it by emphasizing old hatreds the Irish believed should be forgotten. The Orange-controlled Conservative party realized an election could not be won without the Irish vote. An arrangement was made to have religion dropped from the political platform. J.J. Foy, an eminent Irish Catholic lawyer, built an Irish Catholic Conservative Association which initiated in Toronto and spread throughout Ontario to help bring about a Conservative victory. Irish Catholic group cohesion had become a political fact.[82]

Through a process of conflict and consensus, Irish Catholic Tridentinism became a distinctive ethno-religious culture. Merging the best elements of a peasant culture in an urban milieu with traditional Tridentine Catholicism, it was a vehicle for ethnic survival. Urban-born in the economic capital of Ontario, it utilized the communication linkage of the Irish kinship system, the Irish press, separate Irish Catholic schools and the Church's ecclesiastic metropolitanism to penetrate Ontario, and make Toronto a centre for Irish Catholic culture. Ethnic and institutional fusion offered reasons for the perpetuation of group values. The fusion was so complete that, in Victorian Toronto, to be Irish was to be Catholic.

NOTES:

1. Documentation for this paper lies within my unpublished Ph.D. Thesis, "The Catholic Church and the Irish in Victorian Toronto," Department of History, University of Guelph, 1980. I have developed some aspects of this in "The Irish Catholics and Social Action in Toronto 1850-1900," *Studies in History and Politics*, No. 1 (1980); and "Ecclesiastical Metropolitanism and the Evolution of the Archdiocese of Toronto," *Social History* vol. 29 (May, 1982). For a description of the Irish Celtic Frontier see W.C. MacLeod, "Celt and Indian: Britain's Old World Frontier in Relation to the New," in P. Bohannan and F. Plog, eds., *Beyond the Frontier Social Process and Cultural Change* (New York, 1967), pp. 25-42. The problem of traditionalism and change can be seen in L. Hartz, *The Founding of New*

Societies (New York, 1964), p. 3. Traditional societies are discussed in the old but still valuable work, F. Tonnies, *Gemeinschaft and Gesellschaft* (1887), translated by C.P. Loomis as *Fundamental Concepts of Sociology* (New York, 1940). For world view or Weltanschauung see C.G. Jung, *Psychology and Religion: West and East* (Princeton, New Jersey, 1977); and R.R. Davis, *Lexicon of Historical and Political Terms* (New York, 1973), p. 130.

2. Methods of approaching the study of Urban History can be found in, ''The Introduction,'' Alan F.J. Artibise and Gilbert A. Stelter, *Canada's Urban Past: A Bibliography and Guide* (Vancouver, 1981).

3. See, for example: O. Handlin, *Boston's Immigrants A Study in Acculturation* (New York, 1976); D. Clark, *The Irish in Philadelphia Ten Generations of Urban Experience* (Philadelphia, 1973); N. Glazer and D.P. Moynihan, *Beyond the Melting Pot: The Negroes, Puerto Ricans, Jews, Italians, and Irish of New York City* (Cambridge, 1963); and J.P. Dolan, *The Immigrant Church, New York's Irish and German Catholics, 1815-1865* (Baltimore, 1975).

4. For a good analysis of the American parochial school system see J.W. Sanders, *The Education of an Urban Minority. Catholics in Chicago 1833-1965* (New York, 1977).

5. Irish American politics are amply described in Glazer and Moynihan, *Beyond the Melting Pot*.

6. For the socializing aspects of the American system see: J.P. Dolan, *The Immigrant Church*, p. 101; D. Clark, *The Irish in Philadelphia*, p. 104; and J.W. Sanders, *The Education of an Urban Minority*, p. 228.

7. For data on the Irish Catholic and Protestant population in urban and rural Ontario, see: D.H. Akenson, ''Ontario: What Ever Happened to the Irish?,'' in D.H. Akenson, ed. *Canadian Papers in Rural History*, Vol. III, (1982), pp. 204-256.

8. Although there is no solid academic work on the Irish in Hamilton or London see: J.R. Teefy, ed. *Jubilee Volume The Archdiocese of Toronto and Archbishop Walsh* (Toronto, 1892).

9. Although there are as yet no studies available on the Irish in Kingston or Peterborough, see the following church histories: L.J. Flynn, *Built on a Rock The Story of the Roman Catholic Church in Kingston 1826-1976* (Kingston, 1976); and E.J. Boland, *From the Pioneers to the Seventies A History of the Diocese of Peterborough 1880-1975* (Peterborough, 1976).

10. R. Choquette, *Language and Religion A History of English French Conflict in Ontario* (Ottawa, 1975), pp. 81-158.

11. *Ibid.*, pp. 10-43.

12. D.S. Cross, ''The Irish in Montreal 1867-1896,'' M.A. Thesis, McGill University, 1969.

13. Sister Frances Xavier, ''Educational Legislation in Nova Scotia and the Catholics,'' *Canadian Catholic Historical Association Report*, No. 24 (1957), pp. 63-74; P.M. Toner, ''The New Brunswick School Question,'' *Canadian Catholic Historical Association Study Sessions* (1970), pp. 85-95; T. Punch, ''The Irish in Halifax, 1836-71: A Study in Ethnic Assimilation,'' M.A. Thesis, Dalhousie University, 1976.

14. The ethnic composition in the American system can be seen in Sanders, *The Education of an Urban Minority*.

15. G.A. Frecker, ''The Origins of the Confessional School System in Newfoundland,'' *Canadian Catholic Historical Association Study Sessions*, No. 38, (1971), pp. 1-17.

16. See, in particular: M.P. Lupal, *The Roman Catholic Church and the North-West-School Question A Study in Church-State Relations in Western Canada 1875-1905* (Toronto, 1975); and P. Crunican, *Priests and Politicians: Manitoba Schools and the Election of 1896* (Toronto, 1974).

17. See: Brian De Breffny, ''From the Reformation to the Jacobite Defeat,'' in B. De Breffny, ed., *The Irish World The History and Cultural Achievements of the Irish People* (London, 1977), pp. 99-126; R. Kee, *The Most Distressful Country* (London, 1972), pp. 3-21; and M.N. Hennessy, *The Wild Geese The Irish Soldier in Exile* (Old Greenwich, Conn., 1973).

18. D. Bowen, *The Protestant Crusade in Ireland, 1800-1870: A Study of Protestant-Catholic Relations Between The Act of Union and Disestablishment* (Dublin, 1978).

19. K. Neill, *An Illustrated History of the Irish People* (New York, 1979) pp. 126-128; G. Broeker, *Rural Disorder and Police Reform in Ireland 1812-36* (London, 1970); and Lady Gregory, *Visions and Beliefs in the West of Ireland* (Toronto, 1976).

20. G.O. Tuathaigh, "The Distressed Society The Struggle for Emancipation and Independence," in De Breffny, ed., *The Irish World,* pp. 171-198; F.S.L. Lyons, "The Famine to the Treaty," V. Meally, ed., *Encyclopedia of Ireland* (Dublin, 1971), pp. 93-98.

21. J.J. Appel, "From Shanties to Lace Curtain, The Irish Image in Puck, 1876-1901," *Journal of Comparative Studies in Society and History,* Vol. 10 (October 1971), pp. 365-375.

22. C.S. Coon, *The Races of Europe* (New York, 1939), pp. 376-384; S.M. Garn, *Human Races* (Springfield, 1968), pp. 16-17; and L.P. Curtis, *Apes and Angels: The Irishman in Victorian Caricature* (Washington, 1971).

23. The problems of diglossia are described in J.A. Fishman, "Nationality-Nationalism and Nation-Nationalism," in J.A. Fishman, C.A. Ferguson, J. Das Gupta, eds., *Language Problems of Developing Nations* (Toronto, 1968), pp. 39-42.

24. For the poetry of W.P. Macdonald, see the Macdonell Papers, Archdiocese of Toronto Archives (M.P., A.T.A.). As well, see *The Catholic,* April 15, 1832.

25. *The Globe*, February 11, 1858.

26. R. Mumford, "Belonging: A Time for Character Assassination," *The United Church of Canada Bay of Quinte Conference* (Peterborough, 1975) Volume 2, pp. 189-190.

27. For an interpretation of stigma and culture shock, see: P.K. Bock, ed., *Culture Shock* (New York, 1970); E. Goffman, *Stigma Notes on a Spoiled Identity* (Englewood Cliffs, 1963).

28. For the importance of kinship in society, see E.L. Schusky, *Manual for Kinship Analysis* (New York, 1965).

29. G. Broeker, *Rural Disorder and Police Reform in Ireland 1812-36* (London, 1970).

30. S.M. Garn has stated that "Alcoholism and Irish Ancestory are not likely to be related on a purely genetic basis." See: Garn, *Human Races* (Springfield, 1968).

31. See the ledgers of the various institutes under the direction of the Sisters of St. Joseph, Toronto, Ontario, S.S.J.A.

32. Irish Catholic Housing is well described in Toronto Newspapers. See the various Irish Catholic Newspapers, particularly: *The Toronto Mirror, The Canadian Freeman* and *The Irish Canadian, 1840-1885*.

33. For the Church's attack on consanguinity, see the papers of Bishops Power, Charbonnel and Lynch, Archdiocese of Toronto Archives, A.T.A., P.P., C.P., L.P. Although there is no available work on Irish interbreeding and its production of genetic anomalies, the consequence of interbreeding can be seen in R.M. Goodman, *Genetic Disorders Among the Jewish People* (Baltimore, 1979). For the high death rate among Irish children, see The Records of St. Paul's Cemetery, Toronto, A.T.A., Sundry Books, S.B.R. For the killing of changelings in Ireland, which is only recorded orally in Toronto, see K. Briggs, *A Dictionary of Fairies* (Bungay, 1976), pp. 70-73.

34. S. Gmelch and P. Langan, *Tinkers and Travellers* (Montreal, 1976).

35. R. Kee, *The Most Distressful Country* (London, 1976), pp. 19-20.

36. D. Bowen, *The Protestant Crusade in Ireland 1800-70* (Dublin, 1978).

37. G. Broeker, *Rural Disorder and Police Reform in Ireland* (London, 1970), p. 229.

38. K. Duncan, "Irish Famine Immigration and the Social Structure of Canada West," *Canadian Review of Sociology and Anthropology*, Vol. 2, No. 1 (1965), pp. 19-40.

39. Irish Catholic politics are well documented in the papers of the period. See in particular: *The Toronto Mirror, The Canadian Freeman* and *The Irish Canadian*, 1840-1885.

40. J.J. O'Riordain, *Irish Catholics — Tradition and Transition* (Dublin, 1981); E. Larkin, "The

Devotional Revolution in Ireland 1850-75,'' *American Historical Review*, Vol. 77, No. 3 (June, 1972), pp. 625-652.

41. The re-emergence of paganism when traditional Christianity has been eliminated can be seen in W. Kolarz, *Religion in the Soviet Union* (New York, 1961), p. 102.

42. Syncretism is well described in F.S. Herskovits, *The New World Negro* (London, 1966), pp. 57-58. The various elements in Irish Catholic folk religion can be seen in: W.Y. Evans-Wentz, *The Fairy Faith in Celtic Countries* (New York, 1966); and D. MacManus, *Irish Earth Folk* (New York, 1959).

43. The function that various life crises perform can be seen in A. VanGennep, *The Rites of Passage* (Chicago, 1966).

44. The old wakes in Toronto and the Archdiocese when compared to the practices in Ireland show a continuity of form. See S.O. Suilleabhain, *Irish Wake Amusements* (Dublin, 1976).

45. For the complete lack of social institutions in the period prior to 1850, see the Bishops Macdonell's and Power's Papers, A.T.A., M.P., P.P.

46. The Macdonell Papers give much evidence of this little recognized group's activities, A.T.A., M.P.

47. Little has been written on this amazing Irish priest, and his real position in the history of Upper Canada is not as yet established. For some documented evidence, see A.T.A., M.P.

48. Pastoral Letter, December 31, 1846, A.T.A., P.P.

49. J.R. Teefy, "The Life and Times of the Right Rev. Armand Francis Marie Comte De Charbonnel, Second Bishop of Toronto," in J.R. Teefy, ed., *Jubilee Volume, The Archdiocese of Toronto and Archbishop Walsh* (Toronto, 1892), pp. 109-140.

50. Nicolson, "The Irish Catholics and Social Action in Toronto 1850-1900."

51. *The Mirror*, April 18, 1845.

52. E. Kelly, *The Story of St. Paul's Parish Toronto 1822-1922* (Toronto, 1922), pp. 96-99.

53. The records of the Irish Protestant Benevolent Society, Toronto Public Library: *The Globe*, 1850-1860; and Moynihan and Glazer, *Beyond the Melting Pot*, p. 240.

54. The sources for both Tables I and II are: *Census of the Canadas, 1851-1852*; *Census of the Canadas, 1860-1861*; *Census of Canada, 1870-1871*; *Census of Canada, 1880-1881*; *Census of Canada, 1890-1891*; and *Census of Canada, 1901*.

55. See particularly the various church census, A.T.A., S.B.R.

56. For the concept of a universal Catholic society see E. Gilson, "Forward," in V.J. Bourke, ed., *City of God* (New York, 1958), pp. 13-35.

57. Although the concept of an 'Irish Holy' was formed from Sermon Literature and Irish Newspapers, the concept is discussed in R. Otto, *The Idea of the Holy: An Inquiry into the Non-Rational Factor in the Idea of the Divine and its Relation to the Rational* (London, 1968).

58. Circular on Christian Forebearance, June 1853, A.T.A., C.P. See, as well, the first editions of the *Catholic Weekly Review* and the *Catholic Register*, which replaced the *Irish Canadian*.

59. Although there is considerable information on the devotional renewal in the various Bishops' papers, Irish newspapers and oral history, much more detail can be found in retreat manuals. See *The Mission Book of the Redemptorist Fathers: A Manual of Instructions and Prayers* (New York, 1897).

60. M. Barkun, *Disaster and the Millenium* (London, 1974) pp. 63-64.

61. *Ibid*.

62. See particularly Larkin, "The Devotional Revolution in Ireland 1850-75."

63. The concept of the 'Irish New World Millenium' is best seen in H.C. McKeown, *The Life and Labors of the Most Rev. John Joseph Lynch, D.D. Cong. Miss. First Archbishop of Toronto* (Toronto, 1886).

64. *Ibid*. For a contemporary study of Lynch see, G.J. Stortz, "John Joseph Lynch, Archbishop

of Toronto: A Biographical Study of Religious, Political and Social Commitment,'' Ph.D. Thesis, Department of History, University of Guelph, 1980.

65. *Manual of the Society of St. Vincent de Paul* (London, 1851), pp. 50-51.

66. See the Record Books and Reports of the St. Vincent de Paul Society, Toronto, Ontario, A.T.A., S.V.P.

67. See the Records of the Bona Mors Society and the Toronto Savings Banks, A.T.A., S.V.P. and *The Irish Canadian*, 1860-1865.

68. See particularly the Records and Reports of the St. Vincent de Paul Society, A.T.A., S.V.P. and *The Canadian Freeman*, 1855-1865.

69. As well as the Annals of the various religious orders in Toronto, see: M. Theriault, *Les Instituts de vie Consacrée au Canada depuis les débuts de la Nouvelle — France Jusqu'à aujourd'hui* (Ottawa, 1980); J. Moncion, *The Civil Incorporation of Religious Institutes in Canada* (Ottawa, 1979); P.F. Anson, *The Religious Orders and Congregations of Great Britain and Ireland* (Worcester, 1949).

70. *Ibid*.

71. See particularly the various records of the Sisters of St. Joseph, A.T.A., S.S.J. and S.S.J.A.; the institutional records in the Lynch Papers, A.T.A., L.P. In addition see the records of St. Michael's College, Archives of St. Michael's College.

72. *Ibid*.

73. See the records of the various religious orders as well as the Parish and Priests files A.T.A.

74. *Ibid*.

75. See the Hospital File in the Lynch Papers, A.T.A., L.P.

76. There is little comparative work on the Irish family. However, see *The Irish Canadian*, 1860-1880. As well, see the personal correspondence, pastorals and sermon literature in the Bishops' Papers, A.T.A., P.P., C.P., L.P.

77. *Ibid*.

78. Although William Thomas is generally looked upon as an Anglican, because he was buried in an Anglican Cemetery, he stated that he was a Catholic. His departure from the church had much to do with the loss of the contract for St. Michael's steeple. See St. Michael's Cathedral Papers A.T.A.

79. See particularly: the Charbonnel and Lynch Papers, A.T.A., C.P., L.P.; and *The Globe, The Canadian Freeman* and *Irish Canadian*, 1860-1880.

80. *Ibid*.

81. The Irish Catholic newspapers show clearly the lack of block voting until Confederation. See particularly *The Toronto Mirror, The Irish Canadian, The Canadian Freeman*, 1850-1870.

82. For the consolidation of the Irish Catholic vote between 1890 and 1900, see the Whitney Papers, Province of Ontario Archives.

Divided City: The Immigrant in Winnipeg Society, 1874-1921

ALAN F.J. ARTIBISE

Winnipeg was a city of immigrnats. Immigration accounted for over seventy percent of the city's population increase in the years prior to World War I, and without this vast influx of people from all over the world, Winnipeg's growth would have been slow indeed. The city was not only the destination of many who intended to settle in western Canada, it was also the gateway through which all western-bound immigrants passed. To the businessmen who viewed population growth as "the essential and paramount need of the West," the arrival of tens of thousands of immigrants meant prosperity for their real estate and commercial concerns. For Winnipeg was not only the "Gateway to the West," as it boosters advertised, it was also the tollgate of the West. "Nothing — neither people, nor goods, nor chattels — moved into or out of prairie Canada save through Winnipeg, [and] the tolls levied by Winnipeg business, industry, commerce, and labour sparked the Winnipeg boom" and the city's rise to the position of the "Bull's Eye of the Dominion."[1]

Yet for all the advantages of Winnipeg's position it was found that the immigrant was a mixed blessing; for, while he may have been the keystone to economic prosperity, he was often also an economic and even a social liability. It is true, of course, that some immigrants — particularly Ontarians, Englishmen, and Americans — arrived in Winnipeg with adequate capital or with assured employment, and were quickly absorbed into the mainstream of Winnipeg society. But many others were not so well prepared. The Slavs and Jews, for example, usually came to Winnipeg with meagre or even no capital, and with the added handicap of a foreign language and a very different cultural background. From the moment of their arrival in Winnipeg these newcomers had to be housed, fed, employed, and assimilated into the life of the community. Also, since many of the overseas immigrants arrived in Winnipeg infected with contagious diseases, the municipal corporation had to take precautionary measures that often taxed

SOURCE: This is an original article, written expressly for this volume.

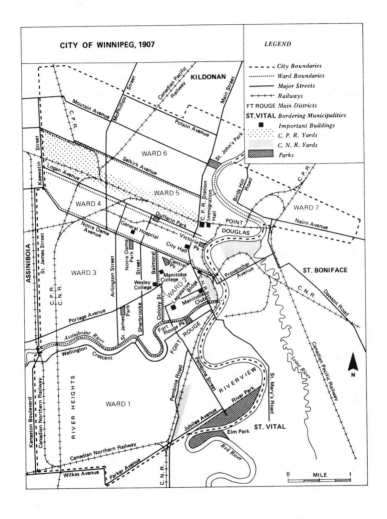

CITY OF WINNIPEG, 1907

LEGEND

- – – – City Boundaries
- · · · · · · · Ward Boundaries
- ——— Major Streets
- +++++ Railways
- FT ROUGE Main Districts
- **ST.VITAL** Bordering Municipalities
- Important Buildings
- C. P. R. Yards
- C. N. R. Yards
- Parks

the city's medical facilities to the full. Many immigrants needed help to see them through the transitional period that lay between the status of immigrant and taxpaying citizens. Thus, while the arrival of tens of thousands of immigrants in Winnipeg may have satisfied the growth ethic of the dominant commercial elite, it also presented this governing group with some of its most serious problems.[2]

One of the most serious of these problems was that by 1921 Winnipeg was — and had been for some time — a divided city, composed of a number of sub-communities separated on the basis of ethnicity, religion, and class.[3] For although most Winnipeggers were firm believers in the virtues of immigration, they did not easily reconcile themselves to the resultant polyglot population. The pride that came with the sharp rise in the size of the city was diminished by the knowledge that much of this growth was caused by "foreign" elements.[4] Only in the years after World War II did the vast majority of residents see the cosmopolitan make-up of Winnipeg as an advantage; a point-of-view that was adopted only after considerable years of outright discrimination against "foreigners."[5]

The role of the immigrnat in the social evolution of Winnipeg is, of course, difficult to examine in isolation. The social conditions experienced by the city's population at any given time were in part a reflection of the age of the community, the state of technology, and general economic conditions. Moreover, the conflict, confusion, tension, and poverty that were inescapable facets of life in Winnipeg in this period were often juxtaposed with examples of co-operation, order, harmony, and great wealth. In short, an account of Winnipeg's evolution into a divided city is complex and full of contradictions. But although it is impossible in a paper of this length to deal with all the events, decisions, and trends that shaped the character and form of 1921 Winnipeg, it is possible to outline the major patterns that led to this result.

At the outset, however, two general observations should be made. First, Winnipeg's population growth rate was not constant throughout the period. Rather, the city grew spasmodically, with bursts of activity interspersed with periods when the city grew quite slowly. Each surge of growth was greeted with predictions that the city would become the "Chicago of the North," rivalling that major American city in size and enterprise, while every slowdown in the growth rate was considered the prelude to stagnation or decline and was usually countered by programs designed to promote population growth. Second, the reaction of established Winnipeggers of "British" origin to the changing ethnic composition of the community went through various phases, depending on the source and number of immigrants arriving in the city during particular periods. The transformation of Winnipeg from a small, compact and ethnically homogeneous city to a large, sprawling and cosmopolitan metropolis is thus best understood by dividing the period from 1874 to 1921 into several, fairly distinct eras of growth and change.

THE FORMATIVE YEARS, 1874-1899

During the first quarter century of its history as an incorporated city, when Winnipeg was growing from a small cluster of wooden stores and residences housing 1800 citizens to a major Canadian city of 40,000 people, three significant population trends were established. First, with the exception of a sharp increase in population in the early 1880's following the arrival of the Canadian Pacific Railway, growth was steady and unspectacular before 1900. Second, virtually all the growth achieved during this early period resulted from the influx of immigrants; natural increase and the extension of the city's boundaries added relatively few citizen's to Winnipeg's population. Third, the flow of immigrants into Winnipeg had its origin in two main sources: Great Britain and Ontario. Of the three trends, the last was most significant, for this early influx of British and Ontario immigrants early established the essentially Anglo-Canadian nature of the city — a quality that was not to be seriously challenged until the post World War II era, despite massive increases in the number of "foreign" migrants.

The rate of population growth in Winnipeg was from the outset far greater that the population growth rate of Manitoba and the other western provinces. At an early date Winnipeg became, and thereafter long remained, the largest urban centre in all of western Canada.[6]

Before 1880, the population of the city increased slowly from about 2,000 in 1874 to just over 6,000 six years later. This was followed by a short burst of activity in the early eighties when the population of Winnipeg climbed to over 20,000 by 1886 (see Table I).[7] By this time the "boom" had already collapsed and for the balance of the period growth was moderate.[8] It was not until the late 1890's that all the conditions necessary for rapid population growth were in place and a sustained boom could take place.[9]

The growth Winnipeg did achieve during this period was primarily because of immigration. Though the city's boundaries were twice enlarged, in 1875 and 1882, these annexations did not substantially increase Winnipeg's population. Combined with other boundary extensions made in 1906, 1907, and 1913, they added only about 3,500 persons to Winnipeg's population.[10] Another source of growth, natural increase, was also of relatively minor importance during this period, when compared to immigration. In the decade from 1891 to 1901, for example, when Winnipeg grew by 16,701 persons, only 4,870 or 29 percent, resulted from natural increase. The remainder, over 70 percent, were immigrants (see Table II).[11]

TABLE I

POPULATION GROWTH IN WINNIPEG, 1871-1921

Year	Population	Increase	
1871	241	—	
1881	7,985	7,744	(3,624.1%)
1886	20,238	12,253	(153.4%)
1891	25,639	5,401	(26.7%)
1896	31,649	6,010	(23.4%)
1901	42,340	10,691	(33.8%)
1906	90,153	47,813	(113.0%)
1911	136,035	45,882	(50.7%)
1916	163,000	26,965	(19.8%)
1921	179,087	16,087	(9.9%)

Indeed, natural increase remained of secondary importance in the population growth of Winnipeg until the outbreak of World War I halted immigration.

Not only did Winnipeg grow primarily because of immigration, it was immigration of a very particular kind. With the exception of small numbers of Jews, Scandinavians and Germans, the bulk of the immigrants arriving in Winnipeg came from Ontario and Great Britain. An analysis of the population according to birthplace in 1891, for example, shows that well over half of the residents of Winnipeg came from these sources (see Table III). The essentially Anglo-Canadian character of Winnipeg during this early period is further confirmed by examining the ethnic origins of the population. Table IV indicates that well over 70 percent of the population gave their ethnicity as "British" in 1901.[12]

TABLE II

NATURAL INCREASE AS A FACTOR IN POPULATION GROWTH, 1891-1921

Years	Total Pop'n Increase	Births	Deaths	Natural Increase	N.I. as % of Total Pop'n Increase
1891-1896	6,010	4,625	2,577	2,048	34.1
1897-1901	10,691	6,396	3,574	2,822	26.4
1902-1906	47,813	16,528	10,985	5,543	11.6
1907-1911	45,882	20,247	9,205	11,042	24.1
1912-1916	26,965	29,395	11,413	17,982	66.7
1917-1921	16,087	29,633	11,507	18,126	112.7

These facts are extremely important in understanding the character and tone of Winnipeg society since the ''British'' early established themselves as the city's dominant or charter group.[13] The entry of Manitoba into Confederation in 1870 was followed by a mass influx of British and Ontario migrants into the province and as early as 1880 the original make-up of the community at Fort Garry — a balance of English, French, and Indian-Métis — was dramatically altered. The new majority of Anglo-Protestants quickly and effectively established their economic, social, political, and cultural beliefs as the norm. Thereafter, all newcomers were expected to conform to the established Anglo-Ontarian mould.[14]

TABLE III

MAJOR GROUPS BY BIRTHPLACE, 1881-1921

Birthplace	Percent of Total Population				
	1881	1891	1901	1911	1921
Ontario	42.5	28.3	24.6	15.1	11.9
Manitoba	12.9	21.5	31.5	23.4	35.2
Britain	21.3	28.4	19.6	29.5	27.9
United States	4.6	3.3	3.3	4.3	3.9
Europe	1.3	8.2	13.9	19.3	14.8
Other	17.4	10.3	7.1	8.4	6.3

This is not to say that the ''British'' majority was a completely homogeneous group. Encompassing, as it did, Ontarians, English, Irish, and Scots elements, the charter group was at one level culturally diverse. Yet more important than this apparent diversity was the feeling among the British-Ontario group that they were no less a unity than was Britain or

TABLE IV

MAJOR ETHNIC GROUPS, 1881-1921

Ethnic Group	Percent of Total Population			
	1881	1901	1911	1921
British	83.6	73.9	62.1	67.1
Slavic	.1	4.2	9.8	12.6
German	2.3	5.4	6.5	2.6
Jewish	.1	2.7	6.6	8.1
Scandinavian	5.1	7.9	3.7	3.5
French	5.6	3.3	2.0	2.2
Other	3.7	2.6	9.3	3.9

Ontario. The diversity that existed among the various elements was almost completely obscured by their common language and British heritage.[15] Moreover, most members of the charter group were also united by their Protestant religion; by 1891, for example over 70 percent of the population of Winnipeg were Protestants (see Table V). And while distinctions between various Protestant churches were quite apparent, they were not nearly so significant as those between, say, Roman Catholics and Methodists. Finally, the various elements of the charter group were further united by common experience: they had all migrated to Winnipeg and were working together to build a new community at the confluence of the Red and Assiniboine Rivers.

TABLE V

MAJOR RELIGIOUS GROUPS, 1881-1921

Religious Denomination	Percent of Total Population				
	1881	1891	1901	1911	1921
Anglican	29.7	26.7	24.0	23.0	24.8
Baptist	4.4	4.2	4.9	3.7	2.8
Methodist	17.3	16.8	15.9	11.3	9.9
Presbyterian	29.6	23.2	24.0	22.3	24.9
Lutheran	3.7	8.9	10.1	8.2	5.5
Roman Catholic	12.7	9.6	12.1	14.5	13.4
Greek Church	—	—	.5	2.5	5.1
Jewish	.3	2.5	2.7	6.6	8.0
Other	2.3	8.1	5.8	7.9	5.6

Even more important, perhaps, than these common traits was the fact that those immigrants who arrived in Winnipeg in the 1870's and 1880's had been a united group even before they emigrated to Manitoba. For they were in large part the "Clear Grits" of Ontario and as such held several basic beliefs with utmost conviction, in particular their conception of the future of Manitoba and the Northwest. To them Manitoba was the new frontier; it was to be a second Ontario or, rather, a second Canada West, embodying their ideas of the separation of church and state and of the absolute need for no special privilege for any group.[16] In other words, unlike some of their contemporaries in eastern Canada — where sheer geographical propinquity, the presence of vocal minority groups, and the demands of political necessity demanded some accommodation between French and English — the charter group in Winnipeg neither believed in nor subscribed to a bilingual or bicultural (much less multilingual or multicultural) view of Canada. On the contrary, cultural uniformity, based, of course, on British traditions, was to be the order of the day.

Thus, very early in Winnipeg's history, two fundamental facts had been established that were to affect all future immigrants. First, the dominance of the British-Ontario group meant that there would be a fundamental difference between this and the various other immigrant groups. Those who arrived in Winnipeg from Britain and Ontario quickly resumed familiar routines and easily merged in interests and activities with established residents. But for those who came from other countries and whose memories and traditions held no trace of recognition for their new surroundings, adjustment was achieved only with the utmost difficulty. Many of these "foreigners" faltered, hesitated, and were overwhelmed, since in their previous experience they found no parallel to guide them in their new life. The sense of alienation experienced by the "foreign" newcomer is clearly revealed in the following penetrating comment on the ethnic divisions of Winnipeg society, a comment made by a Hungarian immigrant:

> "The English," he whispered, ". . . the only people who count are the English. Their fathers got all the best jobs. They're the ones nobody ever calls foreigners. Nobody ever makes fun of their names or calls them 'bologny-eaters', or laughs at the way they dress or talk. Nobody," he concluded bitterly, "cause when you're English it's the same as bein' Canadian."[17]

Secondly, the charter group believed that Winnipeg was, and should remain, British; the concept of cultural pluralism (or a cultural mosaic), used so often to describe Winnipeg society in recent years, was not even contemplated in the city during this period. Rather, the charter group were determined to follow the "melting-pot" approach of the United States, and it was the "British" who were to "provide the recipe and stoke the fire."[18]

This attitude is evident in the reactions of the charter group to various "foreigners." Germans and Scandinavians, for example, did not cause much of a problem. These Northern Europeans, with their familiar Protestant religions, were easily and quickly absorbed into the mainstream of Winnipeg society. The following quotations from the *Manitoba Free Press* makes the point:

> The German is of good stock, and therefore we expect good citizenship to display itself in this element of our foreign population. We look for the virtues of his sturdy teutonic stock to manifest itself in thrift, progressiveness, and prosperity.

> *   *   *

> Like the Scandinavian, the Germans are of the same racial type and original stock as ourselves and have, therefore, kindred habits and institutions and similar ideals and moral standards. They all enhance the value of prospective citizens. Blood will tell and the law of heredity is still active.[19]

In short, the essential characteristic of Winnipeg society prior to 1900 was

TABLE VI

POPULATION OF CITIES AND RANK BY SIZE

1871-1921

City	1921 Population	Rank	1911 Population	Rank	1901 Population	Rank	1891 Population	Rank	1881 Population	Rank	1871 Population	Rank
Montreal	618.506	1	490.504	1	328,172	1	219,616	1	155,238	1	115,000	1
Toronto	521.893	2	381,833	2	209,892	2	181,215	2	96,916	2	59,000	2
WINNIPEG	179,087	3	136,035	3	42,340	6	25,639	8	7,985	17	241	62
Vancouver	117.217	4	100.401	4	27,010	9	13,709	11	—	-	—	-
Hamilton	114.151	5	81,969	6	52,634	5	48,959	4	36,661	4	26,880	5
Ottawa	107.843	6	87,062	5	59,928	4	44,154	5	31,307	7	24,141	7
Quebec	95.193	7	78.710	7	68,840	3	63,090	3	62,446	3	59,699	2
Calgary	63.305	8	43.704	10	4,392	66	3,876	55	—	-	—	-
London	60.959	9	46.300	9	37,976	9	31,977	8	26,266	8	18,000	8
Edmonton	58.821	10	31,064	13	4,176	72	—	-	—	-	—	-

the domination of the city's commercial, political, and cultural life by those of British origin. Led by a core of Anglo-Ontarians, who by 1899 had a full generation to establish themselves as community leaders. Winnipeg would remain in spirit, if not in fact, a "British" city for over fifty years. The experience of moving to the western Canadian frontier changed the attitudes of the British regarding "foreigners" very little, if at all. Although Winnipeg differed greatly from Ontario and British towns and cities in some things, the lifestyle and attitudes of the majority of its citizens were remarkably similar to those of these older centres.

Nothing sums up the nature of Winnipeg society in this period better than the reaction of its citizens to the Boer War. In 1899 thousands of Winnipeggers bid a rousing farewell at a mass rally on Main Street in front of city hall to fifty members of the Canadian contingent. The editor of Winnipeg's social newspaper, *Town Topics*, voiced the sentiments of the city's charter group when he declared: "I know nothing that would bind the empire so strongly together as associations in an enterprise of this kind. It will show the world that . . . when we speak of the 'Soldiers of the Queen', we mean all who carry arms whenever the Union Jack waves from India to Australia, from Windsor Castle to [Winnipeg's] Osborne Street Barracks."[20]

BOOM AND TRANSFORMATION, 1900-1913

While the years before 1900 witnessed relatively slow growth and harmonious ethnic relationships, the decade following the turn of the century was marked by a rapid rate of growth and a sharp increase in tensions between the "British" and the "foreigners." The growth of Winnipeg after 1900 was phenomenal. From a small city of 42,000 in 1901, it swelled to a sprawling metropolis of 150,000 by 1913 and rose from sixth place to third in the ranks of Canadian cities, surpassed only by Montreal and Toronto (see Table VI). Throughout the decade, Winnipeggers witnessed the most spectacular increase their community would ever undergo in such a short period.

James Gray, in his book *The Boy from Winnipeg*, described this period of the city's history:

The Winnipeg of my boyhood was a lusty, gutsy, bawdy frontier boom-town roaring through an unequalled economic debauch. . . . In a single decade more than 500,000 immigrants found their way from the four corners of Europe to Western Canada. All of them passed through Winnipeg, and a good one in ten of them went no further. . . . All summer long, British and European immigrants trudged back and forth between the Canadian Pacific and Canadian Northern stations en route to their new homesteads. Carpenters, bricklayers, stonemasons, tinsmiths, plasterers, and painters worked from dawn to dusk putting up new railway shops, new warehouses for wholesalers, and new homes for the thousands of trainmen, machinists, retail store clerks, bank clerks, and bartenders who were flocking into town on every train from the east.

The official census returns which recorded Winnipeg's growth throughout the period tell only part of the story. Winnipeg also had a "floating population." This group was made up almost entirely of single males who came west in search of work. Since Winnipeg served as the main recruiting centre for railway and bush contractors, farmers and manufacturers, nearly all of these men spent time in the city. Every summer, for example, easterners flocked west to help with the harvest; in 1912 there were 25,000 harvest excursions in the city. Then, in the fall when the men were released from their summer occupations they again trekked to Winnipeg in search of employment. A few received positions in bush camps through the efforts of private employment agencies, but job opportunities during the cold winter months were limited. Some of the slack was taken up by casual work: stoking furnaces, splitting wood, or shovelling snow. Others left Winnipeg for a milder climate. Yet this still left a large number who stayed in Winnipeg, encouraged to remain by the facilities of a large city: its pool rooms, theatres, cheap cafes and rooming houses, and brothels.[21]

TABLE VII

NATIVE AND FOREIGN BORN IN WINNIPEG, 1881-1921

| | Percent of Total Population | |
Year	Foreign-Born	Native-Born
1881	32.5	67.5
1891	42.7	57.3
1901	37.8	62.2
1911	55.9	44.1
1921	47.6	52.4

Although Winnipeg's rapid population growth delighted most residents, it also presented an almost countless series of problems. The ebb and flow of transient workers had an unsettling effect upon Winnipeg's social life, while the rapid increase in the number of permanent residents meant that the maintenance of social order and the protection of the public welfare required endless attention. The difficulties of enforcing laws, safeguarding public health, providing municipal services such as sewer and water, and securing consensus on social values were all magnified as the population grew.[22]

Of all the problems faced during the decade, however, that of assimilating large number of "foreigners" was uppermost in the minds of the city's British majority. Concern intensified when it was found that a large portion of the immigrants arriving in Winnipeg after 1900 were Slavs and Jews; people who were feared as "strangers within our gates." This apprehension on the part of the city's charter group stemmed from the fact that these new arrivals, along with the inevitable difference of background, language, and religion, brought with them a sense of ethnic pride, born at once of oppression and the teaching of their leaders, that was new in Winnipeg. Moreover, large numbers of the newcomers tended to segregate themselves in "foreign ghettos" in the north end.[23] In brief, the overwhelming numbers, the ethnic pride, the different — even strange — religions, and the tendency towards marked residential segregation all led to profound feelings of fear and apprehension on the part of Winnipeg's British charter group.

The dimensions of this hostility and apprehension can perhaps best be understood by recognizing that the dramatic increase in the number and variety of foreign-born in Winnipeg was a unique experience in Canadian urban development. While other cities were also receiving large influxes of immigrants, none received so many from such diverse sources in such a short period of time. The percentage of foreign-born in Winnipeg jumped from just under 38 percent in 1901 to over 55 percent by 1911, an increase of over 60,000. Moreover, a comparison of Winnipeg with other Canadian cities reveals that only two other centres (Victoria and Calgary) had larger proportions of foreign-born in 1911. And in both cases the higher percentages were the result of large numbers of British-born residents rather than European-born or other non-Anglo-Saxon persons.[24]

Comparisons of Winnipeg with other cities in regard to the birthplace and ethnicity of the population also indicates that Winnipeg was unique. In 1911, no other city had a higher proportion of European-born residents. Similarly, Winnipeg had the highest percentage of both Slavs and Jews. What is especially noteworthy, however, is that these high proportions of "European Foreigners" was coupled with one of the lowest proportions of British of any Canadian city. Only three other urban areas — Quebec, Montreal, and Ottawa — had lower percentages.[25] Given these facts, it is hardly surprising that the question of assimilation loomed so large in Winnipeg in the years after 1900.

Winnipeg's charter group, however, was ill-prepared to meet the enormous challenge presented by the newcomers, since they had experienced so little difficulty in their pursuit of a common nationality in the years before 1900. They were particularly unprepared for the large degree of group consciousness that the new wave of immigrants possessed, and this cohesiveness provoked a strong reaction among established Winnipeggers.

The "British" majority became even more entrenched in their own group consciousness as the coherence of the new groups threatened their cherished tenet of cultural uniformity. Uneasy and resentful, the charter group avoided contact with the "foreigners" by withdrawing even farther into a solid, isolated group in the city's south and west ends. By the outbreak of World War I Winnipeg was a partitioned city, separated on the basis of language, religion, and ethnic origin.

Open expressions of bigotry toward the Slav and Jew were voiced frequently in Winnipeg after 1900. "A Ukrainian wedding — that joyful expression of an intense sense of community — was attacked as a debased orgy." The "foreigners" use of alcohol offended many, especially the ladies of the Women's Christian Temperance Union, who invariably linked "foreigners liquor dealers, and politicians in a chain of corruption and degradation."[26] Comments such as "the Slav has not thus far proved himself the equal of the northwestern European as an immigrant," and "they are the unfortunate product of a civilization that is a thousand years behind the Canadian," were both expressed and believed by the charter group.[27] Even J.S. Woodsworth, for all his progressive work among "foreigners," was obsessed with the difficulties facing Winnipeg in its attempt to absorb their immigrants who were "distinctly a lower grade."[28] Some Winnipeggers became so concerned over the presence of large numbers of Slavs and Jews that in a rare abandonment of their belief in the merits of growth they advocated a policy of exclusion or, at the very least, a strictly controlled quota system. The following articles in the *Winnipeg Tribune* and the *Winnipeg Telegram* are typical:

> Increased population, if of the right sort, will be of great benefit. . . . But we should be careful that we do not bring in an imported population of such a character as will be an injury, not a benefit to our people. . . . Anglo-Saxons, Germans, and Scandinavians in general we can take in any number, but we cannot assimilate more than a limited number of immigrants of radically different race. The Galician is as yet an experiment; we do not know how he will turn out; and we cannot afford to make the experiment on too grand a scale.[29]

>   .   .   .

> There are few people who will affirm that Slavonic immigrants are desirable settlers, or that they are welcomed by the white people of Western Canada. . . . Those whose ignorance is impenetrable, whose customs are repulsive, whose civilization is primitive, and whose character and morals are justly condemned, are surely not the class of immigrants which the country's paid immigration agents should seek to attract. Better by far to keep our land for the children, and children's children, of Canadians, than to fill up the country with the scum of Europe.[30]

In spite of these drastic statements, the majority of established Winnipeggers remained convinced that the Slavs and Jews could be assimilated if a sufficient amount of energy and determination was invested in the task.

The key agent in this assimilation process was the public school system. Most "British" Winnipeggers looked to the school "as the mightiest assimilation force for elevating the immigrant to the level of Canadian life."[31] The city's leaders felt strongly that on the school "more than any other agency will depend the quality and nature of the citizenship of the future; that in the way in which the school avails itself of its opportunity depends the extent to which Canadian traditions will be appropriated, Canadian national sentiment imbibed, and Canadian standards of living adopted by the next-generation of the new races that are making their homes in our midst."[32]

From the standpoint of Winnipeg's charter group, however, there were serious problems associated with using the public school system as an assimilating agent. First, there was the problem of providing adequate facilities and teaching staff to serve the rapidly growing student population.[33] The second difficulty, that of language, was even more severe. It was difficult to train a sufficient number of teachers who could speak both English and the language of the immigrants they faced in the classroom. The situation that developed was described by the principal of one North End school:

> Imagine if you can, a young girl, herself only a few years out of school, facing a class of fifty children, none of whom could understand a word she said; nor could the teacher understand a word spoken by her pupils. The children could not converse with each other, excepting in small groups of those who had learned the same language in their homes. Obviously the first task was to get teachers and pupils to understand each other.[34]

The city's charter group realized, moreover, that they had to reach more than school-age children if the process of assimilation through education was to be successful. Accordingly, Mayor Ashdown was instrumental in having the Winnipeg School Board establish a system of evening classes in 1907. During that year ten English-language evening classes were opened for foreigners and six more were soon added, twelve of which were north of the C.P.R. tracks. To attract students to the classes advertisements were run in the city's numerous foreign-language newspapers and handbills in five languages were printed and widely distributed.[35]

The efforts of the Winnipeg School Board to use the educational system as an assimilating agent were frustrated by problems other than facilities and language. One of these was the tendency of the city's ethnic groups to take upon themselves the task of educating their children in the language and culture of their particular group. This was true for almost every nationality, be it Scandinavian, German, Slavic or Jewish. It was estimated that in 1911 at least three thousand foreigners were attending private or separate schools in Winnipeg. Thousands more attended evening or weekend classes conducted by the religious and cultural organizations of the various ethnic groups.[36] In short, it was apparent to all but the most casual observer that many foreigners were either not being "Canadianized" at all, or they were being assimilated at a rate deemed unsatisfactory to the city's Anglo-Saxons.

There were still other problems faced by the charter group in Winnipeg in their attempt to assimilate the "foreigner" through education. The Public Schools Act of Manitoba permitted multilingual instruction and did not provide for compulsory attendance, and these two issues led to a kind of open racism on the part of the city's charter group until these laws were overcome by new legislation during World War I.[37] The clauses of the Public Schools Act dealing with language of instruction had been enacted in 1897.[38] In the first few years of operation the legislation worked as it was intended, to allow French children to be taught in their mother tongue. But since even this compromise was less than satisfactory to most Winnipeggers, it became intolerable when instruction in languages other than English was sought not only by the French but by the Ukrainians, Poles, and others. The editor of the *Manitoba Free Press*, John W. Dafoe, noted with unconcealed horror that this had led by 1907 to some thirteen different languages being used in provincial schools as the language of instruction.[39]

The hostile reaction of Winnipeg's charter group to the use of languages other than English in public schools was intensified when they saw their taxes being used to train teachers to meet the demands for non-English-speaking teachers. During this period the provincial government established at least two special training schools for bilingual teachers in Winnipeg: a Polish Teachers' Training School and a Ruthenian Training School. Indeed, much to the consternation of the charter group, the Ukrainian teachers even established their own teachers' organization, held conventions in the city and published a Ukrainian weekly newspaper,[40] a journal which the *Winnipeg Tribune* described in June 1914 as being "subversive and destructive of Canadian citizenship and Canadian nationality."

The reaction of the charter group of the lack of a school attendance law was equally hostile. Many Winnipeg children were receiving little or no education. To make matters even worse, this was particularly true in the case of new immigrants who, because of economic need or just plain ignorance or fear, kept their chidlren away from classes. Faced with this situation, there arose in Winnipeg a demand for compulsory education as an absolute necessity. The problem was explained as follows:

[Immigrant] children are growing up without an education, save in wickedness. Every day they are becoming a serious menace to the country. The future, if this continues, is very alarming. There must be compulsory education. There must! The party, the parliament, the government which permits a venerable obstacle to stand in the way of this absolute necessity to the very safety of the Dominion, which permits love for office or power to delay the enactment or property enforcement of proper legislation whereby every child shall be compelled to attend school had forefeited all right to the respect of the people, and whatever its merits, must be replaced by those who have vision and courage to discern and do what is imperative.[41]

The opinions expressed here received widespread support among the English community in Winnipeg. In 1902, for example, a delegation headed by Mayor Arbuthnot met with members of the provincial government "and strongly urged the necessity of compulsory education."[42] In 1909 a "Citizen's Meeting," attended by such well-known Winnipeggers as ex-mayors Ashdown and Ryan and Alderman Riley, reported that "thousands of children never attend a school and were growing up absolutely illiterate and that such a condition will work as a menace to the community. The opinion prevailed that the solution of the question . . . lay in the immediate passage by the provincial government of a compulsory education bill."[43] This demand for compulsory education was also supported by such organizations as the Canadian Club and the Orange Order. The latter organization even arranged a mass meeting to protest the provincial government's lack of a school attendance law. The Grand Master of the Orange Lodge in Winnipeg, ex-alderman J. Willoughby, was especially vociferous in his attempts to obtain compulsory education.

J.S. Woodsworth also raised his voice and used his pen with growing insistence for a compulsory school law. In a 1912 report on the educational needs of children employed in shops and factories, he concluded with the blunt statement that "in nearly all cases the workers have very little education." In an address to the Local Council of Women he stated:

One-third of all the children in Manitoba do not attend school, only 25% pass through the entrance, 5% pass through the high school, and 1% go through college. All the rest are practically unprovided for as far as education is concerned. There are few free lectures, concerts and reading rooms. The only public amusements in North Winnipeg are the saloon, the pool-room, theatre and dance hall. The public schools should be put to larger use.[44]

The feelings of Winnipeg's Anglo-Saxon majority were perhaps best summed up, however, in the reaction of the city's school board to the Coldwell amendments of 1912. These amendments, if implemented, would have resulted in a startling change in Winnipeg's public school system. The first amendment provided that for the purpose of the bilingual clause of the Public School Act, every classroom was in fact a complete "school," thus allowing almost every individual class in the public schools of Winnipeg to claim a bilingual teacher. Previously there had just been one or two bilingual teachers in each school. The next amendment compelled the school board to provide space for all children of school age in the city. This clause was intended to force the school board to assume the expense of running existing private schools. The third amendment would have allowed the segregation of children according to religion even during secular school work. This last section would have led to a system diametrically opposed to that established in 1890.[45]

Reaction to the Coldwell amendments was predictable. The *Manitoba Free Press* and the Orange Lodge denounced them, while the Winnipeg School Board stated bluntly and publicly it would not implement the measures in the schools of the city. The strength of the feeling over the issue of bilingualism had come to the point of open defiance of provincial law.

Given this apparently unanimous agreement on the need for compulsory education and unilingual schools among the English majority in Winnipeg, it is necessary to explain why their views were not met by the provincial government. This is not the place for a detailed analysis of the complicated state of provincial politics in Manitoba in this period, but a few basic facts can be stated.[46] The Conservative government headed by Premier Rodmond Roblin, drew heavily on the ethnic vote to maintain its hold on office.[47] Indeed, Roblin had virtially made a compact with the Roman Catholic Archbishop of St. Boniface that stipulated he would not disturb the status quo in return for the relatively small but powerful (in terms of provincial seats) French vote. The agreement was a good one for Roblin and served him well until 1915. The government's only efforts to appease the rising tide of protest in Winnipeg against this attempt to curry favour with the minority groups were the unsuccessful attack on truancy in the city by tightening the enforcement of the provincial Children's Act, and by the passage, in 1906, of flag legislation that symbolically required all provincial schools to fly the Union Jack during school hours.[48]

At the time, in a cynical reference to the lack of a school attendance law, the latter action was treated as a measure designed to make the ensign more visible to the young by not requiring that the flag be inside the school where it could not be so easily seen.[49] The inadequacy of such measures in dealing with the main issue of non-attendance was revealed in 1911 when it was discovered — and widely publicized — that the percentage of illiteracy among foreign-born males in Manitoba (23.3) was the highest in Canada except Quebec, and that Winnipeg stood in eighth place among all cities over seven thousand in its illiteracy rate.

In the face of this unsympathetic attitude on the part of Premier Roblin and the Conservatives, many in the city turned to the provincial Liberal party and its leader, T.C. Norris, who took a firm stand on the education question. Shortly after the Liberal victory in 1915, the new provincial government established a "national" school system and passed a compulsory attendance law. Although the matter of bilingual schools has since remained an issue of some importance in Manitoba, the settlement achieved in 1916 is still in effect. In general, the legislation had the desired effect so far as the charter group was concerned, and in subsequent years all immigrants of school age learned English as a matter of course. On the other hand, the heated rhetoric of the campaign itself impeded cordial social interaction in Winnipeg. While the merits of compulsory education and the utter absurdity of multilingual instruction (though not bilingual) are obvious, the controversy aroused in achieving these aims served to intensify racial divisions in Winnipeg for decades.

The attempts of Winnipeg's charter group to assimilate the "foreigner" were, however, only one side of the story. The other was the formidable adjustment problem faced by the immigrants themselves. From their perspective everything and everyone seemed different; the city was strange and the townspeople strangers. Even with the best intentions, direct and painless entry into the mainstream of Winnipeg's economic and social life was bound to be difficult.[50] For the European immigrant emerging from the C.P.R. or Union Stations after a long railway journey from eastern ports, Winnipeg was both a wonder and a terror. The vast expanse of Main Street was a far cry from the winding alleys of European cities. For the moment, though the street was bustling with activity, it evoked memories of "home" and feelings of loneliness. A fortunate newcomer might have encountered someone who could have told him in his own language of the nearby immigration sheds where he could have stayed until he found more permanent accommodation, or he might have had relatives or old countrymen with whom he could board. More often the newcomers were alone and without much information. One Winnipeg immigrant, Mike Hruska, remembered the experience he shared with a friend:

> After standing there and looking around for a short while, I sat down on the curb, hoping for someone with the familiar sound of my own tongue to come by. Strangely enough, no one paid any attention to us. . . Who cares who we were, where we are going? Nobody, we must have been looked upon as a part of the dirt on the street.

> What a country! In the midst of thousands of people in the big city nobody cared. I thought this would never happen in the old village. Our people were human. In our village someone would certainly stop to talk to strangers by the roadside. . . . Not here.[51]

Once in Winnipeg, the immigrant faced three distinct but related problems. The most pressing concern, of course, was to obtain employment. For those whose background had equipped them with a specific trade or skill there was little difficulty in adjusting to the economic conditions of their new surroundings. Many, however, were poverty stricken peasants with neither training nor capital, and their problems were bound to be more severe. The second major area of adjustment was a broader and more complicated one and more difficult to achieve than was economic security. This was the matter of social and structural assimilations; a process that could be considered complete when the immigrant learned the language and social usages of the city well enough to participate in its economic, political and social life without encountering prejudice. The emphasis here was on external indices, such as the ability to speak English, and the adoption of the dress, manners, and the social ritual of the dominant group with whom the newcomer came in contact. Finally, and most difficult of all, was the matter of cultural assimilation; a process of interpenetration and fusion in which the immigrant acquires the memories, sentiments and attitudes of the city's dominant group, and by sharing their experience and history becomes incorporated with them in a broad and all-embracing cultural life.

In pre-World War I Winnipeg only the process of economic adjustment was achieved to any great extent; social and structural assimilation were just beginning when the tensions of the war and the Winnipeg General Strike temporarily halted the process. Cultural assimilation, the most difficult and gradual process, usually requiring two or three generations, did not get underway until well into the thirties, forties, and fifties.[52]

In the process of economic adjustment all immigrants in Winnipeg were aided by the economic prosperity throughout the period. Except for a few severe but short-lived recessions, such as that in 1907-1908, employment opportunities were plentiful.[53] But finding employment did not necessarily mean that the newcomer achieved economic security. A study conducted by a local minister, J.S. Woodsworth, in 1913, indicated that a normal standard of living in Winnipeg required an income of at least $1200 per year. Yet, Woodsworth continued, "it is difficult to find an actual workingman's family budget which maintains a normal standard. Large numbers of workmen are receiving under $600 per year, many under $500, half of what is necessary."[54] These economic circumstances forced many immigrants to resort to drastic measures in their struggle for survival. Often families broke up as mothers and even children went to work to supplement the incomes of their husbands and fathers. The immigrant, already tested by the new conditions of life in Winnipeg, was further demoralized by the effects of low wages.

The fact that thousands of families had an inadequate standard of living in an apparently prosperous city was brought to the attention of City Council many, many times, particularly after 1900. Private charities, individual investigators, the Trades and Labour Council, and even the municipal health department reported on the manifestations of the maldistribution of income and called for improved health and building by-laws, municipal housing, fair wage schedules, public works programming, and a host of other progressive measures. For the most part these pleas were ignored. Although Winnipeg had a relief committee as early as 1874, its work never extended beyond aiding those in particularly desperate straits and in the period 1900-1913, for example, the city spent, on the average, only $6200 a year on relief.[55]

There are several factors which help explain Winnipeg's failure to deal with its social problems in a progressive manner. First of all, the city's governing elite were obsessed with the need for growth and tended to discourage financial support for any institution which did not promote direct economic returns. The drain of capital, both public and private, into economic enterprises and promotional schemes, such as the Winnipeg Development and Industrial Bureau, left little for community services.[56] There were other factors as well, such as the age-sex ratio of the city's population. The absence of a larger older age-group during these early years may well have relieved the pressure upon health and welfare institutions, but it also removed the steadying influence of tradition and deprived the community of the leadership of those not strenuously engaged in making a living.[57] Similarly, with relatively few children among the early settlers, extensive educational, medical and recreational facilities were not required in the early years. When the situation changed rapidly with the heavy influx of persons in the child bearing group, causing a sharp rise in the number of young children, problems of maternity, infant welfare, and education quickly assumed considerable importance (see Table VIII).[58] Naturally it took time for the city's institutions to adjust, but in the interval many suffered.

The predominance of males in Winnipeg raised even more acute problems (see Table IX).[59] The establishment of social organizations which could serve the needs of the female or child sections of the population were hardly the primary concern of often unmarried "men-on-the-make." In short, as Professor Lower has noted in his social history of Canada, Winnipeg was for much of this period a frontier town. It "was well supplied with frontier characteristics: its bars were numerous, long and rowdy. The men who frequented them were noisily gay with all the vulgarity familiar to anyone who knows the frontier at first hand. . . . The irresponsibilities which all males exhibit when adrift from the order imposed by kinship and association" were very present.[60]

TABLE VIII

AGE COMPOSITION OF WINNIPEG'S POPULATION 1886-1921

Year	0-14	15-44	45-64	65 +	Total Population
1886	7,018 (34.7%)	11,375 (56.2%)	1,647 (8.1%)	194 (0.9%)	20,238
1891	8,734 (34.1%)	14,348 (56.0%)	2,252 (8.8%)	305 (1.1%)	25,639
1901	13,999 (33.1%)	22,602 (53.4%)	4,702 (11.1%)	871 (2.0%)	42,340
1906	24,897 (27.6%)	54,543 (60.5%)	9,155 (10.1%)	1,558 (1.8%)	90,153
1911	38,002 (27.9%)	80,303 (59.9%)	13,698 (10.1%)	2,057 (1.5%)	136,035
1916	52,099 (32.0%)	88,566 (54.3%)	18,934 (11.6%)	3,401 (2.1%)	163,000
1921	56,031 (31.3%)	94,102 (52.5%)	24,244 (13.5%)	4,457 (2.5%)	179,087

Still another element that accentuated the city's social problems was the fact that those persons who had the strongest voice in the direction of institutional policies and community services were the very ones who were least exposed to the disturbing influences faced by the newcomers. Sheltered from these conditions by their lavish homes in Armstrong's Point, Fort Rouge, and Wellington Cresent, and engaged in a social and business life centered around the Manitoba Club, the Board of Trade, and the St. Charles Country Club, the governing elite's callous stance was often the result of ignorance. While some of these people supported social improvement efforts such as mission work, for the most part they gave little serious thought to the problems growing in their midst. "Too often, social improvement was a mere fad or concerned itself with questions that hardly touched the life of the average worker or immigrant."[61] Temperance, direct legislation, the single tax, sabbatarianism, and women's suffrage were middle class diversions which ignored the real problems of poverty, over-crowding, and disease faced by the city's poor.

Fortunately, the process of economic adjustment and assimilation did not rely exclusively on the inadequate agencies of the civic corporation. Both were aided by a host of voluntary associations. Winnipeg's groups were legion. They included the Sons of England, the St. Andrews Society, the Irish Association, the German Society, the Icelandic (Progressive) Society, the (Polish) St. Peter and Paul Society, the Zionist Society, the Ruthenian National Society, and numerous others. Exclusive without being invidious, such clubs served as guideposts for the bewildered immigrant. They identified other residents with like traits and similar interests and encouraged contact on shared grounds and participation in common activities. Coupled with the churches, the unions, the ethnic newspapers, membership in these

TABLE IX
NUMBER OF MALES PER 1,000
FEMALES, 1881-1921

Year	Ratio
1881	1393
1891	1095
1901	1075
1911	1207
1921	1004

organizations of a fraternal and benevolent nature alleviated economic insecurity by providing funds, assistance, and insurance in cases of destitution, illness, and death. Finally, political and commercial bodies promoted aspirations in matters involving municipal authorities and even the federal government. Voluntary organizations often first introduced the immigrant to the community and afterwards linked him to it.[62]

The voluntary nature of these organizations also meant, however, that they had neither the inclination nor the means to help each immigrant, even if the newcomer belonged to a particular ethnic group. The general lack of affluent membership among the Jewish and Slavic organizations, for example, often meant that when need was discovered little could be done.[63] In Winnipeg, as in other cities, the void was partially filled by private charities organized to meet specific needs rather than to serve particular groups.[64]

Winnipeg was fortunate in having several such charitable agencies, led by what can only be called practical idealists. Although the best known as All People's Mission, others such as the Margaret Scott Nursing Mission and the Salvation Army were also active.[65] All People's was founded in 1898 by Miss Dolly McGuire to carry out traditional religious salvation work but by 1910, under the leadership of J.S. Woodsworth, it was doing far more than that. The actual work of the Mission was remarkable, both in scope and the number of people reached. A partial listing of its program includes the running of two kindergartens, visits to immigrants' homes, boys and girls classes and clubs, a fresh-air camp, the provision of swimming and gymnasium facilities, night classes in English and civics, Sunday schools, free legal advice, pressure for a Juvenile Court (established in 1908), hospital visitation, welcoming immigrants at the federal immigration buildings, mothers' meetings, dispensation of relief, concerts and debates, and numerous other activities.[66]

One of the chief values of the work of All People's, and other agencies like it, was the publicity its work gave to conditions in Winnipeg's "foreign ghetto." Winnipeg's daily newspapers gave generous space to the activities of the Mission and until the War — when charges of catering to "enemy aliens" were laid — praised Woodsworth unreservedly. Also, the work of All People's and other such missions is noteworthy since they were usually staffed, led, and financed by the "British." The genuine commitment of such agencies to Winnipeg's poor (of whatever ethnic origin) clearly indicates that not all of the city's charter group were concerned only with economic growth. Rather, those who supported and were involved in these agencies were dedicated to removing, or at least moderating, the depersonalizing and demoralizing aspects of urban life. By so doing they played the important role of communicating to the public at large the great need for caring for all the city's residents, regardless of class, religion, or ethnic origin. In short, through their actual work with the newcomer and in their effect upon established society, the city's private social service agencies helped in no small way to ease the impersonal materialism of the city. At the same time, however, it must be noted that these agencies were no less intent on assimilating the immigrant than was the Winnipeg School Board or the Orange Order. What distinguished these agencies from others was the generally humanitarian and gentle nature of their proselytism.

A DIVIDED CITY, 1914-1921

While the period from 1900 to 1913 was one in which intolerance and hostility toward the "foreigner" in Winnipeg increased, it was in fact an era of relative calm compared to what transpired in the years after the outbreak of World War I in August 1914. In the months and years following Britain's declaration of war a number of issues — some new, others pre-dating the war itself — and events brought into very sharp focus the deep divisions that already existed in Winnipeg between the "British" and the "foreigner." For while the war was certainly a major contributor to the heightening of tension in Winnipeg, other forces also had a significant impact on social relationships between various ethnic groups in the city. Although issues such as temperance, sabbatarianism, compulsory and unilingual education, and unemployment, and events such as the Russian Revolution, the Red Scare and the Winnipeg General Strike had different and usually unrelated causes, they also all managed in their own way to increase or exacerbate ethnic divisions in Winnipeg.[67] Indeed, together with the war, they combined to make the years from 1914 to 1921 the worst in Winnipeg's social history: ethnic discrimination was rampant, "foreigners" lost their jobs and were disenfranchised and even deported, property was destroyed, lives were threatened. But most important of all was that the events of these years left scars on the tissue of Winnipeg society that took decades to heal.[68]

In the years prior to 1914, the charter group in Winnipeg had viewed the "foreigner" and his assimilation to a "British-Canadian" way-of-life as a serious but ultimately solvable problem. The war, however, caused a dramatic change in this attitude. The outbreak of hostilities in Europe brought an immediate heightening of pro-British feelings among members of the city's charter group. At the same time, however, the emotional hysteria that was generated by the war made certain ethnic groups in Winnipeg automatic targets of attack. The most obvious result, of course, was that Germans, who had hitherto been regarded as worthy immigrants, were immediately placed on the list of "undesirable aliens."[69] During the course of the war the natural reaction of "British" Winnipeg to the "German enemy'' was fed by crude but persistent propaganda until, by 1919, the charter group was proclaiming that the term ''Anglo-Saxon'' was a misnomer and that the proper term should be ''Anglo-Celtic.'' The problem with ''Anglo-Saxon,'' of course, was that it signified some relationship with the Germans and this was simply no longer acceptable. Thus the *Winnipeg Telegram* declared: ''All Scottish, Irish and Welsh people, and most English folk, would do well to remember that they are not the descendants of an insignificant German tribe.''[70]

Winnipeggers of German descent were not the only objects of derision during the period 1914-1918. War psychology brought everyone who was not obviously ''British'' under suspicion. The problems faced by European ''foreigners'' in Winnipeg were detailed in a letter printed in the *Winnipeg Tribune* in 1915. Written by a group of Ukrainians, it stated:

> Owing to the unjust classification of all Slavs as Austrians and anti-allies, and owing to irresponsible utterances in the press and otherwise, a certain degree of intolerance and hatred towards everything that is foreign has been transplanted in the public mind, resulting in indiscreet looting of property, disturbing divine service in the churches, raiding of private homes, and personal assaults of the gravest kind, to all those who have the appearance of foreign birth, thus rendering our lives endangered.[71]

The ''alien problem'' in Winnipeg was further intensified as a result of the Russian Revolution of 1917. When the Russian Bolshevists surrendered to the Germans in November, a ''Hun-Bolshevist'' conspiracy designed to destroy ''the civilization of Anglo-Saxonism the world over'' was immediately perceived, with predictable results for Winnipeg's Slavs.[72]

The intense feelings of hostility and hatred generated by the war, moreover, did not soon subside after 1918. Instead, it anything, they became worse. There were several reasons for this. First, the months following the end of the war were marked by an intense fear of a ''combined alien-revolutionary threat'' that plunged most of North America into the infamous Red Scare of 1919. In Winnipeg, manifestations of the general paranoia, fed by pro-alien and pro-revolutionary statements by Winnipeg labour leaders at the founding convention of the One Big Union in March 1919, were even more apparent than in other cities on the continent.[73] Second, the months folloiwng the war saw a severe unemployment problem in Winnipeg, particularly among returned soldiers. ''Frustrated by the fact that many of them were unemployed while Germans and Ukrainians and other 'alien enemies' held down good jobs, it was they who most persistently demanded that the alien-pacifist-Red element be deported immediately.''[74] This bitterness led to serious rioting in January 1919.[75] Third, the Winnipeg General Strike of 1919 was perceived by many in the city as a ''revolution,'' led and supported by the same elements that had proven disloyal during the war. The fact that there was little evidence to support this view (there were no "foreigners" prominent in the labour movement in Winnipeg) mattered little, and the association between strikers and "foreigners" persisted.[76] Finally, throughout the period the supporters of prohibition, sabbatarianism, and compulsory and unilingual education generally perceived the "foreigner" as an opponent of their goals, and these feelings provided a constant undercurrent of anti-alien feeling well into the 1920's.[77]

Whatever the cause, manifestations of "anti-foreigner" feelings were apparent in many fronts during the years 1919 to 1921. Indicative of the mood of Winnipeg's charter group during these years were the actions, in January 1919, of a group of war veterans and opportunistic hoodlums who prowled around the city, smashed the windows of stores in the North End, broke into homes in the "foreign" district and demanded that everyone who had even the appearance of an "alien" kiss the Union Jack. The club building of the Austro-Hungarian society was literally torn to ruins and the Edelweiss Brewery in Elmwood was left in a shambles. Significantly, no charges were laid against the marauders by the authorities.[78]

Winnipeg thus entered the decade of the 1920's with the difficult problem of absorbing the "foreigner" into an all-embracing community life unresolved. When the city emerged from World War I it ran headlong into the question of ethnic relationships, for Winnipeg was best characterized at this time as a city of unassimilated, isolated, and frequently bitter ethnic groups facing a "British" majority with deeply ingrained feelings of prejudice toward "foreigners." It was only slowly that the "British" in Winnipeg learned that the community could survive and even prosper through respect and tolerance.

In this continuing struggle for harmonious relationships between ethnic groups, Winnipeg was aided in the years after 1921 by several general trends that affected both its rate of growth and the characteristics of its population. Most important, perhaps, was the fact that in the years after 1921 Winnipeg grew at a very slow rate compared to the pre-1921 era. Furthermore, many of the people who came to Winnipeg during the decades following 1921 were migrants from rural parts of the country rather than immigrants from abroad. This was significant since in most cases the newcomers in the city had already gone through some of the stages of assimilation and could fit into the community with less difficulty than those who came from foreign countries. The combined effect of these and other factors was a decrease in ethnic hostility. The proportion of British in Winnipeg as compared to other ethnic groups continued to drop throughout the period, but at a much slower rate than during the 1900-1913 era when it declined by over 10 percent in one decade. The city's Anglo-Saxons, more secure in their own positions, were less prone to feel threatened as the years passed, and they gradually lost most of their strident feelings of superiority that had been largely the response to a fear of being overwhelmed by masses of "foreigners." Indeed, as the years passed and the city's other ethnic groups became more settled and secure, they too shed some of the protective coverings that had shielded them from the unknown in earlier years. As the immigrant stream slowed down and ethnic groups no longer received fresh recruits from the mother country, the strength and vitality of these groups slowly waned and increasing numbers were submerged into the broader culture of the community. The Winnipeg-born offspring of the original immigrants identified more with Canada than with their "mother country." They were more adaptive than their parents and easily learned the language and the social customs of the city, and in time even began to participate in its economic, political and social life without encountering prejudice. Indeed, driven on by intense feelings of inferiority that resulted from the essentially "British" nature of Winnipeg, the immigrants' children could not adopt the ways of the city's charter group fast enough. Unlike their parents, the second generation desired, above all, to be accepted by the "British."[79]

Taken together, these trends generally had the effect of improving relationships between various groups in the city, but the process was a slow one and no great changes were evident overnight. While the "foreigner" gained increased acceptance in Winnipeg in the years after 1921, and even the term "foreigner" was replaced by the more positive term "New Canadian," the tone of Winnipeg society changed little. What evolved in Winnipeg was a society that was more diverse but not fundamentally different from that established by 1900. The premises of the city's "British" charter group, and the social instititons which they planted, generally remained intact.[80]

NOTES:

1. James H. Gray, *The Boy From Winnipeg* (Toronto, 1970), p. 2.
2. For a detailed discussion of these problems, and for general background material on Winnipeg during this period, see Alan F.J. Artibise, *Winnipeg: A Social History of Urban Growth, 1874-1914* (Montreal, 1975).
3. See Alan F.J. Artibise, "An Urban Environment: The Process of Growth in Winnipeg, 1874-1914," Canadian Historical Association, *Historical Papers, 1972*, pp. 109-134.
4. The word "foreign" as it is used here and elsewhere in this paper refers to those residents of Winnipeg who were not born in either Canada or Great Britain and whose origin was other than "British." While this usage is not strictly accurate — persons born in Britain are, from one point of view, also "foreign-born" — it does correspond to contemporary usage and had been used in this fashion in the balance of this paper.

It should also be noted at this point that not all Winnipeggers consistently or enthusiastically supported immigration. Organized labour tended to look upon immigrants as cheap labour and their recruitment as a plot by the "plutocracy" to reduce wages. See, for example, *The Voice*, 24 Jan. 1902 and 23 April 1903.

5. See W.J. Carlyle, "Growth, Ethnic Groups and Socio-Economic Areas of Winnipeg," in T.J. Kuz, ed., *Winnipeg, 1874-1974: Progress and Prospects* (Winnipeg, 1974), pp. 27-41.

6. Vancouver did not surpass Winnipeg as Canada's third largest city until the 1920's. See Table VI, below. General discussions of population growth in western Canada can be found in the following: K. Lenz, "Large Urban Places in the Prairie Provinces — Their Development and Location," in R.L. Gentilcore, ed., *Canada's Changing Geography* (Toronto, 1967), pp. 199-211; L.D. McCann, "Urban Growth in Western Canada, 1881-1961," *The Alberta Geographer*, No. 5 (1969), pp. 65-74; Paul Voisey, "The Urbanization of the Canadian Prairies, 1871-1916," *Histoire sociale/Social History*, Volume VII, No. 15 (May 1975), pp. 77-101; and Paul Phillips, "Structural Change and Population Distribution in the Prairie Region: 1911-1961," unpublished M.A. thesis, University of Saskatchewan, 1963.

7. Unless otherwise indicated, the sources for Table I and all other tables are the *Census of Canada* and the *Census of the Prairie Provinces*.

8. Accounts of the Winnipeg "boom" of 1881-1882 can be found in Artibise, *Winnipeg*, pp. 73-74; W.J. Healy, *Winnipeg's Early Days* (Winnipeg 1927), pp. 22-25; and J. Macoun, *Manitoba and the Great Northwest* (Guelph 1882), Chapter 27.

9. See K.H. Norrie, "The Rate of Settlement of the Canadian Prairies, 1870-1911," *Journal of Economic History*, Vol. XXXV (June, 1975), pp. 410-427.

10. Artibise, *Winnipeg*, Chapter 8.

11. The figures for Table II were taken from Reports of the Manitoba Department of Agriculture and Immigration, and from Vital Statistics Registration, Office of Division Registrar, City of Winnipeg. Data was not available for the pre-1891 period. The overwhelming importance of immigration is Winnipeg during this period is also confirmed by birthplace statistics. In 1891, only 5,510 or 21.4% of Winnipeg's population had been born in Manitoba. The figures for Winnipeg would have been even smaller. By 1901, this had only risen to 13,322 or 31.5%. Two of the many reasons for the relative unimportance of natural increase during this period were the shortage of women in the city and high infant mortality rates. See Artibise, *Winnipeg*, Chapter 8.

12. Slavs in Table IV includes Austro-Hungarians, Poles, Ukrainians, and Russians. The terminology "Slav" was commonly used in Winnipeg during this period to refer to all Eastern Europeans. This usage has been followed in this paper.

13. "British" refers both to native-born Canadians of British origin and to the English, Irish and Scots born in Great Britain.

14. A useful analysis of the Manitoba experience that follows the model put forward by Louis Hartz in *The Founding of New Societies* (New York, 1964), is J.E. Rea, "The Roots of Prairie Society," in D.P. Gagan, ed., *Prairie Perspectives* (Toronto, 1970), pp. 46-55.

15. A. Smith, "Metaphor and Nationality in North America," *Canadian Historical Review*, Vol. LI, No. 3 (September 1970), pp. 247-275.

16. Rea, "Roots of Prairie Society"; and V. Jensen, "The Manitoba Schools Question," unpublished paper in possession of author.

17. John Marly, *Under the Ribs of Death* (Toronto, 1957), p. 24.

18. Rea, "Roots of Prairie Society," p. 51. See also G.F. Chapman, "Winnipeg: The Melting Pot," *The Canadian Magazine*, Vol. XXXIII, No. 5 (September 1909), pp. 409-416; and Chapman, "Winnipeg: The Refining Process," *ibid.*, No. 6 (Oct. 1909), pp. 548-554.

19. 16 November and 7 December 1912.

20. *Town Topics*, 17 July 1899.

21. For a discussion of Winnipeg as a labour market see R. Bellan, "Relief in Winnipeg: The Economic Background," unpublished M.A. thesis, University of Toronto, 1941, pp. 46-62.

22. A detailed discussion of these problems can be found in Artibise, *Winnipeg*.

23. *Ibid.*, Chapter 9.

24. The cities with which Winnipeg was compared were Halifax, Saint John, Quebec, Montreal, Toronto, London, Hamilton, Ottawa, Regina, Saskatoon, Edmonton, Calgary, Vancouver and Victoria.

25. The same cities listed above were used for these comparisons. Quebec, Montreal and Ottawa had a lower proportion of British because of the large number of French in these cities.

26. Rea, "Roots of Prairie Society," pp. 51-52. See also John H. Thompson, "The Prohibition Question in Manitoba, 1892-1928," unpublished M.A. thesis, University of Manitoba, 1969.

27. *Manitoba Free Press*, 1 March 1913; and Chapman, "Winnipeg: The Melting Pot," p. 413.

28. J. Woodsworth, *Strangers Without Our Gates* (Toronto, 1909), p. 132 and *passim*.

29. *Winnipeg Tribune*, 29 Jan. 1900.

30. *Winnipeg Telegram*, 13 May 1901.

31. *Manitoba Free Press*, 7 Dec. 1912.

32. "Public School Education in Winnipeg," *Souvenir of Winnipeg's Diamond Jubilee, 1874-1924* (Winnipeg, 1924), p. 65. See also F. Gonick, "Manitoba Public Educational Institutions As An Inculcator of Social Values, 1910-1930," unpublished paper in possession of author.

33. Enrolment jumped from 7,500 in 1900 to 25,814 by 1914. See Artibise, *Winnipeg*, p. 200.

34. W.J. Sisler, *Peaceful Invasion* (Winnipeg, 1944), pp. 19-20.

35. *Ibid.*, pp. 69-70. See also W.G. Pearce, *Winnipeg School Days* (Manitoba Archives, 1951), pp. 24-25; and J.W. Chafe, *An Apple for the Teacher: A Centennial History of the Winnipeg School Division* (Winnipeg, 1967—. pp. 65-66.

36. See, for example, H. Herstein, "The Growth of the Winnipeg Jewish Community and the Evolution of its Educational Institutions," *Manitoba Historical Society Transactions*, Series III, No. 22 (1966-67), pp. 27-66; V. Turek, *The Poles in Manitoba* (Toronto, 1967), Chapters VII-IX; and M.H. Marunchak, *The Ukrainian Canadians: A History* (Winnipeg, 1970), pp. 151-153 and *passim*.

37. Unfortunately, the Manitoba School Question is far too complicated to detail here. See L. Clark, ed., *The Manitoba School Question* (Toronto, 1968). It contains a good bibliography.

38. The "Compromise of 1897" provided that "when pupils in any school spoke French or any language other than English, the teaching of this was to be in French, or other such language, and English upon the bilingual system." W.L. Morton, *Manitoba: A History* (Toronto, 1957), p. 271. It is important to note that Manitoba's school system had originally been bilingual but the "British" had succeeded in 1890 in replacing existing legislation with an act that called for unilingual (English) schools. It was this 1890 legislation that was changed by the compromise of 1897. See Artibise, *Winnipeg*, Chapter 11.

39. M. Donnelly, *Dafoe of the Free Press* (Toronto, 1968), p. 57 and *passim*. In the period 1911-1915, Dafoe published a series of sixty-four articles on the education question in the pages of the *Manitoba Free Press*.

40. Turek, *Poles in Manitoba*, p. 220. See also J.H. Syrnick, "Community Builders: Early Ukrainian Teachers," *Manitoba Historical Society Transactions*, Series III, No. 21 (1965), pp. 25-34.

41. *Winnipeg Tribune*, 22 August 1908. For other representative opinions on behalf of the charter group see *ibid.*, 27 June 1912; and *Manitoba Free Press*, 20 May 1909 and 8 Dec. 1913.

42. *Ibid.*, 12 June 1902.

43. *Winnipeg Tribune*, 20 May 1909.

44. Grace MacInnis, *J.S. Woodsworth: A Man to Remember* (Toronto, 1953), pp. 65, 80.

45. M. Spigelman, "Bilingual Schools in Manitoba and their Abolition" (Manitoba Archives, unpublished paper, 1970), pp. 14-15.

46. See L. Orlikow, "A Survey of the Reform Movement in Manitoba, 1910-1920", unpublished M.A. thesis, University of Manitoba, 1958.

47. See T. Petersen, "Ethnic and Class Politics in Manitoba," in M. Robin, ed., *Canadian Provincial Politics: The Party Systems of the Ten Provinces* (Scarborough, 1972), pp. 69-115.

48. Morton, *Manitoba*, pp. 311-312. The ethnic minorities, particularly the Ukrainians and French, were opposed not only to the abolition of the bilingual clause but also to compulsory attendance legislation. The former were used to having sons and daughters help earn the family living, while the French were afraid such legislation would lead to "godless" institutions. Moreover, the lack of an attendance law meant that any changes in the school laws that were obnoxious could be resisted, at the expense of the children, by refusing to allow them to attend school.

49. James A. Jackson, *The Centennial History of Manitoba* (Toronto, 1970), p. 173. The Children's Act had some serious shortcomings. No child could be forced to attend school unless he was a "neglected child" whose parents ignored their "moral duties" in raising him. Only parents who contributed to "juvenile delinquency" could be prosecuted. Finally, any child apprehended had to be treated under the provisions of the law, in the same manner as criminals, thus tempting the truant officers to ignore rather than arrest young offenders. In short, despite Premier Roblin's statements that the act was an effective alternative to a compulsory attendance law, it was only barely enforced in Winnipeg and not at all in rural areas.

50. This paper makes no pretense about covering all the varied dimensions of the reactions of the "foreigner" to life in Winnipeg. I have, for example, been forced to rely on English sources because of the language barrier and, unfortunately, there are few secondary studies completed that base their findings in whole or in part on non-English sources. This is obviously an area where a great deal of primary research remains to be done. Fortunately, some of this work is underway. One of the products of this type of research, that indicates that not all "foreigners" in Winnipeg during this period accepted their fate in a passive manner, is Orest T. Martynowych, "The Ukrainian Socialist and Working Class Movement in Manitoba, 1900-1918," (Manitoba Archives, unpublished paper, 1973). Another example of this type of research, which attempts to tell the story from the perspective of the immigrant, is R. Harney and H. Troper, *Immigrants: A Portrait of the Urban Experience, 1890-1930* (Toronto, 1975). Although it portrays life in Toronto, many of the experiences depicted in this book could just as easily have been in Winnipeg.

51. Quoted in A.B. McKillop, "Citizen and Socialist: The Ethos of Political Winnipeg, 1919-1935," unpublished M.A. thesis, University of Manitoba, 1970, pp. 24-25.

52. See R.D. Fromson, "Acculturation or Assimilation: A Geographic Analysis of Residential Segregation of Selected Ethnic Groups: Metropolitan Winnipeg, 1951-1961," unpublished M.A. thesis, University of Manitoba, 1965.

53. R. Bellan, "The Development of Winnipeg as a Metropolitan Centre," unpublished Ph.D. thesis, Columbia University, 1958, pp. 71-227.

54. Artibise, *Winnipeg*, Appendix D, pp. 308-319.

55. *Ibid.*, Chapters 10-13.

56. *Ibid.*, Chapter 7 and *passim*.

57. In 1911, for example, when Winnipeg had only 1.5% of its population in the 65+ age group, only Calgary, Regina, and Edmonton had a lower percentage. The percentages for other cities are as follows: Montreal, 3.2%; Toronto, 3.3%; Vancouver, 1.7%; Ottawa, 3.9%; Hamilton, 4.0%; Quebec, 5.0%; Halifax, 4.9%; London, 5.7%; Calgary, 1.1%; Saint John, 5.7%;

Victoria, 3.2%; Regina, 0.7%; and Edmonton, 1.2%. Figures are not available for Saskatoon. A good discussion of the implications of the age distribution of the population can be found in C.B. Davidson, H.C. Grant, and F. Shefrin, *The Population of Manitoba* (Winnipeg, 1938), pp. 78-92 and *passim*.

58. Between 1906 and 1916, for example, the proportion of the city's population aged 0-14 increased by almost 5% while the group 15-44 declined by over 6%. This indicates that the child bearing age group (15-44) were by this time causing a sharp increase in the number of children. Thus the 0-14 age group increased by 27,202 or 109% between 1906 and 1916, while the 15-44 age group increased by 34,023 or only 62% during the same period. The other age groups, 44-64 and 65+ also increased by a greater degree than did the 15-44 group. The rise for 44-64 was 107% over the period 1906 to 1916; for the 65+ group it was 118%. In short, all three groups that were in some sense more dependent on the community than the 15-44 group increased during this crucial period at a faster rate, causing severe strains on Winnipeg's already inadequate social facilities.

59. Comparable figures for other Canadian cities in 1911 are as follows: Montreal, 998; Toronto, 980; Vancouver, 1499; Ottawa, 923; Hamilton, 1059; Quebec, 858; Halifax, 927; London, 898; Calgary, 1550; Saint John, 909; Victoria, 1518; Regina, 1892; Saskatoon, 1507; and Edmonton, 1270.

60. A.R.M. Lower, *Canadians in the Making: A Social History of Canada* (Toronto, 1968), p. 360.

61. K. McNaught and D.J. Bercuson, *The Winnipeg Strike: 1919* (Toronto, 1974), p. 2.

62. Artibise, *Winnipeg*, Chapters 10 and 11. A good survey of the various ethnic newspapers in Winnipeg during this period is Canada Press Club, *The Multilingual Press in Manitoba* (Winnipeg, 1974).

63. See, for example, H. Herstein, "The Growth of the Winnipeg Jewish Community"; Turek, *Poles in Manitoba*; and S. Belkin, *Through Narrow Gates: A Review of Jewish Immigration, Colonization and Immigrant Aid Work in Canada, 1840-1940* (Montreal, 1966).

64. D. McArton, "75 Years in Winnipeg's Social History," *Canadian Welfare*, Volume 25 (October, 1949), pp. 11-19.

65. For discussions of the work of the Margaret Scott Nursing Mission see Artibise, *Winnipeg*, Chapter 10; H. Macvicar, *The Story of the Mission* (Winnipeg, 1939); and K. Pettipas, "Margaret Scott and the Margaret Scott Nursing Mission, 1904-1943" (Manitoba Archives, unpublished paper, 1970).

66. For discussions of All People's Mission see Artibise, *Winnipeg*, Chapter 10; K. McNaught, *A Prophet in Politics: A Biography of J.S. Woodsworth* (Toronto, 1959); and G.N. Emery, "The Methodist Church and the 'European Foreigners' of Winnipeg: The All Peoples Mission, 1889-1914," *Manitoba Historical Society Transactions*, Series III, No. 28 (1971-1972), pp. 85-100.

67. The defeat of the provincial government of Premier R. Roblin in 1915 by the Liberals also added to the problem Roblin had long relied on the ethnic vote for support while the Liberals, led by T.C. Norris, promised to accelerate assimilation of non-British groups. See Peterson, "Ethnic and Class Politics in Manitoba," pp. 73-84. Furthermore, in the years after 1916, both the provincial Liberal and Conservative parties began to decline as effective forces. Since both had acted in their quest for political power "as bonds of society and agents of assimilation," their decline added to the general sense of malaise during this period. See Morton, *Manitoba*, p. 361 and *passim*.

68. It is impossible in a paper of this length to deal in detail with all the complex issues of this period in Winnipeg's social history. Accordingly, the following remarks are meant only to provide an outline of the more significant developments with a view to placing them in the broader context of Winnipeg's social evolution. Fortunately, several detailed studies on this period do exist. The best is Morris K. Mott, "The 'Foreign Peril': Nativism in Winnipeg,

1916-1923," unpublished M.A. thesis, University of Manitoba, 1970. I want to acknowledge my debt to this piece of work for much of the material in this section. Also useful are: Thompson, "The Prohibition Question in Manitoba, 1892-1928"; and Orlikow, "The Reform Movement in Manitoba, 1910-1920." On the Red Scare of 1919-1920 see W. Preston, *Aliens and Dissenters: Federal Suppression of Radicals, 1903-1933* (New York, 1963); and S. Cohen, "A Study in Nativism: The American Red Scare of 1919-29," *Political Science Quarterly*, Vol. LXXIX (March 1964), pp. 52-75. Winnipeg's reaction to the Red Scare is apparent by examining the following: *Winnipeg Tribune*, 29 Jan. 1919; *Winnipeg Telegram*, 9 Jan. 1919; and *Manitoba Free Press*, 6 Feb. 1919.

69. See, for example, *ibid.*, 21 Sept. 1914.

70. *Winnipeg Telegram*, 10 June 1919. On the question of anti-German propaganda see Mott, "The 'Foreign Peril'," pp. 15-17.

71. *Winnipeg Tribune*, 29 January 1915. See also Martynowych, "Ukrainian Socialist and Working-Class Movement in Manitoba, 1900-1918," pp. 24-27.

72. *Ibid.* See also Mott, "The 'Foreign Peril'," pp. 15-18.

73. *Ibid.* See also J.E. Rea, "The Politics of Conscience: Winnipeg After the Strike," Canadian Historical Association, *Historical Papers, 1971*, pp. 276-288.

74. Mott, "The 'Foreign Peril'," p. 23. See also D.C. Masters, *The Winnipeg General Strike* (Toronto, 1950), pp. 29-30; *Winnipeg Tribune*, 31 Jan. 1919.

75. Mott, "The 'Foreign Peril'," pp. 23-26.

76. See, for example, opinions expressed in the following: *Manitoba Free Press*, 20 June 1919; *Winnipeg Telegram*, 3 June 1919; and *Winnipeg Citizen*, 10 May 1919.

77. See, for example, Marunchak, *The Ukrainian Canadians*, pp. 147-150; and Mott, "The 'Foreign Peril'," *passim*.

78. *Ibid.*, pp. 23-25. Other episodes of anti-foreigner feelings are recounted in Winnipeg's newspapers during this period and in the *Canadian Annual Review*.

79. These trends have been discussed in some detail in A.F.J. Artibise, "Patterns of Population Growth and Ethnic Relationships in Winnipeg, 1874-1974," *Histoire Sociale/Social History*, Vol. IX, No. 18 (November, 1976).

80. See, for example, D.C. Masters, "The English Communities in Winnipeg and in the Eastern Townships of Quebec," in M. Wade, ed., *Regionalism in the Canadian Community, 1867-1967* (Toronto, 1969), pp. 130-159.

The Original City of Edmonton: A Derivative Prairie Urban Community

CARL BETKE

This essay explores the urban dimension of life in an early stage of the development of a Canadian prairie city. Were Edmonton not such a new city, for which census data is not yet available, it might be instructive to apply the statistical techniques recently popular in North American urban historical analyses. Their conclusions have to an interesting extent been fashioned by the nature of the data available. Nineteenth century census takers and directory publishers seem to have been captivated by a combination of questions about what people had been before arriving in the city (birthplace, ethnic origin, religious denomination, level of education) and what they became on arrival (occupation, residential location). What difference, they seem to have asked, did the urban context make? The limitations on techniques of mathematical manipulation of such historical data raise a significant methodological puzzle: whether to study a whole large urban population and suffer criticism of sampling reliability, or to work with data for every soul in a smaller community and suffer criticism of the attempt to generalize for large cities.[1] Again the tantalizing question is evident: how to comprehend the collective meaning of an urban society.

The city is of course a special kind of community, or set of associations, to the point that it is sometimes distinguished from the concept of community altogether. In ways which affect both intimate personal interaction and neighbourhood life, urban community implies the consolidation of groups in

SOURCE: This is a revised version of the original which appeared in Alan F.J. Artibise, ed., *Town and City: Aspects of Western Canadian Urban Development* (Regina: Canadian Plains Research Center, University of Regina, 1981), pp. 309-45. Reprinted by permission of the author and editor.

392

a massive project. The cultivation of a habit of voluntary association and the technology of mass communication were important pre-conditions for modern urban development, Richard D. Brown has argued from the Massachusetts example, on the one hand to recognize and organize diverse individual interests, and on the other hand to permit their broader coordination. In studies of the nineteenth century formation of particular small cities in the eastern United States, Michael Frisch and Stuart Blumin have emphasized the practical requirements amidst growing population density for agencies to administer public services and voluntary activities which in the process promoted the conceptual acceptance of an abstract, symbolic urban community, beyond that felt in personal relationships. By the end of the century in an English city, according to Stephen Yeo, many traditional associational activities, especially of leisure, were subject to the mass production and widespread marketing approaches of corporate business, extending the nature of urban community beyond individual cities. In Canada, J.M.S. Careless and Gilbert Stelter have both sought to divide studies of conditions within a city from studies of systems of cities; yet close attention to the first must come up constantly against the second.[2] Investigation of life in a particular Canadian city is a study of Careless' metropolitan theme from the inside out, illuminating the conjunction of local experience with transcendent organizational patterns.

Life in modern North American cities has clearly been affected by a collective spirit, whatever the internal conflicts. Sociologist Leo Schnore has gone so far as to suggest that one may best understand an urban entity as a social organism. A discussion of the origins of western Canadian urban social welfare by John Taylor hints at the degree to which established cities were webs of organization.[3] Those citizens who did not organize themselves adequately to cope with the demands of the community gradually became objects of attention for organizers activating the concept of public or social welfare. The very term emphasizes a dedication to the welfare not so much of individuals as of the organism which they comprised. Misfits often seemed not just peripheral but burdensome, sometimes even dangerous. To put it another way, without commitment (however unwitting) to community, there would be no concern for welfare on a group level, only one to one concerns among individuals. In the study of Edmonton development, one gains the overwhelming impression that individual pursuits and the quality of individual lives came irreversibly to depend on the quality of the urban community. A tyranny of community was exerted, its elimination unimaginable.

To isolate Edmonton in 1906 does not, of course, illustrate the pattern over time, but it does provide an example of the collective process getting underway with future commitments so strong they would not later be easily escaped. The basic requirements for urban community were there: a substantial influx of people responding to a perceived demand for their occupational services. Complexity of occupational specialization in itself needs economic co-ordination in order to work, but beyond that the accompanying concentration of population in close residential proximity forces other levels of cooperation. The stage Edmonton was at in 1906 permits a close look at how pressure for utility and health services, the necessity to resolve sectional tensions, the existence of fraternal and service associations, and mass recreation all contributed to the rapid consolidation of an urban community in Edmonton with characteristics similar to those found in many other North American cities.

I

Edmonton in 1906 had changed dramatically from its nineteenth century village state, and the principal dynamic was immigration. In Edmonton city were counted 11,167 residents; in the attached town of Strathcona situated across the North Saskatchewan River, 2,921: in all, over 14,000 citizens of whom four-fifths were newcomers since the Klondike gold rush of 1898. The late nineteenth century stability suggested by the presence of equal numbers of males and females was replaced by the frontier condition indicated by a clear majority of men over women. Nearly 60 percent of the population was male in 1906 (see Table I). Not just the expansion, but also the expansionism of the place is strikingly illustrated by the escalation which had taken place in the number of men engaged in property development. Real estate agencies (73), building contractors (43), building material merchants (23), and insurance agencies (29) dominated Edmonton business. Expansion of population and accommodation was showing a very specific source of profit. The booming urban centres were set in the midst of a prospering agricultural countryside where two or three times as many farmers laboured in 1906 as in 1901; still, the city — particularly Edmonton proper — outdistanced the country in population growth rate.[4]

The economic development of Edmonton in 1906 was very much a story of railways and real estate. The special advantage acquired by Edmonton which was the main foundation for the rising property values was railway centrality. Before 1902 local rail service, namely the Calgary and Edmonton Railway operated by the CPR, terminated at Strathcona. By 1906, however, not only was there a rail connection of the C&E Railway to the north side, but there were also two new incipient transcontinentals chugging to the Edmonton side of the river: the Canadian Northern Railway of William Mackenzie and Donald Mann, and the Grand Trunk Pacific. Not to be left entirely out of the more northerly east-west traffic, the CPR in the same year constructed its own parallel line from Winnipeg through Saskatoon to Wetaskiwin, forty miles south of Edmonton, where it could connect with the C&E Railway, making Strathcona the terminus.[5] Thus stimulated, real estate agencies multiplied, urban land costs soared and surrounding agricultural land was speedily filled. Sawmills expanded, lumber prices jumped repeatedly, and the demand for coal brought prosperity for another local industry.[6] The first Alberta legislature, dominated by governing Liberals from northern Alberta, delivered to the city the permanent site of the provincial capital. The new Liberal Premier, Strathcona's A.C. Rutherford, quietly negotiated the purchase for the province of a south side land package where he was determined to establish the University of Alberta.[7] The boom created a demand for manpower, and that portion of the general immigration stream which was diverted to the city introduced an ethnic shift in the population along with the growth of a working class population. Prosperity was accompanied by the beginning of social differentiations which would require some effort to overcome.

TABLE I

POPULATION BY SEXES IN EDMONTON, 1901–1911

Year	Male	Female	Total
1901	1,374	1,252	2,626
1906	6,652	4,515	11,167
1911	13,933	10,967	24,900

SOURCES: *Censuses of Canada,* 1901 and 1911. *Census of Population and Agriculture of the Northwest Provinces, 1906.*

Despite the entry of more European immigrants into Edmonton than ever before, the city was, if anything, even more Anglo-Saxon than it had been before the turn of the century. This apparent oddity is explained by the relatively static situation of the French-speaking population, whose strength of more than 500 made up a decreasing proportion of the total. Putting a generous construction on the matter, one might credit to the French population five percent of the whole, whereas all other minority ethnic groups together might already add up to ten percent. Of the latter element, those with Germanic names made up roughly half. These would presumably have been born in German, Austro-Hungarian, American or Canadian territories. A German Community was clearly visible: there were German

Lutheran and Baptist clergymen serving both sides of the river, a thriving German "Edelweiss" Club, a German book store and a locally published German language newspaper called the *Alberta Herold*.

Other groups had so far been almost as unnoticeable institutionally as they were numerically — two or three hundred people of Slavic or other east European extractions, fewer than a hundred each of Scandinavians, Jews, East Asians, and Dutch. But Ukrainians and Jews had just created religious congregations, while the more all-embracing Catholic congregation found it necessary to arrange sermons in seven languages — French, English, German, Polish, Galician, Ruthenian, and Cree. Laundry and restaurant services were favourite and obvious Chinese enterprises, and the Chinese were inevitably curiosities of special interest. Fascination about what might be going on in the back rooms of Chinese restaurants was as keen in 1906 as it had been in the early 1890s.[8]

TABLE II

POPULATION GROWTH IN EDMONTON AND STRATHCONA, 1901–1911

	1901	1906	1911
Edmonton	2,626	11,167	24,900
Strathcona	1,550	2,921	5,579

SOURCES: See Table I.

The Ukrainian population was recognizable mainly in the city's Catholic organizations. Basilian missionaries from late 1902 on attracted Ukrainians to St. Joachim's and Ste. Anne's parishes with Ukrainian language masses and music, and they stimulated the construction of the separate Ukrainian St. Josaphat's church in 1904. In individual homes were established two or three "Chytalnia" societies, in which merchant, real estate dealer and developer Paul Rudyk seems to have been instrumental. Rudyk was a complex individual, however, whose home was also apparently the site for the origin of a Ukrainian Labour Fraternity ("Rivnist").[9] The Edmonton Hebrew Association was even newer, founded by ten Jewish Edmontonians only in August 1906 under the direction of the clothing merchants Abraham Cristall and William Diamond with the assistance of newly arrived Hyman Goldstick. Goldstick had been brought from Toronto specifically to take on the formal teaching and religious leadership duties for the Association and the Edmonton Hebrew Congregation of Beth Israel it fostered. To Goldstick fell the chore of uniting the Edmonton Jewish peoples of sundry geographic origins and religious traditions in the common cause.[10]

The French-speaking community, despite its proportional decline, occupied a far different kind of minority position in Edmonton. Its leadership seemed to react to the diminishing proportion of French people in Edmonton by its most determined organizational effort. Close social contact was maintained by the elite, while Saint Jean Baptiste Day was made an event of fellowship encompassing French-speaking Catholics of the entire district. The memory of the 1905 struggle by Edmonton's St. Jean Baptiste Society to maintain French constitutional rights in education in the new province of Alberta seems to have sustained a vigorous community for some years to follow. A new publication, *Le Courrier de L'Ouest*, was founded by general merchant Prosper Edmond Lessard and Dr. Phillippe Roy, the former soon to become a Liberal provincial cabinet minister, the latter a Liberal senator from the date of Alberta provincial inauguration in September 1905.[11]

These two individuals were examples of a second difference between the French and other minority ethnic groups. The French presence in Edmonton and the surrounding district went back early enough that some had become prominent professionals or businessmen who took their residential place among the substantial dwellings of the west end dominated by a prosperous English-speaking set. Few among the other ethnic newcomers found their homes in that relatively exclusive neighbourhood in 1906; most of them were labourers or tradesmen. Except for the traditional clustering of French-speaking people around St. Joachim's parish in the far west, the city (excluding Strathcona) divided pretty definitely into more and less well-to-do sections. West of First Street, especially the first six streets, and mostly south of Jasper Avenue, close to the North Saskatchewan River banks, was the domain of prosperous businessmen, professionals and senior civil servants. East of First Street and mainly north of Jasper Avenue were the labourers, tradesmen, marginal businessmen and alien ethnic newcomers. Pretty well three-quarters of Edmonton lawyers and doctors, financiers and senior civil servants, as well as a large majority of businessmen, lived in the west end. A larger proportion of the prosperous lived in the east end, however, than could be found of the less well-off in the west end, for many established veterans continued to reside in the area which had once been the village core, but which was now rarely chosen by well-heeled newcomers. Some of the older residents in the east end, however, were less than pleased with the transformation they thought they detected taking place.[12]

The concept of an urban elite[13] had taken hold in Edmonton, though naturally different observers held different opinions about its membership. For our purposes, analysis of three separate sources suggests sufficient overlap to permit certain important generalizations. Biographical sources[14] yield the names of some 175 publicly successful men (mostly north-siders) representing about six percent of greater Edmonton families, but possibly representative of a wider commercial and professional upper class. They were occupationally quite distinct, according to a fairly predictable pattern. Almost nine-tenths of those recorded were directing urban services, as opposed to manufacturing industries: professions (29 percent), commerce (14 percent), real estate and financial services (14 percent), construction-related enterprises (8 percent), assorted other service businesses (10 percent), and the newly-arrived phenomenon, government (11 percent). Government positions in fact outnumbered proprietors of agriculture-related manufacturing and sales enterprises (9 percent).

Members of the elite came as outsiders perceiving vacuums they might successfully fill. Better than three-quarters of them came from birthplaces in other parts of Canada; more than half from Ontario. Most of the remainder were born in Great Britain. Their parents' origins appear to confirm that pattern, with a slight reinforcement of the British background. Their Christian denominationalism was more or less of the Ontario and maritime pattern, more than two-fifths Presbyterian, one-quarter Anglican, one-sixth Methodist and only one-tenth Catholic. These Canadian Protestants grew up mainly in modest rural or village situations, but definitely not in urban poverty. Half of them had some education other than secondary school: in universities (particularly professional schools), trade schools, business colleges or apprenticeship programs. Relatively young (average age 40), but not straight from their education or training, most had left their original occupations and adult locations or had tried two separate livelihoods before arriving in Edmonton or Strathcona. The mean of their years in Edmonton was nine, but the majority had come after the turn of the century.

A second way to isolate an urban elite is to observe members at their ease. During the Christmas season of 1905 there appeared for the first time in Edmonton *The Saturday News*, with a striking and substantial women's section, *The Mirror*.[15] The subsection entitled "Home and Society" was during 1906 devoted to details of the entertainments indulged in principally by those women and the men who associated with one another in the guise of Edmonton's embryo elite. In the columns filled with elaborate description of "At Homes," "recherche" luncheons, parties featuring the card game known as "500," private skating parties, dances, downtown luncheons for the men, the affairs of a genteel cricket club, and the receptions and grand balls of the new Lieutenant-Governor, two things can be perceived. First, these were perfectly intelligent people, who no doubt thought of themselves as civic leaders, and who presented these spectacles in full knowledge of their artificiality. The very care taken to create a veneer of social refinement, to elevate their style of entertainment above the norm, as they thought it, provides a measure of their sense of special importance. And second, a list of some 180 Edmonton and Strathcona family units can be made from the names mentioned in *The Mirror's* columns in 1906. As in the biographical sample, professionals were predominant, particularly doctors and lawyers, while bank and other finance executives, and some senior officials of the federal and new provincial civic services, also stood out. Of the community's businessmen, once again, those associated with property development — contractors, hardware merchants, real estate and insurance agents — were the best represented. Their residential focus was even more definitely in the west end of the city than that of the biographical sample and, for the small group (one-quarter) whose names were also in that sample, biographical details were roughly the same.

A third approach to identifying an Edmonton elite is to study the membership of the exclusive Edmonton Club.[16] For the 106 Edmonton and (very few) Strathcona members in 1906, occupational and residential characteristics corresponded closely with those of the other two clusters. The biographical overlap for this group was only two-fifths, but for those on both this and the biographical lists the proportion of Anglicans (two-fifths) and Catholics (one-quarter) rose at the expense of Presbyterians (less than one-quarter) in the biographical proportions. Though that was the only notable distinction, the overlap among all three groups here isolated was very small, between one-eighth and one-fifth. What is to be made of this lack of unaminity in the identification of Edmonton's socially most important citizens? Perhaps that in so rapidly expanding a centre it was not yet easy to sort out the socially superior from the ordinary, especially given the short residency in Edmonton enjoyed by the majority. The task was not made any simpler by the relatively homogeneous and primarily non-elitist backgrounds of the contenders for the honours. If, however, the question of the community's leadership had been thrown somewhat open by the rapid influx of newcomers, it would still have been obvious that the opportunity did not extend to alien immigrants with a poor grasp of the English language, or to those of poor education and reduced means. A recognizable chasm was being developed by the city's prosperity between two distinguishable sections of the population.

II

A booming economy and multiplication of the urban population exerted unique pressures for collective approaches to a host of new problems. The city's two basic solutions were not exactly innovations, but were borrowed from available examples for their aptness to the condition of rapid growth: public ownership of utilities and a professional executive branch of civic government. Strathcona's response to the situation was dependent upon the nature of Edmonton's; it will be considered separately later. For Edmonton citizens, the task of coping with common requirements was in 1906 understood to comprehend the provision of the following services: modern streets and sidewalks, electricity, telephones, water and sewerage, a street railway, parks, education and, reluctantly, some supervision of public health. On the other hand, obvious growth encouraged optimistic visions of proliferating future good fortune. Civic administration was managed, therefore, not only to cope with an increasing magnitude in collective problems of utility and welfare services after they arose, but also to prepare for the continuing boom to come.

Moreover, the expectation of prevailing growth suggested an apparently logical way to finance urban utility advances: property taxation. Actually there were further implications to property assessment beyond simple taxation. High assessments and low taxation rates were believed to accomplish good civic advertising to attract new business and to boost the limits of civic borrowing. Net Edmonton assessment after exemptions was in 1906 set at more than $17,000,000 which, in the conventional wisdom, permitted borrowing power to 20 percent or $3,400,000. That the city in the fall of 1906 had a debenture liability of just over $1,000,000, half of it in sinking funds, could therefore be interpreted as a "splendid condition" against the possible limits of borrowing power.[17]

Some rather imposing costs could in this atmosphere pass as routine, like a year-end commitment to nearly $300,000 worth of future paying. After 1902 Edmonton's electric light and power had been municipally administered precisely for the purpose of ensuring continued expansion of the service without running out of funds. By 1906, therefore, this public utility could display fine operating profits as long as capital costs of ceaseless construction and equipment purchase were kept in a widely-separated accounting column. It was possible on the one hand to cut power rates in the middle of the year while on the other hand concurrently adding to the city's debt by increasing the number of arc street lights. When a potential plan to build a hydro-electric power development on the North Saskatchewan River fifty miles west of the city threatened to require a capital outlay of $1,000,000 and annual operating funds of $140,000, it is difficult to say which sum caused the more consternation. Capital debt was one thing; operating expenses which would be covered by high power prices was likely the key factor in scuttling the proposal.[18]

The telephone system was another utility which the municipality had taken over from private operators after their original ten-year charter was concluded in 1903. The twin demands for expansion and modernization enabled city council in 1906 to pass a $65,000 bylaw for a new automatic

Jasper Avenue looking west, 1906. (*Courtesy of Provincial Archives of Alberta*)

system with a landslide majority in a poor ratepayers' voting turnout.[19] Nor was there any fuss in July about undertaking the immense financial and managerial burden of a $300,000 expenditure on "the largest public work ever projected in Edmonton, or [for] that matter by any municipality between Winnipeg and the Pacific coast": major extensions of water and sewerage pipelines. The lack of disputation here was even more remarkable considering that the necessity for replacing mains with much larger pipes and for installing a new three million gallon electrically driven pump had tripled what began as a mere $113,000 estimate. Council discussions of sewerage and water plans, however, were typically characterized by opposition to "temporizing" with construction that would be overloaded immediately, and by calls for "the best, not the cheapest" systems to last 50 or 100 years.[20]

It would perhaps be difficult to argue against the importance of proper water distribution and sewerage disposal in relation to sanitation and the reduction of disease. The early history of plans for a street railway, on the other hand, bespoke pure civic and commercial ambition. Though from 1894 to 1905 an Edmonton street railway proved too grand a project for successful private accomplishment, so determined was the Edmonton council to have the system that private failure was interpreted not as reason to abandon the project but as justification for making it a public one. Most of 1906 was consumed by a consulting engineer's study of the likely cost of a twelve-block stretch of street railway along Jasper Avenue (the main street). His report in October predicted that installation of track and purchase of equipment would require over $100,000. The visiting general manager of the Canadian Bank of Commerce thought a current typhoid epidemic emphasized more legitimate fields for municipal expenditure, but ratepayers remained unaffected and in December overwhelmingly approved purchase of street rails and trolley wire for some six miles of street railway. It was the first step to a small system which became operational in 1908.[21]

It was probably no accident either in the halcyon expansion years after city incorporation that the council was frequently presented with offers of new property for park land. Quite apart from any profit the generous donors might earn or deny themselves in the direct sale, there was no doubt that firm establishment of future park land in any area would improve real estate prices in the vicinity. When on one occasion some private citizens took the initiative to secure land for parkland until the city had time to act officially, this was judged a gesture of Edmonton's "public spirited citizens" of the same variety, significantly, as those responsible for securing the city's first bridge and the Canadian Northern Railway depot. On a larger scale, a Board of Trade interested in attracting new business by presenting a favourable picture of residential amenities did not hesitate, in November 1905, to put pressure on city council to extend its park land. One of the Board's suggestions was that council assist the financially strapped Edmonton Industrial Exhibition Association by purchasing the land on which it paid rent to Messrs. McDougall and Secord, successful local businessmen. In June burgesses approved a $46,000 expenditure to obtain for parks 100 acres far to the west and about 250 acres in two eastern river lot packages. Before the end of the year they approved a further $60,000 outlay to purchase the large Exhibition Association grounds, an acquisition which was completed in the following year.[22]

The conclusion cannot easily be avoided that Edmontonians were being loaded with a current and future debt burden with startling rapidity and long-term consequences. A negative sort of collective urban interest was being imposed on Edmonton's people. The point has been made often enough that, in Edmonton as elsewhere before the Great War, shared urban utilities would not only overcome some of the difficulties of residential density, but also satisfy businessmen and speculators in urban and rural property who had opportunities to extract private profit from urban expansion.[23] As long as a bright future beckoned, it was apparently easy to believe that it would handle the mounting debt as well. One of the reasons this cynical view is so easy to hold is the hesitancy with which unprofitable health and social welfare services were approached. Only in 1906 did the requirements of public health and fire prevention finally move council to accept city commissioner's recommendations that "horses and a scavening outfit be purchased and maintained as a street cleaning department," and that a sanitary inspector be appointed (with multiple extra duties as caretaker and nurse of the isolation hospital and quarantine officer). Endemic smallpox, malaria and diptheria were not reason enough to build a decent isolation hospital; it took a typhoid epidemic in 1906 to frighten officials into action. The city's doctors pressed the city to enforce its by-law requiring connections of residences to the city's water and sewer systems; meanwhile council was embarrassed to discover some city-owned houses not only with typhoid cases but also with no sewer and water connections. The epidemic no doubt also increased the overwhelming majority by which the money by-law for an isolation hospital passed in August, even as it conveniently calmed east-end objections to the proposed east-end site.[24]

The transition of hospital administration from private and voluntary to public support and care in other than emergency conditions was not nearly complete by 1906. In Edmonton the voluntary Women's Aid Society of the public hospital was a firmly-entrenched institution with more than 130 members and the desire to be bigger. The Society was still the major fund raiser for the hospital's operations, even if its members did worry about the prospects for voluntarily clearing the hospital of operational debt. At the end of the year, however, plans were underway for the city to build a new public hospital. Rapid expansion of health services threatened to overreach the capacity of the Women's Aid Society to raise enough health care funds privately. By way of contrast, in 1906 Strathcona was just equipping its first tiny temporary hospital in a six-bedroom house, and a Strathcona Ladies' Hospital Aid Society was just being formed by wives of some of Strathcona's prominent citizens. And in terms of social welfare, neither municipality had progressed further than the relief committee method of handling the most extreme financial need.[25] But the plans for a new public hospital and an isolation hospital indicated how health emergencies could push even reluctant leaders into costly health and welfare services.

Education was a far better accepted responsibility. The four school boards (public and separate) of the two municipalities had but one overriding concern in 1906: to provide enough school space for the multiplying pupil enrolment. Their deliberations were uniformly about building programs. Otherwise, even salary adjustments provoked no great controversy: trustees themselves observed that teachers dissatisfied with the inadequate remuneration solved their problem by leaving the profession. Thus, the manifold opportunity in boom-time Edmonton worked its own pressure on the school boards to raise teachers' salaries.[26]

The same unusual opportunity reduced aldermen's anxiety to induce new businesses to locate in the city by offering financial advantages of lower taxes and utility rates or free land. Faced with several applications, councillors eventually worked out a meagre policy to offer water, power and light at cost. There was one enormous exception in 1906. To civic leaders starved for direct transcontinental railway connections from the expectant days of 1881 to 1905, there was no hesitation about bonusing railway companies. For the Grand Trunk Pacific Railway, Edmonton council had city burgesses approve a bonus of $100,000 together with long-term tax exemptions in 1905 even before surveys were completed. That offer went into effect in November 1906, when the necessary federal order-in-council approved the GTP routes through Edmonton, but not before civic officials had spent several more months arranging land purchases to open the desired right of way. Otherwise, Edmonton's council clearly preferred the much more discreet and limited cost of civic grants to the Board of Trade to promote Edmonton opportunities by pamphlets, newspaper advertisements and paid agents at eastern fall fairs.[27]

Nevertheless, Edmonton city council paid its Board of Trade proportionally far more than the Strathcona town council paid its Board for similar services. This was a good indication of the limits on Strathcona boosterism which made all the more believable Edmonton Mayor Charles May's boast that Edmonton and Strathcona would soon form a single more imposing metropolis.[28] For that was the essential difference in the collective Strathcona response to urban service requirements: smaller Strathcona had an alternative not open to Edmonton, simply to attach itself in whole or in part to the larger urban neighbour, to join another community rather than create a separate one. That alternative seems to have gained respectability during 1905 and 1906 when both the CNR and GTP chose to locate terminals in Edmonton rather than in Strathcona.[29]

Strathcona council was left with the CPR, to which it belatedly offered land and tax-exemption inducements to build impressive new terminal facilities and the long-surveyed high level bridge to Edmonton.[30] But even this attempt to improve its traditional rail connections southward had, in the wake of the sudden Canadian Northern and GTP advances into Edmonton, not nearly the impact or purpose it might have had earlier during the period of Strathcona's railway advantage. Moreover, a CPR high level bridge to Edmonton would provide another though more indirect transcontinental route for Edmonton freight besides those of the two competitors. The inevitable result after its eventual completion would be co-operation among the three lines and an additional impetus to amalgamation of the two communities. Hence, promotion of the high level bridge was an ironic response to the disturbing realization that Strathcona as a separate entity had been left out of the northern transcontinental railways. Strathcona council in the fall of 1906 authorized a railway approach route to the proposed bridge site. At that time the citizens of Strathcona, whether oblivious of the consequences or resigned to the inevitable, were pressing even more forcefully than the citizens of Edmonton for addition of a non-railway "traffic floor" level on the bridge.[31]

It was the Strathcona Board of Trade which first sent resolutions in April to the provincial and federal governments requesting healthy contributions to the expected $311,000 extra cost for a traffic floor. As the Edmonton Board of Trade discussed its own endorsation of those resolutions, a leading Strathcona advocate urged the move as a morale booster for a petition circulating in Strathcona. The petition recommended that Strathcona ratepayers take upon themselves fifteen percent of the traffic floor cost up to a maximum of $50,000. In short order that petition, with Premier Rutherford's name at the head of a list of 255, was presented to Strathcona council. When action was not sufficiently prompt a "committee of leading citizens" which included ex-Mayor Davies called on council personally early in May and extracted a promise of a public meeting on the issue. At that public meeting no argument was offered against the traffic floor. The only modification cherished by Mayor W.H. Sheppard was to saddle the

Alberta and Canadian governments with the full cost. A committee of eight, including the mayor, the ex-mayor, Board of Trade President Orlando Bush, and Alderman J.M. Douglas, was created to accomplish the project. When council appeared to relax its efforts through 1906, the Board of Trade kept up pressure by delegation. While satisfactory arrangements were not achieved until 1910, it is not possible to see in the 1906 controversy the least sign of resistance to the submergence of Strathcona identity in an integrated transportation and business system for greater Edmonton.

There were in fact other signs that leading Strathconans now saw Strathcona's future in tandem with Edmonton's. It is true that the old dream of city status was pushed to its conclusion toward the end of 1906, culminating in city incorporation in March 1907, but there were short-term practical considerations to that: for qualified towns, city incorporation gave additional financial power, which was the main argument for it offered by the *Strathcona Plaindealer* and the Board of Trade. That this move did not indicate aggressive championship of a separate Strathcona is confirmed on the one hand by an accompanying failure to solicit assisted location of new businesses in Strathcona, and on the other hand by the trend to share utilities with Edmonton. In several fields — electric power, street lighting, water and sewerage, streets and sidewalks, parks — Strathcona already had systems which its council continued to maintain.[32] In the expensive fields of transportation and communication, however, co-operation with Edmonton seemed to have certain advantages.

Associated with the idea of a high level bridge was the project of the Strathcona Radial Tramway Company, the majority of whose directors were from Edmonton. Since an October 1904 incorporation, the company's intention was to create an integrated system connecting Strathcona, Edmonton and Fort Saskatchewan, with the possibility of future radial extension up to eighty miles from 1904 town boundaries. In September 1906 the directors sought a thirty-year franchise and a ten- to twelve-year taxation exemption from both Strathcona and Edmonton in return "after a time" for sharing profits with the municipalities. The significance of Strathcona council's acceptance of the scheme in principle was not that any action followed immediately — in fact it did not for several years — but that Strathcona officials raised no fierce objection to so close an integration with the commercially more powerful neighbour.[33] The same was true for development of Strathcona's telephone system. Since 1901 it had been an adjunct of the Edmonton system which, since 1903, had been run by the municipality of Edmonton as a public utility. In 1906, when advances in telephone technology and population growth made the old system seem as inadequate in Strathcona as in Edmonton, one alternative for Strathcona was to develop its own modern system. But council swiftly decided to negotiate with Edmonton for the cheaper expedient: simple extension of the new Edmonton automatic system throughout Strathcona according to the terms of a fifteen-year franchise.[34]

Disappointments over rail-lines and strain on Strathcona's capacity to provide urban services were insistently highlighting the easier solution of amalgamation with larger Edmonton at precisely the same time as Edmonton's corporate approach to utility expansion was undergoing extraordinary escalation. Edmonton municipal council became increasingly and irrevocably important to its citizens, not only as expansion emphasized the need for physical and health services, but also as the civic debt mounted. To discharge that debt must mean the continuation or adaptation of the institutions through which it had been accumulated. The eager acquisition of utilities was a financial commitment of the community as a whole; the community as a whole must discharge the cost over a long period of time. Furthermore, the community already had a taste of the way this process was inevitably extended by the requirements for maintenance and improvement of some services. The persistence of problems like epidemic disease and poverty was forcing reluctant community attention to public health and welfare, a commitment equally difficult to retreat from once entered. A corollary to the effect on collective financial commitment was the perception of a need for more sophisticated administrative machinery.

Certain Edmonton leaders were instrumental in adapting the executive branch to cope with the increasing civic business. One of these was William Short, who in 1904 had imposed his ideas on the charter of city incorporation. What he proposed was not unique, but borrowed from recommendations of Ontario municipal government experts, especially former Toronto solicitor W.H. Biggar. The general point was to perfect a form of government which would temper the democracy of an elected council with institutions promoting efficient corporate administration and planning — to modify the voices of individual citizens with the bureaucracy of an organic entity. A town the size of Edmonton could not immediately be said to require the separation of legislative and administrative branches of government. The town had begun with a small council and only one commissioner other than the mayor; but it could be and was argued that provision in this form was farsightedly made for the future. "Business efficiency" characterized also the nature of aldermanic representation. The town opted, not for the ward system (which had been judged corrupt by municipal experts surveying the influence of sectors of the population in major American and central Canadian cities), but for the system in which aldermen represented the city as a whole. In 1906 Alderman W. A.

Griesbach made the Edmonton application unmistakably explicit: "where there is a foreign element, it is often difficult to find a suitable representative."[35]

While Strathcona would at the end of 1906 make plans to follow Edmonton's example, in Edmonton not all aldermen appreciated Short's outlook on the value of the new arrangements. In 1906 — as, indeed, in years to come — Edmonton city council struggled to accommodate the apparently conflicting jurisdiction of the commissioners' branch. The broader issue arose from an unedifying debate about the competence of City Engineer J.H. Hargreaves. Whether or not to dispense with his services, on the basis of charges that he had supervised some cement work of inferior quality, and had grossly underestimated the costs of certain sewerage works, was a question paradoxically solved by creating a new Commissioner of Public Works position for Hargreaves while appointing another chief engineer to work under him. Hargreaves' argument that the expansion of public works in the city's priorities created undue pressure on administrators was obviously a telling one. Here was an advance in the framework of the 1904 charter arrangements: to the first commissioner (Secretary-Treasurer G.J. Kinnaird) was not added a second; to the first all-encompassing correspondence and financial duties of the old town clerk were now added the boom city responsibilities of a Public Works Commissioner to extend utilities as rapidly as possible.[36]

Sorting out the administrative jurisdictions of the new officials occupied several months of wearying squabbles. At about the same time the commissioners were engaged in a confrontation with the voluntary fire brigade — a problem which they solved by replacing the voluntary firemen with a smaller but full-time force. Alderman Griesbach was, however, an "old boy" of the voluntary brigade, and he did his futile best to reinstate the voluntary system.[37] For varying reasons, therefore, some aldermen were in 1906 discontented with the separation of council and commissioners' functions. They stimulated a full debate of the underlying principles. Late in April the new provincial legislature found itself studying a number of amendments to the Edmonton Charter proposed by the Edmonton council, among them two designed to increase council control over the commissioners. One would have reduced the two-thirds majority council required to dismiss a commissioner. The other would have taken all administrative powers from the commissioners and vested them in the council with the latter retaining the option of delegating authority to the commissioners.

As Alderman Griesbach argued the case before the legislative committee of the whole, the question was whether commissioners' powers should be derived from the legislature as embodied in the Charter, or from the city council; as it was, he claimed, the commissioners were out of public control.

Members of the legislature, including Attorney General Cross, himself an Edmonton law partner of William Short, seemed inclined to believe petty quibbling undermined the Edmonton council's principles. Cross' legal partner, Short, was present as well to make with confidence the same points he had in 1904. Business involving $800,000 and more, contended Short, required consistent planning and executive administration. The council changed composition each year and aldermen had not sufficient time to spend on administration. Indeed, he observed, "the better the aldermen the less time they have," for they would properly be addressing their attention to legislating policy. Better that administrative details be left to commissioners responsible to the elected council but free of undue "cajolery." It was the system of the joint stock company that Short advocated, with councillors in the place of directors, commissioners in the place of managers. The amendments requested had not been placed before a public meeting in the city nor, Short was certain, would the businessmen of Edmonton either request or accept them. Noting little urgency, Cross commented that more general municipal legislation was in any case due next year, and the amendments died in committee.

Along the same line, both J.R. Boyle (once an alderman and now a Liberal MLA) and the *Edmonton Bulletin* editor viewed the city as a twenty million dollar "gigantic stock company." For the ratepayers who constituted the stockholders, it was ludicrous that city council as the board of directors should consume so much time debating "a six foot plank sidewalk on the east side of steenth street from Beautiful avenue to Black Stump lane." A general manager should handle the details and, on the basis of regular supervisors' reports, issue monthly statements to council to permit sensible policy decisions.[38]

Nevertheless, in November Alderman Griebach made a suprising suggestion in the form of a by-law to raise the number of aldermen from eight to ten. Twelve would be even better, he argued, both to lighten onerous workloads and also to permit institution of the apparently popular ward system. But if Griesbach seemed to desert his earlier elitist principles in order to counteract increasing bureaucratic power, most of his colleagues maintained theirs. Alderman Bellamy observed wryly that Griesbach's proposition would mean fifty aldermen when the city reached a population of 75,000. Though Griesbach had minority support, he lost his second voluntarist alternative to a paid and expanding civil service.[39] The fact was that debates on the bureacratic arrangement were resolved in 1906 in favour of the streamlined corporate approach to civic business, for the cause of council irritability — increasing work — was simultaneously the chief argument for continuation of commissioners' services.

III

The city's plunge into massive public works did not fail to stimulate some dissent which brought to the attention of civic leaders the existence of Edmonton's social diversity. Some of the outcomes of the boom and the city's corporate response briefly aggravated distinctions in the populace which were both highlighted and dissipated during the year-end municipal elections. On the surface, the strain expressed in the electoral framework was an east-west division of opinions, but there were several layers of complexity. There was some hint of a clash among ethnic groups and between the deprived and the privileged. Signs of animosity for west-enders on the part of east-enders embodied not simply business rivalries but also other frictions which would in later years be aired by labour or "populist" representatives.

In 1906, however, the form organized labour would take in Edmonton was just being hammered into shape, largely because of determined organizational work by the Canadian Trades and Labour Congress and the American Federation of Labour. Late in August travelling organizers of those two associations rallied Edmonton tradesmen and labourers in a series of meetings. They argued not only formation of new unions (there were probably not yet a dozen in Edmonton) and emphasis on the "union label," but also affiliation of the new Edmonton Trades and Labour Council (organized in December 1905) with the Trades and Labour Congress. The resulting enthusiasm carried through the ET and LC's first Labour Day program, but it proved premature to attempt collective participation in the December municipal elections. The ET and LC delegates decided against complicating further the crowded electoral scene.[40]

Working people's concerns were therefore subsumed in the east-west controversy in the last half of 1906. That confrontation derived substantial impetus from fall railway affairs. First veteran alderman Thomas Bellamy reacted with heated animosity to the city's detailed agreement with the GTP in which, among other things, he foresaw problems of citizen access to established east-end streets across which the GTP would be permitted to build. West-enders like Griesbach displayed benign complacency during Bellamy's onslaught,[41] but the tables were neatly turned a few weeks later when it came time to consider the simple request from the CPR for permission to cross several streets on the level from the north end of the proposed high level bridge. These were in the middle of the fashionable west-end residential area.

During the debate of this proposition over the next three months, the Board of Trade was very clear about its recommendations: to force the CPR to cross in the east rather than the west end, a solution condemned by one

View of West End residential area, 1906. (*Courtesy of Provincial Archives of Alberta*)

alderman as blatantly "saving west end property at the deliberate expense of east end property." Not only Board spokesman William Short, but also the leader of a bitter west-end committee of ratepayers, prominent merchant and ex-Mayor John A. McDougall, delved deep into Edmonton business hostility toward the CPR. If the location was not to be moved, then Short, the Board of Trade, and Alderman Griesbach, among others, looked for "an abatement of nuisances" and some way to avoid cutting main streets "to the detriment of the established interests." At the very least, west-enders looked for a complex combination of subway and overhead bypasses, no use of whistles or bells in the vicinity, and the search for "smokeless coal" or "other inoffensive motive power."[42] It would be a long time yet before the details were settled. For the time being one cannot help noticing that east-enders — even those many with long residence and memory in Edmonton — saw no comparable need to refer to old CPR wounds in discussion of the high level bridge location.

They were far less sanguine about the council's selection of a site for the proposed isolation hospital. No sooner had it been made than an east-end property owner objected that he did not want a "pest house" so near the lots he owned. A yard-long east-end petition which followed succeeded in postponing the decision, but other resentments accumulated. A vitriolic letter to the editor of the *Bulletin* in August decried the arrogant assumption of residential superiority in the west end and condemned efforts to move the CPR bridge to the east end. The writer was not the first to recommend an east-end rather than the chosen west-end location for the planned parliament buildings. In November, F.W. Brown, proprietor of the Hub Cigar Store, fostered the notion of a straight east-end aldermanic ticket and listed the year's grievances in vehement style. "If I had may way," he told a *Bulletin* interviewer, "not a man west of First street would go into next year's council, and this business of beautifying the west end with lovely boulevards and elegant drives while labor is too scarce to comply with the hundreds of applications for street connections by east enders should stop." He deplored plans for the expensive new sewer project which seemed to him to place ninety percent of new lateral lines west of First street, and he had similar ideas on the planned streetcar line and paving. He was outraged that the garbage incinerator was slated for construction "right in the middle of the residential section of the east end":

> They tell us that this garbage doesn't smell; that the plant will be a nice place — in fact an ornament. All right. Then we will locate the plant somewhere along McKay or Victoria. I think about a block from the new parliament buildings would suit.[43]

Large and boisterous public meetings in the east-end were followed by petitions against the incinerator location and for water connections to the populous north part of east Edmonton, protesting against ongoing construction of blocks of pipe in parts of the west-end where there were no residents at all. Another meeting chaired by Brown to select east-end aldermanic candidates was hugely attended, allowing organizers to envision a central committee of no fewer than 100 to direct a canvasser for every block in the city. The keynote of the east end aldermanic campaign was expressed by candidate Thomas Daly, who "said that he had no particular grievance against the present council except that they were very dirty housekeepers and that they swept a great deal of dirt into the east end." A fellow candidate, Dr. W. McCauley, attacked another east end concern with his own calculation that there had been at least 500 cases of typhoid in the city during the summer and thirty-five to forty deaths as a consequence.[44]

Other points of discussion — such as the general problem of coping with utilities expansion — did arise, but the basic east-west contest was underlined by the election results. Conveniently for analysis, there were two polling stations, one in the east end, one in the west end. Three of the five east-end aldermanic candidates were successful, and the other two placed sixth (Gustav Koermann, editor of the German language newspaper, the *Alberta Herold*) and seventh in the field of fourteen competing for five seats. Their success was clearly a function of their championing east-end causes: nearly eighty percent of their support came at the east-end poll. By contrast, the other two successful candidates, James B. Walker and Wilfrid Gariepy, drew two-thirds of their votes from the west-end poll.[45] Despite the absence of ward representation in the Edmonton charter, a division of outlook was thus both expressed and contained in the framework of the municipal election.

IV

City councils are by definition charged with community development, but many voluntary associations available to Edmontonians were important, if unwitting, urban community agencies. Most church, fraternal, ethnic, political, professional or elite groups would not have described their purposes in terms of promoting the urban entity of which they were a part, but some of them were undergoing urban transformations and others hardly made sense except in the urban context. Some provided communal comfort, or identity, within the larger urban confusion. Some helped to define the urban elite. Most involved strong links with other similar groups in other places, strengthening the standardization of Canadian and North American life even as they discouraged deviation from the norm within the Edmonton community. Some had the effect of easing the transition from alien lifestyles, and a few beginning but important organizations were formed especially to provide certain services for the community at large.

The demand for pure fraternity, for carving out a smaller yet related social identity, could not be expected to decline while the city expanded. The clubs of ritual rather than service proliferated and grew, age-old Masonic orders and the Oddfellows joined by the brand new orders of Elks and Eagles, all sharing the artificial attempt at exclusivity so apparent in the name of one lesser lodge, the Canadian Order of Chosen Friends. Despite the Canadian content in some of their titles, almost all were extensions of a North American phenomenon. The most recently acquired fraternity, the Canadian Benevolent Order of Elks, owed its Edmonton origin in November to the efforts of a travelling organizer; the Canadian branch was itself a late appendage of a gigantic American organization begun in New York not forty years earlier. The continuing popularity of fraternities was demonstrated by an initial membership list of 280 young Elks in Edmonton, average age twenty-eight, the largest Canadian chapter outside Toronto. Another example of strength, the Friendship Lodge of the Independent Order of Oddfellows, showed a membership of 110 and growing, enough to justify following the Masonic and Orange Lodges in the construction of their own hall. Their national and international dimensions were manifest, just as for other lodges, in their participation in provincial, national and international Grand Lodges.[46]

All the major church denominations (Anglican, Presbyterian, Methodist, Catholic and Baptist) had developed men's, women's and young people's societies, of which several had advanced beyond purely religious worship and fellowship. The Methodist, Presbyterian and Baptist men's and youth groups in particular often met to debate issues of local or national community interest. Entertainment encompassed musical concerts, skating parties, lawn socials and mass organization of the game known as "progressive pedro." In an expanding community, social intercourse was recognized to have value for welcoming strangers. Anglicans showed the broadest community outlook, providing a "Willing Workers Mission Band" to play for 1,00 revellers at Edmonton's annual fancy dress costume skating carnival at Thistle Rink, and at Christmas time sponsoring a program in south side Ross Hall filled with secular items like "Santa Claus and the Mouse" and a "May Pole Drill." Anglican, Methodist, Presbyterian and Baptist congregations supported rather military Boys' Brigades.[47] Despite congregational differences of emphasis, all were equally energetic and undoubtedly contributed a hefty share of Edmonton's community social activities.

The east end was the usual location for an entirely different religious manifestation: the revival meeting. While the Methodist Rev. C.H. Huestis

Paul Rudyk Company store, East End Edmonton, c. 1906. (*Courtesy of Provincial Archives of Alberta*)

detected a demand early in the year when he conducted a series of evening "special revival meetings" himself, the regular denominations were not normally involved. A Free Methodist missionary, the Rev. Oscar L. King, fitted the pattern better. He began early in the year in private homes, then briefly borrowed the facilities of the German Baptist Church, then in the late spring pitched his Gospel Tent at the corner of east-end Syndicate and Clara streets. There he addressed decidedly personal rather than community subjects: one was "Hell — Where it is; What it is; and Who goes there." Without exactly becoming widespread, the phenomenon showed signs of developing into a distinctive urban occurrence.[48] Without too much stretch of the imagination, these services can be seen as appeals to discontented souls with messages of basic truths designed to set them at rest. As such, they had palliative urban social significance.

At the other end of the scale was the Edmonton Club, by 1906 beginning to overshadow the older bastion of the pioneers, the Old Timers' Association. Former in 1899 by fifty-four charter members, the Edmonton Club claimed a membership of about 130 in 1906, enough to enable construction of a spacious new clubhouse. Membership depended upon sponsorship and acceptance by club members coupled with substantial entrance and continuing subscription fees. That it was purely an elite social club of the city, meant to transcend other divisions, was driven home by the very first article of the constitution, which forbade absolutely not only projects but even mere discussions of political or religious import. The Edmonton Club included very few Strathconans. The first session of the Alberta legislature provided an alternative, a charter for a Strathcona Club, but only desultory consideration of this possibility took place in November.[49]

Most of the professional men brought together in the Edmonton Club were simultaneously involved energetically in an expanding range of professional societies — legal, medical, pharmaceutical, architectural and veterinarian. Their purpose was of course primarily self-regulatory, as it was also for the Edmonton District Retail Merchants' Association, an effort to cope collectively with their economic and technical problems and to maintain prominent economic and social status. Occasionally their collective expertise was useful to the city, as when the Northern Alberta Medical Association was consulted on the question of a proper isolation hospital.[50] All these organizations did more than merely co-ordinate local specialists of a kind. Equally important, they introduced provincial, Canadian and international standardization to Edmonton practices; they helped make Edmonton life in certain respects indistinguishable from urban life elsewhere.

The collective homogenization of professional and fraternal organizations also extended to policital associations. In 1906 the overwhelmingly visible provincial and federal political organization was the Liberal Party, which

Edmonton Club, 1907. (*Courtesy of Provincial Archives of Alberta*)

was firmly established in both federal and provincial governments. Quite apart from demonstrating the ease with which they could capture a Strathcona district federal by-election, the Liberals were determined to identify themselves with Edmonton in other ways. On occasion the senior Liberal Association could stage a spectacular civic event designed to impress citizens with the magnitude of the local Liberal prevalence. One took place when the local M.P. and cabinet minister, the Hon. Frank Oliver, visited his constituency in October. He was entertained at a banquet in the Thistle Rink for which nearly 500 tickets were sold. An even more active and regular community prescence was established by the new Young Liberal Club, which expressly added to a political function the social one of fraternity and collective entertainment. An active membership of 185 participated in mock parliaments, debates on women's suffrage or the question of Chinese exclusion from Canada, and the recreation of a well-rehearsed male chorus. Finally, the Liberals paid careful attention to ethnic minorities, including among their officers not only French-speaking individuals but newcomers like Gustav Koermann.[51]

The Liberal Party had sound political reasons for seeking east-end alien ethnic and working-class support, but acculturation for the servant girls, labourers and working-class families of German and Ukrainian descent was promoted by some of their own apparently isolated institutions. Two German Lutheran congregations, one German Baptist church and the Ukrainian Greek Catholic St. Josaphat's church all provided a social buffer against the strangeness of local practices and thus eased the transition. St. John's Lutheran Church early accepted the assimilative implications of splitting its congregation into two for Sunday services in both English and German. Of the new immigrant secular clubs mentioned earlier, the German Club Edelweiss, with its new hall under construction at east end Kinistino Street and its German entertainment flavour, was the most prominent.[52]

Would not this alien cluster point in the city retard rather than promote civic unity? Not likely. For Edmonton in 1906 it is perhaps not easy to prove absolutely the validity of American urban historian Blake McKelvey's perceptive insights on the role of urban ghettoes as assimilative agencies for "self-conscious minorities," but a glance at the activities of all Edmonton's "old country" clubs (most from Great Britain) reveals only the mildest social identification with points of origin. In fact, there is little doubt that they could only have eased whatever social or psychological adjustments were necessary by providing a few of the familiar features of old in the new place. The United Irishmen celebrated St. Patrick's Day. "Lodge Edmonton" of the Sons of England was simply a fraternal order to which membership was restricted by the qualification of a member's birth or his parents' birth in England. The Braemar Circle, the St. Andrew's Society,

St. Josaphats Ukrainian Greek Catholic Church, east end Edmonton, 1908. (*Courtesy of Provincial Archives of Alberta*)

and the Caledonian Society all specialized in bagpipe entertainment, Highland flings, and Scottish reels. Innocent traditional amusements were coupled with occasional gestures of commitment to the larger Edmonton community. The St. Andrew's Society Robbie Burns banquet was attended by the Lieutenant-Governor, provincial cabinet ministers and MLAs as well as civic leaders, and toasts were traded with the "sister societies" of St. Jean Baptiste and the Sons of England.[53]

The Independent Order of Daughters of the Empire displayed an additional dimension still somewhat rare in the new city. The "Westward Ho!" and "Beaver House" chapters formed in Edmonton in 1906 undertook duties "Imperial, Patriotic and Philanthropic." Over and above their promotion of an imperial sisterhood, two of their projects provided significant community services. The "Westward Ho!" chapter sponsored a spring "Bal Poudre" and solicited donations throughout the year to purchase an ambulance for the city. "Beaver House" chapter developed a scheme which would both promote desirable immigration and fill an upper-class demand: to bring "domestic servants from the motherland" who would remain in service six months at low wages less deductions until their transatlantic fares were repaid to their employers. Other family members were expected to be drawn over with them.[54]

Church members had gone further than social clubs into community service. Two institutions stand out: Alberta College and branch of the Young Men's Christian Association. In this short period preceding the opening of the University of Alberta, the Alberta College of the Methodist Church enjoyed its greatest impact on the community. Its annual enrolment of more than 300 students studied high school matriculation, commercial, and university courses (the last in affiliation with McGill University). Its profile in the Edmonton community was enhanced by part-time evening courses in secretarial skills, music and elocution, and by the exploits of its football and hockey teams. The official opening of a new school year in November drew more than 300 onlookers, including the Premier, the Lieutenant-Governor and the mayor.[55]

No other voluntary organization was as significant to the new urbanism as the Young Men's Christian Association. Symbolically, it was in 1904, the year of city incorporation, that Edmonton organizers (a decidedly elite group) resolved to replace the Edmonton Young Men's Institute, so dependent for its sports and instructional facets on voluntary work, with the highly-structured YMCA employing paid staff members. The first to be hired was an executive secretary, R.B. Chadwick, lured in 1906 from a similar position in Belleville, Ontario. Chadwick soon whipped up a large and successful building campaign and recommended further staff additions to develop Edmonton men "mentally, morally and physically" with the help of religious, education, physical, information, employment and relief departments.[56]

During this same year the temperance work of the Women's Christian Temperance Union and like societies took a temporary back seat to the boom-stimulated organization of the YMCA. There had been a shift in Protestant interdenominational energies, one in which prominent laymen of various congregations were far more vitally involved that they had ever been in prohibitionist crusades. Alberta College and the YMCA were inspired not so much by religious considerations as by perceived needs in the development of the city. Similarly, when the Alberta Methodist Conference announced in June its willingness to consider union with other denominations, a *Bulletin* editorial made just two intriguing points: first, that unique western friendliness among denominations for practical reasons favoured such a move; second, that the "primal purpose" would be "that *society* should receive the moral uplift which is the real purpose and mission of all churches."[57] No theological argument here, nor any concern for individual salvation. The urban organism was exerting its collectivizing influence on the nature of church as well as secular associations.

V

Edmontonians and Strathconans were entertained, if not en masse, at least in substantial masses already in 1906, and for a startling proportion of their entertainment they were passive spectators. Without denying the continuation of private recreational activity, it is obvious that the organized variety boomed. Some of it was in the traditional and more active forms of skating carnivals, dances and picnics. Fancy dress skating carnivals in particular attracted up to 1,000 participants. So also did special entertainments planned for holidays. One fitting celebration in this year of railway bonanza was a train trip for 1,200 ticket purchasers to Fort Saskatchewan sporting events and dancing on Victoria Day. Dominion Day, a national event, was submerged in the attractions of the Edmonton Fair, a local extravaganza running four days at the beginning of July. It is likely that businessmen saw the fair's value principally in financial terms. The Exhibition Association directors eagerly anticipated 20,000 attendance, many to be brought to the city by special trains from points as much as a hundred miles away. There were, however, other aspects to it. A *Bulletin* editorial hoped for a successful fair as an advertisement of collective civic and agrarian vitality, and the shopkeepers themselves interrupted their bursting business opportunities for a day at the height of the fair in order to attend. It served as a focus, a symbol of collective effort and, especially, success.[58]

The herd characteristic taking over Edmonton entertainment was even more evident in regular week-to-week offerings in Edmonton's halls, theatres, rinks and playing fields. Very little of the fantasy which Edmontonians paid to take in was provided within their own ranks, even as early as 1906. The few musical variety concerts and fewer amateur theatrical presentations offered by local talent were almost unnoticeable amidst the professionals touring through the city. The Thistle Rink (an arena fitted for theatre), Robertson's Hall before fire consumed it, Ross Hall on the south side, the Empire Theatre built in June, and the Edmonton Opera House after its October opening, all carried well-attended entertainments of decided mediocrity.

There were some exceptions. The serious French Canadian prima donna referred to consistently as "Madame Albani" carried such a reputation and was given such a promotional build-up that the capacity audiences may have come more for the spectacle of celebrity than for her singing. A slightly different example was the touring Harold Nelson Stock Company which mixed popular and lavishly-produced light theatre like *The Virginian, David Garrick's Love* and *The Prisoner of Zenda* with Shakespeare's *The Merchant of Venice*. Nevertheless, the company's leading man, Harold Nelson, who was invariably its main attraction to the crowds of people who attended, soon complained that the popularity of Shakespearian drama had almost disappeared in the face of the demand for visual spectacles associated with the less sophisticated plays.[59]

The rest of Edmonton's theatrical fare made little pretence at cultural elevation. Stock companies showing off melodrama like *The Convict's Daughter, A Foxy Tramp, Rip Van Winkle* and *The Irish Boarder* were merely "merry makers," and musical productions were mainly proven American hit comedies. One company, the Roscian Opera Company, did supplement its fare of recognized operettas, including those of Gilbert and Sullivan, with the operas *Martha* and *Cavalleria Rusticana*. Despite these rarities, the greatest plaudits seemed reserved for the Juvenile Bostonians who produced "the 'excruciatingly funny cannibalistic' musical comedy 'Gee Whiz' "; or Pollard's Lilliputian Opera Company. Some of the specialty groups must have seemed incongruous in this northern setting, with minstrel shows featuring "the latest coon ditties," "the Zulu travesty 'A Dream of Dahomey,' " or endless variations of *Uncle Tom's Cabin*.[60] Some of these groups verged on vaudeville variety shows, supplementing their major features with the contortions of jugglers, unicyclists and Siberian bloodhounds.

One vaudeville troupe, announced the *Bulletin* with relish, presented "no pathos or seriousness anywhere to interrupt the stream of mirth" and did "not aspire to ethics or classics, [taught] no moral lesson, and [did] not attempt to be instructive." Exactly. Edmonton was solidly and happily plugged into the homogeneous North American phenomenon of travelling fantasy and comic entertainment. The first, though temporarily unsuccessful, attempt at opening a theatre (the Empire) for four daily performance of "refined vaudeville" in June was a sign of things to come. The Edmonton Opera House was built in the fall for a steady diet of variety theatre, supplemented in afternoons by roller skating. A prairie Managers' Association was being promoted from Calgary to co-ordinate prairie bookings for North American touring companies, to create a Canadian prairie "circuit," so to speak.[61] The enlivening of hundreds of urban lives nightly had become another business specialty, a service performed for an urban population rather than by themselves, and standard marketing procedure to satisfy the broadest taste promised little fundamental variety or quality. The new urban entertainment was in its standardization of fantasy both a communal force and a communal sign.

Sports entertainment was following a similar pattern, but with the added dimension of competition which led to representative teams for the city. Sports clubs proliferated in the city, launched at first simply for organization of local competition in hockey (men's and women's), cricket, curling, football, lacrosse, baseball, rifle marksmanship and tennis. In most of those sports, however, organization had already transcended local competitions to support civic representative teams carrying the colours of Edmonton or Strathcona into inter-urban contests. The Edmonton Curling Club bonspiel late in January drew more outsiders than members of the Edmonton and Strathcona curling clubs. The Edmonton and Strathcona Rifle Associations, whose members normally occupied themselves with an endless series of shooting practices, combined in June and July to place well in the eight-team Canadian Military Rifle matches. The Edmonton Cricket Club had perhaps proceeded the least distance to external competition in team sports, yet games between teams of married and bachelor members on Good Friday and Arbour Day were matched by games with Wetaskiwin, Fort Saskatchewan and Red Deer, while Edmonton organizers tried to establish a North-West Cricket League for Alberta and Saskatchewan.[62] Both Edmonton and Strathcona as well as Alberta College had lacrosse and football clubs with teams playing at the intermediate and senior levels, and a crack Strathcona lacrosse team was judged worthy to be sent on a B.C. tour promoting Strathcona. But of the team sports, hockey and baseball organization illustrated the trend best.

Hockey organization was not much more complex than that for football or lacrosse, but the range of external challenge exhibition games was greater. For regular local performance, representatives of high school, Alberta College, Printers and the Edmonton Thistle and Strathcona Shamrock intermediate teams organized a city hockey league. Senior Thistle and Shamrock teams for the most part played each other before capacity crowds of around 2,000 spectators. The Thistles fittingly in this year consistently thrashed their counterparts for a trophy known as the Paterson Cup. A Rossland, B.C. team visited to play several games; the obverse of this was a Thistle tour through Calgary, Medicine Hat, Regina, Moose Jaw, Portage la Prairie, Brandon and Winnipeg. Although regular league play was not thought feasible, frequent games before good crowds established hockey as a major recreational spectacle in early Edmonton. Games against outside teams received extensive front-page newspaper coverage, stressing the identification of Edmonton readers with their representative teams even as players began to be imported from as far afield as Quebec.[63]

Baseball was the most vigorously promoted and businesslike spectator sport, drawing 1,200 and more to ''witness the tragedy'' of repeated losses to the major Calgary rival. In a tournament which took place during the Edmonton fair, the potential for the game in Edmonton was demonstrated by the attendance of 1,500 at a final game in which the Edmonton team did not play. A game against a team from Anacortes, Washington drew a similar crowd. During the spring campaign to form and fund an athletic association to promote and secure facilities for summer sports, the *Bulletin* remarked, ''If there is anything that brings into prominence a town or city it is a victorious lacrosse, baseball or football team.'' As soon as it thus became a matter of finding the best to represent the city, it became necessary to transform the organization into a professional and commercial one. Shareholders were quickly found for an athletic company which was first and foremost a baseball club. American players were imported, Bleachers were installed, grounds improved, fences built and tickets sold at the baseball diamond. Bitter complaints were registered when paid players committed too many errors. New players were brought in to replace them. After the 1906 season Edmonton promoters journeyed to the other centres to draw them into a Western Canada League which applied for and received the sanction of the American co-ordinating board for professional baseball leagues.[64]

As for theatrical entertainment, but not quite at the same pace, the organization of Edmonton sports entertainment was becoming a specialized international service for passive consumers on a mass scale. Challenge matches mixing local and touring participants in boxing and wrestling exerted a similar appeal, presumably with the added attraction of laying bets on the outcome. The ultimate gambling sport, horse racing, was the most

Edmonton Fair, July 1905. (*Courtesy of Provincial Archives of Alberta*)

popular feature of the Edmonton fair. In the fall, Edmonton's first "Driving Club" prepared to campaign for funds to build a sophisticated racing speedway.[65] Sports contests and theatrical entertainment displayed the crowd formation of Edmonton behaviour as nothing else could. Here was not independent, let alone unique, initiative: here was transplantation of urban forms into a new setting, the reproduction of an organism.

To put it another way, there was no doubt that Edmonton was a city in 1906, as its promoters so devoutly wished to ensure. Its lack of distinction from other cities, the collective behaviour of its humanity, and its commitment to community all betrayed its urbanity. The individuals and the groups within the city who organized themselves to provide certain collective services simultaneously committed themselves to the form of total urban community which would permit only limited modification. Independent behaviour had been sacrificed in many fields; in taking the collective approach citizens made the city the unit governing much of their individual conduct: not only in their work, but also in their accommodation and utilities, in provision of health care and education, even in their voluntary associations and in their entertainment. Between citizens and city, which now served which?

NOTES:

1. See Richard S. Alcorn and Peter R. Knights, "Most Uncommon Bostonians: A Critique of Stephan Thernstrom's *The Other Bostonians*," *Historical Methods Newsletter*, vol. 8 (June, 1975), 98-114, and Thernstrom's rejoinder, 115-120. For the approach of a massive American project, see Theodore Hershberg, "The Philadelphia Social History Project: An Introduction," *Historical Methods Newsletter*, vol. 9 (March-June, 1976), 43-58. An excellent Canadian statistical exploration is Michael Katz, *The People of Hamilton, Canada West* (Cambridge: Harvard University Press, 1975). A superb study along slightly different lines is Kathleen N. Conzen, *Immigrant Milwaukee 1836-1860: Accommodation and Community in a Frontier City* (Cambridge: Harvard University Press, 1976).

2. Richard D. Brown, "The Emergence of Urban Society in Rural Massachusetts, 1760-1820," *Journal of American History*, vol. 61 (June, 1974), 29-51; Walter S. Glazer, "Participation and Power: Voluntary Associations and the Functional Organization of Cincinnati in 1840," *Historical Methods Newsletter*, vol. 5 (September, 1972), 151-168; Michael Frisch, *Town into City: Springfield, Massachusetts, and the Meaning of Community* (Cambridge: Harvard University Press, 1972); Stuart M. Blumin, *The Urban Threshold: Growth and Change in a Nineteenth Century American Community* (Chicago/London: University of London Press, 1976); Stephen Yeo, *Religion and Voluntary Organizations in Crisis* (London: Croom Helm, 1976); J.M.S. Careless, "Urban Development in Canada," *Urban History Review*, no. 1-74 (June, 1974), 9-10; Gilbert A. Stelter, "The Historian's Approach to Canada's Urban Past," *Histoire Sociale/Social History, vol. 7 (1974), 9-10, 18-20.

3. Leo Schnore, "The City as a Social Organism," *Urban Affairs Quarterly*, vol. 1 (1966), 58-69; John Taylor, "The Urban West, Public Welfare, and a Theory of Urban Development," in A.R. McCormack and Ian Macpherson, eds., *Cities in the West* (Ottawa: National Museum of Man, 1975), 288-290.

4. Canada, Sessional Paper No. 17(a), 6-7 Edward VII, 1907, *Census of Population and*

Agriculture of the Northwest Provinces . . . 1906 (Ottawa: King's Printer, 1907), pp. 70, 77, 101; *Henderson's Manitoba and North West Territories Gazetteer and Directory* (1906) for Edmonton (pp. 459-540) and Strathcona (pp. 1117-23).

5. T.D. Regehr, *The Canadian Northern Railway: Pioneer Road of the Northern Prairies, 1895-1918* (Toronto: Macmillan, 1976), pp. 69-71, 107-23, 164-69, 245; R.A. Christenson,"The Calgary and Edmonton Railway and the *Edmonton Bulletin*," M.A. Thesis (University of Alberta, 1967), pp. 152-56, 160-62, 218-23, 236-49; *Edmonton Journal (EJ)*, January 2, 23, June 19, 1906; *Edmonton Bulletin (EB)*, February 2, 6, 7, June 29, 30, 1906.

6. The Edmonton newspapers were studded with the goods news all year long. See also *The Labour Gazette* (Ottawa, Department of Labour), Vol. 7, No. 6 (December 1906), p. 632 and No. 7 (January 1907), pp. 746-47; R.G. Ironside and S.A. Hamilton, "Historical Geography of Coal Mining in the Edmonton District," *Alberta Historical Review*, Vol. 20 (Summer 1972), pp. 10-11.

7. L.G. Thomas, *The Liberal Party in Alberta* (Toronto: University of Toronto Press, 1959), pp. 34-41, 50; Morris Zaslow, *The Opening of the Canadian North, 1870-1914* (Toronto: McClelland and Stewart, 1971), pp. 210-11; John F. Gilpin, "The City of Strathcona 1891-1912," M.A. Thesis (University of Alberta, 1978), pp. 119-20; Gilpin, "Failed Metropolis," Chapter ten in this volume; and Bruce Kilpatrick, "A Lesson in Boosterism: The Provincial Capital Controversy in Alberta, 1904-1906," *Urban History Review*, Vol. VIII (February 1980), pp. 47-109.

8. E.J. Hart, "The History of the French-Speaking Community of Edmonton, 1795-1935," M.A. Thesis (University of Alberta, 1971), pp. 59-64; Elizabeth B. Gerwin, "A Survey of the German-Speaking Population of Alberta," M.A. Thesis (University of Alberta, 1938), pp. 109-10; *Henderson's Edmonton and Strathcona Directories for 1906* (survey of ethnic names); Ban Seng Hoe, *Structural Changes of Two Chinese Communities in Alberta, Canada* (Ottawa: National Museum of Man, 1976), pp. 74-75, 291; *EB*, February 27, March 5, 7, 10, 24, May 1, June 5, 1906.

9. Michael H. Marunchak, *The Ukrainian Canadians: A History* (Winnipeg and Ottawa: Ukrainian Free Academy of Sciences, 1970), pp. 63-67, 102, 151-52, 167-69; J. Skwarok, *The Ukrainian Settlers in Canada and Their Schools . . . 1891-1921* (Edmonton: Basilian Press of Toronto, 1958), pp. 24-27, 32; *EB*, March 10, 1906.

10. Sid Bursten, "Edmonton: A Jewish Community in Perspective," *The Jewish Post* (March 3, 1966), p. 16; Tony Cashman, *Abraham Cristall: The Story of a Simple Man* (1963), pp. 10-18; Taped interview with Hyman Goldstick by David Nelson, May 30 and June 5, 1973, Provincial Archives of Alberta, Edmonton (PAA).

11. Hart, "The History of the French-Speaking Community," pp. 52-77, 102-04.

12. *Henderson's Edmonton and Strathcona Directories for 1906* were numerically analyzed for occupational distribution according to residential area (addresses are available for Edmonton but not for the much smaller Strathcona) and, in a rough way (by reference to names), for ethnic distribution according to residential area.

13. I am following E. Digby Baltzell's distinction in *Philadelphia Gentlemen* (N.Y.: The Free Press 1958) between upper class and elite, the latter involving exclusivity based on acceptance by members. None of my keys is likely to unlock the door to Edmonton's elite perfectly, but they give sufficient indication of its embryo existence and its distinction from the bulk of the population for what follows.

14. Statistical generalizations are based on analysis of data available for Edmonton names in the following sources: John Blue, *Alberta: Past and Present*, Vols. 2 and 3 (Chicago: Pioneer Publishing Company, 1924); Henry J. Boam, comp., *The Prairie Provinces of Canada* (London: Sells Ltd., 1914); A.O. Macrae, *History of the Province of Alberta*, 2 vols. (The Western Canada History Company, 1912); *Men and Makers of Edmonton, Alberta* (Edmonton: Keystone Press, 1913).

15. The microfilmed copy of *The Saturday News* held at PAA is missing issues between May 19 and September 15, 1906. It was edited by the former editor of the Woodstock (Ontario) *Sentinel-Review*. A. Balmer Watt, who would later transfer to the *Edmonton Journal*. The women's section was written by the editor's wife.

16. The following generalizations are based on the membership list to 1906 in *The Edmonton Club, Act of Incorporation, Constitution, Regulations and List of Members* (Edmonton: Keystone Press, 1913).

17. *EB*, August 18, November 24, 1906. For Canadian interest in a single tax, see Alan F.J. Artibise, "Boosterism and the Development of Prairie Cities, 1871-1913." Chapter eight in this volume, and Ramsay Cook, "Henry George and the Poverty of Canadian Progress," CHA *Historical Papers* (1977), pp. 143-56.

18. *EJ*, May 9, 1906; *EB*, June 2, 12, 13, 20, 29, August 11, 16, November 10, 12, 15, 1906; E.H. Dale, "The Role of the City Council in the Economic and Social Development of Edmonton, Alberta, 1892 to 1966," Ph.D. Thesis (University of Alberta, 1969), pp. 58-61.

19. Dale, "The Role of the City Council," p. 80; *EB* January 3, 20, 24, February 22, March 8, April 6, 9, 14, 25-28, May 23, June 6, 29, August 11, 16, 1906.

20. Dale, "The Role of the City Council," pp. 66-70; *EB*, January 3, February 21, March 8, 9, 14, 31, June 6, 13, 22, July 11, August 20, November 15, December 1, 19, 1906.

21. Dale, "The Role of the City Council," pp. 84-89; *EJ*, January 17, 1906; *EB*, January 19-24, March 8, 9, 14, September 22, October 19, 20, November 7, December 15, 18, 1906.

22. Dale, "The Role of the City Council," pp. 120-24; *EB*, February 1, March 14, April 14, June 29, August 9, 16, 18, 1906.

23. See John C. Weaver, "Edmonton's Perilous Course, 1909-1929," *Urban History Review*, No. 2-77 (October 1977); Artibise, "Boosterism"; and Dale, "The Role of the City Council."

24. *EJ*, January 11, 1906; *EB*, January 3, 10, 24, 27, 30, February 14, April 28, May 2, June 6, 13, 14, 26-29, July 25, August 16, September 19, 22, 26, December 19, 1906.

25. Strathcona Council Minutes, January 2, February 6, 20, March 20, April 13, July 10, 24, October 16, November 6, 1906; Edmonton City Archives (ECA); *EB*, January 3, 16, 24, March 23, June 23, 29, July 6, August 25, September 4-8, December 27, 1906; Gilpin, "The City of Strathcona," p. 74; Taylor, "The Urban West," pp. 294-98.

26. *EB*, January 5, 18, March 9, April 14, August 27, October 12, November 24, 1906; *EJ*, July 2, 1906; Tony Cashman, *Edmonton's Catholic Schools* (Edmonton: Roman Catholic Separate School District No. 7, 1977), pp. 48-49.

27. Gilpin, "The City of Strathcona," p. 135; Minutes, Grand Trunk Pacific (GTP) Directors' meetings, November 8, 1906 and February 7, 1907; Public Archives of Canada (PAC), CNR Papers, RG 30, vol. 1104, pp. 269, 299; Dale, "The Role of the City Council," p. 32; *EB*, February 3, 7, 13, March 10, 28, April 6, 11, 14, 19, June 30, July 11, September 8, November 7, 13, 21, 1906; *EJ*, December 6, 1906.

28. Strathcona Council Minutes, October 30, 1906; ECA; *EB*, February 3, 15, March 28, September 11, 1906.

29. Gilpin, "The City of Strathcona," pp. 108-9, 121-30; GTP Directors' meeting, February 1, 1906, p. 179; PAC.

30. Strathcona Council Minutes, January 20, March 14, May 30, June 4, July 3, 1906; ECA; Gilpin, "The City of Strathcona," pp. 26-27.

31. This paragraph and the following one are drawn from Strathcona Council Minutes, April 17, June 19, September 4, 27, October 15, 23, November 6, 20, 27, 1906; ECA; *EB*, January 2, February 3, 26, April 11, May 3, 7, June 13, 21, 1906; Gilpin, "The City of Strathcona," pp. 140-41.

32. Strathcona Council Minutes, November 21, December 29, 1905, January 3, 16, February 6, March 12, April 3, 9, 17, May 15, June 4, July 6, 17, 1906; ECA; Gilpin, "The City of Strathcona," pp. 70-71, 75; *EB*, March 12, April 9, 11, June 28, 1906.

33. Gilpin, "The City of Strathcona," pp. 139-40; Strathcona Council Minutes, September 11, 18, 1906; ECA.

34. Dale, "The Role of the City Council," p. 80; Strathcona Council Minutes, June 19, October 16, November 6, December 28, 1906; ECA; *EB*, April 28, November 7, 13, December 8, 27, 29, 1906.

35. Weaver, "Edmonton's Perilous Course," pp. 21-23; Artibise, "Boosterism"; Dale, "The Role of the City Council," p. 104; J.D. Anderson, "The Municipal Government Reform Movement in Western Canada 1880-1920," in Alan F.J. Artibise and Gilbert A. Stelter, eds., *The Usable Urban Past: Planning and Politics in the Modern Canadian City* (Toronto: Macmillan, 1979), pp. 73-111; *EB*, August 14, 1906.

36. *EB*, December 8, 1905, February 28, March 8, 9, 24, 31, 1906.

37. *EB*, March 30-April 5, 19, May 12, 25, 28, June 6, 13, 14, 20, 21, September 19, 1906.

38. *EB*, March 7, April 21, May 3, December 3, 1906.

39. *EB*, November 7, 15, 1906.

40. *EB*, August 21, 27, 28, September 1, 4, November 27, 1906; *Alberta Labour News* supplement *Labour Annual*, September 3, 1921, p. 41; Monthly issues of *Labour Gazette*, Vols. 6 and 7, February, 1906-February, 1907; W.R. Askin, "Labor Unrest in Edmonton and District and its Coverage by the Edmonton Press, 1918-1919," M.A. Thesis (University of Alberta, 1973), pp. 6-7; W.J.C. Cherwinski, "Organized Labour in Saskatchewan: The TLC Years, 1905-1945," Ph.D. Thesis (University of Alberta, 1972), pp. 11-13; Robert Babcock, *Gompers in Canada* (Toronto: University of Toronto Press, 1974), pp. 51-53.

41. *EB*, August 18, 25, 1906.

42. *EB*, September 1, 4, 8, 10, 11, November 5, 14, 1906.

43. *EB*, January 3, April 28, May 2, June 6, 13, 14, 26, 27, 29, July 25, August 16, 25, November 9, 1906.

44. *EB*, November 14, 17, 20, 30, December 6, 8, 1906; *EJ*, December 11, 13, 1906.

45. *EJ*, December 6, 10, 11, 1906; *EB*, December 6, 11, 15, 1906.

46. *EJ*, January 6, 1906; *EB*, January 2, 11, February 10, March 26, August 6, 25, November 7, 12, 1906. Reports on meetings of other organizations appeared regularly in the city's newspapers.

47. Frank A. Peake, "The Beginnings of the Diocese of Edmonton, 1875-1913," M.A. Thesis (University of Alberta, 1952), pp. 61-62; *EJ*, January 6, 8, 19, 1906; *EB*, January 2, 5, 11, 15, 22-24, 29-31, February 5, 10, 17, 23, 26, 27, March 5, 7, 12-15, 26, 28, April 23, 25, May 9, June 18, 20, 27-30, July 3, 13, August 25, October 6, 11, November 5, 12, 13, 19, 27, December 21, 26, 31, 1906.

48. *EJ*, January 27, 1906; *EB*, January 18, 22, 27, April 23, May 1, June 12, 16, November 10, 27, 1906.

49. *The Edmonton Club . . . Regulations*, pp. 3-15, 32; *EB*, February 1, November 7, 1906.

50. *EJ*, January 11, 1906; *EB*, February 2, 12, 21, March 8, 21, June 4, 5, 25, July 6, September 8, 1906.

51. *EB*, January 13, 16, 18, February 5, March 14, 17, 22, April 6, 7, 9, June 15, 18, 26, 27, September 8, October 6, November 20, December 5, 1906.

52. *EB*, January 16, 18, February 5, 6, April 9, 23, June 15, 18, September 8, November 20, December 5, 1906; C.C. McLaurin, *Pioneering in Western Canada: A Story of the Baptists* (Calgary: The Author, 1939), pp. 138, 343-44; Emile J. Legal, *Short Sketches of the History of the Catholic Churches and Missions in Central Alberta* (1914), pp. 121-6. A separation of

English from other names in *Henderson's Directory for Edmonton and Strathcona in 1906* confirms the description of German and Ukrainian occupational status reported in the two books cited here.

53. Blake McKelvey, "Cities as Nurseries of Self-conscious Minorities," *Pacific Historical Review*, Vol. 39 (1970), pp. 367-81; *EB*, January 25, 26, February 6, March 6, 14, 16, April 4, 7, 20, June 22, December 8, 11, 15, 21, 29, 1906; *EJ*, January 6, 27, 1906.

54. *EB*, January 5, March 24, 30, April 14, 18, 21, June 30, September 13, November 5, 1906.

55. J.H. Riddell, *Methodism in the Middle West* (Toronto: Ryerson Press, 1946, pp. 271-75; George N. Emery, "Methodism on the Canadian Prairies, 1896-1914," Ph.D. Thesis (University of British Columbia, 1970), pp. 15-6, 347; *EB*, January 2, 16, February 9, 27, June 13, 19, 21, 30, November 12, 24, 1906.

56. Typescript manuscript written from YMCA minutes, "The History of the Edmonton Young Men's Christian Association," pp. 1-8; Edmonton YMCA Papers, PAA; *EB*, January 8, 13, March 12, April 16, 27, 30, June 16, 22, August 27, November 12, 27, 1906.

57. Local Edmonton and Strathcona union reports to the Alberta WCTU convention, October, 1906: WCTU Papers, Box 6, File 34, Glenbow-Alberta Institute Archives, Calgary; *EB*, January 22, 25, April 23, June 20, 1906. Evidently a "mass meeting of Methodists and Presbyterians in Edmonton" had endorsed church union already in 1904, despite the local eminence of "pronounced Presbyterian chauvinist" Rev. D.G. McQueen, later to lead dissenting Presbyterians out of church union in 1925: Emery, "Methodism," 331, 337. The italics in the quotation are added.

58. *EB*, February 10, May 25, June 30-July 6, 1906.

59. James Sheremeta, "A Survey of Professional Entertainment and Theatre in Edmonton, Alberta Before 1914," M.A. Thesis (University of Alberta, 1970), pp. 80-82, 97-103; *EB*, May 9, October 8-13, December 26, 1906; *EJ*, May 9, 1906.

60. Sheremeta, "A Survey of Professional Entertainment," pp. 70-74, 86-88, 112, 142-43; *EB*, April 2-9, June 19-28; July 21, 27, August 11, 24, October 8-13, November 5, 10, 15, 30, December 31, 1906.

61. *EB*, June 21, 26, November 6, 9, 12, 13, 1906; John Orrell, "Edmonton Theatres of Alexander W. Cameron," *Alberta History*, Vol. 26, No. 2 (Spring 1978), pp. 1-4.

62. *EB*, January 2, 22, March 9, 13, April 10, June 29, July 3, August 25, 27, September 5, 1906.

63. *EB*, January 2, 3, 19, 30, February 2, 7, 14-17, 27, March 5-9, 13, 14, 24, November 5, 7, 13, 15, 20, December 26, 27, 1906.

64. *EB*, April 6, 9, 20, 23, May 24, June 13, 16, 26-29, July 5-7, August 4, 27, September 1, 8, 11, 12, October 11, November 5, 27, December 15, 26, 1906.

65. *EB*, June 26-July 6, August 24-27, September 1, 4, 25, October 2, 19, 1906.

VI URBAN REFORM AND MUNICIPAL GOVERNMENT

Attempts to reform urban society, whether in the early nineteenth century or during the urban reform movement of 1890-1920, have generally focused on four distinct but inter-related concerns: social welfare (poverty, crime, disease, etc.); the restructuring of municipal government; planning the physical environment; and public ownership or regulation of municipal utilities. Critical assessments of these reform efforts are now well advanced and there is a substantial body of historical literature by competent and often imaginative scholars on which to build.

An examination of existing literature in the field reveals that Canadian historians have approached the subject from three different perspectives. One group has examined urban reform from the contemporary rhetoric concerning the problems faced by the Canadian city and responses to them.[1] In this approach it is argued that although there have always been a few in the cities who were interested in civic betterment, it was only in the late 1880s and early 1890s that urban reform became a subject of some importance to Canadians. This concern intensified in the following decades as urban politicians, planners, humanitarians, businessmen, and health officials became aware of the massive problems faced by their communities and set out to reconstruct and regulate urban government, society, and the physical environment. It is further argued that the reform movement disintegrated during the 1920s, although it had by that time drastically altered the design of urban Canada.

While this broad approach is obviously fruitful — it does, for example, tell us a great deal about many outstanding publicists and politicians — it also has certain inadequacies since an extensive gap separated reform ideology and practice. This is the conclusion reached by several historians who have approached the topic from the perspective of individual cities.[2]

These studies indicate that behind the contemporary rhetoric lay patterns of behaviour that were at variance with the calls for fundamental reform.[3] Schemes designed to reform municipal government provide an example of this discrepancy. The demands of reformers for changes in the structure of municipal government through the institution of such measures as Boards of Control or Commissions were designed not so much to make government more efficient or "more responsive to the popular will,"[4] but rather to lessen public participation in municipal government by minimizing the effect of ward politicians. Indeed, in nearly every area of urban reform — housing, planning, public ownership, social work, and government — recent studies have shown that reform ideology cannot always be taken as an accurate description of reform practice.

A third approach, which builds on and combines the work found in the first two categories, has recently been adopted. This work has as its perspective a critical comparison of reform rhetoric and practice in a wide variety of cities. By examining both early attempts at reform and the reform movement of the late nineteenth and early twentieth centuries in a number of different contexts, and by comparing not only individual cities but the entire Canadian experience with that of other countries, this approach is generating broad new generalizations about the nature of the reform movement in Canada.[5] Although much work remains to be done in an effort to refine and perhaps revise the basic research already completed, several tentative conclusions are possible. It is clear, for example, that much reform rhetoric, whether at the local or the national level, blended very closely with "booster" ambitions and that it usually arose from businessmen and their organizations, whose goal it was to retain control in municipal affairs.

Canadian urban reformers rarely viewed the city as a human environment requiring attention in the area of human needs and desires. Rather, it was seen as a municipal corporation that called for efficient management. The motives behind most reform measures were not primarily humanitarian. Reformers went about their tasks motivated by a high degree of self-interest; they were intent on manipulating the urban environment as much for their own benefit as for any desire to help others.

It can also be said of urban reform that in nearly all cases the efforts of the reformers to deal with the pressing problems of Canadian cities were inadequate, since long-range goals and consensus as to the best solutions were conspicuously absent. As growth continued, so too did urban compexities and problems. Indeed, the best that can be said about reform efforts prior to 1920 is that they had very limited success. Their greatest influence was in providing information about urban problems.

This emphasis on the conservative nature of urban reform in recent work reveals a continuity that ties the urban reform movement of the period

1880-1920 to both preceding and succeeding reform efforts. It also indicates that the patterns found in Canada bear a striking resemblance to the reform movement of the American Progressive Era.[6]

The urban reform era in Canada also witnessed the beginnings of senior government intervention in local affairs. Here, as in other aspects of municipal government in this period, there were similarities with the United States. The process of intervention and the consequent loss of local autonomy was ragged in terms of quality, quantity, timing, and location. It is not entirely complete even today. Nevertheless, the evolution and decline of local autonomy was one of the most significant and — paradoxically — virtually unnoticed developments of twentieth-century municipal government. As John Taylor demonstrates in his article in this section, and in another publication,[7] municipal governments had reached a stage of virtual impotence by the 1970s.

NOTES:

1. This approach is most ably represented by the work of Paul Rutherford. Besides the essay reprinted in this section, see Paul Rutherford, ed., *Saving the Canadian City: The First Phase, 1880-1920* (Toronto, 1974). This anthology of articles on urban reform contains a good introductory essay and a supplementary bibliography.

2. Unfortunately, most of this work is available only in unpublished form. See, for example, David A. Sutherland, "Gentlemen vs. Shopkeepers: Urban Reform in Early 19th Century Halifax," unpublished paper represented at the Canadian Historical Association's annual meeting at McGill University, Montreal, June 1972; Michael Gauvin, "The Municipal Reform Movement in Montreal, 1886-1914," M.A. thesis (University of Ottawa, 1972); and Daniel J. Russell, "H.B. Ames as Municipal Reformer," M.A. thesis (McGill University, 1971). For published works see: Alan F.J. Artibise, *Winnipeg: A Social History of Urban Growth, 1874-1914* (Montreal, 1975); John C. Weaver, "The Meaning of Municipal Reform: Toronto, 1895," *Ontario History*, Vol. 44 (June 1974); John C. Weaver, "The Modern City Realized: Toronto Civic Affairs, 1880-1915," in Alan F.J. Artibise and Gilbert A. Stelter, eds., *The Usable Urban Past: Planning and Politics in the Modern Canadian City* (Toronto, 1979), pp. 39-72; Terry Copp, *The Anatomy of Poverty: The Condition of the Working Class in Montreal, 1897-1929* (Toronto, 1974); and Stephen A. Speisman, "Munificent Parsons and Municipal Parsimony: Voluntary vs. Public Poor Relief in Nineteenth Century Ontario," *Ontario History*, Vol. LXV, No. 1 (March 1973), pp. 33-49.

3. This conclusion has been reached by American historians as early as 1964. See Samuel P. Hays, "The Politics of Reform in Municipal Government in the Progressive Era," *Pacific Northwest Quarterly*, Vol. 55 (October 1964), pp. 157-159.

4. Rutherford, *Saving the Canadian City*, p. xx.

5. This article by John C. Weaver in this section falls into this category. See also John C. Weaver, "Elitism and the Corporate Ideal: Businessmen and Boosters in Canadian Civic Reform, 1890-1920," in A.R. McCormack and Ian MacPherson, eds., *Cities in the West: Papers of the Western Canada Urban History Conference* (Ottawa: National Museum of Man, 1975), pp. 48-73; T.K. Hareven, "An Ambiguous Alliance: Some Aspects of American Influences on Canadian Social Welfare," *Histoire Sociale/Social History*, Vol. 3 (April 1969), pp. 82-98; and James Anderson, "The Municipal Government Movement in Western Canada, 1880-1920," in Artibise and Stelter, *The Usable Urban Past*, pp. 73-111. See also John C.

Weaver, ed., "Approaches to the History of Urban Reform," Special Issue, *Urban History Review*, No. 21-76 (October 1976), pp. 3-66.

6. A recent article than can serve as a starting point for more comparative work in urban reform history is Samuel P. Hays, "The Changing Political Structure of the City in Industrial America," *Journal of Urban History*, Vol. 1 (November 1974), pp. 6-38. Despite its title, this article offers a conceptual framework which could be useful in comprehending the evolution of the city sicne the early nineteenth century.

7. John H. Taylor, " 'Relief from Relief': The Cities Answer to Depression Dependency," *Journal of Canadian Studies*l, Vol. 14 (Spring 1979), pp. 16-23. See also D.M. Nowlan, "Toward Home Rule for Urban Policy," *Journal of Canadian Studies*, Vol. 13 (1978), pp. 70-79.

Tomorrow's Metropolis: The Urban Reform Movement in Canada, 1880-1920

PAUL RUTHERFORD

Between the census of 1881 and the census of 1921, the urban population of Canada increased in absolute terms from 1.1 million to 4.3 million, and in proportional terms from one-quarter to one-half the total population.[1] This demographic revolution was largely unexpected. True, the Canadians of the 1860's had envisaged a great and populous future, but as an agricultural nation with a vast western frontier, not an urban frontier. As early as the 1870's however, newspapers commented upon the steady drift of population towards the cities and by the turn of the century the theme of rural depopulation had become common throughout eastern Canada. Worse, urban growth led more to the expansion of cities than towns, and threatened to change the whole economic and social character of the Dominion. In a prophetic passage, J.S. Woodsworth warned that the railway, the telephone, and similar technological innovations were carrying the city into the countryside, a process which would ultimately give the whole nation a metropolitan image.[2]

The Canadian response to the urban fact, especially to the appearance of the "big city," was generally unfavorable. At one level, it is true, cities were regarded as the physical embodiment of progress, the home of literature and the arts. Yet many people, looking to the sad experience of Europe and America, feared the further spread of the city.[3] Rural apologists emphasized the debilitating influences of city life upon the individual.[4] Social conservatives inveighed against the rampant materialism of the new culture.[5] Even urban writers admitted that there was a dark side to the city where

SOURCE: Canadian Historial Association, *Historical Papers, 1971*, pp. 203-224. Reprinted by permission of the author and the Canadian Historical Association.

disease, crime, prostitution, and general misery flourished.[6] In the city all the ills of modern society were concentrated and highly visible. By the beginning of the twentieth century, it was widely accepted that urban growth posed a serious menace to the future of the nation.

It is only in retrospect that reform seems the logical solution to the urban crisis. Well into the twentieth century there were public leaders who continued to hope that a new wave of agricultural development would direct the city dweller back to the farm.[7] It took four decades of agitation before the reform movement achieved a national prominence. During the 1880's, various daily newspapers, the exponents of what was called "people's journalism," turned to the idea of urban reform, then attracting considerable attention in the United States.[8] These papers appealed to the expanded reading public of their cities, which was as interested in urban affairs as in provincial and national problems. The Montreal *Star* launched a series of crusades against municipal corruption and incompetence and sponsored such welfare projects as the "Fresh Air Fund" to send poor women and children out of the city in the summer months. The Toronto *World* appeared as the champion of the interests of the people in the city's many battles with local monopolists and utility companies. The Vancouver *News-Advertiser* argued the case of labor and demanded the increased political involvement of all city dwellers (excepting, of course, the Chinese) in civic affairs. Though inspired as much by hopes of a higher circulation as civic spirit, these papers popularized the idea of reform long before intellectuals discovered urban problems.

By 1900, however, the journalist had been replaced by the expert. In 1897 Herbert Ames, a businessman, published "The City Below the Hill," a statistical analysis of social conditions in Montreal. A decade later, another businessman, S. Morley Wickett of Toronto, edited an anthology on municipal government with wide-ranging suggestions for reform. In 1910 in Quebec a somewhat different study of municipal government by a one-time *bleu* journalist and provincial minister, G.A. Nantel, was published postumously by friends. This book, *La Métropole de Demain*, proposed a scheme of metropolitan federation and civic beautification for the island of Montreal, based upon the experience of Paris. And in 1911 appeared J.S. Woodsworth's *My Neighbor*, an impassioned plea for the reform of living conditions in Canada's cities.

These works were only a portion of the material which reached the public. No annual session of the Canadian or Empire Clubs, those so eminent representatives of opinion in English Canada, seemed complete without one address on urban problems — and not only by Canadians, but by visitors from Britain and the United States.[9] These were supplemented by conferences sponsored by the churches, women's organizations, and eventually town planning and civic improvement associations. Specialized magazines, like the *Municipal World* and the *Western Municipal News*, appeared as house organs of municipal government and consistent advocates of reform. Even academics joined the movement: in 1913 the new Canadian Political Science Association held a special seminar on municipal government, involving American and Canadian municipal officials.[10]

Urban reform was less a single creed and more a common approach to a wide variety of urban problems. Early reformers concentrated upon the redemption of the urban environment, a theme which extended back to the mid-century. The old ideal of civic improvement had emphasized the construction of stately buildings, colleges and academies, eventually libraries and museums, to bolster the prestige of the city.[11] But as the cities became more and more congested, this concern was replaced by the attempt to make the city healthy, moral, and equitable.

Public health reform was founded upon the sanitary ideal, a British doctrine long popular in Canada. Originally the sanitarians concentrated upon the issues of pollution and pure water. Even before the acceptance of the germ theory, it was widely recognized that water pollution was a public hazard and waterworks were one of the first utilities subject to direct municipal improvement. In the 1870s Toronto invested some $2,000,000 in the construction of an effective waterworks system.[12] By this time, of course, the city was moving into the general field of health control, with an emphasis upon the prevention of disease. After 1880 reformers tackled the problems of vaccination, pure food, and living conditions, especially as these related to the health of the poor and the proletariat.[13] Such reform was not always welcomed; in 1885 during the short but severe Montreal smallpox epidemic, spokesmen for the francophone proletarian fiercely opposed the whole idea of vaccination.[14] Ideally, reformers hoped to impose a strict code of public health upon all city dwellers. Without pure environment, they warned, the city would soon die. Charles Hastings, the medical officer of Toronto during the war, pointed out that the contamination of any class would soon lead to the infection of the rest of the community. Disease did not respect social standing.[15]

During the 1880's clergymen, temperance societies, and women's organizations set out on a long crusade to purify city life. William Howland, elected in 1885 as Toronto's first reform mayor, was a stout advocate of moral reform — in fact, he founded that city's department of morality — and he left an influential party on city council which carried on his work for decades. These crusaders were most famous for their attacks upon organized sin: the saloon, the gambling den, the house of prostitution, even the theatre. They were convinced that vice was so much a fact of city life that it menaced the national destiny.[16] They managed to persuade provincial and municipal authorities to pass laws to stamp out immorality, to regulate the behaviour of the wealthy as well as the poor and the immigrants, and to protect the youth of Canada.[17] They sponsored a variety of moral clean-up campaigns in each city to enforce these laws, a task which was not always easy or successful. In Winnipeg, after an initial assault on prostitution, the chief of police contacted the leading madam of the day, Minnie Woods, and re-established a segregated red-light district, where the police could at least control the activities of prostitutes.[18] In Halifax war-time prohibition closed down legal bars but left the city to "blind pigs" (illegal saloons), generally in league with brothels, which expanded to meet the needs of thousands of soldiers and sailors.[19] Still it is little wonder that these reformers were despised by many — C. S. Clarke, an opinionated Torontonian, denounced them as a small group of pious fanatics who bothered the respectable and terrorized the weak.[20] Moral reform was an experiment in social engineering, an attempt to force the city dweller to conform to the public mores of the church-going middle class.

In attitude and in personnel, moral reform was closely connected with social welfare. Howland, for example, throughout his civic career, was devoted to the cause of the underprivileged. Traditionally the care of the urban poor was the task of the churches and private charities with some relief services supplied by the municipalities and the provincial government.[21] As with so many other institutions, this welfare system collapsed under the impact of urban growth. In both his books, *My Neighbor* and *Strangers Within Our Gates*, J.S. Woodsworth drew upon his experiences and those of others to paint what to contemporaries must have been an incredible picture of spiritual and physical degradation in Canada's big cities. Some humanitarian reformers like J.J. Kelso of Toronto, who had been active since the 1880's, concentrated upon child welfare. They reasoned that by saving the young, they could ultimately save the future, an idea which particularly appealed to middle-class Canadians. These people saw the child as tomorrow's hope for a better society and invested heavily in education as an instrument of social and moral improvement. Thus the concern for a special children's charter, boys' camp, parks and recreational centres, and new schools, all to protect the innocence of the child and to mold his character according to the rational ethic.[22]

But other reformers, notably J.S. Woodsworth, refused to forget the adult generation of poor. Woodsworth rejected the notion that the majority of the poor were undeserving, that they had failed because of some weakness in their make-up. Rather, social and economic conditions, perhaps the very structure of society, had prevented the poor from achieving any kind of success. Surely the fruits of progress could be more evenly distributed? Woodsworth called upon the well-off to recognize their responsibility to the underprivileged — thus the title *My Neighbor*. In fact, civic authorities did respond to the misery of the poor. Speaking to an Ottawa audience in 1914, Mayor Hocken of Toronto claimed that his city had taken up a wide variety of "human services," such as public recreation, the care of the feeble-minded, food inspection, unemployment relief, and the like.[23] This "new spirit," as Hocken called it, was laying the foundations of the welfare state.

In 1902, in his classic survey of city government, S. Morley Wickett concluded that the "corporation question" in all its manifold aspects was of overshadowing importance to urban reform. By the "corporation question" he meant utility regulation and ownership, issues which had become more and more pressing towards the end of the nineteenth century. Waterworks, street railways, electric power, and the telephone systems, all constituted the physical plant of the city and the basis for continued urban expansion. The "utility base" of the cities had been largely developed by the efforts of private capital, usually on extremely generous terms to the entrepreneurs. Even though most utility companies performed with reasonable efficiency, there seemed an inherent conflict between civic requirements and business profits.[24]

It was this assumption which gave rise to the long controversy over municipal ownership. Drawing upon American and British experience, reformers like Wickett concluded that civic authorities must take control of the utility base. They argued that utility development was very different from other kinds of business endeavor. The utilities were in fact natural monopolies since any competition was both wasteful and expensive. Companies were able to exploit this captive market with little regard for the interest of the city. Because of their wealth, they could thwart any efforts to regulate their activities. Municipal ownership would allow the city to extend utilities into suburban areas, reduce service rates, and increase civic revenues.[25] Of course, not all Canadians agreed with this appraisal. However argued, municipal ownership was an assault upon the national ethic of individual enterprise. Theoretical questions aside, one noted economist, James Mavor of the University of Toronto, warned that public ownership everywhere had failed. Because they were essentially political bodies, subject to the changing impulses of the public mind, governments simply could not manage a business enterprise. Efficient, cheap service was lost in a welter of bureacratic red-tape and noisy rhetoric.[26]

Whatever the merit of his conclusions, Mavor had taken up a losing cause. True, the campaign for municipal ownership was not immediately victorious. In Montreal between 1904 and 1909, the utility companies easily overcame a threat of municipalization and remained largely untouched for the next thirty years.[27] In 1910, after running its power and transport utilities for fifteen years, Moncton returned these facilities to a private company, apparently to save money.[28] But these were exceptions. As early as 1893 Guelph had purchased its gas works and electric light and power plants.[29] In 1901 delegates from Quebec and Ontario, led by O.A. Howland, mayor of Toronto, founded the Union of Canadian Municipalities specifically to combat the machinations of utility companies.[30] In 1905 the new Whitney Government in Ontario organized the Public Hydro Commission to provide cheap power for industries and cities.[31] In 1907 the Manitoba government purchased the young provincial telephone system and expanded it across the province.[32] By 1920 the idea of municipal control, if not always municipal ownership, had won numerous converts in cities and towns.

After 1900 urban reformers, inspired by the town planning craze, became aware of their ability to mold the physical character of Canadian cities. The concept of town planning originated in the so-called City Beautiful and Garden City movements common to Europe, Britain, and the United States and popular ever since the Chicago Exposition of 1893 and the Letchworth experiment in England in 1903.[33] The City Beautiful movement undated the old ideal of civic improvement — the elimination of unsightly civic architecture and its replacement by attractive buildings, widened streets, promenades, parks, and trees. G.-A. Nantel wished to turn Montreal into this kind of City Beautiful. The Garden City and Garden suburb ideas were more drastic attempts to create communities separate from existing urban centres and without their problems. These schemes were an extension and a rationalization of the movement to the suburbs and an attempt to revive the ideal of the village community.[34] In 1912 at the Canadian Club of Montreal, Adam Shortt unveiled a fantastic scheme of urban depopulation to redeem the life of the city dweller throughout Canada. Envisaging a network of rapid transit systems, he imagined the movement of city workers out to country homes where they could enjoy the benefits of rural life and perhaps indulge in a little farming to supplement their incomes.[35] In essence, he was proposing the ruralization of the city. Such nostalgia for country life was implicit in all these schemes.

Many town planning experts, like the influential Thomas Adams, a Scotchman attached to the Commission of Conservation, were very conscious of the need to disassociate their projects from this kind of nostalgia. Their sensibility was injured by the disjointed civic topography left in the wake of the early developers, who in their rush to accommodate new industry, the rural migrant, and the foreign immigrant cared little whether they created a livable environment.[36] These town planners emphasized that they were not merely concerned with the aesthetic but with pressing economic and heatlh problems. Town planning, noted Clifford Sifton, was "a rational scheme of supervising the conditions in which the people of our great cities live.''[37] It was practical and economical, involving the doctor, the engineer, and the businessmen as well as the artist and the architect. Just prior to World War I, more and more municipal and provincial authorities became converts of the movement and an incredible number of town plans were initiated throughout Canada, for example, the proliferation of special zoning by-laws to protect residential areas, the Halifax reconstruction scheme after the disastrous explosion of 1917, and the new steel town of Ojibway projected for Southwestern Ontario.[38]

Perhaps the most publicized scheme was that put forward by the Toronto Harbor Commission. At an estimated cost of twenty-five million dollars, using civic and federal capital, the Commission proposed to redevelop the Toronto waterfront as a multiple-use site with improved warehousing and commercial facilities, room for industrial growth, better housing for workers, and a recreational area, all tied to the rest of the city by means of an expanded rapid transit system. Although controlled by the Commission, the project was in fact an alliance of private and public interests (the all-important railway companies had early given their approval) so that all might profit. It was an expensive investment in the future, but the initial cost would soon be recouped by the attraction of new business to Toronto. Waste lands, then largely valueless, would become industrial areas. And Torontonians as a whole would benefit from the use of the waterfront as a public park.[39]

The Toronto harbor project, of course, stood in a long tradition of developmental schemes with which Canadians and businessmen were very familiar.[40] A more novel concern of town planners was urban congestion and the appearance of the slum and the immigrant ghetto. In the years after 1895 a series of studies by such people as Herbert Ames, J.J. Kelso, J.S. Woodsworth, and Bryce Stewart showed that all major cities, even small centres like Port Arthur and Fort William, housed an urban proletariat, in part foreign-born, generally poor and concentrated in crowded subdivisions, slums, or shanty-towns.[44] Like the United States, suggested Charles Hodgetts, we had ''our Little Italys, our Little Londons, and our Chinatowns, devoid of the simplest of modern sanitary requirements.''[42] These slums were ''cancerous sores'' on the body politic, ''sources of bacteria'' spreading disease, crime, and discontent throughout the city. They menaced the moral and physical character of Canadian manhood and thus the racial future of the whole nation. Some alarmists even feared a red revolution sparked by the disgruntled proletariat and the immigrants. But all reformers charged that slums were a reflection upon the nation; no civilized society could allow its citizens to suffer in this way.[43]

Yet, without tremendous expenditures, how could the nation end the slum problem? Clifford Sifton pointed out that the much-heralded suburban movement was no solution; it was actually a movement of the prosperous, not the poor, away from the urban core.[44] Some reformers tried to meet the problem with new housing laws to control tenements and to maintain minimum standards of hygiene and health — in effect to check the further spread of the slum and to ameliorate conditions within it.[45] Others attempted to get business interests involved in cheap housing, a primitive form of urban renewal. Herbert Ames advocated such a plan of privately financed workers' homes and this was apparently carried out on a limited scale by G. Frank Beer in Toronto. During the post-war reconstruction clamour, there was a demand for direct state involvement in the housing business. In fact Thomas Adams did head a commission which co-ordinated a joint federal-provincial loan scheme for cheap housing, essentially to meet the needs of returned soldiers.[46] All of these reformers, it should be emphasized, were convinced of the moral and physical virtues of the single-family dwelling; they wanted a nation of homes, not of apartment houses.

The steadily expanding services expected of city governments resulted in mounting costs and an increased tax burden, neither of which were popular. In 1907 Wickett pointed out that "the annual expenditure of Winnipeg clearly exceeds that of Manitoba; Montreal's that of the province of Quebec; and until the present year Toronto's that of the province of Ontario."[47] Reformers and municipal officials constantly searched for new methods of meeting tax requirements. Some of the impetus behind the campaign for municipal ownership was this desire for greater revenue. Most cities switched from the confused personal property tax system to a more specific and just business tax. Between 1890 and 1910, western cities experimented widely with variants of Henry George's single tax idea, exempting at least part of the value of improvements upon land.[48] Of course, all civic leaders paid at least lip-service to economy and retrenchment, but it was impossible to implement these axioms with any permanent success. Businessmen were particularly outraged by the casual attitude which civic authorities adopted towards new expenditures. Sir Frederick William-Taylor of the Bank of Montreal insisted that "the outstanding matter calling for municipal reform in this country is with regard to borrowing powers."[49] He believed that Canadian cities, especially in the west, had accumulated debts at a per capita rate out of all proportion to the rest of the world.

The success of the reform idea was heavily dependent upon the active support of municipal government. Only the state had sufficient authority to impose order on the chaos of city life. But even before 1880 it was clear that the existing councils of untrained aldermen were ill-equipped to deal with the multiplicity of new problems. Too often they were dominated by ward-heelers and partymen — individuals who were more concerned with private gain, local interests, and politics than with the city's welfare.[50]

Worse, the expansion of civic responsibilities had vastly increased the opportunities for and the profits of municipal corruption. These evils seemed so pressing that for some time the urban reform movement was closely identified in the mind of the public at large with the reform of municipal government.

In 1885 H. Beaugrand, editor of Montreal's Liberal paper *La Patrie*, and in 1886 W.H. Howland, a business leader and child welfare advocate in Toronto, won the mayoralty of their respective cities as declared reform candidates. But they and later reform mayors found it difficult to realize their promises. It was hard to overcome civic apathy, to maintain reform morale and cohesion, and to get rid of the "old guard" politicians. During the mid-1890's in Montreal, to meet these problems, Herbert Ames and like-minded English civic leaders constructed a political machine to combat the "old guard" at the ward level.[51] Thus began a battle which lasted two decades between, on the one hand, a reform coalition, supported by many English voters, certain businessmen, and French-Canadian progressives such as Bourassa and Asselin, and, on the other hand, a mixed bag of opportunists who had the backing of most French Canadians, especially the clerical and artisan classes. In 1914 this classic battle ended with the victory of Médéric Martin, a colourful and unscrupulous cigar-maker, who during his long rule crushed the reform-progressive coalition.[52] Elsewhere in Canada, the conflict was rarely so fierce or reform so decisively beaten. In fact, municipal politicians generally paid lip-service to reform, though their active support for the idea was offtimes sporadic and self-interested.[53] It was this hypocrisy which Stephen Leacock brutally satirized in his account of "the great fight for clean government."

As the early reformers learned to their chagrin, the mere election of honest men did not ensure the ability of the council to handle the rapacious utility companies or to foster civic improvement. In the 1890's reformers began a search for new governmental structures. To ensure continuity, the ward system was rationalized and the length of term for aldermen increased. To enlarge the powers of the executive, the Board of Control was instituted first in Toronto (1897) and later in several cities as a kind of municipal cabinet. Some enthusiats, for instance the young Frank Underhill, supported the American idea of commission government, rule by a small body of elected or even appointed officials.[55] These measures were an attempt to divide legislative and executive functions and to fix responsibility, thereby reducing political influences. Of course, this emphasis upon structures produced its own reaction. Throughout, some reformers, especially those who were actually involved in municipal government, argued that "good men" were essential, no matter the structure. Ultimately, it was the quality of elected officials who would determine the character of municipal government.[56]

Whether concerned with structures of men, reformers agreed that city government must be more responsive to the interests of the whole community. They looked upon the city as a single entity. Urban society was founded upon interdependence: "City life," claimed J.S. Woodsworth, "is like a spider's web — pull one thread and you pull every thread."[57] Thus all urban problems, not merely those relating to utilities and town planning, had a general import. In the past, argued reformers, too much attention had been paid to particularist interests. Wealthy neighbourhoods had benefitted from local improvement schemes at the expense of slums and suburbs. Entrenched neighbourhood politicians had hindered the implementation of general reform measures necessary to the city's welfare.[58] It was essential to subordinate the neighbourhood to the city. In future, the civic leadership must look to the whole electorate and not to its constituent elements.

Then as now, reformers were continually foiled by civic apathy. Even when they managed to win over municipal officials, they found it difficult to mobilize public support, especially if their suggestions required increased expenditures. Not surprisingly, frustrated reformers were inclined to blame such defeats upon a conspiracy of the cruder elements in municipal politics. There was a significant though muted fear of the urban proletariat and the immigrant vote, both of which could lead to the dominance of American-style city bosses. Some reformers, like Wickett, seemed to favour the restricted franchise which would give the respectable property-holder decisive power in civic affairs.[59] One of the reasons for proposals to rationalize the ward system, particularly by creating enlarged wards, was in the hope of undermining the strength of the lower-class vote.[60] On the whole, though, reformers placed greater emphasis upon popular involvement in municipal politics through civic organizations, a lowered franchise, and the plebiscite — in Regina and Edmonton, civic leaders even experimented with "direct democracy" incorporating the referendum system in their respective city charters.[61] Time after time, reformers called upon municipal leaders to educate the public, to make the electors aware of civic problems. Reformers seemed convinced, at least at the level of rhetoric, that a vigorous "civic patriotism" would eventually overcome particularism and partisanship, freeing municipal government from the corrupting influence of special interests.[62] In reality "civic patriotism" meant a blanket commitment to the schemes of the reformers.

More and more, the reformers placed their final trust in the bureaucratic method, that essential handmaiden of modern collectivism. The bureaucratic method was a radically new approach to society and problem-solving. At the theoretical level, it was founded upon the burgeoning science of statistics. This science, in vogue since the last quarter of the nineteenth century, seemed able to rationalize the complex and mysterious world created by the new urban-industrial order. The statistician broke down situations into their constituent elements, transferred these results to paper, and thereby rendered understandable the "real world."[63] In this study of a particular area in Montreal, Herbert Ames analyzed the inhabitants as an economic class of varying income units, as ethnic groups, and as home-owners, piling category on top of category, and eventually creating a composite picture of their physical needs. Although very ambitious, Ames' survey was only one of the innumerable municipal studies sponsored by reform organizations and individuals, dealing with relief cases, crime and disease, municipal finances, and so on. Such studies were essential as a means of educating the public and projecting sound reform programmes — without statistics, complete and standardized, there could be no effective planning, no slum clearance, no tax reform.[64]

At the institutional level, the bureaucratic method required the creation of an autonomous and trained administration dedicated to the twin ideals of economy and efficiency. To the reformers expert knowledge was a near panacea. This was the beginning of the age of the specialist and the professional. The reformers hoped to minimize the influence of the amateur in all departments of civic government, to take administration out of politics.[65] Wickett pointed to Germany where leading civic administrators were trained before they took office.[66] There were suggestions that Canadian academics become involved in municipal research and the training of municipal experts. Reformers demanded the multiplication of bureaucratic structures, special and permanent commissions, advisory posts and the like, to deal in detail with the community.[67] Responding to reform pleas, especially after 1900, municipal governments did create formidable civic bureaucracies to control police, public health, utilities, parks and recreation, and social welfare.[68] To a degree, this appeared to be a devolution of authority; in fact, it was a centralization of authority in the hands of professions, well-nigh independent of the electorate with a vested interest in the success of the reform movement. This latent authoritarianism was tempered by the assumption that the bureaucrat would move in accordance with a right-thinking public.

The reform idea had an import far beyond the immediate urban setting. Some reformers and municipal officials, it is true, did seem to favour the separation of the city and the wider provincial community. These "home rulers" argued that provincial assemblies were dominated by rural members and therefore the provincial governments were largely indifferent to municipal problems. W.D. Lighthall, secretary of the Union of Canadian Municipalities, believed that the cities must have complete control over all their utilities.[69] W.F. Maclean, owner of the Toronto *World*, argued that Toronto should extend its control over the surrounding countryside and regulate its own affairs without outside interference.[70] Similarly, G.-A. Nantel wished to consolidate all major governmental functions on the island of Montreal under one general scheme of metropolitan federation. Such beliefs led to experimentation with existing incorporation and municipal acts: in Toronto a call for a special charter to meet the city's peculiar needs, in Edmonton a less specific grant of municipal powers to ensure flexibility and freedom.[74]

But "home rule" never secured as much support in Canada as in the United States. As most reformers recognized, it has hardly practicable to establish an inflexible division between civic and provincial affairs. Cities were legal creatures of the provinces and schemes for municipal reorganization, public health, or social welfare required provincial approval. Battles between the cities and utility companies, such as the public hydro controversy in Ontario, the campaign against corporate domination in Montreal, and the drive for provincialization of telephones in Manitoba and Alberta, all involved province-wide interests and consequently these battles were transferred to the legislative assemblies. Thus reformers pressured provincial governments to take an active hand in urban reform. In response, provinces passed special laws and gradually established a new bureaucracy to deal with municipal matters.[72]

Towards the end of the period, more and more reformers demanded a national response to urban problems. Most wanted a federal commission modelled on the British Local Government Board with extraordinary powers to co-ordinate schemes for civic improvement. To a degree, this desire was satisfied by that strange federal body, the Commission of Conservation, which existed between 1909 and 1921. Although in theory only advisory, under the energetic direction of Clifford Sifton the Commission delved into all kinds of issues, not the least being urban reform. It held a number of special hearings on housing and public health, sponsored conferences on town planning and civic improvement, and engineered the founding of the Civic Improvement League of Canada. Between 1914 and 1921, it published a quarterly magazine, *Conservation of Life*, to investigate town planning housing and public health. It attempted to co-ordinate the plans of reformers and provincial and federal administrators and to establish national codes for housing and health. The range of activities included within the purview of the Commission was astonishing. It had tried to deal with all the problems of the new urban-industrial order. Unfortunately, it had also challenged the politicians — the result was its abolition in 1921.[73]

Urban reform should not be considered in isolation. It was part of a movement international in scope and general to Canadian society. Urban problems were common to all industrialized nations. The ties between Canadian reformers and American progressives are obvious. In a lone discussion of American influences on Canadian government, delivered at the University of Toronto in 1929, the Harvard political scientist William Bennett Munro concluded that Canadian city government, if not the idea of municipal reform, was modelled upon the American system with its checks and balances, administrative profusion, and divided authority.[74] While there was some truth in this assertion, Canadian reformers had in fact imported ideas and techniques from everywhere. Much of the theory of town planning in Canada was inspired by the British experience, perhaps because of the influence of Thomas Adams. G.-A. Nantel praised Paris as the prototype for the City Beautiful in the Dominion. Morely Wickett looked upon German cities as a model of efficient government. The advocates of social purity looked to Britain and the United States for inspiration. The idea of reform in Canada, or for that matter anywhere, had only a limited nationalist content.

In his book *The Search for Order, 1877-1920*, Robert Weibe has argued that the challenge of social and economic change during the late nineteenth century led to the disruption of the loosely-knit American society based upon a network of "island communities." In the following decades, he maintains, it was re-ordered, more properly integrated, by the new urban middle class along collectivist lines. There is every reason to believe that a similar process, perhaps not so drastic, occurred in Canada. To control a society both fluid and complex, Canadians searched for some new method of ensuring stability. The answer for many, whether radical or moderate, anglophone or francophone, business, labour, and farm, lay in collectivism. The rise of the professions, the proliferation of business combinations and associations, trade unionism and agarian organizations, all were aspects of the same collectivist urge.[74] Urban reform was only one of many phenomena like civic service reform, the social gospel, and conservation, which together constitute the progressive tradition in Canada.[76] By 1920 organization and bureaucracy flourished at all levels.

Although the idea of urban reform appealed to an everwidening constituency, it drew its leadership from the spokesmen of the new middle class concentrated in Canada's, especially central Canada's big cities. Speaking very generally, this class was itself a collection of at least three elements: old and new professionals proud of their particular expertise; businessmen, committed to the efficient exploitation of the nation's resources; and women, in many cases the wives of professionals and businessmen, determined to carve out their own place in society. Each group saw the ideal city in a somewhat different light. Much of the early initiative came from journalists like Hugh Graham of the Montreal *Star*, John Ross Robertson of the Toronto *Telegram*, and W.F. Maclean of the Toronto *World*. These self-proclaimed tribunes of the people were most conscious of political corruption and vaguely distressed by the squalor of urban life.

Businessmen, like Herbert Ames and S. Morley Wickett, and particularly their fellows in the Boards of Trade, desired an attractive community, run on principles of economy and efficiency. Women's organizations, clergymen, and humanitarians concentrated their efforts upon the moral and social uplift of the underprivileged. And the ultimate victors, the bureaucrats like Thomas Adams, Charles Hastings, and Charles Hodgetts pictured the city as a poorly-functioning mechanism which had to be streamlined and regulated.

Still these people held much in common. The distinction between say, humanitarian and town planner or sanitary and municipal reformer was always blurred, especially in the heat of battle. They were all motivated by a generalized sense of crisis, founded on a variety of fears, such as the spread of moral decay, the threat of class hatreds, and the growth of vested interests. They were inspired by the possibilities of improvement, by a belief in their ability to mold the urban environment and to create a humane, rational society. Though this was an essentially secular goal, their values, moral, humanitarianb, political, and economic — in a phrase, their cultural baggage — was defined within a Christian context and jumbled together in the drive for social reconstruction. They fostered a concept of the public interest based upon the primacy of the civic community, social justice and social order, and good government. They tried to impose this concept upon all city dwellers, rich and poor. More significant, they institutionalized reform at the three levels of government, thereby creating a bureaucracy which systematically carried forward their work.

The story of urban reform does not end here. It would be unwise to assume that reform doctrine was wholly accepted by the urban middle class, much less by other groups within Canadian society. The rural myth, more especially the image of the "evil city", retained a strong hold upon the Canadian mentatlity. Moreover, some critics feared that reform would subvert the individualistic ethos which underlay Victorian Canada, while others warned that it would solidify the class domination of city life. Such attitudes have not died. In fact, the very success of the urban reform government has inspired new anxieties, for the price of order was a reduction in the freedom of the individual and the neighbourhood. Since 1960, centralization, bureaucracy, even expertise have become the targets of a new dissenting movement based upon radically different propositions. Ironically, we are now witnessing a general reaction against collectivism which threatens to undo the work of the urban reformers.

NOTES:

1. M.C. Urquhart, *Historical Statistics of Canada* (Toronto, 1965), pp. 14-15.
2. J.S. Woodsworth, *My Neighbour* (Toronto, 1911), p. 37.

3. A good example of this ambivalent approach to the city can be found in the speech of Martin Burrill, minister of agriculture, to the sixth national conference on town planning: "But we have all got to remember that the cities of the past and many of the cities of the present have been responsible for the building up of the greater forces of our modern and our past civilization, that the impact of mind on mind and the interplay of moral and intellectual forces which are associated closely together in our great centers are responsible for the advance that civilization has made in all ages. It is perfectly true that there is a darker side to our city life, and it is not without some poignancy of regret to every man who believes that from the great country homes of the land the streaming forces that uplife the whole of the national life must and do mainly come, [sic] it must be a matter of regret that in Canada, essentially an agricultural country today, there are 45 per cent of our people living in urban homes. In speaking of that, one cannot forget that the greast cities of the world are characterized too often by squalor and by a dismal poverty that must rob man of his manhood and point to nothing but dismay." *Proceedings of the Sixth Annual National Conference on City Planning* (Boston, 1914), pp. 315-316.

4. See Thomas Conant, *Life in Canada* (Toronto, 1903), pp. 227-243 and W.G. Good, "Canada's Rural Problem," *Empire Club Speeches*, Toronto, 1915-16/1916-17, pp. 299-302.

5. C. Berger, *The Sense of Power* (Toronto, 1970), pp. 177-198.

6. C.S. Clarke's scurrilous account of Toronto in 1898 contains an excellent description of this "dark side." Clarke was particularly intrigued by the extent of the social evil, prostitution and the like in Toronto. C.S. Clarke, *Of Toronto the Good* (Toronto: Coles reprint, 1970).

7. For critical comments on this movement see "The Back-to-the-land Movement," *Conservation of Life*, Toronto, October, 1914, pp. 30-31 and John A. Cormis, "Back to the Land," *University Magazine*, April, 1918, pp. 197-203.

8. These papers were the Montreal *Star*, the Toronto *Telegram*, the Toronto *World*, the Toronto *News*1, The Ottawa *Journal*, the Vancouver *News-Advertiser*, and to a lesser extent the Winnipeg *Sun*. They were less partisan, more sensationalist, more chauvinist, and much cruder than the regular party journals. These people's papers set a new tone in journalism which eventually effected the whole of the urban press. It should be added that regular journals did not neglect municipal affairs, but their concern was rarely so continuous.

9. For example, in 1910 the Canadian Club of Ottawa was addressed by Charles J. Bonaparte, ex-attorney general of the United States, on the purification of city politics and by Henry Vivian, a British M.P., on city planning.

10. Canadian Policitial Science Association, *Papers and Proceedings*, vol. 1, 1913.

11. This had first been championed by the civic booster, the spokesman for local business interests, who was committed to the material growth of his community. But by the late 1870's and early 1880's, when the public library issue arose in Montreal and Toronto, there was a much more obvious reform tone to civic improvement, a concern with popular culture as well as prestige.

12. J.E. Middleton, *The Municipality of Toronto: A History*, vol. 1 (Toronto and New York, 1923), pp. 301-302.

13. For a chronological account of the advance of public health in the city of Toronto, see *Events and Factors in the Advance of Public Health Measures in Toronto, 1866-*, a special report, Department of the City Clerk, September 18, 1968.

14. The English papers in Montreal were the most vociferous advocates of vaccination — the Montreal *Herald* was the target of a riot for its "advanced" views. But so-called respectable francophone opinion, represented by Mayor Beaugrand, was equally committed. Vaccination was as much a class issue as a race issue, involving the physical imposition of the wishes of the educated upon the lower orders.

15. Charles J. Hastings, "The Modern Conception of Public Health Administration," *Conservatism of Life*, October, 1917, p. 88.

16. For an elaboration of the ideas of these moral reformers see G.A. Warburton, "The Moral Conditions of Toronto," Canadian Club, Toronto, *Proceedings*, 1915-16, pp. 17-25 and "Commercialized Vice and the White Slave Traffic," and "Temperance," Social Service Congress, *Report of Addresses and Proceedings*, (Toronto, 1914), pp. 199-237 and 303-326. Another valuable source are the yearbooks of the National Council of Women, especially with regard to the social purity movement. These yearbooks indicate the wide variety of interests involved in moral reform, especially its concern with the immigrants, the underprivileged, and social welfare.

17. These laws related to prostitution and seduction, liquor and prohibition, gambling, night curfew, pernicious literature, tobacco and narcotic sales, sabbatarianism, and the police. The moral reform movement had a national import: the anti-gambling legislation of Blake, Charlton's campaign against seduction, the Dominion Lord's Day Act, and of course prohibition. "Blue Laws" won considerable support in cities, towns, and farming districts — more often from English Canada than Quebec. The moral reform campaigns in the cities were only a part of a movement general throughout English Canada.

18. James H. Gray, *The Boy from Winnipeg* (Toronto, 1970), pp. 5-8.

19. Thomas H. Raddall, *Halifax, Warden of the North* (Toronto, 1948), pp. 260-261.

20. C. Clarke, *Of Toronto the Good*, pp. 86-131.

21. Richard B. Splane, *Social Welfare in Ontario, 1791-1893* (Toronto: University of Toronto Press, 1965).

22. See the comment of W.J. Hanna, an Ontario cabinet minister to the new Civic Improvement League of Canada: "The nation is the individual in the aggregate. Surround the individual with the proper conditions and most of the real problems, the social problems, will cease to exist. Before the individual is born, make such labour laws and establish such conditions as will ensure him a healthy mother. . . . Suitable town-planning and enforced housing laws will give him a home with sunshine and fresh air on all sides. . . . We must also give him supervised playgrounds. Failing playgrounds and open spaces, he should have a quiet street with now and then a hurdy-gurdy. . . . Where he goes to school he should be put in his proper class; he should not have to sit beside a consumptive or a defective. Manual training should be part of his school course. His sister should be taught mothercraft, cooking and sewing; at the same time she ought to be given some practical education that would enable her to become a skilled wage-earner. Give the boy a school bank if you can, that he may learn the first principle of thrift. Introduce him to the public library with its Saturday afternoon story talks and moving pictures and get his parents in to read the magazines. Censor his movies so that he will not choose the wrong hero. Give him compulsory military training. If you launch him with this equipment, he is not likely to prove a serious civic problem. Launch a generation of him and your civic problems are largely solved." Civic Improvement League of Canada, *Report of Conference*, 1916, pp. 31-32. See also J.J. Kelso, "Neglected and Friendless Children," *Canadian Magazine*, vol. 2, 1893-94, pp. 213-216; C.J. Atkinson, "The Boy Problem," Canadian Club, Toronto, *Addresses*, 1909-10, pp. 52-60; and "Child Welfare", Social Service Congress, *Report of Addresses and Proceedings*, (Toronto, 1914), pp. 89-115.

23. H.C. Hocken, "The New Spirit in Municipal Government," Canadian Club, Ottawa, *Addresses*, 1914-15, pp. 85-97.

24. S. Morley Wickett, "City Government in Canada," *Municipal Government in Canada*, ed. S. Morley Wickett (Toronto, 1907), p. 23. This article was first written in 1902. See also A.C. Thompson, "The Taxation of Franchises," *Canadian Magazine*, vol. 24, 1904-05, pp. 463-465.

25. S. Morley Wickett, "Present Conditions," *Municipal Government in Canada*, pp. 157-162; W.F. Maclean, "A Greater Toronto," *Empire Club Speeches*, Toronto, 1907-08, pp. 84-89;

and F.S. Spence, "Some Suggestions as to Toronto Street Railway Problems", Canadian Club, Toronto, *Addresses*, 1908-09, pp. 37-40.

26. James Mavor, "Municipal Ownership of Public Utilities," reprint, a paper read at the joint meeting of the Michigan Political Science Association and the League of Michigan Municipalities (Ann Arbor, 1904); James Mavor, *Government Telephones: The Experience of Manitoba, Canada* (New York: Moffat, Yard and Company, 1916); and Edward Harris, "A Review of Civic Ownership," (Toronto: William Briggs, 1908).

27. For a fuller description of the abortive campaign against corporate dominance in Montreal, see J.I. Cooper, *Montreal: A Brief History* (Montreal and London, 1969), pp. 120-121 and Joseph Levitt, *Henri Bourassa and the Golden Calf* (Ottawa, 1969), pp. 47-56.

28. Lloyd A. Machum, *A History of Moncton, Town and City 1855-1965* (Moncton, 1965), p. 218 and 222.

29. W.J. Bell, a local civic booster, claimed that Guelph was "the first Canadian Municipality to own and successfully operate all of its public utilities," W.J. Bell, "Municipal Ownership and Civic Government" (Guelph, 1909), p. 3.

30. J.E. Middleton, *The Municipality of Toronto*, p. 364 and W.D. Lighthall, "Valedictory of W.D. Lighthall, K.C., On Retiring from the Honorary Secretaryship of the Union of Canadian Municpalities, August, 1919."

31. Even before this, Ontario towns had been purchasing their electric power utilities. According to R.N. Beattie, twenty towns and cities between 1899 and 1902 had commenced operation of their own facilities. R.N. Beattie, "The Impact of Hydro on Ontario," *Profiles of a Province* (Toronto, 1967), pp. 167-168.

32. The telephone question was a problem unto itself. Bell Telephone had a Dominion charter which could not be touched by the provinces. Furthermore, Bell controlled the trunk lines between cities, upon which an efficient and extensive telephone system depended. It seemed almost impossible for cities to handle Bell on their own, thus the interest in provincial and national control.

33. For a discussion of the significance of these movements see Charles N. Glaab and A. Theodore Brown, *A History of Urban America* (New York and London, 1967), pp. 260-263 and 289-291. Jane Jacobs, the noted urban philosopher, argues that the town planners, in fact urban reform generally, never overcame the myths created by the City Beautiful and Garden City ideas. Jane Jacobs, *The Death and Life of Great American Cities* (Toronto: Random House, 1961), pp. 16-25.

34. Henry Vivian, "Garden Suburbs and Town Planning," Canadian Club, Toronto, *Addresses*, 1910-11, pp. 35-40 and G. Trafford Hewitt, "Canada and the United States as a Field for the Garden City Movement," *Proceedings of the Sixth National Conference on City Planning* (Boston, 1914), pp. 180-189. Hewitt was the president of the Province of Nova Scotia Land Corporation, Limited and he claimed that he planned to build a Garden City in Canada. Purportedly, Lindenlea, outside Ottawa, was a garden suburb. See B. Evan Parry, "Ottawa a Garden Suburb," *Town Planning and Conservation of Life*, July-September, 1920, p. 68.

35. Adam Shortt, "The Social and Economic Significance of the Movement from the Country to the City," Canadian Club, Montreal, *Addresses*, 1912-13, pp. 70-71.

36. James Gray gives an amusing description of the chaos left by the developers in Winnipeg after the boom in the early twentieth century. James H. Gray, *The Boy from Winnipeg*, pp. 1-5.

37. Clifford Sifton, "Address of Welcome," *Proceedings of the Sixth National Conference on City Planning* (Boston, 1914), p. 12. One writer argued that Canadians were following the broader scheme of town planning along the British model rather than the American, which tended more towards the aesthetic. "The Meaning and Practical Application of Town Planning," *Conservation of Life*, July, 1915, pp. 74-76.

38. As an appendix, the magazine *Conservation of Life* carried a summary of town planning exploits throughout the nation.

39. R.S. Gourlay, "Some Aspects of Commercial Value to the City of Toronto of the Proposed Harbor Improvements," *Empire Club Speeches*, Toronto, 1912-13/1913-14, pp. 129-145; R.S. Gourlay, "Basic Principles of Water Front Development as Illustrated by the Plans of the Toronto Harbor Commission," *Proceedings of the Sixth National Conference on City Planning* (Boston, 1914), pp. 17-31; and L.H. Clarke, "Putting a New Front on Toronto," *Canadian Magazine*, vol. 42, 1913-14, pp. 205-15.

40. The CPR and the Grand Trunk had sponsored development schemes in Moncton, Toronto, Winnipeg and Vancouver, though these railway companies had not been especially concerned with the idea of town planning.

41. For a short but effective description of the problem of immigrant ghettoes see Bryce Stewart, "The Housing of Our Immigrant Workers," Canadian Political Science Association, *Proceedings and Papers*, vol. 1, 1913, pp. 98-111.

42. Charles Hodgetts, "Unsanitary Housing," Commission of Conservation, *Addresses, 1911*, p. 33. See also G.F. Chipman, "Winnipeg: The Melting Pot," and "The Refining Process," *Canadian Magazine*, vol. 33, 1909, pp. 409-416 and 548-554.

43. P.H. Bryce, "Civic Responsibility and the Increase of Immigration," *Empire Club Speeches* (Toronto, 1906-7), pp. 186-197; W.D. Lighthall, "Toronto and Town Planning," *Empire Club Speeches, 1910-11*, pp. 233-234; and J.W. Macmillan, "Problems of Population," *Empire Club Speeches*, 1911-12, pp. 75-79. It seems that the prosperous urbanities who attended Empire Club proceedings were interested in the slum problem. Comment after Bryce's paper, however, revealed that at least three members were more concerned with keeping out undesirable immigration than with solving the existing problem.

44. Clifford Sifton, "Address of Welcome," *Proceedings of the Sixty National Conference on City Planning* (Boston, 1914), p. 8. The suburban movement had been a feature of Canadian life for some years by 1914. Developers had been quick to realize the possibilities of exploiting the dissatisfaction of prosperous urbanities with their cities. But in terms of urban reform, the suburban movement further fragmented the city into poor and rich districts and did not solve the problem of congestion within the poor districts.

45. Charles Hodgetts discussed the character of housing laws in Canadian provinces. They usually established regulations with regard to space, ventilation, and sanitation and they made provision for some kind of permanent inspectorate. Hodgetts noted that where applied these acts had the desired effect, but unfortunately many boards of health had not exercised their powers to the fullest extent. Charles Hodgetts, "Unsanitary Housing," *Addresses, 1911*, Commission of Conservation, pp. 43-51. For a more general discussion of town planning and slum reform see G. Frank Beer, "A Plea for City Organization," *Addresses, 1914*, Commission of Conservation.

46. Thomas Adams, "The Housing Problem," Canadian Club, Montreal, *Addresses*, 1918-19, pp. 178-187 and C.B. Sissons, "A Housing Policy for Ontario," *Canadian Magazine*, vol. 53, 1919, pp. 241-248.

47. S. Morley Wickett, "Present Conditions," *Municipal Government in Canada*, p. 343.

48. For a long discussion of the conversion to business taxes and the single tax experiment, see J.H. Perry, *Taxes, Tariffs, and Subsidies; A History of Canadian Fiscal Development* (Toronto, 1955), pp. 124-136. The western variant of single tax was not in fact a true application of Henry George's principles and it was based upon an extravagant land boom which constantly raised the value of land. There were many absentee landowners and speculators in the west, not the least being the Canadian Pacific Railway. When the land boom ended after 1910, western towns soon turned to the business tax and other more regular taxation systems. There was some discussion of the western variant in Ontario, especially in Toronto where it received approval in principle in a plebiscite, but the provincial government

refused to allow its adoption. Perry indicates, however, that in practice improvements were under-assessed in many municipalities.

49. Civic Improvement League of Canada, *Report of Preliminary Conference at Ottawa*, 1915, p. 8.

50. For example, municipal politics in Toronto in the 1880s seems to have been based upon a network of localist influences, religious and ethnic factions like the Orange Order, and sporadic business interest all overlayed by the partisan loyalty of civic leaders and the press to the Conservatives or Liberals.

51. H.B. Ames, "The Machine in Honest Hands," *Canadian Magazine*, vol. 3, 1894, pp. 101-109.

52. See W.H. Atherton, *Montreal, 1535-1914* (Montreal, 1914), vol. 2, pp. 184-191; Leslie Roberts, *Montreal: From Mission Colony to World City* (Toronto, 1969), pp. 263-270 and 304-316; and J.I. Cooper, *Montreal*, pp. 96-103, 119-121, and 130-144.

53. E.A. Macdonald, mayor of Toronto in 1900, is an excellent example of this kind of "reform" politician. Throughout the 1880s he constantly sniffed out scandal among his opponents in a finally successful campaign to secure the mayoralty. An account of his chequered career, albeit inadequate, can be found in J.E. Middleton, *The Municipality of Toronto*, vol. 1, pp. 339-357.

54. This innovation was peculiar to Canadian cities. It spread from Toronto to Hamilton and Ottawa and was temporarily adopted by Montreal, Winnipeg, and London. S. Morley Wickett, "City Government in Canada," *Municipal Government in Canada*, pp. 12-13 and H.L. Brittain, *Local Government in Canada* (Toronto, 1951), pp. 52-53.

55. F.H. Underhill, "Commission Government in Cities," *The Arbor* (University of Toronto), vol. 1-2, 1910-11, pp. 284-294; W.J. Bell, "Municipal Ownership and Civic Government by Commission"; Oliver Asselin, "Le Problème Municipal" (Montreal, 1909); and Goldwin Smith "Municipal Government: A Letter to the World", reprint, 1905(?).

56. During the 1880's, when certain reformers were trying to change the structure of city government, the Toronto *Telegram* constantly argued the case for "good men" over reformed institutions. Toronto *Telegram*, January 12, 1893, p. 4; February 27, 1896, p. 4; and March 28, 1896, p. 5. Mayor R.D. Waugh of Winnipeg told the Civic Improvement League of Canada in 1916 much the same thing: "The citizen does not, as a rule, take any of the blame or responsibility for mismanagement himself. It is almost invariably "the system" or "the Council" that is wrong. But you hear it in Ottawa, Toronto, Montreal, Winnipeg, everywhere, that old story, "The city government is no good." There is always a clamour more or less loud for a change. We all know that there is room for great improvement, but when we get down to the question of "How?" one says one thing, one another, but it is just threshing out the same old straw. We try new schemes, elect new men, but still the main result is the same.

No, the system is not altogether to blame for the result. It matters little about the system after all — the man is the main consideration. Poor men with a good system will not insure good government, but good man may, no matter what the system." Civic Improvement League of Canada, *Report of Conference*, 1916, p. 22.

57. Woodsworth, *My Neighbor*, p. 26.

58. Underhill, "Commission Governments in Cities," pp. 286-287.

59. Wickett, "City Government in Canada," *Municipal Government in Canada*, pp. 9-11.

60. In Toronto, there was a proposal that all wards be drawn from the harbour to the northern city limits. Such would create "hetergeneous" wards and break down the influence of lower-class neighbourhoods.

61. Wickett, "Present Conditions," *Municipal Government in Canada*, p. 351.

62. This point was continually raised at the two conferences on civic improvement; Civic Improvement League of Canada, *Report of Preliminary Conference at Ottawa*, 1915, p. 12 (Thomas Adams) and pp. 35-36 (S. Morley Wickett); and Civic Improvement League of Canada, *Report of Conference*, 1916, pp. 24-25 (R.D. Waugh, mayor of Winnipeg) and pp. 35-36 (W.J. Hanna).

63. See "Community Engineering," The Citizen's Research Institute of Canada, Ottawa, 1920. This was a pamphlet put out by the Institute to attract interest in statistical research into municipal problems. For a price the Institute was willing to carry out studies of particular communities.

64. S. Morley Wickett, "Municipal Publicity Through Uniformity in Municipal Statistics," Eighth Annual Convention of the Union of Canadian Municipalities, Montreal, 1908 and J.A. Cooper, "The Municipal Survey." *Canadian Political Science Association*, vol. 1, 1913, pp. 124-131.

65. Mrs. Adam Shortt: "But I think none of us will disagree in this, that in almost all municipal councils, at least, so far as we have known, from Halifax to Vancouver, there is an element of politics which enters into municipal administration and sometimes ties up the machinery, which, at its best and without politics, might be more efficient. Moreover, this entrance of politics into the municipal situation frequently leads to the appointment of men for outstanding positions which affects our morality, our beauty and our efficiency — not because they are men fitted for the positions, but because they are men who, for some reason or other, it is thought must have a job. It is, in many cases, as has been said, not the man's fitness for the occupation, but there is an occupation to which they may fit the man who needs a job." Civic Improvement League of Canada, *Report of Preliminary Conference at Ottawa*, 1915, p. 2.

66. S. Morley Wickett, "The Problems of City Government," *Empire Club Speeches*, Toronto, 1907-08, p. 113.

67. Initially this demand was only for a special post like City Engineer and Medical Officer or a commission for police or waterworks. But after 1900 reformers were concerned with the development of a complete municipal civil service. See J.O. Miller, "The Better Government of Our Cities," in *The New Era in Canada*, ed. J.O. Miller (Toronto, 1917), pp. 368-370.

68. For example, in 1919 a handbook on Ottawa listed 10 permanent officials — city clerk, commissioner of works, city collector, city treasurer, city auditor, fire chief, assessment commissioner, city solicitor, charity officer, and market inspector. J.H. Putnam, "City Government Ottawa" (Ottawa: James Hope & Sons, Limited, 1919).

69. W.D. Lighthall, "Valedictory. . . .", 1919.

70. W.F. Maclean, "A Greater Toronto," *Empire Club Speeches* (Toronto, 1907-08), pp. 81-90.

71. S. Morley Wickett, "Civic Charters: The Question of a Charter for Toronto and of Civic Charters in General," *The Municipal World*, January, 1905, pp. 8-10. Wickett claims that the act incorporating Edmonton was written by the editor of *The Municipal Manual*, a former city solicitor of Toronto — Wickett, "Present Conditions," *Municipal Government in Canada*, pp. 151-152.

72. These included liquor licensing and prohibition, public health, municipal financing, utilities and highways, town planning and housing.

73. J.W. Dafoe, *Clifford Sifton in Relation to His Times* (Toronto, 1931), pp. 444-445. Dafoe deals mainly with the involvement of the commission in resource development.

74. W.B. Munro, *American Influence on Canadian Government* (Toronto, 1929), pp. 99-142.

75. For a discussion of the collectivist urge and economic groups see J. M. Bliss, "The Protective Impulse: An Approach to the Social History of Mowat's Ontario," a paper delivered at the Mowat Seminar, Kingston, November, 1970.

76. Recently historians have begun to investigate this progressive tradition. R. Craig Brown has pointed out that Robert Borden expressed the ideals of bureaucratic reform in national policies. R.C. Brown, "The Political Ideas of Robert Borden," *The Political Ideas of the*

Prime Ministers of Canada, ed. M. Hamelin (Ottawa, 1969), pp. 87-97. Joseph Levitt has argued that one can find a progressive response to social and economic problems in French Canada in the writings of Bourassa and the *nationalistes*. J. Levitt, *Henri Bourassa and the Golden Calf* (Ottawa: Les Editions de L'Université d'Ottawa, 1969). And of course, Richard Allen has discussed in some detail the rise and decline of the social gospel in Canada. R. Allen, ''The Social Gospel and the Reform Tradition in Canada, 1890-1928,'' *Canadian Historical Review*, vol. 59, Dec. 1968, pp. 381-399.

"Tomorrow's Metropolis" Revisited: A Critical Assessment of Urban Reform in Canada, 1890-1920

JOHN C. WEAVER

The crises experienced by Canadian cities between 1890 and 1920 triggered an urban reform movement whose goal was to save the country's cities with a "utopian vision of tomorrow's metropolis." Throughout the period, urban reformers deluged the public with progressive rhetoric, using such diverse methods of publicity as clergymen's civic sermons, articles in newspapers and journals, special technical reports, and speeches to conferences.[1] This abundant propaganda has led to sympathetic appraisals of the urban reform movement, for historians have accepted the statements of the reformers at face value. An analysis of urban reform, however, must go beyond the declarations of key reform figures, for the printed and spoken record does not wholly convey the meaning and significance of the reform movement.

Reformers were often excessively enthusiastic and biased in reporting. Their addresses to Canadian Clubs, municipal Associations, and similar gatherings seem remote from the realities of problems in particular communities. Distant experiments received praise without a full understanding of their origins or aims. Most reformers relied heavily on the data and proposals of foreign authors, and accurate information on Canadian urban problems was an elusive commodity even in the writings of such well known individuals as child-welfare reformer J.J. Kelso, planner Thomas Adams, and social critic J.S. Woodsworth.[2]

Reform measures were not always implemented for the professed idealistic purposes. Public ownership at times complemented unregulated private aspirations, while restructured civic governments were designed to afford business interests a greater opportunity to mould city development.[3]

SOURCE: This article is a revised version of a paper presented at the Canadian Historical Association's annual meeting held at Quebec City, June, 1976.

Reform, therefore, must be viewed from two different perspectives. Social and sanitary reformers genuinely sought to alleviate misery by dealing with very real social and health problems. But they also sought to perpetuate a stratified society based upon traditional patterns of deference and morality, patterns which clashed with the ways of the newcomers who resided in urban slums.

Specific urban reforms did not often indicate an interest in substantive change or utopian vision.[4] Certain actions generously accorded a reform label blended all too completely with booster ambitions or arose from attempts of a local business elite to retain direction in municipal affairs. Declining interest in urban reform during the twenties, therefore, did not represent a rude break. Considering the conservative intent of many reforms, and the close bonds between them and a business and booster ethos, the transition reveals, rather, a fundamental continuity. This is not to deny a distinct period of intense intellectual interest in prospects for an urban, industrial Canada. It does stress, however, that motives for local reform initiative had as least as much in common with forces in previous and subsequent eras in Canadian urban development as they did with a progressive outlook inspired by new urban professions, a growing middle-class, a rising social gospel, or the local labour movement. Among the long-term considerations that appeared in the implementation of reforms, the striving after ever greater growth, the erosion of personal liberty in favour of regulatory powers (weighing heavily on newcomers and the poor), and government by the haphazard expansion of civic bureaucracies are most prominent. They imparted an ambiguity to reform acts, a complexity all but obscured by declarations of progress.

A critical assessment of urban reform, if it is to go beyond an examination of reform rhetoric, must deal with local perspectives rather than national or international ones. It must examine motives (other than idealism) and consider continuity instead of change. It is these shifts in emphasis that will guide this revisiting of "tomorrow's metropolis."

PUBLIC OWNERSHIP AND THE GROWTH ETHIC

Reform criticism of private utility companies rang loud and, in most regards, true. Aside from their often poor level of service, corporations had helped to debase civic politics. Prominent reform leaders, therefore, promoted public ownership as a matter of principle capable, not only of improving service, but of injecting virtue into civic affairs. Social gospel leaders, for example, felt "public ownership was indeed . . . a movement of divinity in the modern world."[5] Building momentum for their cause, exponents of public ownership extolled pioneer efforts in the aggressive communities west of Superior, communities such as Port Arthur, Winnipeg, Brandon, Regina, Saskatoon, Lethbridge, Edmonton, and Calgary. Civic officials from public ownership communities, meanwhile, eagerly publicized their efforts; they seemed intent on outbidding one another when enumerating civic owned ventures in orations that read like booster tracts, which in fact they were. If western cities were "laboratories of reform,"[6] they were also real estate casinos and the two features proved complementary. Alderman M.C. Costello, publicity commissioner, claimed that "Calgary is now known as the city of Public Utilities and people out of curiosity come here to see what we are like."[7] The Secretary of Port Arthur's Board of Trade, a composer of promotional literature, found public ownership useful in advertizing.

> As a city where municipal ownership is king, Port Arthur stands supreme on the American continent. She owns her own street railway, telephones, electric lighting and waterworks, does her own paving and sidewalk construction, and is able to make out of her utilities a handsome profit.[8]

To claim that a profit and high level of service had been achieved was something of a misrepresentation. In 1909, it has to be admitted that with respect to the electric lighting, telephone, and streetcar systems, "the public patience has been well tested with disorganized conditions and bad service."[9]

The Port Arthur experience is a good example of the complexities of the public ownership issue.[10] The city's streetcar system was the first in Canada to operate under municipal ownership. One of the earliest electrified lines in the Dominion, the Edison company installed it as a practical test for new equipment. A double innovation, it reflected a daring on the part of town council which attracted outside attention. Nonetheless, a very traditional consideration, civic rivalry, had inspired the action. The late 1880's posed challenges for Port Arthur's Establishment as its rival Fort William became an ever more dynamic centre. While Port Arthur continued to boast fine shops and lower retail prices, employment opportunities in construction and manufacturing beckoned from across the bay. Labourers found it more convenient to move to the scene of their work. "They left Port Arthur like rats desert a sinking ship."[11]

Alarmed, boosters schemed to retain their residents by subsidizing a stagecoach line between the twin cities. When practical electric streetcars became widely publicized by 1890, limited capacity and discomfort soon made the existing service appear inadequate. But no entrepreneurs would risk initiating the desired service, regarding the scheme "with a sneer at its certain failure."[12] Fort William opposed improved access since community leaders there understood the purpose of a streetcar service.

Our friends across the ferry don't exactly like to see our little boom . . . and they want to pull things their own way a little and . . . they propose patronizingly to help us along a trifle by offering to build us an Electric Railway. . . . The electric road from Port Arthur would enable Port Arthur people to keep all those workmen as citizens.[13]

Furthermore, a line would have had to traverse a sparsely settled area providing few fares. With no attraction for private investment, merchants and civic boosters suggested municipal ownership and relied on local chauvinism to carry municipal elections against opponents who warned of mounting tax burdens.[14] Circumstances at the head-of-the-lake did not apply elsewhere; the twin cities rivalry was not a typical case. Nevertheless, the broader issue, the use of public ownership to achieve business rather than public ends, had wide play.

Public ownership also often came by default since many new or medium size communities either failed to attract or were unable to hold private companies. This inability concerned local businessmen, who worshipped streetcars with a rapture approximating that apparent during the railway-mania of fifty years earlier. What "golden hub" anticipating new industries and residents could neglect a trolley system without jeopardizing its future? The ambitious little railway centre of St. Thomas, Ontario, for example, longed for and annually expected an industrial boom. To round out a base of attractive services, it readily granted a streetcar franchise in 1897. With low revenue and some equipment seized by creditors, the London owners forfeited the franchise in 1902 and willingly gave up their slender assets. No other syndicate could be induced to operate the line; private capital, a clear first choice, stayed away and public ownership came on the rebound, not with a crusade.[15]

A combination of booster ambition and default of private enterprise brought Edmonton its municipal trolleys. Franchises had been granted, but construction was never undertaken. This was a major problem for a city eager to develop the image of a potential metropolis. The notion of public ownership, therefore, provoked no controversy on principle. Instead, debate focussed on streetcar routes, indicating the real estate concerns of civic leaders. In a bustling centre like Edmonton, there was little cautious talk about limiting operations to congested and therefore profitable streets. A complete network would symbolize maturity and a degree of parity with eastern giants. An extensive streetcar network would also resolve the developers' problem of luring residents out to their surveys.[16] While there was agreement in Edmonton that rails should extend to barren suburbs where operations would necessarily lose money, disagreement came on details. One faction led by ex-Mayor William Short, acknowledged for his reform views as a "Progressive" who "would not clog the wheels of progress,"[17] organized a petition requesting a far ranging system. Short pressed for a line to the Clover Bar coal mine, claiming it would reduce bulk coal rates, and hence attract industry. The line would, he maintained, "meet with favour with nine-tenths of the money interests of the city."[18] Members of Council hedged but finally agreed to construct a far flung network.[19]

Only Alderman George Armstrong questioned operating lines in almost vacant suburbs, noting "the fact that it would serve to promote speculation." In a curious denial, actually verifying Armstrong's fears, Alderman Robert Manson claimed that this should be no obstacle since "all the property in question had already been secured by speculators." Armstrong felt that a vast streetcar undertaking would escalate the price of suburban lots, placing them "beyond the reach of workingmen."[20] The morning after Council's stated policy of expansion, the city's major real estate boomers, Magrath, Hart and Company, placed a full page advertisement in the *Bulletin*:

STREETCARS TO
BELLEVUE
PROPOSED EXTENSION OF STREETCARS TO VIEWPOINT
AT A SPECIAL MEETING HELD LAST NIGHT
-BELLEVUE-
IS NOW ASSURED OF THE FOLLOWING ADVANTAGES
ELECTRIC LIGHT, TELEPHONES,
WATERWORKS, SEWERS
AND STREETCARS[21]

The promoters' bandwagon almost collapsed during a credit crisis in 1907[22] but with the return of prosperity in 1909 real estate developers again found a pliable council. One council member, Alderman Tipton, himself a speculator, summed up the mood: "I believe that street railway extensions are the greatest of city builders."[23] This attitude resulted in several dubious agreements between the city and private businessmen. In the fall of 1909, a syndicate with west end holdings in the Glenora tract requested a streetcar extension which would require bridging ravines. The principals, James Carruthers and H.R. Round, reached an agreement later duplicated by competitors. They shared the expense of bridge and rail construction with the city, while the city assumed all operating costs.[24] Still the critic, Alderman George Armstrong protested that the agreement was "merely a money making proposition of Messrs. Carruthers and Round." At a subsequent meeting, however, Council suspended procedures and passed the agreement at one sitting. The crisp report of the *Bulletin* stated that there was "very little discussion and no dissenting voice".[25] The precedent set, Council rubber-stamped other accords with Carruthers and Round, as well as with the Robertson Davidson Company and the Magrath, Holgate Company.[26]

As the severe 1913 slump began, the speculator's honeymoon with public ownership experienced strains. A greatly over-expanded system rumbled along in near chaos, drawing complaints about inadequate downtown service and the city's refusal to permit use of workmen's tickets at mid-day. A tremendous debt burden had been accumulated and desperate stop-gap measures were introduced. A special rate was arranged with the municipal power plant and labour costs were cut by reducing employees.[27] Ironically, the overcrowded cars and labour practices of private companies had figured in arguments for public ownership in eastern cities. Edmonton's civic street railway did not appear to provide service superior to that of private operations in the east, but, significantly, it did contribute to a loose pattern of light density development. The statement of a Trades and Labour Council Alderman concerning one developer's agreement for a trolley line had wider application. He maintained that it would result in "getting people to go some nineteen blocks south of Whyte Avenue to live. This would mean that utilities of every description would have to be carried out there, while parts of the city closer in would have to wait."[28] When the boom ended in 1913, pockets of serviced but unoccupied property left Edmonton with a high fixed debt and a sagging tax base.

The struggle for civic streetcars in Toronto paralleled the situation found in most thriving new western cities in many respects, but it also had several distinctive features. Transit issues in Toronto were exceedingly complex and the combination of interests and arguments favouring public ownership were extensive. Still, the question of property development was central. Among early public ownership supporters was E.A. Macdonald, a real estate developer whose east-end holdings had not had benefit of service from the cautious Toronto Street Railway Company.[29] Despite discussions on public ownership in 1890, the franchise continued to be held by a private syndicate. For years the company found itself pitted against City Hall's persistent but not formidable legal resources. Much litigation concerned the City's on-going attempt to force the company to run more cars and lay more track. On one occasion, city health officials carted petrie dishes onto rush-hour cars hoping to develop germ cultures proving that overcrowding spread disease.[30] By late 1909, criticism of the private streetcar utility was such that a publicly owned system seemed inevitable. Numerous publicly owned ventures elsewhere and the publicity generated by public ownership advocates contributed to the mood, yet more fundamental circumstances account for the inception of a Toronto civic line.

The specific crisis forcing the city of Toronto into the streetcar business was the issue of suburban extension. Reaping profits on heavily travelled routes and shunning capital risks required to service white elephant pastures, the T.S.R. declined to run tracks into recently annexed areas in the north. The General Manager, Robert J. Fleming, gave sound enough reasons: "In two or three years," he wrote, "the physical conditions of the City may vary considerably, and streets which at present appear important to the City Council may in two or three years appear comparatively unnecessary."[31] Fleming had a point. Suburban tracts were plentiful and it took years for them to fill to their capacity; the precise direction of substantial urban growth was difficult to predict. But restraint, a poorly received virtue in heady times, inconvenienced those few who had settled on "the crab grass frontier" and it certainly annoyed influential property developers. Major property developers actually would initiate steps "to create an artificial demand for a direct street car line" in order to secure service for their surveys.[32] City leaders, too, pondered means to encourage construction in the annexed areas and hence broaded the city tax base.

To the delight of the legal profession, the familiar antagonists paraded to the Courts once more. Ultimately, the judicial Committee of the Privy Council denied that the City had authority to compel the T.S.R. to provide the desired tracks; the 1891 franchise agreement, according to the Courts, did not apply to districts then outside the city.[33] This decisive judicial statement and the interests it adversely affected did more to force public ownership in Toronto than capable arguments from men of principle who long had denounced private franchises. Conflicting designs, one represented by an expansion-minded civic leadership and the other by a capital-cautious utility company, meant eventual elimination of private traction. To William Maclean, champion of suburbanites, a Donlands real estate speculator and editor of the Toronto *World,*[34] the issue was inextricably related to Toronto progress. The blocking of suburban extensions was . . . not only intolerable for present citizens, but constitutes a serious limitation on the growth of the city. Cheap and rapid transportation means plentiful labour, well-houses, well-fed, and intelligent labour. Good labour of this kind means satisfactory conditions for the employer and manufacturer. This reacts on retail business, and the development of the modern community follows, all as a result of rapid transport.[35]

A blend of naive optimism and bald commercial ambition, not idealism alone, secured Toronto a civic owned streetcar line by early 1912.[36] The fledgling civic line on Gerrard Street, St. Clair, and Danforth Avenues failed to provide the desired links, adding to the confusion, since one suburban area, North Toronto, had chartered its own line prior to annexation. No transfer agreements existed among the Toronto Suburban Railway Company, the T.S.R., and the civic line. Real estate developers complained, hoping for a rationalization of the system:

> The proposed purchase of the Toronto Street Railway by the city [1913] has roused considerable interest among real estate leaders in Toronto who are interested in suburban property. It is uniformly believed that the purchase of the railway will give a great impetus to outside property. Real estate men are confident that under municipal control, transportation facilities will anticipate rather than lag behind demand. It is also believed that one-fare lines will ultimately result.[37]

Pressures and appeals of a practical nature continued through the war years and concluded with complete rationalization by civic ownership when the T.S.R. franchise expired in 1921.[38]

Public ownership caught hold where private enterprise could not be secured, retained, or where its lack of expansionist zeal frustrated important civic interests. Conversely, when a private company moved with an alacrity satisfying to business and real estate interests, it weathered challenges. The British Columbia Electric Railway Company is a case in point. London-based, with access to London finance, and possessing diverse interests — electric power, streetcars, and heavier interurbans — the B.C.E.R. had expanded from Vancouver into South Vancouver, Burnaby, Point Grey, and New Westminster by 1912. Unlike the cautious T.S.R., it risked poor short-term returns on suburban lines in favour of planning for long-term profits. As Patricia Roy has noted,

> . . . the board had . . . sought to devise a building program which, if it did not forestall municipal competition, would at least mitigate its effects. Because of their British experience with municipal ownership of utilities they were particularly sensitive to all talk of public ownership.[39]

The B.C.E.R. could take a reasonably expansionist position since it had obtained forty year franchises from North and South Vancouver. Also, subdivision companies eased losses with the cash bonus. For their extension, Vancouver Heights developers paid $56,000.[40] Montreal's advocates of expansion also found private tram lines compatible. Suburban extensions, for example, represented prime features of the Park and Island Railway which participated in the real estate development of Notre Dame de Grace West.[41]

Reformers sincerely interested in the public-weal compiled their briefs against private franchises, but public ownership was achieved when it assisted real estate promotion and the aspirations of municipalities eager to have tracks and trams, harbingers of urban advance. To appreciate issues in Canada's "Progressive era," therefore, the issue of public or private ownership as discussed by reformers must be brought into step with the self-interest by businessmen.

Striving for accelerated growth was a touchstone for innumerable aspects of North American urban history before and after the "reformers." It figures prominently in the achievement of civic streetcars; it appeared, as well, in campaigns for public owned electric power. A quest for cheap and reliable power, an obvious asset in municipal promotion and in realizing the ambitions of local manufacturers, encouraged communities to embrace public ownership of electric power. In Ontario, Boards of Trade from communities with manufacturing interests led the clamour for a public-owned power-distribution system. The exception that illustrates the rule was Hamilton. Extremely successful in attracting industry in the post-Confederation period,[42] Hamilton repeated the achievement in the early 1900's. Among its assets, the city claimed an inexpensive supply of power from the Cataract Power Company with generating facilities near St. Catharines. The company assumed an important role in Hamilton's publicity efforts, setting it apart from Toronto and the lesser industrial centres in the Grand River Valley region. Hamilton, "the Birmingham of Canada," became Hamilton, "the electric city."[43] The prospect of a public-owned power grid for Southern Ontario failed to excite local businessmen to the same degree that it interested Boards of Trade in Toronto, Berlin, Preston, Galt, and London.[44] Cataract shareholders included influential Hamiltonians such as publisher W.J. Southam, but another feature of the cool reception devolved from a calculation that Hamilton stood to forfeit one of its competitive advantages. Only when Ontario Hydro became a fact and rivals secured lower power rates did a Council dedicated to business efficiency seek a Hydro contract.[45]

No Niagaras brightened expectations for prairie communities. The urban businessmen of the West could not use the rationalized Ontario Hydro scheme as a model because the prairies lacked a great power source and a compact cluster of urban centres. Civic "socialism" in power was realized piecemeal, community by community. In Saskatchewan, "municipally owned power plants sprang up in no less than twenty municipalities."[46] By 1910, one western city, Edmonton, did show modest interest in having a Provincial scheme and passed a resolution for Provincial take-over of power sites. Nonetheless, the motive was local and boom-oriented: "Cheap power is essential in order to induce manufacturing establishments to locate in the City of Edmonton."[47] Publicly owned power actually had been established in Edmonton during 1902. And, like streetcar episodes, the circumstances do not present a clear portrayal of idealism and triumph. The company possessing the private franchise hesitated to improve its faltering plant; its inaction was considered a blot on Edmonton's reputation and hence an impediment to its growth. An impatient Council purchased the plant, inheriting a malfunctioning engine and antiquated transformers.[48] By unloading a disaster, the company gave the city public power by default. In Winnipeg, take-over was not so swift and effortless, but it had a strikingly similar purpose. As Alan Artibise has shown, in the struggle for cheap power "public good was simply a dividend; it was not the operating principle."[49] Across Saskatchewan, "many small municipalities were creating public utilities suitable for municipalities several times their size and the general idea seemed to be to let the future take care of itself."[50] The future, however, did not take care of itself and many municipal utilities were far from successful. The adoption of municipal ownership was a new tactic in the long established tradition of North American city-building which valued dynamic growth.

The connection between public power and promoting manufacturing surfaced at a 1907 meeting of the Union of Alberta Municipalities. Budding western cities had been luring industry by fair means and foul. What constituted a legitimate device became a matter of controversy. Cash bonuses were criticized at the convention, in part because of the risk, but it was agreed that favourable utility rates could be offered. Mayor Griesback of Edmonton insisted on having the issue clarified: "A town or city owning its own utilities would be allowed to give special rates to industries using large quantities of water or light . . . [and] would be allowed to give sites at a cheap rate in an industrial area."[51] Western civic leaders were overwhelmingly in favour of public ownership since it placed the community in a better position to offer inducements to industry. The Mayor of Medicine Hat summed it up: "The town with something to offer which is equivalent to a bonus, frequently escapes being required to put up a cash bonus. Municipal ownership and industrial progress go hand in hand."[52]

Rather than illustrating substantive change, the early achievements in public ownership demonstrated the crude accuracy of one side of the maxim, "socialism for the rich, but free enterprise for the poor." The validity of the second half can be tested by responses to the housing crisis.

SOCIAL ILLS AND THE REGULATORY IMPULSE

The same well-to-do civic leaders who supported public ownership because it would foster communal and individual prosperity harboured fears about threats to order and health introduced by the same rapid urban expansion that they so enthusiastically wanted. Planning actually encompassed this ambivalent perception of growth. On one side, planning in the form of city beautiful movements complemented booster endeavours; on the other, housing codes and land-use regulations aimed at patching up and sorting out rough features of urban booms. Codes and regulation, more influential than the grandiose plans of City Beautiful in the long-term, were joined by another form of planning. Suburban developers laid out planned communities with restrictive covenants. These practical applications of planning reveal more about its complex role in urban Canada than do the tracts and speeches of prominent planners. What they suggest is that public and private attempts to shape an orderly city abetted a natural process of social segregation which had been in progress since the latter decades of the nineteenth century. Further, enforcement of regulations, which kept multiplying "like Topsy" beyond 1920, added to an administrative maze and contributed to the conversion of local government into a realm for technical experts.

Civic enhancement briefly provided an influential motif in planning in the years before the war. During its 1910 convention, the Union of Canadian Municipalities hosted a series of papers on "town planning and embellishment."[53] The two terms had, at this stage in the nascent planning profession, a certain interchangable quality. Indeed, interest in planning on the grand scale by some city councils was inspired by the ever present ambition of boosters, "embellishment" to their ears had a promising ring. In Calgary this resulted in Council hiring Thomas H. Mawson of Liverpool to prepare a master plan. His plan for parks, playground, boulevards and a civic centre was solicited, in part, for promotional reasons. Council believed that it would prove of "great value to us from a publicity standpoint." True to this objective, the report went out to every prominent newspaper and magazine.[54] Wishing to enhance Edmonton, that city's Council hired Montreal landscape architect, Frederick Todd. They baulked, however, when Todd suggested in late 1906 that legislation be obtained "to control the subdivision of land in such a manner as to secure uniformity of surveys having regard to a general scheme." It was one thing to plan with promotional objectives, using ravines and river banks, quite another to impinge upon real estate development.[55] In Winnipeg, a few supporters of planning were wholly sincere and concerned about social issues, but the bulk of those active looked on planning "as a distinctly business proposition, just another means to boost Winnipeg's image outside the city's borders."[56] Even lesser centres, like Berlin (Kitchener), Ontario, had Civic Improvement Associations devoted to embellishing their communities with new public buildings which would excite admiration and attract attention.[57] City Beautiful had its aesthetic appeal, but many adopted it as a tactic, like public ownership, for achieving further publicity. In any case, with the collapse of the urban boom in 1913 and the long term debts incurred by many cities, most features of beautification schemes were shelved.[58]

The long-term impetus for planning came from another direction. Certain basic tools of planning — invoking the police power to eliminate "nuisances," the related evolution of zoning, and the appearance of building codes — sprang from sanitary officials backed by middle-class concern about both health and property values. The consequences of their efforts were a mixed blessing for the Canadian city.

In the course of their regular work, municipal health officers exposed concentrations of misery and provided a wealth of information on slums across the country. Publicity from their condemnations of unhealthy environments and subsequent remedial actions proved constructive in improving the health of the poor. One of their recommendations was an attempt to remodel private life through the passage of regulations. Considering the precious stakes, imposition of controls seemed worthwhile; intervention into the moral habits and daily routines in slum districts transpired, it seems, for compelling reasons. However, regulatory measures found acceptance for other than purely health considerations. Imposing restrictions, after all, was not the sole means of working toward achievement of a robust community. Other remedies, curbing urban growth or establishing civic supported housing projects, had scant appeal. More plausible measures such as providing improved water and sanitary facilities for all sections of the city lagged behind, due to lead-times required to plan, finance, and execute large public works. Moreover, these undertakings were primarily designed to service suburbs and there existed an optimistic faith that the new residential districts would house the working class, rendering pest-ridden slums obsolete. Reformers ranging from medical authorities to clergymen claimed for suburbs the status of a social remedy.[59] The free-market in property, complemented by public transportation, could resolve the housing and health crisis. Old slums would vanish under demolition for naturally expanding business and industrial facilities.[60] But one set of props was required. Slum residents had to be divested of their wasteful habits and forced to vacate overcrowded tenements. In short, the suburb would render substantive social change unnecessary by operating as a natural agent for improvement when the poor and the newcomers became proper middle-class citizens. Logical within the assumptions of middle-class reformers, the approach contained oversight and problems.

Civic and provincial efforts to tackle health problems owed something to a concern about the well-being of slum residents, but they also derived from a broadened understanding of self-interest by the middle and upper clases. The germ theory made it clear that a city's health was no better than the health and sanitation of all its districts, including its slums. For example, one of the few dimensions of life to improve in Montreal's "city below the hill" was health. As Terry Copp indicates, efforts "were not directed specifically at the working class. Indeed, it may be argued that progress was possible precisely because health problems affected the entire society, not just the working class."[61] Port Arthur's health officer claimed that in his city there existed a very direct bridge between rich and poor in matters of health. His men badgered "ignorant and careless" foreigners because from their homes "come a large proportion of the servant girls, who may contract and pass the fever along into the homes where they work."[62]

The regulatory impulse also surfaced as a response to the housing crisis, even though some observers condemned regulations as inadequate. J.S. Woodsworth observed that, by themselves, "the issuing of regulations or the passing of by-laws will not clean up a congested district." Still, his complementary measure, "the active co-operative of a score of social agencies," seems to have under-estimated the extent of the shelter crisis.[63] He drew upon the American philanthropic and voluntary tradition, rather than the British Council housing experience and garden city experiments.

By the end of 1913, however, with the acute housing crisis intensified by depression and unemployment, a few reformers turned to public housing. J.O. McCarthy, a businessman and reform-minded Toronto Controller, shifted away from an earlier faith in suburbs and the ideal of a city of private homes. Social service investigator Bryce Stewart and local health officers began to recommend public housing in their reports.[64] But while some success with limited-dividend housing was realized,[65] it proved too expensive for low income families.[66] The question of expense combined with the feeling that the poor did not merit civic assistance precluded serious interest. Instead, reforms which attacked poor housing rather than addressing the shelter storage were accorded wide-spread acceptance. A Hamilton sanitary reformer who rejected "municipal housing" because he had witnessed the poor squandering money proposed that the city hire a vigilant corps of health and building inspectors who, rather than waiting for complaints, would receive authority to systematically go about "looking for trouble." Inspection would be "followed by prompt closure where immediate steps are not taken for . . . remedial measures."[67]

The attitude and remedy were common. Both in the United States and Canada important steps were taken in the Progressive era to restrict use of private property. For reasons of health and fire protection, these actions had ample justification, but the tone of execution and the failure to harness restrictions with resettlement or low-cost dwellings exacerbated housing problems. Winnipeg authorities boasted that they met the "overcrowding evil by dint of stern repression and frequent prosecutions."[68] With "the whole-hearted support of . . . Police Magistrates," Winnipeg inspectors ordered removal of beds from overcrowded lodgings. To apprehend offenders they occasionally conducted night inspections, claiming that nocturnal raids should upset only those possessing "a guilty conscience."[69]

Oriental shacktowns in Vancouver and New Westminster received similar inspections, and when they could, officials arranged for their destruction while displaying no apparent concern for the plight of the occupants.[70] The latter, after all, were guilty of living in an unhealthy environment and endangering the health and moral well-being of the city.

The legislation which supported inspection and condemnation reflected more than a concern that disease would reach out to menace from slums. The Manitoba Tenement Act of 1909, according to one of its supporters, also concerned protection of property values. Since tenement houses "may . . . to a large extent spoil the appearance of a neighborhood," they were excluded from "certain restricted areas in order to protect the rights of owners of dwellings."[71] As for new tenements, restrictions defined the area of the lot to be covered, room dimensions and fire precautions.[72] The Ontario Public Health Act of 1914 among other ingredients, included an adaptation of the pseudo-scientific "Denver by-law." This model piece of legislation prescribed a formula for the number of cubic feet required per resident in boarding houses. Saskatchewan had had a similar measure since early 1910. Ontario's Act also gave the Medical Officer of Health power to close a house which in his judgment was unfit.[73]

The strategy of housing betterment through codes and stringent code enforcement did not come to terms with the central social affliction of Canadian cities since it did not increase the supply of inexpensive housing. On the contrary, codes raised costs and reduced the supply of low income housing by discouraging tenement builders and boarding house conversions. In a sense, housing or sanitary reforms with their emphasis on codes helped to direct these aspects of civic affairs into narrow technical considerations. In a 1914 Social Service address, Reverend Walter A. Riddell described the valuable "housing reformer" as one who "should be able to judge adequate ventilation and proper sanitation."[74] Few reflected upon or understood the scope of the housing issue, though many eventually came to know and supervise the codes that only met the problem half-way. The press, public health officials, assorted lay and clerical reformers felt slum districts represented an evil, scarcely appreciating that requirements for better construction, more space and improved sanitary facilities would result in higher rents. Of course, the restrictions on house size and against multi-family dwellings that developers placed on suburban surveys produced similar consequences. Suburbs functioned as social fillers rather than as hoped-for social remedies.[75]

Enforcement of standards, moreover, augmented resentment against authority, especially when accompanied by intrusive zeal. With paternalistic dismay, Port Arthur's health officer could not understand why the foreigners should "look upon the health officials as their natural enemies, whose aim and desire is to interfere and make life unpleasant for them.''[76] An anonymous critic of social workers in Toronto suggested why friction existed between social improvement enforcers and their "clients." Regulations, orders and friendly advice on everything from dwelling size to bathing and bedding did not touch "the fundamental cause." Instead, the author of "A Kick at Slum Workers" recommended getting after "the employers . . . where the poor man works from sunrise to sunset for a few paltry dollars and is driven like an animal instead of a human being; see that the poor man gets better pay . . . then he will have time to think of home conditions, to know his children, see more of them and his eyes will be opened to his environment.''[77]

The claim that reformers felt compelled to regulate the city for the benefit of all is simply not accurate. Instead, the regulatory impulse, with its counter productive and unpleasant implications, must be viewed as stemming as much from prejudice, self-interest and a concern for property values as from idealism and vision.

MUNICIPAL REFORM AND THE LEGACY OF CONFUSION

Municipal government was also a target of urban reformers. Careless administrative practices, corruption, and patronage quickly eroded respect for the municipal government system and it soon became the "whipping boy" for urban reformers. In particular, the Council-committee structure of civic government was singled out as the cause of all manner of urban problems ranging from the difficulties of a civically owned power plant to the inability of Council to guarantee services equal to the demands of developers. Because of the hasty developments caused by booster ambitions, many of these problems were unavoidable and government structure alone could not be blamed. Nonetheless, government structure was blamed for problems by many in progress-conscious communities. Something other than the buoyant drive for growth had to bear the blame for inefficiency.

In Toronto, reformers responded by creating a Board of Control (1896). Later, other Canadian cities followed this example: Winnipeg (1906), Ottawa (1907), Montreal (1909), Hamilton (1910), London (1914). Calgary had the essentials of a Board of Control in 1908 but called it a Commission. Edmonton (1904), Regina, Saskatoon and Prince Albert (1911-1912) adopted a Commission form of civic executive in which administrators were to be hired to guide Council. Saint John, New Brunswick followed the American reform example and established a Commission elected at large (1912). In Vancouver a campaign for a Commission form of government, led by the Board of Trade, was almost successful. In a referendum, a majority of eligible voters (just over 5,000 voted) favoured an elected Commission to a Council-committee or Board of Control system but the proposal died under consideration by Council.[78]

Municipal reformers chipped away at Council in other ways, advocating that certain urban services be placed under special boards and commissions: police, parks, water, electric, transportation and planning. In fact, Ontario communities had a precedent for the creation of commissions since in 1856 a statute for Upper Canada created Boards of Commissions for Police, consisting of the senior judge of the county, the Police Magistrate and the Mayor elect. The purpose of this measure was identical to that behind the proliferation of such bodies between 1890 and 1920, namely, to take an important area of decision-making out of the hands of neighbourhood politicians who might well intervene for political reasons. The wedge between politics and administration had put in an appearance. However, with pressure from temperance associations, anti-vice leagues, ministerial associations, and a host of other special interests, it was impossible to keep police forces beyond political debate and tampering. The distinction between a political or policy issue and an administrative act was never the precise matter that reformers so readily maintained. When service responsibilities expanded through growth and public ownership in the early 1900's, the attempt to separate the political from the administrative became an obsession complicating the structure of urban government. The combination of public ownership and government by special bodies truly commenced a new era in urban experience, one composed of attempts to rationalize expansion. For years poor service and rate increases raised the ire of civic leaders against private utilities. The same issues, alas, were to persist in the new era, but criticism involved administrators of public services. Unlike entrepreneurs, the managerial bodies could and did protect their decisions with references to the public good and to the highly technical nature of their task.

Formulas for selecting members on the various commissions differed; some consisted of appointees, others of elected officials, and still others had mixed membership. If elected, it was to be on a city-wide basis thus negating the influence of ward politicians. One can surely sympathize with reformers in their campaign against corruption, but it is necessary to realize that this was not their sole consideration; nor did assaults on Council and proliferation of new institutions necessarily generate decency and efficiency. A fortified executive branch was no guarantee against self-interest. Toronto's Board of Control would, through the years, contain many of the men whom reformers had sought to purge. Boards and commissions did not necessarily increase efficiency. In fact, they established new forms of inefficiency and indecision. Reports and recommendations bounced back and forth among Council, Council's committees, and the Board of Control. Hired Commissioners, confident of their rectitude and the merit of their decisions, were not always willing to cooperate with Council.

Municipal reformers, with justification, had expressed dismay over the lack of a city-wide view in the old style civic government, contending with some justification that aldermen concentrated efforts on securing benefits for their ward and therefore engaged in log-rolling. Schemes for boards and commissions with a city-wide jurisdiction thus attracted support as devices which would centralize decision-making. Two reform projects, one successful and the other not, illustrate the objective. To improve drainage and sewer systems in Vancouver and in surrounding independent suburbs, the foremost Canadian civic engineer of the day, R.S. Lea of Montreal, was retained to draft plans for a comprehensive metropolitan network. His final report called for a commission that would manage the expansion and maintenance of this greater Vancouver drainage project.[79] His recommendations shaped provincial legislation. In 1913, municipal reformer S. Morley Wickett drafted a plan for a metropolitan Toronto government that would achieve a rationalization of services. The new body would have consisted of appointed administrators, each responsible for a technical area.[80] The all-encompassing perspective, cutting across ward and municipal lines, had much to recommend it. However, innovations also implied a decentralization of authority and accountability by establishing more governmental bodies where decisions would be reached. A carved-up geographic arrangement of power was to be replaced by an administrative carving-up of tasks. At least one civic official saw the irony and concluded that "decentralization has been carried too far. Town Planning Commissions, Suburban Road Commission, Railway Commission, Police Commissions, Boards of Education, Hospital Trusts, Utilities Commissions have usurped Council powers. The Council today is little more than a tax-levying body with little or no control."[81] Since neither reform plans nor existing arrangements wholly dictated the evolution of Canadian municipal government, the resulting mix contributed to citizen confusion and generated new political games which narrowed community involvement. Log-rolling obstruction now included a collection of bureaucratic officials as well as the old practitioners, aldermen.

Reform attempts to reduce involvement of aldermen, ostensibly to eliminate corruption, inefficiency and fragmentation, were accompanied by other considerations. Sewers, pumping stations, streetcars, power systems, street paving, building codes and many other concerns made the city appear as a special area best understood by engineers and experts; a field of government coping with issues too complex to be trusted to aldermen and the general public. Related complications in civic finance — assessments, department budgets, tenders, debentures and sinking funds — called for fiscal expertise. Reformers did not just wish to see requisite professional skills introduced on a consultative basis; they wanted them placed in policy-making positions with considerable discretionary powers. When S. Morley Wickett criticized the volume of provincial legislation that encumbered city government, he did so because he ultimately hoped that Canadian cities would be managed by professional administrators who would require a wide operating latitude. Likewise when Port Arthur's publicly owned utilities were foundering, the response was to appoint a "commissioner" who was "not amenable to control, discipline, or dismissal by the mayor or council." Only the chairman of the Federal Board of Railway Commissioners could remove him for cause.[82] The slogans, speeches and articles of reformers as much as the helter-skelter alterations in government furthered the belief that civic affairs was properly a technical or business realm. For example, Hamilton's reforming Mayor, Captain McLaren, ran as an independent summarizing his policy as "civic business is not politics." What this meant in practical terms is reflected by his tangible reform contributions which included the hiring of an industrial commissioner and the purchasing of property for an industrial park."[83] The notion that the city constituted a community, a human environment, was pushed further into the background with the rise of overwhelming technical and business concerns. Civic government was moving away from the ideal described by the author of the 1849 Municipal Corporations Act, Robert Baldwin, who had suggested that local government should serve as a school for democracy.[84]

One further aspect of municipal reform thinking merits critical scrutiny. Since ethnic and working class areas were clustered in certain wards, the movement for city-wide boards and commissions and at-large elections reduced their already slight role in civic affairs. With "foreigners" in their midst and American experiences with ethnic voting in mind, municipal reformers feared an "excess of democracy". Progressive Mayor Short of Edmonton, for example, struck a common chord when he stated that "if the city owned all its utilities, the old system of government by council-committee would no longer be feasible". He decided to pay no heed to "the cry that you must not take away powers from the direct control of the people".[85] His was a widespread attitude and the reduction of public participation implied in special purpose bodies and in efforts to separate the executive and legislative branches constituted a deliberate policy.

The present state of our knowledge about Canadian urban reform allows two generalizations to be made. First, the conclusions reached by Samuel Hays concerning the American municipal reform movement can be applied to Canada. "Innovations in government . . . narrowed the actors in the decision-making process and the range of alternatives and debate; the authorities continued this process. Once given a grant of power it became difficult to render the authority accountable to any other governmental body.''[86] Second, reforms which encompassed public ownership, planning and social welfare can be interpreted in several ways. A few sincere idealists did seek change for humanitarian motives. On the other hand, actual implementation of reform disclosed manipulation of growth for the benefit of the "better classes".

NOTES:

1. Paul Rutherford, "An Introduction," *Saving the Canadian City; The First Phase, 1880-1920* (Toronto: University of Toronto Press, 1974), p. xxii.

2. The lack of serious investigation is disappointing; *a priori* notions appear to have guided many social reformers. The pamphlets of J.J. Kelso held by the Public Archives of Ontario are void of information on Toronto; his observations are general and depend on American reports. His reports in the Ontario Sessional Papers concerning the Bureau of Neglected Children are somewhat superficial and they reflect a strong anti-urban sentiment similar to that of Children's Aid founder Charles Loring Brace. Thomas Adams planned with *a priori* concepts and his major writings on planning were prepared after he left Canada to settle in the United States. *My Neighbour* and *Strangers within Our Gates* by J.S. Woodsworth are filled with ideas and observations drawn from the United States. One might state that they contain a multitude of proposals, but they at times resemble grabbags. Woodsworth's modest appraisal of *My Neighbour* is worth keeping in mind. "With slight equipment, with limited time and many distractions, the author is very conscious of the roughness of his work." All three can be said to have spread a spirit of reform, but the depth of their perception, the nature of their remedies and the origins of the concepts they advanced contain negative as well as positive features. They accepted certain biases and stereotypes commonly held by other Anglo-Saxon Protestants. For a discussion of the positive and negative in town planning and public housing, as they were applied, see John Weaver, "Reconstruction of the Richmond District in Halifax: A Canadian Episode in Public Housing and Town Planning, 1918-1921," *Plan Canada* (March, 1976).

3. John Weaver, "Businessmen and Boosters: Elitism and the Corporate Ideal in Canadian Municipal Reform," in R. McCormack and I. MacPherson, eds., *Cities in the West* (Ottawa: National Museum of Man, 1975); A.F.J. Artibise, *Winnipeg: A Social History of Urban Growth* (Montreal: McGill-Queens, 1975), pp. 43-58.

4. Rutherford, *Saving the Canadian City*, p. xx.

5. Richard Allen, *The Social Passion: Religion and Social Reform in Canada, 1914-1928* (Toronto: University of Toronto Press, 1971), p. 355.

6. Rutherford, *Saving the Canadian City*, p. xiii.

7. Alderman M.C. Costello, "City Publicity," *Canadian Municipal Journal*, vol. 10 (October, 1914), p. 406.

8. H.S.H. Goodier, Secretary, Board of Trade, "The City of Port Arthur," *Public Health Journal*, vol. 5 (January, 1914), p. 57. From an address to the Canadian Union of Municipalities.

9. "Municipal Ownership at Fort William," *Canadian Municipal Journal*, Vol. 5 (July, 1909), p. 306. For similar evaluations of other publicly owned enterprises, see *Labour Gazette*, February, 1905, p. 793; May, 1905, p. 1173; *Edmonton Bulletin*, October 8, 1907, p. 8; Reginald G.J. Smith, "Municipal Affairs in Alberta," *Canadian Municipal Journal*, Vol. 13 (April, 1917).

10. For a discussion of the Port Arthur experience see clipping from *Mail and Empire*, January 8, 1901, in Edmonton Council clippings on Municipal Ownership.

11. *Fort William Journal*, January 17, 1891, p. 2, quoting *Port Arthur Sentinel*. See also *Journal*, August 22, 1891.

12. Joshua Dyke, Ex-Mayor of Fort William, "The Twin Cities Experiences," *Canadian Municipal Journal*, Vol. 1 (June, 1905), p. 183.

13. *Journal*, August 22, 1891, p. 1.

14. *Journal*, March 21, 1891, p. 1; August 6, 1891, p. 1; October 3, 1891, p. 2; March 5, 1892, p. 1; March 9, 1892, p. 2.

15. *London Free Press*, September 23, 1902, p. 7; October 1, 1902, p. 6; November 26, 1902, p. 2. *St. Thomas Evening Journal*, October 1, 1902, p. 1; October 28, 1902, p. 2; November 18, 1902, p. 1.

16. For the background on Edmonton's streetcar franchise, see *Bulletin*, August 17, 1907, p. 8; September 27, 1907, p. 1. For an example of developers' transportation worries, see Phyllis R. Blakeley, *Glimpses of Halifax, 1867-1900* (Halifax: Public Archives of Nova Scotia, 1949), pp. 103-104.

17. *Bulletin*, November 26, 1912, p. 1.

18. *Ibid.*, March 8, 1907, p. 1; March 20, 1907, p. 1.

19. *Ibid.*, March 8, 1907, pp. 1, 6. For the cautious view, see March 6, 1907, p. 1.

20. *Ibid.*, March 8, 1907, p. 6.

21. *Ibid.*, March 9, 1907, p. 11.

22. *Ibid.*, October 4, 1907, p. 4.

23. *Ibid.*, April 16, 1913, p. 2.

24. *Edmonton City Council Minutes*, April 20, 1909; October 13, 1909; November 23, 1909; December 14, 1909; December 28, 1909.

25. For Armstrong's comment, see *Bulletin*, November 24, 1909, p. 3. Coverage on the conclusion of the issue appeared in the *Bulletin*, December 29, 1909, p. 1.

26. See, for example, *Edmonton City Council Minutes*, August 30, 1911; September 3, 1911; March 25, 1913.

27. *Edmonton City Council Minutes*, November 6, 1913; November 11, 1913; November 18, 1913. These were emergency meetings to consider the city's financial burden and to reduce street car losses.

28. Alderman East quoted in *Bulletin*, April 26, 1913, p. 2.

29. *Toronto World*, May 28, 1889, p. 1.

30. G.G. Nasmith, Director of City of Toronto Laboratory, "The Value of a Health Laboratory to a Municipality," *Public Health Journal* (January, 1913), p. 35.

31. Robert J. Fleming, General Manager, T.S.R., to C.H. Rust, City Engineer, June 21, 1909. "Board of Control Report No. 19," Appendix A, *Toronto Council Minutes*, 1909.

32. The practice was well enough known by 1919 that it figures prominently in the strategy of a Hamilton developer who held a 700 acre tract. His advisers had had Toronto experience. "Report of Survey and Recommendations, McKittrick Properties, February 1, 1919", McMaster University, Special Collections (typescript).

33. "Judgement of Judicial Committee of Privy Council Re. Street Railway Extensions," Appendix C, *Toronto Council Minutes*, 1910.

34. See Paul Rutherford, "The People's Press: The Emergence of the New Journalism in Canada, 1869-99," *Canadian Historical Review*, Vol. 56 (June, 1975). Maclean's real estate speculation is mentioned by the rival *Globe*, November 23, 1909, p. 6.

35. *Toronto World*, November 27, 1909, p. 6.

36. *Labour Gazette*, September, 1913, p. 247.

37. *Financial Post*, May 3, 1913, p. 5. Also see September 24, 1910, p. 18; October 23, 1910, p. 10; November 5, 1910, p. 4.

38. For some of the requests for nationalization by public ownership see *Toronto Council Minutes*, 1911, December 6, 1911; "Board of Control Report No. 1," Appendix A, *Toronto Council Minutes*, 1912, January 8, 1912.

39. Patricia E. Roy, "Direct Management from Abroad: The Formative Years of the British Columbia Electric Railway," *Business History*, Vol. 47 (Summer, 1973), 251.

40. *Vancouver Daily Province*, January 29, 1910, p. 18; December 14, 1910, p. 18; December 14, 1910, p. 22; January 7, 1911, p. 8; January 9, 1912, pp. 3, 26; January 12, 1912, p. 36; January 30, 1912, p. 28; December 11, 1912, p. 13.

41. I am indebted to Michel Gauvin for this reference. See John Irwin Cooper, *Montreal, A Brief History* (Montreal: McGill-Queen's University Press, 1969), p. 126.

42. Michael Katz, *The People of Hamilton, Canada West* (Cambridge, Mass.: Harvard University Press, 1975), pp. 2-6.

43. *Hamilton: The Electric City of Canada, Souvenir Edition* (Magazine of Industry and Daily Times, 1910).

44. Ontario Hydro's origins are discussed in W.R. Plewman, *Adam Beck and the Ontario Hydro* (Toronto: Ryerson, 1947), and H.V. Nelles, *The Politics of Development: Forests, Mines, and Hydro-Electric Power in Ontario, 1849-1941* (Toronto: Macmillan, 1974).

45. Hydro Electric System of Hamilton, Scrapbook, Hamilton Public Library, Reverence Station.

46. Clinton O. White, *Power for a Province: A History of Saskatchewan Power* (Canadian Plains Research Centre, University of Regina, 1976), p. 7.

47. *Edmonton City Council Minutes*, October 25, 1910.

48. For accounts of the takeover see the *Bulletin*, January to March, 1902; for details on subsequent problems, see *Edmonton City Council Minutes*, October 14, 1902.

49. Artibise, *Winnipeg*, p. 101.

50. Saskatchewan Local Government Board, *Annual Report, 1915*, quoted in White, *Power for a Province*, p. 11.

51. *Bulletin*, January 10, 1907, p. 1.

52. Mayor Forster, Medicine Hat, "Development of Natural Resources Under Municipal Ownership," *Canadian Municipal Journal*, Vol. 2 (April, 1906).

53. *Labour Gazette*, October, 1910, p. 384.

54. *Calgary City Council Minutes*, October 11, 1912.

55. *Edmonton City Council Minutes*, November 14, 1906; October 12, 1912; Costello, "City Publicity."

56. Artibise, *Winnipeg*, p. 274. A "Beautiful Winnipeg" movement was launched in 1908 by Charles E. Roland, "the enterprising Publicity Commissioner." *Canadian Municipal Journal*, Vol. 4 (June, 1908), p. 231.

57. W.V. Uttley, *A History of Kitchener, Ontario* (Kitchener, 1937), p. 399.

58. Walter Van Nus, "The Fate of City Beautiful Thought in Canada, 1890-1930," Canadian Historical Association, *Historical Papers*, 1975. (Reprinted in this volume as chapter 7.)

59. Speech by Commissioner Coombes of the Salvation Army quoted in *Vancouver Daily Province*, January 24, 1910, p. 24; Dr. Charles A. Hodgetts, *Unsanitary Housing* (Ottawa, 1911), 52-53; J.E. Laberge, Superintendent, Department of Infectious Diseases, Montreal, "Town Planning and Civic Authorities," *Public Health Journal*, Vol. 3 (March, 1912), p. 128.

60. See for example Bureau of Municipal Research, Toronto, *What is "the Ward" Going to do with Toronto* (Bureau of Municipal Research, 1918), p. 18.

61. Terry Copp, *The Anatomy of Poverty: The Conditions of the Working Class in Montreal, 1897-1929* (Toronto: McClelland and Stewart, 1974), p. 140.

62. Lt.-Col. C.N. Laurie, M.O.H., Port Arthur, Ontario, "Sanitary Work Among the Foreign Population," *Public Health Journal*, Vol. 4 (July, 1913), p. 455.

63. J.S. Woodsworth, "The Significance of Human Waste in Modern Life and its Causes," *Public Health Journal*, Vol. 5 (January, 1914), p. 21.

64. J.O. McCarthy, "We try to regulate overcrowding, and we enact a building code or by-law; but this is not dealing with the housing problem," in "The Problem of the City — Factors in its Solution — Municipal Departments," Social Service Congress, Ottawa, 1914, *Report of Addresses and Proceedings* (Toronto: Social Service Council of Canada), p. 125. Also see Bryce Stewart, *A Preliminary and General Social Survey of Hamilton* (National Council of Churches, 1913); James Roberts, *Annual Report of the Board of Health, Hamilton, 1912* (Spectator Printing Company); and Artibise, *Winnipeg*, pp. 244-45.

65. Shirley Spragge, "The Toronto Housing Company: A Canadian Experiment," unpublished paper delivered at the Canadian Historical Association Annual Meeting in Edmonton, June, 1975.

66. The Toronto District Labour Council condemned the scheme since few working men could afford the $250 initial payment. *Labour Gazette*, March, 1912, p. 856.

67. James Roberts, "Insanitary Areas," *Public Health Journal*, Vol. 3 (April, 1912), p. 180.

68. Ernest W.J. Hague, Assistant Chief Sanitary Inspector, Winnipeg, "The Housing Problem," *Public Health Journal*, Vol. 5 (June, 1914), pp. 375-76.

69. *Ibid.*, p. 376.

70. *Vancouver Daily Province*, January 27, 1910, p. 28; December 6, 1910, p. 11; December 8, 1910, p. 1.

71. Hague, "The Housing Problem," p. 373.

72. Artibise, *Winnipeg*, p. 243.

73. J.W.S. McCullogh, Chief Officer of Health for Ontario, President Elect, Canadian Public Health Association, "The Ontario Public Health Act," *Public Health Journal*, Vol. 5 (September, 1914), pp. 554; Hodgetts, *Unsanitary Housing*, p. 48; Woodsworth, "The Significance of Human Waste," p. 21.

74. Rev. Walter A. Riddell, "The Value of the Social Survey," Social Service Congress, Ottawa, 1914, *Report of Addresses and Proceedings* (Toronto, 1914), p. 54-55.

75. Developers across Canada set minimum housing standards to protect their unsold lots. The social consequences of this are being examined in a quantitative analysis of the Hamilton suburb of Westdale, established in 1912. I am directing this study.

76. Laurie, "Sanitary Work Among the Foreign Population," p. 455.

77. "Fiat Justita: A Kick at Slum Workers," *Canadian Therapeudist and Sanitary Engineer*, Vol. 1 (July, 1910).

78. John Weaver, "Toronto, 1895: The Meaning of Municipal Reform," *Ontario History* (June, 1974); *Labour Gazette*, October, 1909, p. 775; *Vancouver Daily Province*, December 2, 1910, p. 2; December 3, 1910, p. 6; January 13, 1911, p. 9; January 20, 1912, p. 25.

79. *Vancouver Daily Province*, December 11, 1911, p. 1.

80. S. Morley Wickett, *Memorandum Re Metropolitan Area* (Toronto, 1913).

81. S.M. Baker, "Municipal Government Reform," *Municipal World*, Vol. 27 (October, 1917), p. 154.

82. Wickett, "Civic Charters," *Municipal World*, Vol. 15 (January, 1915), pp. 8-9. For Port Arthur episode, see *Financial Post*, January 6, 1912, p. 2.

83. *Globe*, January 5, 1909, p. 1; January 12, 1909, p. 2.

84. J.H. Aitchison, "The Municipal Corporations Act of 1849", *Canadian Historical Review*, 30 (June, 1949), p. 121.

85. *Bulletin*, November 26, 1912, p. 1.

86. Sam Hays, "The Changing Political Structure of the City in Industrial America," *Journal of Urban History*, Vol. 1 (November, 1974), p. 28.

Urban Autonomy in Canada: Its Evolution and Decline

JOHN H. TAYLOR

Much was paradox in "A Nation Transformed,"[1] and not the least among the paradoxes was the urban expansion that held within it the loss of local autonomy. As cities and towns grew in number, size, power and complexity in twentieth-century Canada they lost control of their affairs and became increasingly subject to senior levels of government. The dynamic of that process remains obscure. The contours of the process are, however, somewhat clearer. What happened and when can be outlined and the process speculated on.

By 1900 urban Canada was expanding rapidly as measured by raw population and economic growth, and this expansion was only the most dramatic and obvious aspect of a more complicated metamorphosis.[2] The process by which the expansion and its attendant changes was achieved is yet not well understood.[3] This complex process also occurred in a generally *laissez-faire* environment, one in which a major emphasis was placed on growth and a relatively minor one on control.[4] At the turn of the century, much of urban Canada was growing like Topsy, with warts. Growth combined problems with its undoubted rewards, especially in the large centres. Whatever was magistral had a noisome and seamy side. With growth came complications, with splendour also came squalor. Growth, for example, led to a continuous and more complex reformulation of urban infra-structure and the environment, especially with respect to the supply of services and to planning. Services and planning implied the use of public money and public control.[5] On the social side, growth led either to an increase in the number of people vulnerable to the ravages of uncertain employment, disease, old age and infirmity, or, possibly, growth led to a

SOURCE: This is an original paper, prepared especially for this volume.

heightened concern for these problems.[6] Certainly the problems were exacerbated by the close of the frontier safety valve in the 1920s, and by the diminished capacity of some support systems of long standing, such as the family, the church and the private charity. Individuals lived in an increasing artificial, interlocking and dangerous environment. As time went on, the difficulties proved less and less susceptible to private sector solution and implied the use of public money and public control.

Just as urban centres were largely left free, in the last part of the nineteenth century, to pursue their policies of growth, so too were they left largely free to evolve policies of physical and social amelioration. Certainly the senior governments posed few obstacles to such activities. Most statutory legislation applicable to early twentieth-century localities was open-ended. There was an abundance of "may" clauses and very few "must" ones. In addition, such legislation was not generally trenched on by other statutes that were concerned with specific problems like welfare. Finally, most senior governments as a matter of political policy were non-interventionist. Local governments were, by and large, left alone to deal with both the progress and the problems of late nineteenth and early twentieth-century society and economy.

Services, such as utilities and public works, were expanded in this era either by public bodies or under their franchises.[7] Social services, especially for the indigent and the unemployed, were elaborated or expanded.[8] Efforts were made in some centres to introduce planning, and in many cities elaborate schemes emerged from the drawing boards of early consultants.[9] Efforts were made to provide housing, parks, and other amenities. Local governments, for all their *ad hocery* and at times reluctance, did make some provision for the improvement of the conditions in which their citizens lived and did business, though there was perhaps more stress on the latter than on the former. And, a matter of some significance, they did so largely out of their own pocketbooks.[10] By the late 1920s, however, many local governments were finding it difficult to sustain such efforts and were beginning to call for a re-adjustment among all levels of government of revenues and responsibilities, including abandonment by the federal government of the income tax field.[11]

Though local governments were left largely to their own devices in this period, the beginnings of senior government intervention in local affairs was also apparent: ". . . avec le tournant du siècle, les interventions législatives abandonnnment, en effet, leur caractère essentiellement libéral pour adopter une orientation plus impérative et plus centralisée."[12] The process of intervention and consequent loss of local autonomy was a ragged one in terms of its quality, quantity, timing and location. It is not entirely complete even today. The process appears to have taken place in two phases, the first beginning in the nineteenth-century and the second, and more significant, about the time of the Great War.

In the first phase, beginning about 1880 in Ontario and apparently following an American pattern, "new functions of local government were assigned to newly created boards rather than to the established municipal councils."[13] Such boards included library boards, park boards, and health boards. In addition to restricting local control over certain functions, there was also the nineteenth century phenomenon of restricting local control over certain officials, like the medical health officer, assessor, and sanitary inspectors.[14] In certain highly sensitive areas, like policing, a buffer, usually in the form of a commission, was often placed between the politicians and the functioning department. This last scheme, in various forms, was also used to control indulgent political behaviour with respect to utilities and sometimes with respect to private enterprise in general.[15] Finally, there was the creation of bodies to provide a service to an aggregation of municipalities and such bodies generally had a quasi-independent status. The Vancouver Water and Drainage Districts were an example of this phenomenon with respect to physical services, and the Montreal Metropolitan Commission with respect to the provision for and control of borrowing.[16] In this phase, certain functions or offices were removed from the direct control of city council, but both the functions and the offices were retained at the local level and both were almost always funded from the local level. Senior government supervision was imposed, in effect, by fragmenting or diluting local authority.

The second phase in the erosion of local autonomy, beginning about the time of the Great War, was the more significant. In this phase senior governments imposed function and office on the local authority but retained most (if not all) control over funding and regulation. In the period between the two wars, the practice had become solidly entrenched. By 1940, K.G. Crawford could write:

> It has become almost standard practice that a portion of the cost of almost every "social service" which, in its wisdom, the provincial government sees fit to undertake, shall be passed on without consultation to the municipalities and thence to the owners of real estate, whether or not the service is one which might logically be classed as a municipal service or a legitimate charge to be based on the ownership of real property.[17]

The practice, it might be added, extended into areas other than "social service."

This changed relationship between local and senior governments was uneven in its quality and pace of application, but in broad terms tended to depend on exigencies (most notably the Great Depression), the extent and impact of the change to urban-industrial and post-industrial society in the various regions,[19] and the composition and attitudes of governments at all levels.[20] The changed pattern of the relationship, despite its unevenness, can be seen in at least four inter-related developments of the inter-war and immediate post-war period: changes in provincial statutory control; changes in administrative and regulatory control at the senior levels; changes in local finance; and the expansion of the conditional grants system. All trenched on local autonomy.

CHANGES IN PROVINCIAL STATUTORY CONTROL

Though it is almost unquestioned that in Canada the provinces have exclusive powers to "make laws in relation" to "municipal institutions,"[21] the sort of laws existing in the first decades of the twentieth-century were not very restrictive. An examination of provincial statutes in this period provides fairly clear evidence that the provinces conferred on local governments (at least the larger and more mature ones) almost "residual powers" to make laws affecting their communities. Indeed, such powers in at least one jurisdiction, Saskatchewan, were expanded in the first decades of the century. "The City Act" of that province, passed in 1908, asserted that a city council "may" make regulations and bylaws "for the peace, order, good government and welfare of the city," but specifically enumerated some obligatory responsibilities.[22] In 1915 these general powers were somewhat widened, mainly by removing references to specific responsibilities,[23] and thereby made to conform to the more general practice in the Dominion. Ontario was not untypical. The "General Provisions Applicable to all Municipalities" in Ontario in 1914 were as follows:

> Every council may pass such by-laws and make such regulations for the health, safety, morality, and welfare of the inhabitants of the municipality in matters not specifically provided for by this Act, as may be deemed expedient and are not contrary to law, and for governing the proceedings of the council, the conduct of its members and the calling of meetings.[24]

Similar clauses can be found in the statutes of most of the provinces in the period. The broad, almost residual nature of local powers, and their discretionary quality, was coupled with rather loose and rather little provincial control. In the main, concurrent legislation affecting local government was aimed mainly at preventing abuse rather than controlling function, and most of the preventative legislation was concerned with audit of local revenue and expenditure, with control over borrowing and lending, and, in some instances, with control of "public" utilities, including funding and promotion of railways, and manufacturing.

Perhaps the most extensive set of pre-1914 statutes affecting local government can be found in Quebec; but though extensive, it was not highly restrictive. Municipal governance fell under the rubric of the Provincial Secretary (and later a number of other ministers). The Provincial Secretary superintended the administration or the execution of the laws govering the municipal system, in addition to a number of other duties.[25] Quebec municipalities were also required to inform this minister when they required an expansion of borrowing powers,[26] but made the application to the Lieutenant-Governor.[27] The statutory limit on borrowing came into effect only when interest and sinking fund payments absorbed up to half the annual revenue of the municipality.[28] Fiscal control was exerted under "The Municipal Accounts Act" dating to at least 1909,[29] and under "The Municipal Debt and Loan Act" of 1918,[30] and a series of amended versions of it in the following five years.[31] These acts were concurrent with another series of acts to control aid to or sale of utilities. There were few other significant statutory or ministerial restraints on Quebec municipalities at this time.

At the other end of the statutory spectrum, New Brunswick, Nova Scotia and British Columbia had almost no explicit legislation (outside the municipal and other incorporation acts) to circumscribe their local governments, apart from some control over audit. In the middle of the spectrum was Ontario, with legislation similar to that of Quebec, but perhaps less extensive.[32] Only two provinces, Alberta and Saskatchewan, had departments of municipal affairs under the direction of a cabinet minister.[33] Though statutes gave the department of both provinces fairly broad powers of supervision, the main intent of the legislation was clearly to supervise finances, debt, and audit. Manitoba had what approximated a department in the form of the Municipal Commissioner's Department. It was established under "The Municipal Commissioner's Act" of 1890,[34] and had functions similar to those of the departments in the neighboring prairie provinces.

Beginning about the Great War there was a perceptible increase in the legislation affecting municipalities, both in terms of its quantity and quality. This legislation not only told local governments what they were required to do in respect of their omnibus powers, but began, particularly in the 1930s — as the provinces became more intervention in the social sector and the municipalities more financially strapped — to trench on those omnibus powers. The growth of provincial statutory control as it relates to local government can be observed most clearly in four areas: general municipal supervision through departments of municipal affairs, social welfare, planning and housing, and finance and audit.

In terms of general municipal supervision, every province (apart from Prince Edward Island) had by 1936, operational departments of municipal

TABLE I

GOVERNANCE OF MUNICIPALITIES BY THE PROVINCES*

Province	Official	Date	Act
Manitoba	Commissioner	1890	Manitoba, 53 Vic, c. 51 (1890)**
Saskatchewan	Minister	1908	Saskatchewan, 8-9 Edw. VII, c. 15 (1908-9)
Alberta	Minister	1912	Alberta, 2 Geo V, c. 11 (1911-12)
British Columbia	Minister	1934	British Columbia, 24 Geo V, c. 52 (1934)
New Brunswick	Commissioner	1934	New Brunswick, 24 Geo V, c. 14 (1934)***
Ontario	Minister	1935	Ontario, 25 Geo V, c. 16 (1935)
Quebec	Minister	1935	Quebec, 25-26 Geo V, c. 45 (1935)
Nova Scotia	Commissioner	1936	Nova Scotia, 25-26 Geo V, c. 5 (1935)****

NOTES:

*In all jurisdictions municipalities reported to a provincial minister but who was not a minister of municipal affairs and did not run a department of municipal affairs, as such. In Ontario, for example, it was for many years the Provincial Secretary. My concern here is the point at which local government was placed under the authority of a provincial department, created by statute and concerned solely with municipal affairs, either directly under a minister of municipal affairs, or under a commissioner of municipal affairs, operating a department and reporting to a minister, as in Manitoba, Nova Scotia, and New Brunswick.

**Made a Department under a minister by *Statutes of Manitoba*, 2 Eliz. II, c. 37 (1953 — 2nd Session).

***A complete overhaul of municipal affairs was only carried out in 1966.

****This act, though passed in 1935, was not proclaimed until 1936, after amended by Statutes of Nova Scotia, 1 Edw. VIII, c. 53 (1936). A ministry and a minister was provided for in 1945 by *Statutes of Nova Scotia*, 9 Geo VI, c. 6 (1945).

affairs, most with extensive powers to supervise, influence and pass money on to local governments (Table 1). Furthermore, both prior to and after the establishment of such ministries there was an expansion of legislation providing for greater provincial control over many local government functions. Ontario provides perhaps the most spectacular example of this phenomenon, though it was endemic in the Dominion. The Municipal Act entry in the index of the *Revised Statutes of Ontario* for 1950 contains cross-references to sixty-five other provincial acts affecting local government.[35] Some date prior to 1914 and are generally prohibitive or guiding in nature, but most date after 1914 and trench on the omnibus powers of local government. Chief among these later statutes were: The Planning and Development Act (1918), The Ontario Housing Act (1919), The Municipal Housing Act (1920), The Department of Public Welfare Act (1913), The Factory, Shop and Office Building Act (1932), The Ontario Municipal Board Act (1932), The Federal District Commission Act (1934), The Department of Municipal Affairs Act (1935), The Municipal Employees Pensions Fund Act (1937), The Department of Planning and Development Act (1944), The Municipal Health Services Act (1944), The Planning Act (1946), The Department of Reform Institutions Act (1946), The Department of Public Welfare Act (1948), The Housing Development Act (1948), The Vital Statistics Act (1948), and the Ontario Municipal Improvement Corporation Act (1950).[36]

Perhaps the most significant development in this legislative outburst were those acts relating to public welfare and ultimately the creation of provincial departments in this area, an area clearly within the general powers of most municipal acts and charters (and specified responsibilities of Vancouver and the Alberta cities in the 1920s and the Ontario municipalities in the 1930s).[37] Of nearly equal significance was the legislation relating to town planning, development control, and housing.[38] What gives all this legislation such importance is that it not only represented an interventionist commitment on the part of the senior government in certain policy areas and the concurrent growth of bureaucracies to implement such policy, but also a commitment in most instances to three-level conditional cost-sharing as the means of funding such interventionist ventures. With these developments, and with local financial problems associated with the depression, fiscal supervision also became much more close and much more strict.[39] It was also tied to senior, not local, government policy.

Oddly enough, despite these statutory changes, the general powers of local government remained virtually untouched. For example, the general powers of city councils in Ontario were precisely the same in 1950 as they had been in 1914.[40] But by 1950 legal power and real power were no longer co-incident. Other provincial statutes now trenched on the general powers of local government, and so did provincial (and federal) administrations.

CHANGES IN ADMINISTRATIVE AND REGULATORY CONTROL

While legislative changes can be charted with some degree of accuracy, changes in administrative structures and powers are not nearly so susceptible to analysis, which perhaps explains why so little analysis has been done. But administrative changes were nonetheless significant insofar as they affected the loss of local autonomy. Not only were the new provincial and federal administrators able to exert control over municipal decisions through their statutory and discretionary powers, but they were also in a position to lay down or influence new policy directions that tended both to concentrate authority at a central point and to homogenize (usually in the name of equity) the type and amount of services delivered.[41] Growth of senior government administration, as it affected local government, seems to have been particularly strong from the 1930s on, even though much of it was haphazard, often temporary, and *ad hoc*. Its influence could be pervasive. In the 1930s, for example, the unemployment relief branch of the federal Department of Labour, operating on a year-to-year basis and with questionable constitutional powers to provide relief to the indigent unemployed, could exert considerable control on provincial and local authorities in its efforts to protect the federal treasury. "These controls [were] manifested in federal approval not only of projects and contracts for public works but also of schedules of families to be assisted under the relief settlement agreements; in inspectional and investigational activities; in reporting requirements; in departmental rulings and interpretations; and in audits."[42] Provincial administrative controls over local governments could obviously be even more direct. Grants brought bureaucracies in their train.

CHANGES IN LOCAL FINANCE AND THE EXPANSION OF THE CONDITIONAL GRANT

Along with a loss of autonomy through the growth of statutory control and changes in its quality, local government also lost much of its autonomy to innovate through the erosion of its tax base, both absolutely and in relation to the services it was expected to provide. The contraction of the local tax base was mainly a phenomenon of the 1930s and 1940s when provincial authorities (at various times) eliminated local income taxes, sales taxes, and personal property taxes; eliminated or reduced the local share of liquor and motor vehicle taxes; and in some instances placed restrictions on untrammelled exploitation of the property tax.[43] By the end of the 1930s, the major remaining tax field left to local government, the property tax, was approaching the limits of exploitation. The costs of services local government was expected or required to provide continued, however, to rise. The result was a growing gap between what local governments could raise on their own and the total amount of revenue they required (see Table II). The

TABLE II

MUNICIPAL REVENUES AND TRANSFERS
1926 to 1956
(Millions of Dollars)

	1926	1928	1930	1932	1934	1936	1938	1940	1942	1944	1946	1948	1950	1952	1954	1965
Total Municipal Revenues	336	367	403	385	366	380	381	393	412	452	496	640	796	1027	1206	1463
Total Transfers [1]	29	32	46	48	36	37	37	36	44	65	86	138	182	228	274	361
Municipal Revenue Less Transfers	307	335	357	337	330	343	344	357	368	387	410	502	614	799	932	1102
Revenue Less Transfers as a percentage of Total Revenues [2]	91	91	89	88	90	90	90	91	89	86	87	78	77	78	77	75

NOTES:

1. Transfers from municipalities to provinces and transfers from provinces to municipalities. Municipal revenue less transfers thereby represents net available revenue obtained from local sources.

2. By the mid-1970s this percentage, by some accounts, had fallen to almost 50%. See David M. Nowlan, "Towards Home Rule for Urban Policy," *Journal of Canadian Studies*, Vol. 13, No. 1 (Spring 1978), p. 70.

SOURCE: DBS, National Accounts, *Income and Expenditure, 1926-1956* (Queen's Printer, Ottawa, 1962), Table 36, pp. 74-75.

transfer payment, usually in the form of a conditional grant, was the device used to close the gap.

The federal conditional grant came into use in Canada in 1913 (the first one was for agricultural instruction) and, until the unemployment and farm relief grants of the 1930s, was used for only six programs that involved relatively small amounts of money. Its use has been traced, at the outset, not to financial exigency, but "to get the provinces started in certain activities having a national interest."[44] Until the depression, its significance was far outweighed by the unconditional federal subsidies passed on to the provinces under the terms of the British North America Act and subsequent agreements. By 1934, largely because of the relief grants, conditional transfers amounted to almost $44 million while the direct subsidies, or unconditional transfers, came to just over $15 million.[45] Perhaps more important, the relief grants were in response to financial need more than functional need, and, though given to the provinces, were in effect administered and disbursed by the local authorities. By the 1940s they had become an important and apparently permanent feature of inter-governmental finance and policymaking.

Provincial conditional grants to local governments have a somewhat longer history than those made by the federal governments.[45] But like the federal grants they were usually *ad hoc*, and often temporary.[46] Also, they were, like the federal ones, used for emergency purposes, or, as in the case of Ontario's housing legislation of 1919, designed to encourage local governments to move into new areas. There has been little analysis of their impact on the policy and financing of local governments, but it appears that until the 1930s it was slight.

So long as the grants were not allied with broad interventionist policies at the senior levels, so long as control remained loose, and so long as the grants were deemed temporary measures, there was no appreciable impact on local autonomy. But once the grants were allied with permanent interventionist policies, and once they became an important and permanent part of local revenues, compulsion and control by the senior governments, for good or ill, necessarily followed. Local governments lost autonomy over their activities in two ways. They were told what to do and given the money (or some of the money) to do it. Or they were given the option of taking money on certain conditions or not at all. In the former case the compulsion was explicit; in the latter implicit. In either case, local autonomy was compromised. Identification of problems and the establishment of priorities could not be determined in the locality. Responsibility for problems and the power to solve them (especially fiscal power) was separated. And power of elected officials at the local level was diluted or constricted by discretionary powers of non-elected officials at the senior levels.

PERCEPTIONS OF CHANGE

Changes in the relationship of the local governments with the senior ones, however ragged and incomplete, did not pass without some alarm. One of the earliest warnings to local governments in Canada was made by an American, Mayor Joseph Carson, of Portland Oregon, in an address to the Union of Canadian Municipalities annual convention in 1936.

> I tell you gentlemen frankly, that in the United States we are facing a loss of self government. I am not in any way criticizing the present federal government in my country. What I say is that local governments, head over heels in debt and with their credit exhausted, have begged the superior governments to come in and take over our responsibilities. Now we find ourselves faced with the danger of losing our local self government rights.
>
> I warn you in Canada, whose local problems parallel our own, that cities must cease being political mendicants at the feet of federal government. For just as surely as you accept handouts from the superior authority, you will see a corresponding loss of your own local autonomy.[47]

Though the Canadian representatives to the convention paid little heed to the American guest, he clearly perceived that something was happening or had happened already to the autonomy of Canadian local government. Rather similar fears, for perhaps different motives, were expressed in 1938 by Commissioner Mary Sutherland in a dissenting memorandum to parts of the *Final Report* of the National Employment Commission that called for federal assumption of administrative responsibility for the unemployed. Depression exigencies, she argued, perhaps reflecting Kingsian policy, were no excuse for federal assumption.

> The fact that Municipalities and Provinces are at the moment distraught and harassed by their financial incapacity to meet their primary responsibilities is entirely beside the point. Indeed if relevancy can be claimed it should be to caution against the capitalizing of their distress and difficulties for the purpose of securing an assignment of any of their Provincial rights or powers to a central government.[48]

She also argued that alleged abuses in the delivery of relief at the provincial and local levels would not necessarily be cleaned up by federal assumption. A Dominion system, she said, "is also liable to many abuses."[49] Finally, and in a philosophical vein, she questioned the desirability of separating government from the individual. An individual, she argued, has a more responsible attitude toward a government he pays taxes to directly and can see functioning for him.[50] Other opinions, however, were to prevail.

The changing nature of local government was also noted, with varying degrees of trepidation, by the academic community, and appears to have precipitated a debate on the relationship of local government and democracy, a debate, at bottom, that constituted a new rationalization for the existence of local government in a subjected form.

Among the first to make a comprehensive analysis of the changing "Independence" of municipal councils was K.G. Crawford in an article in 1940. He concluded that the more serious encroachment was from the provincial direction.

> This is a movement which is not only increasing, but increasing at a greatly accelerated rate. It is characteristic both of legislative bodies and governmental boards and bureaux that they will endeavour constantly to widen their field of control and operation. In Ontario, the tendency towards increasing interference with municipal independence, and the imposition of financial burdens by the Province, has covered a period of many years and all varieties of governments. It is a trend which is not likely to be arrested until the situation becomes so acute as to overshadow other provincial issues.[51]

Crawford was followed in short order by Alan Van Every, who in 1943 saw some potential benefit in what he termed "enlarged provincial oversight of Canadian municipalities."[52] Perhaps less sanguine was C.A. Curtis. In an article in 1942 he dealt with what he perceived to be the major problems facing local government: the inappropriate division of fiscal resources and responsibilities,[53] the fragmentation of municipal functions that inhibited the entry of good men into local politics because they would not make themselves available "unless the functions and powers of Council are worthwhile and sufficiently important,"[54] inadequate planning, irrational delineation of boundaries, insufficient housing, and the increasing impact of provincial administration and control. In an address in 1951 he outlined a program of reform aimed at dealing with the problems he had identified earlier.[55] A similar, tentative effort was made in the same year by Keith B. Callard.[56] Other discussion on more specific areas of concern also made their way into print: a series of articles in the 1940s on control of local finances in *Municipal Finance*,[57] A.E. Buck's chapter on the subject in *Financing Canadian Government* in 1949,[58] Eric Hardy on provincial-municipal relationships and Fred R. MacKinnon on local government and welfare in the same volume of *Canadian Public Administration* in 1960,[59] and Lionel Feldman's discussion of "Legislative Control" in 1961.[60]

For the most part, these writers, and others like George Mooney of the Canadian Federation of Mayors and Municipalities,[61] asserted a fundamental belief in the virtue of local government on grounds that it served not only a functional good, but also a political good in the sense that it was a support of and a training ground for democracy.

The view was apparently widespread in the North Atlantic community, for its challenge at the International Political Science Association meeting at The Hague in 1952 by Georges Langrod[62] provoked considerable debate,[63] and precipitated what appears to have been a rather sudden change in perspective of Canadian writers in the field, notably Hugh Whalen, who in 1960 published two somewhat contradictory articles on the subject.[64] Whatever one's position in the debate, the fact that it occurred at all indicates a recognition that the place of local government in an urban-industrial society had undergone a significant and substantial change. As Whalen pointed out:

> Local self-government as it exists in most industrial democracies today can no longer be considered a major instrument of control. In an era of expanding communities, growing mass publics, and intricate and rapidly expanding technologies, mechanisms of democratic control must be located at the vital centres of power of each national community.[65]

By 1970 Whalen and many others had noted or accepted a diminished role for local government, and, depending on their inclinations, were offering prescriptions either for its continued existence in an atrophied form or for its rejuvenation. Among those beginning to prescribe rejuvenation were the municipalities themselves, which in the 1960s broke a virtual silence that extended back to the early 1930s. Planners and economists, more recently, have also called for the reversal of the drift to dimunition. There seems little doubt that a significant loss of local autonomy occurred in twentieth century Canada and that the pressures created by an urban-industrial and post-industrial society — by ''A Nation Transformer'' — were fundamentally related to that loss. Just how they related has been more a matter of speculation than investigation.

THE PATTERN OF CHANGE

One possible, and perhaps too easy explanation for the altered circumstances of local government is that secular change of itself dictated that ''mechanisms of democratic control must be located at the vital centres of power of each national community.'' Vital centres, however, can be made as well as materialize, and in Canada, at least, the senior governments (slowly and often relunctantly) arrogated to themselves the power to control the changed national community, and from the local point of view the provincial actions were the more significant and the more vital.

As a general proposition, Whalen's dictum has much to recommend it, and as an explantory device parallels, in a broad sense, Marxist explanations,[66] the vital shifts in the latter analysis relating to the emergence of corporations and the corporate city in the twentieth century, a change in Canada more commonly referred to as the second industrial revolution. But elaboration of the elements of that change, and provision of an analytical framework, in Canada at least, has been rare.[67] Some understanding can be gained by considering the birth of local autonomy in Canada and its subsequent development.

The birth of autonomous local government in Canada has usually been traced to the events of the 1840s, in particular to the Baldwin Municipal Act of 1849, and parallel legislation in Nova Scotia, and somewhat later, in Quebec. Though individual charters had been given some cities in the Canadas and Maritimes as early as the 1830s, they were spotty and to some extent intended to broaden police powers and make possible certain acts of amelioration, though in the agitation, if not in the legislation, they were part of a widening effort to develop the commercial city of that day into an instrument of expansion for the commercial classes. In other words, certain groups of merchants and retailers were attempting to use the city as a vehicle or lever to expand their own fortunes through, primarily, provision of infrastructure in the form of railways, roads, harbour improvements and the like. Typically in the period of the commercial city, most municipally-related improvements were in the area of transportation. But charters were not widespread and generally not comprehensive in their powers. Rather, such legislation seems to have been part and parcel of the great economic and political events of the 1840s that treated the autonomous, national, as opposed to the dependent, of imperial, commercial city in Canada.

The Baldwin Act, the act incorporating Halifax, and the scattered town and city charters of the 1830s and 1840s seem to have had two over-riding objectives in common. All wished to break the centralized and oligarchic form of local government in the form of the justices of the peace and grand jury systems, and create independent centres of local power. They were in that sense a political reform. And all seem, with some ambivalence, to have wanted to do so to give effect to an economic independence, one not beholden to the Imperial commercial system within which they then operated. In that sense they were operating within the times and were to some extent at one with the British reformers, who wanted to dismantle the Imperial and mercantilist system; and with the British North American reformers who were agitating for political independence in the form of responsible government, especially after it became clear in the 1840s, with the repeal of the Corn Laws and timber duties, that they were going to get economic independence, willy nilly.

The agitation for responsible government in Nova Scotia, for example, was at least in part directly related to the emergence of a new retail class and its desire for a charter for the city of Halifax, one that would both recognize its new economic importance and wrest some of the political control from the merchants who had political and economic roots in the imperial system.[68]

The Baldwin Municipal Act, too, seems to have stemmed from some of the same concerns. As Whebell noted the "principle of responsible government was a facet of [the reform], but underlying it was the deeper reality of a rising middle class struggling for a share of political power. The Municipal Corporations Bill or Baldwin Act was a weapon in this struggle, especially as it demolished the magistracy as a perpetual power base for the Tories."[69] But it was also the occasion or the opportunity for the "rising middle class" to weld their futures and fortunes to those of their towns and cities and produce the phenomenon of boosterism in its commercial and early industrial phase.[70] In both the political and the economic sense, local communities were freed, at the same time, from provincial and from imperial control.

The development of local autonomy also appears to have meshed neatly with the desire of Francis Hincks, and perhaps others, to underwrite the financing of railway construction in the 1840s and 1850s. One device was his Railway Guarantee Act of 1849. A second was to encourage municipal support of railway projects, in effect a scheme to use the property tax base to underwrite railway development. Both were more or less failures, and a prelude to direct granting of Crown land to supply collateral for railway ventures. But the desire to use the municipal "state" to support railway building necessarily implied the development of a municipal "state."[71] He thus supported the passage of the Baldwin Act, as he had supported the earlier municipal legislation of Sydenham.

In this way, the opportunity was provided to make supreme in local government a local business group whose focus was on development of localities, regions and, in case of metropolitan centres, a nation; and the concurrent displacement of a gentility whose fortunes were more tied up with Imperial prerogatives. To some extent this was accomplished, at least in the case of the Baldwin Act, with a new residency qualification that was attached to the property qualification in the franchise. That, too, reinforced identification with place. The property franchise, nonetheless, remained intact. Control of local governments, though in theory broadened, was in reality shifted from one elite to another. There was apparently at no time an intent to admit popular democratic control of local governments in the nineteenth century, and such tendencies were resisted in most jurisdictions until well after World War Two.[72]

This pattern or mode of local autonomy was easily adapted to the industrial phase of economic development in Canada, perhaps because the British municipal model of 1835, one designed for an industrial society, was used in Canada. Or perhaps because the older commercial enterprises found the new system as much to their liking as the newer industrial ones.

There is some indication that commercial and industrial capital found itself at odds in terms of the development of some Canadian cities, but generally there seems to have been an inter-locking of the commercial and industrial groups except where one group or the other attempted monopoly control of development policy, like the successful commercial group in Saint John,[73] or the power and traction capitalists of much of Ontario, who were defeated by provincial intervention at the behest of urban business.[74] That is to say, there was a fairly fluid transition, as far as local government went, from the commercial to the first industrial stage, except in areas that "privatism" handled badly: for example the social ills stemming from industrial development; health problems; matters of fiscal control; and audit. In these areas, the provincial governments began stepping in in the 1880s, the period in which control was exerted by main force and through administrative fragmentation. But the essential identification by a booster elite of its fortunes with the fortunes of its place was not seriously impaired. Local governments, controlled by a small body of men operating under a property franchise largely raised and disposed of their own funds for their own purposes and in their own interests. Political tensions were vented by various forms of "conventional factionalism."[75]

By the twentieth-century, and especially in the inter-war period, serious problems were beginning to appear in this scenario as a result of the development of corporate structures: expansion of welfare; exhaustion of local fiscal resources; social segregation; expansion of democracy; and proletarian political organization. Probably the three most critical of these were the breaking of the booster nexus, a result of development of corporations not identified with places; its obverse, in the form of the geo-social-political identification in cities of a democratized urban proletariat; and third, the exhaustion of the property tax as the major source of independent municipal revenue. The opportunity in these circumstances was ripe for fiscal, social, and economic fragmentation and the assumption of indirect control of the cities by the corporate sector and its political allies, the provinces, this at a time when a minimum and equitable standard of social welfare, education and the like was becoming a strong political cry in the country and a political justification for managing the city. The era has been termed one of unstable equilibrium between the liberal decentralizers of the nineteenth-century and the interventionism of the twentieth-century.[76] Functionally, the cities could not manage — their mentalité and competitive instincts did not admit it — and in terms of power, their organization was morphologically incompatible with the corporate and provincial phase.

Corporations are merely in cities, they are not of cities. And their role grew in the twentieth century to the point that they overshadowed the industrial and commercial elites who had dominated in the nineteenth. Of most importance is the fact that corporations have no special loyalty to place. Their fortunes are not tied to the fortunes of a city or town, and indeed such ties can even be seen as counter-productive. The loyalty is to the organization, or at best to the corporate headquarters city.

For the lower social classes, the case in the twentieth-century was the reverse of the nineteenth, when the property franchise had effectively shut them out of local government. In the nineteeth, their transiency and their poverty apparently gave them a relatively weak association with place, and if they did have one, it was likely with a cultural not a class community within a city, for example the French in Montreal or the Roman Catholics in Ottawa. The segregation of cities in the industrial phase and the identification of class, and sometimes culture and class, with discreet geographic or social areas within cities, coupled with the widening of the franchise — through legislation or prosperity — gave rise to organization, political as well as other. By the crisis of the 1930s, an organized proletariat was seen as having the potential to control local government.[77] It is this sort of threat that Marxist scholars in the United States see as prompting the flight of corporate capital to the suburbs; to the fragmentation of corporate and therefore working class functions; and as putting their businesses beyond the influence of a local government run by the lower classes. Some evidence of this phenomenon is seen in Canada, and it perhaps proved most hurtful in Montreal.[78] But generally other strategies were employed. Perhaps the most important of these was the emergence of the alphabet parties as a counter to socialist impulses in the city. The old business groups, supported by the corporate sector, organized to combat (successfully) socialist organization. Conventional factions stopped being factious, especially in western cities. Provincial governments, accidentally or on purpose, did their part to mute political radicalism. Many set up regional governments or agencies that limited radical activity. Such agencies also pitted the generally more conseravative suburbs and urban areas — home of the expanding white collar class — against the radical core areas. Conservatism was bred in many cities, especially west of the Ottawa River, by the widespread nature of property ownership and the almost exclusive use of the property tax as the chief tax resource of local government. Urban voters and the city itself can become hyper-sensitive to the burden of property tax and its visible effect on the individual. Much social conservatism can be bred by such an identification, especially when owners are usually paying the social benefits of a non-owning group, a group which is often in a geographically different part of the city.[79]

As for the property tax itself, it had been a most lucrative source of revenue until about the 1930s, and arguably the most lucrative of all the tax bases in Canada for more than a century. Certainly by 1929, the property tax was generating more tax revenue than any other single source. But as the depression of the 1930s was to demonstrate, it was very nearly at a point of exhaustion. Few additional demands could be placed upon it in its monolithic and regressive form without creating unwarranted inequalities, without creating a capital crisis, and without creating more of a tax dodge communities to which many corporations were beginning to flee.[80] Provincial resistance to provision of new sources of revenue meant, in effect, that future funding of local government would be in the form of transfer payments, which were, as indicated, usually in the form of the conditional grant. Inter-governmental transfers would thus effectively control inter-class transfers, and senior governments effectively controlled the inter-governmental transfers. Proletarian control of a city was thereby made redundant because the city had been made impotent. Any effort by a radical local government to develop, for example, income support policies, could only be done at the expense, for example, of cutting the water off. Local health officers, operating under a provincial act, could prohibit that, as part of the minimum standard guaranteed to rich and poor alike.

By the 1960s city governments had basically one resource left: a bureaucracy more expert than that of the senior governments. Reliance on this liberal-professional class proved a weak reed. Provincial and federal governments, and even some corporations, by the 1970s had hired experts of their own and had often had hired away the expertise the cities had developed. Small local business elites were crippled along with their cities. The complex of zoning, planning, building and other regulations that made its way into city bylaws, especially after 1945, could be navigated by big business, which could afford the cost of legal, planning and other experts, to chart the way. Small business was, and is, swamped in a tide of regulation. The cities last hope, that of superior knowledge and intelligence, withered.

An explanation for the loss of autonomy is complex, but if one single factor had to be pointed to it would be the loss of identification of elite with place and its replacement of elite identification with organization. Cities as a special kind of place for doing business have ceased to exist. As a special kind of place for living, they may only now be on their way to fulfilling their potential.

NOTES:

1. R.C. Brown and G.R. Cook, *Canada, 1896 to 1921: A Nation Transformed* (Toronto: McClelland and Stewart, 1975).

2. Changes in population growth are outlined in Leroy Stone, *Urban Development in Canada* (Ottawa: Dominion Bureau of Statistics, 1967), pp. 26-42. Complete and comparable historical runs of data on economic changes in urban Canada are not available, but fragmented analyses clearly indicate a major change in scale and quality. See, for example, sections on "Public Finance" in the *Canada Year Book* for the first three decades of the century; K.A. Buckley and H. Urquhart, eds., *Historical Statistics of Canada* (Toronto: Macmillan, 1965);

R.H. Coates, "Preface," in Canada, Dominion Bureau of Statistics, General Statistics Branch, *Economic Fluctuations in Canada During the Post-War Period* (Ottawa: King's Printer, 1938); and *The Rowell-Sirois Report*, Book I, ed. D.V. Smiley (Toronto: McClelland and Stewart Ltd., 1963), esp. p. 24, where it is noted that in 1870 the three leading urban centres contributed about one-quarter of the total net value of Manufactures while in the 1930s they contributed nearly one half. Changes in the occupational patterns in seven major cities between 1921 and 1931 are revealed in *Census of Canada*, 1931, Vol. VII, Table 9 and *Census of Canada*, 1921, Vol. IV, Table 1. In general the censuses are difficult to use to chart changes in urban economic growth, especially before 1921 because of a lack of comparability. See also K.C.R. D'Arcy, "The Occupational Trends of the Male Labor Force in Canada and Canadian Urban Areas, 1911-1961," M.A. Thesis, Department of Sociology (University of Saskatchewan, 1967), esp. p. 234 and Table Series A.1, pp. 244-64.

3. Stone, *Urban Development in Canada*, pp. 17-24.

4. See the burgeoning literature on "enterprise" at the turn of the century, including: Brown and Cook, *A Nation Transformed*; Martin Robin, *The Company Province* (Toronto: McClelland and Stewart, 1972); H.V. Nelles, *The Politics of Development* (Toronto: Macmillan, 1974); Glenn Porter and Robert Cuff, *Enterprise and National Development* (Toronto: Hakkert, 1973); J.M. Bliss, *A Living Profit* (Toronto: McClelland and Stewart, 1974); and articles such as John C. Weaver, "Elitism and the Corporate Ideal," J.E. Rea, "How Winnipeg was Nearly Won," and Paul Phillips, " 'Power Politics': Municipal Affairs and Seymour James Farmer," all in *Cities in the West*, ed. A.R. McCormack and Ian MacPherson (Ottawa: National Museum of Man, Mercury Series, 1975).

5. See, for example, *The Rowell-Sirois Report*, pp. 128-29, 142-47.

6. *Ibid.*, pp. 142-3 and 174. Also, see a growing body of literature on what might be called a growing social conscience on the problem, Richard Allen, *The Social Passion* (Toronto: University of Toronto Press, 1971) and Terry Copp, *The Anatomy of Poverty* (Toronto: McClelland and Stewart, 1974) are only the most recent. It should be noted that Michael Katz, "The People of a Canadian City, 1851-2," in *The Canadian City: Essays in Urban History* (Toronto: McClelland and Stewart, 1976), pp. 227-254 has demonstrated quite conclusively that a large, fluid lower class was typical of at least one mid-century city. Whether the quality of that group changed, became endemic in Canada, or was only really noticed at the end of the nineteenth century, is not known.

7. See the *Rowell-Sirois Report*, pp. 142-147. Francis Hankin and T.W.L. MacDermot, *Recovery by Control* (Toronto: J.M. Dent and Sons, 1933), claim in Chapter V that all but 90 of 585 waterworks in Canada to 1928 were owned and operated by public bodies, one-third in the hands of public utility commissions; and in 1929, 21 of 59 electric railways in Canada were owned by municipalities in Canada, including all the major ones in Ontario and the Prairies. See also J.E. Rea, "How Power was Nearly Won," in *Cities in the West*, and C.O. White, "Moose Jaw Opts for Private over Municipal Ownership of its Electrical Utility," in *ibid*.

8. See *The Rowell-Sirois Report*; Copp, *Anatomy of Poverty*; Serge Mongeau, *Evolution de l'assistance au Quebec* (Montreal: Editions du Jour, 1967); Richard B. Splane, *Social Welfare in Ontario, 1791-1893* (Toronto: University of Toronto Press, 1965); Margaret K. Strong *Public Welfare Administration in Canada* (Chicago: University of Chicago Press, 1930); John H. Taylor, "The Urban West: Public Welfare and a Theory of Urban Development" in *Cities in the West*; and a large body of thesis material that has emanated from the Schools of Social Work, particularly at the University of Toronto and the University of British Columbia.

9. Usually in the form of Town Planning Commissions that were permitted under legislation passed in nearly all the provinces in the late 1910s and 1920s as a result of efforts of the federal government's Commission of Conservation. Some were anaemic ventures, like Ottawa, others quite thorough, like Vancouver, and yet others, like Calgary, which planned to

establish a "Venice of the West," quite utopian. Much work remains to be done on the history of planning in Canada, though a number of commendable efforts have been produced recently. See, for example, Alan F.J. Artibise, "Winnipeg and the City Planning Movement, 1910-1915," in D.J. Bercuson, ed., *Western Perspectives I* (Toronto: Holt, Rinehart and Winston, 1974); Walter Van Nus, "The Architect and City Planning in Canada, 1890-1930," paper presented to the Canadian Historical Association, Annual Meeting, Edmonton, 1975; and Alan F.J. Artibise and Gilbert A. Stelter, "Conservation Planning and Urban Planning: The Canadian Commission of Conservation in Historical Perspective," in *Planning for Conservation: An International Perspective*, ed. by Roger Kain (London: Monsell, 1981), pp. 17-36.

10. See Table I. In 1926, less than nine percent of local revenue was received from sources other than the local tax base.

11. Notably the Union of Canadian Municipalities. See Resolution Five of their 1929 Annual Convention as reported in *The Municipal Review of Canada*, Vol. XXV, No. 9 (Sept. 1929), p. 369, a resolution reiterated in its substance in the 1930 and 1931 conventions. Similar sentiments were expressed in speeches and resolutions at the annual meetings of the Ontario Municipal Association.

12. Centre de recherche en droit public, Université de Montréal, *Droit et Societe Urbaine au Quebec: Rapport Synthese*, sous la direction de P.A. Coté, A. Lajoie, J. Leveillée, *et al* (Montreal, March 1981), p. 3.

13. K.G. Crawford, "The Independence of Municipal Councils in Ontario," *Canadian Journal of Economics and Political Science* (hereafter *CJEPS*), Vol. VI, No. 4 (November 1940), p. 543.

14. *Ibid.*, pp. 548-9.

15. See "The Ontario Railway and Municipal Board Act," *Statutes of Ontario*, 6 Edw. VII (1906), c. 31; "The Municipal Aid [to industrial or commercial establishments] Prohibition Act," 1925, c. 116, as examples.

16. *Revised Statutes of Quebec*, Montreal proper operated outside the commission, but most of its suburbs were embraced by it. The commission membership was dominated by representatives of the richer suburban municipalities like Westmount and Outremont.

17. Crawford "The Independence of Municipal Council," p. 547.

18. For example, in the Maritimes the changed relationship was rather slower than elsewhere, especially in New Brunswick where a complete overhaul did not occur until the 1960s.

19. Contrasts could be made here between Quebec with its generally anti-statist inclinations and the Prairie provinces, which with little historical overburden, seemed quite willing to experiment and did so. For one discussion of the Prairie experience see Alan F.J. Artibise, "Continuity and Change: Elites and Prairie Urban Development 1914-1950," in *The Usable Urban Past: Planning and Politics in the Modern Canadian City*, ed. by Alan F.J. Artibise and Gilbert A. Stelter (Toronto: Macmillan, 1979), pp. 130-154.

20. Note the sudden changes, especially with respect to municipal control and welfare, with the changes to Liberal governments in B.C. in 1933 and Ontario in 1934. At the federal level quite dramatic changes can be observed in the attitudes of R.B. Bennett in January of 1935, Mackenzie King in December of 1935, and King again in the war period. For the latter evolution, see J.L. Granatstein, *Canada's War* (Toronto: Oxford University Press, 1974), esp. chs. 6 and 7.

21. "The British North America Act," s. 92, head 8.

22. *Statutes of Saskatchewan*, 8-9 Edw. VII, c. 16, s. 184 (1908-9).

23. *Statutes of Saskatchewan*, 6 Geo. V., c. 16 (1915).

24. *Statutes of Ontario*, 3-4 Geo. V., c. 43, s. 250, (1912).

25. *Revised Statutes of Quebec*, 1909, Title XI, Art. 777.

26. *Ibid.*, Arts. 5889-90.

27. *Ibid.*, Arts. 5776-89.

28. *Ibid.*

29. See *Revised Statutes of Quebec*, 1909, Art. 5956 (i).

30. *Statutes of Quebec*, 8 Geo. V., c. 60, (1918).

31. See *Statutes of Quebec*, 9 Geo. V., c. 59 1919; 10 Geo. V., c. 67 1920; 11 Geo. V., c. 48 1921; 12 Geo. V., c. 60 1922; and 13 Geo. V., c. 84 1923. These acts were administered under the terms of "The Quebec Municipal Commission Act," *Revised Statutes of Quebec*, 1925, c. 111A.

32. By 1914, the main legislation affecting municipalities was "The Municipal Act," *Revised Statutes of Ontario*, 1914, c. 192; "The Ontario Railway and Municipal Board Act," *Revised Statutes of Ontario*, 1914, c. 186; "The Municipal and School Accounts Audit Act," passed in 1914, *Revised Statutes of Ontario*, c. 290.

33. "The Department of Municipal Affairs Act," *Statutes of Alberta*, 2 Geo. V., c. 11 (1911-12); "The Department of Municipal Affairs Act," *Statutes of Saskatchewan*, 8-9 Edw. VII, c. 15 (1908-9).

34. "The Municipal Commissioner's Act," *Statutes of Manitoba*, 53 V, c. 51 (1890).

35. "The Municipal Act," Index Heading, *RSO* (1950).

36. *Statutes of Ontario*, 8 Geo. V, c. 38 (1918); 9 Geo. V., c. 54 (1919); 10-11 Geo. V., c. 84 (1920); 21 Geo. V, c. 5 (1931); 22 Geo. V., c. 35 (1932); 22 Geo. V, c. 27 (1932); 24 Geo. V, c. 16 (1934); 25 Geo. V, c. 16 (1935); 1 Geo. VI, c. 50 (1937); 8 Geo. VI, c. 16 (1944); 8 Geo. VI, c. 41 (1944); 10 Geo. VI, c. 71 (1946); 10 Geo. VI, c. 22 (1946); 12 Geo. VI, c. 23 (1948); 12 Geo. VI, c. 44 (1948); and 12 Geo. VI, c. 47 (1948).

37. Manitoba, "The Health and Public Welfare Act," 1928; New Brunswick, 1944, established a minister responsible in the field but under no specific legislation; Saskatchewan, "The Bureau of Labour and Public Welfare Act, 1934-35; Nova Scotia, 1944, a minister but no act; Ontario, "The Department of Public Welfare Act," 1931; Quebec, "The Health and Social Welfare Act," 1936; Alberta, "The Bureau of Public Welfare Act," 1939; and British Columbia, "The Department of Health and Welfare Act," 1946.

38. For example, in Ontario there were no planning or housing acts in 1914. Their proliferation is indicated above, note 36. Perhaps the earliest example of planning legislation was in Alberta under "The Town Planning Act," *Statutes of Alberta*, 1913(1), c. 18. For a discussion of the Alberta experience, see P.J. Smith, "The Principle of Utility and the Origins of Planning Legislation in Alberta, 1912-1975," in Artibise and Stelter, *The Usable Urban Past*, pp. 196-225. By the 1940s, such acts as the Alberta one existed in nearly every province, in part it seems to provide a channel through which federal money under the National Housing Act could flow. For example, Ontario's "Housing Development Act," *Statutes of Ontario*, 12 Geo. VI, c. 44 (1948), provides under section 6(1) for federal and provincial agreements "as contemplated" in section 35 of "The National Housing Act," 1944 (Canada).

39. For a general overview and other references, see A.E. Buck, *Financing Canadian Government* (Chicago: Public Administration Service, 1949), pp. 209-332.

40. Compare *Statutes of Ontario*, 3-4 Geo. V., c. 43, s. 250 with *Revised Statutes of Ontario*, 150, c. 243, s. 260.

41. A phenomenon clearly evident, for example, in the flow of regulations from the provinces to most cities with respect to relief administration in the 1930s.

42. Luella Gettys, *The Administration of Canadian Conditional Grants* (Chicago: Public Administration Service, 1938, pp. 156-7).

43. See Crawford, "The Independence of Municipal Councils," p. 548, and Buck, *Financing*, pp. 321-5.

44. Gettys, *The Administration*, p. 13.

45. Richard Splane, *Social Welfare in Ontario*, pp. 284ff.

46. *Ibid.*, p. 15, n. 30.

47. *The Municipal Review of Canada* (November 1936), p. 6.

48. Mary Sutherland, ''Memorandum of Reservations Containing the Reasons for Dissent,'' Canada, National Employment Commission, *Final Report* (Ottawa: King's Printer, 1938), p. 47.

49. *Ibid.*, p. 50.

50. *Ibid.*, p. 49.

51. Crawford, ''The Independence of Municipal Councils,'' p. 543.

52. Alan Van Every, ''Trends in Provincial-Municipal Supervision,'' *Public Affairs*, Vo. 6, No. 4 (Summer 1943), pp. 211-15.

53. C.A. Curtis, ''Municipal Government in Ontario,'' *CJEPS*, Vol. VIII, No. 3 (August 1942), p. 418.

54. *Ibid.*, p. 421.

55. C.A. Curtis, ''Municipal Finance and Dominion-Provincial Relations,'' *CJEPS*, Vol. XVII, No. 3 (August 1951), pp. 297-306.

56. Keith B. Callard, ''The Present System of Local Government in Canada: Some Problems of Status, Area, Population and Resources,'' *CJEPS*, Vol. XVII, No. 2 (May 1951), pp. 2-17.

57. For example, Emile Morin, ''Municipal Debt Supervision in Quebec,'' *Municipal Finance* (November 1944), pp. 16-20; W.R. Cottingham, ''Provincial Supervision of Municipal Debts,'' *Municipal Finance* (August 1940), pp. 20-33; and G.A. Lascelles, ''Financial Organization of the City of Toronto, Canada,'' *Municipal Finance* (November 1942), pp. 17-22.

58. Buck, *Financing*.

59. Eric Hardy, ''Provincial-Municipal Relations: With Emphasis on the Financial Relationships Between Provinces and Local Governments,'' and Fred R. MacKinnon, ''Local Government and Welfare,'' both in *Canadian Public Administration*, Vol. III (1960), pp. 14-23 and 31-41, respectively.

60. ''Legitlative Control of Municipalities in Ontario,'' *Canadian Public Administration*, Vol. IV (1961), pp. 294-301.

61. ''The Canadian Federation of Mayors and Municipalities: Its Role and Function,'' *Canadian Public Administration*, Vol. III (1960), pp. 82-92.

62. ''Local Government and Democracy,'' *Public Administration*, Vol. XXXI (Spring 1953), pp. 25-34.

63. See Keith Panter-Brick, ''Local Government and Democracy — A Rejoinder,'' *Ibid.*, pp. 344-48; Leo Moulin, ''Local Self-Government as a Basis for Democracy: A Further Comment,'' *Ibid.*, pp. 433-37; and Panter-Brick, ''Local Self-Government as a Basis for Democracy: A Rejoinder,'' *Ibid.*, pp. 438-40.

64. Hugh Whalen, ''Democracy and Local Government,'' *Canadian Public Administration*, Vol. III (1960), pp. 1-13; and ''Ideology, Democracy, and the Foundations of Local Self-Government,'' *CJEPS*, Vol. XXVI, No. 3 (August 1960), pp. 377-95.

65. Whalen, ''Ideology, Democracy,'' p. 394.

66. See for example, W.K. Tabb and M. Sawer, *Marxism and the Metropolis* (New York: Oxford University Press, 1978).

67. One of the few is Gilbert Stelter, ''The City Building Process in Canada,'' in Stelter and Alan F.J. Aritibise, eds., *Shaping the Urban Landscape: Aspects of the Canadian City Building Process* (Ottawa: Carleton University Press, 1982).

68. David Sutherland, ''The Merchants of Halifax, 1815-1850: A Commercial Class in Pursuit of Metropolitan Status,'' Ph.D. Thesis (University of Toronto, 1975).

69. C.F.J. Whebell, ''Robert Baldwin and Decentralization 1841-9,'' in F.H. Armstrong, et al., eds., *Aspects of Nineteenth-Century Ontario* (Toronto: University of Toronto Press, 1974), p. 61.

70. For studies of the booster phenomenon, see Carl M. Wallace, ''Saint John Boosters and

Railroads in Mid-Nineteenth Century," *Acadiensis*, Vol. 6, No. 1 (1976), pp. 71-91; Elizabeth Bloomfield, "Municipal Bonusing of Industry: The Legislative Framework in Ontario to 1930," *Urban History Review*, Vol. IX, No. 3 (1981), pp. 59-77; and articles by J.W. Brennan, A.F.J. Artibise, B. Potyondi, P. Voisey, John Gilpin, and Max Foran in Alan F.J. Artibise, ed., *Town and City: Aspects of Western Canadian Urban Development* (Regina: Canadian Plains Research Centre, 1981).

71. My thanks to Michael Piva, whose current investigations into public finance in pre-Confederation Canada led to this important insight.

72. A comprehensive study of the municipal qualification and franchise would be useful. In lieu of such, the Ontario experience is instructive. In the nineteenth century, the qualification for citry office required a $400 freehold or $800 leasehold and residence in or within two miles. The franchise was restricted to those with a freehold or leasehold rated at $400 or a business income of $400 annually. See *Revised Statutes of Ontario*, 1887. Plural voting was also permitted, once in each ward, for candidates elected by ward, in each ward where sufficient property was owned or leased. In the 1920s qualification was equated with franchise, but only householders with rateable property could run (see *RSO*, 1927, c. 233, s. 52). The $400 franchise persisted, and so did plural voting. And so powerful was the use of property that "highest assessment" was used to break tie votes in some situations (see *RSO*, 1960, c. 249, s. 149(2)). Only in the 1970s was the property qualification and franchise done away with in Ontario.

73. T.W. Acheson, "The Great Merchant and Economic Development in Saint John, 1820-1850," *Acadiensis*, Vol. VIII, No. 2 (Spring 1979), 3-27.

74. H.V. Nelles, *The Politics of Development* (Toronto: Macmillan, 1975), *passim*.

75. J.H. Taylor, "Mayors à la Mancha: An Aspect of Depression Leadership in Canadian Cities," *Urban History Review*, Vol. IX, No. 3 (February 1981), pp. 3-14.

76. *Droit et Societe Urbaine*.

77. Taylor, "Mayors à la Mancha."

78. See, for example, Terry Copp, "Montreal's Municipal Government and the Crisis of the 1930s," in Artibise and Stelter, *The Usable Urban Past*, pp. 112-129.

79. J.H. Taylor, "Relief from Relief: The Cities' Answer to Depression Dependency," *Journal of Canadian Studies*, Vol. 14 (Spring 1979), pp. 16-23.

80. See, for example, Artibise, "Continuity and Change: Elites and Prairie Urban Development," in Artibise and Stelter, *The Usable Urban Past*.

Notes on Editors

Gilbert A. Stelter and Alan F.J. Artibise have co-authored and co-edited numerous books and articles, including *The Usable Urban Past: Planning and Politics in the Modern Canadian City*, Carleton Library Series #119 (Toronto: Macmillan, 1979) and *Shaping the Urban Landscape, Aspects of the Canadian City-Building Process*, Carleton Library Series #125 (Ottawa: Carleton University Press, 1982); *Canada's Urban Past: A Bibliography to 1980 and a Guide to Canadian Urban Studies* (Vancouver: University of British Columbia Press, 1981); "Canadian Resource Towns," Special Issue, *Plan Canada*, Vol. 18 (1978); and "Conservation Planning and Urban Planning: The Canadian Commission of Conservation in Historical Perspective," in R. Kain, ed., *Planning for Conservation: An International Perspective* (London: Mansell, 1981), pp. 17-36.

Gilbert A. Stelter is Professor of History at the University of Guelph. He co-ordinated two important urban history conferences: the Guelph Urban History Conference in May, 1977; and the Canadian-American Urban History Conference in August, 1982. His publications include numerous articles on Canadian urban historiography, on frontier and resource towns, and on early Canadian urban development. He has also co-edited *Urbanization in the Americas: The Background in Comparative Perspective* (Ottawa: National Museum of Man, 1981). He is chairman of the Urban History Committee of the Canadian Historical Association and a member of the editorial boards of the *Urban History Review* and the *Urban History Yearbook*.

Alan F.J. Artibise is Director, Institute of Urban Studies, University of Winnipeg. He is general editor of the *History of Canadian Cities Series* and the *Urban History Review*. He is the author of *Winnipeg: A Social History of Urban Growth, 1874-1914* (Montreal: McGill-Queen's University Press, 1975); *Winnipeg: An Illustrated History* (Toronto: James Lorimer and National Museum of Man, 1977); *Western Canada Since 1870: A Bibliography and Guide* (Vancouver: University of British Columbia Press, 1978); and numerous other books and articles on western Canadian urban history. He has also edited *Town and City: Aspects of Western Canadian Urban History* (Regina: Canadian Plains Research Center, 1981). Artibise is a member of the editorial board of the *Journal of Urban History* and serves as urban consultant to the *New Canadian Encyclopedia*.

Notes on Contributors

T.W. Acheson is Professor of History at the University of New Brunswick. He has published widely in the field of business and economic history and is currently engaged in research on the early development of Saint John, N.B.

F.H. Armstrong is Professor of History at the University of Western Ontario in London. A pioneer in the study of Canadian urban history, he has published numerous articles on early Toronto and on London, Ontario.

Carl Betke is a researcher for Alberta Heritage. He has taught at the University of Victoria and at Camrose Lutheran College, and has done historical research in the R.C.M.P. Historical Section, Ottawa. He recently completed his Ph.D. thesis for the University of Alberta on the development of Edmonton to 1929.

Suzanne Cross teaches in the History Department of Vanier College in Montreal. Her current research concerns the development of Montreal in the nineteenth century.

Chad M. Gaffield is an Associate Professor in the History Department at the University of Victoria. He is a social historian interested in the history of the family and education.

Peter G. Goheen is a member of the Geography Department at Queen's University. His current research interests involve the study of the relationship between industrialization and urbanization.

Alan Gowans is a Professor in the Department of History in Art at the University of Victoria. His publications, including *Church Architecture in New France* (1955) and *Building Canada: An Architectural History of Canadian Life* (1967), have become standard works in the field of Canadian architectural history.

Robert F. Harney is a Professor of History at the University of Toronto and Director of the Multicultural History Society of Ontario. He is the co-author of *Immigrants: A Portrait of the Urban Experience, 1890-1930* (1975) and of numerous books and articles on the Italians in North America.

Deryck Holdsworth is a graduate of the University of British Columbia and is currently a full-time research associate with the *Historical Atlas of Canada* project.

502

Michael Katz is Professor of History at the University of Pennsylvania. Prior to this, he directed the Canadian Social History Project and led the way in discovering new methods for understanding family and class in nineteenth-century urban society. His most notable publication is *The People of Hamilton, Canada West: Family and Class in a Mid-Nineteenth Century City* (1975).

Paul-Andre Linteau is a Professor of History at the University of Quebec at Montreal. A noted Quebec historian, Linteau's most recent major publication is *Maissoneuve: Comment les promoteurs fabriquent une ville, 1883-1918* (1981). He is also an Associate Editor of the *Urban History Review*.

Sheva Medjuck is an Assistant Professor at Mount Saint Vincent University. She completed her Ph.D. in Sociology at York University in 1978 on ''Wooden Ships and Iron People: The Lives of the People of Moncton, New Brunswick, 1851-1871.''

Murray Nicolson recently completed his Ph.D. in History at the University of Guelph. He has published several articles dealing with the Irish in Toronto.

Jean-Claude Robert is a Professor of History at the University of Quebec at Montreal. Together with P.-A. Linteau, he directs the Research Group on Montreal Society in the Nineteenth-Century. He is also the co-author of *Histoire du Québec contemporain Confédération à la crise* (1979).

Paul Rutherford is a member of the History Department at the University of Toronto. His publications in the field of urban reform include the anthology *Saving the Canadian City: The First Phase, 1880-1920* (1974).

John Taylor teaches in the History Department at Carleton University. An Associate Editor of the *Urban History Review*, he is currently preparing an urban biography of Ottawa for the *History of Canadian Cities Series*.

Walter van Nus is a member of the History Department at Concordia University. His article in this volume is part of a more extensive examination of urban planning in Canada during the early decades of the twentieth-century.

John C. Weaver is an Associaste Professor at McMaster University. His most recent publication is *Hamilton: An Illustrated History* (1982), a volume in the *History of Canadian Cities Series*.

THE CARLETON LIBRARY SERIES

CARLETON CONTEMPORARIES

AN INDEPENDENT FOREIGN POLICY FOR CANADA? Edited by Stephen Clarkson
THE DECOLONIZATION OF QUEBEC: AN ANALYSIS OF LEFT-WING NATIONALISM by Henry Milner and Sheilagh Hodgins Milner
THE MACKENZIE PIPELINE: ARCTIC GAS AND CANADIAN ENERGY POLICY Edited by Peter H. Pearse
CONTINENTAL COMMUNITY? INDEPENDENCE AND INTEGRATION IN NORTH AMERICA Edited by W.A. Axline, J.E. Hyndman, P.V. Lyon and M.A. Molot
THE RAILWAY GAME: A STUDY IN SOCIO-TECHNOLOGICAL OBSOLESCENCE by J. Lukasiewicz
FOREMOST NATION: CANADIAN FOREIGN POLICY AND A CHANGING WORLD Edited by N. Hillmer and G. Stevenson

GENERAL LIST

1. DICCIONARIO DE REFERENCIAS DEL ''poema de mio cid'', compiled and arranged by José Jurado
2. THE POET AND THE CRITIC: A Literary Correspondence Between D. C. Scott and E. K. Brown, edited by Robert L. McDougall